Sri Lanka

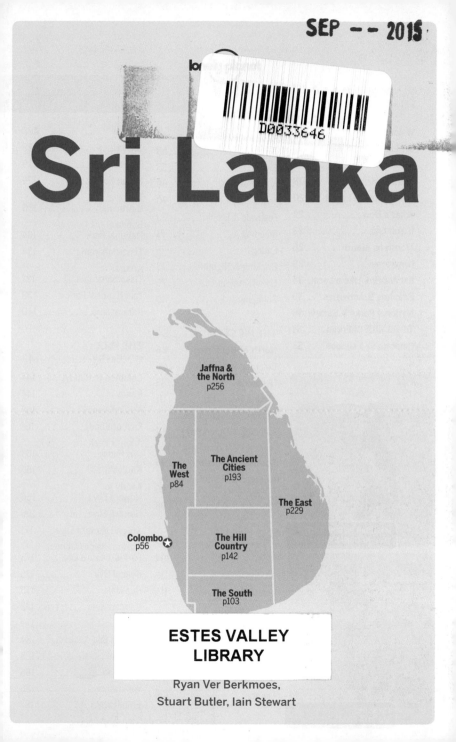

Jaffna & the North
p256

The Ancient Cities
p193

The West
p84

The East
p229

Colombo
p56

The Hill Country
p142

The South
p103

Ryan Ver Berkmoes,
Stuart Butler, Iain Stewart

PLAN YOUR TRIP

MALABAR PIED HORNBILL,
YALA NATIONAL PARK P138

SARANGA DEVA DE ALWIS /GETTY IMAGES ©

FRESCOES,
SIGIRIYA P200

ERIC L WHEATER /GETTY IMAGES ©

ON THE ROAD

Contents

PETTAH MARKETS P60,
COLOMBO

Welcome to Sri Lanka

Endless beaches, timeless ruins, welcoming people, oodles of elephants, rolling surf, cheap prices, fun trains, famous tea and flavourful food describe Sri Lanka.

The Undiscovered Country

You might say Sri Lanka has been hiding in plain sight. Countless numbers of travellers have passed overhead on their way to some-place else, and years of war and challenges, such as tsunamis, have kept Sri Lanka off many itineraries.

But now Sri Lanka is finding its way onto the itineraries of ever more travel-lers. Several years since the war ended, the country is moving forward quickly, even as questions about the hostilities continue to spark debate. Lying between the more trodden parts of India and Southeast Asia, Sri Lanka's myriad appeals are undeniably alluring.

So Much in So Little

Few places have as many Unesco World Heritage Sites – eight – packed into such a small area. Sri Lanka's 2000-plus years of culture can be discovered at ancient sites, where legendary temples boast beautiful details.

Across the island, that thing that goes bump in the night might be an elephant heading to a favourite waterhole. Safari tours of Sri Lanka's pleasantly relaxed national parks encounter leopards, water buffaloes, all manner of birds and a passel of primates.

Rainforests & Beaches

When you're ready to escape the tropical climate of the coast and lowlands, head for the hills, with their temperate, achingly green charms. Verdant tea plantations and rainforested peaks beckon walkers, hikers and those who just want to see it during a spectacular train ride.

And then there are the beaches. Daz-zlingly white and often untrod, they ring the island so that no matter where you go, you'll be near a sandy gem. Should you beat the inevitable languor, you can surf and dive world-class sites without world-class crowds.

It's So Easy

Distances are short: see the sacred home of the world's oldest living tree in the morning in Anuradhapura, and stand awestruck by the sight of hundreds of elephants gather-ing in the afternoon at Minneriya. Discover a favourite beach, meditate in a 2000-year-old temple, exchange smiles while stroll-ing a mellow village, marvel at birds and wildflowers, try to keep count of the little dishes that come with your rice and curry. Stroll past colonial gems in Colombo, then hit some epic surf. Sri Lanka is spectacular, affordable and still often uncrowded. Now is the best time to discover it.

Why I Love Sri Lanka

By Ryan Ver Berkmoes

My fascination with Sri Lanka began when I read Paul Theroux's *The Great Railway Bazaar* as a child. His wonderment at the island's endless contradictions stayed with me. In 2004 I was in the west and south in the weeks after the tsunami. I was struck by the stories of the survivors and deeply moved by their efforts to rebuild. In the years since I have been endlessly amazed by the Sri Lankans' ability to overcome disaster, war and myriad other challenges as they work tirelessly to make their country match its potential, while remaining some of the most charming people on the planet.

For more about our authors, see page 336.

Above: Statue of Buddha, Maligawila (p232)

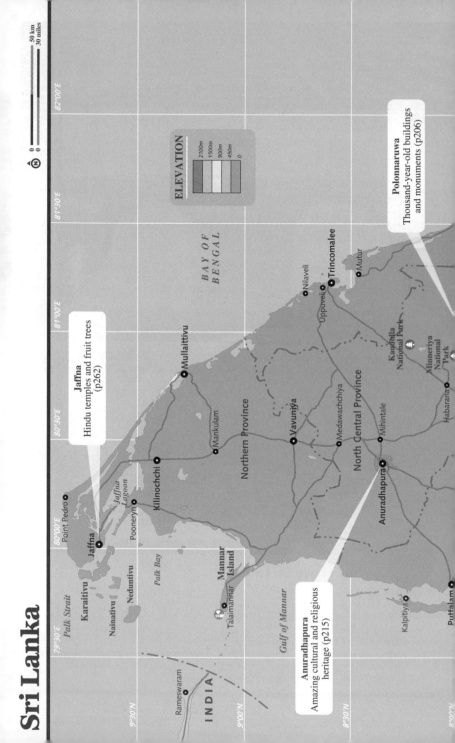

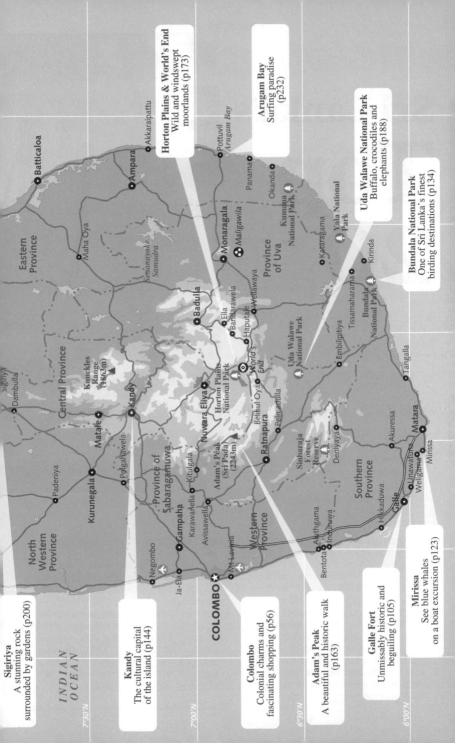

Sigiriya
A stunning rock surrounded by gardens (p200)

Horton Plains & World's End
Wild and windswept moorlands (p173)

Arugam Bay
Surfing paradise (p232)

Uda Walawe National Park
Buffalo, crocodiles and elephants (p188)

Bundala National Park
One of Sri Lanka's finest birding destinations (p134)

Kandy
The cultural capital of the island (p144)

Colombo
Colonial charms and fascinating shopping (p56)

Adam's Peak
A beautiful and historic walk (p163)

Galle Fort
Unmissably historic and beguiling (p105)

Mirissa
See blue whales on a boat excursion (p123)

INDIAN OCEAN

Batticaloa

Akkaraipattu

Ampara

Pottuvil
Arugam Bay

Panama

Okanda

Kumana National Park

Eastern Province

Maha Oya

Senanayake Samudra

Monaragala

Maligawila

Province of Uva

Yala National Park

Kataragama

Kirinda

Tissamaharama

Bundala National Park

Badulla

Ella
Bandarawela
Haputale
Wellawaya

Uda Walawe National Park

Embilipitiya

Tangalla

Sigiriya
Dambulla

Central Province

Knuckles Range (1863m)

Kandy

Matale

Polgahawela

Kurunegala

Padeniya

North Western Province

Negombo

Ja-Ela

Province of Sabaragamuwa

Kitulgala

Avissawella

Karawanella

Kegalle

Gampaha

Mt Lavinia

Western Province

COLOMBO

Nuwara Eliya

Horton Plains National Park

World's End

Adam's Peak (Sri Pada) (2243m)

Ratnapura

Belihul Oya

Pelmadulla

Sinharaja Forest Reserve

Deniyaya

Akuressa

Matara

Weligama
Unawatuna

Mirissa

Galle

Hikkaduwa

Ambalangoda

Induruwa

Bentota
Aluthgama

7°30'N

7°00'N

6°30'N

6°00'N

Sri Lanka's
Top 20

Stunning Beaches

1 There are long, golden-specked ones, there are dainty ones with soft white sand, there are wind- and wave-battered ones, and ones without a footstep for miles. Some have a slowly, slowly vibe and some have a lively party mood, but whichever you choose, the beaches of Sri Lanka (p39) really are every bit as gorgeous as you've heard. And we guarantee that after you've returned home, every time you sit in rush-hour traffic on a wet and cold Monday morning, an image of palm trees and azure Sri Lankan waters will float into your mind! Tangalla beach (p131)

Travelling by Train

2 Sometimes there's no way to get a seat on the slow but oh-so-popular train to Ella (p179), but with a prime standing-room-only spot looking out at a rolling carpet of tea, who cares? Outside, the colourful silk saris of Tamil tea pickers stand out in the sea of green; inside, you may get a shy welcome via a smile. At stations, vendors hustle treats, including some amazing corn and chilli fritters sold wrapped in somebody's old homework paper. Munching one of these while the scenery creaks past? Sublime.

PETER BARRITT / GETTY IMAGES ©

Uda Walawe National Park

3 This huge chunk of savannah grassland centred on the Uda Walawe reservoir (p188) is the closest Sri Lanka gets to East Africa. There are herds of buffalo (although some of these are domesticated!), sambar deer, crocodiles, masses of birds and elephants – and we don't just mean a few elephants. We mean hundreds of the big-nosed creatures. In fact, we'd go so far to say that for elephants, Uda Walawe is equal to, or even better than, many of the famous East African national parks. Blue-tailed bee-eater

Ancient Anuradhapura

4 Here bits of Sri Lanka's cultural and religious heritage sprawl across 3 sq km. In the centre is one of the world's oldest trees, the more than 2000-year-old Sri Maha Bodhi. That it has been tended uninterrupted by guardians for all those centuries is enough to send shivers down the spine. The surrounding fields of crumbling monasteries and enormous dagobas attest to the city's role as the seat of power in Sri Lanka (p215) for a thousand years. Biking through this heady past is a thrilling experience. Isurumuniya Vihara (p220)

Soaring Sigiriya Rock

5 If it was just the rolling gardens at the base of Sigiriya, it would still be a highlight. Ponds and little man-made rivulets put the water in these water gardens and offer a serene idyll amid the sweltering countryside. But look up and catch your jaw as you ponder this 370m-high rock (p200) that erupts out of the landscape. Etched with art and surmounted by ruins, Sigiriya is an awesome mystery, one that the wonderful museum tries to dissect. The climb to the top is a wearying but worthy endeavour.

5

Surfing at Arugam Bay

6 The heart of Sri Lanka's growing surf scene, the long right break at the southern end of Arugam Bay (p233) is considered Sri Lanka's best. From April to September you'll find surfers riding the waves; stragglers catch the random good days as late as November. Throughout the year you can revel in the surfer vibe: there are board-rental and ding-repair joints, plus plenty of laid-back cheap hangouts offering a bed on the beach. And if you need solitude, there are fine breaks at nearby Lighthouse Point, Whiskey Point and Okanda.

ASANKA BRENDON RATNAYAKE / GETTY IMAGES ©

6

Adam's Peak Pilgrims

7 For more than 1000 years, pilgrims have trudged by candlelight up Adam's Peak (Sri Pada; p163) to stand in the footprints of Buddha, breathe the air where Adam first set foot on earth and see the place where butterflies go to die. Today, tourists join the throngs of local pilgrims and, as you stand in the predawn light atop this perfect pinnacle of rock and watch the sun crawl above waves of mountains, the sense of magic remains as bewitching as it must have been for Adam himself. Buddhist temple at Adam's Peak summit

Visiting a Tea Plantation

8 It wasn't really all that long ago that Sri Lanka's Hill Country was largely a wild and ragged sweep of jungle-clad mountains, but then along came the British who felt the need for a nice cup of tea. So they chopped down all the jungle and turned the Hill Country into one giant tea estate. And you know what? The result is mighty pretty! Sri Lankan tea is now famous across the world, and visiting a tea estate (p302) and seeing how the world's favourite cuppa is produced is absolutely fascinating. Pedro Tea Estate (p167)

IDRIS AHMED / GETTY IMAGES ©

MARGIE POLITZER / GETTY IMAGES ©

Fabulous Galle Fort

9 Man and nature have joined forces in Galle Fort (p105) to produce an architectural work of art. The Dutch built the streets and buildings, the Sri Lankans added the colour and style, and then nature got busy covering it in a gentle layer of tropical vegetation, humidity and salty air. The result is an enchanting old town that is home to dozens of art galleries, quirky shops, boutique cafes and guest-houses, plus some splen-did hotels. For tourists it's, without doubt, the number one urban attraction in the country. Clock tower and fort walls (p110)

Bundala National Park

10 With all the crowds heading to nearby Yala National Park, the Ramsar-recognised Bundala National Park (p134) often gets over-looked. But with the park's huge sheets of shimmering wetlands singing to the sound of birdsong, skip-ping it is a big mistake. Bundala has a beauty that other parks can only dream of, and is one of the finest birding destinations in the country. Oh, and in case herons and egrets aren't glam enough for you, the crocodiles and resident el-ephant herd will put a smile on your face. Monitor lizard

Feel the Healing: Ayurveda

11 If you start to feel the burden of the centuries while in Sri Lanka, you might appreci-ate an irony while you feel the tensions melt out of your body in an Ayurvedic sauna (p96): the design is more than 2500 years old. Ayurveda is an ancient practice and its devotees claim enormous benefits from its therapies and treatments. Herbs, spices, oils and more are used on and in the body to produce balance. Some people go on multiweek regimens in clinics, others enjoy a pampering afternoon at a luxury spa. Ayurvedic medicines

GRANT FAINT / GETTY IMAGES ©

Polonnaruwa's Stupendous Structures

12 Arrayed around a vast grassy quadrangle like the chess pieces of giants, these intricately carved buildings and monuments offer a visitor-friendly briefing on what was the centre of the kingdom some thousand years ago (p206). Handy plaques are loaded with information, although you may find the buildings too extraordinary to switch your concentration to signage. Catch sight of the ruins at sunrise and sunset, when the rosy rays of light bathe the complex in a romantic glow. Reclining Buddha, Gal Vihara (p210)

Exploring Undiscovered Beaches

13 No longer off-limits due to war, or in-accessible due to primitive roads, the truly magnificent east coast beaches are ready to lure travellers away from their more famous counterparts in the west and south. Just take one look at these beautiful ribbons of sand and you won't want to leave. And you may well have them to yourself. A few areas to consider: Navalady (p242), Kalkudah (p245), the islands near Batticaloa Lighthouse (p245) and beaches down the strip from Uppuveli and Nilaveli (p251). Uppuveli beach

Richly Spiced Food

14 Venture into the entertaining pandemonium of a large Sri Lankan market, such as those found in Colombo and Kandy, and you'll soon see and smell the rich diversity of foods and flavours that come from this fertile land. An average Sri Lankan cook spends hours each day tirelessly roasting and grinding spices while mincing, slicing and dicing all manner of foods (p34). A seemingly humble rice and curry can consist of dozens of intricately prepared dishes, each redolent of a rich and, yes at times, fiery goodness. Spices

Horton Plains & World's End

15 The wild, windswept Horton Plains (p173), high, high up in Sri Lanka's hill country, are utterly unexpected in this country of tropical greens and blues, but they are far from unwelcome. You'll need to wrap up warm (a morning frost isn't uncommon) for the dawn hike across these bleak moorlands – it's one of the most enjoyable walks in the country. And then, suddenly, out of the mist comes the end of the world and a view over what seems like half of Sri Lanka. Horton Plains National Park from World's End

Kandy: Cultural Capital

16 Kandy (p144) is the cultural capital of the island and home to the Temple of the Sacred Tooth Relic, said to contain a tooth of the Buddha. For the Sinhalese, this is the holiest spot on the island, but for tourists Kandy offers more than religious satisfaction: there's a pleasing old quarter, a pretty central lake, a clutch of museums and, in the surrounding vicinity, some beautiful botanical gardens. In case you need further blessings from the gods, there's also a series of fascinating ancient temples. Interior, Temple of the Sacred Tooth Relic (p145)

15

16

Jaffna & the Rediscovered North

17 In Jaffna (p262), everything seems different, especially the language: the rapid-fire staccato of spoken Tamil is a real change from singsong Sinhala. So too the cuisine: singularly spiced and, in season, complemented by legendary mangoes. And perhaps even the light: it has a distinctive quality, reflected as deep garden greens in Jaffna's suburbs. Revel in the uniqueness of Jaffna, including the towering, ornate Hindu temples. And don't miss Jaffna's isolated islands and their end-of-the-earth appeal. Hindu temple, Jaffna

Colonial Legacy

18 Yes, the Brits were chased out at independence in 1948, but their legacy lives on in much more than an often impenetrable bureaucracy addicted to forms. Colombo (p56) has wide, tree-shaded streets where you'll see the structures of the empire at their most magnificent. The National Museum building is redolent with empire. Look around a little and you'll find the colonial legacies of the Dutch and Portuguese as well. Just head to restored quarters of Fort and wander, pausing at the hugely popular Old Dutch Hospital. Cargills main store (p59), Colombo

ASANKA BRENDON RATNAYAKE / GETTY IMAGES ©

Whale-Watching at Mirissa

19 People once visited the beaches of southern Sri Lanka to laze under palm trees and maybe go and peer at a few little fish on a diving excursion. Then somebody realised that the deep blue was home to more than just schools of workaday fish. It turns out that the waters off Sri Lanka are home to the planet's biggest creature, the blue whale (not to mention the somewhat smaller sperm whale). Now, every morning in season, boats leave Mirissa (p124) in search of these creatures unlike any other.

Shopping in Colombo

20 Part of the magic of Colombo – yes, you read that right – is going on a retail binge (p80). We don't necessarily mean the kind where you buy more than will fit in a fleet of three-wheelers; rather we mean bingeing on the experience itself. Even as parts of the world race to a big-box future, Colombo's markets in Pettah heave and hurl with goods and general chaos. And if you'd like something a bit more stylish, Colombo has a growing collection of chic boutiques, stores and malls to choose from. Manning Market (p60), Colombo

Need to Know

For more information, see Survival Guide (p303)

Currency
Sri Lankan Rupee (Rs)

Language
Sinhala, Tamil and English

Visas
Thirty-day visitor visas cost US$30, apply in advance online (www.eta.gov.lk).

Money
ATMs available in cities and large towns. Credit cards accepted at some midrange and all top-end hotels.

Mobile Phones
Local SIM cards cheaply available for unlocked phones.

Time
Sri Lanka Standard Time (GMT/UTC plus 5½ hours)

When to Go

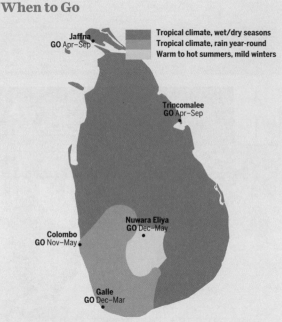

Jaffna
GO Apr–Sep

Tropical climate, wet/dry seasons
Tropical climate, rain year-round
Warm to hot summers, mild winters

Trincomalee
GO Apr–Sep

Nuwara Eliya
GO Dec–May

Colombo
GO Nov–May

Galle
GO Dec–Mar

High Season
(Dec–Mar)

➡ The Hill Country plus west- and south-coast beaches are busiest – and driest.

➡ With beds in demand, prices peak.

➡ The Maha monsoon season (October to January) keeps the East, North and Ancient Cities wet.

Shoulder
(Apr & Sep–Nov)

➡ April and September offer the best odds for good weather countrywide.

➡ New Year's celebrations in mid-April cause transport to fill beyond capacity.

➡ A good time to wander without a set schedule of bookings.

Low Season
(May–Aug)

➡ The Yala monsoon season (May to August) brings rain to the south and west coasts plus the Hill Country.

➡ The weather in the North and East is best.

➡ Prices nationwide are at their nadir.

Websites

Lonely Planet (www.lonely planet.com/sri-lanka) Destination information, hotel bookings, traveller forum and more.

Ceylon Today (www.ceylon today.lk) News, sports, entertainment and a handy ticker with exchange rates.

Gossip Lanka (www.english. gossiplankanews.com) Gossip and entertainment news.

Yamu (www.yamu.lk) Excellent restaurant reviews, sights listings and more.

Government Information Centre (www.gic.gov.lk) A huge amount of info, from transport to visas to health matters and more.

Meteo (www.meteo.gov.lk) Weather forecasts nationwide.

Important Numbers

All regions have a three-digit area code followed by a six- or seven-digit number. Mobile numbers usually begin with 07 or 08 and have up to 12 digits.

Country code	☑94
International access code	☑00
Emergencies	☑118/119

Exchange Rates

Australia	A$1	Rs 121
Canada	C$1	Rs 119
Europe	€1	Rs 174
Japan	¥100	Rs 127
New Zealand	NZ$1	Rs 110
UK	UK£1	Rs 217
US	US$1	Rs 130

For current exchange rates see www.xe.com.

Daily Costs

**Budget:
Less than Rs 5500**

➡ Simple guesthouse: Rs 1500–4000

➡ Local rice and curry: Rs 150–400

➡ Bus fares: under Rs 300 per day

**Midrange:
Rs 5500–20,000**

➡ Double room in a nice place: Rs 4500–12,000

➡ Meals at hotel/restaurant: Rs 1500–2500

➡ Hire bikes, ride trains and use a car and driver some days: average per day Rs 2500

**Top End:
More than Rs 20,000**

➡ Top-end hotel: Rs 12,000 and up

➡ Meals at top-end places: from Rs 3000

➡ Daily use of car and driver: from Rs 5500

Opening Hours

Outside of tourist areas much is closed on Sunday.

Bars Usually close by midnight, last call is often a sobering 11pm.

Restaurants and cafes 7am to 9pm daily, later in areas popular with travellers.

Shops 10am to 7pm Monday to Friday, 10am to 3pm Saturday

Shops and services catering to visitors 9am to 8pm

Arriving in Sri Lanka

Bandaranaike International Airport (CMB; www.airport.lk) Sri Lanka's one main airport is 30km north of Colombo.

Taxis to Colombo Prepaid about Rs 2600 depending on destination; one hour to Fort via expressway.

Hotel car & driver to Colombo Rs 3000 to Rs 4000.

Bus to Colombo Air-con bus via expressway to Central Bus Station Rs 130, under one hour.

Getting Around

Bus Sri Lanka's buses are the country's main mode of transport. They cover most towns, are cheap and are often crowded. Only a few routes have air-con buses. Private buses can offer a bit more comfort than government buses.

Car Many travellers use a hired car with a driver for all or part of their trip. This allows maximum flexibility and is the most efficient way to get around. Many drivers are delightful characters and founts of local knowledge.

Train The improving railway network serves major towns and can be more comfortable than buses (excepting third-class carriages). Some routes, such as Haputale to Ella and Colombo to Galle, are renowned for their scenery.

For much more on **getting around**, see p313.

First Time Sri Lanka

For more information, see Survival Guide (p303)

Checklist

➡ Make sure your passport is valid for at least six months past your arrival date

➡ Check on the need for vaccinations

➡ Arrange for appropriate travel insurance (see p308)

➡ Check the airline baggage restrictions

➡ Inform your debit-/credit-card company

What to Pack

➡ A good pair of earplugs

➡ Mosquito repellent – hard to find in Sri Lanka (unlike mosquitoes)

➡ Sunscreen – another surprisingly hard-to-find item

➡ Tampons – impossible to find outside Colombo

Top Tips for Your Trip

➡ Explore the beaches: especially in the south and east there are vast, deserted and beautiful swaths of sand. If you see a road heading towards the coast, take it and see what you find.

➡ Ride the trains: you'll enjoy the scenery, have comfort greater than buses and you will travel with a cross-section of locals.

➡ Hit the markets: even if you don't want 100 bananas, you'll see the country's bounty, meet people and get caught up in the bargaining frenzy.

➡ Eat with the locals: a busy cafe in a town centre or near a bus terminal will serve rice and curry that's properly spicy, something impossible to find at any place catering to tourists.

➡ Watch the calendar: *poya* (full moon) nights are when celebrations take place across the country.

What to Wear

Shorts and a T-shirt will work most of the time, but bathing suits and bikinis are never proper off tourist beaches. Bring a cover-up for shoulders and arms, and a long skirt, sarong or light pants for visiting temples. Sandals are always fine and are good for slipping off quickly when visiting temples. Something slightly dressy is required for the very best restaurants in Colombo. For the elements, a lightweight waterproof jacket or poncho is handy in case of sudden downpours, and pack a warm layer if spending time high in the temperate mountains.

Sleeping

See p304 for more accommodation information.

➡ **Guesthouses** Family-run guesthouses are found everywhere; they can provide good value and offer a great way to interact with locals.

➡ **Hotels** Coming in all flavours, hotels range from modest to grand and from backroad to beachfront.

➡ **Resorts** Offering one-stop luxury, the best resorts are found on the west and south coasts and in the national parks.

➡ **Ayurvedic spas** Stay at a spa for accommodation and wellness in a single package.

➡ **Rented villas** Villas offer some grand accommodation, some even with their own private beach.

Local Economics

Although Sri Lanka's economy is quickly expanding, people still work very hard to get by. Earnings compared to First World nations are low.

➡ Minimum wage on plantations: Rs 515 per day

➡ Minimum wage for servers/hotel staff: Rs 7500 per month

➡ Annual salary for a manager or accountant: US$12,000

Bargaining

See the box on shopping (p310) for information regarding bargaining.

Tipping

Although a 10% service charge is added to food and accommodation bills, this usually goes straight to the owner rather than the worker.

➡ **Restaurants & Bars** Up to 10% in cash to servers beyond the 'service charge'

➡ **Drivers** 10% of total fee

➡ **Room cleaners** Up to Rs 100 per day

➡ **Bag carriers/porters** Rs 50 per bag

➡ **Shoe minders at temples** Rs 20

➡ **Guides** Varies greatly; agree to a fee in parks and religious sites *before* you set out

Language

Many Sri Lankans speak English but your efforts to speak their language are always appreciated. See p318 for some useful phrases to learn.

MICK ELMORE / GETTY IMAGES ©

Food sellers, Galle Face Green (p61), Colombo

Etiquette

➡ Remove shoes and hats at temples (but socks are OK for walking sun-scorched pavements).

➡ Cover shoulders, arms and legs at temples as directed.

➡ Never pose beside or in front of a statue of the Buddha (ie with your back to it) as this is considered extremely disrespectful.

➡ Displaying any kind of body art that includes an image of the Buddha can get you arrested and deported.

➡ Ask permission before photographing people. A few business-oriented folk, such as the stilt fishers at Koggala or the mahouts at the Pinnewala Elephant Orphanage, will ask for payment.

➡ Raising your voice is very rude and won't help your dispute.

➡ Nude and topless sunbathing are not allowed on beaches.

➡ Modesty is the rule: overt displays of affection are frowned upon.

➡ Answer the personal questions that are common – Are you married? Do you have children? Where are you from? – with good cheer and even creativity.

➡ Don't hand somebody something with your left hand (which is considered unclean), use both hands or just your right.

What's New

Restored Buildings, Colombo

The lavishly restored 17th-century Old Dutch Hospital and other renovated grand old buildings are bringing real appeal to Colombo's historic Fort area. (p58)

New Hotels & Malls, Colombo

A number of huge hotel (p71) and mall (p80) complexes are set to open facing Galle Face Green and around Slave Island and Union Place.

Colombo–Galle Trains

Newly renovated tracks have sped up trains on this very scenic route. It's easily the best way to travel between these two key points. (p115)

Renovations, Galle

New paving stones on its once-dirt streets and lavishly renovated buildings, such as the Dutch Hospital, are making Galle a showplace. (p104)

New Restaurants & Hotels, Galle

Smart new boutique hotels such as Fortaleza (p110), and great restaurants including Elita (p113), are making it hard to leave the Fort walls.

Beach Hotels, Tangalla

The vast, often-unexplored beaches east of Tangalla are seeing many new and excellent beachfront hotels, such as Serein Beach. (p133)

Lakeside Walk, Tissamaharama

Stroll along the new lakeside walkway at Tissa Wewa (p134), the centrepiece of town and a romantic spot for sunsets.

Galway's Land National Park

Sri Lanka's newest national park is opening up to nature lovers who revel in the great bird-spotting. It's a temperate, tropical adventure. (p167)

Uda Walawe National Park Accommodation

Renowned for its elephant spotting, this national park (p188) now has many more sleeping options, such as the safari-experience at Athgira River Camping.

Wilpattu National Park Accommodation

This park received few visitors during the war years but now is opening right up. New guesthouses and hotels are appearing outside the gates. (p93)

The A9 road, Jaffna Peninsula

Repaved and fully reopened, the A9 highway across the Tamil Eelam region and on to Jaffna allows for exploration of these fascinating lands. Watch, too, for the resumption of the Colombo–Jaffna train service. (p267)

Beach Hotels, Arugam Bay

The beautiful beaches at this surfer and sun-seeker hangout have great new places to stay, including the Sandy Beach Hotel. (p235)

For more recommendations and reviews, see lonelyplanet.com/srilanka

If You Like...

Beaches

If Sri Lanka looks outlined in white from space, it's due to the beaches that encircle the island. You can rarely travel any part of the coast for long without coming upon a simply stunning stretch of sand. More amazing is that many are almost empty.

Thalpe With its smattering of comfy guesthouses and quiet sands, this beach is a welcome respite from over-subscribed Unawatuna. (p120)

Marakolliya Beach So what if the swimming isn't always safe? The beach itself is simply stunning. (p131)

Rekawa Beach Long and windswept, this beach attracts turtles and folks who love a lonely, dramatic landscape. (p130)

Arugam Bay Classic hangout for surfers and anyone who likes mellow, easy vibes. (p232)

Uppuveli & Nilaveli Beautiful beaches in a still-quiet corner of the East; the location has kept them quiet and natural. (p251)

Batticaloa Most of the coasts around here are totally isolated; for explorers, adventurers and dreamers only. (p242)

Diving & Snorkelling

Sri Lanka's diving scene is developing along with its tourist scene. Excellent places for diving and snorkelling can be found right around the coast but most are still seldom visited. The west coast south of Colombo has been the centre of diving but other, better areas like the South and East are coming on strong.

Bar Reef Little-exploited and near-pristine reefs where dolphins play in their hundreds. (p92)

Great Basses Reefs It's tricky to access and conditions are fickle but this might be the finest dive site in Sri Lanka. (p137)

Pigeon Island National Park A shallow coral reef, with tons of fish and sharks, that's equally satisfying to snorkel or dive. (p253)

Batticaloa The HMS *Hermes*, a WWII-era wreck, is for Tec divers, but the rock dives around here are for everyone. (p242)

Walking

Sure it's a bit hot during the day and it might rain, but there are oodles of places where you can stretch your legs and appreciate Sri Lanka's remarkable natural beauty, rich culture and ancient monuments.

Colombo The main streets may be choked but other roads in the capital are tree-lined and have a genteel charm. Stroll the buzzing neighbourhoods from Cinnamon Gardens to Galle Face Green. (p56)

Polonnaruwa The ancient monuments here are in a lush park-like setting that rewards walkers ready to explore. (p206)

Adam's Peak On Adam's Peak you can walk in the footsteps of the Buddha with hundreds of pilgrims. (p163)

Knuckles Range Rain soaked and densely vegetated, the Knuckles Range is no walk in the park, but it offers the most exciting hiking in the country. (p161)

Galle After you've explored the endlessly walkable Fort, continue on around the bay to the tropical fantasy of Jungle Beach. (p104)

Buddhist Temples

More than 2000 years of religious heritage can be found in the temples, great and small, that dot this small island. Time your visit with a festival for an extraordinary experience.

Gangaramaya Temple One of several temples in the capital that have high-profile celebrations through the year. (p63)

Mulkirigala Hiding inside a series of cleft-like caves and dangling off a rocky crag is this beautiful and little-visited temple. (p128)

Temple of the Sacred Tooth Relic Containing a tooth of the Buddha, this is the heart and soul of Sri Lankan Buddhism. (p145)

Sri Maha Bodhi The world's oldest documented human-planted living tree is the focus of this very sacred site in the heart of Anuradhapura. (p215)

Mihintale This temple of legends has more than 1800 legendary steps to its mountaintop location. (p223)

Nagadipa A simple temple on a little island in the far north where the Buddha, legend goes, once visited. (p275)

Wildlife

The island may be small but the animals are big, especially the herds of Asian elephants that live inside and outside the national parks. Leopards and water buffaloes are just some of the other creatures.

Yala National Park Drawing crowds like only a spotty big cat can, a leopard safari in Yala National Park is a Sri Lankan highlight. (p138)

Uda Walawe National Park If you've ever wanted to see a wild elephant, you're unlikely to find a better place to do so than at this park. (p188)

Minneriya National Park Already a good place to see elephants and other animals, this park is the site of 'the Gathering', when more than 400 pachy-

Top: Making an offering to Buddha, Galle (p104)
Bottom: Beach, Batticaloa lighthouse (p245)

derms gather in an awesome spectacle. (p213)

Kumana National Park Leopards, elephants and birds galore at this park that's much less crowded than its popular neighbour, Yala. (p213)

Pottuvil Lagoon safaris can bring you titillatingly close to elephants, monitor lizards and crocodiles. (p237)

Shopping

Being a lush country, it's not surprising that some of Sri Lanka's best goods are what it grows. Tea is an obvious purchase; all manner of spices another. In addition there are various handicrafts and a growing range of designer items.

Colombo Of course the capital has good shopping. What's surprising is just how good it is. Stylish designer boutiques, galleries and markets galore sell just about anything you might want, with plenty of surprises on offer. (p80)

Negombo Charming and ramshackle Negombo has a busy town centre full of shopping Sri Lankans, and a beachfront lined with tourist souvenir shops. (p86)

Galle With a surfeit of classy little galleries, independent designer boutiques and quirky bric-a-brac shops, Galle is a fascinating place for shoppers to explore. (p114)

Hill Country At tea plantations and factories you can buy excellent teas – many hard to find elsewhere – at good prices. (p142)

Ayurveda

Ayurveda is an ancient system of medicine and therapies designed to heal and rejuvenate. It's widely used in Sri Lanka for a range of ailments and draws many visitors each year; some stay in clinics and spas for weeks.

Spa Ceylon (p69) and **Siddhalepa Ayurveda** (p70) Rejuvenate in luxury and enjoy a full range of treatments in Colombo; the capital's market district of Pettah also has Ayurveda shops.

Sanctuary Spa A hard day swimming in the energetic surf of Unawatuna can be followed by long sessions getting your inner balance restored. (p116)

Ayurveda Pavilions In Negombo, Pavilions offers rooms that include spa treatments. (p90)

Barberyn Reef Ayurveda Resort A complete health resort in Beruwela, offerings include yoga and meditation. (p96)

Heritance Ayurveda Maha Gedara A west coast retreat where the quality of the resort matches the quality of the treatments. (p96)

Heritage Sites

Unesco has recognised eight World Heritage Sites in Sri Lanka, an impressive number for a small island.

Galle Fort The Dutch fort forms Sri Lanka's most beautiful urban environment: stroll the walls at sunset. (p105)

Kandy The Royal City and temples are the heart of Sri Lankan culture. (p144)

Sinharaja Forest Reserve One of the last remaining slabs of dense montane rainforest in Sri Lanka is a birdwatcher's dream. (p189)

Dambulla The cave temples and their extraordinary paintings are works of art. (p197)

Sigiriya The rock monastery which, yes, many people still think was a fort or temple; on a clear day you can see forever from the top. (p200)

Polonnaruwa A vast range of surviving structures of the medieval capital. (p206)

Anuradhapura The sacred and the secular come together in a sprawling precinct that spans centuries of history. (p215)

Central Highlands The forests and peaks of Sri Pada Peak Wilderness (p163), Horton Plains (p173) and Knuckles Range (p161) house outstanding biodiversity.

Colonial Architecture

The Dutch, the Portuguese and the British all literally left their marks on Sri Lanka. Their legacies are today's atmospheric sights.

Colombo The Dutch-built Old Dutch Hospital is just one of many colonial beauties you can enjoy in the capital. The National Museum is in an old British compound. (p56)

Galle Fort Take a sunset walk along the perimeter of Galle's Dutch-built fort walls and you can almost feel history seep out of the ground around you. (p105)

Nuwara Eliya Stay in one of the grand old hotels of Sri Lanka's favourite colonial hill station, and the days of the Raj seem to come flickering back to life. (p166)

Jaffna Nineteenth-century homes and Portuguese-era churches, though damaged in the war, pepper the city's suburbs. (p262)

Month by Month

January

At the peak of the tourist season, when crowds are at their largest, many popular towns have special events such as the fast-growing literary festival at Galle.

✯ Duruthu Perahera

Held on the *poya* (full-moon) day at the Kelaniya Raja Maha Vihara in Colombo, and second in importance only to the huge Kandy *perahera* (procession), this festival celebrates the first of Buddha's three visits to Sri Lanka.

✯ Thai Pongal

Held in mid-January, this Hindu winter-harvest festival honours the sun god Surya. It is important to Tamils in Sri Lanka and South India. Look for the special sweet dish, *pongal*, which is made with rice, nuts and spices.

February

The tourist crowds continue with wintering Europeans baking themselves silly on the beaches. A busy month for Sri Lankans also, with an important national holiday.

✯ Independence Day

Sri Lanka gained independence on 4 February 1948 and this day is commemorated every year with festivals, parades, fireworks, sporting events and more across the nation. In Colombo, motorcades shuffle politicians from one event to the next.

✯ Navam Perahera

First celebrated in 1979, Navam Perahera is one of Sri Lanka's biggest and most flamboyant *peraheras*. Held on the February *poya*, it starts from Gangaramaya Temple and travels around Viharamahadevi Park and Beira Lake in Colombo.

March

This is an important month for many of Sri Lanka's Buddhists and you'll see them observing Maha Sivarathri in the Ancient Cities areas and portions of the west coast where they are in the majority.

✯ Maha Sivarathri

In late February or early March the Hindu festival of Maha Sivarathri commemorates the marriage of Shiva to Parvati with all-night vigils and more. It's the most important day for Shaivites, who comprise the majority of Sri Lanka's Hindus.

April

Although Christians comprise only 6% of Sri Lanka's population, secularised versions of Christian holidays are popular. Don't be surprised when you see an Easter bunny at the mall.

✯ Aurudu (New Year)

New Year's Eve (13 April) and New Year's Day (14 April) are nonreligious holidays. There is a period between the old and new year called the 'neutral period'; all activities are meant to cease, although buses and trains are jammed.

May

The Yala monsoon blows in for five months, bringing huge rains from the Indian Ocean that drench the Hill Country and the beach towns in the southwest.

Vesak Poya

This two-day holiday commemorates the birth, enlightenment and death of the Buddha. Amid the festivities, the high point is the lighting of paper lanterns and displays of coloured lights outside every Buddhist home, shop and temple. Night-time Colombo is a riot of colours.

June

Sri Lanka's Buddhists barely have a chance to catch their breath after Vesak before another major religious event occurs – and they'll want to catch their breath...

Poson Poya

The Poson *poya* day celebrates the bringing of Buddhism to Sri Lanka by Mahinda. In Anuradhapura there are festivities in the famous temples, while in nearby Mihintale thousands of white-clad pilgrims ascend the lung-busting 1843 steps to the topmost temple.

July

Light-bulb vendors do a huge business as Buddhists gear up for Esala Perahera, which begins at the end of the month. Light displays are an integral part of the Kandy festivities, with a parade of light-bulb-decorated elephants.

Vel

This festival is held in Colombo and Jaffna. In Colombo the gilded chariot of Murugan (Skanda), the god of war, is ceremonially hauled from Pettah to Bambalapitiya. In Jaffna the Nallur Kandaswamy Kovil has a 25-day festival.

Kataragama

Another important Hindu festival is held at Kataragama, where devotees put themselves through a whole gamut of ritual masochism. It commemorates the triumph of the six-faced, 12-armed war god Skanda over demons here.

August

The Kandy Esala Perahera is important but smaller versions are held across Sri Lanka. Many celebrations feature dancers and other performers such as stilt-walkers who practise all year.

Kandy Esala Perahera

The Kandy Esala Perahera, Sri Lanka's most spectacular and prominent festival, is the climax of 10 days and nights of celebrations during the month of Esala. This great procession honours the sacred tooth relic of Kandy and starts in late July.

Nallur Festival

Jaffna's Nallur Kandaswamy Kovil temple is the focus of an enormous and spectacular Hindu festival over 25 days in July and August, which climaxes on day 24 with parades of juggernaut floats and gruesome displays of self-mutilation by entranced devotees.

October

This is a month of meteorological mystery as it falls between the two great monsoon seasons. Rains and squalls can occur almost any place, any time.

POYA

Every *poya* (full-moon) day is a holiday. *Poya* causes buses, trains and accommodation to fill up, especially if it falls on a Friday or Monday. No alcohol is supposed to be sold on *poya* days, and some establishments close. Some hotels and guesthouses discreetly provide thirsty guests with a cold beer 'under the table'.

Note that the official full-moon day for *poya* does not always coincide with the same designated full-moon day in Western calendars. Because of the religious time used to calculate the exact moment of full moon, the *poya* day may be a day earlier or later than that shown on regular calendars.

✹ Deepavali

The Hindu festival of lights takes place in late October or early November. Thousands of flickering oil lamps celebrate the triumph of good over evil and the return of Rama after his period of exile.

December

Sri Lanka's second annual monsoon season, the Maha, brings huge rains to the northeast part of the island.

✹ Adam's Peak

The pilgrimage season, when pilgrims of all faiths (and the odd tourist) climb Adam's Peak near Ella, starts in December and lasts until mid-April. The trek begins shortly after midnight so that everyone can be in place for sunrise.

✹ Unduvap Poya

This full-moon day commemorates Sangamitta, who brought a cutting from the sacred Bodhi Tree in India in 288 BC to Anuradhapura. The resulting tree, the Sri Maha Bodhi, is considered the oldest living human-planted tree in the world. The ceremonies attract thousands in their finest.

✹ Christmas

Outside of Sri Lanka's Christian communities – mostly around Colombo – this day has become a popular secularised holiday. Ersatz versions of Western Christmas traditions can be found across the nation, from bone-thin Santas in strange masks to garish artificial trees.

Top: Nallur festival (p267), Jaffna
Bottom: Pilgrims, Temple of the Sacred Tooth Relic (p145), Kandy

Itineraries

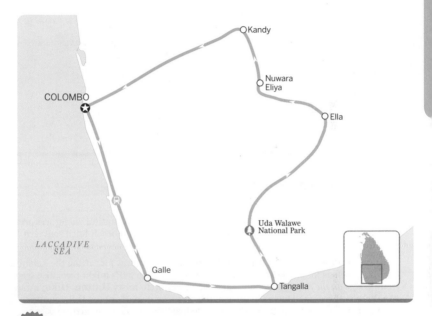

COLOMBO

Kandy

Nuwara Eliya

Ella

Uda Walawe National Park

Galle

Tangalla

LACCADIVE SEA

1 WEEK Essential Sri Lanka

This compact trip covers a core selection of Sri Lanka's must-see sights.

Start in **Colombo**, exploring the markets and visiting the city's vibrant Buddhist temples. Then take the train south along the coast to amazing **Galle**, avoiding the often traffic-clogged road on the west coast and the ho-hum towns along it.

From Galle, go get some beach time. The **Tangalla** region has a growing selection of lovely beach places on its beautiful and uncrowded ribbon of sand. Head inland and venture up to **Uda Walawe National Park**, where you'll see dozens of elephants and many other animals. Take the winding road up into the heart of the Hill Country and put down roots for a few days in **Ella**, a cool town with a fun travellers' vibe.

Take one of the world's most beautiful train rides to the stop for the British colonial heritage town of **Nuwara Eliya**, where you'll enter a time warp. Visit tea plantations and stop in iconic **Kandy** for temples and gardens. From here it's an easy jaunt back to Colombo or the airport.

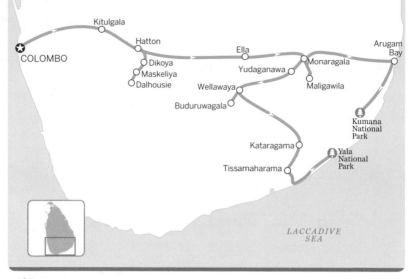

 **Natural South**

It's not a big island but Sri Lanka still manages to have some beautiful wilderness areas, especially in the tropical peaks and valleys, national parks and beach-lined southern coast.

Start in **Colombo**. On your way east, **Kitulgala** is a gateway for rafting the Kelaniya Ganga, as well as for jungle hikes and birdwatching. Movie buffs might recognise scenes from *Bridge on the River Kwai* here. Take the short hop to misty **Hatton**, **Dikoya** and **Maskeliya**, three small towns in some of the most scenic parts of the Hill Country. Spend a few days tasting fragrant single-estate teas and bed down in luxurious ex-colonial tea planters' bungalows, or cosy guesthouses in **Dalhousie**, the traditional starting point for the pre-dawn ascent of Adam's Peak.

Head east to **Ella** for more hiking, wonderful views and guesthouses renowned for having some of Sri Lanka's tastiest home-cooked food. Continue to **Monaragala**, a low-key gateway to the east and the jumping-off point for one of Sri Lanka's most atmospheric ancient Buddhist sites at **Yudaganawa**. Also nearby, **Maligawila** is home to an 11m-tall standing Buddha that's more than a thousand years old.

On the coast is the ever-more-popular **Arugam Bay**, with its easygoing surfers' vibe and excellent seafood. It's easy to spend an extra day or three here, swinging in a hammock at one of the beach guesthouses. Don't miss a boat trip exploring the nearby Pottuvil Lagoon. Explore the seldom-visited wilds of **Kumana National Park**, then veer back inland via Monaragala to **Wellawaya**, and find time for a brief detour to Sri Lanka's tallest standing Buddha at **Buduruwagala**. Soak up the beauty of the tiny lakes and listen to the birds.

Descend from Wellawaya to the coastal plains of **Kataragama**, the terminus of the Pada Yatra, a pilgrimage that begins at the other end of the island. Nearby **Tissamaharama** has a lovely lakeside setting, which is also a convenient entry point for the hugely popular safaris into **Yala National Park**, where you can spot elephants, leopards and most of Sri Lanka's other iconic critters.

Top: Newburgh Green Tea Factory (p180), Ella

Bottom: Cave temples, Dambulla (p197)

CHRISTIAN KOBER / GETTY IMAGES ©

Emerging North

Visitors are now discovering the beauty, beaches and culture of Sri Lanka's north, which was off-limits for many years. Roads and rails services have been greatly improved.

Start at **Kalpitiya**, the main town on the long finger of land that juts up into the Indian Ocean. The beaches here are just OK but the kitesurfing and reef diving are spectacular. Hook your way around north to **Wilpattu National Park**. This treasure has leopards and many other large mammals.

Next, explore another beautiful spit of Sri Lanka extending into the sea: **Mannar** is technically an island but feels like a peninsula. It has white beaches and African baobab trees. From remote **Talaimannar**, Adam's Bridge, a chain of reefs and islets, almost forms a land bridge to India.

Hook around again to the Jaffna peninsula. On the mainland near the coast, 13km east of Mannar Town, imposing **Thirukketeeswaram Kovil** is one of the *pancha ishwaram*, the five historical Sri Lankan Shiva temples established to protect the island from natural disaster.

As you head north on the much-improved A9 highway, stop at Murukandy's tiny **Ankaran Temple**. Locals believe that a prayer here will ensure a safe journey. Further on, marvel at the wetlands beauty as you cross the **Elephant Pass** causeway to **Jaffna**, where the rich Tamil culture is rebounding and temples on shady backstreets await exploration.

Visit **Keerimalai Spring**, a sacred site with legendary bathing pools. It's close to the Naguleswaram Shiva Kovil, which traces its past to the 6th century BC. Your next destination is **Point Pedro**, with its long swath of lonely white sand at Munai Beach.

Jaffna has nearby islands well worth exploring for their sheer minimalistic beauty, including **Nainativu**, a tiny speck of sand with Buddhist and Hindu temples, and **Neduntivu**, a windswept place beyond the end of the road where wild ponies roam.

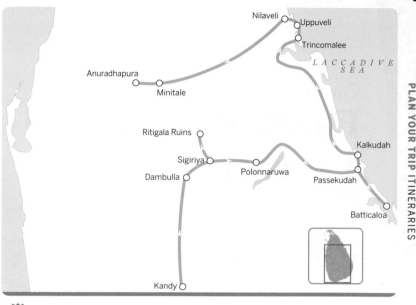

 The Cultured Centre

This tour covers the uncrowded middle of Sri Lanka, which is at the heart of the country's rich culture. You'll see ancient temples and towns, along with some of the natural beauty that has inspired generations.

Start in **Kandy**, which has a lakeside setting with real natural beauty and was the capital of the last Sinhalese kingdom until the early 19th century.

Head north to **Dambulla**, with its series of cave shrines painted with vivid Buddhist murals. From here it's a short jaunt to **Sigiriya**, a 200m-tall rock outcrop that was once a monastery and is truly one of the island's most amazing sights. A short drive northwest will bring you to the Ritigala Strict Nature Preserve. Deep inside this land is one of Sri Lanka's most mysterious sites: the **Ritigala Ruins**. Your inner Indiana Jones will enjoy exploring the remains of this once vast and ancient place.

Further east the former royal capital of **Polonnaruwa** offers an inspiring collection of Buddhist sculptures and monastery ruins dating back nearly a thousand years. Continue east to the coast and the beaches at **Kalkudah** and **Passekudah**. The former is a deserted and beautiful broad strip of sand. The latter is seeing much development.

Follow the coast south to **Batticaloa**, a historic port that has provided refuge to ships for years. It has a Dutch fort, while offshore is one of Sri Lanka's most fabled dive sites: the HMS *Hermes*, a British aircraft carrier sunk in WWII.

Going north you'll pass through nature preserves and deserted beaches until you reach the idyllic natural harbour of **Trincomalee**. It has a colourful history going back centuries. Continue on to the beach towns of tiny **Uppuveli** and buzzy **Nilaveli**.

Now head due west into the heart of the country. Prepare for a steep climb up the hillside at **Minitale** to appreciate the Buddhist history here that dates back to the 3rd century BC. A mere 13km further west brings you to **Anuradhapura**, one of the top sights in all of South Asia. Wander or bike around this sprawling landscape of temples, ruins and more.

Plan Your Trip

Eat & Drink Like a Local

Combining intricate flavours, incredibly fresh produce and a culinary heritage that blends indigenous and extraneous influences Sri Lanka is perhaps the original Spice Island. Eating out here is a delight, whether it's tucking into an authentic roadside rice and curry or enjoying surf-fresh seafood from an oceanfront restaurant table.

The Year in Fruit

Sri Lanka's diverse topography means that the variety of fruit is staggering.

Year-Round

Many fruits including bananas (more than 20 varieties!), papayas and pineapples are available year-round.

Apr–Jun

The first mangoes appear in April in the north: the Karuthakolamban (or Jaffna) mango thrives in dry parts of the island and is prized for its golden flesh and juicy texture. Rambutans (peculiar-looking red-skinned fruits with hairy skin), meanwhile, are at their best in June. They taste like lychees; you'll see them stacked in pyramids by the roadside.

Jul–Sep

It's peak season for durian, that huge spiky yellow love-it-or-hate-it fruit that smells so pungent that it's banned on the Singapore metro – you won't find this one on the breakfast buffet. Mangosteens, delicately flavoured purple-skinned fruit, are also harvested at this time. The fruit do not travel well, so it's best to sample these at source in the tropics.

Food Experiences

Seafood Heaven

➡ **Elita Restaurant** (p113), Galle. For lighthouse views and seafood to die for.

➡ **Crab** (p253), Uppuveli. Beachside dining, great local crab and a romantic atmosphere.

➡ **Bu Ba** (p78), Colombo. With candlelit tables right on Mt Lavinia beach.

➡ **Cool Spot** (p101), Hikkaduwa. Family-run and serves a superb seafood platter.

Meals of a Lifetime

➡ **Ministry of Crab** (p75), Colombo. A highly atmospheric seafood institution inside the capital's Old Dutch Hospital.

➡ **Fortaleza** (p113), Galle. Delicious Western or Sri Lankan food in the historic Fort quarter of Galle.

➡ **Hill Club** (p172), Nuwara Eliya. A classic baronial-style dining room with British menu and adjacent billiards room.

Colonial Class

➡ **The Sanctuary at Tissawewa** (p222), Anuradhapura. Refined dining in the former residence of a British governor.

➡ **Fits Margosa** (p268), Jaffna. This 19th-century manor house makes a sublime setting for a memorable meal.

➡ **Olde Empire Cafe** (p154), Kandy. A revamped menu and renovated premises make this place a winner.

➡ **Royal Dutch Cafe** (p113), Galle. Sip fine teas and coffees or enjoy a meal in this elegant colonnaded structure.

Cafe Cool

➡ **Hansa Coffee** (p78), Colombo. Arguably Colombo's best coffee, sourced from a renowned island estate.

➡ **Pedlar's Inn Cafe** (p113), Galle. Order a cappuccino and enjoy the historic surrounds.

➡ **Dutch Bank Cafe** (p250), Trincomalee. Great snacks and meals in a converted colonial building that faces the harbour.

➡ **Dambulla Heritage Resthouse Cafe** (p200), Dambulla. Tour the caves, then recharge with a coffee here.

➡ **Queens Art Cafe** (p119), Unawatuna. An inviting shady spot for a bite and a drink, just off the beach.

➡ **Barefoot Garden Cafe** (p76), Colombo. Stylish courtyard cafe in the Barefoot gallery.

Time for Tea

➡ **High Tea at the Grand** (p171), Nurwara Eliya. For cucumber sandwiches, dainty cakes and a vast selection of different teas.

➡ **Ceylon Tea Moments** (p76), Colombo. Upmarket tea emporium with plush furnishings and speciality teas.

➡ **T-Lounge** (p75), Colombo. An atmospheric setting for a cuppa in a landmark building.

➡ **Chaplon Tea Centre** (☑034 493 7293; Galle Rd), Bentota. Take tea and biscuits on the terrace, then browse the high-grade leaf teas for sale.

➡ **Mlesna Tea Centre** (p179), Bandarawela. Acclaimed tea shop in the heart of tea country.

Cheap Treats

➡ **Kotthu** A stir-fried combo of chopped *rotti* bread, vegies and spices. Try it at the Hotel De Pilawoos (p77) in Colombo.

➡ **Paratha** A filling flatbread that's pan-fried on a hot plate. Those at Mangos (p269) in Jaffna are excellent.

➡ **Vadai** Generic term for disc or doughnut-shaped deepfried snack, usually made from lentils.

➡ **Coconut Rotti** Sold by street vendors, locals eat this toasted minibread with a chilli salt topping.

➡ **Samosa** The ubiquitous snack, usually stuffed with spicy cooked vegies.

Cooking Classes

Sri Lanka does not have an abundance of places offering cooking classes, but as interest grows the possibilities are expanding.

➡ **Barberyn Reef Ayurveda Resort** (p96), south of Colombo.

➡ **Mamas Galle Fort** (p112), Galle.

➡ **Serendipity Arts Cafe** (p113), Galle.

➡ **Sonjas Health Food Restaurant** (p117), Unawatuna.

➡ **Rice Villa** (p212), Giritale.

➡ **Rawana Holiday Resort** (p181), Ella.

Sri Lankan Specialities

Rice is the staple of Sri Lankan cuisine and the national dish (rice and curry), and rice flour is also a basis for some unique foods. Many Sri Lankans are vegetarian, so meat-free eating is easy and vegetables are plentiful. Coconut is also added to most dishes. 'Devilled dishes' are any type of meat or fish cooked in a spicy, sweet-and-sour style sauce with onion and peppers.

Rice

Hoppers Bowl-shaped pancakes (also called *appa* or *appam*) made from rice flour, coconut milk and palm toddy. If eggs are added it becomes an egg hopper. *Sambol* (a condiment made from ingredients pounded with chilli) is often added for flavouring.

Dosas *(thosai)* Paper-thin pancakes made from rice batter and usually served stuffed with spiced vegetables.

Kola kanda A nutritious porridge of rice, coconut, green vegetables and herbs.

Rice and curry The national dish is a selection of spiced dishes made from vegetables, meat or fish.

Top: Jackfruit
Bottom: Masala dosa

Biryanis Fragrant basmati rice cooked with plenty of turmeric, garlic and cardamom, often with chunks of chicken or lamb.

Vegetable Dishes

Mallung Slightly like a tabbouleh, this salad combines chopped local greens (such as kale), shredded coconut and onion.

Jackfruit curry The world's biggest fruit combines beautifully with rich curry sauces, as its flesh actually has quite a meaty texture.

Breads

Bakeries are common throughout the country, but can be disappointing.

Rotti Thick flatbreads cooked on a hot plate and served with sweet or savoury filling.

Kotthu Chopped *rotti* fried with vegetables and/or egg, cheese or meat on a hot plate. Try Hotel De Pilawoos (p77) in Colombo.

Uttapam A Tamil speciality, this thick pancake is prepared with onion, chillies, peppers and vegetables.

Seafood

Jaffna crab Recipes vary but in the north tamarind and coconut are key ingredients to bring out the flavour of this unique dish.

Ambulthiyal This fish curry is a southern speciality, made with *goraka*, a fruit which gives it a sour flavour.

Condiments

Pol sambol Shredded coconut, lime juice, red onions, chilli and spices.

Lunu miris Red onions, salt, chilli powder, lime juice and dried fish.

Desserts & Sweets

Wattalappam (*vattalappam* in Tamil) A coconut milk and egg pudding with jaggery and cardamom.

Pittu Steamed in bamboo, these cylindrical cakes are made from flour and coconut.

Curd Slightly sour cream that tastes like natural yoghurt; it's served drizzled with *kitul* treacle made from raw palm sugar.

Pani pol A small pancake made with a sweet topping of cinnamon and cardamom-infused jaggery.

Bolo fiado A layered cake said to have been first introduced by the Portuguese.

How to Eat
Where to Eat

Compared with most Asia countries, Sri Lanka is quite unusual in that most locals prefer to eat at home. Things are different in beach resorts and the capital but in many towns there are actually very few restaurants, or even street food stalls. See p306 for the price ranges used throughout this guide.

Accommodation You'll usually eat breakfast in your hotel. Evening meals are often available too,

RICE & CURRY

The national dish, Sri Lankan rice and curry is a complex, intricately spiced array of individual vegetable (and often meat and fish) dishes, served with rice. Chutneys and *sambol* (a condiment made from ingredients pounded with chilli) add heat and additional flavour. Pappadoms are usually present too.

Virtually all Sri Lankan curries are based on coconut milk and a blend of spices: chilli, turmeric, cinnamon, cardamom, coriander, *rampe* (pandanus leaves), curry leaves, mustard and tamarind. Dried fish is also frequently used to season dishes.

As you're travelling around the country, you're likely to pull over at many a local restaurant for a rice and curry feed. Some of the best places are simple family-owned roadside restaurants with a selection of around five to 10 individual dishes (mainly vegetarian but there's usually a meat or fish option too).

Many restaurants only serve rice and curry at lunchtime. Guesthouses will often prepare it for dinner but you'll need to order it early in the day and leave the cooks to work their magic.

though guesthouses will ask you to order ahead, so they can purchase ingredients. Larger hotels usually offer buffet lunches and dinners with Western and local food.

'Hotels' When is a hotel not a hotel? When it's in Sri Lanka. Confusingly, restaurants here are also called 'hotels'. Usually these places are in towns and cities, pretty scruffy, and will consist of a store at the front selling snacks and drinks and tables at the rear for sit-down meals. Rice and curry is the lunchtime staple, for dinner *kotthu*, rice and noodle dishes are popular.

Restaurants In Colombo, beach resorts and tourist-geared towns (such as Galle) you'll find excellent restaurants offering everything from Italian to gourmet local cuisine.

Bakeries These sell what locals call 'short eats', essentially an array of meat-stuffed rolls, meat-and-vegetable patties (called cutlets), pastries and *vadai*. At some places, a plate of short eats is placed on your table, and you're only charged for what you eat. Many bakeries (and some restaurants) also offer a 'lunch packet', which is basically some rice and a couple of small portions of curry.

When to Eat

Sri Lankans generally eat three meals a day. Interestingly, the type of food consumed at each meal is quite distinct, so you usually won't find lunch foods (like rice and curry) available at dinner time.

Breakfast A typical local breakfast might take place around sunrise, and consist of hoppers and some fruit. Milky tea is usually taken with breakfast; in the cities some favour coffee. In hotels and guesthouses popular with tourists, Western-style breakfasts are almost always available.

Lunch Eaten between midday and 2.30pm. Rice and curry, the definitive Sri Lankan meal, is an essential experience which simply can't be missed – it can be quite a banquet or simple pitstop depending on the place.

Dinner Usually eaten between 7pm and 9pm. If you really don't fancy a hot curry for dinner, you'll find seafood and fish usually very lightly spiced, and fried rice is mild.

Drinks

Sri Lanka's heat means that refreshing beverages are an important – and vital – part of the day's consumption.

Tea & Coffee

Tea with spoonfuls of sugar and hot milk is the locally preferred way to drink the indigenous hot drink. If you don't have a sweet tooth, be very assertive about lowering the sugar dose.

Coffee, while not traditionally favoured, is now literally a hot commodity in Colombo and areas popular with tourists. Cafes with full-on espresso machines are catching on, though are not widespread as yet. Out in the sticks be prepared for instant, or something fresh-ish that tastes like instant.

Other Soft Drinks

Lime juice is excellent. Have it with soda water, but ask for the salt or sugar to be separate. If not, you could be in for another serious sugar hit. Indian restaurants and sweet shops are a good spot for a *lassi* (yoghurt drink). Ginger beer is an old school, very British option, offering refreshment with a zing – look out for the Elephant or Lion brands. *Thambili* (king coconut) juice still in the husk can be found on sale at roadside stalls everywhere.

Beer

Locally brewed Lion Lager is a crisp and refreshing brew that is widely sold. Lion also sells a very good stout, with coffee and chocolate flavours. Three Coins and Anchor are less delicious local lagers. The licensed versions of international brands like Carlsberg, Heineken and Corona offer no surprises at all.

Other Alcoholic Drinks

Toddy is a drink made from the sap of palm trees. It has a sharp taste, a bit like cider. There are three types: toddy made from coconut palms, toddy from *kitul* palms and toddy from palmyra palms. Toddy shacks are found throughout the country, but are very much a male preserve. Arrack is a fermented and (somewhat) refined toddy. It can have a powerful kick and give you a belting hangover. The best mixer for arrack is the local ginger ale.

Fishing boats, Mirissa (p123)

Plan Your Trip
Beaches & Activities

From remote pristine beaches to whale-watching tours and a whole host of water-based activities, the Sri Lankan coast has something to offer everyone. Lie back, hang 10 or simply breathe deeply – we have all options covered.

Best for ...

Diving & Snorkelling

Pigeon Island, off Nilaveli beach, offers crystal waters, shallow reefs, colourful fish, and diving and snorkelling that's great for a beginner or the experienced.

Whale-Watching

Whales can be seen all along the Sri Lankan coast but Mirissa is the best base for seeing the blue whales that splash past Dondra Head.

White-Water Rafting

As the Kelaniya Ganga tumbles out of the mountains and passes through Kitulgala it produces the best white-water rafting in the country.

Indulgence

Bentota beach has an unrivalled collection of sublime boutique hotels, and when you're done with pampering, the beach itself ain't bad.

Solitude

We almost want to keep this one to ourselves, but seeing as you asked nicely... Talalla beach is utterly empty and utterly divine – for the moment.

When to Go

Sri Lanka is pretty much a year-round beach destination. When it's raining in the East, it's normally sunny in the West and vice versa.

➡ The main tourist season coincides with the northeast monsoon, which runs from December to March. At this time the beaches on the west and south coasts are bathed in sunshine and the tourist industry for this part of the country is in full swing. The east coast, by contrast, is often wet and many hotels are closed.

➡ Between May and September, when the stronger southwest monsoon hits the island and the southwest coast is drenched, head straight for the east coast, which sits in the rain shadow of the highlands and will be sunny and idyllic.

➡ Don't take the seasons as gospel: even during the height of the southwest monsoon it can often be sunny in the morning on the west-coast beaches before afternoon thunderstorms roll in.

➡ The north of the island is generally much drier so you could come here any time and get your beach towel out.

Beaches

For many people the beach *is* Sri Lanka, and, small though the island is, it really is no slouch in the sand and sea department.

➡ The west coast is the most developed beach area and is where the majority of the package-tour resorts can be found, but don't let that put you off because some of the beaches here are up there with the best in the country.

➡ With its stunning beaches, good selection of accommodation and activities that range from diving to sunning to surfing, it's no surprise that the south coast of the island is the most popular area with beach-bound independent travellers. However, heavy development is bringing more package tourists.

➡ For years war and unrest had kept the east coast beaches largely off the radar of all but the most adventurous, but with peace a coastline littered with excellent beaches is now ripe for the picking for all comers. New hotels are springing up fast but the east is still much less developed than the west or south.

➡ Finally, there's the far north, where a beach to yourself isn't just a possibility but more of a given. However, tourist development up here remains minimal and locals aren't used to foreign beach worshippers.

Safe Swimming

Every year drownings occur off Sri Lanka's beaches. If you aren't an experienced swimmer or surfer, it's easy to underestimate the dangers – or be totally unaware of them. (Don't worry, not all Sri Lanka's beaches are surf battered: Unawatuna, Passekudah and Uppuveli all vie with one another for title of calmest, safest swimming beach and are perfect for less confident swimmers and children.) There are few full-time lifesaving patrols, so there's usually no one to jump in and rescue you. A few common-sense rules should be observed:

➡ Don't swim out of your depth. If you are a poor swimmer, always stay in the shallows.

➡ Don't stay in the water when you feel tired.

➡ Never go swimming under the influence of alcohol or drugs.

➡ Supervise children at *all* times.

➡ Watch out for rips. Water brought onto the beach by waves is sucked back to sea and this current can be strong enough to drag you out with it. Rips in rough surf can sometimes be seen as calm patches in the disturbed water. It's best to check with someone reliable before venturing into the water.

➡ If you do get caught in a rip, swim *across* the current towards the breaking waves. The currents are usually less where the waves are actually breaking and the surf will push you shoreward. Never try and swim against the current. If it's too strong for you to swim across it, keep afloat and raise a hand so that someone on shore can see that you are in distress. A rip eventually weakens; the important thing is not to panic.

➡ Exercise caution when there is surf.

➡ Beware of coral; coming into contact with coral can be painful for the swimmer and fatal for the coral. Always check with someone reliable if you suspect the area you're about to swim in may have coral.

GILLIANNE TEDDER / GETTY IMAGES ©

Kitesurfer

➡ Never dive head-first into the water. Hazards may be lurking under the surface or the water may not be as deep as it looks. It pays to be cautious.

BEACH CULTURE IN THE NORTH & EAST

By and large Sri Lankans are an easygoing and accepting lot, and on the south and west coasts they are also very used to foreign tourists and their skimpy beachwear. For much of the East and North, though, the situation is a little different: women in bathing suits, even modest one-piece numbers, can attract a lot of unwelcome attention. Even in the now very popular east-coast beach resorts such as Arugam Bay and the beaches north of Trincomalee the attention can be excessive (and there have been sexual assaults). On these beaches and especially in more remote locations, women will not want to travel alone, and should consider wearing a T-shirt and shorts into the water. Even in the more trodden beaches in the south and west it's worth remembering that the vast majority of Sri Lankans remain very conservative and that few local women would dare wear a bikini, so although nobody is likely to say anything to you about wearing one on a tourist beach you will risk causing offence, and possibly worse, if you leave the beach and venture off around the village or town in skimpy clothing.

Surfers, Hikkaduwa (p98)

Surfing

Sri Lanka has consistent surf year-round, but the quality of waves is far lower than the nearby Maldives and Indonesia. You visit Sri Lanka more for the culture, climate and ease of travelling than for the chance to get barrelled.

On the east coast, surf's up from April to October. On the west and south coasts, the best surfing is from November to April, with the start and end of this season more consistent than January and February when, bizarrely, most surfers choose to visit. On the flip side, however, the swells at this time can be less clean and come with a more easterly wind to them, which can badly affect some spots.

Sri Lanka is a superb place to learn how to surf or for intermediate surfers to get their first reef-break experiences. Many of the spots are very close to shore and surf access couldn't be easier, which also makes Sri Lanka an ideal destination for a surfer with a nonsurfing partner. Boards can be hired (expect to pay Rs 300 to Rs 500 per hour) and lessons are available at most

BEST SURF SPOTS

Arugam Bay (p233) Sri Lanka's best-known wave is at Arugam Bay on the east coast. Surf's up at this long right point from April to October.

Weligama (p123) On the south coast, Weligama seems custom-made for learning to surf, and a number of surf schools and camps have recently sprung up there.

Hikkaduwa (p99) The reefs here on the west coast are a long-time favourite, although more for the ease of living than for the quality of the waves.

Midigama (p121) This area is the best spot along the south coast, with a mellow left point, a nearby consistent beach break and a short and sharp right reef, which offers about the only frequently hollow wave in Sri Lanka.

White-water rafting, Kelaniya Ganga (p165)

Back on salty water you can organise boat or catamaran trips for sightseeing, birdwatching and fishing around Negombo, Bentota and most east-coast beach resorts.

Windsurfing & Kitesurfing

Sri Lanka isn't renowned for its windsurfing or kitesurfing but that doesn't mean there's no action. Negombo has a well-run kitesurfing school (p87) that runs trips up and down the coast. Further north, the Kalpitiya area has gained a reputation as one of the best kitesurfing areas in South Asia and there are plenty of board hire places and experienced kitesurfing (p92) schools. On that note, the far north of Sri Lanka, around Munnar Island and the islands off Jaffna have good windsurfing potential, but they remain very much off the beaten track.

Some top-end hotels and a couple of private water-sport operators around the Bentota area hire beaten-up sailboards. It's a good place for learners and lessons are possible; windsurfing courses cost around US$130.

beach towns; courses start at around €30. **Low Pressure Stormrider Guides** (www.lowpressure.co.uk) offers good advice on surfing Sri Lanka.

White-Water Rafting, Canoeing & Boating

You don't have to be a beach babe to enjoy Sri Lankan water sports. High up in the hills, rivers tumble down mountains to produce some memorable rafting conditions.

Currently the best-known white-water rafting area is near Kitulgala, where a number of different operators can take you out on gentle river meanders (around US$30 per person) or, for experienced rafters, exciting descents of Class 4–5 rapids. Adventure Sports Lanka (p316) is the biggest player in Sri Lankan rafting and organises rafting expeditions to Kitulgala and elsewhere from its Colombo base. The Belihul Oya area of the Hill Country is also gaining a reputation for kayaking and other river-borne sports.

Whale- & Dolphin-Watching

Sri Lanka is fast gaining a reputation for being a world-class whale-watching location. The big attraction is big indeed – blue whales, the largest of all creatures. Mirissa (p124) is the best place from which to organise a whale-watching trip. On the east coast, Uppuveli and Nilaveli offer quieter but less-reliable whale-watching and in the northwest the Kalpitiya area (p92) is popular, although here schools of dolphins are more common than whales.

In all these places local boat tours are available, but it pays to go with someone who really knows what they're doing. **Eco Team Sri Lanka** (☑011-583 0833; www.srilankaecotourism.com; 20/63 Fairfield Gardens, Colombo) is first-rate and offers whale-watching (and dolphin-watching) tours to all of these places.

SARANGA DEVA DE ALWIS / GETTY IMAGES ©

Top: Unawatuna (p115)
Bottom: Dolphins

BEST DIVE SPOTS

Great Basses Reefs (p137) Several kilometres off the southeast coast, these remote reefs are ranked by divers as about the best in the country. Eagle rays and white-tip sharks are the big fish to see here. And just in case you're interested, treasure from sunken ships has been found here too... But take note – the reefs are for experts only.

Bar Reef (p92) These offshore reefs in the northwest of the country offer pristine reef systems, masses of fish and dolphins and whales to boot, but again it's for experienced divers only.

Pigeon Island (p253) Accessible for beginners but still rewarding for experts, the beautiful, colour-splashed reefs off this pinprick of an island put a smile on everyone's face. Around 300 species of fish and other marine life have been seen in the waters around here. Also a great snorkelling spot.

Unawatuna (p117) It's all about wreck diving here – one boat was even sunk exclusively for the purpose of improving the diving. Several dive schools, lots of facilities and good for all levels of experience.

Batticaloa (p243) Calm waters and exploring the wreck of HMS *Hermes*, a WWII British naval ship.

Negombo (p87) Looking at the rather brown waters here you might not expect it to be a very good dive area, but that brown water hides reefs bustling with fish just offshore.

The season for whales (and dolphins) off the south coast and Kalpitiya is from January to April, while on the east coast it runs from May to October.

Diving & Snorkelling

There are plenty of opportunities to live like a fish in Sri Lanka. Dive schools can be found all along the coast (except the far north) and you can slap on a snorkel almost anywhere. Diving and snorkelling in Sri Lanka is more about the fish than the reefs, but there are a few exceptions and wreck diving is also possible. Sri Lanka has the full dose of tropical Indian Ocean fish species including such pretty little numbers as angel fish, butterfly fish, surgeon fish and scorpion fish. Higher up the gnashing-teeth scale come the black- and white-tip sharks.

Along the west coast, the best time to dive and snorkel is generally from November to April. On the east coast, the seas are calmest from April to September. But at none of these times can underwater visibility be described as breathtaking.

Diving shops can be found in the major west-coast resorts. They hire and sell gear, including snorkelling equipment. PADI courses cost around €265 to €340 and are also available with the following respected dive schools:

➡ **Poseidon Diving Station** (p98), Hikkaduwa.

➡ **Unawatuna Diving Centre** (p117), Unawatuna.

➡ **Sport Diving** (p123), Weligama.

➡ **Sri Lanka Diving Tours** (p243), Batticaloa.

➡ **Poseidon Diving School** (p254), Nilaveli.

➡ **Colombo Divers** (p87), Negombo.

Safety Guidelines for Diving

Before embarking on a scuba-diving trip, carefully consider the following points to ensure a safe and enjoyable experience:

➡ Possess a current diving certification card from a recognised scuba-diving instructional agency.

➡ Be sure you are healthy and feel comfortable diving.

➡ Obtain reliable information about physical and environmental conditions at the dive site (eg from a reputable local dive operation).

➡ Dive only at sites within your realm of experience; if available, engage the services of a competent, professionally trained dive instructor or dive master.

Plan Your Trip

National Parks & Safaris

Sri Lanka is one of the finest wildlife-watching countries in South Asia. The island may be small in size, but the variety of habitats, and the wildlife found there, would do justice to a country many times its size. Even a visitor with only the most casual of interest can't help but be overawed by the sight of great herds of elephants, enormous whales, elusive leopards, schools of dolphins, hundreds of colourful birds, and reefs teeming with rainbow-coloured fish.The Sri Lankan tourism industry hasn't been slow to cotton on to the country's wildlife-watching potential, and an impressive array of national parks, protected zones and safari options exist that allow anyone, from dedicated naturalists to interested lay persons, to get out there with a pair of binoculars and make the most of the Sri Lankan wilderness.

Wildlife by Region

West, South & East

The west is best for marine life, but Wilpattu National Park has large mammals, and birders will like Muthurajawela Marsh. The south coast is home to whales and turtles, and Yala National Park is one of the best places in Asia to see leopards. In the east there are quiet national parks and bird species that prefer drier climates than the west and south.

The Hill Country

The hills have rainforests, moorlands and savannah parks with everything from elephants to endemic high country birds.

The Ancient Cities

Numerous national parks are filled with big ticket mammals and offer great dry country birding. Even the region's ruined cities provide ideal habitat for many creatures.

Wildlife

For its size, Sri Lanka boasts an incredible diversity of animalia: 92 mammal species, 242 butterflies, 435 birds, 107 fish, 98 snakes and more. Given the fragility of the environment in which they live, it should come as no surprise that quite a few are vulnerable.

Mammals

Sri Lanka's mammals include some of the most easily observable of the country's animal species, as well as some of the most invisible. Hard to spot are the solitary and mostly nocturnal leopard, Sri Lanka's top predator; the scavenging golden jackal; the shaggy sloth bear; the civet (a catlike hunter related to the weasel); the mongoose; and the shy, armour-plated Indian pangolin, with overlapping scales made from modified hair.

Very audible, but not always visible, are troops of tree-bound cackling primates, such as common langurs, also known as Hanuman or grey langurs; endemic

BEST PLACES FOR ELEPHANTS

Uda Walawe National Park (p188) With around 500 elephants present year-round, this park offers the most reliable elephant-spotting in the country.

Minneriya National Park (p213) Each August hundreds of elephants home in on this park in an elephant spectacle known as 'the Gathering'.

Kaudulla National Park (p213) More than 250 elephants call this park home.

Bundala National Park (p134) Consistent elephant sightings in a beautiful watery setting.

Yala National Park (p138) Lots of elephants but surprisingly hard to see.

purple-faced langurs; hairy bear monkeys; and toque macaques, notable for their distinctive thatch of middle-parted hair. The slow movements of the slender loris belie its ability to snatch its prey with a lightning-quick lunge.

More often seen, albeit at different times of the day, are the majestic Asian elephant; the omnivorous and tusked wild boar of Sri Lanka; and cervine creatures like the big, maned sambar and smaller white-spotted Axis deer. The bushy-tailed, five-striped palm squirrel is commonly seen scurrying around gardens and town parks. These are often also the locations of the large trees in which Indian flying foxes (large fruit-eating bats) camp by the hundreds.

Mammals don't just hide out in the forests and savannahs. The biggest of all mammals are to be found in the waters off Sri Lanka. Blue whales and slightly smaller sperm whales swim along migration corridors off the coast here. The area around Dondra Head, at the southern tip of the country, is being hyped as the best place in the world to see blue whales.

Birds

A tropical climate, long isolation from the Asian mainland and a diversity of habitats have helped endow Sri Lanka with an astonishing abundance of birdlife. There are more than 400 species, 26 of which are unique to Sri Lanka; others are found only in Sri Lanka and adjacent South India. Of the estimated 198 migrant species, most of which are in residence from August to April, the waders (sandpipers, plovers etc) are the long-distance champions, making the journey from their breeding grounds in the Arctic tundra.

Birders may wish to contact the **Field Ornithology Group of Sri Lanka** (www. fogsl.net), the national affiliate of Birdlife International.

Tips for Birdwatchers

➡ Visit a variety of habitats – rainforest, urban parks and bodies of water in the dry zone – to see the full diversity of birdlife in Sri Lanka.

➡ February to March is the best time for birdwatching. You will miss the monsoons, and the migrant birds will still be visiting.

➡ Waterbirds are active for most of the day.

➡ Although morning is always the best time to go birdwatching, in the evening you will see noisy flocks of birds preparing to roost.

➡ Consider taking a tour with a specialist if you're keen to see the endemic species and achieve a healthy birdwatching tally, particularly if time is short.

BEST PLACES FOR BIRDS

Sinharaja Forest Reserve (p189) A slab of rainforest with around 160 bird species.

Knuckles Range (p161) Little-known montane forests filled with hill-country and forest birds.

Bundala National Park (p134) This wetland park is the classic Sri Lankan birdwatching destination.

Yala (p138) **& Kumana** (p239) **National Parks** Superb low-country birdwatching with around 150 species present.

Muthurajawela Marsh (p86) Excellent wetland birding close to Colombo.

Pottuvil Lagoon (p237) Numerous waders and waterbirds in this little-visited east-coast wetland.

ADITYA SINGH / GETTY IMAGES ©

Top: Elephant, Yala
National Park (p138)

Bottom: Leopard,
Wilpattu National Park,
(p93)

MAJOR NATIONAL PARKS & RESERVES

PARK	AREA	FEATURES	BEST TIME TO VISIT
Bundala National Park	62.2 sq km	coastal lagoon, migratory birds, elephants	year-round
Gal Oya National Park	629.4 sq km	grasslands, evergreen forest, deer, Senanayake Samudra (tank), elephants, sloth bears, leopards, water buffaloes	Dec-Sep
Horton Plains National Park	31.6 sq km	Unesco World Heritage Site, montane forests, marshy grasslands, World's End precipice, sambars	Dec-Mar
Kaudulla National Park	66.6 sq km	Kaudulla Tank, evergreen forest, scrub jungle, grassy plains, elephants, leopards, sambars, fishing cats, sloth bears	Aug-Dec
Knuckles Range	175 sq km	Unesco World Heritage Site, traditional villages, hiking trails, caves, waterfalls, montane pygmy forest, evergreen forest, riverine forest, grasslands, scrub, paddy fields, 31 mammal species	Dec-May
Kumana National Park	181.5 sq km	grassland, jungle, lagoons, mangrove swamp, waterfowl	May-Sep
Lunugamvehera National Park	235 sq km	grasslands, reservoir, elephants	May-Sep
Minneriya National Park	88.9 sq km	Minneriya Tank, toque macaques, sambars, elephants, waterfowl	May-Sep
Sinharaja Forest Reserve	189 sq km	Unesco World Heritage Site, sambars, rainforest, leopards, purple-faced langurs, barking deer, 147 recorded bird species	Aug-Sep & Jan-Mar
Sri Pada Peak Wilderness Reserve	192 sq km	Unesco World Heritage Site, Adam's Peak, hiking trails	Dec-May
Uda Walawe National Park	300.2 sq km	grassland, thorn scrub, elephants, spotted deer, water buffaloes, wild boar	year-round
Wasgomuwa National Park	393.2 sq km	evergreen forest, hilly ridges, grassy plains, elephants, leopards, sloth bears	Jun-Sep
Wilpattu National Park	1317 sq km	dry woodland, scrub, saltgrass, leopards, sloth bears, deer, crocodiles	Jan-Mar
Yala National Park	141 sq km	tropical thornforest, lagoons, elephants, sloth bears, leopards, water buffaloes, lesser flamingos	Nov-Jul

Planning Your Safari

Where to Go

Where to go depends entirely on what you want to see and what kind of safari you want to take. For example Yala National Park in the far southeast is the most popular overall park and is fantastic for leopards, but it's also very busy and can become something of a circus with minibuses chasing each other around in search of cats. If you want your leopard-spotting quieter (and less certain), try Wilpattu National Park.

National Parks & Reserves

More than 2000 years ago, enlightened royalty declared certain land areas off limits to any human activity. Almost every province in the ancient kingdom of Kandy had such *udawattakelle* (sanctuaries). All animals and plants in these reserves were left undisturbed.

Today's system of parks and reserves is mostly an amalgamation of traditionally protected areas, reserves established by the British, and newly gazetted areas set aside for things like elephant corridors. There are more than 100 of these areas under government guard, covering approximately 8%

FIELD GUIDES & WILDLIFE BOOKS

There are plenty of good field guides out there. These are some of our favourites:

A Photographic Guide to Mammals of Sri Lanka (Gehan de Silva Wijeyeratne) This well-known Sri Lankan naturalist has also published extensively on the country's birds and butterflies, among other things.

A Selection of the Birds of Sri Lanka (John and Judy Banks) A slim, well-illustrated tome that's perfect for amateur birdwatchers.

A Field Guide to the Birds of Sri Lanka (John Harrison) A pricier hardback with colour illustrations; one of the best field guides available.

The Nature of Sri Lanka With stunning photographs by L Nadaraja, this is a collection of essays about Sri Lanka by eminent writers and conservationists.

What Tree Is That? (Sriyanie Miththapala and PA Miththapala) Contains handy sketches of common trees and shrubs in Sri Lanka, and includes English, Sinhala and botanical names.

of the island. They are divided into three types: strict nature reserves (no visitors allowed), national parks (visits under fixed conditions) and nature reserves (human habitation permitted). Sri Lanka also has two marine sanctuaries – the Bar Reef (west of Kalpitiya peninsula) and Hikkaduwa National Park.

Off the Beaten Track

A full 82% of Sri Lanka's land is controlled by the state in some form or another, and is therefore subject to a raft of legislation to combat destructive activity and protect sensitive areas like the scores of natural forests. The table above only includes information about 11 of the national parks and three other green spaces from among the 63 sanctuaries, a long list of forest reserves and countless wetlands both with and without official titles.

Given the overcrowding at some of the better-known natural areas, new attention has been directed to other deserving national parks, such as Lunugamvehera (which serves as a link between Yala and Uda Walawe National Parks and allows elephants to pass between the two) as an alternative to Yala, and Wasgomuwa, instead of Gal Oya or Minneriya.

Sri Lanka is a signatory to the Ramsar Convention on Wetlands, which currently recognises three coastal zones. These include Bundala National Park and the 915-hectare Madu Ganga Estuary near Balapitiya, which is 80km south of Colombo on the A2, and site of one of the last pristine mangrove forests in Sri Lanka. There is also the Annaivilundawa Tanks Wildlife Sanctuary, just west of the A3 and about 100km north of Colombo, a cluster of ancient, manmade, freshwater reservoirs that are now a safe haven for awesome wetland biodiversity.

For further listings of out-of-the-way green escapes, contact the government conservation departments or consult *LOCALternative Sri Lanka* (www.local ternative.com).

When to Go

Sri Lanka is a year-round wildlife-watching destination but generally the best times correspond with the main November-to-April tourist season. At this time of year all the big parks are open and the dry conditions mean that animals start to gather around water holes, making them easier to spot (this is especially so between February and early April). If you come in the May-to-October southwest monsoon season, head to the parks around the Ancient Cities and in the east of the island.

How to Book

For all the major national parks and other protected areas, organising a safari couldn't be easier. Groups of safari jeep drivers can normally be found in the nearest town or gathered outside the gates, and hotels can also organise safaris. It's normally just a case of turning up the evening before and discussing a price and your needs. Entry fees to all parks are paid directly at entrance gates.

Plan Your Trip

Travel with Children

Like a good rice and curry, Sri Lanka offers a dazzling array of choices. This is obviously not a first-world country, so the child who expects a packaged Disneyland experience won't be happy, but any bumps along the way are more than compensated for by the Sri Lankans themselves and their love of children.

Eating with Kids

Sri Lankan hospitality means that people will go to any length to please young and finicky eaters; most places have a few Western-style dishes.

To ease your children into Sri Lankan food, try a breakfast of *pittu*. The coconut-rice combination will be kind to their palates. Also try hoppers (bowl-shaped pancakes), especially the string variety, or nice and mild *rotti*. flatbreads with filling. The profusion of fresh and exciting varieties of fruit should mean that everybody will find something they like.

Children's Highlights

There aren't many attractions dedicated solely to children in Sri Lanka, but there are a lot of sights they'll love.

➡ **Pinnewala Elephant Orphanage** (p144) A home for elephants near Kandy, with up to 80 ready to interact with visitors.

➡ **Uda Walawe** (p188) One of the best national parks for wildlife-spotting safaris.

➡ **Elephant Transit Home** (p188) Not far from Uda Walawe, this is a well-regarded halfway house for injured and orphaned elephants.

➡ **Minneriya** (p213) A national park renowned for its herds of elephants.

Best Regions for Kids

The West
It's beaches all along this sandy coast. There are all manner of child-friendly resorts where you can relax and maybe build a castle or two. Overall, this is probably the most child-friendly area.

The South
More beaches, lots of water-based activities and in the east there's elephants.

The Hill Country
Many of the attractions here are more adult orientated, but the mild temperatures are a good respite from the heat elsewhere. Tea plantations and trains are an unbeatable day out.

The Ancient Cities
Ancient temples, forts, ruins, jungles and elephants. Hello, Indiana Jones!

TRAVELLING WITH A TODDLER

We travelled with our 22-month-old son around the west and south coasts and the Hill Country. I'd be lying if I said it was all plain sailing and a perfectly relaxing holiday! However, it was certainly rewarding; travelling with him was a real ice-breaker with both local people and other tourists.

A few points to note: few places have baby beds. We knew this and came with our own, but we met many other couples with young children who ended up sleeping in the same bed as their toddler for the whole time. It was, in their words, 'Not as romantic a holiday as we hoped!' You should also bring an extra mosquito net as hotels rarely have spares.

Always order your child's meal well in advance, otherwise by the time the food arrives they'll be too tired to eat. Our son loved the food, but for children who don't then pasta is normally available in tourist areas.

Some people travel by public transport but we hired a car and driver for the duration, which had the added bonus of meaning we had a babysitter on hand!

Without any doubt it was easier to travel along the coast than the hills, where attractions are more for adults. If you really want to make things easy for yourself then just choose one beach, make a base and take day trips from there.

Nappies (diapers), even if they're the same brand you use at home, don't seem to work as well and they rarely make it through the night. The size scale is also smaller, so if you buy mediums at home you'll need large in Sri Lanka.

Stuart Butler

➡ **Turtle hatcheries** (p94) On the west coast, these are popular.

➡ **Unawatuna** (p115) Fringing reefs mean the beach here is safe and shallow for little ones.

➡ **Polonnaruwa** (p206) Kids can literally run themselves silly at the vast and car-free ancient heritage sites such as this one, with its very cool ruins.

➡ **Three-wheelers** (p316) Buzzing, blowing and completely unlike a ride anyplace else, these ubiquitous transport options are good for a thrill.

➡ **Hill Country Train Rides** (p316) Kids will love hanging out the doors of chugging trains (and giving their parents heart attacks!).

Planning & Practicalities

➡ Sri Lankan hotels and guesthouses invariably have triple and family rooms, plus extra beds can be supplied on demand. Baby beds and highchairs (in restaurants), however, are in short supply.

➡ For very young children, the dilemma is to bring either a backpack carrier or a pram/stroller. If you can, bring both. Prams are tough going on uneven or nonexistent footpaths, but are worthwhile in Colombo and Kandy.

➡ Check if your hired car (with driver) has a child's seat. If not, you can get one in Colombo.

➡ Buy pharmaceutical supplies, imported baby food and disposable nappies at Cargills Food City and Keells supermarkets throughout the country.

➡ Breastfeeding in public is accepted, but parents will struggle with finding dedicated baby-changing rooms. It's not a major problem as it's acceptable for toddlers to be naked in public.

➡ Rabies and animal-borne parasites are present in Sri Lanka, so keep children away from stray animals, including cats, dogs and monkeys.

➡ Bring suncream and children's mosquito repellent with you; you won't find it in Sri Lanka.

Regions at a Glance

✪

Colombo

Sunsets
Urban Life
Shopping

Amazing Colours

Built right up to the shores of the Indian Ocean, Colombo faces west into the setting sun. Many evenings begin with an explosion of magenta and purple on the horizon that you can share with others at a hotel bar or with the real people along the shore.

Pettah Market

The first time you almost get run down by a madman with a cart full of goods in the markets of Pettah, you may regret your decision to come. But soon you'll be in the chaotic thick of things and on the ride away, you'll be urging your three-wheeler driver to go faster, faster!

Retail Therapy

From artwork to tea, you can find unique and desirable goods and gifts in Colombo, especially along the leafy streets of Cinnamon Gardens.

p56

The West

Beaches
Activities
Lodging

Sand for All

From all-inclusive package-tour resorts to former hippy hangouts and little-visited sands, the beaches of the west coast span all the spectrums and keep everyone happy.

Watery Pleasures

Ride the waves and dive the reefs of Hikkaduwa, birdwatch on the marshes, explore the back blocks and see the dolphins in the north, and get pampered in a spa and take a boat safari around Bentota.

Top Resorts

The beaches around Bentota are home to some breathtaking boutique hotels that rank among the finest in the country. Cheerful Negombo also contains some memorable accommodation.

p84

The South

Beaches
Activities
Wildlife

Stunning Strands

There are beaches here with a real traveller vibe and there are beaches with barely another person in sight, but the uniting factor is that they're almost all stunning.

Surfing

The area between Galle and Matara is arguably the finest slice of surf country in South Asia. Ahangama, Midigama and Weligama are known to surfers everywhere – or should be.

Creatures Galore

Monkeys crash through the trees, whales splash through the seas, leopards slink through the night, birds flap through the skies, turtles emerge on the beach and animal lovers can't stop smiling.

p103

The Hill Country

Walking
Wildlife
Eating

Verdant Hikes

Hack through jungles, shiver over high plateaus, traipse to vertigo-inspiring viewpoints, tip-toe through tea plantations and walk in the footsteps of gods.

Elephants & More

No other part of Sri Lanka offers such varied wildlife habitats. There's steamy rainforests filled with noisy birds, grassland savannahs ruled by elephants, and highland forests covered in delicate lichens and moss.

Guesthouse Dining

Eating in Sri Lanka is rarely anything but a pleasure, but it's in the Hill Country where the preparation and consumption of food becomes an art form, and the best food comes from your guesthouse kitchen.

p142

The Ancient Cities

Monuments
Temples
Cycling

Ancient Treasures

The Polonnaruwa Quadrangle, the ancient quarter of Anuradhapura, the jaw-dropping sight of the rock monastery at Sigiriya: just some of the remarkable ruins ready for exploration.

Sri Maha Bodhi

Amid the leaf-shrouded ruins of Anuradhapura is Sri Maha Bodhi, a tree that has seen history and devotion for 2000 years. Nearby, a welter of temples and monuments will inspire your own devotion.

Biking the Temples

The ruins of the Ancient Cities are sited within much larger parks and reserves. You can pedal between the wonders along palm-shaded paths and never see a car. Guesthouses have bikes for hire.

p193

The East

Beaches
Activities
Wildlife

Lonely Sands

Most of the east coast's miles of beaches are untouched, but even those that are developed are sandy wonderlands, with just the right amounts of palm trees, white sands and low-key scenes.

Snoozing & Diving

The East provides activities to alternate with napping on hammocks. The ocean here isn't just calm and gorgeous, but it has the reefs and wrecks for great snorkelling and diving, and the right waves for surfing.

Kumana National Park

Kumana National Park doesn't have the size (or the leopard population) of its neighbour Yala. However, it does lack Yala's tourist population, which means the leopards, elephants and birds here are all yours.

p229

Jaffna & the North

Discovery
Temples
Seashores

Off the Beaten Path

All but shut down to travel for years, the North is now ready to be explored. The going is greatly improved, while seeing glimpses of war history is powerfully moving.

Religious Discoveries

Hindu gods and goddesses painted in exquisite riots of colour animate towering temple gateways all over the North. Even better, though, are the friendly priests and devotees who will welcome you to *puja* (prayer).

Jaffna's Coasts

Seemingly endless coastlines curl around the Jaffna region's mainland and islands. Coast roads, causeways and wooden-boat rides to isolated islands are only second to the islands' sublime beauty.

p256

On the Road

**Jaffna &
the North**
p256

The West
p84

**The Ancient
Cities**
p193

The East
p229

Colombo
p56

**The Hill
Country**
p142

The South
p103

Colombo

🎵 011 / POPULATION 4.6 MILLION

Best Places to Eat

➜ Ministry of Crab (p75)
➜ Hotel De Pilawoos (p77)
➜ Ceylon Tea Moments (p76)
➜ Bu Ba (p78)

Best Places to Stay

➜ Lake Lodge (p72)
➜ Cinnamon Grand Hotel (p73)
➜ Havelock Place Bungalow (p74)
➜ Colombo Courtyard (p73)

Why Go?

Although reclaiming its 19th-century moniker 'the garden city of the East' is unlikely, Colombo is rapidly emerging as a must-see stop in Sri Lanka. No longer just the sprawling city you have to endure on your way to the southern beaches, it has become a worthy destination in its own right.

The legacies of colonial Colombo's garden roots are still very much intact along its often shady boulevards. Fort is in the midst of widespread historic restoration of its landmark colonial architecture, while Pettah brims with markets and rampant commerce. Even traffic-clogged Galle Rd is getting spiffier with glossy new hotel complexes, while the seafront benefits from new roads that are spurring hotel construction.

Colombo's cosmopolitan side supports ever-more stylish eateries, galleries and museums. Surprises abound in its old quarters where you can find great local food and discover a characterful shop or tiny, convivial cafe. The capital is an excellent start – or finish – to your Sri Lankan adventures.

When to Go
Colombo

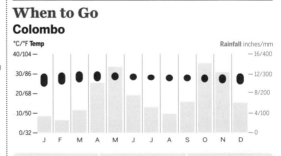

Jan–Mar The driest season, with cool evening breezes. More tourists, so book hotels in advance.

May The important religious celebration of Vesak sees the city come alive in colours, lights and festivities.

Dec Although Christians are a minority, Christmas is popular and festive decorations abound.

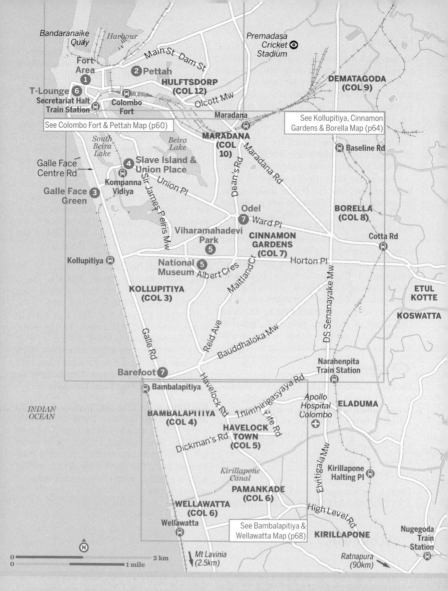

Colombo Highlights

1 Revelling in the restoration of the historic **Fort area** (p58)

2 Plunging into the commercial madness of the shops, stalls and markets of age-old **Pettah** (p60)

3 Catching a sunset amid families and courting couples on Colombo's front lawn, **Galle Face Green** (p61)

4 Strolling the ancient quarters of **Slave Island** and **Union Place** (p62) before they fall to new glitzy developments

5 Walking through Sri Lanka's history in the remarkable **National Museum** (p67), before exploring the grounds of lively **Viharamahadevi Park** (p67)

6 Enjoying some of the best Sri Lankan tea at **T-Lounge** (p75), one of Colombo's new stylish tea cafes

7 Shopping at stores such as **Odel** (p80) and **Barefoot** (p80), where you can browse for creative and interesting local merchandise

History

As far back as the 5th century, Colombo served as a sea port for trade between Asia and the West. During the 8th century Arab traders settled near the port, and in 1505 the Portuguese arrived. By the mid-17th century the Dutch had taken over, growing cinnamon in the area now known as Cinnamon Gardens, but it wasn't until the British arrived that the town became a city. In 1815 Colombo was proclaimed the capital of Ceylon.

During the 1870s the breakwaters were built and Fort was created by flooding surrounding wetlands. Colombo was peacefully handed over when Sri Lanka achieved independence in 1948. A new parliament was built in Sri Jayawardenepura-Kotte, an outer suburb of Colombo, in 1982.

Bomb attacks in Fort over the years of war caused Colombo's major businesses and institutions to disperse across the city. With peace, Colombo is growing fast, with much development north and south along the coast, a building boom of highrises in the centre and relentless – and mostly charmless – sprawl eastward.

◉ Sights

Lacking signature must-see sights, Colombo's real appeal lies in its many neighbourhoods, which span an era from the earliest colonial days to the city's present nascent boom. Start in Fort and Pettah and work your way south.

◉ Fort

During the European era Fort was indeed a fort, surrounded by the sea on two sides and a moat on the landward sides. Today it's literally at the centre of Colombo's resurgence, with grand old colonial-era buildings being restored amid a mix of modern structures, such as the World Trade Center.

Security remains in evidence in this area as the walled-off **President's House** (Map p60) and various government ministries are here. You may have to detour around a bit but it's a compact area and can be appreciated on a short stroll, starting at the Old Galle Buck Lighthouse.

The busy harbour on the north side of Fort is mostly walled off but you can enjoy sweeping views from the tiny terrace of the otherwise humdrum top-floor cafe of the once-grand Grand Oriental Hotel (p71).

★**Old Dutch Hospital**   HISTORIC BUILDING
(Map p60; Bank of Ceylon Mawatha, Col 1) Centrepiece of the ever-more vibrant Fort, this colonial-era complex dates back to the early 1600s. Lavishly restored, it is home to shops, cafes and restaurants run by some of Colombo's best operators. Enjoy a pause for a cold drink amid the incredibly thick columns of its arcades. An annex has now opened in a 19th-century British building on the backside that faces Chatham St.

Old Galle Buck Lighthouse   LIGHTHOUSE
(Map p60; Marine Dr, Col 1) It was built in 1954 and is surrounded by old cannons. Climb up onto the large central terrace for views of the ocean and the rapidly expanding commercial port. The immediate area is getting a bit of a polish, with some modest stops for refreshments.

COLOMBO IN...

One Day

Start at the bustling markets of **Pettah**, taking time for small Hindu temples and the Dutch Period Museum (p61). Head west to **Fort** and pause to appreciate the restoration of colonial gems like the Old Dutch Hospital (p58). Rub elbows with busy locals over a spicy curry and rice at New Palm Leaf Hotel (p75).

In the afternoon visit the eclectic Buddhist Gangaramaya Temple (p63) and wander down to Viharamahadevi Park (p67). Later, take a stroll along the oceanfront with Sri Lankan families at Galle Face Green (p61) as the sun sets and enjoy a snack from a vendor.

Two Days

Grab a *kotthu* (a *rotti* chopped and fried with a variety of ingredients) at Hotel De Pilawoos (p77) before tackling the excellent National Museum (p67). Afterwards, go shopping at the many excellent stores and boutiques in leafy **Cinnamon Gardens** and **Kollupitiya**. For dinner, enjoy scrumptious local crab prepared Jaffna style at Yaal Restaurant (p78).

COLOMBO'S MAIN NEIGHBOURHOODS

Colombo is split into 15 postal-code areas, which are often used to identify the specific districts. Pettah, for example, is also referred to as Colombo 11 (or just Col 11) and so on. The main areas of interest:

DISTRICT	SUBURB
Col 1	**Fort** The revitalised centre of the city; historic and chic
Col 2	**Slave Island** Not an island at all (though it really was used for keeping slaves in the Dutch colonial era); some of Colombo's oldest – and most threatened – historic areas are here, including Union Pl
Col 3	**Kollupitiya** The dense commercial heart of the city, with myriad shops, hotels and businesses along Galle Rd
Col 4	**Bambalapitiya** An extension of Col 3
Col 5	**Havelock Town** Gentrifying southern extension of Col 4
Col 6	**Wellawatta** More commercial sprawl south along Galle Rd; inland, **Pamankade** is a newly stylish enclave
Col 7	**Cinnamon Gardens** Colombo's swankiest district has the National Museum, Viharamahadevi Park, old colonial mansions and trendy shops and cafes
Col 8	**Borella** The quieter eastern extension of Cinnamon Gardens
Col 11	**Pettah** Old quarter just east of Fort, with thriving markets
Col 13	**Kotahena** Alongside the port north of Pettah; home to old neighbourhoods and important religious buildings

Sambodhi Chaitiya SHRINE
(Map p60; Marine Dr, Col 1) Just north of the lighthouse, you won't be able to miss this bombastic white dagoba (stupa) perched about 20m off the ground on huge, incongruous curving concrete 'legs' so that sailors could see it from offshore.

Clock Tower LANDMARK
(Map p60; Janadhipathi Mawatha, Col 1) The clock tower at the junction of Chatham St and Janadhipathi Mawatha (once Queen St) was originally a lighthouse that was built in 1857. It's now right at the heart of officialdom and you can expect a few watchful guards.

Central Point HISTORIC BUILDING
(Map p60; Chatham St, Col 1; ⊘ museum 8.30am-4pm Mon-Fri) FREE Chatham St is seeing a lot of renovation of old buildings, one of the grandest being the old colonnaded 1914 Central Bank building called Central Point. The beautifully restored interior is a riot of Greco-Roman detailing and features the tallest chandelier in Asia. There's also a museum of local money that's worth the time simply for the display on why bartering a cow for fish was a bad idea, thus leading to the invention of currency.

Lloyd's Buildings HISTORIC BUILDING
(Map p60; Sir Baron Jayatilaka Mawatha, Col 1) Sir Baron Jayatilaka Mawatha has the grandly restored Lloyd's Buildings. Several other imposing colonial piles on the street are also being renovated, recreating the regal air of when this was the fiscal heart of Ceylon.

Cargills Main Store HISTORIC BUILDING
(Map p60; York St, Col 1) Local retail giant Cargills once had its main store on York St. The now mostly empty ornate 1906 red building still shows its faded elegance in its long arcades with old store signage such as the one noting 'toilet requisites'. Ground-floor colonnades like those found here were once a feature across colonial Colombo, allowing people to get around sheltered from monsoon deluges.

St Peter's Church CHURCH
(Map p60; Col 1; ⊘ 7am-5pm Tue-Sun) Reached along the arcade on the north side of the Grand Oriental Hotel, this converted Dutch governor's banquet hall was first used as a church in 1821. Inside it has an original wood ceiling and myriad plaques attesting to its work with seamen through the years.

Colombo Fort & Pettah

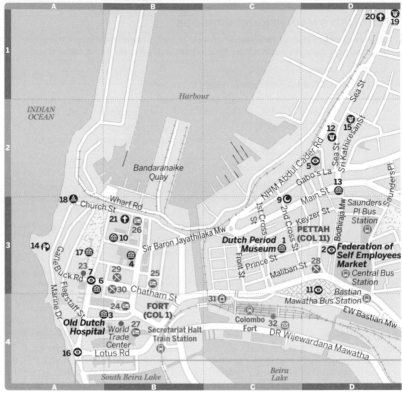

◉ Pettah

Immediately inland from Fort, the bustling bazaar of Pettah is one of the oldest districts in Colombo and one of the most interesting places to spend a few hours. It is the most ethnically mixed place in the country. Large religious buildings represent a plethora of faiths, while more earthly pursuits can be found in market stalls and shops selling seemingly everything.

The crowds in Pettah can become overwhelming during the morning and late-afternoon rush hours but the streets are still thronged during most daylight hours. Vendors hurrying with carts piled high with impossible loads, zooming three-wheelers, cars trying to fit down narrow lanes and people rushing hither and yon can make for an exhausting experience. Your best bet is to find a shady spot out of traffic and just observe the timeless swirl around you.

Wolfendhal Lane is a typical side-street refuge: wander past its pirated-DVD and textile stores and exchange gentle 'hellos' with the locals.

Pettah Markets MARKETS
(Col 11) The concentrated and manic commerce of Pettah is concentrated even further in its markets. The one not to miss is the **Federation of Self Employees Market** (Map p60; off Olcott Mawatha, Col 11; ⊙ 7am-4pm), which stretches along 5th Cross St and is a hive of household goods and food. Admire the artful displays of fruit and veg, like the pyramids of limes.

Just east of Fort train station, **Manning Market** (Map p60; Olcott Mawatha, Col 11; ⊙ 6am-2pm) is ripe with everything grown in Sri Lanka. It's the city's wholesale fruit and veg centre and is a monkey's dream of bananas. The modernised **Central Market** (Map p60; Market St, Col 11; ⊙ 7am-3pm) lacks the charm of the others.

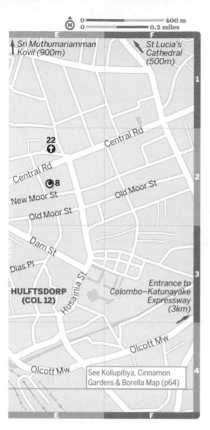

and you'll discover something of a wax-works in the old council chambers. There, covered in dust, are replicas of the town's first councillors in 1906.

It's slightly comic and ghoulish, especially given the green glow from the stained glass. Views from the windows put you above the hubbub outside.

Pettah Hindu Temples TEMPLES
Known as *kovils,* Hindu temples are nu-merous in Colombo, with a particularly high concentration in Pettah. On Sea St, the goldsmiths' street, **Old Kathiresan Kovil** (Map p60; Sea St, Col 11; ⊕6am-6pm) and **New Kathiresan Kovil** (Map p60; Sea St, Col 11; ⊕6am-6pm) are both dedicated to the war god Murugan (Skanda), and are the starting point for the annual Hindu Vel festival held in July/August, when the huge *vel* (trident) chariot is dragged to various *kovils* on Galle Rd in Bambalapitiya.

Pettah Mosques MOSQUES
In the heart of Pettah, the decorative 1909 **Jami-Ul-Alfar Mosque** (Map p60; cnr 2nd Cross & Bankshall Sts , Col 11) is a show-stopper with its candy-striped red-and-white brickwork. Guards will usually let you in for a look, ex-cept during peak prayer times on Friday. Afterwards have a coffee at one of the Halal cafes across the way. The modern **Grand Mosque** (Map p60; New Moor St, Col 11) is the most important of Colombo's many mosques.

Wolvendaal Church CHURCH
(Map p60; Wolvendaal Lane, Col 11; ⊕9am-4pm) The 1749 Wolvendaal Church is the most important Dutch building in Sri Lanka. When the church was built, this area was a wilderness beyond the city walls. The Euro-peans mistook the packs of roaming jackals for wolves, and the area became known as Wolf's Dale, or Wolvendaal in Dutch. The church is in the form of a Greek cross, with walls 1.5m thick, but the real treasure is its Dutch furniture.

The Dutch governors had a special pew made with elegant carved ebony chairs, and the workmanship in the wooden pulpit, bap-tismal font and lectern is just as beautiful. The stone floor includes the elaborate tomb-stones to long-forgotten Dutch governors and colonists.

★**Dutch Period Museum** MUSEUM
(Map p60; ☎ 244 8466; 95 Prince St, Col 11; adult/child Rs 500/300; ⊕9am-5pm Tue-Sat) This unique museum was originally the 17th-century residence of the Dutch governor and has since been used as a Catholic seminary, a military hospital, a police station and a post office. The mansion contains a lovely garden courtyard and has a nice faded feel since a 1977 restoration. Exhibits include Dutch colonial furniture and other artefacts.

It's here in 1638 that King Rajasinghe II of the Kingdom of Kandy signed the treaty that opened up Ceylon to the Dutch.

★**Old City Hall** HISTORIC BUILDING
(Map p60; Main St , Col 11; ⊕8am-5pm Mon-Sat) Dating to 1865, this municipal building from the British era is mostly empty today, save for some old trucks and municipal equip-ment on display in the ground-floor galler-ies. But let the attendants lead you up the vintage mahogany stairs (tip them Rs 100)

◉ **Galle Face Green**

Colombo's front porch is immediately south of Fort. **Galle Face Green** (Map p64) is a

Colombo Fort & Pettah

long stretch of lawn facing a narrow beach and the sea. It was originally cleared by the Dutch to give the cannons of Fort a clear line of fire. Today its broad lawns and seaside promenade are a popular rendezvous spot. On weekdays it's dotted with kite flyers, canoodling couples and families, and (especially Sunday evening) **food vendors** (Map p64; Galle Face Green) at the south end along the surf offer up all manner of deep-fried and briny snacks. Try a fresh *isso wade,* a shrimp fritter with the shrimp still whole and cooked right in, then wash it all down with a fresh lime juice.

Kids jump from the small **pier** (Map p64; Galle Face Green) into the rather dubious waters below. Note the **pelicans** (Map p60; Galle Face Green) perched atop the light poles at the north end.

The remaining structures of the 1871 **Colombo Club** (Map p64; Galle Face Centre Rd) face the green from the grounds of Taj Samudra hotel; the club's rooms are still used for functions and there's still a few members from British times. At opposite ends of the green are the delightful old Galle Face Hotel and the monolithic and ageing hotels of Fort. Note the rapidly changing backdrop to the east as a row of posh new hotels rises up.

◎ Slave Island & Union Place

After Pettah, Colombo's oldest neighbourhoods are found here. Slave Island was once mostly surrounded by water and it's where the Dutch kept slaves during colonial times. Largely a backwater during the war, its proximity to Fort and Galle Face Green make it the centre of vast new developments. While multilevel malls, posh condos and the Lotus Tower are rising up, you can still find streets of timeless character, but don't delay.

Already in the shadow of new buildings, Union Place is on the cusp of transformation. But until bulldozers arrive, its narrow lanes pulse with life little changed in centuries. Start at the row of **colonial storefronts** (Map p64; Union Pl, Col 2) on Union Pl (and consider a snack from one of the myriad storefront vendors) then plunge into the neighbourhood by walking south on **Church St** and prowling random alleys to the west. Tiny shopfronts sell goods of uncertain provenance and each alley holds a surprise. Wind your way south until you reach Nawam Mawatha and South Beira Lake.

Lotus Tower ARCHITECTURE
(Map p64; DR Wijewardana Mawatha, Col 2) Casting a shadow over Slave Island, the 350m Lotus Tower is set to open sometime in 2016. With a bulbous top meant to resemble the namesake blossom, this soaring erection (24m taller than the Eiffel Tower) will have telecommunications equipment and an array of tourist attractions including an observation deck at the top and a water park at the base. Like most other recent mega-projects in Sri Lanka, it is being financed by China.

⊙ South Beira Lake & Around
South Beira Lake is a pretty centrepiece to the city. Pelicans vie with rental paddle boats (in the shape of huge swans) for space on the water. The latter are popular with courting couples looking for a little privacy. Stroll the waterside walk with local families, while their children race out to the playground on the small island.

Gangaramaya Temple BUDDHIST TEMPLE
(Map p64; ✒ 232 3038; www.gangaramaya.com; Sri Jinaratana Rd, Col 2; ⊙ 5.30am-10pm, museum donation Rs 100) Run by one of Sri Lanka's more politically adept monks, Galboda Gnanissara Thera, this bustling temple complex has a library, a **museum** and an extraordinarily eclectic array of bejewelled and gilded gifts presented by devotees and well-wishers over the years (plus one lonely and chained temple elephant named Ganga). Gangaramaya is the focus of the Navam Perahera on the February *poya* (full-moon) day each year. This is the centre for the most extravagant Vesak celebrations in Colombo.

Seema Malakaya Meditation Centre SPIRITUAL PLACE
(Map p64; South Beira Lake, Col 2; ⊙ 6am-6pm) One of Colombo's most photographed sights is on an island on the east side of the lake. This small but captivating meditation centre was designed by Geoffrey Bawa in 1985 and is run by Gangaramaya Temple. The pavilions – one filled with Thai bronze Buddhas, the other centred on a bodhi tree and four Brahmanist images – are especially striking when illuminated at night.

⊙ Kollupitiya
This long commercial strip along traffic-choked Galle Rd is jammed with all manner of shops, businesses and hotels both modest and grand. It makes for a good stroll as surprises abound. Several places popular for snacks are along here as well. Improvements to Marine Dr are harbingers for seaside development but it will be a while before Colombo – sunsets aside – becomes Miami Beach.

Geoffrey Bawa House MUSEUM
(Map p64; www.geoffreybawa.com; 11 33rd Ln, Col 3; admission Rs 1000; ⊙ tours 10am, noon, 2pm & 4pm, confirm in advance) At the end of this quiet little street is the house where renowned architect Bawa lived from 1960 to 1970. The house combines his usual love for traditional local forms with the stark white architectural palette he favoured. Tours take in the interior, with his custom furnishings, and the small gardens.

Temple Trees LANDMARK
(Map p64; Galle Rd, Col 3) The official prime minister's house has also been the residence for several recent presidents, including Mahinda Rajapaks. It's heavily protected and they might not even let you walk along the sidewalks nearby.

⊙ Cinnamon Gardens
About 5km south of Fort and inland from Kollupitiya, Cinnamon Gardens is Colombo's most gentrified area. A century ago it was covered in cinnamon plantations. Today it contains elegant tree-lined streets with

---

ℹ NAVIGATING COLOMBO
Colombo's spine is Galle Rd, which starts just south of Fort and runs all the way to its namesake city in the south. Along the way, it passes the old beach resort of Mt Lavinia, which isn't officially part of Colombo but is definitely within its urban sprawl. Development is frenzied all the way to the airport 30km north.

Note that street numbers start again each time you move into a new district. Thus there will be a '100 Galle Rd' in several different neighbourhoods.

Some Colombo streets have both an old English name and a post-independence Sinhala name. Ananda Coomaraswamy Mawatha is also known as Green Path, for example, while RA de Mel Mawatha is still known as Duplication Rd. For longer stays, the 96-page *A-Z Street Guide* is useful; Google Maps is up to date and accurate.

Kollupitiya, Cinnamon Gardens & Borella

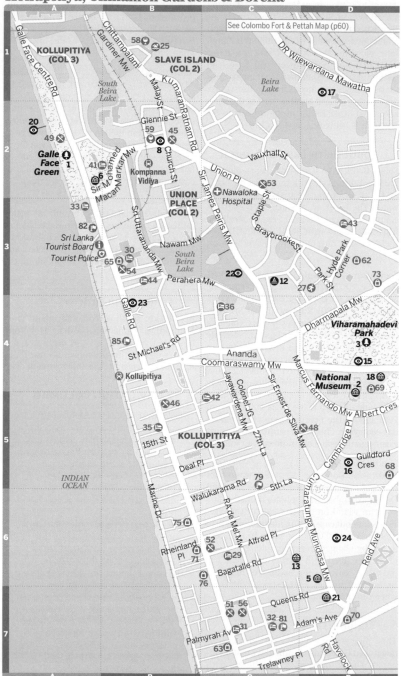

COLOMBO

See Colombo Fort & Pettah Map (p60)

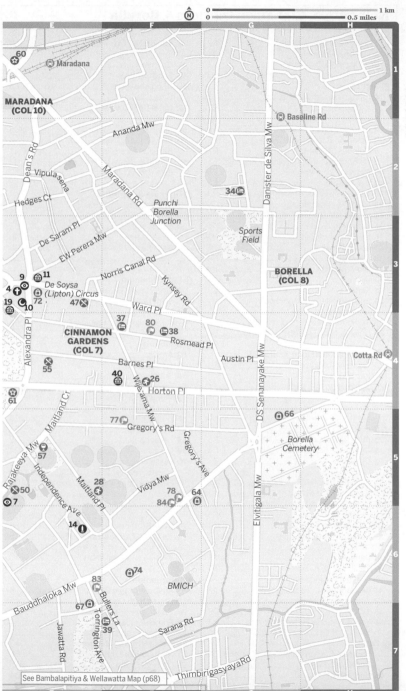

MARADANA
(COL 10)

BORELLA
(COL 8)

CINNAMON
GARDENS
(COL 7)

BMICH

Borella
Cemetery

Sports
Field

Punchi
Borella
Junction

De Soysa
(Lipton) Circus

See Bambalapitiya & Wellawatta Map (p68)

Kollupitiya, Cinnamon Gardens & Borella

posh mansions, embassies, stylish cafes and shops, sports grounds and a cluster of museums and galleries.

Colombo's vivid white and domed 1928 **Old Town Hall** (Map p64; FR Senanayaka Mawatha, Col 7) overlooks the area's heart, Viharamahadevi Park. To the south is the striking Nelum Pokuna Mahinda Rajapaksa Theatre (p79), which opened in 2011.

★ National Museum   MUSEUM
(Map p64; ☑ 269 4767; Albert Cres, Col 7; adult/child Rs 250/150; ☺ 9am-6pm, last entrance 5pm) A large 9th-century stone Buddha greets you with an enigmatic smile as you enter Sri Lanka's premier cultural institution. In galleries dating back as far as 1877, you'll encounter all manner of art, carvings and statuary from Sri Lanka's ancient past, as well as swords, guns and other paraphernalia from the colonial period. There are fascinating 19th-century reproductions of English paintings of Sri Lanka, and an excellent collection of antique demon masks.

Look for the magnificent royal throne made for King Wimaladharma in 1693, as well as the 9th-century bronze Bodhisattva Sandals. The grounds are shaded by magnificent banyan trees.

De Soysa (Lipton) Circus   LANDMARK
(Map p64; De Soysa (Lipton) Circus, Col 7) One corner of this bustling roundabout is occupied by the popular Odel (p80) department store. Opposite is the **Cinnamon Gardens Baptist Church** (Map p64; De Soysa (Lipton) Circus, Col 7), which dates to 1877. Located just south of the church is the **Dewata-Gaha Mosque** (Map p64; Alexandra Pl, Col 7), a rambling structure dating to 1802 that bustles with people following the Friday afternoon prayers. Meanwhile, the ragtag confection of red and white bricks that was once the **Eye Hospital** (Map p64; De Soysa (Lipton) Circus, Col 7) now houses the Coroner's Court while awaiting its own rescue from fate.

★ Viharamahadevi Park   PARK
(Map p64; Col 7) Colombo's biggest park was originally called Victoria Park but was renamed in the 1950s after the mother of King Dutugemunu. It's notable for its superb flowering trees, which bloom in March, April and early May. Elephants used for ceremonies sometimes spend the night in the park, chomping on palm branches. It has been given a major sprucing up and now boasts new benches (often occupied with caressing couples), walkways, landscaping and playgrounds.

Saskia Fernando Gallery   ART GALLERY
(Map p64; ☑ 742 9010; www.saskiafernandogallery. com; 41 Horton Pl, Col 7; ☺ 10am-7pm) Some of the best contemporary Sri Lankan artists are displayed in this white-washed compound. Look for the huge elephant sculpture, created from old mechanical parts. The namesake owner is the daughter of local design maven Shanth Fernando, of Paradise Road fame.

National Art Gallery   ART GALLERY
(Map p64; 106 Ananda Coomaraswamy Mawatha, Col 7; ☺ 9am-5pm) **FREE** The grandest thing about the National Art Gallery is its name. Next to the National Museum, it has a small collection of portraits and landscapes shown without labels or air-conditioning.

Lionel Wendt Centre   ARTS CENTRE
(Map p64; ☑ 269 5794; www.lionelwendt.org; 18 Guildford Cres, Col 7; ☺ 9am-1pm & 2-5pm Mon-Fri, 10am-noon & 2-5pm Sat & Sun) With a constantly changing lineup of cultural events and regular art exhibitions as well as performances, it's worth turning up just to see what's on.

Colombo Racecourse   HISTORIC SITE
(Map p64; Phillip Gunawardena Mawatha) Once the centre of harness racing in Colombo (and a WWII airfield), the landmark grandstands here now face a new rugby ground, while the buildings themselves house a large collection of up-scale shops and cafes.

University of Colombo   UNIVERSITY
(University of Ceylon; Map p64) The 50-acre University of Colombo campus, which originally opened as the Ceylon Medical School in 1870, is surrounded by long tree-lined avenues lined with colonial-era mansions. Of note is Cumaratunga Munidasa Mawatha along the southwest side of the sporting green. Ponder the gracious lives of the people who built the Italianate Baroque **Saifee Villa** (Map p64; Cumaratunga Munidasa Mawatha) in 1910 and the nearby turreted **College House** (Map p64; Cumaratunga Munidasa Mawatha) in 1912.

Independence Memorial Hall   MONUMENT
(Map p64; Independence Sq, Col 7) Really a large memorial building to Sri Lanka's 1948 independence from Britain, the huge stone edifice is loosely based on Kandy's Audience Hall. This is a good place to escape Colombo's crowds as it always seems almost empty.

Bambalapitiya & Wellawatta

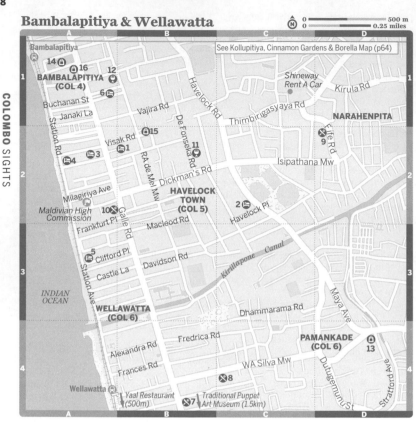

N 0 ————— 500 m
0 ————— 0.25 miles

See Kollupitiya, Cinnamon Gardens & Borella Map (p64)

Southern Colombo

South of Kollupitiya and Cinnamon Gardens is more of the same, only less so. The commercial strip of Galle Rd continues south through Bambalapitiya and Wellawatta. Inland, Havelock Town is a more relaxed version of Cinnamon Gardens. It has several midrange hotels. The one area here with buzz is **Pamankade**, which has some interesting shops and cafes along Stratford Ave.

Traditional Puppet Art Museum   MUSEUM
(☑ 573 5332; www.puppet.lk; Anagarika Dharmapala Mawatha, Col 5; admission Rs 500, performances vary; ⊙ 9am-5pm, call first) Puppet shows were long a part of traditional entertainment in Sri Lankan villages. Performing troupes would stage shows with intricate plots that lasted for hours. This engaging museum keeps the traditional puppet arts alive.

Dozens and dozens of colourful puppets – some quite huge – are displayed. Many are surprisingly animated even when still.

Call to arrange a performance (or to get directions). It's about 200m east of Galle Rd, about midway between Wellawatta and Mt Lavinia.

Mt Lavinia

Long Colombo's beach retreat, Mt Lavinia makes for a good respite from the city's cacophony and fumes. The **beach** is not bad, although some rivers just north empty dodgy water into the ocean after rains and the undertow can be prohibitive. If you're heading to the famous beaches in the south there's no need to stop here. Otherwise Mt Lavinia's many beachside cafes are lovely places to laze away the hours until sunset. It's only 15 minutes by train from Fort, a ride that's a joy itself.

Bambalapitiya & Wellawatta

◉ Kotahena

Kotahena, immediately northeast of Pettah, is closely linked to Colombo's port, which forms the west boundary. It's not as rampant with commerce as Pettah but also boasts many old buildings and streets. You could easily visit the sights listed here with the services of a taxi or three-wheeler.

Hindu Temples HINDU TEMPLES
(Col 13) During the harvest festival of Thai Pongal (held in January), devotees flock to **Sri Ponnambalam Vanesar Kovil** (Map p60; Srimath Ramanathan Mawatha, Col 13), which is beautifully built of South Indian granite, and **Sri Muthumariamman Kovil** (Kotahena St, Col 13). The latter's namesake goddess is thought to be responsible for many miracles.

St Anthony's Church CHURCH
(Map p60; www.stanthonysshrinekochchikade.org; St Anthony's Mawatha, Col 13; ⊙6am-6pm) One of the city's most interesting shrines is St Anthony's Church. Outside it looks like a typical Portuguese Catholic church, but inside the atmosphere is distinctly subcontinental. There are queues of devotees offering *puja* (offerings or prayers) to a dozen ornate statues; a statue of St Anthony said to be endowed with miraculous qualities is the centre of devotions from people of many faiths.

Mothers often bring pubescent daughters here to pray for protection from evil spirits that might take advantage of the girls' nascent sexuality. The current church is built on the sight of an 18th-century chapel that was a mud hut. Photography is frowned upon.

St Lucia's Cathedral CHURCH
(St Lucia's St, Col 13; ⊙5.30am-noon & 2-7pm) This enormous 1887 cathedral lies in the Catholic heart of the Kotahena district. The biggest church in Sri Lanka has an exterior inspired by St Peter's in Rome. It can hold up to 5000 worshippers in its rather plain interior.

◉ North & Northwest of Colombo

The busy old commercial road linking Colombo with Negombo and the north is often traffic-choked and is lined with an untidy mishmash of strip malls aimed at Sri Lanka's burgeoning middle class. It's much the same for the first few kilometres of the road to Kandy, although lush green landscapes soon provide relief.

Kelaniya Raja Maha Vihara BUDDHIST TEMPLE
(www.kelaniyatemple.org; Biyagama Rd) It's believed Buddha visited the site of this temple on his third visit to Sri Lanka. Suitably grand and labyrinthine, it has a dramatic past. The original temple was destroyed by Indian invaders, then restored and destroyed again by the Portuguese in the 16th century. The Dutch restored it again in the 18th century in order to curry favour locally.

The dagoba, which (unusually) is hollow, is the focus of the Duruthu Perahera in January each year. The complex is some 7km northeast of Fort, just off the Kandy Rd.

🏃 Activities

Spa Ceylon SPA
(www.spaceylon.com; massage per hr from Rs 2800) With branches at Old Dutch Hospital (p58) and **Park St Mews** (Map p64; ☑230 7676; www.spaceylon.com; Park St, Col 2; ⊙10am-11pm), this chain of luxury spas offers both Ayurveda treatments and regular spa services in chic surrounds. It has numerous luxe therapies.

Dehiwala & Mt Lavinia

Dehiwala & Mt Lavinia

🛏 Sleeping

1 Blue Seas Guest House	B1
2 Haus Chandra	A1
3 Mount Lavinia Hotel	A3
4 Tropic Inn	B2

🍴 Eating

5 Bu Ba	A3
6 La Voile Blanche	A2
7 Lavinia Breeze	A1

👉 Tours

★ Trekurious TOURS

(📞778 8778; www.trekurious.com; tours from Rs 5500 per person) Learn the fascinating secrets of Fort on a walking tour, or tour Colombo by bike at night; these are just two of the excellent tours offered by this group which represents several fine independent operators. Other activities include cooking and art classes.

Colombo City Tour BUS TOUR

(📞281 4700, 077 759 9963; www.colombocity-tours.com; tour US$25; ⏰5pm Mon-Fri, 8.30am & 4.30pm Sat & Sun) Tour Colombo's sprawl from high above the traffic in an open-top double-decker bus. The narration is in English and snacks and water are included. The four-hour tours cover the city and stops include the National Museum.

🎊 Festivals & Events

Special events, such as street rally races and open-air concerts by the ocean, are blossoming in Colombo.

Duruthu Perahera RELIGIOUS FESTIVAL

(⏰Jan) Held at the Kelaniya Raja Maha Vihara on the January *poya*.

Navam Perahera RELIGIOUS FESTIVAL

(⏰Feb) On the February *poya* and led by 50 elephants; it starts from Gangaramaya Temple and is held around Viharamahadevi Park and South Beira Lake.

★ Vesak Poya RELIGIOUS FESTIVAL

(⏰May) The birth, enlightenment and the death of Buddha is celebrated across Colombo (and Sri Lanka) but the festivities around Gangaramaya Temple and South Lake Beira are mind-blowing. Huge eruptions of coloured light displays vie with hundreds of smaller displays made by competing groups. *Dansala* stands, where food and treats are given away, are everywhere.

Kemara SPA

(Map p64; 📞269 6498; www.kemaralife.com; 12 Barnes Pl, Col 7; ⏰10am-8pm) This spa offers holistic health treatments and luxurious beauty and health products, many based on fruits and herbs. A long list of therapies and spa treatments is available.

Siddhalepa Ayurveda SPA

(Map p64; 📞269 8161; www.siddhalepa.com; 33 Wijerama Mawatha, Col 07; therapies from Rs 2000; ⏰9am-9pm) This full-service Ayurvedic spa offers all manner of treatments and therapies. It also has a small spa that usefully treats jetlag, at Bandaranaike International Airport in the departure concourse.

Kanduboda Siyane Meditation Center SPIRITUAL RETREAT

(📞240 2306; www.insight-meditation.org; Kanduboda) This is a major centre for meditation instruction in the style of the late Mahasi Sayadaw. Accommodation and meals are offered free of charge, though donations are expected. Most meditators stay for an initial three-week training period, after which they can meditate on their own for as long as they like. Located 25km east of Colombo in Delgoda, the Pugoda bus 224 passes the centre and can be caught from the Central Bus Station.

Vel RELIGIOUS FESTIVAL

(☉ Jul or Aug) During the Vel, the gilded chariot of Murugan (Skanda), the Hindu war god, is ceremonially hauled from the Kathiresan *kovil* to a *kovil* at Bambalapitiya.

🛏 Sleeping

Like many other aspects of life in the capital, the accommodation scene in Colombo is awakening from a long slumber. New top-end hotels with names like Hyatt and Shangri-La are being built and older ones refurbished. Luxurious boutique hotels are proliferating in the city's leafier neighbourhoods and there's a new selection of high-quality mid-range places.

Amid this new hostelry energy, some older properties continue to limp along on past glories. Fort and Galle Rd in particular have shabby hotels that are little changed – or improved – in decades. As visitor numbers in Sri Lanka soar, it's worth booking ahead – especially for that first night in Colombo – so you don't end up at an inferior option.

Negombo is a short drive from Bandaranaike International Airport and has a full range of sleeping options, many right on the beach.

🛏 Fort & Pettah

Fort is home to international-style highrise hotels, some of which are decidedly long in the tooth. This is also where you can find historic hotels with rates that make their miscues palatable.

SWIMMING

Skip the polluted waters off Galle Face Green; the only place you might consider an ocean dip is at Mt Lavinia.

Rather, if you are staying someplace without a pool – or just want a change of scenery – consider paying to swim at a hotel with a pool. Many will allow you to use the facilities for a fee of Rs 1000 to 2000. Two good choices are the pool at the **Cinnamon Lakeside** (Map p64; ☎ 249 1000; 115 Sir Chittampalam A Gardiner Mawatha, Col 2; adult/child Rs 1200/750) hotel and the magnificently positioned pool at Mount Lavinia Hotel (p74).

Colombo YMCA GUESTHOUSE $

(Map p60; ☎ 232 5252; 39 Bristol St, Col 1; dm Rs 1050, s/d from Rs 2050/2600; ☎) This old Y is a bit shabby, but if you're on a very tight budget this could be it. It offers male-only dorms, and a few very basic single and double rooms that are open to both men and women: some share bathrooms and some have fans.

Grand Oriental Hotel HOTEL $$

(Map p60; ☎ 232 0391, 232 0392; www.grand oriental.com; 2 York St, Col 1; r 🌐 🛜) Opposite the harbour, this was Colombo's finest hotel a century ago, a place to see and be seen. Although that is no longer the case, there's a certain frumpy charm here. Rooms have a tired, generic look. There are superb harbour views from the fourth-floor restaurant and terrace; go for a drink, skip the food.

Colombo City Hotel HOTEL $$

(Map p60; ☎ 534 1962; www.colombocityhotel. com; Level 3, 33 Canal Row, Col 1; r US$60-100; 🌐 🛜) This hotel has reasonable rates and a fine location next to the Old Dutch Hospital, but the hotel can be very noisy and service is unpolished. The 32 rooms have fridges but are rather small and most lack decent views. The sea views from the restaurant roof are outstanding, even if the food is not.

Hilton Colombo HOTEL $$$

(Map p60; ☎ 249 2492; www.hilton.com; 2 Sir Chittampalam A Gardiner Mawatha, Col 2; r from US$160; 🌐 @ 🛜 🌐) This large, international business-class hotel buzzes with activity around the clock. It has 382 rooms in regular- and executive-floor flavours, six restaurants, a pub, a 24-hour business centre, a fully equipped sports-and-fitness club and an attractive garden and pool area.

🛏 Kollupitiya

Colombo's best large hotels (with many new ones being built) are in this central area, near the ocean and noisy Galle Rd. On back roads to the east you'll find numerous interesting choices.

Clock Inn HOTEL $

(Map p64; ☎ 250 0588; www.clockinn.lk; 457 Galle Rd; dm/r from US$15/50; 🌐 🛜) This clean and well-run hotel is great value, in a great location. The four-bed dorm rooms have a dash of style, while the regular rooms have queen-size beds with cable TV and private bathrooms.

★Lake Lodge GUESTHOUSE $$
(Map p64; ☎232 6443; www.taruhotels.com; 20 Alvis Tce, Col 3; r US$80-120; ❄📶) This hotel gets everything just right. The 13 rooms are well equipped and stylish in a minimalist way. Long concrete counters are good for work and the rooftop terraces have views of South Beira Lake. Service is excellent and the hotel is well managed. You can easily walk to much of what's interesting in Colombo.

★YWCA GUESTHOUSE $$
(Map p64; ☎232 4181; ywcacolombo@gmail.com; 393 Union Pl, Col 2; s/d from Rs 4500/5000, air-con extra Rs 1000 ; ❄📶) Of the several Ys offering budget accommodation in Colombo, this is easily our favourite. Enjoy modest colonial splendour in this leafy compound in a busy and popular part of town. The nine rooms are basic but you can lounge on comfy rattan chairs on the shady porch. The breakfast room is an oasis of serenity.

YWCA National Headquarters GUESTHOUSE $$
(Map p64; ☎232 3498; natywca@sltnet.lk; 7 Rotunda Gardens, Col 3; r from Rs 5000; ❄@) This place has eight tidy, very basic rooms (most fan-only) that surround a leafy courtyard. It's a secure refuge for female travellers; men can stay if they're with a female companion. There's a cheap cafeteria (meals Rs 150 to Rs 350), open from Monday to Saturday.

Hotel Renuka & Renuka City Hotel HOTEL $$
(Map p64; ☎257 3598; www.renukahotel.com; 328 Galle Rd, Col 3; r US$70-90; ❄📶) The well-run Renuka is bifurcated into two different buildings. Its 99 rooms are well maintained and have safes, fridges and 24-hour room service. Decor is somewhat basic; get a room not facing Galle Rd (and ask to see a couple). The staff are good, as is the Palmyrah restaurant, known for its Jaffna dishes.

Alfred Court HOTEL $$
(Map p64; ☎257 6677; www.alfredcourt.lk; Alfred Pl, Col 3; r US$55-85; ❄📶) A good no-frills midrange option in a central location. Rooms in this multistorey building come in two flavours: superior, which have standard hotel amenities; and deluxe, which are larger and have balconies.

Whitehouse Residences GUESTHOUSE $$
(Map p64; ☎077 413 2832; whitehousecolombo@gmail.com; 265/2 RA De Mel Mawatha, Col 3; r from US$80; ❄📶) Self-sufficient travellers will appreciate the large rooms and limited staff interface at this multistorey guesthouse, down a small lane. It's all spick and span.

GEOFFREY BAWA – 'BRINGING POETRY TO PLACE'

The most famous of Sri Lanka's architects, Geoffrey Bawa (1919–2003) fused ancient and modern influences in his work. Architect Ranjith Dayaratne described it as 'bringing poetry to place'.

Using courtyards and pathways, Bawa developed pleasing connections between the interior and exterior of his structures. These connections frequently included contemplative spaces, as well as framed areas that enabled glimpses of spaces yet to be entered. His designs were based within the environment. And he was not averse to the environment claiming his structures – at times he encouraged jungle growth along walls and roofs.

While Bawa created aesthetic beauty, he was also concerned with the functional aspects of architecture, opening and exposing structures to air and light while ensuring shelter and protection from harsh climatic elements. His approach was important not only for its originality but also for its influence on architecture in Sri Lanka and abroad.

Bawa's work outside Colombo includes the landmark Heritance Kandalama Hotel (p199) near Dambulla. In Colombo, don't miss the following:

Gallery Cafe (p76) The historic building used to be Bawa's office and is now used as an exhibition space for art and photography.

Seema Malakaya Meditation Centre (p63) A gem-like space on an island on South Beira Lake.

Geoffrey Bawa House (p63) The house where Bawa once lived is now a museum.

Parliament of Sri Lanka (www.parliament.lk; Kotte; admission by prior arrangement) Bawa's grand masterpiece is located on a lake island in Kotte, 11km southeast of Fort.

Some rooms have bright views and balconies, especially the top-floor suite.

★ Cinnamon Grand Hotel
HOTEL **$$$**

(Map p64; 243 7437; www.cinnamonhotels.com; 77 Galle Rd, Col 3; r US$130-200; ❋@🛜≋) Colombo's best large hotel has a central location well back from Galle Rd. It buzzes with energy as there always seems to be an elite wedding on while some high-profile politician strolls the huge, airy lobby. The 501 rooms are large; ask for a high floor to enjoy views. Service is excellent.

There's a fitness centre, big outdoor swimming pool, numerous top-notch restaurants and a lobby cafe.

★ Colombo Courtyard
BOUTIQUE HOTEL **$$$**

(Map p64; 464 5333; www.colombocourtyard.com; 32 Alfred House Ave, Col 3; r US$105-160; ❋🛜≋) All the comforts you could ask for (huge TVs, work areas, rain showers and more) are appealingly packaged at this new small hotel. Some rooms look onto the pool area. The entire property feels more like a posh urban retreat than mere hotel. Need some action? The rooftop bar, Cloud Cafe, is a trendy hangout.

Taj Samudra
HOTEL **$$$**

(Map p64; 244 6622; www.tajhotels.com; 25 Galle Face Centre Rd, Col 3; r US$140-250; ❋@🛜≋) Part of the well-regarded Indian chain, this vast edifice has elegant public areas and a lovely 11-acre garden, as well as myriad restaurants and bars, including a 24-hour cafe. The 270 rooms have recently been given a luxe refurb.

Galle Face Hotel
HOTEL **$$$**

(Map p64; 254 1010, 254 1016; www.galleface hotel.com; 2 Kollupitiya Rd, Col 3; r US$110-250; ❋@🛜≋) The *grande dame* of Colombo faces Galle Face Green to the north and the sea to the west. The sweeping staircases and trademark checked-tile floors recall the hotel's opening in 1864. Ongoing renovations are meant to restore the former grandeur in the main building to match the newish Regency wing. Service can be hit or miss.

Look for the huge plaque near the entrance with the names of the famous who've bedded down here, from Noel Coward to Richard Nixon to 'Carrie Fisher "*Star Wars*"'.

🛏 Cinnamon Gardens

The tree-lined streets here offer at least the allusion of genteel charm.

Parisare
HOMESTAY **$**

(Map p64; 269 4749; 97/1 Rosmead Pl, Col 7; r Rs 3300-4000) It's not the most luxurious guesthouse in town, but it's probably the most interesting. Parisare is a modern split-level home with few walls so that many of the common spaces are open-air. It's cluttered but clean and down a small alley next to the French embassy. Parisare's three rooms book up early.

Ranjit's Ambalama
GUESTHOUSE **$$**

(Map p64; 250 2403, 071 234 7400; www.ranjits ambalama.com; 53/19 Torrington Ave, Col 7; r Rs 5000-8000; ❋🛜) This guesthouse is modern and airy, with a small leafy courtyard and a wealth of books on Buddhism. There are seven rooms, three with private bathroom. All rooms have air-con (for an extra Rs 1500).

Finding the house is a bit tricky. Coming down Torrington Ave from Bauddhaloka Mawatha, look for the mosque on the right, then take the first left at a small playground and then the first right. It's the second house on the left.

Paradise Road Tintagel Colombo
BOUTIQUE HOTEL **$$$**

(Map p64; 460 2122; www.tintagelcolombo.com; 65 Rosmead Pl, Col 7; r US$150-350; ❋@🛜≋) Set inside an old mansion with a notorious past when it was a home for local politicians, this stylish hotel dazzles with its dark, minimalist design, elegant contours and idiosyncratic artworks. Part of the Paradise Road design empire, each of the 10 rooms is unique and some include private splash pool. Prince Charles and Camilla bunked here in 2013.

🛏 Borella

This middle-class neighbourhood is both quiet and rather far from the rest of Colombo to the west. There are several comfy family-run guesthouses scattered about here and nearby Mardana.

Garden Guest House
GUESTHOUSE **$$**

(Map p64; 269 7919; www.gardenguesthouse colombo.com; 7 Karlshrue Gardens, Col 10; r €40; ❋🛜) The modern home of Mrs Chitrangi de Fonseka bubbles with eccentricity, including chintzy decor, lots of porcelain and an indoor fountain. The three spacious rooms have TVs and a pink colour scheme that would delight a preteen girl. Bus 103 or 171 from Fort will drop you nearby; get off at Punchi Borella Junction.

Bambalapitiya, Havelock Town & Wellawatta

South of the centre, you realise some savings in both money and, at least on the side streets, noise.

Mrs Marie
Barbara Settupathy's HOMESTAY $
(Map p68; ☑ 258 7964; jbs@slt.lk; 23/2 Shrubbery Gardens, Col 4; r Rs 2000-4000; ⬛) The voluble Mrs Settupathy offers four clean and tidy rooms (three with private bathroom). There's a sitting area with TV, a full guest kitchen and a minuscule pebble courtyard. To find the house, look for the Church of Christ on the left as you come down Shrubbery Gardens.

Tropic Inn GUESTHOUSE $$
(Map p68; ☑ 250 6838; www.tropicinn.com; 19 De Vos Ave, Col 4; s/d from US$30/40; ⬛⬛) A new good-value guesthouse from the owners of the well-run hotel of the same name in Mt Lavinia. The five rooms here are in a three-storey house that hides behind a gate off a small lane. Everything is tidy and basic.

Hotel Sunshine HOTEL $$
(Map p68; ☑ 451 7676; www.hotelsunshine.lk; 5A Shrubbery Gardens, Col 4; r fan/air-con from Rs 2000/5000; ⬛⬛) This small budget hotel is tall and narrow and hemmed in by even taller neighbours. It has 24 clean but plain rooms at reasonable rates (cheaper ones are fan-only), just a half-block from the sea. The staff are professional and the address will appeal to Monty Python fans everywhere.

★ Havelock Place
Bungalow GUESTHOUSE $$$
(Map p68; ☑ 258 5191; www.havelockbungalow. com; 6-8 Havelock Pl, Col 5; r US$110-140; ⬛⬛⬛⬛) This appealing guesthouse has seven rooms in two sizes spread across two colonial houses. Modern luxury is matched with antiques that feel authentic to the period. It's on a quiet lane and has lush gardens and a small lap pool. The outdoor cafe is a good place to while away the hours.

Casa Colombo BOUTIQUE HOTEL $$$
(Map p68; ☑ 452 0130; www.casacolombo.com; 231 Galle Rd, Col 4; r from US$250; ⬛⬛⬛) This vast 200-year-old mansion sits in isolated splendour behind a row of shabby storefronts on Galle Rd. Protected from the noise, it's an urban refuge with huge old trees and a rather infamous pink-hued swimming pool. Designed by Lalin Jinasena, the 12 large suites are all decorated in colonial colours that mix modern and minimalist with the odd Moorish touch.

Ozo Colombo HOTEL $$$
(Map p68; ☑ 255 5570; www.ozohotels.com; 36-38 Clifford Pl, Col 4; r from US$110; ⬛⬛⬛⬛) This new hotel is a harbinger for the future of Colombo's waterfront. It has 158 rooms spread over 14 floors of a boldly blue highrise across from Wellawatta's beach (and train station). There are comforts and modern tech gadgets aplenty, while the rooftop has the perfect cafe/bar for sundowners.

Mt Lavinia

If you want a quieter alternative to Colombo but don't want to go as far as large beach towns such as Negombo, Mt Lavinia is a 30-minute drive from Fort and has a modest beachy charm. There are simple guesthouses aimed at local weekend travellers along the aptly named Hotel Rd as well as De Saram and College Rds. Inspect a couple before deciding. The Mt Lavinia train station is central to all the hotels listed here.

Blue Seas Guest House GUESTHOUSE $
(Map p70; ☑ 271 6298; info@footstepsthrough srilanka.com; 9/6 De Saram Rd; r Rs 2500-4500; ⬛⬛) This well-managed large house down a quiet lane has 15 clean and spacious rooms, some with balconies. There's a large sitting room and a garden. Budget rooms are fan-only.

Haus Chandra BOUTIQUE HOTEL $$
(Map p70; ☑ 273 2755; www.plantationgroup hotels.com; 37 Beach Rd; r US$50-70; ⬛⬛⬛⬛) Tucked along a quiet lane, this colonial-era residence-turned-hotel has 30 rooms spread across two buildings. Other options include a charming villa that sleeps six and a suite with antique furnishings and a fully equipped kitchen that's a good choice for tropical fantasies. The pool has ocean views.

Tropic Inn GUESTHOUSE $$
(Map p70; ☑ 273 8653; www.tropicinn.com; 30 College Ave; s/d from US$30/40; ⬛⬛⬛) This multistorey hotel features 16 clean rooms. There's an internal courtyard and many of the rooms have a balcony. The engaging staff are helpful.

Mount Lavinia Hotel HOTEL $$$
(Map p70; ☑ 271 5221, 271 5227; www.mountlavinia hotel.com; 100 Hotel Rd; r US$120-150; ⬛⬛⬛)

Part of this grand seafront hotel dates to 1806, when it was the residence of the British governor. The appropriately named 'governor's wing' has colonial decor and rather small rooms; the remainder is modern and rooms have balconies. There's a private sandy beach and a beautifully positioned pool and terrace. Service can be purely average.

✖ Eating

Colombo boasts a good and growing selection of restaurants. Besides great Sri Lankan food, you'll find food from across the region and further afield. There are upscale and stylish cafes aimed at the well-heeled but perhaps even more interesting are the many high-quality places aimed at Colombo's burgeoning middle class.

For cheap, tasty food it's hard to beat a lunch packet (about Rs 150). Sold between about 11am and 2pm on street corners and from carts all over the city, the lunch packet contains rice and curry, usually made from vegetables, with fish or chicken as optional extras. Also look for open-front shops displaying short eats (snacks to eat on the go) fresh from the kitchen.

The websites www.yamu.lk, www.tasty.lk and www.lankarestaurants.com are good resources for the fast-changing Colombo dining scene.

✖ Fort & Pettah

Hordes of office workers, traders, commuters and residents support excellent snack stands and restaurants, most aimed at the masses. In the Fort's high-profile Old Dutch Hospital you'll find an array of chic restaurants and outdoor cafes.

★ New Palm Leaf Hotel   SRI LANKAN $
(Map p60; 237 Olcott Mawatha, Col 11; meals Rs 200-300; ⊗6am-10pm) Like elsewhere in Sri Lanka, 'hotel' here means 'simple eating place'. Across the very busy road from Fort station and close to Pettah's market madness, pause here for a tea and cake or one of many excellent curries that are properly fiery.

★ T-Lounge   CAFE $
(Map p60; ☑244 7168; www.dilmaht-lounge.com; Chatham St, Dutch Sq; snacks Rs 200-500; ⊗11am-11pm; ❋🖥) A product of Sri Lanka's best tea producer, Dilmah, this gem of a cafe is in an annex to the hugely successful Old Dutch Hospital. The interior compliments the restored colonial exterior. The walls are lined with books about Sri Lanka and tea, while the menu has a range of tasty snacks like crepes, sandwiches and desserts, plus cocktails.

Pagoda Tea Room   BAKERY $
(Map p60; ☑232 5252; 105 Chatham St, Col 1; mains Rs 200-300; ⊗9am-8pm) Hungry like the wolf? Duran Duran filmed its classic 1980s video for that very song in this venerable establishment opened in 1884 (sadly, there are no monkeys or snake charmers at Pagoda these days). Although rice and curry is on the menu, the main focus is inexpensive pastries.

Heladiv Tea Club   CAFE $$
(Map p60; ☑575 3377; Old Dutch Hospital, Col 1; mains Rs 600-1500; ⊗9am-midnight; ❋) Tapas standards, spicy local nibbles, burgers, salads and much more are served at this good casual cafe. Choose from fine teas (the peach iced tea is plummy) or settle back on the porch with a cocktail.

★ Ministry of Crab   SEAFOOD $$$
(Map p60; ☑234 2722; www.ministryofcrab.com; Old Dutch Hospital , Col 1; mains Rs 800-4000; ⊗6-11pm Mon-Fri, noon-11pm Sat & Sun; ❋) Crabs are a major income earner for Sri Lanka's fishing industry but most are exported. This high-profile restaurant (two owners are former captains of the Sri Lanka cricket team plus there's famous chef Dharshan Munidasa) rectifies this loss by celebrating the

---

DON'T MISS

SUNSET

The Indian Ocean can yield up sunsets so rich in vivid colours that your eyes and brain can't quite cope. Many people opt for the outdoor bars in the cloistered surrounds of the Galle Face Hotel, but you can have a much more authentic experience joining Colombo's great and many on Galle Face Green. Nature's beauty is a moment best shared with others and you can enjoy a local snack from the many vendors. The beachside cafes of Mt Lavinia are also good sunset venues. Note that the day's weather is no indication of sunset quality, a dreary grey day can suddenly erupt in crimson and purple at dusk.

crustaceans in variations ranging from Singaporean chilli crab to locally spiced crab curry.

A couple can easily drop Rs 10,000 on a truly superb meal.

Curry Leaf SRI LANKAN $$$
(Map p60; ☑ 249 2492; Hilton Colombo, 2 Sir Chittampalam A Gardiner Mawatha, Col 1; buffet from Rs 2500; ⏱ 7pm-midnight) Tucked away in a lovely garden that has the motif of a Disney-fied traditional village, the buffet here has a vast range of Sri Lankan foods prepared with top-quality ingredients.

✖ Kollupitiya, Slave Island & Union Place

Old favourites can be found along Galle Rd. Head east for restaurants and cafes along quieter and often tree-lined streets. The back streets of Union Island reward snackers.

Green Cabin SRI LANKAN $
(Map p64; ☑ 258 8811; 453 Galle Rd, Col 3; meals Rs 150-400; ⏱ 7.30am-11.30pm) This local institution is famous for baked goods and an inexpensive array of rice and curry variations, all served in a leafy dining area. The lunchtime vegetarian buffet (Rs 280) is excellent value – the mango curry, if it's on, is very good.

For a snack, try the short meals from the bakery area such as the deep-fried peppers. At breakfast, hope they have string hoppers (pancake tangles of steamed noodles).

Burger's King BURGERS $
(Map p64; www.burgerskingsl.com; cnr Malay St & Union Pl, Col 2; mains from Rs 200; ⏱ 8am-11pm) Don't for one second confuse this Sale Island institution with the bland worldwide chain with the copycat name. The smiling dudes behind the big windows here dish up 15 kinds of very tasty burgers (beef, chicken, shrimp and vegie), plus kebabs and more.

Carnival ICE CREAM $
(Map p64; 263 Galle Rd, Col 3; cones under Rs 100; ⏱ 10am-9pm) Unchanged in decades, you don't visit Carnival for the ice cream (which is more icy than creamy) but rather for the timeless ice-cream-parlour surrounds. Still, where else can you get a banana split for Rs 200? And many do love the mint-chocolate chip.

Keells SUPERMARKET $
(⏱ 8am-10pm) Western-style supermarket popular for its large selection of imported goods. Locations at **Crescat Blvd** (Map p64; 89 Galle Rd, Crescat Blvd, Col 3) and **Union Place**

(Map p64; 199 Union Pl, Col 2), the latter with a big range of ready-meals.

Barefoot Garden Cafe CAFE $$
(Map p64; ☑ 258 9305; 704 Galle Rd, Col 3; meals Rs 600-1200; ⏱ 10am-11pm) Located in the courtyard of the splendid Barefoot gallery, this casual but stylish cafe serves sandwiches, salads and daily specials that usually include Sri Lankan and Asian dishes. The wine list is good and some nights there's special events like trivia contests or book readings. On Sunday there's live jazz.

Park Street Mews CAFE $$
(Map p64; www.parkstreetmewsrestaurant.com; 50/1 Park Rd, Col 2; mains Rs 500-2200; ⏱ 9am-11pm; 🐾) The namesake cafe of the smart little lane of designer shops has a suitably hip vibe with an industrial motif and pillows on the concrete floor for lounging – along with tables, chairs and more traditional seating. The menu mixes burgers, salads and Asian fare. Partiers will bless the restorative 'morning after' juice.

Paradise Road Gallery Cafe ASIAN FUSION $$$
(Map p64; ☑ 258 2162; www.paradiseroad.lk; 2 Alfred House Rd, Col 3; mains Rs 500-1500; ⏱ 10am-midnight; 🐾) The trim colonial bungalow that houses Shanth Fernando's Gallery Cafe used to be the office for Sri Lanka's most famous architect, Geoffrey Bawa. The open-air dining area looks over an intimate courtyard and reflecting pool. The Sri Lankan–inspired dishes focus on fresh ingredients and bold, clean flavours.

Curries made with black pork and prawns are popular. There's a huge range of luscious cakes you can snack on through the day.

✖ Cinnamon Gardens

Stylish little cafes and more ambitious restaurants can be found along the genteel streets of Colombo's classiest district.

★ Ceylon Tea Moments CAFE $
(Map p64; ☑ 269 5917; Phillip Gunawardena Mawatha, Colombo Racecourse, Col 7; mains Rs 100-500; ⏱ 7am-11pm; ▣) One of the best of the upscale tea emporiums sweeping Colombo, this rather opulent cafe gets everything right. Settle back into a plush armchair and ponder the glitter from the gold leaves hanging overhead. Try a speciality tea drink like the cinnamon tea shake while you ponder the

huge menu. *Rottis*, such as the crab number, win raves.

Boulevard
FOOD COURT **$**

(Map p64; Odel, 5 Alexandra Pl, Col 7; meals Rs 200-600; ☉10am-8pm) Fronting the entrance to the popular and chic Odel department store is this silver-hued swath of food stalls in a sleek outdoor food court. Outlets of well-known local vendors serve up sandwiches, Indian fare, health food, pizza, various snacks and gelato. Fans keep things breezy and cool.

Good Market
MARKET **$**

(Map p64; www.goodmarket.lk; Phillip Gunawardena Mawatha, Colombo Racecourse, Col 7; ☉10am-6pm Sat) Definitely not a bad market, this organic and artisan food market is held in the northeast parking lot of the Colombo Racecourse and is quickly attracting a range of high-quality vendors. Breads, prepared foods, organic fruit and veg, smoothies, snacks and much more are on offer.

Milk & Honey Cafe
VEGETARIAN **$$**

(Map p64; ☎269 6286; 12 Barnes Pl, Col 7; meals Rs 300-500; ☉9am-6pm Mon-Sat) Eating vegetarian never tasted so good; in a simple house shared with a kids' bookstore and Kemara spa, this groovy little cafe has an ever-changing menu of fresh fare such as slow-roasted veggies with pesto and a scrumptious mushroom and cream cheese focaccia. Enjoy one of many fresh juices outside in the garden.

Commons
BISTRO **$$**

(Map p64; ☎269 4435; 39A Sir Ernest de Silva Mawatha, Col 7; meals Rs 400-600; ☉7.30am-midnight; ❇🖙) This cafe has a strong following among Colombo's iPad-wielding set (who may well hail from the Russian embassy across the road). Customers lounge in soft seats around low tables and enjoy popular breakfasts, *rotti,* excellent burgers, pastas, desserts and more. The garden at the back is a shady urban retreat. Now if management would stop blocking the doors with their cars!

Coco Veranda Cafe
CAFE **$$**

(Map p64; www.cocoveranda.com; 32 Ward Pl, Col 7; meals Rs 500-1000; ☉8am-midnight; ❇🖙) In a small building with designer clothing shops, this cool little cafe has an extraordinarily long menu of teas, coffee drinks, frappes and fresh juices. There are sandwiches and pasta as well as very alluring desserts like the chocolate cake. This is a good late-night stop for a snack.

Paradise Road Cafe
CAFE, DELI **$$**

(Map p64; ☎011 268 6043; 213 Dharmapala Mawatha, Col 7; meals Rs 250-500; ☉10am-7pm; ❇) Part of the designer empire, this smart cafe serves coffee drinks, milkshakes, luscious cakes and a plethora of teas. Mains include sandwiches and pasta. Get upscale picnic fare from the deli and enjoy it in Viharamahadevi Park.

✕ Wellawatta

Local favourites dominate the options of this southern quarter, which has Galle Rd as its spine. Look for a dose of hip over on Stratford Ave in Pamankade.

★Bombay Sweet Mahal
CANDY **$**

(Map p68; 195 Galle Rd, Col 6; treats from Rs 50; ☉9am-7pm) Galle Rd boasts many vendors

DON'T MISS

HOTEL DE PILAWOOS

Just known as **Pilawoos** (Map p64; 417 Galle Rd; meals Rs 200-400; ☉24hr), this open-fronted purveyor of short eats is renowned for what may be the best *kotthu* in town. Starchy, savoury and very addictive, this purely Sri Lankan dish starts with *rottis* (preferably day-old), which are then rather dramatically sliced up along with vegetables, meats or some such combination thereof. The results are cooked on a very hot iron sheet and served steaming.

Possibly invented here, although no one is sure, cheese *kotthu* are rapidly becoming the most popular version. Expect the mighty and the humble to drop by anytime to grab one, often with a fresh juice. In the wee hours, many customers are clearly looking for absorbent fare, of which *kotthu* is ideally suited; in the morning, you'll see bleary eyed customers looking for the restorative magic for which *kotthu* is known.

Note that this is the true and original Pilawoos. As is often the case in Sri Lanka, their success has inspired dozens of competitors to adopt some version of their name; ersatz Pilawoos abound.

of Indian sweets but this tiny open-fronted shop is the best. An array of treats sits colourfully in the display cases. We especially like the thick and chewy nut musket. Buy by weight to go or grab a cool juice at a table at the back. The engaging staff will explain the many offerings.

★ Hansa Coffee
CAFE $

(Map p68; ☏ 311 6579; 24 Fife Rd, Col 5; snacks from Rs 200; ⊙9am-7pm; ❄) Colombo's best cup of coffee? We think so. Away from the Starbucks clones of Cinnamon Gardens, this simple storefront brews up any kind of coffee you can imagine using beans of the cafe's namesake owner, Sri Lanka's best coffee producer.

Katpaham Restaurant
SRI LANKAN $

(Map p68; ☏ 725 3157; 244 Galle Rd, Col 6; mains Rs 100-200; ⊙8am-10pm) Curries of every kind plus hoppers (bowl-shaped pancakes) are perfectly spicy at this storefront cafe which specialises in Jaffna cuisine. Beautiful roast chickens in display cases await consumption.

★ Yaal Restaurant
JAFFNA $$

(56 Vaverset Pl, Col 6; mains Rs 400-600; ⊙10am-10pm) The unique spicy cuisine of Jaffna's Tamils features at this simple yet very tidy restaurant across from the seashore. The speciality is the truly unique *odiyal kool,* a famous Jaffna dish consisting of vegetables and seafood combined in a creamy porridge. Also popular is the crab curry.

A nearby competitor named Yarl is cheaper and less polished.

Curry Leaves
INDIAN $$

(Map p68; ☏ 566 3322; 68 WA Silva Mawatha, Col 6; mains Rs 400-800; ⊙11am-3pm, 5-11pm; ❄) South Indian is served in well-mannered surrounds at this very popular restaurant. Besides good versions of the standards it has a good selection of crab at popular prices. The once Catholic (1853) and now Anglican St Paul Milagiriya is across the road.

✗ Mt Lavinia

The beachfront here is lined with cafes offering up drinks (cold Lions at sunset are Rs 200 to Rs 400), simple meals and seafood. Cross the tracks at any of many points and see what you find.

★ Bu Ba
CAFE $$

(Map p70; ☏ 273 2190; Mt Lavinia beach; mains Rs 800-3200; ⊙8am-midnight) With candlelit

tables right on the sandy beach, this seafood pub is a hidden treat. In the heat of the day you can retreat under the grove of palm trees; at night let the sky open overhead and the starlight rain down. Weekend dance parties are sometimes held here. To find it, walk south alongside the tracks from Mt Lavinia train station – about 100m.

Lavinia Breeze
SEAFOOD $$

(Map p70; ☏ 420 3781; off De Saram Rd; mains Rs 800-2000; ⊙11am-11pm) One of the more appealing of the Mt Lavinia beach cafes, the tables here are in a nice compound near the surf. If you want to caress something firmer with your toes there is an upstairs terrace. The long menu boasts cocktails and seafood in profusion.

La Voile Blanche
CAFE $$

(Map p70; 43/10 Beach Rd; mains from Rs 500; ⊙11am-11pm) Amid the often rather shabby Mt Lavinia beachfront cafes, this vision in white stands out. Under seven iconic palm trees, a range of comfy chairs and loungers beckons. The drinks list is long and the menu offers up sandwiches, pasta and seafood. Look for the cafe across the tracks behind the Mount Breeze Hotel.

🍷 Drinking & Nightlife

Finding a spot for sunset drinks is an essential experience (try Galle Face Green or Mt Lavinia); otherwise, many of the best cafes are good for a drink (notably T-Lounge, Barefoot Garden Cafe and Ceylon Tea Moments). Note that last call comes early: technically 11pm, although many places keep pouring much later.

Colombo's club scene is burgeoning with the rest of the capital's nightlife. Indie locations are thriving.

★ Qbaa
MUSIC BAR

(Map p68; ☏ 077 711 5011; 2 De Fonseka Rd, Col 5; ⊙6pm-late) Some of Colombo's best bands are booked in this exposed-brick-walled venue nightly. It's the kind of place where patrons swap tales of their favourite don at Oxbridge while knocking back good wines and champagne cocktails. The bar is tiny, the ho-hum adjoining restaurant isn't.

41 Sugar
LOUNGE

(Map p64; ☏ 268 2122; 41 Maitland Crescent, Col 7; ⊙6pm-midnight) Rise above it all at this stylish rooftop cocktail lounge. Long tables have views of the ever-growing Colombo skyline. Inside there's lots of low leather sofas for slouching and looking cool. There's a long list of frilly drinks and basic food to chase away the munchies.

Cloud Cafe
COCKTAIL BAR

(Map p64; ☑ 464 5333; 32 Alfred House Ave, Col 3; ☺ 6pm-midnight) The rooftop bar atop the hip Colombo Courtyard hotel is popular most nights for its breezy, sweeping views. Cute little chairs cradle your rump while you enjoy fine cocktails and upscale bar snacks. There's live jazz on Friday night and classic movies on other nights.

7° North
COCKTAIL BAR

(Map p64; Cinnamon Lakeside Hotel, 115 Sir Chittampalam A Gardiner Mawatha, Col 2; ☺ 5pm-1am) The one compelling reason to visit this otherwise forgettable hotel is this sprawling posh bar that overlooks Beira Lake from a large deck. Enjoy high-end cocktails under the stars.

Castle Hotel
BAR

(Map p64; Masjid Jamiah Rd, Col 2; ☺ 10am-late) Right off gritty Union Pl, this timeless boozer offers up cheap drafts of Lion in once-posh surrounds that have borne witness to generations of drinkers, from politicians to railway workers. It's a genial place, good for catching up on current Colombo events while munching on the very good French fries.

Galle Face Hotel
BAR

(Map p64; ☑ 254 1010; 2 Kollupitiya Rd, Col 3; ☺ 11am-midnight) The venerable hotel has the iconic Veranda bar area with its trademark chequered tiles and lawn tables under palms. Popular with G&T-seeking tourists, everyone gets slack-jawed at sunset. Service can be mediocre.

Taphouse by RnR
PUB

(Map p60; ☑ 077 377 3844; Old Dutch Hospital, Col 1; ☺ 11am-11pm) Cheap beer is the highlight at this upscale pub in the Old Dutch Hospital. It can get mobbed on Friday night as hundreds mill about the courtyard, mugs of cold beer in hand while air kisses are blown and intercepted.

Silk
CLUB

(Map p64; ☑ 077 151 2933; 41 Maitland Cres, Col 7; ☺ 9pm-5am Wed-Sat) Near other nightspots like 41 Sugar, this club is among the city's most popular.

Rhythm & Blues
LIVE MUSIC

(R&B; Map p68; ☑ 536 3859; 19/1 Daisy Villa Ave, Col 4; ☺ 6pm-very late) This place has live music nightly. It can get rowdy at the pool tables. Despite the Daisy Villa Ave address, it's on RA de Mel Mawatha.

B52
CLUB

(Map p60; ☑ 232 0320; Grand Oriental Hotel, 2 York St, Col 1; ☺ 9pm-4am Thu-Sun) Somewhat cramped, this club draws a mixed crowd of locals, sailors and lost visitors who take to the dance floor to thump the night away till nearly dawn.

☆ Entertainment

Colombo's after-dark entertainment is still nascent but is starting to blossom.

Nelum Pokuna Mahinda Rajapaksa Theatre
VENUE

(Map p64; www.lotuspond.lk; Ananda Coomaraswamy Mawatha, Col 7) This glossy venue, built largely with Chinese aid, is located in a high-profile spot south of Viharamahadevi Park. Its stunning design is based on the Nelum Pokuna, the 12th-century lotus pond in Polonnaruwa. Look for important productions here.

(When it first opened in 2011, named simply the 'Performing Arts Theatre', it was a popular sport among locals to see how long it would take Mahinda Rajapaksa to add his name to the building.)

Lionel Wendt Centre
CULTURAL CENTRE

(Map p64; ☑ 269 5794; www.lionelwendt.org; 18 Guildford Cres, Col 7; ☺ gallery & office 9am-1pm & 2-5pm Mon-Fri, 10am-noon & 2-5pm Sat & Sun) Among other cultural events, this gallery occasionally hosts live theatre and other events at night.

Elphinstone Theatre
THEATRE

(Map p64; ☑ 243 3635; Maradana Rd, Col 10) This restored 80-year-old theatre maintains a busy program that includes music, drama and films.

CASINOS

Gaming is legal in Colombo, but only for holders of foreign passports. Most of the clientele is from the region and the casinos – despite adopting names familiar to Vegas high rollers – are very modest affairs with no connection to their famous namesakes. although some big-ticket operators have been vying to change this.

Sri Lanka Cricket
CRICKET

(Map p64; ☎ 267 9568; www.srilankacricket.lk; 35 Maitland Pl, Col 7; ⊙ticket office 8.30am-5.30pm) The top sport in Sri Lanka is, without a doubt, cricket. You can buy tickets for major games from Sri Lanka Cricket, at the office near the oval. Major matches are played at Premadasa Cricket Stadium, northeast of the centre.

🛍 Shopping

Colombo's markets, with their vast selection of everyday goods, are much more compelling as places to visit than venues for finding gifts and goods to take home. Otherwise, Colombo has many stores making that extra bag essential, and several glossy new malls are expected to open in the next few years as the economy booms. In the meantime the pick of the city's (somewhat tired) malls include **Crescat Boulevard** (Map p64; 89 Galle Rd, Col 3) and **Majestic City** (Map p68; Galle Rd, Col 4).

Sri Lanka has a thriving weaving industry that produces both hand- and machine-woven fabrics, and is a major garment manufacturer. All manner of clothing, ranging from beachwear to padded jackets, is sold in Colombo.

Ceylon tea is sold in just about every place that sells foodstuffs. For the best quality and selection, however, visit a specialist shop.

★Barefoot
CRAFTS, BOOKS

(Map p64; ☎ 258 0114; www.barefootceylon. com; 704 Galle Rd, Col 3; ⊙10am-7pm Mon-Sat, 11am-5pm Sun) Designer Barbara Sansoni's beautifully laid-out shop, located in an old villa, is justly popular for its bright hand-loomed textiles, which are fashioned into bedspreads, cushions, serviettes and other household items (or sold by the metre). You'll also find textile-covered notebooks, lampshades and albums, and a large selection of stylish, simple clothing.

Within the much-lauded designer shop is an excellent book department. This is where you'll find a carefully selected range of locally published books, the full range of Michael Ondaatje's works and much more. The courtyard cafe is a lovely stop for something refreshing.

★Odel
DEPARTMENT STORE

(Map p64; www.odel.lk; 5 Alexandra Pl, Col 7) A high-profile department store that combines international and top local brands in one glitzy labyrinth. From fashions to homewares to cosmetics and gift items, Odel's selection is tops. It's always crowded with both visitors and the local elite.

Paradise Road
HOMEWARES

(Map p64; ☎ 268 6043; www.paradiseroad.lk; 213 Dharmapala Mawatha, Col 7) In addition to a variety of colonial and Sri Lankan collectables, you'll find a good selection of original homewares and designer items in this high-style boutique from famous designer Shanth Fernando.

Elsewhere, the Paradise Road Gallery Cafe adjoins the noted restaurant and is tightly packed with small, artistic goods. Both are excellent places to look for small gifts to take home.

Gandhara
HOMEWARES

(Map p68; www.gandharacrafts.com; 28 Stratford Ave, Col 6) This stylish designer shop on the trendy stretch of Stratford Ave sells everything from candles to coffee tables. Gift items pegged to the season are displayed in profusion and there is a good selection of books on Sri Lankan art.

House of Fashions
CLOTHING

(Map p64; ☎ 250 4639; www.houseoffashions.lk; cnr RA de Mel Mawatha & Visak Rd, Col 4; ⊙10am-8pm, till 5pm Mon) A sign of the times: Colombo's legendary surplus outlet for the nation's garment industry has gone upscale and now has a new multistorey building. It still has unbeatable textile and clothing prices but now it's cultivating its own style too.

KT Brown
CLOTHING

(Map p64; ☎ 205 5751; 7 Coniston Pl, Col 7) Noted local designer Kanchana Thalpawila offers a range of women's clothing, from casual garb to haute couture. Her inspirations are traditional fabrics and costumes that reflect the ethnic groups of Sri Lanka.

PR
CLOTHING

(Map p64; ☎ 269 9921; 41 Horton Pl, Col 7) The fashion branch of the Paradise Road design conglomerate is run by Annika Fernando and is housed with her sister Saskia Fernando's eponymous gallery. All the clothing is from Sri Lankan and Indian designers.

Melache
CLOTHING

(Map p68; ☎ 259 5405; 29/3 Visaka Private Rd, Col 4) 'Where dressing chic is an art', is the slogan at this shop which stocks the work of a half dozen local designers. A quick browse and you'll see that Colombo's fashion scene is flourishing. Better, you can easily find a unique frock for under Rs 2000.

Sri Lanka

Cashew Corporation   FOOD
(Map p64; 518 Galle Rd, Col 3) Cashews were brought by the Portuguese to Sri Lanka from Brazil in the 16th century. They've clearly found the climate agreeable as the nuts are now a major export item. This small shop is packed full of fulsome cashews of a size and quality that are usually hard to find, especially in that dodgy bag of mixed nuts.

Raux Brothers   HOMEWARES, ANTIQUES
(The Colonial; Map p64; 259 4494; www.raux brothers.com; 137 Bauddhaloka Mawatha, Col 4) This 55-year-old design firm has a gorgeous showroom in a large, beautiful colonial storefront, which stocks an impressive range of furniture and artworks crafted from wood. There are genuine antiques and handcrafted new pieces. This is possibly the best antiques house in the city.

Laksala   HANDICRAFTS
(www.laksala.gov.lk) Large government-run chain of arts & crafts and souvenir shops popular with groups. With a **main store** (Map p64; 215 Bauddhaloka Mawatha, Col 7; 9am-9pm) in Cinnamon Gardens, plus a **National Museum store** (Map p64; National Museum, Nelum Pokuna Rd), it offers cheap carved elephants, well-crafted handicrafts, and handmade jewelry and clothing compete for attention.

Sri Lanka Tea Board Shop   TEA
(Map p64; 574 Galle Rd, Col 3) A large but unflashy shop which has many of the smaller brands of Ceylon tea that can be hard to find. It also has the full range of top brands such as Mackwoods and all sorts of tea-related merchandise.

Mlesna Tea Centre   TEA
(www.mlesnateas.com) High-end boutiques at **Crescat Boulevard** (Map p64; 89 Galle Rd, Crescat Boulevard, Col 3) and **Majestic City** (Map p68; Galle Rd, Majestic City, Col 4), with teas and tea-making wares in addition to the house-brand teas.

Noritake Showroom   CHINA
(Map p64; www.noritake.lk; 546-A Galle Rd, Col 3) The famous Japanese creator of fine chinaware has had factories in Sri Lanka since 1972. At this lovely showroom, you can browse the company's products, which are priced much cheaper here than you'll find post-export.

Lakpahana   ARTS & CRAFTS
(Map p64; 269 8211; www.lakpahana.lk; 14 Phillip Gunawardena Mawatha, Col 3) *The* place for mass-produced carved elephants in bulk so you can show *everyone* back home you care. Traditional souvenirs are sold in profusion and this vast store is a cathedral of unintentional kitsch.

Arpico   SUPERSTORE
(Map p64; Hyde Park Corner, Col 2) A huge store that's good for replacing almost anything you left at home. Imported foods (get your Tim Tams here), cosmetics, sunscreen, a pharmacy, travel gadgets like plug adapters and much, much more. It has a good, casual cafe where you can hone your shopping list.

Dilmah Tea Shop   TEA
Sri Lanka's top tea brand has its own posh shops, at **Cinnamon Gardens** (Map p64; Odel, 5 Alexandra Pl, Col 7), **Crescat Boulevard** (Map p64; 89 Galle Rd, Crescat Boulevard, Col 3) and **Majestic City** (Map p68; Galle Rd, Majestic City, Col 4).

Vijitha Yapa Bookshop   BOOKS
Branches at **Crescat Boulevard** (Map p64; 011 551 0100; 89 Galle Rd, Crescat Boulevard, Col 3) and **Unity Plaza** (Map p68; 011 259 6960; Galle Rd, Unity Plaza, Col 4) stock a comprehensive collection of foreign and local novels, guidebooks and pictorial tomes on Sri Lanka.

PETTAH'S SHOPPING STREETS

Pettah's market stalls and shops sell seemingly everything. When plunging into the age-old district's commercial madness, it's handy to note that many thoroughfares have their own shopping specialities:

1st Cross St at Bankshall St
plastic flowers

2nd Cross St at Bankshall St
lace & ribbons

2nd Cross St jewellery

Gabo's Lane at 5th Cross St
Ayurvedic medicines

Dam St bicycles

Sea St sapphires

DON'T MISS

KALA POLA ART MARKET

Every Sunday morning the broad avenue Ananda Coomaraswamy Mawatha, south of Viharamahadevi Park, comes alive with colour as local artists display their works at the **Kala Pola Art Market** (Map p64; Ananda Coomaraswamy Mawatha, Col 7; ⊙ Sunday 8am-noon). This weekly explosion of colour is an outgrowth of the original market, a huge annual event still held the third Sunday of January when up to 500 artists display their work. The market is a kaleidoscope of creativity from across the nation and you might just find a bargain-priced treasure.

Bazaar SOUVENIRS
(Map p60; off Olcott Mawatha, Col 11) A large collection of stalls just west of Fort station, selling items aimed at tourists. Cheap prices for Lion beer T-shirts.

Buddhist Book Centre BOOKS
(Map p64; ☑ 268 9786; 380 Bauddhaloka Mawatha, Col 7) Filled with books on Buddhism; about a third of the stock is in English.

ⓘ Information

DANGERS & ANNOYANCES

Crime Violence towards foreigners is uncommon, although you should take the usual safeguards. Solo women should be careful when taking taxis and three-wheelers at night; if, as sometimes happens, your taxi turns up with two men inside, call another.

Scams & Touts Colombo has its share of touts and con artists. You may be approached by someone who, after striking up a conversation, asks for a donation for a school for the blind or some such cause – these people are invariably con artists. Street offers for guides and 'special' tours should also be shunned.

EMERGENCY

Fire & Ambulance (☑ 242 2222, 110)
Medi-Calls Ambulance (☑ 534 3343, 255 6605; www.medicallsonline.com) Private ambulance company.
Police (☑ 243 3333, 119)
Tourist Police (Map p64; ☑ 242 1052, 1912; 80 Galle Rd, Col 3; ⊙ 24hr)

INTERNET ACCESS

Many cafes and most hotels in Colombo offer wi-fi.

MEDIA

The daily English-language newspapers, the *Daily Mirror*, the *Daily News* and the *Island* all have local news and entertainment listings.

Good websites:
Ceylon Today (www.ceylontoday.lk) News, sports and entertainment.
Daily Mirror (www.dailymirror.lk) Best of the newspaper websites.
Gossip Lanka (www.english.gossiplankanews.com) Gossip and entertainment news.
Yamu (www.yamu.lk) Good source for events, dining out, sights and more.

MEDICAL SERVICES

Avoid government hospitals, such as Colombo General.
Nawaloka Hospital (Map p64; ☑ 557 7111; www.nawaloka.com; 23 Deshamanya HK Dharmadasa Mawatha, Col 2) This private hospital has a good reputation and English-speaking doctors.

MONEY

There are banks and ATMs all over the city. Exchange services are in the arrivals hall at Bandaranaike International Airport, in Fort and along Galle Rd.

POST

Sri Lanka Post (Map p60; ☑ 011 232 6203; DR Wijewardana Mawatha, Col 1; ⊙ 7am-6pm) has branches around the city.

The major international express shipping services all have locations in Colombo.

TOURIST INFORMATION

Sri Lanka Tourist Board (SLTB; Map p64; ☑ 243 7059; www.srilanka.travel; 80 Galle Rd, Col 3; ⊙ 9am-4.45pm Mon-Fri, to 12.30pm Sat) The country's national tourism office has lavish brochures and maps, and can answer questions.

ⓘ Getting There & Away

Note that the roads in and around Colombo are very congested.

AIR

Although Bandaranaike International Airport (p312##) is at Katunayake, 30km north of the city, it is called Colombo (CMB) in airline schedules. Arriving by air – especially late at night – it is easiest to spend your first night in Negombo or the city. You can then easily move on by road, rail or bus.

BUS

Colombo's bus stations are chaotic, but have frequent buses going in all directions. The city has three main bus terminals, all just east of

Fort train station on the south edge of Pettah. Long-distance buses leave from **Bastian Mawatha** (Map p60; Olcott Mawatha) and **Saunders Pl** (Map p60; Saunders Pl). The following table details which buses leave from which station:

FROM BASTIAN MAWATHA	FROM SAUNDERS PL
Ambalangoda	Anuradhapura
Galle	Badulla
Hikkaduwa	Haputale
Kandy	Jaffna
Kataragama	Kurunegala
Matara	Negombo
Nuwara Eliya	Ratnapura
Tangalla	Polonnaruwa
	Trincomalee

➜ **Central Bus Station** (Map p60; Olcott Mawatha) has suburban buses.

There are fast buses that leave from the southern suburbs for Galle via the Southern Expressway (see p114).

TRAIN

The landmark main train station, **Colombo Fort** (Olcott Mawatha), is very central. Trains in transit often stop only for two or three minutes.

JF Tours & Travels (☑ 244 0048; Galle Fort Train Station; ☺ 9am-5pm) has an office at the front of Fort station; the helpful staff know everything about transport in and out of Colombo. Or you could try the information desk in the station. There is **left-luggage storage** (Map p60; per bag per day Rs 60; ☺ 5.30am-9.30pm) at the extreme left-end as you face the station. See the Transport chapter, p312, for more on train travel in Sri Lanka.

❶ Getting Around

TO/FROM THE AIRPORT

Completion of the **Colombo–Katunayake Expressway** has greatly reduced travel time between Bandaranaike International Airport and the city. From its start 4km northeast of Fort at Kelani Bridge, you can reach the airport in 30 minutes. Unfortunately the city streets remain as congested as ever during the day so add plenty of time for navigating Colombo itself. Avoid the old Colombo–Negombo Rd as it can take up to two hours.

Bus Fast airport buses using the expressway depart from Central Bus Station around the clock, take about 45 minutes and cost Rs 130. At the airport you'll find buses in the parking lot at the far left end of the terminal as you exit the arrivals hall.

Car You can arrange an airport car with most Colombo-area hotels for Rs 3000 to Rs 5000. Hotels as far as Galle and beyond also often arrange airport transport. Drivers will meet you in the arrivals area of the airport.

Taxi You can book a car into Colombo (or elsewhere in Sri Lanka) at the desks when you arrive in the arrivals hall. Or you can use the hassle-free taxi service outside. Rides cost Rs 2600 to about Rs 3200 depending on where you are going in Colombo. Be sure to specify you want to use the expressway and pay the Rs 300 toll.

PUBLIC TRANSPORT

Bus The *A-Z Street Guide* contains a detailed table and a map showing bus routes in Colombo, but the best way to find out which bus to take is just to ask people at the nearest stop. Buses going down Galle Rd from Fort or Pettah include the 100. Fares vary from Rs 5 to Rs 40, depending on distance. Service is frequent; there is usually an English-language destination sign on the front of the bus.

Taxi Most taxis are metered, but often the driver won't use the meter – agree on the fare before setting off. A taxi from Fort train station to Galle Face Hotel (a little over 2km) should cost about Rs 250; Mt Lavinia should cost around Rs 1300.

Dispatched cabs are popular and good value. Reliable companies include:

Ace Cabs (☑ 281 8818; www.acecabs.lk)
Budget Taxi (☑ 729 9299)
Kangaroo Cabs (☑ 258 8588; www.2588588.com)

Three-wheeler Also known as tuk-tuks and trishaws, these are ubiquitous. Although you're likely to get wet if it rains and the cramped back seats have limited views out, a ride in a three-wheeler is part of the Colombo experience. Drivers dart fearlessly between huge buses, an experience that's exhilarating for some and frightening for others.

Many three-wheelers now have meters and are the cheapest means of getting around. However some drivers will try not to use the meter or won't have one. Agree to a price before setting out. From Fort, expect to pay Rs 300 to get to Cinnamon Gardens, Rs 600 to Bambalapitiya and Rs 1000 to Mt Lavinia. Avoid drivers who are parked as they'll charge more; hail one passing by instead.

Train You can use the train to get to the suburbs dotted along Galle Rd – Kollupitiya, Bambalapitiya, Wellawatta, Dehiwala and Mt Lavinia; as a bonus, the line follows the seashore. Timetables are clearly marked at the stations, though service is frequent. If you board the train at Fort train station, double-check that it stops at all stations or you may end up in Galle. Train fares are about the same as bus fares.

The West

Includes ➡

Best Places to Eat

➡ Lords (p90)

➡ Home Grown Rice & Curry (p101)

➡ Petit Restaurant (p90)

➡ Spaghetti & Co (p101)

Best Places to Stay

➡ Ging Oya Lodge (p91)

➡ Shangri-Lanka Villa (p97)

➡ Villa Araliya (p89)

➡ Saman Villas (p97)

➡ Aditya Resort (p101)

Why Go?

You don't have to be on Sri Lanka's west coast for long to realise that the coastline has something of a multiple personality. North of the capital is Negombo, a cheerful beach town crowned with church spires that is, thanks to its proximity to the airport, a staple of almost every visitor's Sri Lankan journey. Head further north, though, and you enter a wild and little-visited region that seems to consist of nothing but coconut plantations and lagoons, sparkling in the sun and filled with dolphins.

South of Colombo's chaos is a world that oscillates between the dancing devils of traditional Sri Lankan culture in Ambalangoda, the chic boutique hotels and uncluttered golden sands of Bentota and the down-at-heel but ever-popular backpacker party town of Hikkaduwa.

Whichever part of the west coast you choose, you can be sure you'll end up spending longer here than planned.

When to Go
Negombo

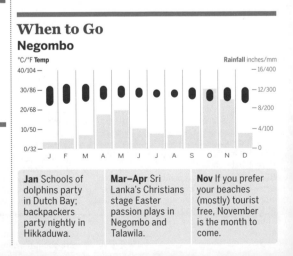

Jan Schools of dolphins party in Dutch Bay; backpackers party nightly in Hikkaduwa.

Mar–Apr Sri Lanka's Christians stage Easter passion plays in Negombo and Talawila.

Nov If you prefer your beaches (mostly) tourist free, November is the month to come.

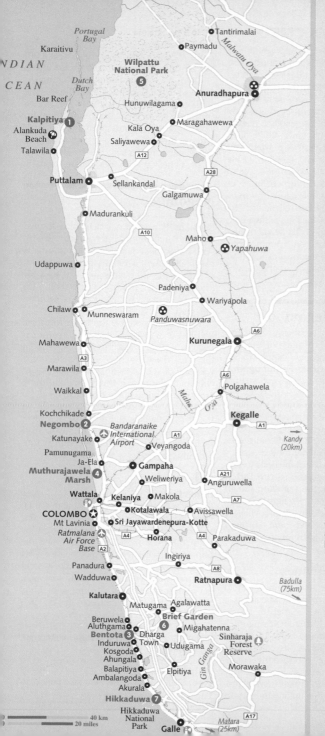

West Coast Highlights

1 Scanning the horizon for schools of playful dolphins in the waters off **Kalpitiya** (p92)

2 Finding your feet after a long flight in charming but ramshackle **Negombo** (p86)

3 Feeling the stress levels drop under the palm trees of lovely **Bentota** (p95), and booking in for a pampering in one of the area's boutique hotels

4 Ticking off egrets and herons during a waterborne birdwatching safari through the **Muthurajawela Marsh** (p86)

5 Scouring the undergrowth for leopards and spotted deer at **Wilpattu National Park** (p94)

6 Getting all green-fingered in the **Brief Garden** (p95) near Bentota

7 Raising a toast to the sunset after a hard day's diving and surfing in lively **Hikkaduwa** (p98)

NORTH OF COLOMBO

Leaving Colombo most eyes look south, but for those with time on their hands and a sense of curiosity, or for those on the slow road towards Anuradhapura, then the northbound A3 heads out of Colombo, skirts some charming old Dutch canals, slides past some sandy beaches and gets utterly lost among a matted tangle of coconut groves and wildlife-filled woodlands. It all adds up to a wonderful sense of discovery. For the moment, aside from workaday Negombo, which sits close to Bandaranaike International Airport, much of this area remains fairly unexplored by tourists, but things are on the cusp of change. The government, inspired by the kind of high-end, exclusive beach tourism of the neighbouring Maldives, has embarked on an ambitious tourism project around the town of Kalpitiya at the end of the long peninsula that separates Dutch Bay from the ocean.

Colombo to Negombo

The narrow belt of land between the gulf and the lagoon that stretches much of the way from the northern suburbs of Colombo to Negombo is sometimes called **Pamunugama**, after its biggest settlement. It's a lovely strip of coconut palms, old Portuguese-style churches, cross-dotted cemeteries on dunes, and pockets of tidy houses. There are some small hotels along here. Unfortunately, though, the beach is steep, with a sheer reef drop-off that makes swimming perilous no matter the sea's state.

This is also home to one of the best stretches of the old and straight-as-an-arrow **Dutch Canal** (also known as the Hamilton Canal) that runs along this entire length of coast. It's lined with small factories, fishing villages, mansions, nature areas and more. Hiring a bike in Negombo is an ideal way to tour this area.

◉ Sights & Activities

The evocatively translated 'Supreme Field of Pearls', or **Muthurajawela Marsh**, is a little-known gem of a wetland at the southern end of Negombo's lagoon. It's Sri Lanka's biggest saline wetland and home to 75 bird species including purple herons, cormorants and kingfishers, as well as crocodiles, monkeys and even some rarely seen otters.

The marsh is under threat from a proposed high-speed rail line linking the airport to Colombo.

★ Muthurajawela
Visitor Centre   BIRDWATCHING

(☏ 011 403 0150; boat trip per person Rs 1000) The Muthurajawela Visitor Centre is at the southern end of the road along Pamunugama, next to the Hamilton Canal. It has some moth-eaten displays and a 25-minute video on the wetland's fauna; but much more interestingly, it also runs two-hour boat trips through the wetlands. It's a very good idea to call and reserve a boat ride in advance, as it can get busy at weekends and on holidays.

Negombo

☏ 031 / POPULATION 141,000

Negombo is a modest beach town located close to Bandaranaike International Airport. With a stash of decent hotels and restaurants to suit all pockets, a friendly local community, an interesting old quarter and a reasonable (though polluted) beach, Negombo is a much easier place to get your Sri Lankan feet than Colombo.

The Dutch captured the town from the Portuguese in 1640, lost it, and then captured it again in 1644. The British then took it from them in 1796 without a struggle. Negombo was one of the most important sources of cinnamon during the Dutch era, and there are still reminders of the European days.

The busy centre of Negombo town lies to the west of the bus and train stations. Most places to stay, however, line the main road that heads north from the town centre, running almost parallel to the beach.

◉ Sights

Dutch Fort   RUINS

(Map p87) Close to the seafront near the lagoon are the ruins of the old Dutch fort, which has a fine gateway inscribed with the date 1678. Also here is a green, called the **Esplanade**, where cricket matches are a big attraction. As the fort grounds are now occupied by the town's prison, the only way you'll get a peek inside is by stealing something. You'd need to be very interested in old Dutch forts to go to such lengths, however.

Several old Dutch buildings are still in use, including the **Lagoon Resthouse** (Map p87; Custom House Rd).

Main Fish Market   MARKET

(Map p87) Each day, fishermen take their *oru-vas* (outrigger canoes) and go out in search of the fish for which Negombo is well known.

Negombo (Town)

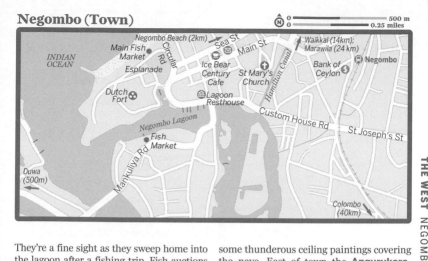

They're a fine sight as they sweep home into the lagoon after a fishing trip. Fish auctions on the beach and sales at the fish market near the fort are a slippery and very smelly sight, but one that's well worth forgoing some swimming pool time for.

The catch is not all from the open sea: Negombo is at the northern end of a lagoon that is renowned for its lobsters, crabs and prawns. Across the lagoon bridge there's a second **fish market** (Map p87). If you can stagger out of bed at 6am, it's a good place to watch much bigger fishing boats return with their catches.

Beach   BEACH
(Map p88) Even though it could never compete in a beauty contest against many Sri Lankan beaches, Negombo's beach, which stretches north from the town right along the hotel strip before fading into a palm-tree distance, has been recently tidied up and, in front of the big hotels, is now quite pleasant. Sadly, the water does have a distinct brown colour thanks to estuary run-off and pollution, but it's no longer bad enough to stop people swimming.

Foreign tourists can often access the beach in front of most big hotels even if you're not staying, but for a more colourful (and noisier) scene join the locals at what is known as **Negombo Beach Park** (Map p88).

Religious Buildings   RELIGIOUS
(Map p87) Negombo is dotted with churches, and so many locals converted to Catholicism that the town is sometimes known as 'Little Rome'. The fading pink chamber of **St Mary's Church**, in the town centre, has

some thunderous ceiling paintings covering the nave. East of town the **Angurukaramulla Temple**, with its 6m-long reclining Buddha, is also worth seeing. The island of **Duwa**, joined to Negombo by the lagoon bridge, is famed for its Easter passion play.

Canals   CANALS
The Dutch showed their love of canals here like nowhere else in Sri Lanka. Canals extend from Negombo all the way south to Colombo and north to Puttalam, a total distance of over 120km. You can hire a bicycle in Negombo from various hotels and ride the canal-side paths for some distance, enjoying the views and small villages along the way.

🏃 Activities

Colombo Divers   DIVING
(Map p88; ☎ 077 736 7776; www.colombodivers. com; Jetwing Blue, Ethukala) The waters around Negombo offer much better diving than many people imagine, and this regarded agency, inside the Jetwing Blue hotel, can take you to meet the fish at more than 40 different dive sites. They charge US$100 for a Discover Scuba course and US$450 for a full PADI open water course.

Kite Centre Negombo   EXTREME SPORTS
(Map p88; ☎ 492 7744; The Pearl, 13 Porutota Rd) Want to skim like a flying fish over the surface of the ocean? Kitesurfing courses using decent equipment and run by experienced surfers are available through the Kite Centre Negombo based inside the Pearl guesthouse (p89). A three-day course costs €340 or one short hour is €49.

Negombo (Beach Area)

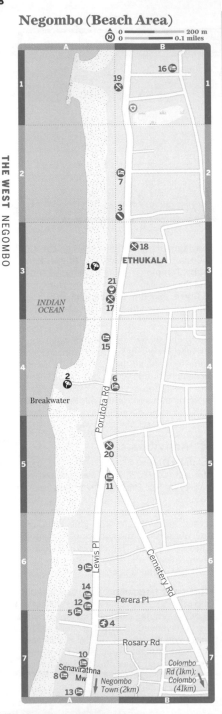

Lucky Tours   BIRDWATCHING
(Map p88; ☎ 223 3733; lucky-tour55@hotmail.com; 146 Lewis Pl) Specialist birdwatching tours in the Negombo region including half-day tours (one person Rs 5000, two people Rs 7000 incl transport) to the Muthurajawela Marsh (p86).

**Serendib Watersports
Paradise**   DIVING
(Map p88; ☎ 077 738 5505; www.dive-srilanka. com; The Pearl, 13 Porutota Rd) Housed inside the Pearl guesthouse (p89), this is a long-established and reputable dive outfit. They charge €380 for the PADI open water dive course.

⌇ Sleeping

There are masses of places to stay in all price bands. However, because so many people spend their first or last Sri Lankan night in Negombo, it pays to book ahead at the more popular places. Generally, the closer the accommodation is to town, the rougher around the edges it is.

Beach Villa Guest House
GUESTHOUSE **$**

(Map p88; ☑ 222 2833; www.beachvillanegombo.
com; 3/2 Senavirathna Mawatha; r Rs 1500-2500;
✻ ✽ 🛜) This backpacker classic has dark but
otherwise decent rooms, and is so close
to the sea that you might want to consider
snoozing in your swimwear. There's a cheap
and pleasant cafe-restaurant, a wealth of
travel advice and loads of other backpackers.
Cheaper rooms are fan only.

Jeero's Guest House
GUESTHOUSE **$**

(Map p88; ☑ 223 4210; 239 Lewis Pl; r from
Rs 3200) With latticework window frames,
comfortably worn-in furniture and breezy
balconies, this is a well-priced and friendly
option set around a pleasing garden just
back from the beach.

Dion's Guest House
GUESTHOUSE **$**

(Map p88; ☑ 223 7373; dionsguesthouse@hotmail.
com; 137 Lewis Pl; r Rs 4500; 🛜) A relative new-
comer, the rooms here, which are large and
screeching white with excellent bathrooms,
border on flashpacker cool rather than backpacker hardcore. There's a nice roadside garden, which is neon-lit at night. Breakfast is
Rs 500 extra.

Hotel Silver Sands
HOTEL **$**

(Map p88; ☑ 222 2880; www.silversands.go2lk.com;
229 Lewis Pl; r Rs 3000-4700; ✻) An excellent,
cheap beachfront option with neatly tiled
rooms that have crazy tent-like mosquito
nets and are decorated with bunches of plastic flowers. Fishy fans will love the rows of
aquariums full of guppies, mollies and goodness knows what else.

★ Villa Araliya
BOUTIQUE HOTEL **$$**

(Map p88; ☑ 227 7650; www.villaaraliya-negombo.
com; 154/10 Porutota Rd; r without air-con US$60, r
with air-con US$80-120; ✻ 🛜 ✽) This standout
choice has a variety of modern rooms – some
dashed up in multihued colours and others
with exposed red-brick walls – but the uniting
factor is that they're all supremely comfort-
able, with big beds, high ceilings and bath-
rooms that you'll be happy to splash about in.
The crystal-clean swimming pool will likely
entice you in for a few pre-breakfast laps.

The hotel is family-friendly (it has chil-
dren's toys, cots and high chairs) and is on
a quiet side street that's a five-minute walk
from the beach. Rates include breakfast.

Ice Bear Guest House
GUESTHOUSE **$$**

(Map p88; ☑ 071 423 7755; www.icebearhotel.
com; 103/2 Lewis Pl; s €23-35, d €44-67; ✻ 🛜)
A gorgeous traditional villa with lots of

colour and flair (or 'Swissness', as the sign
says – to which you could also add 'and a
little eccentricity'). This 'budget boutique'
hotel has a variety of rooms thrown about
the beautiful dog- and duck-filled gardens.
The rooms have flower-sprinkled beds and
homey touches.

There's also a beachside cafe with tasty
treats like homemade muesli, and classical
music often wafts through the palms.

Holiday Fashion Inn
GUESTHOUSE **$$**

(Map p88; ☑ 223 3936; 109 Cemetery Rd; d incl
breakfast US$55; ✻ 🛜) There's an inviting
family vibe to this very smart guesthouse a
short stroll back from the main strip. Rooms
are spacious and immaculate and have little
kitchenettes (minus a cooker).

Angel Inn
GUESTHOUSE **$$**

(Map p88; ☑ 223 6187; 189/17 Lewis Pl; r with/
without air-con US$40/35; ✻ 🛜) This is one of
the most inviting cheap guesthouses in Negombo. Its seven rooms (with more under
construction) might not have beach views,
but in every other way it's truly excellent value with flawlessly clean and shiny rooms set
around a small garden.

Blue Water Boutique Hotel
HOTEL **$$**

(Map p88; ☑ 223 7233; 281/1 Lewis Place; d incl
breakfast US$79; ✻ 🛜) Very new at the time of
research, this place, if it keeps its prices low
and its standards up, has the potential to be
one of the better deals in Negombo. The spa-
cious rooms are all sleek minimalism and
guests can use the pool of the neighbouring
Paradise Beach Hotel.

Breakfast is served on the sun-blasted
roof terrace.

The Pearl
GUESTHOUSE **$$**

(Map p88; ☑ 492 7744; www.pearl-negombo.com;
13 Porutota Rd; s/d €39/52; ✻ 🛜) This small
beachfront pad might be discreet, but it
packs enough flair and comfort to gladden
the heart of any weary traveller. The six immaculate rooms are full of cheeky modern
art and are well maintained. If you're into
watersports, it's a good bet as it's the home
base of well-regarded diving and kitesurfing
outfits.

Beach
RESORT **$$$**

(Map p88; ☑ 227 3500; www.jetwinghotels.com;
Porutota Rd; s/d incl breakfast US$360/380;
✻ @ 🛜 ✽) With its imposing entrance and
echoey corridors, this place feels like a
temple – a temple to minimalist luxury, that
is. The rooms are close to perfect and the

bathrooms, with walk-in showers and circular baths, actually are perfect. There's an impressive pool complex (which is a hit with children) that's lit up at night by flaming torches.

There's even an in-house naturalist who will happily answer all of your birds-and-bees questions.

Ayurveda Pavilions BOUTIQUE HOTEL **$$$**
(Map p88; ☑ 227 6719; www.ayurvedapavilions.com; Porutota Rd; villa s/d incl breakfast from US$245/265; ✴@🛋🏊) Beautiful mud-wall villas with minimalist yet luxurious furnishings. The bathrooms are the real highlights and soaking in one of the steamy, flower-petal-covered outdoor baths with someone special on a rainy afternoon is every bit as romantic as you'd expect. There's a large range of treatments (available to nonguests from US$35), which are included in the room price.

✗ Eating

There are lots of very so-so restaurants and cafes stringing the main road along the beach, with more exciting options in between.

Petit Restaurant SRI LANKAN, SEAFOOD **$$**
(Map p88; ☑ 077 628 7682; 100/7 A Palangathuraya; mains around Rs 750; ⊙11am-10pm) Potted plants and flowers surround the entrance of this suitably small, family-run restaurant. The menu skips through most of the Sri Lankan classics but is especially strong on seafood; there are some more unusual dishes on offer such as the 'prawn fiesta' (essentially prawns dusted in coconut shavings).

It's very popular so reservations are a good idea; be warned that the wait for your meal can be a long one.

Dolce Vita ITALIAN **$$**
(Map p88; ☑ 227 4968; Porutota Rd 27; mains around Rs 650; ⊙9am-10pm Tue-Sun) This simple Italian-owned beachside cafe and restaurant is the kind of place where people end up frittering away half a day, sitting in the breezy shade, drinking real coffee and fruit juice, and tucking into fair pizza and pasta dishes (as well as some local offerings).

Tusker Restaurant SEAFOOD **$$**
(Map p88; ☑ 222 6999; 83 Ethukala Rd; mains Rs 700-1000; ⊙5-11pm Sun-Fri, 2-11pm Sat) The contemporary, elephant-lined Tuskers is one of the smarter places to eat in town. Although its menu is wide ranging in its geo-culinary diversity, it's strong point is seafood. It would be amiss not to mention

the warm welcome extended by the couple who own it.

★Lords FUSION **$$$**
(Map p88; ☑ 227 5655; www.lordsrestaurant.net; 80B Porutota Rd; dishes Rs 850-1400; ⊙11.30am-2.30pm & 6-10pm) By far Negombo's most creative eating experience with dishes that are a hybrid of Western and Eastern flavours. Martin, the British owner of this restaurant–gallery, is a rare thing among expat restaurant owners in that he actually works on the floor and in the kitchen, making sure that everything is just spot on.

🍷 Drinking

Rodeo Pub PUB
(Map p88; ☑ 227 4713; 35 Porutota Rd; ⊙10am-around midnight) Graffiti-sprayed bar busy with expats and tourists. There's live music on Tuesday nights, DJs the rest of the time and a long list of cocktails with sexy names. They also do a range of classic Western and Sri Lankan dishes.

Ice Bear Century Cafe CAFE
(Map p87; ☑ 223 8097; 25 Main St; ⊙9am-6pm) In a lovingly restored peach-pink colonial-era townhouse, this calm retreat in the heart of Negombo offers a touch of refined class, all manner of Sri Lankan brews, mountains of homemade cakes and biscuits, and lunch specials such as Thai noodle soups and Hungarian goulash.

Cafe J CAFE
(Map p88; Jetwing Blue, Ethukala; ⊙7.30am-9pm) Part of the Jetwing Blue hotel complex, Cafe J is a sunny, open-plan street-side cafe and juice bar (it also sells stronger tipples). With its poppy Western coffeeshop vibes, it's about as far removed from a typical Sri Lankan working man's tea shop as you can get.

ℹ Information

There are numerous internet and telephone offices scattered along Lewis Pl and Porutota Rd, as well as near the bus and train stations. If this is your first stop in Sri Lanka, hotels can fix you up with guides and drivers for trips elsewhere in the country.

Bank of Ceylon (Map p87; Broadway) In the centre of town; with ATM.

Post Office (Map p87; Main St) This post office is in the centre of town.

Tourist Police (Map p88; ☑ 227 5555; Ethukala; ⊙24hr) At the northern end of the hotel strip, the tourist police should be your first port of call in an emergency.

Getting There & Away

Central Transport Board (CTB), private and intercity express buses run between Negombo town and Saunders Pl, Colombo (regular/air-con Rs 57/100, one to two hours, every 20 minutes). A faster bus goes via the new highway (Rs 150). Long queues form at the bus station on weekend evenings, when daytrippers return to the capital. There are also trains to Colombo (2nd/3rd class Rs 70/40, two hours), but they're slower and rarer than the buses.

For Kandy, buses run between 4.30am and 5.15pm every hour (Rs 153); the journey takes from three to four hours.

Getting Around

Bus 240 for the Bandaranaike International Airport (Rs 24, 40 minutes) leaves from the bus station in town every 15 minutes between about 6am and 7pm. A three-wheeler costs about Rs 500 from Negombo town or Rs 800 from Lewis Pl. A taxi costs around double this. The journey takes about 20 to 30 minutes and all hotels can arrange transport. Three-wheelers may not pick up passengers from the airport terminal, but you can catch one on the road outside the airport.

To get from the bus station to Lewis Pl or Porutota Rd, catch a Kochchikade-bound bus or splash out Rs 300 on a three-wheeler.

Around Negombo

Waikkal & Marawila

☎ 031

The towns of Waikkal and Marawila lie about 3km inland of the coast on the A3 north of Negombo. It's a very different scene here from the bars and tourist shops at Negombo and while there are several self-contained package tour hotels in the area, the places we have listed here are generally more suited to independent travellers and offer a far more intimate, nature-based experience. A huge plus for this area is that the nearby beaches are long, golden and generally fairly untarnished in comparison to Negombo.

Most people reach Waikkal and Marawila by taxi or car and driver.

Sleeping

★Ging Oya Lodge LODGE **$$**
(☎ 227 7822; www.gingoya.com; Kammala North, Waikkal; s/d incl breakfast €45/52; ❄ 📶 🏊) The Belgium artist-owners of this place were inspired by the safari lodges of Africa, and they've done a sterling job of replicating the rustic-chic luxury. There are 10 spacious cottages with antique doors, filigree window carvings, beautiful four-posters and semi-open plan bathrooms. There's a wonderful pool, birds and butterflies everywhere, and total and utter peace.

Set three-course dinners (€10) are served in an open-sided thatched dining room. The beach is a shady 1km walk or cycle away (bikes available) or you can paddle a kayak down to the sea.

Ranweli Holiday Village RESORT **$$$**
(☎ 227 7359; www.ranweli.com; Waikkal; full-board s/d from US$172/224; ❄ @ 📶 🏊) On the coast near Waikkal, the Ranweli Holiday Village, with its beautifully appointed rooms and unmistakable air of exclusivity, is a show-piece ecofriendly hotel that has won dozens of environmental awards. Away from recycling, tree planting and community development, you'll find that the gentle punt over the canal separating it from the mainland sets a romantic mood.

Negombo to Kalpitiya

Although the A3 stays close to the coast, there are few ocean views from the road. Rather, you'll pass through an endless series of coconut plantations, which have their own rhythmic beauty.

Roughly halfway between Negombo and Kalpitiya, **Chilaw** has a strong Roman Catholic flavour, with elaborate statues of religious figures and local cardinals in the centre.

Munneswaram, 5km to the east of Chilaw, has a rather interesting Hindu temple that is an important centre of pilgrimage. There are three shrines at this complex; the central one is dedicated to Shiva. A major festival, also featuring fire walking, occurs here in August.

The tiny village of **Udappuwa**, 12 km north of Chilaw, has a hectic morning fish market and an important Hindu temple with a large gorpum. A colourful festival is held here in August, when devotees test their strength by walking on red-hot coals.

Buses are frequent all along the A3.

Kalpitiya & Dutch Bay

Dolphins and kitesurfing are what bring people to the Kalpitiya peninsula. Schools of dolphins, hundreds strong, can often be seen jostling and playing in the offshore waters, and boat safaris offer close-up views of these aquatic mammals. Meanwhile, for those who want to act like a dolphin dancing through the waves, Kalpitiya, with its near constant strong winds, is widely considered to have the best kitesurfing conditions in South Asia.

Until recently, this was an intensely rural backwater that saw very few visitors. But it's not just thrill seekers and nature lovers who've discovered Kalpitiya. The government, looking to expand the island's tourist industry, is engaged in a project to turn the peninsula and its string of offshore islands into one of Sri Lanka's prime beach tourism destinations. The blueprints call for investment in projects as diverse as luxury accommodation for more than 10,000 people, a domestic airport, theme parks, an underwater amusement park (!), golf courses, high-speed boat safaris and much more. Environmentalists are concerned about the impact these projects will have on the populations of dolphins, sperm whales and dugongs, which use the waters around Dutch Bay.

More importantly, though, a large number of local people are concerned that their needs are being overlooked in favour of grandiose tourist developments. In addition to the banning of fishing in certain areas, they also have concerns about the development process itself (the minister of economic development has admitted that land deeds have been forged in some places). According to the Law and Society Trust, an independent Sri Lankan body, there is, among other issues, a 'lack of transparency and duplicity in the state's process of land acquisition', a 'violation of land tenure rights and customary rights' and 'forceful land acquisition, violation of private ownership, and illegal land grabbing taking place in Kalpitiya area'.

However, considering the windy beaches, the tendency towards overpriced accommodation and the relatively brown waters of Dutch Bay and the surrounding ocean (in comparison with the crystal blues of the south coast), we do wonder if it will all turn into a bit of a white elephant.

◉ Sights & Activities

At **Talawila**, halfway up the peninsula, there's a Catholic shrine to St Anne. The church features satinwood pillars and is pleasantly situated on the seafront. Thousands of pilgrims come here in March and July, when major festivals honouring St Anne are held. The festivals include huge processions, healing services and a fair.

The two main beaches are **Kalpitiya beach** and **Alankuda beach** a short way to

the south. Alankuda is the busiest and best for non-kitesurfing beach bums. If you squint your eyes and blot out the string of giant wind turbines stretched right out along the length of the beach, the massive coal-fired power plant at the far end and its long and ugly jetty, then Alankuda would be a lovely beach. But let's face it, you're not going to be able to blot that lot out!

Kalpitiya beach, which can only be reached after crossing a lagoon, is certainly the nicer of the two, but its status as a kitesurfing hotspot means that it can get very windy here – too windy to really enjoy lying about on the sand.

Dolphin & Whale Watching   DOLPHIN WATCHING
Boat safaris to watch schools of hundreds of spinner dolphins run most mornings between November and March. Every hotel can organise a safari, but try and suss out how knowledgeable your captain is about dolphins beforehand. Prices start from US$40 per person.

Dolphins (and even whales) are seen around 80% of the time in the October-to-May season.

Snorkelling & Diving   DIVING
There are some spectacular offshore reefs here with plenty of big fish. The prime dive site is Bar Reef, which sits several kilometres off the northwest tip of the peninsula and is said to be one of the finest dive sites in Sri Lanka. Despite its remote location, it's also considered to be a good snorkelling spot. Most hotels can organise snorkelling and diving trips, with prices starting at about €100.

Kitesurfing   KITESURFING
Kalipitya beach is fast gaining a reputation for having excellent kitesurfing conditions and there are schools and board rental places attached to all the hotels as well as dedicated kitesurfing camps.

🛏 Sleeping

There's been a surge of hotel construction in the past two years, including a number of very luxurious options. However, generally speaking, the cost of accommodation is almost universally overpriced and completely out of sync with the rest of the country. There are two main areas to stay: Alankuda beach and Kalpitiya beach.

As well as all the water sports activities, most places can also organise Wilpattu National Park safaris, but it's a fairly long drive and you'll miss dawn, which is the best time for seeing animals.

Omeesha Beach Hotel   HUT $$

(☑ 072 787 8782; Alankuda beach; huts with/without air-con US$75/65; ❀ ☎) Situated right under a giant wind turbine (and we mean *right* under), the rooms here are in rough-walled huts. Though dark and gloomy, the price makes them more interesting than most other choices. The bathrooms (cold water only in the non-air-con rooms) are open-plan affairs. Breakfast is included.

Sethawadiya Dolphin
View Eco-Lodge   HUT $$

(Kalpitiya; full-board r €38-78; ☎) Down a maze of confused tracks from Kalpitiya town, this place, which is very popular with long-staying kitesurfers, has rustic and rather basic palm-thatch huts of varying quality. The cheapest ones have shared bathrooms and are very basic indeed, while the pricier ones are fairly comfortable.

Big pluses are the warm staff, sociable restaurant area, and lagoon-front location with good kiting on tap.

Rosaanne Beach Resort   HUT $$$

(☑ 072 251 3224; www.rosaanne-kalpitiya. com; Alankuda beach; huts with/without air-con US$100/90; ☎) Probably the best bet around Alankuda beach, this very friendly and helpful family-run place has five whitewashed, thatched cottages huddled under the palms. No hot water in the non-air-con rooms.

❶ Getting There & Away

There are frequent buses to Negombo from Kalpitiya (Rs 180, three hours). Buses between Alankuda and Kalpitiya cost Rs 50.

Wilpattu National Park

Wilpattu means 'natural lakes' in Sinhala and '10 lakes' in Tamil and lakes are exactly what you'll find at Wilpattu National Park, which at 1085 sq km is Sri Lanka's largest national park. As well as lakes you'll also find huge swaths of dense, dry country woodland, masses of birds and, with a little luck, an impressive array of wildlife including leopards (this is the second-best park after Yala for leopards), sloth bears, spotted deer, wild pigs and crocodiles.

A safari in Wilpattu is very different from any of the other major national parks. Visitor numbers remain very low and even in high season it's common for there to be no more than a handful of tourist jeeps in the park at any one time. This gives Wilpattu a wonderful, and genuine, wilderness feeling. On the flipside though, the dense forest and general skittishness of the animals means that actually sighting wildlife is less of a sure thing than in the country's more visited parks. This is truly a place for the more dedicated safari-goer. Birders in particular will love Wilpattu with its abundance of dry forest, water and even coastal birds.

🛌 Sleeping & Eating

There's an increasing array of accommodation in the vicinity of the park, although most are a good 15- to 20-minute drive from the entrance. All sleeping options provide meals.

Uthpalawanna
Holiday Resort   GUESTHOUSE $

(☑ 072 432 2085, 075 510 2159; Saliyawewa; s/d Rs 2500/3000) Rooms in this family home are tidy and simple, but the welcome is grand.

Palpatha Eco Lodge   LODGE $$$

(☑ 077 031 0310, 077 360 0710; www.palpatha. com; Saliyawewa; half-board s/d €81/162, tents from €70) ☾ First, a warning. If you don't like camping or open-air living, you won't like this place. If, however, the idea of sleeping on a raised platform with nothing but a mosquito net and a thatch roof between you and the forest appeals, then you will adore this camp.

There are three open-air 'chalets' as well as a safari tent, which offers a little more protection, but lacks the romance. All have open-air bathrooms with showers coming out of tree trunks. The shady grounds are full of birds, squirrels and monkeys, the staff are fabulous and the food is good. The only real downside is the bugle call from the nearby army camp at some ungodly hour in the morning.

Mahoora Safari Camp   LODGE $$$

(☑ Colombo 011-583 0833; www.mahoora.lk; full-board s US$622-869, d US$814-1134) ☾ This is safari the old-fashioned, decadent way. Mahoora offers a 'mobile' camp on the edge of Wilpattu Park. In reality the camp doesn't actually move, but the type of accommodation can be changed depending on customer needs. Whatever safari tent type you opt for, you can expect a bush-chic luxury stay and quality safari jeeps and guides. Full board includes all activities for one night and two days.

It's essential to book in advance – not only do they not accept walk-ins, but the camp itself may not even be set up.

ℹ Information

Wilpattu National Park & Safaris (adult/child US$15/8, service charge per group US$8, jeep entry Rs 250, VAT 12%; ☉6am-6.30pm, last entry 4.30pm) Jeeps can be organised for a safari from beside the park entrance gate and ticket office, but most people organise transport through their accommodation. This also saves you having to get to the park first!

The going rate for a decent jeep is Rs 5000 for about a half-day.

ℹ Getting There & Away

The turnoff to the park on the Puttalam–Anuradhapura road (A12) is 26km northeast of Puttalam and 20km southwest of Anuradhapura. From here it's a further 8km to the park entrance at the barely discernible village of Hunuwilagama.

The nearest main village and site of most accommodation is Saliyawewa. Buses run from here to Puttalam (Rs 80 to 100) and from there to Negombo (Rs 150).

HATCHING TURTLES

Five species of sea turtles lay eggs along the coast of Sri Lanka. The green turtle is the most common, followed by the olive ridley and the hawksbill. The leatherback and loggerhead are both huge, reaching 2m or more in length. During what should be long lives (if they don't end up in a net or soup pot), female turtles make numerous visits to the south coast to lay eggs in the sand of the same beach where they themselves were born. A few weeks later, hundreds of baby turtles make a perilous journey back to the water.

Most of the tiny turtles are quickly gobbled up by birds, fish, people and other critters with gullets. And many never hatch at all, since human egg-poachers work overtime to satisfy the demand for turtle omelettes. However, the turtle hatcheries on the coast around Bentota and Kosgoda claim to increase the odds for the turtles by paying locals for the eggs at a rate slightly above that which they would fetch on the market. The eggs are then incubated by the hatchery. After a short stay in a tank (supposedly for protection against parasites, although many biologists say these tanks actually increase disease and parasite infection), the babies are released under the cover of darkness (in the wild, the babies also emerge at night).

The reality of the situation is that the turtle hatcheries might be doing more damage than good. When a baby turtle hatches it retains a part of the yolk from the egg, which acts as a vital energy source when the turtles first swim out to sea. By keeping the babies for even a very short time in a tank, they do not gain the benefit of this first food source. In addition, mature female turtles like to return to the beach where they hatched in order to lay their own eggs: if they have been born in captivity, they will not have obtained a 'magnetic imprint' of their beach of birth and thus they are thought to be unable to return to shore to lay their eggs. For a truly sustainable turtle conservation effort, it's better that the eggs are simply left on the beach where they were laid and given protection there. For more on this see www.srilankaecotourism.com/turtle_hatchery_threat.htm.

Although the conservation benefits of the hatcheries are limited, there's no denying that the turtles are awfully cute and make for an entertaining visit. Visits rarely last more than about 20 minutes. Expect to see babies, as well as adults, who have been injured by nets or in other calamities. Many environmental groups recommend you do not visit the hatcheries around Bentota area.

Kosgoda Sea Turtle Conservation Project (☎091-226 4567; admission Rs 500; ☉8.30am-6pm) On the beach side of Galle Rd, just north of Kosgoda, this volunteer-run operation has been here for 18 years. It's a very simple affair.

Kosgoda Turtle Hatchery (☎091-225 8667; admission Rs 500; ☉8am-7pm) Turn down a small track on the A2 at the 73 Km marker to find this operation, located in a quiet spot right on the beach. Arrive at 6.30pm and you can help release the day's hatchlings into the ocean.

Sea Turtle Project (☎034-227 1062; www.seaturtleszone.com; Induwara; admission Rs 500; ☉6am-6.30pm) This facility feels more commercial than the Kosgoda operations.

SOUTH OF COLOMBO

Escaping the frenetic and sticky capital for the road south is a giant sigh of relief. Out go the congested streets and dark clouds of exhaust fumes and in come the sultry beaches of the Sri Lankan dream. Most independent travellers focus on surf-obsessed Hikkaduwa, but the Bentota area offers quieter, and even more stunning, beaches, as well as a bizarre twinning of package-holiday hotels and sumptuous boutique hideaways.

Aluthgama, Bentota & Induruwa

034

Protected from noisy Galle Rd by the sluggish sweep of the Bentota Ganga, the ribbon of golden sand that makes up Bentota beach is a glorious holiday sun-and-fun playground. While it's primarily dominated by big package hotels, it also has a number of smaller places catering to independent travellers. There are more such places in Aluthgama, a small town on the main road between Beruwela and Bentota. Many of the pricier places to stay listed here also have respected Ayurveda centres.

Aluthgama has a raucous fish market, local shops and the main train station in the area. Induruwa doesn't really have a centre – it's spread out along the coast.

In 2014, clashes erupted between supporters of a militant Buddhist group (Bodu Bala Sena) and the local Muslim population, following a rally organised by the Buddhist hardliners. Up to four people were killed, many were injured, and a number of properties were destroyed. At the time of research, there had been no further incidents.

◉ Sights

If it's a **beach** you want, then it's a beach you're going to get; the Bentota area is home to some of the best beaches in all the country. Yet there is something altogether odd about these magnificent stretches of sand – despite the huge number of hotels and the fact that most people come to Sri Lanka for the three S's of sun, sand and surf, the beaches at the southern end of this strip are remarkably empty of people. Quite why this is we're not sure, but if the sands of nearby Hikkaduwa are a bit too trodden for your liking, then Bentota might be the place for you. Further watery fun is also available on the calm waters of the **Bentota Ganga**, though pollution can be an issue here.

Aluthgama has a bustling **market** every Monday, located across the train line, towards Dharga Town. A few kilometres inland on the south bank of the river is the **Galapota Temple**, which is said to date from the 12th century. To reach it, cross the bridge and take the side road to your left after 500m.

Brief Garden   GARDENS
(☏ 227 4462, 077 350 9290; www.briefgarden.com; admission Rs 1000; ⊙ 8am-5pm) Ten kilometres inland from Bentota is the Brief Garden. A barely controlled riot of a garden out of *The Jungle Book*, the grounds are a lovely place to get lost. The house, which used to be the home of Bevis Bawa, brother of renowned architect Geoffrey Bawa, has an eclectic range of artwork on display – from homoerotic sculpture to a wonderful mural of Sri Lankan life in the style of Marc Chagall.

To get here, follow the road south from Aluthgama to Matagama Rd and turn inland to the village of Dharga Town. From here you will periodically see yellow signs saying 'Brief', but as everyone knows this place, it's easy enough to ask directions. There's no public transport.

🏃 Activities

The vast lagoon and river mouth make this an excellent area for water sports. Windsurfing, waterskiing, jet-skiing, deep-sea fishing and everything else watery are offered by local operators. **Sunshine Water Sports Center** (☏ 428 9379; www.srilankawatersports. com; Riverside Rd, Aluthgama; ⊙ 9am-sunset) and **Diyakawa Water Sports** (☏ 077 916 5330; 10 Riverside Rd) are independent operators that are both right on the riverfront. Besides renting out a wide range of equipment, they also run courses, which include windsurfing (US$130) and waterskiing (US$30). There are also snorkelling tours, canoeing, deep-sea fishing and diving courses.

Boat journeys along the **Bentota Ganga** (per group US45) are a peaceful, popular and bird-filled way to pass a late afternoon. Tours travel through the intricate coves and islands on the lower stretches of the river, which is home to more than a hundred bird species. Most trips last for three hours. Both of the above companies organise trips, otherwise all hotels can point you to operators.

🛏 Sleeping & Eating

In among the package-holiday resort bubbles are a number of divine boutique hotels and guesthouses, as well as one or two very rare budget offerings.

Almost all the hotels and guesthouses double as restaurants, and seafood is generally at the top of the list of offerings. The **Wunderbar Hotel and Restaurant** (227 5908; Galle Rd) has an enjoyable 1st-floor restaurant open to non-guests and sea breezes, and has a decent selection of seafood and Western dishes (Rs 500 to 800).

If you want to escape the confines of your hotel, then there are a number of busy, tasty and cheap places in Aluthgama town.

Aluthgama

Hotel Hemadan GUESTHOUSE **$$**
(227 5320; www.hemadan.dk; 25 Riverside Rd; s/d incl breakfast from Rs 4345/5335;) A cosy Danish-owned guesthouse that has 10 large, clean rooms in an ageing building. There's a leafy courtyard and prime river-viewing opportunities. Better rooms have balconies. There are free boat shuttles across the river to the oceanside beach and a babycot for those travelling with little ones.

Anushka River Inn GUESTHOUSE **$$**
(227 5377; www.anushka-river-inn.com; 97 Riverside Rd; s/d incl breakfast €35/50;) This hotel's large rooms contain wooden beds, dressing tables and hot-water showers. The rooms without river views, with their shiny new feel, are actually the better deal as some of the others have a musty odour.

Bentota

Dedduwa Boat Hotel GUESTHOUSE **$$**
(077 027 6169, in Colombo 011-452 9901; Dedduwa Junction; s/d incl breakfast US$50/60;) Head inland a couple of kilometres and you'll find this hidden little offering in a lush, green lakeside setting of utter tranquillity. The rooms are carefully tended, and you could spend hours just watching the birdlife on the neighbouring lake or walking the squelchy tracks between houses full of smiling locals.

DON'T MISS

AYURVEDA IN PARADISE

For more than 2500 years the inhabitants of the subcontinent have enjoyed the restorative effects of Ayurveda treatments. More than just a way of treating illnesses using natural medicines, Ayurveda is based on the idea of balance in bodily systems and uses herbal treatment, diet and yogic breathing to achieve this.

Today, Ayurveda treatments are a big attraction in Sri Lanka and there are seemingly hundreds of Ayurveda 'hospitals'. Many have qualified Ayurveda doctors, but some are decidedly more dodgy – this is especially true in popular backpacker towns. You should always ask advice from locals about the authenticity of Ayurvedic hospitals in such places, as well as asking to see the doctors' qualifications.

The west coast is a particular hotspot for such treatments, and almost all the larger hotels, as well as some cheaper places, have a treatment centre. The area around Beruwela, a short way north of Bentota, has a number of regarded Ayurveda resorts, including several of the centres that we have recommended here:

Barberyn Reef Ayurveda Resort (034-227 6036; www.barberynresorts.com; Beruwela; s/d full board from €75/125, plus per person, per day for compulsory Ayurveda treatments €70;) One of the best regarded Ayurveda resorts in Sri Lanka with the full complement of treatments and excellent doctors. It also offers yoga, meditation and Ayurveda cooking classes.

Heritance Ayurveda Maha Gedara (034-555 5000; www.heritancehotels.com; Beruwela; r full board from US$185;) You only have to visit a few Ayurveda hotels to realise that the quality of the accommodation often plays second fiddle to the treatments. Not here. At the Heritance the treatments are first rate and they only use very experienced doctors, while the hotel itself is a wonderful luxury retreat tucked under the palms.

Ayurveda Pavilions (p90) In Negombo.

Temple Tree Resort & Spa (p98) In Indurwa.

Saman Villas (p97) In Bentota.

Aditya Resort (p101) Just south of Hikkaduwa.

Hotel Sasantha   GUESTHOUSE **$$**
(🖉227 5324; Bentota; s with/without air-con Rs 6350/4950, d with/without air-con Rs 6950/6350; ✹@🛜) Shady gardens, traveller-savvy staff, easy access to the northern part of Bentota beach and an array of colourful rooms make this a very popular place to drop your backpack for a few days. You can walk to it straight down the platform of Bentota train station. Breakfast is included in the rates.

⭐**Shangri-Lanka Villa**   GUESTHOUSE **$$$**
(🖉227 1181; www.shangrilankavilla.com; 23 De Alwis Rd, Bentota; s/d incl breakfast UK£60/70; ✹🛜🏊) The peaceful, rural setting of this intimate and beautiful boutique guesthouse, a kilometre inland from the main road and beach, means you fall asleep at night to the sound of cicadas singing to the moon rather than honking buses. The rooms are enormous, the beds covered in pink and orange tropical blooms, and there's tasteful art on the walls.

The food and the service are as good as the accommodation and the centre piece of the garden is an immaculate pool.

⭐**Saman Villas**   BOUTIQUE HOTEL **$$$**
(🖉227 5435; www.samanvilla.com; r US$600-980; ✹@🛜🏊) We would love to tell you just how incredible this place is, but the truth is that there are no words to describe the sheer opulence of this hotel complex. How opulent? Well, some of the rooms have private swimming pools – inside the bathroom!

If you prefer more communal swimming, there's also a heavenly infinity pool that merges into an ocean horizon, and everywhere you go, you will walk on flower petals. But the real clincher is the setting: situated on the headland at the southern end of Bentota beach, the sea views are simply overwhelming.

Nisala Arana   BOUTIQUE HOTEL **$$$**
(🖉077 773 3313; www.nisalaarana.com; 326/1 Circular Rd, Kommala; d incl breakfast US$150-200, houses US$464; ✹🛜🏊) For the ultimate in gracious and exotic Sri Lankan living come to this outstanding boutique guesthouse 3km inland from the beach where everything is easy living: egrets stand sentry by the pool, butterflies flutter and rooms are packed with beautiful dark-wood antique furnishings. There are, however, an inordinate number of mosquitoes at certain times.

Paradise Road –
The Villa   BOUTIQUE HOTEL **$$$**
(🖉227 5311; www.villabentota.com; 138/18 Galle Rd; r incl breakfast from US$264; ✹@🛜🏊) Fab-ulous and intimate boutique hotel decorated in black-and-white zebra stripes and adorned with karma-enhancing Tibetan Buddhist artefacts. Speaking of the Buddha, you can recline like him on one of the oh-so-soft sofas, swirl up the pool like a koi carp or just take things easy with a pot of tea in the shade of a garden pagoda.

Club Villa   BOUTIQUE HOTEL **$$$**
(🖉227 5312; www.club-villa.com; 138/15 Galle Rd; half-board s/d US$231/275; ✹@🛜🏊) Ever wondered what happened to the hippies who bummed across Asia in the 1960s and '70s? Well, while some dropped out of life completely, others went home and became investment bankers, who now spend their dollars reminiscing in hotels like this Bawa-designed masterpiece.

From the tie-dye pillows and cushions to the blissed-out Buddha and Shiva statues, everything about this place reeks of hippy chic. Even the giant catfish that haunt the numerous ponds seem to cruise about in a stoned state of permanent indolence.

Amal Villa   BOUTIQUE HOTEL **$$$**
(🖉077 603 7541; www.amal-villa.com; Galle Rd; half-board s €70/75, d €80-85; ✹🛜🏊) This beautifully maintained German-run villa and hotel, which merges tropical vibes and central European efficiency, is split into two, with one beachside building and one landside one. The simple rooms, full of pure white lines, have views inland over the rice paddies or poking out over the palms towards the sea.

The inland building has a gorgeous swimming pool, but the beachside building, which doesn't have a pool, is more sheltered from road noise (anyway it has direct access to a really big pool otherwise known as the Indian Ocean).

Wunderbar Hotel
and Restaurant   HOTEL **$$$**
(🖉227 5908; www.hotel-wunderbar.com; Galle Rd; d incl breakfast from €75; ✹🛜🏊) In among the surrounding luxury is this solid, much cheaper option that has spacious and well-thought-out rooms with a taste for vaguely erotic art. Some rooms have balconies with sea views, and the pool is more inviting than many others in town.

🛏 Induruwa

Long Beach   HOTEL **$**
(🖉227 5773; www.longbeachcottageinduruwa.com; 550 Galle Rd; tw Rs 2420; ✹🛜) The rooms might

be basic, but if you can't stretch to hotels with private pools, this place might just fit the bill. The rooms are located in the upstairs of a family house. There are green, shady gardens and – with a feature that matches all the big-boy hotels – a gorgeous beach on the doorstep.

Temple Tree Resort
& Spa   BOUTIQUE HOTEL **$$$**
(⌨ 227 0700; www.templetreeresortandspa.com; 660 Galle Rd; s/d incl breakfast from US$146/165; ❄ 🛜 ⛱) Picture a minimalist Manhattan apartment translocated to a tropical beach and you get the Temple Tree Resort. The grey-stone rooms with electric-white walls have whirlpool baths, rain showers and every possible comfort.

❶ Information

Commercial Bank (339 Galle Rd) Just north of the river; has an international ATM.
Tourist Office (⌨ 091-393 2157; ⊙ 8.30am-4.30pm Mon-Fri) Outside the Bentota Beach Hotel.

❶ Getting There & Around

Beruwela and Bentota are both on the main Colombo–Matara railway line, but Aluthgama, the town sandwiched between them, is the station to go to as many trains don't make stops at these smaller stations. Aluthgama has five or six express trains daily to Colombo (2nd/3rd class Rs 110/51, 1½ to two hours), and a similar number to Hikkaduwa (2nd/3rd class Rs 70/35, one hour).

When you get off the train at the unusual middle-platform station, you'll hear the usual tales from the touts and fixers that the hotel of your choice is closed, vanished or has 'magically turned into the Statue of Liberty'. Just ignore them.

Aluthgama is also the best place to pick up a bus, although there is no trouble getting *off* any bus anywhere along the Galle Rd. There is frequent service to Colombo (regular/air-con Rs 85/160, two to three hours depending on traffic). Buses to Hikkaduwa (regular/air-con Rs 57/120, one hour) are just as regular.

Hikkaduwa & Around

⌨ 091

Hikkaduwa has been a firm fixture on the Sri Lankan tourist map since the 1970s. This long exposure to international tourism has left it a little worse for wear. Uncontrolled and unplanned development has meant that the swaying palms of yesteryear have given way to an almost unbroken strip of cheap guest-houses and restaurants that vie among themselves to be the closest to the lapping waves. This in turn has led to terrible beach erosion, and, in parts, the once-famous sand has now been almost completely replaced with sand bags fighting a vain battle to retain what little beach remains (although in recent years sand does seem to be beginning to return to large parts of the beach – a trend we can only hope continues). To make matters worse, the appalling Colombo–Galle road, with its as-phyxiating smog and crazy bus drivers, runs right through the middle of it all, which can make stepping outside of your guesthouse as deadly as a game of Russian roulette!

Bad as it sounds, though, there are glim-mers of hope. There's an increasing range of activities on offer and more and more higher-class places to stay and eat. Finally, and maybe most importantly, at the time of research there was much talk about a pos-sible new bypass road around the edge of Hikkaduwa, which would do much to bring a semblance of peace and tranquillity back to this paradise lost.

◉ Sights & Activities

For many people, a visit to Hikkaduwa begins and ends on the beach and you can't really fault them for that! The widest bit of sand ex-tends north and south from Narigama. Here you'll find a few simple lounge chairs that you can rent or even use for free if they're part of a cafe. But don't expect a chaotic scene: there are a few vendors, but it's pretty relaxed.

The sands at Wewala are narrower and steeper, but this is where the best surf is.

Hikkaduwa National Park   NATIONAL PARK
(adult/child Rs 30/15; ⊙ 7am-6pm) Hikkaduwa's marine park stretches along the northern end of the beach and is a fun and easy way to get a glimpse of some of Sri Lanka's undersea life. Snorkelling gear can be rented from plac-es around the park ticket office for around Rs 300 to 500 a day. Glass-bottomed boat rides (not an ideal way to see the reef) are available for Rs 1750 (plus 10% tax) per half-hour. The boats can be hired from beside the national park ticket office.

Scuba Diving

The diving season runs from November to April. Professional Association of Diving In-structors (PADI) courses (open water €265), plus a selection of wreck dives, night dives and trips for first timers are available from **Poseidon Diving Station** (Map p99; ⌨ 227 7294; www.divingsrilanka.com; Galle Rd).

Hikkaduwa & Around

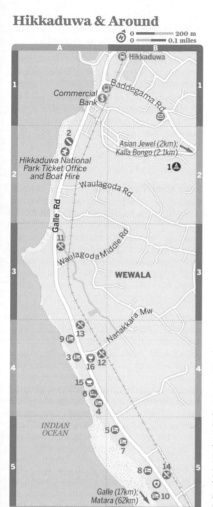

Hikkaduwa & Around

◎ Sights
1 Gangarama Maha Vihara....................B2

◆ Activities, Courses & Tours
2 Poseidon Diving Station......................A2

◉ Sleeping
3 Blue Ocean Villa.................................A4
4 Dewasiri Beach Restaurant &
   Hotel..A4
5 Hotel Drifters....................................B5
6 Hotel Moon Beam...............................A4
7 Hotel Ritas.......................................B5
8 Neela's...B5
9 Time 'n' Tide Beach Resort A4
10 Top Secret.......................................B5

◉ Eating
11 Cool Spot...A3
12 Home Grown Rice & Curry
    Restaurant....................................A4
13 No 1 Roti Restaurant A4
14 Spaghetti & Co B5

◉ Drinking & Nightlife
15 Coffee Shop.....................................A4
16 Sam's Surfers...................................A4

better known surf schools are more interested in looking cool than teaching.

Inland Attractions

Seenigama Vihara BUDDHIST
About 2km north of Hikkaduwa is the Seenigama Vihara, perched on its own island. It's one of only two temples in the country where victims of theft can seek retribution. People who have been robbed visit the temple and buy a specially prepared oil made with chilli and pepper. With the oil they light a lamp in their homes and recite a mantra. Sooner or later the thief will be identified when they're struck down with misfortune.

Gangarama Maha Vihara BUDDHIST
(Map p99) Just off Baddegama Rd is this interesting Buddhist temple that has lots of popular educational paintings that are the work of one man over nearly a decade. The monks are happy to show you around.

Hikkaduwa Lake LAKE
Hikkaduwa Lake, with its monitor lizards and numerous birds, makes for a pleasant excursion away from the beach. Boat tours can sometimes be organised on the lake; ask around. To get there head along the Baddegama Rd.

Surfing

The conditions for surfing are at their best from November to April. The Wewala and Narigama areas of the beach have a handful of tame reef breaks as well as a beach break, all of which are perfect for beginner- to intermediate-level surfers. These waves, combined with the energetic nightlife, has made Hikkaduwa easily the most popular surf spot in Sri Lanka.

Most guesthouses rent out surfboards for around Rs 300 to 400 per hour and there are several places offering surf lessons, but pick carefully because the 'teachers' at some of the

TSUNAMI PHOTO MUSEUM

This ramshackle **private museum** (Galle Rd, Telwatta; ⏱ 8am-6.30pm), halfway between Hikkaduwa and Ambalangoda, tells the story through photographs and newspaper features of that dreadful day in 2004 when the Indian Ocean tsunami struck Hikkaduwa and Sri Lanka. Everything is very badly lit and displayed, but that is of no matter because the images displayed here will render you silent.

Close to the Tsunami Photo Museum is a small memorial to the roughly 40,000 people who lost their lives just in Sri Lanka and the hundreds of thousands of others whose lives were changed forever. It was also around here that the tsunami washed away a packed commuter train with the loss of over 1200 lives – the world's worst ever train disaster and just a small story from that day. Entrance is by donation. Opening hours can be a little flexible.

🛏 Sleeping

Virtually all of Hikkaduwa's accommodation is strung out along Galle Rd.

Most plots of land along the strip are quite narrow, which means that guesthouses will only have a few pricey rooms with views of the water. In contrast, rooms closest to the road get a lot of noise, so be sure to get a room well away from the traffic. Many places are jammed right up against each other.

An increasing number of plush, luxury hideaways are springing up in the environs of Hikkaduwa.

Dewasiri Beach
Restaurant & Hotel   HOTEL $
(Map p99; 472 Galle Rd; tw with fan Rs 1800-2500, with air-con Rs 2800; 🛜) Ideal for surfers on a budget, this place overlooks Main Reef and has a variety of clean, shiny white rooms, but it's the lovely family and their skills in the kitchen that really make it standout from the budget pack.

Blue Ocean Villa   HOTEL $
(Map p99; ☏ 227 7566; blueoceanvilla420@gmail. com; 420 Galle Rd; r Rs 3000-5000; ❄🛜) Smart people rock up to this friendly place in the heart of the action and score themselves a classy room that comes with wicker chairs,

hot water and a rock-and-water-world fantasy in the reception area. Only the more expensive rooms have air-conditioning.

Top Secret   GUESTHOUSE $
(The Harmony; Map p99; ☏ 227 7551; www.srilanka-holiday.info; Galle Rd; r Rs 2000-3000; 🛜) Right at the eastern end of the tourist strip and on an appealing patch of beach is this stylish guesthouse. The rooms themselves are fairly plain, and like most places it only has cold-water showers. But move away from the rooms and you'll discover an Arabian-style lounge area and a decent bar-restaurant.

Hotel Moon Beam   HOTEL $$
(Map p99; ☏ 505 6800; hotelmoonbeam@hotmail. com; 548/1 Galle Rd; s/d with fan Rs 4000/5000, s/d with air-con Rs 5000/6000; ❄🛜) A smart midrange option with numerous spick-and-span rooms that are enlivened by pictures and wooden decorations. Piping-hot water gushes forth from the showers and some rooms have balconies with surf views. Rates include breakfast.

Hotel Drifters   HOTEL $$
(Map p99; ☏ 912 275 692, 077 706 7091; www. driftershotel.com; 602 Galle Rd; r US$40-60; 🛜🖥) Sitting at the heart of this beachside property is a well-kept pool. That alone makes this hotel worth the money, but add in large and nicely presented rooms and a decent patch of beach out front, and you have an all-around winner. The same management also has an inferior (but not bad) hotel on the landward side of the road – don't get them mixed up.

Hotel Ritas   GUESTHOUSE $$
(Map p99; ☏ 227 7496; Galle Rd; r Rs 3000-6500; ❄🛜) Keeping passing travellers' content for years, Rita's has tidy back rooms for those on a budget while midrange cruisers will find the fancier ocean-facing rooms, which are larger and have more attention to detail, to their liking.

Time 'n' Tide Beach Resort   HOTEL $$
(Map p99; ☏ 227 7781; www.time-n-tide.com; 412 E Galle Rd; r with/without air-con US$70/50; ❄🛜) A smart but sterile place with welcoming staff. The more expensive rooms are enormous, which could make them worth considering for families. A big plus is the shady terrace and grassy lawn. The in-house restaurant serves wood-fired pizzas (Rs 900 to 1400).

Neela's   GUESTHOUSE $$
(Map p99; ☏ 438 3166; www.neelasbeach.com; 634 Galle Rd; r Rs 3500-8500; ❄🛜) This excellent

and very welcoming choice has something for everybody. Even the cheapest rooms come with pleasing decorations and lots of cleanliness while the more expensive ones are really quite impressive. Breakfast is included with the more expensive rooms.

★Aditya Resort — BOUTIQUE HOTEL $$$
(📞226 7708; www.aditya-resort.com; 719/1 Galle Rd, Devenigoda; r incl breakfast US$410-490, ste US$1000; ✳🛜🏊) This sublime place is crammed with statues of Hindu gods, tropical flowers and masses of high-quality antiques. The huge rooms have carved wooden bedheads and the semi-open air bathrooms are filled with foliage and plunge-pool baths that double as jacuzzis. The hotel overlooks an empty stretch of beach but most of its small number of lucky guests just relax by the pool and indulge in spa and Ayurveda treatments. It's a couple of kilometres south of Hikkaduwa.

Kalla Bongo — BOUTIQUE HOTEL $$$
(📞438 3234; www.kallabongo.com; 22/8k Field View, Baddegama Rd; r incl breakfast from Rs 11,500; ✳🛜🏊) A serene Buddha greets new arrivals at this beautiful lakeside hideaway and the sense of calm continues throughout the property. The rooms themselves, which are in individual cottages, are surprisingly simple but very tastefully decorated. The lake views are exquisite.

Kayaks are available for lake excursions.

Asian Jewel — BOUTIQUE HOTEL $$$
(📞493 1388; www.asian-jewel.com; 3 Field View Lane, Baddegama Rd; r incl breakfast from US$130; ✳🛜🏊) This small boutique hotel close to Hikkaduwa lake has eye-catching rooms (which some may describe as a bit bling), a beautiful pool, lake views and excellent food, but despite all this what really makes a stay here special are the staff and owners – within seconds of arriving they'll have memorised your name and be bending over backwards to help. It's 3km inland, just off Baddegama Road.

✗ Eating & Drinking

Most of Hikkaduwa's places to eat are connected to hotels and guesthouses; few are all that memorable. Down on the sandy shores of Narigama, you can table-hop from one spot to the next throughout the night. Many places are good just for a drink, and a few stay open past 11pm.

★Home Grown Rice & Curry Restaurant — SRI LANKAN $
(Map p99; 📞072 440 7858; 140/A Wewala; mains Rs 350; ⊘10am-9pm) Half-buried under palm trees and flowering pants, this is a sweet little garden-terrace restaurant on a quiet (at least compared to the main road) side street. The family who run it are as lovely as the setting, and dish up fresh, tasty homemade curries and seafood for an unbeatable price.

There are only around half-a-dozen tables and it's very popular, so get there early or book ahead.

Spaghetti & Co — ITALIAN $$
(Map p99; Galle Rd; meals Rs 700-900; ⊘6-11pm) The lush gardens that surround this colonial-style villa go some way to hiding busy Galle Rd, which helps enhance the enjoyment of the ultra-thin-crust pizzas and creamy pastas served here.

Cool Spot — SEAFOOD $$
(Map p99; 327 Galle Rd; mains Rs 250-800) This family-run place has been serving up fresh seafood from a canary-yellow vintage roadside house at the north end of the strip since 1972. There's a cool verandah where you can peruse the blackboard menu and delight in specialities such as garlic prawns and the bulging seafood platter. It's some way north of the main independent tourist strip.

No 1 Roti Restaurant — SRI LANKAN $
(Map p99; 📞491 1540; 373 Galle Rd; ⊘meals Rs 100-150) Away from the beach and a whole world away from the beach restaurant scene, this hole in the wall is right on the road and sells over 60 kinds of *rotti* (doughy pancake), ranging from garlic chicken to banana. There are also fresh shakes and lassis.

Coffee Shop — CAFE $
(Map p99; 536 Galle Rd; ⊘7am-7pm) Real Italian coffee, including hangover-busting espresso, give a pre-surf morning boost at this fashionable cafe.

Sam's Surfers — BAR
(Roger's Garage; Map p99; 403 Galle Rd) A laid-back bar with pool tables that shows recent movies and big sports events. It has a variety of different beers on tap and is basically about as far removed from a typical Sri Lankan bar as you can get!

ⓘ Information

Commercial Bank (Map p99; Galle Rd) ATM.

WORTH A TRIP

AMBALANGODA & THE DEVIL MASK MUSEUMS

Ambalangoda is a sweaty, workaday town, which is completely overshadowed by nearby Hikkaduwa as a tourist destination. The main reason for visiting – and it's a good one – is to dig under the surface of the Sri Lankan souvenir scene and discover the magical meanings behind the ubiquitous 'devil' masks. Genuine devil dances, which drive out spirits causing illness, still occur irregularly in the hinterland villages.

Ambalangoda is on the main transport route between Colombo and Hikkaduwa and buses and trains are frequent.

Ariyapala Mask Museum (☎091-225 8373; www.masksariyapalasl.com; 426 Main St; ☺8.30am-5.30pm) The Ariyapala Mask Museum, with its dioramas and explanations in English, gives an excellent insight into Sri Lankan masks and the meanings behind them. It also sells the booklet *The Ambalangoda Mask Museum,* a useful publication if you want to delve into the mysterious world of dance, legend and exorcism, and the psychology behind the masks.

Ariyapala Traditional Masks (☎091-493 3319; 432 Galle Rd; ☺8.30am-5.30pm) Ariyapala Traditional Masks has a small museum and a shop selling utterly captivating pieces.

Bandu Wijesooriya Dance Academy (☎091-225 8948; www.mask.lk; 1st fl, 426 Main St) The Bandu Wijesooriya Dance Academy teaches the southern forms of traditional Sri Lankan dance such as *kolam* (masked dance-drama), Kandyan and Sabaragamu. Officially dance courses last a year but it's often possible for foreigners to arrange shorter one-on-one courses.

Main Post Office (Map p99; Baddegama Rd) A five-minute walk inland from the bus station.

Tourist Police Station (Map p99; ☎227 5554; Galle Rd; ☺24hr) At the southeastern end of the tourist strip, although not all the police here speak English – which rather defeats the purpose of the place!

ℹ Getting There & Away

BUS

There are frequent buses from Colombo (normal/luxury Rs 127/190, three hours). Buses also operate frequently to Galle (Rs 37, 30 minutes). Buses to Galle or beyond will drop you south of the bus station along the guesthouse strip. When leaving Hikkaduwa, your chances of getting a seat are best if you start at the bus station.

CAR

There are two roads connecting Hikkaduwa with Galle and Colombo. The old Colombo–Galle road runs right through the middle of Hikkaduwa. Travelling along this road to central Colombo takes at least three hours and you should allow four or five hours to get to the airport (at quiet times you can do it faster than this). Galle is 30 minutes away. It's not worth taking the Southern Expressway (the toll road running 15 minutes inland from the coast) to Galle, but you can shave a great chunk of time off the journey taking it to the southern edge of Colombo. There is talk of a new bypass being built around Hikkaduwa.

TRAIN

The trains can get very crowded; avoid the really slow ones that stop everywhere. Check at the station for express departure times. Service on the coast line is fairly frequent; destinations include Colombo (2nd/3rd class Rs 160/85, two to three hours), Galle (2nd/3rd class Rs 40/20, 30 minutes) and beyond to Matara. Air-conditioned carriages are available on some trains with the price a fixed Rs 1000 to anywhere along the line.

ℹ Getting Around

A three-wheeler from the train or bus stations to Wewala or Narigama costs about Rs 150.

The South

Includes ➡

Best Beaches

- ➡ Goyambokka Beach (p129)
- ➡ Marakolliya Beach (p131)
- ➡ Mirissa Beach (p124)
- ➡ Rekawa Beach (p131)
- ➡ Talalla Beach (p128)

Best Places to Stay

- ➡ Amanwella (p130)
- ➡ Fort Printers (p112)
- ➡ Fortaleza (p110)
- ➡ Frangipani Tree (p120)
- ➡ Lonely Beach Resort (p132)

Why Go?

A sense of romance and wonder sweeps up all visitors to Sri Lanka's south coast; after all, this is the land where people dance across fire on monsoon nights, fishermen float on stilts above the waves, and turtles crawl up onto moonlit beaches.

Prepare your senses for overload. The landscape is one of utter beauty; the radiant-green rice paddies and forests of swinging palm trees contrast with endless beaches of ivory-coloured sand and an ocean of rich turquoise. People drift past in clouds of bright colours, especially in the colonial bastion that is Galle's Fort.

No matter what you're after you'll find it here. You can dive across glowing coral reefs or learn to surf on gentle sandbars. The culturally inclined can soak up works of Buddhist-inspired art in lonely caves; for the naturalist there are huge whales splashing through offshore swells, and leopards moving like spirits in the night.

When to Go
Galle

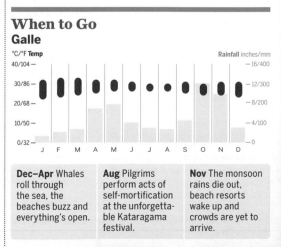

Dec–Apr Whales roll through the sea, the beaches buzz and everything's open.

Aug Pilgrims perform acts of self-mortification at the unforgettable Kataragama festival.

Nov The monsoon rains die out, beach resorts wake up and crowds are yet to arrive.

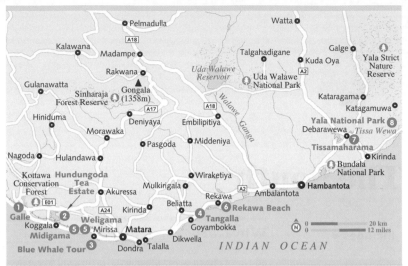

The South Highlights

1 Taking the train south to Unesco-recognised **Galle** (p105) and strolling its sculptured streets

2 Learning the tea trade at **Hundungoda Tea Estate** (p121)

3 Staring in slack-jawed amazement at the biggest creatures alive today on a **blue whale tour** (p124)

4 Trying to find your perfect beach in the sweet sands around **Tangalla** (p131)

5 Speeding through the tube at **Midigama** (p121) or learning to surf at **Weligama** (p123)

6 Watching the first faltering flipper-flaps of a

tiny baby turtle on **Rekawa Beach** (p131)

7 Watching the mist rise off Tissa Wewa in the pink glow of sunset at **Tissamaharama** (p134)

8 Spotting a spotty leopard and listening for ear-flapping elephants in **Yala National Park** (p138)

Galle

♪ 091 / POPULATION 100,200

Galle (pronounced 'gawl' in English, and '*gaar*-le' in Sinhala) is the big unmissable destination in the south. It's at once endlessly exotic, bursting with the scent of spices and salty winds, and yet also, with its wonderful collection of Dutch-colonial buildings, a town of great beauty. Classic architecture melds with a dramatic tropical setting to create a reality that is endlessly interesting.

Above all else, Galle is a city of trade and, increasingly, art. Today the historic Fort area is crammed full of little boutique shops, cafes and hotels owned by local and foreign artists, writers, photographers, designers and poets – a third of the houses are owned by foreigners.

Built by the Dutch, beginning in 1663, the 36-hectare Fort occupies most of a promontory that's surrounded on three sides by

the ocean. Just wandering the old walls and streets at random yields one architectural surprise after another as you explore the amazing collection of structures dating back through the centuries. Its glories have earned the Fort status as a Unesco World Heritage Site.

A key part of the Fort's allure, however, is that it isn't just a pretty place. Rather, it remains a working community: there are administrative offices, courts, export companies, lots of regular folks populating the streets and a definite buzz of energy in the air.

Galle is easily reached as a day trip from Colombo and is a quick drive from the nearby beach towns of Hikkaduwa and Unawatuna, but to really savour the place, stay within the atmospheric walls of the Fort.

History

Although Anuradhapura and Polonnaruwa are older than Galle, they are effectively abandoned cities – the modern towns are divorced from the ancient ruins. In contrast, both old and new Galle have remained vibrant.

Some historians believe Galle may have been the city of Tarshish – where King Solomon obtained gems and spices – though many more argue that a port in Spain seems a more likely candidate. Either way, Galle only became prominent with the arrival of the Europeans. In 1505 a Portuguese fleet bound for the Maldives was blown off course and took shelter in the harbour. Apparently, on hearing a cock (*galo* in Portuguese) crowing, they gave the town its name. Another slightly less dubious story is that the name is derived from the Sinhala word *gala* (rock).

In 1589, during one of their periodic squabbles with the kingdom of Kandy, the Portuguese built a small fort, which they named Santa Cruz. Later they extended it with bastions and walls, but the Dutch, who took Galle in 1640, destroyed most traces of the Portuguese presence. After the construction of the Fort in the 17th century, Galle was the main port for Sri Lanka for more than 200 years, and was an important stop for boats and ships travelling between Europe and Asia. However, by the time Galle passed into British hands in 1796, commercial interest was turning to Colombo. The construction of breakwaters in Colombo's harbour in the late 19th century sealed Galle's status as a secondary harbour, though it still handles some shipping and yachts.

The 2004 tsunami hit Galle's new town badly. In contrast, the solid walls of the Fort helped limit damage in the old quarter. More usefully, the Dutch love of good drainage meant that the Fort area quickly drained of floodwaters thanks to the still efficient 18th-century storm sewers.

◉ Sights

The Fort area is home to about 400 historic houses, churches, mosques, temples and old commercial and government buildings. Galle is an experience to savour, taste and touch; revel in its surprises. And don't neglect the new town where you'll find interesting shops and markets. A large Muslim community lives and works inside the Fort, particularly at the southern end of the walled town. Many shops close for a couple of hours around noon on Friday for prayer time.

◉ The Fort Walls

Locals and visitors alike enjoy walking the Fort walls at dusk. As the daytime heat fades away, you can walk almost the complete circuit of the Fort along the top of the wall in an easy hour or two. You'll be in the company of lots of residents, shyly courting couples and plenty of kids diving into the protected waters. At any time of day, you'll make discoveries inside and out, including hidden beaches.

Note that you can tell which parts of the walls were built by the Portuguese and which parts were Dutch-built: the latter designed much wider walls to allow for cannons to be mounted.

★ Old Gate   HISTORIC SITE
A beautifully carved British coat of arms tops the entrance to the Old Gate on the outer side. Inside, the letters VOC, standing for Verenigde Oostindische Compagnie (Dutch East India Company), are inscribed in the stone with the date 1669, flanked by two lions and topped by a cock. This portion of the old wall also served as a warehouse for spices waiting to be exported.

★ Flag Rock   HISTORIC SITE
(Rampart St) Flag Rock, at the southernmost end of the Fort, was once a Portuguese bastion. Today it is easily the most popular place to catch a sunset. During daylight hours you may see daredevil locals leaping into the water from the rocks. Numerous vendors sell good street food, such as fresh papaya with chilli powder, from carts.

During the Dutch period, approaching ships were signalled from the bastion atop Flag Rock, warning them of dangerous rocks – hence its name. Musket shots were fired from Pigeon Island, close to the rock, to further alert ships to the danger. Later, the Dutch built a lighthouse here; since removed, the nearby street name survives.

Main Gate   HISTORIC SITE
(Lighthouse St) The Main Gate in the northern stretch of the wall is a comparatively recent addition – it was built by the British in 1873 to handle the heavier flow of traffic into the old town. This part of the wall, the most intensely fortified because it faced the land, was originally built with a moat by the Portuguese, and was then substantially enlarged by the Dutch who split the wall in 1667 into separate Star, Moon and Sun Bastions.

Point Utrecht Bastion   HISTORIC SITE
(Hospital St) The eastern section of Galle's wall ends at the Point Utrecht Bastion, close to the powder magazine, which bears a Dutch

Galle

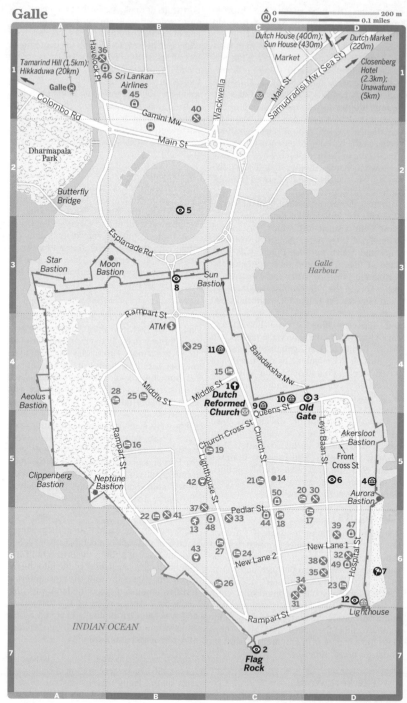

THE SOUTH

N
0 _____ 200 m
0 _____ 0.1 miles

Tamarind Hill (1.5km);
Hikkaduwa (20km)

Galle

Colombo Rd

Havelock Pl

36
46 Sri Lankan
      Airlines
45
Gamini Mw
40
Main St

Wackwella

Market

Main St

Samudradisi Mw (Sea St)

Dutch House (400m);
Sun House (430m)

Dutch Market (220m)

Closenberg
Hotel
(2.3km);
Unawatuna
(5km)

Galle
Harbour

Dharmapala
Park

Butterfly
Bridge

Esplanade Rd

Star
Bastion

Moon
Bastion

Sun
Bastion

5

8

Rampart St
ATM

29   11

15

Middle St

28   25

Aeolus
Bastion

Rampart St

16

Clippenberg
Bastion

Neptune
Bastion

22   41

37

Pedlar St
33

13   48

43

27   24

New Lane 2

26

Middle St

Dutch
Reformed
Church

Church Cross St

19

Lighthouse St

42

21   14

50

Church St

Queens St

9   10   3
Old
Gate

Baladaksha Mw

Akersloot
Bastion

Front
Cross St

6   4

Aurora
Bastion

Leyn Baan St

20   30

18   17
44

39   47

32
38   49
35

34

23

31   12
Lighthouse

New Lane 1

Hospital St

7

INDIAN OCEAN

Rampart St

2
Flag
Rock

Galle

THE SOUTH GALLE

inscription from 1782. The bastion is topped by the landmark 18m-high **lighthouse** (Hospital St), which dates to 1938 and is still in use.

Lighthouse Beach   BEACH
(off Hospital St) A nice little swath of sand right on the east side of the Fort, it's a good place for a dip after a day's sweaty explorations.

◉ Inside the Fort

Most of the older buildings within the Fort date from the Dutch era. Many of the streets still bear their Dutch names, or are direct translations. The Dutch also built an intricate sewer system that was flushed out daily by the tide. With true Dutch efficiency, they then bred musk rats in the sewers, which were exported for their musk oil.

Visitors to Galle 20 years ago will be surprised by what they find today: crumbling streets resurfaced with tidy paving stones and myriad historic building renovations both completed and ongoing. And just when it all

seems a bit upscale, a screaming monkey will go leaping overhead.

★**Dutch Reformed Church**   CHURCH
(Groote Kerk, Great Church; cnr Church & Middle Sts; ⊙9am-5pm) Originally built in 1640, the present building dates from 1752 to 1755. Its floor is paved with gravestones from the old Dutch cemetery (the oldest dates from 1662); the friendly caretaker will tell you where remains are held in the walls and under the floor. The organ from 1760 still sits in the building and the impressive pulpit, made from calamander wood from Malaysia, is an imposing piece. It also makes for a shady place to pause.

Marine Archeological Museum   MUSEUM
(Church St; adult/child Rs 650/325; ⊙9am-4.30pm) With an entrance behind the iconic old Bell Tower, this updated facility is easily the more engaging of Galle's two maritime museums. Exhibits include lots of videos and interactive displays that illuminate the town's maritime past, including the many shipwrecks in the

surrounding waters. It covers two levels that snake though the old walls.

National Maritime Museum
MUSEUM
(Queens St; adult/child US$3/1.50; ⊘9.30am-4.30pm Tue-Sat) Nestled in the old walls, this small museum is worth a quick look for its skeleton of a Brydes whale and a very useful model that explains how tsunamis occur. There are also some dusty mannequins demonstrating old fishing techniques.

Historical Mansion
HISTORIC SITE
(31-39 Leyn Baan St; ⊘9am-6pm) If you think you've got a lot of clutter filling up the shelves at home, then just wait until you get a load of the Historical Mansion, which is the private collection of a longtime Fort family. Set in a restored Dutch house, it's not really a museum, as many of the exhibits have price tags. Look for oodles of colonial artefacts, including collections of antique typewriters, VOC china, spectacles and jewellery.

Don't miss the places where plaster has been removed to show how the building was constructed.

Amangalla
HISTORIC BUILDING
(10 Church St) The Amangalla was built in 1684 to house the Dutch governor and officers. Later, as the New Oriental Hotel, it was the lodging of choice for 1st-class P&O passengers travelling to and from Europe in the 19th century. During much of the 20th century, it was in a decades-long slow decline and was run by the legendary Nesta Brohier, a grand lady who was actually born in room 25.

The hotel has a memorable and comic role in Paul Theroux's iconic *The Great Railway Bazaar*. It was massively restored and reopened as the luxurious Amangalla in 2004. Public areas like the bar, lobby and restaurants are open and worth a look.

Dutch Hospital
HISTORIC BUILDING
(Hospital St) This vast, colonnaded colonial landmark dates to the 18th century. Its size was necessary as both the voyage to Ceylon and life in the tropics proved very unhealthy to the Dutch, who died in droves from various diseases and the tropical heat (their preference for seldom-washed wool clothes didn't help matters). Recently restored, there are plans for shops and cafes that take advantage of this prime waterfront site.

National Museum
MUSEUM
(☑223 2051; Church St; adult/child Rs 300/150; ⊘9am-5pm Tue-Sat) The National Museum is housed in a perfectly realised 1686 Dutch

building. The museum has displays of traditional masks, information on the lace-making process, a few examples of the luxury items that once passed through the port, and religious items, including a relic casket.

◎ New Town

Although the Fort rightfully gets most of the attention, Galle's new town is also worth a stroll. Shops and markets are hives of activity throughout the day. Havelock Place, near the railway station, is attracting interesting businesses that can't afford the ever-ascending rents inside the Fort.

Dutch Market
MARKET
(Main St) Look for the Dutch Market, with its displays of fruits and vegetables under a 300-year-old columned roof. There are other food and spice markets along Main St, as well as a busy row of shops that make for interesting browsing.

Galle International Cricket Stadium
STADIUM
(Main St) Once a racecourse for wagering British colonials, Galle's cricket grounds were established over 100 years ago. Since 1998 it has been used for international matches; in 2010 it was the site of the legendary last appearance of Sri Lanka's great cricket player, Muttiah Muralitharan.

⯅ Activities

Head to nearby Unawatuna for dive shops, snorkelling tours and yoga studios. Unawatuna also has some good spas.

Galle Fort Spa
SPA
(☑077 725 2502; 63 Pedlar St; massage per hr from Rs 5500; ⊘8am-6pm) A top-end spa run by the people behind the Fortaleza hotel, you can enjoy a range of therapies and services here, all with top-end products, potions and lotions.

⌲ Tours

★ Galle Fort Walks
WALKING TOUR
(☑077 683 8659; www.sriserendipity.com; Serendipity Arts Cafe, 60 Leyn Baan St; tours from US$25) Author and photographer Juliet Coombe leads fun 90-minute walking tours of the Fort. The walks come in several themes, including a Mystical Fort Tour, which delves into local legends and myths; a Meet the Artists tour (24 hours' notice required), which introduces you to the town's large artist community; and a range of culinary tours.

Galle Fort Tours TOURS

(Church St; tours from Rs 3000; ☺9am-5pm)
Several of Galle's tuk-tuk drivers offer tours
around the Fort and town. You can find them
waiting across from the Galle Fort Hotel.
Rates are negotiable, as are the itineraries.
These guys are real characters, so expect to
have fun as you careen about in the back of a
three-wheeler. Longer trips in air-con cars are
also available.

☀ Festivals & Events

Galle Literary Festival CULTURAL FESTIVAL

(www.galleliteraryfestival.com) A somewhat annual event this festival usually brings together renowned Asian and Western writers, although the schedule can vary depending on
the mood of the volunteers.

🛏 Sleeping

Each year brings new places to stay within
the walls of the Fort; everything from simple
homestays to enticing boutique hotels. In
high season it's best to book as demand keeps
spiralling ever upward. The surrounding region also has a vast range of options.

🛏 Fort

Pedlar's Inn Hostel GUESTHOUSE $

(☐222 7443; www.pedlarsinn.com; 62 Lighthouse
St; dm US$12-15, r US$50-60; ☎) The Pedlar's
empire has expanded to this new and bright
guesthouse which features very good hostel
rooms. Each has three or four beds and is fan-
cooled. Two private rooms have air-con. You
can rent bikes and serve yourself from the
breakfast bar.

Hotel Weltevreden GUESTHOUSE $

(☐222 2650; piyasena88@yahoo.com; 104 Pedlar
St; r Rs 2500-5000; ☎) A heritage-listed Dutch
building, the Hotel Weltevreden has 10 basic
rooms painted in bright colours set around a
well-loved courtyard garden. Plenty of friendly chit-chat with the elderly owner is included
in the room price. Cheaper rooms have shared
bathrooms and are fan-only.

Mrs ND Wijenayake's

Guest House GUESTHOUSE $

(Beach Haven; ☐223 4663; www.beachhaven-galle.
com; 65 Lighthouse St; r Rs 2000-5500; ❋☎) The
wonderful Mrs Wijenayake has been playing
host to grateful backpackers forever and her
knowledge of their needs shows in this comfy guesthouse. The 12 rooms range from the
clean and simple, with shared bathrooms, to
fancier air-con rooms. The family still talk of
the extended stay by Lonely Planet cofounder
Tony Wheeler in 1977.

Frangipani Motel GUESTHOUSE $

(☐222 2324; www.frangipanigroup.com; 32 Pedlar
St; r US$24-40; ❋☎) Modern and kitsch, this
family-run guesthouse has eight rooms in two
buildings that straddle Pedlar St. The large
rooms upstairs are airy and bright, with ocean
breezes billowing through the roof slats and a
flower-bedecked bed. There's a garden full of
songbirds, where you can eat and relax. Some
rooms have balconies.

★Seagreen Guest House GUESTHOUSE $$

(☐224 2754; www.seagreen-guesthouse.com; 19B
Rampart St; r Rs 4500-8000; ❋☎) The five
whitewashed rooms here feature colourful
Indian textiles and rainwater showers. The
bathrooms are some of the best in this price
range and the rooftop terrace has sublime
sunset views off over the ramparts and far,
far away over a salt-spray Indian Ocean. Some
rooms are fan-only while others have excellent ocean views.

Fort Dew Guesthouse GUESTHOUSE $$

(☐222 4365; www.fortdew.com; 31 Rampart St; r Rs
4000-9000; ❋☎) Set close to the ancient city
walls, this five-room guesthouse is a real find.

THE SOUTH GALLE

HOLIDAY RENTALS

Sri Lanka's beautiful southern beaches have been drawing people for decades, many of
whom find leaving harder than they thought and put down roots more permanently. Scores
of private villas and holiday homes dot the sands east and west of Galle. Most are the very
definition of discretion, with high walls keeping the hubbub of the coast road away.

Many of these beautiful properties are available for rent at prices that may surprise: for
as little as US$150 a night, you can have your own beach house. And as you pay more, the
amenities only proliferate, from pools to staff and beyond. Some of the grander properties
are no strangers to the pages of *Hello* magazine.

Good sources for rentals include the following websites: www.villsinsrilanka.com, www.
lankarealestate.com and www.vrbo.com.

It's whitewashed in a classic Mediterranean style and beautifully maintained; the motif extends to the rooms which have a simple white wall and dark wood design. The rooftop terrace cafe and bar have stunning views. Some rooms are fan-only.

Light House View Inn GUESTHOUSE $$
(☑ 223 2056; www.lighthouseviewinn.com; 44 Hospital St; basic r Rs 2000, fan/air-con r Rs 3200/7000; ❄☎) The name aptly describes the view of the Galle's landmark as the lighthouse is right in front. Views of it and the ocean are highlights of the very nice and breezy terrace. The cheapest of the five rooms share a toilet; all have simple decor. The genial owner is proud of her corner room which has sunrise and sunset views.

New Old Dutch House HOTEL $$
(☑ 223 2987; www.newolddutchhouse.lk; 21 Middle St; r US$35-55; ❄☎) This place with the timeless name might well be the most immaculate guesthouse in all of southern Sri Lanka. The eight spacious rooms have creaky, polished wooden floors and lovely soft beds. Breakfast can be enjoyed under the courtyard's pawpaw trees. Amenities include satellite TV and fridge.

Fort Inn GUESTHOUSE $$
(☑ 224 8094; rasikafortinn@yahoo.com; 31 Pedlar St; r Rs 2500-5000; ❄@☎) The ever-beaming owner of this ever-expanding 11-room guesthouse offers good, basic rooms and a perfect people-watching balcony. The decor is simple but you can enjoy amenities like a fridge and air-con in the more expensive rooms.

Ocean View Guest House GUESTHOUSE $$
(☑ 224 2717; www.oceanviewlk.biz; 80 Lighthouse St; r US$30-60; ❄) The small and pleasingly old-fashioned rooms (some fan-only) come in as many styles and flavours as there are curries in Sri Lanka. The real clincher, though, is the beautiful rooftop garden. The guesthouse is entered from Rampart St.

⭐ **Fortaleza** BOUTIQUE HOTEL $$$
(☑ 223 3415; www.fortaleza.lk; 9 Church Cross St; r US$110-200; ❄☎) This former spice warehouse has been transformed into a fabulous small hotel. Although there are only four rooms, each exudes relaxed luxury, with furnishings that have a colonial feel, without the pomp. The bathrooms are large and nicely kitted out. Opt for the Library Room, which has a huge round window that bathes the interior in light.

🏃 Town Walk
The Historic Fort

START CLOCK TOWER
FINISH CLOCK TOWER
LENGTH 2.75KM; THREE TO FOUR HOURS

This walk will take you past many of Galle's highlights as you traverse four centuries of history. One of the Fort's great charms is that detours and aimless wanderings are rewarded, so don't hesitate to stray from the following walk.

Start at the ❶ **Clock Tower**, which unlike so many worldwide, actually displays the correct time thanks to the fine engineering of the 1882 British mechanism inside. Pause and look out across the cricket field to the New Town, with its ceaseless bustle. Walk down along the inside of the wall and pause at the British-built ❷ **Main Gate** (p105). Avoid the careening three-wheelers and cross Lighthouse St, following the walls to the ❸ **Sun Bastion**, with its fine views of the harbour.

Curve back down off the wall and proceed up Church St to the heart of old Dutch Galle. Admire the deep porches of the ❹ **Amangalla** (p108) hotel. Cross Middle St to the cool confines of the ❺ **Dutch Reformed Church** (p107). Across from the church is a ❻ **bell tower** (built in 1901) which rings for tsunami warnings. Continue south on Church St to ❼ **All Saints Anglican Church** at the corner of Church Cross St. Built from 1868–71, its solid rock construction would look right at home in an English village. Leave some money in the donation box as it needs a lot of restoration. About 50m further on is the ❽ **Old Lloyd's Office**, with its preserved ship arrival board, in the 19th-century commercial building just north of Galle Fort Hotel.

Retrace your steps and turn east on Queens St. Admire the 1683 ❾ **Dutch Governor's House**. A slab over the doorway bears the date 1683 and Galle's ubiquitous cock symbol. Walk down the gentle hill and stop to admire both sides of the ❿ **Old Gate** (p105). Now make your way back up the walls to the Fort's northeast corner and the ⓫ **Zwart Bastion** (Black Bastion), thought to be Portuguese-built

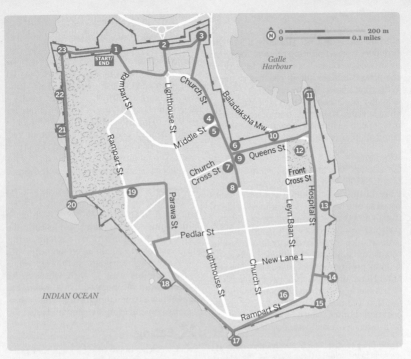

and the oldest of the Fort bastions, with some portions dating to 1580.

Make your way down to the vast leafy expanse of ⑫ **Court Square**. As the name implies, various courts and related offices ring the sides. On weekdays you'll see people in the shade of the huge banyan trees nervously awaiting their turn in court. Follow Hospital St south and you'll encounter the lavishly restored ⑬ **Dutch Hospital** (p108), which once was filled with victims of the plague. This part of the wall is the shadiest and most pleasant in the heat of the day. You might even consider a dip at ⑭ **Lighthouse Beach** (p107).

At the southeast corner of the Fort you can't miss the British-built ⑮ **Lighthouse** (p107). Just west along Rampart St is the bright white and imposing ⑯ **Meeran Mosque**, the centre of Galle's vibrant Muslim community. Continue west to have fun and frolic at ⑰ **Flag Rock** (p105), a good place to see so many of the submerged rocks that have claimed dozens of ships through the centuries. Walk the walls northwest to ⑱ **Triton Bastion**, a great place to be at sunset.

Now come down off the wall to the cafe-lined Pedlar St and make a quick turn north

on Parawa St. These two narrow blocks have some of the most typical of the old Dutch colonial houses, complete with characteristic thick columns and shaded porches. Curve west and at the corner of Rampart St you'll find ⑲ **Sudharmalaya Temple**, with its compact dagoba. If you have the good fortune to be here on a full moon day, you can expect to see all sorts of ceremonies, many featuring coloured lights and candles after dark.

Head back up onto the wall at ⑳ **Clippenberg Bastion**. In the usually gentle surf surging around the rocks and sand below you may well see sea turtles feeding at dusk. Head north along the walls and enjoy the vast grassy expanse that until very recently was part of Galle's modern-day army base. Today you're more likely to see a cow chewing its cud than a recruit standing at attention.

North of ㉑ **Aeolus Bastion**, look for the small ㉒ **tomb of the Muslim saint** Dathini Ziryam outside the wall. At the northwest corner of the Fort, pause at the ㉓ **Star Bastion**, which has ample evidence of the area's dark past; the fortifications were used at various times by the Dutch as a prison and slave quarters. Now complete your circuit at the Clock Tower.

★ Fort Printers
BOUTIQUE HOTEL **$$$**

(📞 224 7977; www.thefortprinters.com; 39 Pedlar St; r US$140-200; ✳ @ 🛜 ☀) This large 1825 structure once housed printing presses. Today, the enormous wooden beams used to support the presses remain but all else has changed. With great respect for the building's heritage, a luxury hotel has been created within the vintage walls. The style is traditional but with just enough lashings of modern style to avoid being another colonial cliche.

★ Amangalla
BOUTIQUE HOTEL **$$$**

(📞 223 3388; www.amanresorts.com; 10 Church St; r from US$500; ✳ @ 🛜 ☀) Enjoy colonial opulence in this lavishly kitted out resort that's based in one of the Fort's most famous buildings. The opening scene is one of massive, polished wooden floors and spiffily dressed staff, who lead you like royalty into luxurious rooms you may have a hard time leaving.

In its previous incarnation as the New Oriental Hotel, the building housed generations of travellers. You can recall those days – and the Dutch family who ran the place – in the beautiful library, which, like the gorgeous pool, offers a reason to leave your room.

★ Galle Fort Hotel
BOUTIQUE HOTEL **$$$**

(📞 223 2870; www.galleforthotel.com; 28 Church St; r from US$200; ✳ @ 🛜 ☀) This former 17th-century Dutch merchant's house is home to a breathtaking boutique hotel. The rooms are all different: some have two levels and others stretch across entire floors. Linens are exquisite and there are antiques everywhere. What you won't find are distractions like TVs – rather, you can enjoy the large courtyard pool and the pervasive serenity.

🛏 Around Galle

★ Dutch House
BOUTIQUE HOTEL **$$$**

(📞 438 0275; www.thedutchhouse.com; 23 Upper Dickson Rd; r from US$250; ✳ 🛜 ☀) After a game of croquet on the lawn and a swim in the dreamy pool, retire to one of only four rooms high in the hills above Galle to write a novel or sketch a masterpiece. Then take a break by clambering into the towering four-poster or by blowing bubbles of love in the bath.

★ Sun House
BOUTIQUE HOTEL **$$$**

(📞 438 0275; www.thesunhouse.com; 18 Upper Dickson Rd; r US$140-250; ✳ 🛜 ☀) This gracious old villa, built in the 1860s by a Scottish spice merchant, is located on the shady hill above the new town. The eight rooms vary in size, although even the smallest is a crisply decorated gem. Colours are muted and there are nice accents of colonial elegance. It's part of the same group that runs the nearby Dutch House.

★ Tamarind Hill
BOUTIQUE HOTEL **$$$**

(📞 222 6568; www.asialeisure.lk; 288 Galle Rd; r/ste from US$150/450; ✳ 🛜 ☀) This 19th-century former British Admiral's mansion has been converted into a small boutique hotel with 10 luxurious rooms, fine service and a jungle-fringed pool. Rooms are set in long colonnaded wings, with remarkably thick walls. The public spaces recall the days of the Royal Navy. It's 2km west of the new town.

★ Closenberg Hotel
HISTORIC HOTEL **$$$**

(📞 222 4313; www.closenburghotel.com; 11 Closenberg Rd; r US$100-200; ✳ @ 🛜) Built as a 19th-century P&O captain's residence in the heyday of British mercantile supremacy, this rambling hotel sits on a promontory with views over Galle harbour and the Fort (which is five minutes' west by three-wheeler). It's a grand work in progress: the 20 rooms are mostly modern in convenience, while a new infinity pool jazzes up the outdoor bar.

🍴 Eating

Every week seems to bring a great new place to eat in the Fort, but be sure to find a table by 9pm as the town gets sleepy fast. Also, many places do not serve alcohol (yes, that means beer!).

🍴 Fort

★ Dairy King
DESSERTS **$**

(📞 222 5583; 69A Church St; treats from Rs 250; ⊙ 11am-10pm) If no one is around at this window-front outlet attached to a house, ring a bell and soon one of the King's family will appear to offer you a choice of Galle's best ice cream. The passion fruit is simply divine.

★ Mamas Galle Fort
SRI LANKAN **$**

(📞 223 5214; off Church St; mains from Rs 350; ⊙ 11am-9pm) Malini Perera is the true 'Mama' of Mama's fame. She and her daughters are now cooking up their much-loved and dead-simple rice and curries at this small house. Everything is ultra-fresh and you can learn how to prepare these meals yourself at her cooking classes (US$30) which include a trip to the new town market.

★ Anura's Restaurant
INTERNATIONAL **$**

(📞 222 4354; 9 Lighthouse St; mains from Rs 350; ⊙ 8am-9pm) This tiny bright-orange hole-in-the-wall place caters to backpackers and serves curries, various pasta dishes and pretty good pizzas. The paintings on the wall give it something of a cafe-gallery feel.

★Spoon's Cafe   SRI LANKAN $$
(☑ 077 938 3340; 100 Pedlar St; meals from Rs 450; ⏰ 11am-9pm) Shamil Roshan Careem hails from one of the Fort's oldest families and he loves to cook. Lucky us! In his new and tiny cafe he serves up some superb curries; his takes on old family recipes. Save room for dessert as his superb 'Silk Route Toffee' may be the best thing to cross your lips in Sri Lanka.

★Elita Restaurant   SEAFOOD $$
(☑ 077 242 3442; 75 Hospital St; meals from Rs 500; ⏰ 11am-9pm) Thirteen years of work as a chef in Belgium gave Krishantha Suranjith myriad skills in preparing seafood. His new two-level restaurant has great views out to the lighthouse and harbour and is a great place to sample the local salt-water bounty. Opt for a table out front or upstairs in the cute dining room.

★Royal Dutch Cafe   CAFE $$
(☑ 077 177 4949; 72 Leyn Baan St; meals from Rs 450; ⏰ 8am-7pm) Owner Fazal Badurdeen puts 'storyteller' right on his business card and he has a million of stories. He also seems to have almost that many teas and coffees, from cinnamon to cardamom to ginger. There's a small menu of curries and good banana pancakes at breakfast. Enjoy the day from the colonnaded porch.

Serendipity Arts Cafe   INTERNATIONAL $$
(☑ 224 6815; 65 Leyn Baan St; meals from Rs 350; ⏰ 8am-9pm; 🛜) This art-crammed cafe has a fusion menu that includes Western sandwiches and Eastern curries, fresh juices and shakes, bacon-and-egg hoppers and filter coffee. It's a very casual place, with a big table outside, and is the home of Galle Fort Walks. Ask about cooking classes.

Heritage Cafe   INTERNATIONAL $$
(☑ 224 6668; 53 Lighthouse St; mains from Rs 800; ⏰ 8am-10pm; 🛜) This boutique-style cafe stands out for its array of unusual salads and a menu that encircles half the planet, although the focus is on South Asian. Choose between eating on the sunny terrace, under the lazy interior fans or out in the courtyard garden. The fresh juices and shakes are tops on a typically sultry day.

Cafe Punto   SRI LANKAN $$
(42 Pedlar St; meals from Rs 500; ⏰ 11am-9pm) The praise for this rice and curry joint is far wider than its narrow dining room. There's the usuals but also some more obscure creations such as a very tasty cabbage and eggplant number. They'll make your dishes appropriately spicy once you convince them you won't be a wimpy tourist and whinge.

Pedlar's Inn Cafe   SRI LANKAN $$
(☑ 077 314 1477; 92 Pedlar St; meals Rs 600-1200; ⏰ 8am-10pm; 🛜) A very popular cafe in an old colonial house. Shakes, coffee and sandwiches can be enjoyed at long tables that are good for lounging. More complex meals include the expected array of good rice and curries plus some excellent seafood.

Mama's Roof Café   INTERNATIONAL $$
(☑ 222 6415; 76 Leyn Baan St; mains from Rs 400; ⏰ 11am-9pm) Eat under the twinkling star-lit sky with views of a spinning lighthouse. The food is fine, but note that the original 'mama' has moved with her recipes to another location nearby.

★Fortaleza   INTERNATIONAL $$$
(☑ 223 3415; 9 Church Cross St; mains from Rs 800; ⏰ 8am-10pm; 🛜) The large courtyard at this old spice warehouse is surrounded by deep colonnaded porches. It's a quiet and classy scene and the menu matches the mood. Elegant takes on local fare are joined by a changing lineup of dishes such as lamb chops and seafood. The small bar mixes some fine drinks; breakfast is a treat.

✕ New Town

The new town, especially the canalside strip along Havelock Place, is attracting new businesses wary of the Fort's ever-increasing rents.

South Ceylon Bakery   SRI LANKAN $
(☑ 223 4500; 6 Gamini Mawatha; mains Rs 100-300; ⏰ 8am-9pm) Opposite the bus station, this highly popular lunch spot, with its impossible-to-resist sweet and savoury short eats and tasty curries, is the most authentic place to eat in the new town.

★Old Railway Cafe   CAFE $$
(☑ 077 626 3400; 42 Havelock Pl; meals Rs 300-800; ⏰ 9am-6pm Mon-Sat) Right across the small canal from the namesake station, this upstairs cafe has an enticing and changing menu of creative soups, salads and mains. Have some good coffee or juice with wonderful warm banana cake.

🍷 Drinking

Galle is not known for its nightlife, but you can find a few spots for a relaxing beverage.

Living Room
LOUNGE

(50A Lighthouse St; ⊙from 5pm) Easily Galle's most stylish spot for a tipple, this is a beautiful bar-cum-lounge-cum-designer shop. The owners have a Colombo flower business and exquisite examples of their wares are displayed in fragrant profusion. Dramatic and whimsical art abounds, which you can ponder over a G&T.

Pilgrims Lounge
BAR

(Rampart St; ⊙noon-late) Climb the rickety stairs to enjoy the ocean views from the one place in the Fort you can get a cold beer at 11pm. The jovial young guys who run this open-air joint have a nominal menu, but really you're here to make new friends.

Amangalla
COCKTAIL BAR

(☑ 223 3388; 10 Church St; ⊙11am-11pm; 🌐) Sip an exquisite mixed drink or fine wine in colonial splendour on the large porch at Galle's landmark hotel. It's amazing how the minutes just drift right on by while you recline in the plush wicker chairs.

🔒 Shopping

Galle's history makes it a natural spot for antique shopping. You'll also find a growing number of designer-owned shops. Note that many stores in the new town close on Sunday.

★ Shoba Display Gallery
ARTS & CRAFTS

(☑ 222 4351; www.shobafashion.org; 67A Pedlar St; ⊙9am-6pm) Beautiful lacework made right here. The shop teaches local women dying crafts and ensures them a fair price for their work. Even if you're not buying, pop in to witness the process of making lace. Ask about the excellent lace- and paper-making classes. The small cafe is a treat.

Old Railway
BOUTIQUE

(☑ 077 626 3400; 42 Havelock St; ⊙9am-6pm Mon-Sat) An eclectic shop with a fine cafe upstairs, look for all manner of tasteful (not pricey) locally made clothes, decor items and souvenirs.

Barefoot
ARTS & CRAFTS

(☑ 222 6299; www.barefootceylon.com; 41 Pedlar St; ⊙10am-7pm Mon-Sat, 11am-5pm Sun) Stylish takes on local clothing, jewellery, high-quality house decorations, crafts and gifts are the hallmarks of the Galle outlet of this excellent chain of shops. The book section has an excellent selection of Sri Lanka–centric titles.

Stick No Bills
ART

(☑ 224 2504; 35 Church St; ⊙9am-6pm) Postcards and posters covering Sri Lanka through the decades. Many of the beautiful vintage airline images for Ceylon sell a tropical paradise of fantasy.

Olanda Antiques
ANTIQUES

(☑ 223 4398; 30 Leyn Baan St; ⊙9am-6pm) A vast Aladdin's cave of antique furniture and clocks that stopped ticking in 1929 are among the treasures you'll find in this Dutch colonial house. There's also an attached cafe.

Orchid House
JEWELLERY

(☑ 545 3344; 28A Hospital St) A teashop with a sideline in jewellery and the sweet smells of incense.

Small Antique Shop
JUNK

(Hospital St; ⊙vary) Even tinier than the name implies, this little hole-in-the-wall has goods washed up on the beach across the road, found on the street and rescued from dusty old attics. The owner is a chatty charmer (and he thought up the name for his shop right after we asked him).

Cargills Food City
SUPERMARKET

(2rd fl, 26 Gamini Mawatha; ⊙9am-9pm) A convenient stop for useful items such as plug converters or bug spray.

ℹ Information

There is no shortage of banks and ATMs, both in the Fort and the new town. Wi-fi is common in hotels and cafes

Galle has a few scammers, a firm 'I have no interest in anything you have to offer' should do the trick. Dark corners of the ramparts are best avoided by women at night.

ATM In the Fort.

Main Post Office (Main St) It's near the market.

Post Office (Church St) A small branch office.

Sri Lankan Airlines (☑ 224 6942; 3rd fl, 16 Gamini Mawatha) You can book flights here; it also offers a full range of travel services.

ℹ Getting There & Around

BUS

There are plenty of buses linking the towns along the coastal road. They leave from the bus station in the centre of Galle, opposite the cricket stadium. Major destinations include the following:

Colombo via the coast road and Hikkaduwa, regular/air-con Rs 150/300, three hours

Hikkaduwa Rs 37, 30 minutes

Matara Rs 67, one hour

Air-con buses using the Southern Expressway from Colombo (Rs 420) take 75 minutes and depart from the southern Colombo suburb of

Maharagama near Kottawa. Buses run constantly from 5am to 8pm.

CAR

Galle is an exit on the Southern Expressway, which ends at Matara (30 minutes). It takes about 75 minutes to travel from the Galle entrance to Kottawa (the current northern terminus and a short way northeast of Colombo). This saves at least two hours compared to taking the road along the west coast. Note that it can take up to 2½ hours to drive from Galle to Bandaranaike International Airport, but this will shorten as additional sections of expressway are opened.

TRAIN

The railway route along the coast from Colombo Fort to Galle's vaguely art-deco train station is easily the most scenic and atmospheric way to journey between the cities. There are up to 10 express trains a day and they take slightly over two hours on the recently rebuilt tracks (2nd/3rd class Rs 180/100). Local trains serve Hikkaduwa (2nd/3rd class Rs 40/20, 30 minutes) and Matara (Rs 80/40, one to 1½ hours). There's a daily express to Kandy (Rs 320/175, 6½ hours).

Around Galle

The area around Galle is dotted with sights, both religious and natural. You can easily visit several in half a day by tuk-tuk.

Rumassala Peace Pagoda   BUDDHIST

On the west end of the peninsula of the same name, the Rumassala Peace Pagoda was built by Japanese Buddhist monks of the Mahayana sect in 2005, as part of their scheme to build peace temples in war-torn places worldwide (the Sri Lankan war was raging at the time). The glistening white stupa is easily seen from Galle Fort and can be reached via a narrow 1.6km road along the east end of the bay. There is another built by the same monks in Ampara, on the east coast.

Jungle Beach   BEACH

One of those 'secret' spots it seems everyone knows about, Jungle Beach is indeed reached through a tropical forest at the east end of Galle's bay. The sand is good and there is plenty of shade, along with a very basic cafe. Most drivers know the spot; take the road to Rumassala Peace Temple for about 1km and look for the signs.

Kottawa Conservation Forest   PARK

(Kottawa) Explore untouched jungle at this 14-hectare wet evergreen forest about 15km northeast of Galle. There are walking tracks in the forest, but first get permission from the forest department office near the gate. Wear good walking shoes and trousers: the leeches are ravenous. Trees are identified with their botanical names. In the small-sized park is a swimming spot fed by a waterfall.

Yatagala Raja Maha Viharaya   BUDDHIST

(donation Rs 100) Just 4km inland from Unawatuna, the Yatagala Raja Maha Viharaya is a quiet rock temple with a 9m reclining Buddha. The mural-covered walls are painted in the typical style of the Kandyan period. Monks have been living here for at least 1500 years. You'll seldom find crowds here, which only adds to the appeal. As you ascend the long flights of stairs, there are good views over the rice fields.

Unawatuna

🎧 091

Unawatuna is a cautionary tale for the rest of Sri Lanka's south coast. Where there was once a flawless crescent of golden sand that swept along a palm-lined shore with turquoise waters that had just enough surf to make for ideal swimming conditions, there is now one of Sri Lanka's less appealing beach towns.

The beautiful water is still there and you can still find decent patches of sand, but in several places greed has replaced good taste and common sense. Bulldozers have pushed huge boulders right up to and beyond the high tide line, allowing for the construction of some especially ugly hotels and cafes. Ironically, authorities have actually enforced setbacks on the west half of Unawatuna's beach and the result is much more salubrious.

Unawatuna makes for a good, quick beach escape from Galle's Fort: it's only 6km southeast. Otherwise it offers a cheap and cheerful sandy idyll, at least on the bulldozer- and boulder-free west end.

🏃 Activities

Most people spend a lot of their time lying around the beach or slouching in cafes. The small **Buddhist temple** at the west end of the beach has a vigilant monk ready to chase away anyone who is hoping to feign some piety in return for a shady rest.

Spas & Yoga

⭐ **Yoga with Asiri**   YOGA

(📱 077 176 4662; 6 Wella Dewala Rd; sessions from Rs 1000) The namesake owner of this yoga studio has become something of a legend with yoga

Unawatuna

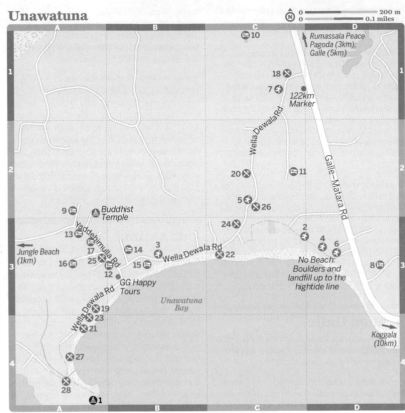

Unawatuna

◉ Sights
1 Buddhist Temple A4

✛ Activities, Courses & Tours
2 Ocean Dive Centre.............................. C3
3 Sanctuary Spa..................................... B3
4 Sea Horse Scuba Diving Centre........... D3
Secret Garden.............................(see 14)
5 Sonjas Health Food Restaurant........... C2
6 Unawatuna Diving Centre.................... D3
7 Yoga with Asiri C1

⊜ Sleeping
8 Black Beauty Guest House................... D3
9 Dream House A2
10 Nooit Gedacht C1
11 Palm Grove C2
12 Primrose Guest House......................... B3
13 Saadhana Bird House A3

14 Secret Garden..................................... B3
15 Villa Hotel B3
16 Village Inn A3
17 Weliwatta House................................. A3

⊗ Eating
Dream House .... (see 9)
18 Fruit Market.. C1
19 Hot Rock A3
20 Jinas Vegetarian and Vegan
   Restaurant.......................................C2
21 Kingfisher Restaurant......................... A4
22 Koko's on the Beach C3
23 One Love Restaurant A4
24 Pink Elephant C3
25 Queens Art Cafe A3
26 Roti Shop C2
27 Shekira Restaurant A4
28 Sunrise Seafood Restaurant................ A4

pros and beginners alike. He wins plaudits for
his teaching style and general enthusiasm.

Sanctuary Spa SPA
(☏ 077 307 8583; 136 Wella Dewala Rd; one-hour

spa sessions from Rs 3200) If a holiday means doing nothing more strenuous than being utterly pampered, the Sanctuary Spa should be music to your knotted muscles. It's also an Ayurveda centre. The serenity starts at the tidy entrance.

Secret Garden YOGA
(☑ 077 761 4119; off Wella Dewala Rd; yoga sessions from Rs 1000; ☺ yoga classes 9am & 5pm) Find your inner peace – and muscles you never knew you had – on one of the recommended yoga sessions in the yoga pavilion of the Secret Garden hotel's yoga dome. It also offers Ayurveda treatments.

Water Sports

Unawatuna doesn't have a lot in the way of surf breaks thanks to a fringing reef, though there is a gentle break right at the western end of the bay that a few locals ride. However, there are some decent waves along the beach, good for frolicking and body-surfing.

You can easily rent gear to **snorkel** the reefs a short distance from the west end of the beach.

There are several interesting **wreck dives** around Unawatuna, as well as reef and cave diving. The wreck dives include the *Lord Nelson,* a cargo ship that was wrecked about 10 years ago; it has a 15m-long cabin to explore. The 33m-long *Rangoon* is one hour south of Unawatuna.

Ocean Dive Centre DIVING
(☑ 077 721 3559; www.oceandive.asia; equipment rental from €30 per day) Offers a full range of tours and trips plus PADI courses.

Sea Horse Scuba Diving Centre DIVING
(☑ 228 3733; www.seahorsedivinglanka.com; snorkel gear hire Rs 800 per day, dive trips from €25) A well-regarded and long-standing outfit. Offers a range of snorkelling and dive tours, including ones to popular Jungle Beach on the north side of the peninsula.

Unawatuna Diving Centre DIVING
(☑ 224 4693; www.unawatunadiving.com; off Galle–Matara Rd; two tank boat dives from €40, PADI courses from €215) The only dive shop with a decompression unit. Offers discovery dives for novices for €25.

Walking

There are numerous good walks in and around Unawatuna. None of the following are more than 2km.

➡ Up the hill behind Yaddehimulla Rd to catch views to the other side of the

promontory with Galle Fort far in the distance.

➡ Walk north around the rocky outcrop at the west end of the beach to **Rumassala**, known for its protected medicinal herbs – legend has it that Hanuman, the monkey god, dropped herbs carried from the Himalaya here. The **temple** right on the promontory is fenced off, but you can wander up to the Rumassala Peace Pagoda (p115) on top of the hill.

➡ Isolated Jungle Beach (p115) on the north side of the peninsula is a popular destination, and if you don't feel up for the 2km walk over the hill through dense canopy to the beach, numerous boat operators will take you around the point on a day trip.

☙ Courses

★ **Sonjas Health Food Restaurant** COOKING
(☑ 077 961 5310, 224 5815; Wella Dewala Rd; courses from Rs 3000) These highly recommended day-long cookery courses tutor you in the finer points of Sri Lankan cuisine and will have you mixing your own curry powder in no time. The course is led by the lovely Karuna and a trip to Galle market is included in the price. Book at least a day in advance.

⌂ Sleeping

Unawatuna is home to a huge number of small budget guesthouses. There are some midrange options as well, many in the shady and pleasant small lanes back off the beach. Most of the beachside hotels are unattractive and several are built atop landfill which destroys the remaining beauty of the beach. There are a growing number of budget places right on busy Galle–Matara Rd, avoid them.

Saadhana Bird House GUESTHOUSE $
(☑ 222 4953; www.birdhouse.8k.com; Yaddehimulla Rd; r from Rs 3500; ❊ ☎) A charming – and yes, a bird-loving – family run this three-room guesthouse. It's simple, clean and close to the beach. The road is quiet. You can spot the local fowl from the rooftop terrace and there's plenty of feathered-friend spotting info on offer. Tasty local fare is also on offer.

Village Inn GUESTHOUSE $
(☑ 222 5375; unavillageinn@gmail.com; off Yaddehimulla Rd; r from Rs 1200) A very simple guesthouse that can't be beaten on price. All 11 rooms have bathrooms and a balcony or verandah, which are perfect for watching the

quarrelsome monkeys leaping about in the trees.

Weliwatta House GUESTHOUSE $$
(☑222 6642; www.weliwattahouse.com; Yaddehimulla Rd; r with fan/air-con from US$35/50; ✴🐱) This attractive century-old buttercup-yellow villa has loads more character than most of its competition. It has a couple of spacious and tidy rooms with hot-water bathrooms in the main building, and newer and more comfortable rooms behind. Enjoy relaxing in the lush garden in a comfy chair with a cold drink.

Secret Garden GUESTHOUSE $$
(☑224 1857; www.secretgardenunawatuna.com; off Wella Dewala Rd; r US$50-135; ✴🐱) Creak open the door and, like the name suggests, step into hidden gardens featuring a riot of colourful flowers. This renovated 140-year-old house has a range of rooms that are colour coordinated with the posies outside. Besides the four rooms, there are two good-value bungalows. Various yoga and Ayurvedic sessions are on offer.

Nooit Gedacht HISTORIC HOTEL $$
(☑222 3449; www.nooitgedachtheritage.com; Galle–Matara Rd; r US$45-80; ✴@🐱🐱) At the heart of this compound is an atmospheric 1735 Dutch colonial mansion, which is slightly tumbledown but perfectly enchanting. Rooms are divided between an old wing and newish two-story block (the latter have outside seating areas). There's a well-regarded Ayurvedic treatment centre and two pools.

Palm Grove GUESTHOUSE $$
(☑225 0104; www.palmgrovesrilanka.com; off Wella Dewala Rd; r with/without air-con from US$40/35; ✴🐱) Rummage through the masses of houseplants and hanging baskets and you'll discover a little English-run gem of a guesthouse. The four spacious rooms are very comfortable and have nice, private outdoor porches. Upstairs is a roof terrace filled with hammocks.

Dream House GUESTHOUSE $$
(☑438 1541; www.dreamhouseunawatuna.com; off Yaddehimulla Rd; r US$50/65; 🐱) Set well back from the hustle of the beach, this Italian-owned house has four intimate rooms that have been restored and decorated in a Rome-meets-the-tropics fusion. It's got a large terrace that's great for relaxing while you count the monkeys leaping overhead.

Villa Hotel HOTEL $$
(☑224 7253; www.villa-unawatuna.com; Wella Dewala Rd; r US$60-70; ✴@🐱) A waterfront hotel built in a vaguely traditional, but very tall, style. The twirling wooden window slats have an Arabic feel and the interiors of the rooms are attired in Indian art and ancient furnishings. The highlight is the garden full of ornate 1920s English garden furniture.

Primrose Guest House GUESTHOUSE $$
(☑222 4679, 077 607 4428; www.primrose.wz.cz; Yaddehimulla Rd; r with/without air-con US$40/35; ✴🐱) This bright three-storey guesthouse is close to the beach. The tidy and spacious rooms are well maintained; each has a little balcony overlooking a mass of bamboo plants.

Black Beauty Guest House GUESTHOUSE $$
(☑077 658 2909; www.black-beauty-sri-lanka.com; Galle–Matara Rd; r fan/air-con from US$27/33; ✴@🐱🐱) The tranquil gardens feature a pool, and the bright-orange tower of a guest-

---

HIGH TIDE HIGHJINKS

After the 2004 tsunami, laws were passed forbidding construction within 100m of the high tide line on any beach. Unfortunately, a quick drive along any part of Sri Lanka's developed coastal areas will show that the law has been widely ignored. This is especially apparent on the south coast, where the tsunami's destruction was so complete that most structures date from the last decade.

While places such as the east end of Unawatuna's beach have suffered greatly from developments built not only up to the ocean's edge but right out into the water, there are examples for all to see of the many positive benefits of the setback rule. To the surprise of many, regional authorities swooped in on the west end of Unawatuna in 2011 and demolished several offending structures. The result is a greatly improved beach for one and all (the cafes which rebuilt in compliance with the law now enjoy good business from beach-goers drawn to the unspoiled sand).

And rumours continue that the government could again take decisive action against offending properties at any time. Other areas where demolitions have been discussed include Mirissa and Hikkaduwa.

house has equally colourful rooms. It's good for people travelling with children as there are lots of kids' toys (although you do have to cross the busy road to reach the beach).

🍴 Eating & Drinking

Almost all places to stay provide meals or have restaurants. The best way to choose from the many cafes lining the beach may be to simply stroll around and see what you like. Most places are good for a drink – see which ones are in favour when you're there. Just don't expect much past midnight.

Shekira Restaurant   SEAFOOD $
(off Wella Dewala Rd; meals from Rs 500) With boats bobbing like ducks on the water just a few metres away, this wooden fisherman's shack is at the best end of the beach. There are just a few candlelit tables and it's perfect for a cold sunset beer and a cheap fried-fish dinner punctuated by the owner's friendly banter.

Hot Rock   SRI LANKAN $
(☑224 2685; Wella Dewala Rd; meals Rs 300-800; ☺9am-10pm) One of several beachside cafes that all but merge into one. Enjoy local fare plus seafood and cheap beer on the sand. The menu trumpets the many pork dishes, which are indeed not common on menus.

Queens Art Cafe   CAFE $
(Yaddehimulla Rd; mains from Rs300; ☺8am-9pm; ☎) A real travellers' cafe in a nice shady spot off the beach. Enjoy wi-fi, fine coffee and good snacks from the woodsy, open-air main room. There are numerous vegetarian options.

Roti Shop   SRI LANKAN $
(Wella Dewala Rd; mains Rs 250; ☺10am-10pm) Dozens of sweet and savoury *rotti* jammed full of cheeses, fruits and more make for a tasty snack or lunch. Wash it down with a fresh banana lassie.

Fruit Market   MARKET $
(Wella Dewala Rd; ☺7am-5pm Mon-Sat) The vast array of Sri Lanka's fruit and veg bounty is on display here.

★ Jinas Vegetarian and
Vegan Restaurant   VEGETARIAN $$
(Wella Dewala Rd; meals Rs 500-800; ☺11am-9pm) Set back from the road, this enjoyable garden restaurant offers a wide array of classic Indian dishes such as thalis and masala dosas as well as European vegetarian dishes, including veggie burgers. You'll find nirvana with the fresh passion fruit juice and the organic banana cake. Ask about the meditation lessons.

Kingfisher Restaurant   SEAFOOD $$
(Wella Delaya Rd; meals Rs 800-2000; ☺9am-midnight Tue-Sun) This seafront restaurant has a wide-ranging menu that, no surprise, focuses on seafood. The lobster is a treat, as are the many forms of shrimp. Many dishes have Thai or Italian accents. In high season waits for a table on the sand are long; book ahead.

Koko's on the Beach   BURGERS $$
(Wella Dewala Rd; meals from Rs 500; ☺9am-11pm) The beach bar for those who literally can't wait to get home for a burger or fish and chips. Gary the owner runs a tight ship and curry-weary customers rave about the warm welcome and quality of those very chips.

Pink Elephant   MIDDLE EASTERN, BAR $$
(Wella Dewala Rd; meals from Rs 500; ☺11am-midnight) Sure you can taste some Middle Eastern fare, but really this place is all about achieving the name through partying. Slouch with a shisha on a sofa or knock back a papaya mojito. There's regular live music.

Sunrise Seafood Restaurant   SEAFOOD $$
(Beach; mains from Rs 500; ☺11am-9pm) Cross the little stream at the west end of the beach and you'll find this simple place next to the temple. It's got a great location away from the hordes and a fine view back across the surf. The menu reflects whatever has been culled from the fishing boats resting on the sand. Order your shrimp with plenty of garlic.

One Love Restaurant   SRI LANKAN $$
(Wella Devala Rd; meals from Rs 400; ☺9am-10pm) Once hung right over the high tide line, now relocated well back on the beach, One Love has a nice spread of tables on the sand. Amidst a plethora of shrimp-grilling cafes, this is the local option for a classic rice and curry. Be sure to emphasise you want it spicy.

Dream House   ITALIAN $$
(☑438 1541; off Yaddehimulla Rd; mains from Rs 500; ☺5-9pm) Eat alfresco while being serenaded by classical music at this Italian restaurant. The secret to enjoyment here is remembering that Rome is 7700km west, so order simply (lots of good pasta dishes, no pizza) and appreciate the change from local fare.

ℹ️ Information

You'll find most goods and services in Galle. There are simple grocery stores on the inland portion of Wella Dewala Rd. Wi-fi is common in guesthouses, uncommon at cafes.

GG Happy Tours (☑223 2838; www.gghappy tours.com; Yaddehimulla Rd; ☺9am-10pm)

Internet access, and a good place to arrange tour and car-hire services.

ℹ Getting There & Away

Coming by bus from Galle (Rs 20, 10 minutes) you can get off at small Wella Dewala Rd at the 122 Km marker, which leads into town, or get off at the next stop, where the ocean meets the main road, and walk in along the beach (when the tide is down and you can get past the landfill boulders). A three-wheeler to or from Galle costs between Rs 400 and 500.

Unawatuna to Koggala

♪ 091

Beyond Unawatuna, the road runs close to the coast through Thalpe, Dalawella and Koggala, and on to Ahangama and beyond. This is posh country, with beautiful albeit narrow beaches and a long stretch of walled estates and hotels. Along this part of the coast you will see **stilt fishermen** perching precariously like storks above the waves at high tide. Each fisherman has a pole firmly embedded in the sea bottom, close to the shore, on which they perch and cast their lines. Stilt positions are passed down from father to son and are highly coveted. You'll be amazed at how fast they can get off those stilts and run up to you for payment if you even vaguely wave a camera in their direction.

◉ Sights & Activities

★ Martin Wickramasinghe Folk Art Museum   MUSEUM

(off Galle–Matara Rd; admission Rs 200; ⊗ 9am–5pm) This surprisingly interesting museum includes the house where respected Sinhalese author Martin Wickramasinghe (1890–1976) was born. The exhibits are well displayed, with information in English. Among them is a good section on dance (including costumes and instruments), puppets, *kolam* (masked dance-drama) masks (including one of a very sunburnt British officer), kitchen utensils and carriages. Don't miss the kitchen goods, including the multipurpose 'mill stone'. Look for the turn near the 131 Km marker, across from the Fortress Hotel. The bookshop sells Wickramasinghe's works, which are lauded for their exploration of local cultures and the roots of all the people on the island.

Koggala Lake   LAKE

Next to the road, Koggala Lake is alive with birdlife and dotted with islands, one of which features a Buddhist temple that attracts many visitors on *poya* (full moon) days and another that contains an interesting cinnamon plantation.

You can take a 90-minute **boat tour** of the lake and islands for about Rs 4000 in a four-passenger motor boat. Besides the main sights, you'll stop at a small island village and see a lot of birds (hawks, herons, egrets etc). Look for the Bird Island Boat Tours sign just east of the 132 Km marker.

Kataluwa Purwarama Temple   BUDDHIST

Rarely crowded, this feels like the temple time forgot. Dating from the 13th century, it has some recently restored murals, including some large ones depicting foreigners in flowing robes. A friendly monk will open the building and explain the murals. Some of the painted Jataka tales (stories from the Buddha's lives) are 200 years old. Turn inland and drive for 1.2km right at the 134 Km marker.

🛏 Sleeping & Eating

🏖 Thalpe

Thalpe is popular with those looking for a more sedate alternative to Unawatuna. There are a number of very exclusive places to stay as well as a few cheaper options. The beach is largely hidden from the road by a solid line of villas, houses and hotels, each with thick walls and massive gates. Many beach rentals can be found here.

★ Frangipani Tree   BOUTIQUE HOTEL $$$

(☑ 228 3711; www.thefrangipanitree.com; Galle–Matara Rd; ste from US$250; ❋ ☎ ☀) Cement, of all things, is the basis for this starkly modern vision of contemporary architecture on the beach. There are nine suites in three beach houses here and you can pick various sizes. All have soaring ceilings, private verandahs and views of the ocean. The narrow beach is the very picture of a palm-shaded cliche.

Why House   BOUTIQUE HOTEL $$$

(☑ 222 7599; www.whyhousesrilanka.com; off Galle–Matara Rd; r from US$250; ❋ ☎ ☀) Well, why not? You'll feel like you're staying at a private estate at this small hotel set inland in a green respite. Rooms are in the colonial main house or cottages. Personal service is emphasised, children are catered to and all manner of meals can be prepared. Look for the turn off the main road at the 124 Km marker.

Era Beach Hotel   BOUTIQUE HOTEL $$$

(☑ 228 2302; www.jetwinghotels.com; Galle–Matara Rd; r US$90-200; ❋ ☎ ☀) Small boutique hotel where wood and stone create a Zen-like sense

DON'T MISS

HUNDUNGODA TEA ESTATE

Sri Lanka's tea industry can seem like one vast outdoor factory, with workers toiling end-lessly for little money to produce a product that's been stripped of any cachet. That's not the case at the Hundungoda Tea Estate (✆ 077 329 0999; www.virginwhitetea.com; off Katha-luwa Rd; ⊗ 8am-6pm), an exquisite tea plantation in the hills above Koggala, 6km inland via Kathaluwa Rd from the Galle–Matara Rd near the 131km marker.

Here tea isn't a commodity to be off-loaded in bulk to the highest bidder, rather it is a simple indulgence to be savoured. Presiding over this small plantation is Herman Gunaratne, one of the legends of the island's tea industry. On a free one-hour tour you'll sample and learn how they produce more than 25 varieties of tea. Of these the most cov-eted is Virgin White tea, a delicate brew made from the tiniest and newest leaves. Where the average large plantation worker will pick 23kg of black tea in a day, the workers here manage but 150 grams of the virgin white leaves. Be sure to pick up a copy of Gunaratne's autobiography, *The Suicide Club: A Virgin Tea Planter's Journey*, which is a remarkably entertaining and insightful read about his life, tea and Sri Lanka, from the waning days of the British Raj to today.

of happiness (the beachside setting and gor-geous pool help out with this too). However, some of the six rooms catch a little road noise. The pool is vast and angles around the public spaces. The beach is dreamy.

★ Wijaya   INTERNATIONAL $$
(✆ 228 3610; Galle–Matara Rd; mains from Rs 800; ⊗ 9am-11pm; 🛜) The high-class option along the coast, Wijaya is hugely popular with lo-cal expats, who flock in for its pizza cooked in wood-burning ovens. Many never quite get past the dramatic views at this seaside loca-tion just 2km east of Unawatuna. The bar is skilled and the seafood specials also win raves.

🛏 Koggala

Koggala is home to a long, wide, but wave-lashed stretch of beach. The road runs quite close to the shore but most of the time it re-mains just out of sight, hidden by the high walls of estates.

The Fortress   HOTEL $$$
(✆ 438 9400; www.thefortress.lk; Galle–Matara Rd; r from US$280; 🅿️🛜🏊) From the outside this vast place, with its high walls, looks ex-actly like a prison. But inside you'll find it's all wide open in the one direction it should be: the sea. Revel in infinity pools, 53 chic urban-style rooms with whirlpool baths and rain showers, superb dining and more.

Ahangama & Midigama

✆ 091

The Ahangama and Midigama area are home to the most consistent, and possibly

best, surf in Sri Lanka. It's a very low-key area with plenty of cheap surfer-friendly accommodation and a scattering of pretty beaches (though the road often runs very close to the shore).

🏃 Activities

The first surf spot heading east is the consist-ent beach break at **Kabalana Beach**, which normally has something to ride even when it's tiny elsewhere.

In **Midigama** itself, a spicepot-sized village built beside a curve of sand, there are a couple of reef breaks. Lazy Left is the apt-ly named wave that bends around the rocks and into the sandy bay – it's perfect for that first reef experience. A few hundred metres further down is Ram's Right, a hollow, shal-low and unpredictable beast. It's not suitable for beginners.

Note that the water covers loads of rocks, coral and other hazards. Also, besides a few guesthouses offering battered boards for rent (Rs 600 to 1000 per day), there are no places selling surf gear or offering repairs – you'll have to go to Hikkaduwa.

★ Subodinee Surf School   SURFING
(✆ 077 765 9933; www.subodinee.com; off Galle–Matara Rd, Midigama; two-hour course €30, three courses €75) Yannick Poirier, a Frenchman, is something of a local legend and runs one of the better surf schools in the area, in con-junction with the Subodinee Guesthouse. He also has the best range of boards for hire (from €10 per day).

🛏 Sleeping & Eating

🛏 Ahangama

Many surfers stay in Ahangama and ride the waves in Midigama. Stilt fisherman offshore add colour, while the short commercial strip has services and ATMs. Some of the guesthouses are quite isolated.

Haus Sunil GUESTHOUSE $
(📞 228 3988; sunil.walgamage@yahoo.com; Galle–Matara Rd; r from Rs 3500; 🛜) A little jewel box of a guesthouse with two basic second-floor rooms with the kind of ocean views (including a small island) you can ponder for days. The modest building is well off the road and there is a tiny beach. Food is available. It's just east of the 137 Km marker.

Azure Beach Villa GUESTHOUSE $
(📞 499 3844; Galle–Matara Rd, 136 Km marker; r from Rs 4000; ❄🛜) Somewhat faded from it's once more ambitious self, this small guesthouse has two large rooms, one of which has good views of the pounding waves. There's very little beach here and there's no in-house restaurant, but if you want wave-tossed solitude, this is it.

Ahangama Easy Beach HOTEL $$
(📞 228 2028; www.easybeach.info; Galle–Matara Rd, 136 Km marker; r US$45-80; ❄@🛜) Popular with surfers, the eight rooms here (some fan-only) are decent and have nicely tiled bathrooms and four-poster beds. All have balconies facing the surf. The waterfront garden has hammocks and tables for lounging about. Note that there's little in the way of a beach.

🛏 Midigama

This tiny town has a few basic services and a couple of worthwhile cheap guesthouses.

Subodinee Guesthouse GUESTHOUSE $
(📞 228 3383; www.subodinee.com; off Galle–Matara Rd; r Rs 1500-2500, cabanas from Rs 5000; @) Longtime owners Jai and his wife Sumana offer 19 very different rooms, from hot concrete cubes with shared bathrooms to pleasing individual cabanas and rooms in a modern building over the road with hot water. Surfers are catered to. Turn inland off the main road at the 139 Km marker and go just past the clock tower and the train station.

Rams Guesthouse GUESTHOUSE $
(📞 225 2639; Galle–Matara Rd; r from Rs 2000; @) The 15 rooms at this ever-popular surfers'

beachfront hangout are basic, but they are clean and have private bathrooms, although road noise is invasive. Many surfers barely leave here for months on end, which gives it a friendly community vibe. It's located just west of the 140 Km marker, right in front of the best wave on the island.

🛏 Midigama Beach

Just west of Weligama and right at the 140 Km marker, look for a tiny road heading 100m towards the water from the main road. At the end you'll discover a splendid oasis of calm. There's a long beach and a wide grassy expanse that's kept tamed by a few cud-munching cows. The several places to stay are all real finds. The area is also called Gurubebila.

★ Villa Naomi Beach HISTORIC HOTEL $$
(📞 041-225 4711; www.villanaomibeach.com; Midigama Beach; r from €50; 🛜) A beautiful colonial villa with five whitewashed rooms, antique furnishings, plush bathrooms and a verandah with rattan rockers that's perfect for a sundowner. All up it offers exceptional value for money and looks out at the ocean through a strip of coconut trees.

Lion's Rest GUESTHOUSE $$
(📞 225 0990; www.lions-rest.com; Midigama Beach; r €50-90; 🛜) This new hotel has eight very attractive rooms set in a two-story complex surrounding a pool. Upper-floor units have ocean views across the green. The decor is all whitewashed plaster and dark wood. Beds are comfortable and the fittings are high quality. There's a small seafood restaurant.

Villa Tissa HISTORIC HOTEL $$$
(📞 041-225 3434; www.villatissa.net; Midigama Beach; r from US$90; 🛜🏊) Set in pleasant beachfront gardens, the six huge and well-appointed rooms line a colonnaded terrace and recall bygone days. There's a good large swimming pool, a narrow patch of beach out front and a cute little cafe.

ℹ Getting There & Away

There are frequent buses along the coastal road connecting Ahangama and Midigama with other towns between Galle and Matara and points beyond. The bus from Galle costs Rs 35 to Midigama. Many Colombo–Galle–Matara trains stop at Ahangama. Only a few local trains stop at Midigama.

Cinnamon Air (www.cinnamonair.com; one-way US$231) runs daily scheduled flights from Koggala airstrip to Colombo's Bandaranaike International Airport.

Weligama

📞 041

Weligama (meaning 'Sandy Village') is located about 30km east of Galle and is an interesting and lively blend of international beach resort and raucous Asian fishing town. You can spend a happy day wandering around, getting a feel for local life, dipping your toes in the ocean and marvelling at the denizens of the deep, who end their days being hacked up and sold from roadside fish stalls.

◎ Sights & Activities

Scenic though the bay is, Weligama Beach is a bit shabby and not geared for sunbathers. It's primarily a fishing village, with boats lining the western end of the bay. This all makes the appearance of the enormous new Marriott resort at the east end of the beach all the more ironic. It's out of all scale with anything around it and has many worried that others will follow. Weligama is known for its **lacework**, and stalls are located on the main road by the coast.

Taprobane   ISLAND
(www.taprobaneisland.com; island rental from US$1800 per day) Close to the shore – so close that you can walk out to it at low tide – is this tiny island. It looks like an ideal artist's or writer's retreat, which indeed it once was: novelist Paul Bowles wrote *The Spider's House* here in the 1950s. The island was developed in the 1920s by the French Count de Maunay-Talvande who perched his mansion on the tiny rock. You can stay or dine on the island with advance planning.

Surfing   SURFING
Weligama is a good place to learn to surf with soft, sandy beach waves that rarely exceed one metre. Both the Samaru Beach House and the Weligama Bay View, next door, rent boards (from Rs 1500 per day), offer lessons (from Rs 2500) and arrange for surf guides (from Rs 300 per hour).

Weligama Bay Dive Center   DIVING
(📞 225 0799; www.scubadivingweligama.com; 126 Kapparathota Rd; boat dives from €35, snorkel gear rental €10) Snorkelling and diving at Weligama is good. This operation, close to the harbour at the western end of the beach, runs PADI courses as well as excursions such as wreck dives. It also organises whale and dolphin diving and snorkelling trips.

🛏 Sleeping & Eating

Accommodation is spread out along the beach road; there is no reason to stay on the charmless inland side of the road.

For eating, tuck into some fresh-from-the-ocean seafood at one of the waterfront joints opposite Taprobane Island.

Samaru Beach House   HOTEL $$
(📞 225 1417; www.guesthouse-weligamasamaru.com; 544 New Matara Rd; r US$35-80; ❄ 🤶) Located at about the middle of the bay, this traveller-savvy place is on the beach and has 14 light and airy rooms (some fan-only) that are sheltered from road noise. The better rooms have a verandah. Bikes and surfboards can be rented and the genial owner can organise local tours and activities.

Weligama Bay View   GUESTHOUSE $$
(📞 225 1199; www.bayviewlk.com; Galle-Matara Rd; r US$30-60; ❄ 🤶) The ocean is your pool at this beachside hotel that adjoins other similar venues. The 14 rooms are basic but comfortable, and some have air-con. Upstairs units enjoy better views. Surfers are served with board rentals and lessons.

AVM Cream House   ICE CREAM $
(3 Samaraweera Pl; treats from Rs 20; ⊙ 11am-9pm) For dessert head to this wildly popular ice cream cafe opposite the bus station in the town centre. There's a huge range of fresh fruit flavours; a big glass of fresh-squeezed orange juice is a mere Rs 20.

ℹ Information

Weligama's busy commercial centre is inland from the coast road. It has supermarkets and ATMs in the streets around the bus station.

ℹ Getting There & Away

There are frequent buses to Galle (Rs 52, one hour) and Matara (Rs 28, 30 minutes).

Weligama is on the Colombo–Matara train line; destinations include Colombo (2nd/3rd class Rs 220/120, four hours), Galle (Rs 60/30, one hour) and Matara (Rs 30/15, 30 minutes). There are seven to 12 trains daily between Galle and Matara.

Mirissa

📞 041

Crack open a coconut, slip into a hammock and rock gently in the breeze, allowing the hours, days and even weeks to slip calmly by. Welcome to Mirissa, which is 4km southeast of Weligama, and is another quickly developing crescent of beach.

Modest guesthouses abound and there are a string of simple cafes along the sand that seem to come and go with the tides. So far the government has stopped the kinds of sand-encroaching construction as seen at Unawatuna, but only time will tell as visitor numbers just keep growing.

You'll need to go to Weligama or Matara for most services, although there are internet and phone places, and small markets near the 149 Km marker.

◉ Sights & Activities

The west end of Mirissa's **beach** is the nicest and is separated from the main road by streets lined with guesthouses. As the sand curves gently around to the east, it meets up with the roar of the Galle–Matara road. However, there is also a much-photographed tiny peninsula of sand at this end which juts out to a tiny island you can walk to at low tide.

There are some pleasant walks. One heads up a steep series of steps from the main road to the small **Kandavahari temple**, while the headland is a good spot to view Weligama Bay. **Mirissa Harbour**, across the peninsula from the west end of the beach, is always buzzing with boats.

The one very popular activity is a whale-watching boat trip.

Secret Root Spa   SPA
(☏ 077 329 4332; www.secretroot.yolasite.com; off Galle–Matara Rd; massage Rs 2500 per hr) Secreted away at the end of a jungle lane, 200m inland from the east end of the beach, is this family-run sanctuary of calm. It's an Ayurvedic centre (male masseurs only) where your big release will be your tension.

BLUE WHALE TOURS

Only in recent years have marine biologists realised that blue whales – the world's largest living mammal – are remarkably similar to many holidaying humans: they like Sri Lanka's coast. In fact, the waters off Mirissa and Dondra Head to the east often host some of the world's largest number of blue whales. (On the east coast, Trincomalee is another excellent place for blue whale spotting.)

The stats for blue whales are as extraordinary as their size: 30m long and weighing 170 tonnes (which makes them heavier than any known dinosaur by a significant amount). They are thought to live for more than 80 years, but this is not well understood as research has been scant, primarily because there were so few blues whales left after whaling finally ended in the 1970s (maybe 5000 whales were in the world's oceans then, 1% of the population just 200 years before).

Mirissa-based boat tours to spot blue whales are a major draw for visitors and there are many competing operators. Besides the blues, it's common to spot their smaller cousins, sperm whales (20m long, 57 tonnes), and various dolphins. A few points to consider:

➡ Although blue whales have been spotted throughout the year, December and April seem to be the peak months.

➡ Avoid May to July as monsoon season makes the waters very rough.

➡ Tours usually depart at 6.30am and last about two to seven hours, depending on how long it takes to find whales. This can make for a long day if seas are rough.

➡ Established tour boats have at least two levels for viewing, plus proper toilet facilities.

➡ Look for tours which respect international conventions about approaching whales. Ask about this before you book.

➡ Avoid rogue operators or chartered fishing boats as many of these are known to harass whales, for example by boxing one animal between two boats.

➡ Ask about food and drink availability. Find out if there are binoculars for passengers' use.

Recommended operators include the following:
Raja and the Whales (☏ 077 695 3452; www.rajaandthewhales.com; Mirissa Harbour; adult/child Rs 6000/3000) Uses a two-level trimaran for trips, follows international guidelines for approaching whales.

Paradise Beach Club (☏ 225 1206; www.paradisebeachmirissa.com; Gunasiri Himi St; tours US$50) The small beach resort runs its own tours on a good, custom-built boat.

🛏 Sleeping

You'll find a thicket of good-value guesthouses and modest beach hotels at the west end on and off tiny Gunasiri Himi Rd. Inland, there are some excellent family-run places along tiny lanes a short walk from the beach. Beware of road noise at the east end of the beach, and loud and late music near the beach cafes.

Poppies GUESTHOUSE **$**
(☏ 077 794 0328; poppiesmirissa@yahoo.com; off Galle–Matara Rd; r fan/air-con from Rs 2500/3500; ❄️🛜) The pristine rooms here are set around a grassy courtyard; each has a nice outside sitting area and hammock. It's just inland from the eastern end of the beach.

Calidan HOMESTAY **$**
(☏ 077 754 7802; calidan.mirissa@gmail.com; Sunanda Rd; r fan/air-con from Rs 2500/3500; ❄️🛜) This welcoming two-storey homestay features five basic rooms painted in cheery colours and big smiles from the owners. It's a five-minute walk back from the west end of the beach.

★ Rose Blossom HOMESTAY **$$**
(☏ 077 713 3096; mirissa.roseblossom@gmail.com; off Galle–Matara Rd; s/d with fan Rs 3000/4800, r with air-con Rs 7500) This cute little five-room place has smallish but well-decorated rooms and wonderfully charming owners. It's a leafy five-minute walk inland from the eastern end of the beach.

Point GUESTHOUSE **$$**
(☏ 077 151 4710; www.thepointmirissa.com; cnr Sanunda Rd & Gunasiri Himi Rd; r from US$45; ❄️🛜) The six rooms at this new two-storey guesthouse offer a hip vibe on a budget (some are fan-only). The owner is a local surfer and he offers advice, lessons, board rental and more. The west end of the beach is 200m away.

Palm Villa GUESTHOUSE **$$**
(☏ 225 0022; www.palmvillamirissa.com; Galle–Matara Rd; r fan/air-con from €45/55; ❄️🛜) The best option at the beach's east end, each of the eight lovely rooms in this colonial-style manor is uniquely decorated in a bright and modern fashion. The more expensive rooms are set right on the beach. At the excellent in-house restaurant you can eat at a candlelit table under the stars. There's a two-night minimum.

Amarasinghe Guest House GUESTHOUSE **$$**
(☏ 225 1204; www.amarasingheguesthouse.com; off Galle–Matara Rd; r from US$40; @🛜) This de-lightful place, adrift in a web of rural lanes five minutes inland from the beach, is ideal. A range of 10 agreeably ramshackle rooms and cottages lie scattered throughout the gardens. The owners grow all their own organically produced vegetables and spices, and the food receives rave reports.

Surf Sea Breeze HOTEL **$$**
(☏ 071 404 8084; www.surfseabreezemirissa.com; Gunasiri Himi Rd; half-board r fan/air-con from US$60/70; ❄️🛜) On its own shady plot of sand at the west end of the beach, this compact hotel has 19 basic rooms spread between a three-storey main building and small bungalows. The former have balconies with trees obscuring the views. The real appeal here is the location.

★ Mirissa Hills BOUTIQUE HOTEL **$$$**
(☏ 225 0980; www.mirissahills.com; off Galle–Matara Rd; r US$80-300; ❄️🛜🏊) Ponder buffalo wallowing in the ever-green rice paddies, peacocks strutting their stuff, and high above, on a hill in the heart of a working cinnamon farm, you can live royally here. Accommodations include a renovated estate house, rooms in the plantation's museum building and a modern hilltop retreat. The entrance is 1.1km inland from the main road's 148 Km marker.

Imagine Villa Hotel BOUTIQUE HOTEL **$$$**
(☏ 223 2088; www.imagine.lk; off Galle–Matara Rd; s/d from US$95/120; ❄️🛜🏊) This colonial-style, colonnaded L-shaped two-storey hotel is right on its own patch of beach. The nine rooms are nicely furnished and have fridges and private outdoor seating areas (upstairs ones have the best views). It's about 5km in either direction for the nightlife of Mirissa and the attractions of Matara. Look for the turn at the 154 Km marker.

Aussie Swiss Beach Resort HOTEL **$$$**
(☏ 225 4662; www.aussieswissbeachresort.com; 23 Modarawatta Rd; s/d from US$95/125; ❄️🛜) You get no points for guessing the nationalities of the owners of this immaculate six-room hotel on its own little beach west of Mirissa Beach. Rooms feature king-size beds, balconies or patios with sea views, and fridges. You can enjoy Ayurvedic treatments and menus. Look for the turn at the 147 Km marker on the main road.

Palace Mirissa RESORT **$$$**
(☏ 225 1303; www.palacemirissa.com; off Gunasiri Himi St; s/d half board from €75/90; ❄️🛜🏊) With the dominant position on the headland

at the western end of the bay, this is a very appealing top-end option. The 13 raised cottages have Hindu accents and nice porches with views. There's a pleasant fresh-water swimming pool and stunning views from the restaurant.

✖ Eating & Drinking

Numerous cafes set up plastic tables and chairs right up to the tide day and night. Wander and compare which one has the freshest seafood. All are good for a beer (invariably served to a reggae and rock soundtrack).

★ No1 Dewmini Roti Shop   SRI LANKAN $
(off Galle-Matara Rd; meals from Rs 200; ☺8am-9pm) The original and still the best local *rotti* shop. It also produces *kotthus* (*rotti* chopped up and mixed with vegies) and delicious, more substantial rice and curry–style dishes – don't miss the pumpkin. The ever-smiling chef and owner offers cooking classes (Rs 2000 for six curries). It's 200m inland past the Amarasinghe Guest House.

❶ Getting There & Away

The bus fare from Weligama is Rs 15; a three-wheeler costs Rs 350. From Matara the bus fare is Rs 25. If you're heading to Colombo, it's better to catch a bus to Matara and change, as many buses will be full by the time they pass through Mirissa.

Matara

📓 041 / POPULATION 69,300

Matara is a busy, booming and sprawling commercial town that owes almost nothing to tourism – which makes it a fascinating window on modern Sri Lankan life. Matara's main attractions are its ramparts, a well-preserved Dutch fort and, most of all, its street life.

◉ Sights

You can spend half a day wandering Matara. The long strip of beach along Sea Beach Rd is somewhat tatty, commercial and missable.

★ Dutch Rampart   HISTORIC SITE
(off Main St) The smallish Dutch rampart occupies the promontory separating the Nilwala Ganga from the sea. Built in the 18th century to protect the VOC's *kachcheri* (administrative office), its structure is a little peculiar – it was originally meant to be a

fort, but accountants, with their pesky cost-cutting exercises, dictated otherwise.

Inside the rampart are quiet vestiges of old Matara. Wander the narrow streets and you'll see the odd colonial gem. The river bank at the west corner is serene; see if you can spot one of the rumoured crocodiles.

★ Star Fort   FORT
(Main St; ☺10am-5pm) About 350m from the main rampart gate, Star Fort was built by the Dutch to compensate for deficiencies in the rampart. However, it's so small it could only have protected a handful of bureaucrats. The construction date (1765) is embossed over the main gate, along with the VOC company insignia and the coat of arms of the governor of the day.

Look for the two carved lions that guard the entrance gates. You can also spot the slots that once secured the drawbridge beams.

Parey Dewa   BUDDHIST
(off Sea Beach Rd) A pedestrian bridge near the bus station leads to a small island, Parey Dewa (Rock in Water), which is home to a tiny Buddhist temple with a very fancy modern bridge leading out to it. The beach on which it sits is a great place to go for an evening walk and enjoy an ice cream with many of the town folk.

Polhena Beach   BEACH
(Polhena Rd) The best beach in the area is hugely popular with locals at weekends who rent goofy inflatable toys and frolic in the surf. It's just west of town.

Weherahena Temple   BUDDHIST
(Weherahena Rd; admission by donation; ☺dawn-dusk) On the east side of Matara, turn inland 1km off the main road for this gaudy temple that features an artificial cave decorated with about 200 cartoon-like scenes from the Buddha's life. There's also a huge Buddha statue.

During the late-November or early December *poya*, a *perahera* (procession) of dancers and elephants is held at the temple to celebrate the anniversary of its founding.

🛏 Sleeping

Southwest of the centre, beachy Polhena has a number of budget guesthouses scattered amidst the warren of small tracks; you may need to ask for directions. A three-wheeler from central Matara costs Rs 350. Otherwise, Mirissa is just 9km west.

Matara

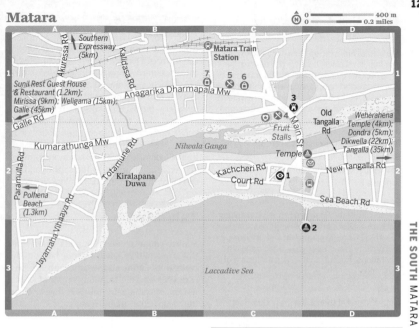

Sunil Rest Guest House &
Restaurant   GUESTHOUSE **$**

(☏ 222 1983; sunilrestpolhena@yahoo.com; 16/3A Second Cross Rd; r from Rs 2500; ☏) About 150m from the beach, the plain rooms in the main building at cheery Sunil's are a bit run down, but the owners operate a couple of other establishments with plusher rooms (up to Rs 7000) nearby. Note that they don't pay commission, so many three-wheeler drivers will tell you it's closed – it's not.

🍴 Eating

Just north of the bridge, on the main road, you'll see **food markets** (off Main St) and several fruit vendors with gorgeous displays of produce. There are also lots of simple storefronts with quick eats.

Galle Oriental
Bakery Restaurant   SRI LANKAN **$**

(41 Anagarika Dharmapala Mawatha; meals from Rs 200; ⊙ 8am-8pm) The best central option is a snazzy old place with a wooden interior and display cases bulging with baked and savoury treats. The soups and curries are good.

🛍 Shopping

Matara has the widest range of shops in the south.

Matara

⦿ Sights
1 Dutch Rampart...C2
2 Parey Dewa...D3
3 Star Fort...C1

⊗ Eating
4 Food Markets C1
5 Galle Oriental Bakery
   Restaurant...C1

ⓐ Shopping
6 Cargills Food City....................................C1
7 Vijitha Yapa Bookshop C1

Cargills Food City   SUPERMARKET

(☏ 222 9815; Anagarika Dharmapala Mawatha; ⊙ 8am-10pm) One of several large supermarkets on the main road, this place has traveller supplies and a pharmacy.

Vijitha Yapa Bookshop   BOOKS

(78 Anagarika Dharmapala Mawatha; ⊙ 9am-6pm Mon-Sat) Good selection of novels, magazines, maps and guidebooks.

ℹ Information

All the main roads in the centre have banks and ATMs.

Post Office (New Tangalla Rd) Near the bus station.

ℹ️ Getting There & Away

BUS

The Matara **bus station** (New Tangalla Rd) is a vast multilevel place. Look for tiny destination signs over the queuing pens. As Matara is a regional transport hub, services are frequent in all directions. At the time of research there were no services using the new expressway to Colombo but this may change. Major destinations include the following:

Colombo regular/air-con Rs 200/395, five hours
Galle Rs 67, two hours
Ratnapura Rs 215, 4½ hours
Tangalla Rs 60, 1½ to two hours

CAR

The section of the Southern Expressway linking Matara to Galle (30 minutes) and Colombo's suburbs (1¾ hours) opened in 2014. It follows a pretty route inland through rice fields and tea plantations. The entrance is 5km northwest of the centre.

TRAIN

Matara's train station is the present terminus of the coastal railway, although work is progressing on an extension as far as Kataragama which may open later in the decade. Destinations include the following:

Colombo 2nd/3rd class Rs 230/130, four hours
Galle Rs 80/40, one to 1½ hours
Kandy Rs 360/195, seven hours

Dondra

About 5km southeast of Matara you come to the town of Dondra, which is dominated by the important **Tanaveram Buddhist temple**, which was one of the island's primary places of worship until a previous – and grander – incarnation was destroyed in 1587.

Travel south from the centre for 1.2km and you'll reach the southernmost point of Sri Lanka. The landmark **Dondra Head Lighthouse** (admission Rs 600; ⊙ hours vary) provides an exclamation mark to the setting and you can climb the interior for fabulous views.

Talalla

📷 041

Squirreled away down muddy dirt tracks, this is one of those near-pristine beaches that really does define all the tropical-beach postcard clichés. This 1km-long curve of sand is mostly unspoiled by tourism development; the major man-made feature here is small fishing boats.

You can reach Talalla's narrow access road from two points on the main road; the best is at the 171 Km marker.

🛏️ Sleeping & Eating

There are several simple guesthouses back off the beach. There are just a couple of

---

WORTH A TRIP

MULKIRIGALA

Dangling off a rocky crag 16km northwest of Tangalla and nestled away among a green forest of coconut trees are the peaceful rock temples of **Mulkirigala** (Mulkirigala Rd; admission Rs 200; ⊙ dawn-dusk). Clamber in a sweat up the many steps and you'll encounter a series of seven cleft-like caves on five different terraced levels. You'll discover a number of large reclining Buddha statues interspersed with smaller sitting and standing figures.

Vying with these for your attention are some fantastical wall paintings depicting sinners pleasuring themselves with forbidden fruit on Earth and then paying for it with an afterlife of eternal torture – apparently it was worth it! Further on up, and perched on top of the rock some 206m from the base, is a small dagoba with fine views over the surrounding country.

Temples, in some form or another, have been located here for over 2000 years but the current incarnation, and their paintings, date from the 18th century. Nearby is a Buddhist school for young monks.

Pali manuscripts found in the monastic library here by a British official in 1826 were used for the first translation of the Mahavamsa (Great Chronicle), which unlocked Sri Lanka's early history for Europeans. For much more info on the site, see the website www.srilankaview.com/mulkirigala_temple.htm.

Mulkirigala can be reached by bus from Tangalla via either Beliatta or Wiraketiya. (Depending on the departures, it might be quicker to go via Wiraketiya than to wait for the Beliatta bus.) A three-wheeler from Tangalla costs about Rs 2000 for a return trip.

places for snacks and drinks on the sand; all accommodations have their own cafes.

Secret Bay Hotel GUESTHOUSE $$
(☏438 1089; www.secretbayhotel.jimdo.com; off Matara–Tangalla Rd; r from US$60; ✹☏) Set well back from the beach, this guesthouse has rooms split between humble bungalows (best) and a rather looming three-storey main building. Decor is simple but accented with vivid blues to reflect the bay. The top-floor restaurant has sweeping views.

Talalla Retreat RESORT $$$
(☏225 9171; www.talallaretreat.com; off Matara–Tangalla Rd; r with shared bath from US$60, r with private bath US$85-130; ☏✖) This unassuming resort is about a 100m walk from the beach. Half the rooms are open-plan, allowing you to live an alfresco life of outdoor showers and nights peering at the stars. The other rooms are more enclosed. Yoga courses are available, the restaurant serves organic food and there's a 20m pool in the middle of the expansive grounds.

Dikwella
☏041
Little more than a wide spot in the road with a few shops useful to locals, Dikwella – 22km east of Matara – is close to a couple of interesting sights and some fine beachfront hotels.

◉ Sights & Activities

★**Wewurukannala Vihara** BUDDHIST
(Wewurukannala Rd; admission Rs 100; ⊙dawn-dusk) A 50m-high seated Buddha figure – the largest in Sri Lanka – is a highlight of this temple, which is often thronged with worshippers. Before reaching the Buddha you pass through a hall of horrors full of life-sized models of demons and sinners. The punishments depicted include being dunked in boiling cauldrons, sawn in half and disembowelled. The temple is 1.5km inland from Dikwella, towards Beliatta.

Ho-o-maniya Blowhole LANDMARK
(admission Rs 250; ⊙dawn to dusk) Do you feel lucky? The Ho-o-maniya blowhole is sometimes spectacular and other times a fizzle. During the southwest monsoon (June is the best time), high seas can force water 23m up through a natural chimney in the rocks and then up to 18m in the air. At other times the blowhole will leave you limp. From the park-

ing area, its a 300m up-and-down walk past numerous vendors.

Driving, look for the 1km-long access road about 6km northeast of Dikwella, just west of the 186 Km marker.

🛏 Sleeping & Eating
This low-key stretch of coast features some beautiful beaches in perfect little coves off the main road.

★**Dickwella Beach Hotel** HOTEL $$
(☏225 5522; www.dickwellabeach.lk; 112 Mahawela Rd; r fan/air-con from US$30/60; ✹☏) This family-run beachfront hotel is a real find. Rooms have a certain vintage charm but are basic. However, everything is clean and well-run. You'll enjoy the ocean views through the cross-hatched coconut palms, while the only real noise here is the sea itself. Look for the turn off on the main road about 1km east of Dikwella.

Surya Garden Guest House BOUTIQUE HOTEL $$
(☏077 714 7818; www.srilanka-vacanze.com; Pubudu Mawatha; r from US$65) Sri Lankan charm meats Italian flair at this personable little place, set on large shady grounds 100m back from an idyllic beach. The three cabanas here have a mud-hut-meets-high-style motif and feature lovely decor and outdoor bathrooms. The excellent restaurant serves local and Italian dishes. Look for the turn at the 189 Km marker.

Goyambokka
☏047
The beautiful little coves around Goyambokka, with their turquoise waters and gentle waves, are almost a cliché of what tropical beaches are supposed to look like. Look for narrow Goyambokka Road just west of the 194 Km marker. Any bus travelling between Matara and Tangalla will drop you at the turnoff. A three-wheeler from Tangalla bus station costs Rs 400.

🛏 Sleeping & Eating
Quiet, leafy Goyambokka Road, behind the shore, is lined with several guesthouses and hotels, although they are widely scattered and the overall atmosphere is much more natural than commercial. At the main beach below Palm Paradise Cabanas you'll find a few shacky beach cafes.

Green Garden Cabanas
HOTEL **$**

(☏ 077 624 7628; www.greengardencabanas.com; Mahawela Rd; r fan/air-con from US$28/35; ❄ ☎) Set back from the beach, this hotel has a range of rooms, including well-kept cabanas with wooden floors and tidy bathrooms. Rooms in the main building have private terraces with views out to the fruit-filled gardens. The turn is at the 196 Km marker.

Palm Paradise Cabanas
CHALETS **$$**

(☏ 224 0338; www.beach.lk; Goyambokka Rd; r from US$80; ☎) Set on Goyambokka's beautiful main cove, the wooden cabanas and villas are hidden behind a veil of coconut palms. The units are of various vintages but the overall property is well-maintained. Being tucked up in your wooden hut listening to the waves is undeniably romantic.

Rocky Point Beach Bungalows
GUESTHOUSE **$$**

(☏ 077 497 7033; www.srilankarockypoint.com; Goyambokka Rd; dm/r from US$20/35, bungalow from US$40; ☎) There's a range of accommodation at the sunny compound back off the beach. You can opt for one of the four-bed dorm rooms or a private room in the main building, or a bungalow. All rooms have nice private terraces and balconies.

Goyambokka Guest House
GUESTHOUSE **$$**

(☏ 077 790 3091; www.goyambokkaguesthouse. page.tl; Goyambokka Rd; r Rs 4400-6000; ☎) This whitewashed colonial villa set under a ceiling of dancing palm trees is back off the beach. It offers 10 pleasant and well-priced rooms, some of which come with outdoor showers.

★ Amanwella
LUXURY HOTEL **$$$**

(☏ 224 1333; www.amanresorts.com; off Matara–Tangalla Rd; ste from US$550; ❄ @ ☎ ⊠) One of the most luxurious beach resorts in Sri Lanka, each of the Amanwella's 30 suites has its own private plunge pool and is so sybaritic that you may need to be prised out on checkout day. All of the units have ocean views, and some are right on the beach. The entrance is just east of the 193 Km marker.

Tangalla & Around

☏ 047

Tangalla is the gateway to the wide-open spaces and wide-open beaches of southeast Sri Lanka. It's the last town of any size before Hambantota and has some old world charm.

But you're really here to find your perfect beach and revel in it.

◉ Sights & Activities

Tangalla's harbour is an interesting place for a minor exploration. There's evidence of the Dutch all around here. Follow Harbour Road around the point and into the military area (which is usually wide open); there are great vistas from the **viewpoint** (Harbour Rd) along the grassy verge.

Rest House
HISTORIC BUILDING

(Harbour Rd) The shady Rest House was once home to the Dutch administrators. It's one of the oldest rest houses in the country, and was originally built (as a plate on the front steps indicates) in 1774.

★ Turtle Watch Rekawa
ECOTOUR

(☏ 076 685 7380; www.tcpsrilanka.org; Rekawa Beach; adult/child Rs 1000/600; ⊙ from 8pm, days vary) From April to September, green, hawksbill and occasionally even leatherback turtles struggle ashore at night to lay their eggs on Rekawa Beach. Tours are run by volunteers from the non-profit Turtle Conservation Project and locals. The emphasis is on protecting the turtles, so camera flashes and other lights aren't allowed. Call ahead to check conditions; if no turtles are sighted, you can return another night. A three-wheeler from Tangalla costs around Rs 1500; you'll need a driver to find this place. Unlike the turtle hatcheries on the west coast the eggs here are left undisturbed in the sand and are protected in situ. The visitor centre has good displays.

⌂ Sleeping

There are several areas in and around Tangalla in which to stay. As you go east, many are very remote and lie at the end of rough tracks off the Hambantota Road.

⌂ Tangalla

The following option is above the beach, just southwest of the centre.

Moonstone Villas
HOTEL **$$**

(☏ 077 675 8656; www.moonstonevillas.com; 336 Matara Rd; s/d from US$72/90; ❄ ☎ ⊠) A Canadian-run complex with modern and pleasantly decorated rooms. It's a slick operation and the grounds are pretty, although a bit cramped. The beach is down and across the busy main road.

TANGALLA AREA BEACHES

Tangalla marks the dividing line between the picture perfect tropical coves that dominate much of the south coast and the long, wind- and wave-lashed beaches that dominate the southeast of the island. Amidst this long strip of sand are several distinct beach zones, each with a distinct character.

The following are listed geographically, from Tangalla east to Rekawa.

Tangalla

The town beaches south of the centre are pretty, but sadly the busy main road runs very close to the edge of the sand, meaning lots of fascinated bus passengers watching you lounge about in a bikini.

Medaketiya Beach

The long sandy beach here, which extends northeast away from the town, is lined with both good and bad budget guesthouses and cafes. The sand is golden but dumping waves can make swimming dangerous. At the northeast end, the busy road turns inland and it becomes quieter. Unfortunately, some businesses are now building breakwaters out into the water, which is screwing up the flow of the beach.

Marakolliya Beach

Virtually a continuation of Medaketiya Beach, but much further out of town, the beach here is utterly breathtaking. Unfurling along the coast is a seemingly endless tract of soft sand backed by palms, tropical flowers and mangrove lagoons. At night, turtles lumber ashore to lay eggs; by day, a lone traveller scours the sands for seashells.

You'll find plenty of ways you can arrange for lagoon tours, bird-watching or kayak and canoe rental. Note that the dramatic surf which pounds the beach here has undertows, and it's frequently too dangerous to swim.

Rekawa Beach

Around 10km east of Tangalla, this is another corker of a beach. Like Marakolliya but even less developed, it's an endless stretch of wind- and wave-battered sand that isn't safe for swimming. An access road wanders off the Hambantota Road at the 203km marker.

THE SOUTH TANGALLA & AROUND

🛏 Medaketiya Beach

A popular area for budget travellers, this long beach, which extends north from town, offers a mixed bag of places to stay. Some are decades old and depressing, but there are also some sprightly new additions, especially along the narrow streets closer to town.

Starfish Beach Cafe   GUESTHOUSE $
(☑ 224 1005; starfishtangalle@gmail.com; Vijaya Rd; r Rs 2000-5000; 🛜) Run by a bunch of energetic and music-loving young guys, this guesthouse has large and airy rooms that are as neat as a pin. It's probably the most popular backpacker hangout on this strip. As the name implies, this is the place to get a *rotti* from their seaside stand.

King Fisher   GUESTHOUSE $
(☑ 224 2472; chrisandolli@hotmail.de; Vijaya Rd; r from Rs 2000) Bright colours abound at the best ultra-cheap option on the strip. The very basic rooms are adequate and, for the price, great value.

★ **Frangipani Beach Villas**   GUESTHOUSE $$
(☑ 071 533 7052; www.frangipanibeachvilla.com; NU Jayawardana Rd; r US$40-80; ❄🛜) Located close to town and on the nicest stretch of Medaketiya Beach, this guesthouse is a real find. The eight rooms (some fan-only) are spotless and are spread between a house and a nearby two-storey block. The management is very enthusiastic and friendly, and organises a variety of activities. The beachside cafe is a delight.

★ **Villa Araliya**   GUESTHOUSE $$
(☑ 224 2163; www.villa-araliya.net; Vijaya Rd; r from US$45) Set in back of luxuriant gardens are two bungalows decorated with vintage furniture, including lovely carved wardrobes. The compound has a charm that's lacking nearby and there are also more remote villas on offer.

Tangalla

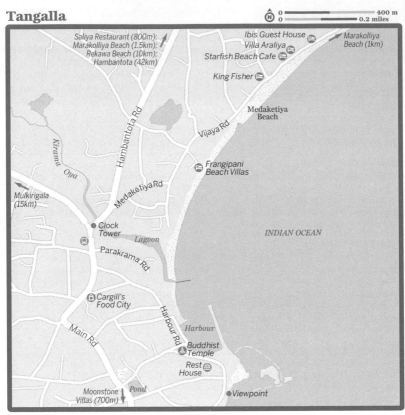

Saliya Restaurant (800m);
Marakolliya Beach (1.5km);
Rekawa Beach (10km);
Hambantota (42km)

Ibis Guest House
Villa Araliya
Starfish Beach Cafe

Marakolliya
Beach (1km)

King Fisher

Medaketiya
Beach

Vijaya Rd

Hambantota Rd

Kirama Oya

Frangipani
Beach Villas

Mulkirigala
(15km)

Clock
Tower

Lagoon

Medaketiya Rd

INDIAN OCEAN

Parakrama Rd

Cargill's
Food City

Main Rd

Harbour Rd

Harbour

Buddhist
Temple

Rest
House

Moonstone
Villas (700m)

Pond

Viewpoint

Ibis Guest House GUESTHOUSE **$$**
(☎ 567 4439; www.guesthouse-ibis.de; Vijaya Rd; r from Rs 4000) Despite its chain-hotel name, this rambling place is all local. The six spacious rooms are filled with heavy wooden furnishings, four-poster beds and easy chairs. There's a secluded splash of sandy beach outside and a general lazy tropical ambience about the place.

🛏 Marakolliya Beach

Marakolliya Beach has a lot of good midrange accommodation and it's all very lowkey and peaceful. There are two access roads: Madilla Rd is an at times rough continuation of Vijaya Rd in Tangalla, while another partially paved track extends from the main Hambantota Road at the 200 Km marker.

★ Lonely Beach Resort BUNGALOW **$**
(☎ 071 816 4804; www.lonelybeachresort.com; off Hambantota Rd; r US$25-45) Let the huffers and

puffers blow the other bungalows down, the substantial beachside units here are made from brick and have nice outdoor terraces. And while the planet is not lonely, this corner of the beach near the lagoon certainly is. The cafe has lovely views and you can ponder it all from a hammock strung between palm trees.

Cinnabar Resort BUNGALOW **$**
(☎ 077 965 2190; www.cinnabarresort.wordpress.com; Madilla Rd; r US$20-50; ☞) Everything you need to know about this fantasy of palm thatch is that one of the seven rooms is a treehouse (the others are bungalows). If you're bored it wouldn't be much effort to find driftwood on the beach to build an eighth room – this really is a rustic experience. The cafe has tables right on the sand.

Panorama Rock Cafe BUNGALOW **$**
(☎ 224 0458; www.panoramarockcafetangalla.com; Madilla Rd; r Rs 2000-4500; ☞) This older property has nine rooms in bungalow-style units that are solidly built from cement. The site is

nicely shaded with mature plants while the open-front cafe has a good water's edge view along the narrow beach. You can arrange mangrove outings here.

★ Serein Beach   BOUTIQUE HOTEL $$
(☑224 0005; www.sereinbeach.com; Madilla Rd; r US$55-90; ☎) An excellent newcomer, this well-run hotel has a three-storey main building with a wonderful rooftop deck. The nine rooms feature recycled materials and solar energy is used to heat water. The location is sun-drenched and the beach out front is unspoiled.

Mangrove Beach Cabanas   BUNGALOW $$
(☑077 790 6018; www.beachcabana.lk; off Hambantota Rd; r from €40; ☎) On a breathtaking stretch of near-deserted beach, this superb place has several rustic but chic cabanas hidden under the trees. Inside the cabanas virtually everything is made of twisted driftwood. Some units have bathrooms inconveniently located below ground, while the newest ones have snazzy outdoor showers and outdoor lounging areas with fab views. The open-air bar/cafe is good.

Mangrove Chalets   BUNGALOW $$
(☑077 790 6018; www.beachcabana.lk; off Hambantota Rd; r from €47; ☎) A sibling of the nearby Mangrove Beach Cabanas, you'll find these large bungalows in an utterly serene setting close to the beach. It's a good spot for families as the mangrove waters are clear and calm for swimming. You can access the site by a very Hollywood-feeling creaky bamboo bridge.

Ganesh Garden   BUNGALOW $$
(☑224 2529; www.ganeshgarden.com; Madilla Rd; r US$35-80; ☎) Choose from an array of different sizes and styles of cabanas – some have mud walls, some are built from twisted palm thatch and others are straight concrete, but all are comfortable and well designed. It's on a nice bit of beach, although we like the views from the lagoon-side rooms.

Suwaya Villa   RESORT $$
(☑224 0844; www.suwayavilla.com; Madilla Rd; r US$40-80; ✳☎☒) This plush place, with 25 rooms that verge on luxurious, feels a little out of place in rustic Tangalla. At the very end of Madilla Rd, it is surrounded by beach and mangroves. The swimming pool is a tempting alternative to the often dangerous ocean.

Sandy's   GUESTHOUSE $$
(☑077 622 5009; www.sandycabana.com; off Hambantota Rd; r from US$40) This is one of those classic Robinson Crusoe–style beach hangouts with seven palm-thatch open-air cabanas (some have bedrooms open to the stars and the sea breezes). Conditions can be basic (and you may have to inspect a couple to find a clean unit) but that can be the allure. The dinner buffet (Rs 1200) is excellent.

🛏 Rekawa Beach

A few top-end resorts are starting to appear out in these very isolated sands. The Hambantota Road is as much as 4km inland along here.

Buckingham Place   RESORT $$$
(☑348 9447; www.buckingham-place.com; Rekawa Beach; r from US$200; ✳☎☒) This gated compound holds an excellent resort set back from the beach on a small knoll. The grounds are as spacious as the rooms. Service is tops, as is the bar and restaurant. It's close to the turtle-viewing area.

The drive out winds through mangroves on narrow tracks – you'll want to spend more than one night.

✕ Eating

Just about all the places to stay serve meals. Many have cafes with dreamy ocean views. Among the best options are Frangipani Beach Villas, Lonely Beach Resort, Mangrove Beach Cabanas, Ganesh Garden and Sandy's.

Saliya Restaurant   SEAFOOD $
(☑224 2726; Hambantota Rd; meals Rs 250-500; ⊘7am-10pm; ☎) Sitting on wobbly stilts, 1.5km east of the town centre, near the 198 Km marker, this eccentric wooden shack, stuffed full of old clocks and radios, has great seafood as well as rice and curry. This is a great lunch stop and there are nice views over the mangroves.

ⓘ Information

You'll find plenty of banks and ATMs in the centre. There's a popular **Cargills Food City** (Main Rd; ⊘8am-10pm).

ⓘ Getting There & Away

Tangalla is an important bus stop on the main coastal road. Major destinations include the following:

Colombo regular/semi-luxe Rs 248/350, six hours

Galle Rs 116, two hours

Matara Rs 460, 1½ to two hours

Tissamaharama Rs 110, two hours

THE SOUTH TANGALLA & AROUND

Bundala National Park

Much less visited than nearby Yala National Park, **Bundala National Park** (entrance west of 251 Km marker; adult/child US$10/5, plus per vehicle Rs 250, service charge per group US$8, VAT 12%; ⊙ 6am-6pm, last entrance 4.30pm) is a fantastic maze of waterways, lagoons and dunes that glitter like gold in the dying evening sun. This wonderland provides a home to thousands of colourful birds ranging from diminutive little bee-eaters to memorably ugly open-billed storks. It shelters almost 200 species of birds within its 62-sq-km area, with many journeying from Siberia and the Rann of Kutch in India to winter here, arriving between August and April (December to March is the peak time). It's also a winter home to the greater flamingo, and up to 2000 have been recorded here at one time.

The park also has a small but very visible population of elephants (between 15 and 60 depending on the season, December is the best month), as well as civets, giant squirrels and lots of crocodiles. Between October and January, four of Sri Lanka's five species of marine turtles (olive ridley, green, leatherback and loggerhead) lay their eggs on the coast.

Bundala stretches nearly 20km along a coastal strip between Kirinda and Hambantota. Most people access the park (and hire 4WDs) from Tissamaharama and Kirinda; Hire rates and details are the same as for Yala, but unlike Yala, Bundala is open year-round, allowing wildlife junkies to get a wet-season fix. There's a breezy visitors centre at the main gate which has views over the marshes; check out the skeleton of a fearsome, huge crocodile.

There's no accommodation in the park itself and most people stay in Tissamaharama. The **Lagoon Inn** (⏀ 071 631 0173; lagooninn@ yahoo.com; off Tissa Rd; r from Rs 2600) is a friendly homestay on the edge of the village of Weligaththa (halfway between Tissamaharama and Hambantota) and an excellent alternative base for the park as it's only 2km from the park's northern entrance gate. The upstairs rooms overlook the marshes, allowing you to birdwatch without leaving your seat. The owner is an experienced birdwatcher who organises park tours.

Tissamaharama

⏀ 047

In Tissamaharama (usually shortened to Tissa), eyes are automatically drawn upwards and outwards. Upwards to the tip of its huge, snowy-white dagoba and outwards, beyond the town's confines, to a wilderness crawling with creatures large and small, Yala National Park. With its pretty lakeside location, Tissa is a mellow and ideal base for the nearby Yala and Bundala National Parks.

⊙ Sights

Tissa is surrounded by rice fields backed by misty mountains in the distance. It's a good place to get a bike and go exploring, peddling past lotus-filled ponds and prowling peacocks.

★ Tissa Wewa   LAKE
The centrepiece of the town and its surrounds is the lovely Tissa Wewa (Tissa Tank), a huge man-made lake about 1.5km from the town centre. In the evening, check out the huge flocks of egrets that descend onto the trees around the lake to roost. The road along the southern edge has a wide new **Lakeside Walkway** for strolling.

★ Yatala Wehera   BUDDHIST
Lotus ponds surround this site, which has a wealth of elephant details in the carvings. There's a small **museum** (⊙ 8am-5pm) **FREE** next to the dagoba. Amidst the dusty artefacts dug up from around the site, look for an ornate, ancient bidet sitting outside. Note the carved footpads. It's an easy walk from town.

It was built 2300 years ago by King Mahanaaga in thanks both for the birth of his son, Yatala Tissa, and for his safe escape from an assassination attempt in Anuradhapura.

★ Tissa Dagoba   BUDDHIST
This large much-restored dagoba looming between Tissa town centre and the *wewa* is believed to have been originally built around 200 BC by Kavantissa, a king of Ruhunu, which was centred on Tissamaharama. The white dagoba has a circumference of 165m and stands 55.8m high. It is thought to have held a sacred tooth relic and forehead bone relic. It's attractively lit up at night.

Next to the dagoba is a statue of Queen Viharamahadevi. According to legend, Viharamahadevi was sent to sea by her father, King Devanampiya Tissa, as penance after he killed a monk. Unharmed, the daughter landed at Kirinda, about 10km south of Tissa, and subsequently married Kavantissa. Their son, Dutugemunu, was the Sinhalese hero who liberated Anuradhapura from Indian invaders in the 2nd century BC.

Within the site is the much smaller **Sandagiri Wehera** dagoba and the remains of

Tissamaharama

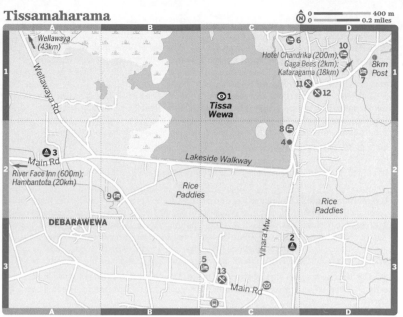

a monastery complex thought to date back around 2000 years.

🛏 Sleeping

There are pleasant hotels and guesthouses scattered all about Tissa. Lakeside ones have obvious appeal. Just about every place has a restaurant. Note that for Yala tours, hotels along the park access roads and near the beach in Kirinda are also good options.

🛏 Tissa Wewa & Town Centre

Vikum Lodge   GUESTHOUSE $
(☑ 071 464 7254; www.vikumlodge.com; off Kataragama Rd; r with/without air-con from US$24/18; ❄🛜) Hidden down a muddy side street in a peaceful location is this flowery gem of a guesthouse. The 10 rooms are set in lush gardens. The small restaurant serves Chinese dishes and Sri Lankan standards.

★ My Village   GUESTHOUSE $$
(☑ 077 350 0090; www.myvillagelk.com; 69 Court Rd; r US$30-60; ❄🛜) Arriving at this lovely three-room guesthouse, hidden away behind unassuming plain walls, you won't be surprised to learn that this is the dream creation of a local designer. There is a stylish open-plan cafe and communal area where the free breakfast is served. The shady grounds are

peaceful and have hammocks. Guests can use bicycles for free.

Gaga Bees   BUNGALOW $$
(☑ 071 620 5343; www.gagabeesyala.com; Sandagirigama; r Rs 4500-6000; ❄🛜) This new compound of bungalows is in a serene setting surrounded by rice fields that are home to

HAMBANTOTA

Once Hambantota was a dusty little workaday fishing town where nothing much ever happened. But today this formally sleepy place is now the site of the biggest urban construction project in Sri Lanka. And it's all thanks to Sri Lanka's president, Mahinda Rajapaksa, who hails from the region and still has a web of family and business ties here.

The bumpy two-lane coast road gives way to huge freeway interchanges as you enter Hambantota. The new roads are peppered with huge new projects including a hospital, cricket stadium, wind farms and much more. However, two of the largest projects have been controversial, even in a country where Rajapaksa's whims are seldom questioned.

Mattala Rajapaksa International Airport Named for the president's family, this vast new facility is 28km north of Hambantota and has cost well over US$200 million. It's a gleaming facility that lacks one thing: passengers. Since its opening in 2013, flights have been limited to a couple of face-saving daily services by state-run Sri Lankan Airways.

Magampura Mahinda Rajapaksa Port Also named for the president's family, this huge new port near the centre of town has cost upwards of US$400 million and construction continues. It is meant to relieve Colombo's container port, although the low-capacity roads surrounding Hambantota have restricted use. There has also been much controversy around the port's depth: some international organisations claim the port is too shallow for modern container ships, while the Rajapaksa government claims that dredging has solved the problem.

Most of the new projects are being funded by China. In addition, work is progressing on extending the railway line east from Matara to Katagama via Hambantota. The first sections may open by 2017.

---

a few water buffalo. The 12 rooms have a thatched decor and small sitting patios. There's a small on-site cafe. It's 1.7km east of the main road after a turn at the Hotel Chandrika.

Hotel Chandrika HOTEL $$
(☑ 223 7143; www.chandrikahotel.com; Kataragama Rd; r US$80-120; ❉ ☀) This very modern hotel is very popular with tour groups and is a fine option with 40 comfortable rooms set around a palm-lined courtyard and good pool. A newer wing of rooms have added style. The staff are attentive and the restaurant does a tasty curry. There's an Ayurvedic spa.

Hotel Tissa GUESTHOUSE $$
(☑ 077 501 5100; www.hoteltissa.com; Main Rd; r US$35-60; ❉ @ ☎) The eight rooms here are divided between the main building and quieter block out back. All have air-con, while more deluxe units have fridges and hot water. Overall it's very basic, but it does offer a popular pool table.

Traveller's Home GUESTHOUSE $$
(☑ 223 7958; www.yalasafarisrilanka.com; Main Rd; r Rs 2000-6000; ❉ @ ☎) Near the workaday town centre, this traveller-aware guesthouse is just off Main Rd, about halfway between Tissa and Debarawewa. It has a wide variety of rooms that range from cheapies with fans and cold water, to ones with air-con and more.

There are free bicycles for guests and a good restaurant. Expect pressure to book a safari.

Priyankara Hotel HOTEL $$$
(☑ 223 7206; www.priyankarahotel.com; Kataragama Rd; r US$100-160; ❉ ☎ ☀) The rooms here, with their high wooden ceilings, dashes of style, hardwood furnishings and balconies, have lots of colonial style as well as views over the gorgeous pool, which in turn has views over the gorgeous rice fields and duck-filled ponds.

The Safari HOTEL $$$
(☑ 567 7620; www.ceylonhotels.lk; Kataragama Rd; r US$90-200; ❉ ☎ ☀) Run by the same group as Colombo's Galle Face Hotel, this large hotel is Tissa's most mainstream option. The 50 rooms are large and comfortable, albeit slightly bland. Most have unbeatable views over Tissa Wewa (especially at sunset). The open lobby leads to a large pool. The included morning breakfast buffet is quite good (try the curry juice).

Hibiscus Garden Hotel BUNGALOW $$$
(☑ 223 9652; www.hibiscus-garden.com; off Kataragama Rd; r Rs 9600-13,500; ❉ ☎ ☀) The 20 rooms aren't flashy, but they are large, comfortable and set in separate bungalow blocks. There's good birdwatching in the nearby marshes and pools, and afterwards the birds can watch you as you relax around the swim-

ming pool. It's towards the northeastern end of the lake; head toward Hotel Chandrika, then go 700m off the main road.

Debarawewa

West of Tissa, there are some good choices amidst lush rivers and wide lakes.

★ River Face Inn　　　　GUESTHOUSE **$**
(📞 077 389 0229; www.yalariverfaceinn.com; off Hambantota Rd; r Rs 3000-5000; 🌀 🛜) The real highlight at this riverside guesthouse is the huge covered terrace where an array of tables with chairs, comfy loungers and hammocks await the weary big-game-spotter. Rooms are comfy and there is good food available at night. It's 3km west of Tissa; some rooms are fan-only.

Tissa Inn　　　　HOTEL **$$**
(📞 223 7233; www.tissainn.com; Wellawaya Rd; r Rs 3500-5500; 🌀 🛜) About 1500m from the landmark Debarawewa clock tower, this is a very friendly hotel. It's worth checking out a few of the 10 high-ceilinged rooms as quality varies, but at its best it's a spotless place of starched sheets and whirling fans.

Flower Garden Lake Resort　　　　HOTEL **$$**
(📞 223 9980; www.flowergardenlakeresort.com; off Wewa Rd; r US$50-80; 🌀 🛜 🌀) In a very quiet and remote location about 2km west of Tissa, this small hotel has a grand setting on Wirawila Wewa. There's nothing other than the song of birds to interrupt the quiet. Rooms have satellite TVs and there is a small pool. The cafe is good.

Eating

★ Royal Restaurant　　　　SRI LANKAN **$**
(📞 071 085 1361; Main St; mains Rs 250-700; 🕗 8am-10pm) Cheap and tasty curries draw local families plus smiling travellers. Although in the centre, it is off the road, so the open-sided dining rooms are quiet. Don't miss the fried garlic.

New Cabanas Restaurant　　　　SRI LANKAN **$$**
(Kataragama Rd; mains Rs 300-1200; 🕗 11am-10pm) A simple, open-sided restaurant with well-priced rice and curry. There are regular fresh seafood specials that are delicious right off the grill.

Refresh Hotel　　　　INTERNATIONAL **$$**
(📞 223 7357; Kataragama Rd; mains Rs 800-1500; 🕗 11am-10pm) This Western-style restaurant always has a few tourist vans parked out front. The setting is peaceful, and its even got a bit of style. Food spans the gamut from pizzas to pasta to local favourites (which have been tamed down for the timid).

ℹ Information

Banks, ATMs and markets are easily found on Main Rd in the centre of town.

ℹ Getting There & Around

Few buses go directly to the Hill Country, and if you can't get one you'll need to change at Wirawila junction (Rs 19, 30 minutes) and/or at Wellawaya (Rs 80). There are no buses to Yala National Park. Three-wheelers around town and out to Tissa Wewa and beyond will cost Rs 100 to Rs 200. Other major bus destinations from Tissa include:

Colombo Rs 540, eight hours (buses start in Kataragama, so may be crowded when they reach Tissa).

Tangalla Rs 110, two hours

Around Tissamaharama

Wirawila Wewa Bird Sanctuary

West of Tissa, the Hambantota–Wellawaya road runs on a causeway across the large Wirawila Wewa. This extensive sheet of water forms the Wirawila Wewa Bird Sanctuary. The best time for birdwatching is early morning.

Kirinda

📞 047

Oceanside Kirinda, 12km south of Tissa, is a place on the edge. On one side its sandy streets and ramshackle buildings give way to a series of magnificently bleak and empty beaches (heavy undertows make swimming here treacherous but they're perfect for long evening walks). In the other direction, tangled woodlands and sweeps of parched grasslands merge into the national parks.

◉ Sights & Activities

The village itself centres on a Buddhist shrine dramatically perched atop huge round rocks right at the shore. Visible offshore are the wave-smashed **Great Basses** reefs with their lonely **lighthouse**.

The **diving** out on these reefs is ranked as about the best in the country, but it's not for inexperienced divers – conditions are often rough. The best time is only between mid-March and mid-April.

Kirinda Temple
BUDDHIST

Kirinda centres on this Buddhist shrine piled atop huge round rocks. It is dedicated to Queen Viharamahadevi, who lived in the 2nd century BC and is at the heart of an old favourite story. When raging waters threatened Ceylon, King Kelanitissa ordered his youngest daughter, then a princess, into a boat as a sacrifice. The waters were calmed and the princess miraculously survived. Some 2000 years later, the temple was a place of refuge during the 2004 tsunami.

🛏 Sleeping

Guesthouses and hotels are scattered all around the Kirinda area. Some are at Yala Junction, 1.6km north of town where the road to the national park branches off from the Tissa–Kirinda Rd. Others are strung along the wave-tossed beaches to the west.

Temple Flower Guesthouse
GUESTHOUSE $

(☑077 881 4679, 492 2499; www.templeflower19yala.com; r Rs 2500-3000; ☎) A delicious guesthouse in town with a wonderful green colonial-style verandah shared between five tidy rooms, some with sea views. The cafe is good and the welcome is warm.

★ Suduweli Beauties of Nature
GUESTHOUSE $$

(☑072 263 1059; www.beauties-of-nature.net; Yala Jct; r US$22-52; @) Accommodation at this rural idyll consists of basic but clean rooms in the main house and a handful of comfortable, vaguely alpine-style cottages in the gardens. There's a small lake on the grounds; wildlife abounds. The owners are a Swiss–Sri Lankan couple who met through his work as a driver when he was recommended in an earlier edition of this guidebook.

★ Kirinda Beach Resort
HOTEL $$$

(☑077 020 0897; www.yalawildlifebeachresortsrilanka.com; r from $100; ☎☀) Located 1km west of town, this quirky compound is on a dramatic stretch of beach. Gaze upon the pounding surf from the uniquely elevated swimming pool and enjoy a meal in the large, airy cafe before retiring to a comfortable room in either a wood chalet or earthy mud hut. It's a good area for riding the free bikes.

Elephant Reach
RESORT $$$

(☑077 106 5092; www.elephantreach.com; Yala Jct; r US$100-120; ☀☎☀) The stylish communal areas at this small resort have a free-form style that fits the rustic setting. Rooms include huge showers, stone floors, hemp curtains and TVs. Outside, the large pool curls like a water snake around the gardens. Avoid rooms in the down-market rear.

ℹ Getting There & Away

There is a bus from Tissa to Kirinda every half-hour or so (Rs 30); a three-wheeler is Rs 600.

Yala National Park

With monkeys crashing through the trees, peacocks in their finest frocks, elephants ambling about and cunning leopards sliding like shadows through the undergrowth, Yala National Park (also known as Ruhunu) is the *Jungle Book* brought to glorious life. This vast region of dry woodland and open patches of grasslands is the big draw of this corner of Sri Lanka. A safari here is well worth all the time, effort, crowds and cost.

👁 Sights

Yala combines a strict nature reserve with a national park, bringing the total protected area to 1268 sq km of scrub, light forest, grassy plains and brackish lagoons. It's divided into five blocks, with the most visited being Block I (141 sq km). Also known as Yala West, this block was originally a reserve for hunters, but was given over to conservation in 1938. It's the closest to Tissa.

With around 25 leopards thought to be present in Block I alone, Yala is considered one of the world's best parks for spotting these big cats. *Panthera pardus kotiya,* the subspecies you may well see, is unique to Sri Lanka. The best time to spot leopards is February to June or July, when the water levels in the park are low.

The park's estimated 300 elephants can be more elusive, although some regularly appear in the most visited areas. Other animals of note include the shaggy-coated sloth bear and fox-like jackals. Sambars, spotted deer, boars, crocodiles, buffaloes, mongooses and monkeys are also here, along with startlingly large crocodiles.

Over 200 species of birds have been recorded at Yala, many of which are visitors escaping the northern winter, such as white-winged black terns, curlews and pintails. Locals include jungle fowl, hornbills, orioles and peacocks by the bucketload.

Despite the large quantity of wildlife, the light forest can make spotting animals quite hard; however, small grassy clearings and lots of waterholes offer good opportunities. The

NATIONAL PARK TOUR ESSENTIALS

Tours of Yala and Bundala National Parks are by jeep. Most people opt for half-day tours that start with a Tissa hotel pick-up at 5.30am followed by a one-hour drive to the park for a dawn start. You are usually back by 11am. Dusk tours run about 3pm to 7pm. Full day tours run 5.30am to 5pm and include stops at beaches and other sights.

You can arrange for drivers at your accommodation, at the **Independent Jeep Association** car park by the lake or at the park entrances. Expect operators to find you as they look for business. Standards between the jeeps vary greatly, although almost all are open-sided, with a high roof for shade. Broadly, the operators and their jeeps fall into three groups:

Normal Often very old vehicles, these often have inward-facing seats along the sides which is very bad for animal spotting. Rates average Rs 4500 per half-day.

Luxury Usually three rows of two forward-facing seats that are stepped up towards the back so you can see over the heads of those in front of you. The seats may be worn or in a few cases broken. Rates average Rs 5000 per half-day.

Super Luxury The newest jeeps are usually Range Rovers or Toyotas and have two or three rows of comfortable seats. Rates average Rs 5500 per half-day.

The differences between luxury and super luxury can be minor; the most important consideration is that the jeep is in good shape (new models have better suspensions which are essential as you go racing across the countryside) and that the seats are comfortable. Avoid any jeep with middle seats. Shop around as prices are negotiable. Other considerations:

➡ Are the services of a guide included? This is not always necessary as many of the drivers are very good at animal-spotting. You will also usually be offered the services of a tracker inside the park; these guys work for tips (for a half-day tour, tip the driver and any guide Rs 500 each).

➡ Does your prospective driver seem in a rush? One common complaint is about drivers who zip across the countryside reducing the tour to a gut-wrenching blur.

➡ Does the driver provide binoculars? Also ask about water and snacks.

➡ Hoping for tips, drivers aim to please, perhaps too much so. The merest hint of a large animal can spark a stampede of jeeps. You can do your part to keep things calm by asking your driver to refrain from madcap chases. The resulting quiet is more conducive for spotting anyway.

end of the dry season (March to April) is the best time to visit, as during and after the rains the animals disperse over a wide area.

As well as herds of wildlife, Yala contains the remains of a once-thriving human community. A monastic settlement, **Situlpahuwa**, appears to have housed 12,000 inhabitants. Now restored, it's an important pilgrimage site. A 1st-century BC *vihara* (Buddhist complex), **Magul Maha Vihara**, and a 2nd-century BC *chetiya* (Buddhist shrine), **Akasa Chetiya**, point to a well-established community, believed to have been part of the ancient Ruhunu kingdom.

Yala is a very popular park: there were over 330,000 visitors in 2013, a number that grows each year. At times jeeps can mimic a pack of jackals in their pursuit of wildlife. It's a good idea to discuss with your driver and/or guide where you can go to get away from the human herd. Be sure, however, to make time for the park's **visitor centre** at the western entrance. It has excellent displays about the park and a good bookstore.

🛏 Sleeping

There has been no accommodation inside the park since the 2004 tsunami. However, there are several top-end resorts off the 12km road that runs into the park from Yala Jct; some are on the long untrodden beach.

One way you can sleep inside the park is on an organised **camping trip**. These can be arranged with guides, as part of a package with a local guesthouse or simply by reserving space in one of the often-luxurious campgrounds. One good organiser is **Nandika** (☑ 077 975 3203; lal_nandika@yahoo.com; camping packages from Rs 38,000 for two people), a longtime guide who provides tours, a BBQ dinner, breakfast, a tent and more. For extra fees, you can get a tent that has its own attached private toilet. Another option is a night in a treehouse (from Rs 22,000 for two), where you can spot animals wandering below.

Cinnamon Wild Yala　　　　　LODGE **$$$**
(☑ 047-223 9449; www.cinnamonhotels.com; r US$130-200; ✱@🛜🏊) 🍃 Near the park

entrance, this lodge run by the noted Cinnamon hotel group offers the ultimate in bush-chic accommodation. Rooms are in individual luxe bungalows. The hotel runs on solar power, some of the waste water is recycled and there's a tree-planting scheme. At night elephants often wander through the grounds. Breakfast and full-board options are available.

Jetwing Yala RESORT **$$$**
(☑ 047-471 0710; www.jetwinghotels.com; r US$100-200) Only 4km from the park entrance, this posh new resort is set amidst the dunes near the beach. What the modern design lacks in character, the staff make up for in service. Arrange for a sunset picnic for two on the beach or go wild with all the animal spotting you can schedule.

ⓘ Information

The entrance fees for **Yala National Park** (adult/child US$15/8, jeep & tracker Rs 250, service charge per group US$8, plus overall tax 12%; ☺ 5.30am-6pm mid-Oct–Aug) are payable at the main office, which is near the west entrance. The only practical way to visit the park is as part of a tour or safari (see p139).

ⓘ Getting There & Away

The drive to Yala National Park takes about one hour (due to road conditions) whether you take the 22km route via Yala Jct from Tissa, or a somewhat shorter road past some remote and pretty lakes.

Kataragama

☑ 047

Sheltered in the foothills 15km northeast of Tissa is Kataragama. This most holy of towns is a compelling mix of pomp and procession, piety and religious extravagance. Along with Adam's Peak (Sri Pada), this is the most important religious pilgrimage site in Sri Lanka and is a holy place for Buddhists, Muslims and Hindus alike. It is one of those wonderful places where the most outlandish of legends becomes fact and magic floats in clouds of incense. Many believe that King Dutugemunu built a shrine to Kataragama Deviyo (the resident god) here in the 2nd century BC, and that the Buddhist Kirivehera dagoba dates back to the 1st century BC, but the site is thought to have been significant for even longer.

In July and August, the predominantly Hindu **Kataragama festival** draws thousands of devotees who make the pilgrimage over a two-week period. Apart from festival time, the town is busiest at weekends and on

poya days. At these times it may be difficult to find accommodation, and the place will be buzzing; at other times it possesses a tranquillity befitting its sacred status. It's easily visited from Tissa.

⊙ Sights

The sacred precinct is set on the other side of Menik Ganga, a chocolate-coloured river in which pilgrims wash themselves before continuing towards the shrines. The site's wide promenades are lined with grey monkeys always on the lookout for a handout – or a dropped personal item.

Shrines RELIGIOUS
The most important shrine, **Maha Devale**, features the lance of the six-faced, 12-armed Hindu war god, Murugan (Skanda), who is seen as identical to the Kataragama Deviyo. Followers make offerings at daily *puja* at 4.30am, 10.30am and 6.30pm (no 4.30am offering on Saturdays). Outside this shrine are two large boulders, against which pilgrims smash burning coconuts while muttering a prayer.

The **Kirivehara** dagoba and **Sivam Kovil** shrines are dedicated to the Buddha and Ganesh (the remover of obstacles and champion of intellectual pursuits) respectively; there is also a **bodhi tree**.

Kataragama

THE LONG WALK TO KATARAGAMA

Forty-five days before the annual Kataragama festival starts on the Esala *poya* (full moon) in July, a group of Kataragama devotees start walking the length of Sri Lanka for the Pada Yatra pilgrimage. Seeking spiritual development, the pilgrims believe they are walking in the steps of the god Kataragama (also known as Murugan) and the Veddahs, who made the first group pilgrimage on this route.

The route follows the east coast from the Jaffna Peninsula, via Trincomalee and Batticaloa to Okanda, then through Yala National Park to Kataragama. It's an arduous trip, and the pilgrims rely on the hospitality of the communities and temples they pass for their food and lodging. Although often interrupted during the war years, the walk is now hugely popular.

Pilgrims arrive in Kataragama just before the festival's feverish activity. Elephants parade, drummers drum. Vows are made and favours sought by devotees, who demonstrate their sincerity by performing extraordinary acts of penance and self-mortification on one particular night: some swing from hooks that pierce their skin; others roll half-naked over the hot sands near the temple. A few perform the act of walking on beds of red-hot cinders – treading the flowers, as it's called. The fire walkers fast, meditate and pray, bathe in Menik Ganga (Menik River) and then worship at Maha Devale before facing their ordeal. Then, fortified by their faith, they step out onto the glowing path while the audience cries out encouragement.

The festival officially ends with a water-cutting ceremony (said to bring rain for the harvest) in Menik Ganga.

Ul-Khizr Mosque — MOSQUE

The Muslim area near the river features this beautiful mosque with coloured tile work and wooden lintels, and tombs of two holy men.

Kataragama Museum — MUSEUM

(admission Rs 650; ☺8.30am-4.30pm Tue-Sun) This archæological museum inside the complex has a collection of Hindu and Buddhist religious items, as well as huge fibreglass replicas of statues from around Sri Lanka. However, you'll need a guide to provide context as the labelling is woeful.

Mahinda Rajapaksa National Tele-Cinema Park — STUDIO

(www.serendibstudio.com; off Tissa–Kataragama Rd; admission foreigner US$10) Named for its patron, the gift-bearing Sri Lankan president, this studio located halfway between Tissa and Kataragama is only mentioned because some drivers and tours will suggest you visit. Don't. There's a small soundstage and a tiny backlot meant to recreate colonial Bombay (which is already crumbling in the tough local climate). The foreigner admission fee is pure rip-off.

🛏 Sleeping & Eating

Kataragama's accommodations are limited. You'll find simple snack stands along Tissa Rd and at the parking lots.

★ Sunhil's Hotel — GUESTHOUSE $

(☑567 7172; Tissa Rd; r with/without air-con Rs 3000/2500; ❄) This cheery little guesthouse is right on the main drag of the quiet strip that passes for Kataragama's centre. The eight rooms are brightly painted and have attached bathrooms.

Mandara Rosen — HOTEL $$$

(☑223 6030; www.mandararesorts.com; Tissa Rd; r from US$100; ❄🛜🏊) The smartest address in town, Rosen is 3km west of the centre. The rooms are good, but the hotel's best asset is the pool, which has an underwater music system. Out the front, near the road, is a good, shady cafe open to all.

ℹ Information

You'll find ATMs in the centre along Tissa Rd.

ℹ Getting There & Away

There are frequent buses to Tissamaharama (Rs 37, 30 minutes). Should you arrive by car, you'll set off frenzied competition from the owners of various snack, offering, toy and garish souvenir stands who will try to get you to park on their patch in the hope you'll buy something.

The Hill Country

Best Places to Eat

➜ Sharon Inn (p154)

➜ Grand Indian (p172)

➜ High Tea at the Grand (p171)

➜ Olde Empire Cafe (p154)

Best Places to Stay

➜ Baramba House (p160)

➜ Planters Bungalow (p181)

➜ The Kandy House (p160)

➜ Ferncliff (p171)

➜ Tea Trails (p166)

Why Go?

Picture Sri Lanka and visions of golden beaches probably dance before your eyes. But there's another side to this island. It's a side where mists slowly part to reveal emerald carpets of tea plantations and montane forests clinging to serrated ranges bookended by waterfalls. This is Sri Lanka's Hill Country; a place where you can wear a fleece in the daytime and cuddle up beside a log fire in the evening. A region where you can walk to the end of the world, stand in the footsteps of the Buddha, paddle a raft down a raging river, enjoy the drumbeat of traditional dance and be surrounded by a hundred wild elephants.

With a hit list like that it's perhaps hardly a surprise that when many visitors look back on their Sri Lankan adventures it's not the beaches that make them smile fondly, but rather it's the surging, rolling highlands.

When to Go
Nuwara Eliya

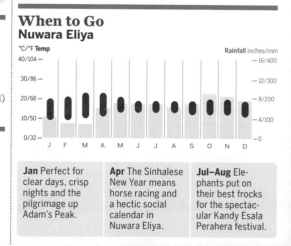

Jan Perfect for clear days, crisp nights and the pilgrimage up Adam's Peak.

Apr The Sinhalese New Year means horse racing and a hectic social calendar in Nuwara Eliya.

Jul–Aug Elephants put on their best frocks for the spectacular Kandy Esala Perahera festival.

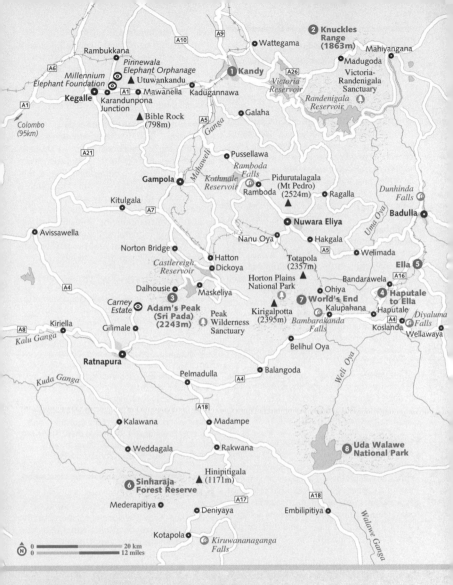

The Hill Country Highlights

1 Experiencing the excitement of elephants, drummers and dancers at the **Kandy Esala Perahera** (p149)

2 Getting away from Sri Lanka's energetic buzz by hiking the montane forests of the **Knuckles Range** (p161)

3 Joining devout pilgrims and following flickering torchlight to ascend the sacred heights of **Adam's Peak** (p163)

4 Rattling and rolling with Tamil tea-pickers on a slow, slow train journey from **Haputale to Ella** (p184)

5 Winding down in **Ella** (p179), combining excellent home-cooked food and spectacular walks

6 Discovering your inner birdwatcher amid the tangled perfection of the **Sinharaja Forest Reserve** (p189)

7 Rising before dawn for a view from the stunning heights of **World's End** (p174)

8 Counting elephants by the dozen in the **Uda Walawe National Park** (p188)

Colombo to Kandy

The **Henerathgoda Botanic Gardens** near Gampaha, off the Colombo–Kandy road about 30km northwest of Colombo, are where the first rubber trees planted in Asia were grown. Some original plantings dot the 37-acre gardens, together with 400 other plant varieties.

About 50km from Kandy is **Cadjugama**, famous for its cashew nuts. Brightly clad sellers beckon passing motorists with nuts they've harvested from the surrounding forest. At the 48km post is **Radawaduwa**, notable for woven cane items.

Kegalle, 77km from Colombo, is the nearest town to the **Pinnewala Elephant Orphanage**. Several spice farms that are open to visitors can also be found around here. Nearby is **Utuwankandu**, a rocky hill from where the 19th-century Robin Hood-style highwayman, Saradiel, preyed on travellers until the British executed him.

At **Kadugannawa**, just after the road and railway make their most scenic climbs – with views southwest to the large Bible Rock – is a tall pillar erected in memory of Captain Dawson, the English engineer who built the Colombo–Kandy road in 1826.

Cadjugama, Kegalle and Kadugannawa are on the A1, easily accessible by bus between Colombo and Kandy. Catch a train to Kadugannawa and the Henerathgoda Botanic Gardens at Gampaha.

Pinnewala Elephant Orphanage   ZOO
(adult/child Rs 2500/1250; ☉8.30am-6pm) Initially created to protect abandoned or orphaned elephants, this government-run elephant orphanage near Kegalle is one of Sri Lanka's most popular attractions, but today some people think it seems to have largely lost sight of its original aims and is more a zoo than anything else. Some people love the place and the opportunity it gives to get up close and cuddly with elephants, but many more find it an out-and-out rip-off with no conservational value whatsoever.

There are around 80 elephants here of all ages. The creatures are largely well looked after, but conservationists have expressed some concern over the amount of contact elephants have with the public and the fact that the facility has been used for breeding, contrary to its status as an orphanage.

The elephants are controlled by their mahouts, who ensure they feed at the right times and don't endanger anyone. Otherwise the elephants roam freely around the sanctuary area. The elephants are led to a nearby river for bathing daily from 10am to noon and from 2pm to 4pm. Meal times are 9.15am, 1.15pm and 5pm. For Rs 350 you can bottle feed a baby elephant, although take note of the concerns about tourist-elephant contact as the elephants can become easily stressed.

Millennium Elephant Foundation   ZOO
(☑035-226 3377; www.millenniumelephant foundation.org; adult/child Rs 1000/500, elephant rides Rs 1000-4000; ☉9am-4pm) Two kilometres from Pinnewala, on the Karandupona–Kandy road, the Millennium Elephant Foundation houses a number of elephants rescued from various situations, such as aggressive mahouts, or elephants retired from working in temples. Volunteers are welcome at the foundation and the facility also supports a mobile veterinary service.

❶ Getting There & Away

The elephant orphanage is a few kilometres north of the Colombo–Kandy road. From Kandy take a bus to Kegalle. Get off before Kegalle at Karandunpona Junction (Rs 45). From the junction, catch bus 661 (Rs 18) going from Kegalle to Rambukkana and get off at Pinnewala. A three-wheeler from the junction to Pinnewala is around Rs 350. It's about an hour from Kandy to the junction and 20 minutes from the junction to Pinnewala. Buses also link Colombo and Kegalle.

Rambukkana station on the Colombo–Kandy railway is about 3km north of the orphanage and all trains travelling this route stop there. From Rambukkana get a bus (Rs 18) going towards Kegalle or a three-wheeler for around Rs 300.

Kandy

☑081 / ELEVATION 500M / POPULATION 109,000

Some days Kandy's skies seem perpetually bruised, with stubborn mist clinging to the hills surrounding the city's beautiful centrepiece lake. Delicate hill-country breezes impel the mist to gently part, revealing colourful houses and hotels amid Kandy's improbable forested halo. In the centre of town, three-wheelers careen around slippery corners, raising a soft spray that threatens the softer silk of the colourful saris worn by local women. Here's a city that looks good even when it's raining.

And when the rain subsides – and it does with frequency and alacrity – Kandy's cobalt-blue skies reveal it as this island's other real 'city' after the brighter coastal lights of Colombo. Urban buzz is provided by busy spontaneous street markets and even busier

THE HISTORY OF THE TOOTH

The sacred tooth of the Buddha is said to have been snatched from the flames of the Buddha's funeral pyre in 483 BC and smuggled into Sri Lanka during the 4th century AD, hidden in the hair of a princess. At first it was taken to Anuradhapura, then it moved through the country on the waves of Sri Lankan history before ending up at Kandy. In 1283 it was carried back to India by an invading army but it was retrieved by King Parakramabahu III.

The tooth gradually grew in importance as a symbol of sovereignty, and it was believed that whoever had custody of the tooth relic had the right to rule the island. In the 16th century the Portuguese apparently seized the tooth, took it away and burnt it with devout Catholic fervour in Goa. Not so, say the Sinhalese. The Portuguese had actually stolen a replica tooth while the real incisor remained safe. There are still rumours that the real tooth is hidden somewhere secure, and the tooth kept here is only a replica.

The Temple of the Sacred Tooth Relic was constructed mainly under Kandyan kings from 1687 to 1707 and from 1747 to 1782, and the entire temple complex was part of the Kandyan royal palace. The imposing pinky-white structure is surrounded by a moat. The octagonal tower in the moat was built by Sri Wickrama Rajasinha and used to house an important collection of *ola* (talipot-palm leaf) manuscripts. This section of the temple was heavily damaged in the 1998 bomb blast.

The main tooth shrine – a two-storey rectangular building known as the Vahahitina Maligawa – occupies the centre of a paved courtyard. The eye-catching gilded roof over the relic chamber was paid for by Japanese donors. The 1998 bomb exposed part of the front wall to reveal at least three layers of 18th- to 20th-century paintings depicting the *perahera* (procession) and various Jataka tales (stories of the Buddha's previous lives).

Sri Lankan Buddhists believe they must complete at least one pilgrimage to the temple in their lifetime, as worshipping here improves one's karmic lot immeasurably.

bus stations and restaurants. History and culture are on tap, and 115km from the capital and at an altitude of 500m, Kandy offers a cooler and more relaxed climate.

Kandy served as the capital of the last Sinhalese kingdom, which fell to the British in 1815 after defying the Portuguese and Dutch for three centuries. It took the British another 16 tough years to finally build a road linking Kandy with Colombo. The locals still proudly see themselves as a little different – and perhaps a tad superior – to Sri Lankans from the island's lower reaches.

Kandy is renowned for the great Kandy Esala Perahera, held over 10 days leading up to the Nikini *poya* (full moon) at the end of the month of Esala (July/August), but it has enough attractions to justify a visit at any time of year. Some of the Hill Country's nicest boutique hotels nestle in the hills surrounding Kandy, and the city is a good base for exploring the underrated terrain of the nearby Knuckles Range.

◉ Sights

Kandy Lake   LAKE
(Map p146) Dominating the town is Kandy Lake. A leisurely stroll around it, with a few stops on the lakeside seats, is a pleasant way to spend a few hours, although buses careening around the southern edge of the lake can mar the peace somewhat. The nicest part to walk along is the area around the Temple of the Sacred Tooth Relic. Due to some reports of harassment, single women should not walk here alone after dark.

The lake is artificial and was created in 1807 by Sri Wickrama Rajasinha, the last ruler of the kingdom of Kandy. Several minor local chiefs protested because their people objected to labouring on the project. In order to stop the protests they were put to death on stakes in the lake bed. The central island was used as Sri Wickrama Rajasinha's personal harem. Later the British used it as an ammunition store and added the fortress-style parapet around the perimeter. On the south shore, in front of the Malwatte Maha Vihara, the circular enclosure is the monks' bathhouse.

**Temple of the
Sacred Tooth Relic**   BUDDHIST TEMPLE
(Sri Dalada Maligawa; Map p146; adult/child Rs 1000/free, video camera Rs 300, World Buddhism Museum admission Rs 500; ⊙ temple 5.30am-8pm, puja 5.30-6.45am, 9.30-11am & 6.30-8pm, World Buddhism Museum 8am-7pm, Sri Dalada Museum 7.30am-6pm) Just north of the lake, the

Kandy

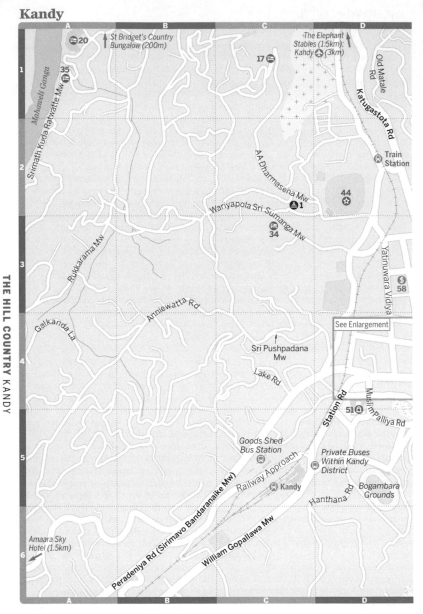

golden-roofed Temple of the Sacred Tooth houses Sri Lanka's most important Buddhist relic – a tooth of the Buddha.

During *puja* (offerings or prayers), the heavily guarded room housing the tooth is open to devotees and tourists. However,

you don't actually see the tooth. It's kept in a gold casket shaped like a dagoba (stupa), which contains a series of six dagoba caskets of diminishing size.

The entire temple complex covers a large area and as well as the main shrine there

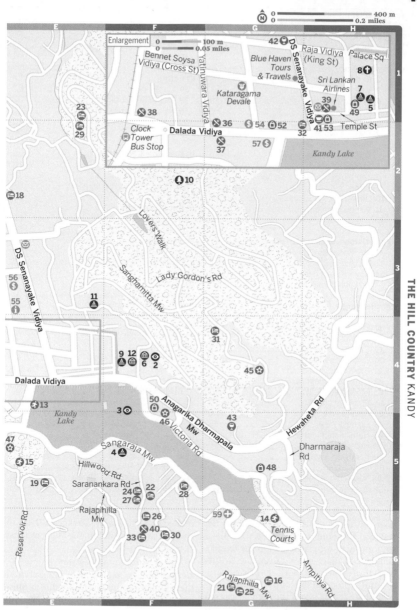

are numerous other temples and museums within the complex. The following are some of the key sites.

⇒ **Alut Maligawa**

Behind the shrine stands the three-storey Alut Maligawa, a newer and larger shrine hall displaying dozens of sitting Buddhas donated by Thai devotees. The design resembles a Thai Buddhist shrine hall in tribute to the fact that Thai monks re-established Sri Lanka's ordination lineage during the reign of King Kirti Sri Rajasinha. The upper two

THE HILL COUNTRY KANDY

Kandy

⊙ Sights
Alut Maligawa .... (see 12)
1 Asgiriya Maha Vihara C2
Audience Hall .... (see 12)
2 Kandy Garrison Cemetery....................F4
3 Kandy Lake..F4
4 Malwatte Maha Vihara F5
5 Natha Devale...H1
6 National Museum..................................F4
7 Pattini Devale..H1
Rajah Tusker Hall......................... (see 12)
Sri Dalada Museum .... (see 12)
8 St Paul's Church H1
9 Temple of the Sacred Tooth
Relic..F4
10 Udawattakelle Sanctuary F2
11 Vishnu Devale..E3
12 World Buddhism Museum.....................F4

⊙ Activities, Courses & Tours
13 Joy Motorboat Service...........................E4
14 Playpark G6
15 Royal Palace Park E5
Sri Lanka Trekking.........................(see 22)

⊟ Sleeping
16 Anna Shanthi Villa..................................G6
17 Blue Haven Guesthouse C1
18 Burmese Rest...E2
19 Castle Hill Guest House E5
20 Cinnamon Citadel..................................A1
21 Day's Inn..G6
22 Expeditor Guest House..........................F5
23 Forest Glen E1
24 Freedom Lodge......................................F5
25 Helga's Folly...G6
26 Highest View...F6
27 Hotel Mango Garden F5
28 Hotel Suisse...F5
29 Kandy Cottage E2
30 McLeod Inn...F6
31 Nature Walk Resort...............................G4
32 Queens Hotel..G2

33 Sharon Inn..F6
34 St Bridget's Country Bungalow.............C3
35 Villa Rosa A1

⊗ Eating
36 Bake House...G2
37 Devon Restaurant G2
38 Kandy Muslim Hotel...............................F1
39 Olde Empire Cafe H1
40 Sharon Inn..F6

⊙ Drinking & Nightlife
41 National Coffee.......................................H1
42 Royal Bar & Hotel G1
43 Slightly Chilled Lounge Bar...................G5

⊕ Entertainment
44 Asgiriya Stadium D2
45 Kandy Lake Club.....................................G4
46 Kandyan Art Association &
Cultural Centre F5
47 Mahanuwara YMBA E5

⌂ Shopping
48 Buddhist Publication Society G5
49 Cultural Triangle Office..........................H1
50 Kandyan Art Association &
Cultural Centre F4
51 Main Market...D5
52 Odel Luv SL G2
53 Rangala House Gallery H1
Selyn ....(see 39)

ⓘ Information
54 Bank of Ceylon......................................G2
55 British Council E3
56 Commercial Bank...................................E3
Cultural Triangle Office................(see 49)
57 Hatton National Bank G2
58 HSBC..D3
59 Lakeside Adventist Hospital G6
Sri Lanka Cricket Office...............(see 44)
Tourist Information Office...........(see 37)

floors of the Alut Maligawa contain the **Sri Dalada Museum** (☉ 7.30am-6pm), with a stunning array of gilded gifts to the temple. Letters and diary entries from the British time reveal the colonisers' surprisingly respectful attitude to the tooth relic. More recent photographs reveal the damage caused by a truck bomb set off by the LTTE in 1998 that destroyed large parts of the temple.

➡ Audience Hall
To the north inside the compound, and accessible only via the Temple of the Sacred Tooth Relic, is the 19th-century Audience Hall, an open-air pavilion with stone columns carved to look like wooden pillars.

Adjacent in the **Rajah Tusker Hall** are the stuffed remains of Rajah, the Maligawa tusker who died in 1988.

➡ World Buddhism Museum
Just behind the main temple, but still inside the complex, is the World Buddhism Museum. Housed inside the former High Court buildings, the museum contains lots of photographs, models and displays illustrating Buddhism around the world. Note that a large number of the statues and other exhibits are actually reproductions.

Freelance guides will offer their services around the entire temple complex for around Rs 500, and free audio guides are available at the ticket office. An elevator facilitates access for travellers with disabilities.

The shrine receives many worshippers and tourists, with fewer tourists in the morning. Wear clothes that cover your legs and your shoulders, and remove your shoes.

★ Ceylon Tea Museum   MUSEUM

(Map p159; ☏ 070 280 3204; www.ceylontea museum.com; Hantane; adult/child Rs 500/200; ⏱ 8.30am-4.30pm Tue-Sun) An essential stop on any Sri Lankan tea tour, this museum occupies the 1925-vintage Hantane Tea Factory, 4km south of Kandy on the Hantane road. Abandoned for more than a decade, it was refurbished by the Sri Lanka Tea Board and the Planters' Association of Sri Lanka. There are exhibits on tea pioneers James Taylor and Thomas Lipton, and lots of vintage tea-processing paraphernalia. Knowledgeable guides are available and there's a free cuppa afterwards in the top-floor tearoom.

National Museum   MUSEUM

(Map p146; ☏ 222 3867; adult/child Rs 500/300, camera/video camera Rs 250/1500; ⏱ 9am-5pm Tue-Sat) This museum once housed Kandyan royal concubines and now features royal regalia and reminders of pre-European Sinhalese life. There are some interesting objects housed here and it could be a very interesting museum, but it's sadly let down by very poor lighting, labelling and general layout.

One of the displays is a copy of the 1815 agreement that handed over the Kandyan provinces to British rule. This document announces a major reason for the event.

...the cruelties and oppressions of the Malabar ruler, in the arbitrary and unjust infliction of bodily tortures and pains of death without trial, and sometimes without accusation or the possibility of a crime, and in the general contempt and contravention of all civil rights, have become flagrant, enormous and intolerable.

Sri Wickrama Rajasinha was declared 'by the habitual violation of the chief and most sacred duties of a sovereign,' to be 'fallen and deposed from office of king' and 'dominion of the Kandyan provinces' was 'vested in... the British Empire.'

The tall-pillared audience hall hosted the convention of Kandyan chiefs that ceded the kingdom to Britain in 1815.

The museum, along with four *devales* (complexes for worshipping deities) and two monasteries – but not the Temple of the

KANDY ESALA PERAHERA

This *perahera* (procession) is held in Kandy to honour the sacred tooth enshrined in the Temple of the Sacred Tooth Relic (Sri Dalada Maligawa). It runs for 10 days in the month of Esala (July/August), ending on the Nikini *poya* (full moon). Kandy's biggest night of the year comes after these 10 days of increasingly frenetic activity. A decline in elephant numbers has seen the scale of the festival diminish in recent years – in earlier times more than 100 elephants took part – but it is still one of Asia's most fascinating celebrations.

The first six nights are relatively low-key. On the seventh night, proceedings escalate as the route lengthens and the procession becomes more splendid (and accommodation prices increase accordingly).

The procession is actually a combination of five separate *peraheras*. Four come from the four Kandy *devales* (complexes for worshipping Hindu or Sri Lankan deities, who are also devotees and servants of the Buddha): Natha, Vishnu, Kataragama and Pattini. The fifth and most splendid *perahera* is from the Sri Dalada Maligawa itself.

The procession is led by thousands of Kandyan dancers and drummers beating drums, cracking whips and waving colourful banners. Then come long processions of up to 50 elephants. The Maligawa tusker is decorated from trunk to toe. On the last two nights of the *perahera* it carries a huge canopy sheltering the empty casket of the sacred relic cask. A trail of pristine white linen is laid before the elephant.

The Kandy Esala Perahera is Sri Lanka's most magnificent annual spectacle. It's been celebrated annually for many centuries and is described by Robert Knox in his 1681 book *An Historical Relation of Ceylon*. There is also a smaller procession on the *poya* day in June, and special *peraheras* may be put on for important occasions.

It's essential to book roadside seats for the main *perahera* at least a week in advance. Prices range from Rs 5000 to 7000. Once the festival starts, seats about halfway back in the stands are more affordable.

OFF THE BEATEN TRACK

DEGAL DORUWA RAJA MAHA VIHARA

Hidden away in Kandy's leafy outskirts is the little visited **Degal Doruwa Raja Maha Vihara** (Map p159; Lewella; entry by donation) cave temple, constructed (with the help of some obliging boulders) in the 18th century. The interior of the cave is painted head to toe in slightly faded but captivating murals. These fine Kanyan-era paintings depict scenes from the Jataka stories (tales from the previous lives of the Buddha). In among these are some out-of-place paintings depicting men with guns. These are likely to have been inspired by the first guns to have arrived in Sri Lanka. Alongside the paintings is a large reclining Buddha. Visitors are likely to be shown around by one of the five resident monks.

Sacred Tooth Relic itself – make up one of Sri Lanka's Cultural Triangle sites.

St Paul's Church   CHURCH
(Map p146; Deva Veediya; by donation) Construction of this red brick colonial-era church began in 1843 and was completed five years later. It originally served as a garrison church for British troops based nearby. Today it stands in solemn contrast to the boisterous comings and goings in the next door Temple of the Sacred Tooth relic.

Kandy Garrison Cemetery   CEMETERY
(Map p146; 8am-6pm) FREE This cemetery, which is a short walk uphill behind the National Museum, contains 163 graves dating back to colonial times. The most striking aspect of a visit to this melancholy place is just how young most people were when they died – if you made it to 40 you were a very ripe old age. Some of the deaths were due to sunstroke, elephants or jungle fever.

Kandy Monasteries   BUDDHIST TEMPLE
The principal *viharas* (Buddhist complexes) in Kandy have considerable importance – the high priests of the two best known, Malwatte and Asgiriya, are the most important in Sri Lanka. They are the headquarters of two of the main *nikayas* (orders of monks). The **Malwatte Maha Vihara** (Map p146; Sanagaraja Mawatha) is across the lake from the Temple of the Sacred Tooth Relic, while the

Asgiriya Maha Vihara (Map p146; Wariyapola Sri Sumanga Mawatha) is off Wariyapola Sri Sumanga Mawatha, northwest of the town centre. It has a large reclining Buddha image.

Udawattakelle Sanctuary   FOREST
(Map p146; adult/child Rs 650/375; 6.30am-6pm, last tickets issued at 4.30pm) North of the lake, this forest has huge trees, good bird-watching and loads of cheeky monkeys. Birdwatchers can arrange guides (Rs 500) at the ticket office. Be careful if you're visiting alone. Muggers are rare but not unknown; solo women should take extra care.

Enter by turning right after the post office on DS Senanayake Vidiya.

Devales

There are four Kandyan *devales* to the gods who are followers of Buddha and protect Sri Lanka. Three of the four *devales* are near the Temple of the Sacred Tooth Relic.

Natha Devale   BUDDHIST TEMPLE
(Map p146; 24hr) The 14th-century Natha Devale is the oldest of Kandy's *devales*. It perches on a stone terrace with a fine *vahalkada* (solid panel of sculpture) gateway. Bodhi trees and dagobas stand in the *devale* grounds.

Pattini Devale   BUDDHIST TEMPLE
(Map p146; 24hr) The simple Pattini Devale is dedicated to the goddess of chastity.

Vishnu Devale   BUDDHIST TEMPLE
(Map p146; 24hr) The Vishnu Devale is reached by carved steps and features a drumming hall. The great Hindu god Vishnu is the guardian of Sri Lanka, demonstrating the intermingling of Hinduism and Buddhism.

Activities

Visitors can learn or practise meditation and study Buddhism at several places in the Kandy area. Ask at the Buddhist Publication Society (p155) for details about courses.

There are many walks around Kandy, including the Royal Palace Park (p153), constructed by Sri Wickrama Rajasinha and overlooking the lake. Further up on Rajapihilla Mawatha are even better views over the lake, the town and the surrounding hills. For longer walks, there are paths branching out from Rajapihilla Mawatha. Ask at your guesthouse.

Amaya Hills
AYURVEDA

(Map p159; ☑447 4022; www.amayaresorts.com; Heerassagala; facial from Rs 2500, oil massage & steam bath Rs 6000) Outside Kandy and the nicest Ayurveda centre in the area is the colourful ambience of the treatment centre at Amaya Hills. Also a resort, Amaya Hills is high in the hills on a winding road. A three-wheeler from Kandy costs around Rs 1000 return. Make a day of it, have lunch and spend a few hours around the stunning pool.

Victoria Golf & Country Resort
GOLF

(☑237 6376; www.golfsrilanka.com; green fees US$70, caddy per round Rs 650) This resort is located 20km east of Kandy and is surrounded on three sides by the Victoria Reservoir, with the Knuckles Range as a backdrop. It's worth coming here for lunch at the clubhouse and to savour the views. Claimed to be the best golf course in the subcontinent, it's a fairly challenging 18 holes.

Joy Motorboat Service
BOATING

(Map p146; 20min Rs 2000; ☺9am-6pm) Put on an eye patch and set sail like a pirate into the great blue...lake. Little puttering boats can be hired from this place on the jetty at the western end of the lake.

Sri Lanka Trekking
HIKING

(Map p146; ☑075 799 7667, 071 499 7666; www. srilankatrekking.com; Expeditor Guest House, 41 Saranankara Rd) Sumone Bandara and Ravi Kandy can arrange trekking around Kandy, and camping and trekking (and birdwatching) expeditions to the rugged Knuckles Range. They can also arrange mountain-biking and rafting trips in other parts of the Hill Country. For a standard overnight trek in the Knuckles expect to pay €69. The per-person price decreases with group size.

🛏 Sleeping

Kandy has many good guesthouses, and the more comfortable hotels often occupy spectacular hilltop locations. There's an increasing range of smaller, boutique-style accommodation within around 45 minutes' drive of Kandy. These places enjoy quiet locations, but you will need your own transport.

At the time of the Kandy Esala Perahera, room prices can treble or quadruple, and usually book out in advance. Booking far ahead may secure you a better deal.

The highest concentration of accommodation is along or just off Anagarika Dhar-

mapala Mawatha and Saranankara Rd; buses 654, 655 and 698 will get you there (or just ask for 'Sanghamitta Mawatha' at the clock-tower bus stop).

At the time of research a monstrous 100-plus room, seven-storey hotel (which is against local building regulations that only allow for four storeys) was going up on Saranankara Rd and blocking the views of many a guesthouse. Rumour has it that it's owned by a friend of the president's family.

Most places have in-house restaurants.

Hotel Mango Garden
GUESTHOUSE $

(Map p146; ☑223 5135; www.mangogarden.lk; 32/A Saranankara Rd; r Rs 3000-3500, with shared bathroom Rs 2500; ✱☎) Manager Malik and his French wife run a tight ship here. Rooms are plain but spacious with pristine bedding. The bathrooms let the side down a bit but it's a minor quibble. There's a lovely wooden terrace restaurant for end-of-day drinks and excellent meals (open to all).

The Mango Garden can arrange car hire and local tours.

Day's Inn
GUESTHOUSE $

(Map p146; ☑224 1124; www.daysinn-kandy.com; 66A Rajapihilla Mawatha; r US$31; ✱☎) Staying at this intimate six-room guesthouse is a pleasure. It's bursting with pictures, colour and decorations and has a warm homely feel. However, if you want a lie-in avoid the rooms close to the dining area, which can get noisy at breakfast time.

St Bridget's Country Bungalow
HOMESTAY $

(Map p146; ☑221 5806; www.stbridgets-kandy. com; 125 Sri Sumangala Mawatha, Asgiriya; r from Rs 2700; ◉) Hemmed in by jungly forest filled with birds, this gorgeous family house has rather plain rooms, a very warm welcome, superb home-cooking (dinner Rs 700) and a guestbook full of happy comments. It's a 20-minute uphill walk from town or Rs 200 in a three-wheeler.

Expeditor Guest House
GUESTHOUSE $

(Map p146; ☑490 1628, 223 8316; www.expeditor kandy.com; 41 Saranankara Rd; r Rs 2000-5000; ✱☎) Lots of potted plants, balconies with views, a warm welcome, spotless rooms and the opportunity to share the living areas with the guesthouse owners give Expeditor a cosy bed-and-breakfast feel. The owners offer fantastic treks in the Knuckles Mountains and can provide good advice.

WORTH A TRIP

HELGA'S FOLLY

Helga's Folly (Map p146; ☑ 223 4571; www.helgasfolly.com; 32 Frederick E de Silva Mawatha; r US$200, nonguest admission US$3; ✼🛜🛏) could easily have been dreamt up as a joint project between Gaudí and Dalí. This 35-room hotel/art gallery/surrealist dream has to be the most over-the-top and truly extraordinary hotel in Sri Lanka. It's run and designed by the outlandish Helga da Silva, who grew up in a world of 1950s Hollywood celebrities, artists, writers, politicians and general intrigue, and she has to be one of the only hotel owners we've ever met who prefers her property not to be full. The rock band Stereophonics famously wrote a song about her and her creation has surely led to a thousand twisted nightmares for her guests. As extraordinary as it all is, once you've peeled through all the decorations you'll see that the place is actually looking pretty tatty. Rather than stay here we'd recommend just popping past for a poke about and a drink – for many people it's actually one of the most interesting sights in Kandy.

McLeod Inn   GUESTHOUSE $
(Map p146; ☑ 222 2832; mcleod@sltnet.lk; 65A Rajapihilla Mawatha; r Rs 3000-4000; 🛜) The stupendous lake views make up for the very basic rooms and there's a relaxed family atmosphere and a balcony for the essential end-of-the-day combination: a good book and a cold drink.

Burmese Rest   GUESTHOUSE $
(Map p146; ☑ 223 3261; 274 DS Senanayake Vidiya; s/d Rs 400/700) Considering the price (it's by far the cheapest place in Kandy) you might expect this former pilgrims' guesthouse to be awful, but in fact it's all very clean and well looked after and the building itself is an absolute gem. All the rooms share bathrooms. The monks are friendly and the courtyard is a slowly crumbling haven filled with tortoises.

★**Freedom Lodge**   HOMESTAY $$
(Map p146; ☑ 222 3506; freedomomega@yahoo. com; 30 Saranankara Rd; r incl breakfast Rs 4500-5500; 🛜) We really like this place! It's owned by a friendly family, surrounded by towering palm trees and has eight spotless rooms, excellent food and an authentic family atmosphere. The bathrooms are what you'd expect from somewhere much flasher. When you take everything into account you can see why this has been considered one of Kandy's best guesthouses for many years.

If you want to eat dinner here then book by 2pm at the latest – space is limited.

Kandy Cottage   GUESTHOUSE $$
(Map p146; ☑ 220 4742; www.kandycottage.com; 160 Lady Gordon Dr, Sri Dalada Thapowana Mawatha; r incl breakfast Rs 5060-6820; ✼🛜) Tucked away in a forested valley, the cool and beautiful, whitewashed Kandy Cottage has three rooms (including a family room suitable for four people) with chunky wooden furniture, polished concrete floors and a bohemian, artists' vibe. It's all total peace and tranquility but central Kandy is just a 10-minute stroll away.

Anna Shanthi Villa   GUESTHOUSE $$
(Map p146; ☑ 222 3315; 203 Rajapihilla Terrace; s/d incl breakfast US$49/55; ✼🛜) An awful lot of thought has gone into this guesthouse. Its seven rooms have good quality furnishings and a lot more style than many similarly priced places. The standard of service is also worthy of talking about with staff going out of their way to help. A very good deal.

Sharon Inn   HOTEL $$
(Map p146; ☑ 220 1400; www.hotelsharoninn.com; 59 Saranankara Rd; r incl breakfast Rs 6500-8500; ✼@🛜) One of Kandy's longest established guesthouses and still one of the best. Excellent views and scrupulously clean rooms decorated with Sri Lankan arts and crafts add up to a relaxing place to stay. Not surprisingly it's one of the town's busiest hotels and the owners are fully on the ball with travel information and tours.

It's a good bet for those travelling with young children as they have baby cots as well as a family room sleeping up to five people (Rs 12,000). The nightly buffet dinner, served at 7.30pm under the starlit rooftop restaurant (Rs 1100), is a tasty shortcut to falling in love with Sri Lankan cuisine. Dinner is open to outside guests, so phone to make a booking.

Nature Walk Resort   GUESTHOUSE $$
(Map p146; ☑ 077 771 7482; www.naturewalkhr.net; 9 Sanghamitta Mawatha; r incl breakfast US$35-50; ✼🛜) Terracotta tiles and French doors lead to balconies with, from some rooms, excellent forest views. The rooms are spacious

and airy, and you can look forward to troops of monkeys in the morning and squadrons of bats at dusk.

Castle Hill Guest House HOMESTAY $$
(Map p146; ☑ 222 4376; 22 Rajapihilla Mawatha; s/d incl breakfast Rs 4950/6050, cabins Rs 5000; ☎) This place has beautiful gardens with views over the lake, town and distant mountain peaks playing peek-a-boo with the clouds. The guest rooms don't quite live up to the high expectations that the gardens instil but they're peaceful, well away from the tourist hustle and full of authentic 1930s architecture and decor.

It also has some newer cabins out in the garden but these are grossly overpriced. If these are all they have available then look elsewhere.

Highest View GUESTHOUSE $$
(Map p146; ☑ 223 3778; www.highestview.com; 129/3 Saranankara Rd; r Rs 4000-5000; ☎) It's not quite the 'highest view' but we won't quibble because the views are pretty darn good. Pastel-coloured rooms, quiet shared areas, and a spacious restaurant and bar add up to a good choice on winding Saranankara Rd.

Blue Haven Guesthouse GUESTHOUSE $$
(Map p146; ☑ 222 9617; www.bluehavenguesthouse.com; 30/2 Poorna Lane, Asgiriya; r incl breakfast Rs 3500-5000; ☎ ☎) The rooms here are rather ordinary, but the location is peaceful, the pool a big plus and there are fantastic views out over the Knuckles Range. The proprietor, Mr Linton, is an entertaining host who can arrange car hire and tours of the country. A three-wheeler ride from town to the guesthouse costs Rs 250 to Rs 300.

Forest Glen GUESTHOUSE $$
(Map p146; ☑ 222 2239; www.forestglenkandy.com; 150/6 Lady Gordon's Dr, Sri Dalada Thapowana Mawatha; r Rs 4000-5500; ☎) Simple, somewhat faded, but very quiet rooms feature at this wonderfully secluded family guesthouse on a winding road on the edge of Udawattakelle Sanctuary. The lovely woman who runs it also works as a nanny and if you're travelling with young children they'll be delighted to know that there's a small playground.

Kandy's bright lights are just a 10-minute walk away.

★ Villa Rosa BOUTIQUE HOTEL $$$
(Map p146; ☑ 221 5556; www.villarosa-kandy.com; Asigiriya; s US$90-150, d US$160-240; ☎) Dotted with antiques, and with stunning views over a secluded arc of the Mahaweli Ganga, Villa Rosa is the kind of place you'd build if you moved to Sri Lanka (and had deep pockets!). Spacious wooden-floored rooms in cool, neutral tones share the limelight with relaxing lounges and a what-do-I-read-next reading room. A separate pavilion houses yoga and meditation centres.

The Elephant Stables BOUTIQUE HOTEL $$$
(Map p159; ☑ 743 3201; www.elephantstables.com; 46 Nittawela Rd; r incl breakfast US$250; ✴ ☎ ☎) This colonial-era villa has been lovingly converted into a beautiful boutique hotel, with excellent service, earthy tones, polished concrete and gnarled wood. Two of the rooms have balconies overlooking a rather inviting pool and the not-so-distant mountains.

True to its name elephants used to be stabled up here and staff can arrange for an elephant to come trumpeting past.

Queens Hotel HISTORIC HOTEL $$$
(Map p146; ☑ 223 3026; queenshotel1938@gmail.com; Dalada Vidiya; s/d incl breakfast from US$139/145; ✴ ☎ ☎) Ambience and location are the key reasons for checking in here. While other Asian colonial hotel landmarks have been gussied up, the Queens Hotel hangs in there with an array of old-school rooms with charming floral decor, sharply polished floorboards and a lobby that's big enough for a one-day cricket match.

It's only a short walk from the Temple of the Sacred Tooth Relic (p145) and **Royal Palace Park** (Map p146; admission Rs 100; ⊘8.30am-4.30pm) and it's the place to be during the Kandy Esala Perahera. Try and get a room away from the noisy road though.

Amaara Sky Hotel BOUTIQUE HOTEL $$$
(Map p159; ☑ 223 9888; www.amaarasky.com; 72/22 AB Damunupola Mawatha; s/d incl breakfast US$140/150; ✴ ☎) Flash new boutique hotel atop the hills of Kandy. The rooms are probably the largest in town and while there's little that can be faulted about the place, it is rather business-hotel sterile with little Sri Lankan character.

Cinnamon Citadel RESORT $$$
(Map p146; ☑ Colombo 223 4365; www.cinnamonhotels.com; 124 Srimath Kuda Ratwatte Mawatha; s/d incl breakfast US$190/200; ✴ ☎ ☎) Designer-chic rooms in chocolate tones and grey slate incorporate a riverside location with a breezy lobby and poolside bar at one of Kandy's nicest package-tour resorts. It's

5km west of Kandy; a taxi costs around Rs 600 one way. Nonguests can use the pool for Rs 700.

Hotel Suisse
HISTORIC HOTEL $$$

(Map p146; ☑ 223 3024; www.hotelsuisse.lk; 30 Sangarajah Mawatha; d incl breakfast US$160; ❇☎✱) This is one of those grand old creaky colonial properties, with huge rooms and a lakeside location. It has lots of old-fashioned charm but in reality is only really held together by all the polish on the wooden floors and furnishings.

✖ Eating

For years the restaurant scene in Kandy has been a bit of a nonevent revolving around eating in your guesthouse or at one of a handful of fairly basic restaurants in the town centre. However, in the last couple of years change has been afoot with the opening of some fancier places to eat in the town centre.

Even so, most people eat their evening meal in one of the guesthouses. Most are open to nonguests, but you usually need to inform the hotel a few hours in advance. Particularly good is **Sharon Inn** (Map p146; ☑ 220 1400; buffet Rs 1100), with a buffet comprising up to a dozen dishes (try the aubergine curry) at 7.30pm. It's often possible to just turn up

---

KANDY FOR CHILDREN

Kandy isn't as obvious a child-friendly destination as Sri Lanka's beaches and national parks, but there are a few sights and activities that'll keep little ones – and therefore you as well – happy and sane.

Renting a boat from Joy Motor Boat Services (p151) for a putter about the lake and burning off some energy in the Udawattakelle Sanctuary (p150) and Peradeniya Botanic Gardens (p158) are both likely to be hits. With their elaborate costumes and fire eaters, Kandy's various **dance shows** (p156) will surely meet with approval. The Temple of the Sacred Tooth Relic (p145) has enough exotica to capture the imagination of most children and a day trip to the Pinnewala Elephant Orphanage (p144) is an obvious one. Finally, there's a surprisingly good children's **playpark** (Map p146; Sanagaraja Rd; ⊙ Tue-Sun) at the eastern end of the lake.

---

and eat without booking in advance here. Hotel Mango Garden (p151) has a lovely decked terrace restaurant and no early reservation required. Freedom Lodge (p152) has room for just a handful of people for some of the best curries in town and St Bridget's Country Bungalow (p151) also whips up excellent curries for a limited number of people.

Kandy Muslim Hotel
SRI LANKAN $

(Map p146; Dalada Vidiya; mains Rs 200-350) No, it's not a hotel, but it is an always bustling eatery that offers Kandy's best samosas, authentically spiced curries and heaving plates of frisbee-sized, but gossamer-light, naan. However, what people really come for are the *kotthu* (*rotti* chopped and fried with meat and vegetables), which come in a variety of styles and flavours, and are legendary throughout town. Foreigners are often hustled up the stairs, but for more local character eat downstairs with the locals.

Devon Restaurant
INTERNATIONAL $

(Map p146; 11 Dalada Vidiya; mains Rs 225-450) This large and busy restaurant and bakery has a long menu of Sri Lankan and Chinese staples, a few lacklustre Western offerings and some 'healthy' salads (the bacon, egg and chip butty 'salad' being a particularly healthy offering!).

The main dining hall is a smart canteen-like affair that's a step up in the posh stakes from many of the other town-centre restaurants. It has high chairs and is popular with young families.

Bake House
SRI LANKAN $

(Map p146; ☑ 223 4868; 36 Dalada Vidiya; mains Rs 80-250) Bake House is versatility plus, with tasty baked goodies out the front and a more formal dining room concealed under the building's whitewashed colonial arches. Pop in just after 3pm, when the second bake of the day comes out and the short eats are still warm.

★ Olde Empire Cafe
SRI LANKAN, INTERNATIONAL $$

(Map p146; ☑ 223 9870; 21 Temple St; mains Rs 380-500; ⊙ 8.30am-8.30pm) People who know the Olde Empire from just a couple of years back will be shocked by the recent transformation from musty old relic to a flamboyant, modern and very inviting restaurant where diners sit under a bevy of fluoro paintings and tuck into great rice and curries, pastas, salads and juices.

🍷 Drinking & Nightlife

In this sacred city, the legislation for pubs, bars and discos is very strict. The typical Kandyan goes to bed early, but there are a few places for an end-of-day gin and tonic. All the top hotels also have decent bars.

Kandy's two nightclubs are in hotels. At both, entry for women is free and for mixed couples Rs 500, and there's usually no entry allowed for unaccompanied men from outside the hotel. Long trousers, covered shoes and a collared shirt are mandatory for the lads.

Royal Bar & Hotel   BAR
(Map p146; 222 4449; 44 Raja Vidiya (King St); mains Rs 700-1500) One of the nicer places in town for an oh-so-civilised drink. This recently opened place, in a beautifully renovated colonial building, recalls pith helmets and British stiff upper lips, and its courtyard bar couldn't be a better place for an evening G&T. Happy 'hour' runs from 5.30pm to 7.30pm.

It's also a restaurant and hotel, and while the food isn't bad, it's not great either. The rooms are overpriced.

Slightly Chilled Lounge Bar   BAR
(Map p146; 29A Anagarika) With views out over the lake, pool tables, premiership football, decent Chinese food and a 6pm-to-7pm happy hour, this place is a winner on many accounts. It's a big British expat hang-out. It's sometimes still known by its old name of Bamboo Garden.

National Coffee   CAFE
(Map p146; 220 5734; 5 Temple St; 8am-7pm) Bright and cool environment for a freshly ground, organic caffeine pick-me-up.

☆ Entertainment

The modest **Asgiriya Stadium** (Map p146), north of the town centre, hosts crowds of up to 10,000 cheering fans at international one-day and test matches. The compact stadium is reckoned to be one of the most attractive used for international cricket. Ticket prices depend on the popularity of the two teams. India versus Sri Lanka matches are the most valued. Tickets are also sold on the day, or you can book grandstand seats up to a month in advance through the **Sri Lanka Cricket office** (Map p146; 223 8533) at the stadium.

Rugby is played between May and September at the Nittawella rugby grounds.

Alliance Française   CULTURAL CENTRE
(Map p159; 222 4432; www.afkandy.org; 642 Peradeniya Rd; 8.30am-6pm Mon-Sat) The Alliance hosts film nights (often with English-subtitled films), and has books and periodicals. Good coffee is available. Non-members can browse in the library.

🛍 Shopping

Central Kandy has shops selling antique jewellery and silver belts, and you can buy crafts in the colourful **main market** (Map p146; Station Rd).

Selyn   CLOTHING, JEWELLERY
(Map p146; 223 7735; 7/1/1 Temple St) High-quality, fair-trade textiles, clothing and jewellery made of recycled paper and other materials.

Rangala House Gallery   GALLERY
(Map p146; 2nd fl, 7/1/1 Temple St) The works of local and Colombo-based artists are displayed and sold here. It also sells a range of organic jams made in the hills surrounding Kandy.

Kandyan Art Association & Cultural Centre   HANDICRAFTS
(Map p146; Sangharaja Mawatha; 9am-5pm daily) Has a good selection of local lacquerware, brassware and other craft items in a colonial-era showroom with a patina of age. There are some craftspeople working on the spot. Prices are slightly inflated.

Buddhist Publication Society   BOOKS
(Map p146; 223 7283; www.bps.lk; 54 Victoria Rd; 9am-4.30pm Mon-Fri, to 12.30pm Sat) The Buddhist Publication Society, on the lakeside 400m northeast of the Temple of the Sacred Tooth Relic, is a nonprofit charity that distributes the Buddha's teachings. Local scholars and monks occasionally give lectures, and there is a comprehensive library. See online for free information downloads. It's a good place to ask about meditation courses.

Odel Luv SL   CLOTHES, SOUVENIRS
(Map p146; shop L3-3, 5 Dalada Veediya; 10am-7pm) T-shirts, tacky tourist goods and some good souvenirs: this shop under the arcades of the Queens Hotel has the lot.

Cultural Triangle Office   BOOKS
(Map p146; 8am-4.15pm) Has a selection of books on the Ancient Cities for sale. *Kandy,* by Dr Anuradha Seneviratna, is an

DON'T MISS

KANDYAN DANCERS & DRUMMERS

With elaborate costumes, gyrating dance moves and show-stopping fire-breathing stunts, a Kandyan dance performance is one of the defining experiences of a stay in Kandy. Calling it a traditional Kandyan dance performance is something of a misnomer as the shows are very much aimed at audience entertainment, and feature dance routines and costumes from across the country, including the famous 'devil' dances of the west coast (which are sadly very hard to see in their home region).

There are three different venues. All have nightly performances that last an hour (get there 30 minutes in advance to get a better seat).

Kandy Lake Club (Map p146; Sanghamitta Mawatha; cover Rs 500; ⊙ show starts 5pm) Located 300m up Sanghamitta Mawatha, this place has arguably the best costumes of any of the venues staging traditional Sri Lankan dance shows. The front seats are usually reserved for groups, so arrive early for good seats.

Kandyan Art Association & Cultural Centre (Map p146; Sangharaja Mawatha; cover Rs 500; ⊙ show starts 5pm) This is the busiest dance-show venue and in high-season it can be overwhelmingly crammed with tour groups. However, the auditorium makes it easier to take photographs than at other venues. It's on the northern lake shore. Seeing as though it is so busy, the earlier you arrive the better.

Mahanuwara YMBA (Map p146; ☑ 223 3444; 5 Rajapihilla Mawatha; cover Rs 500; ⊙ show starts 5.30pm) Southwest of the lake, the YMBA guesthouse is a low-key venue for Sri Lankan dance, but the performance is the equal of the other venues and the crowds somewhat less.

You can also hear Kandyan drummers every day at the Temple of the Sacred Tooth Relic (p145) and the other temples surrounding it – their drumming signals the start and finish of the daily *puja* (offering or prayers).

informative guide to the city's heritage. Also available is *The Cultural Triangle,* published by Unesco and the Central Cultural Fund, which provides background information on the ancient sites.

ℹ Information

DANGERS & ANNOYANCES

The back alleys of the town centre are worth avoiding after dark. Most habitués are local guys searching out gambling dens and late-night bars.

Touts mooch around the train station and the lake. It's best to book ahead with a guesthouse; most will pick you up from the Kandy train station.

While researching we also heard of solo women travellers being hassled around the lakeside at dusk and after dark. Get a three-wheeler back to your guesthouse to keep safe.

INTERNET ACCESS

There are internet cafes throughout the town centre (Kotugodelle Vidiya has a glut of such places). All charge around Rs 60 per hour. Virtually every hotel also has wi-fi access.

MEDICAL SERVICES

Lakeside Adventist Hospital (Map p146; ☑ 222 3466; 40 Sangaraja Mawatha) Has English-speaking staff.

MONEY

The following all have ATMs and exchange facilities.

Bank of Ceylon (Map p146; Dalada Vidiya)

Commercial Bank (Map p146; Kotugodelle Vidiya)

Hatton National Bank (Map p146; Dalada Vidiya)

HSBC (Map p146; Kotugodelle Vidiya)

POST & TELEPHONE

The main post office is opposite the train station. A more central post office is at the intersection of Kande Vidiya and DS Senanayake Vidiya. There are numerous private communications bureaus for IDD (International Direct Dial) calling.

TOURIST INFORMATION

British Council (Map p146; ☑ 222 2410; www.britishcouncil.lk; 88/3 Kotugodelle Vidiya; ⊙ 9am-5.30pm Tue-Sat, to 4pm Sun) British newspapers, CDs, videos and DVDs, and occasional film nights, exhibitions and plays. Nonmembers may read newspapers on presentation of a passport.

Cultural Triangle Office (Map p146; ☎222 2661; 16 Deva Vidiya; ⏱8am-4.15pm) Located in a colonial building near the Temple of the Sacred Tooth Relic. Sells the Cultural Triangle round-trip tickets that cover many of the sites of the Ancient Cities. Within Kandy the ticket covers the four Hindu *devales* – Kataragama, Natha, Pattini and Vishnu – two monasteries (Asgiriya and Malwatte) and the National Museum.

Tourist Information Office (Map p146; ☎222 2661; Level 2, Kandy City Centre, Dalada Vidiya; ⏱8.30am-4.15pm) The main tourist office can dish up a lot of smiles but not so much information. It's inside the flash Kandy City Centre shopping mall.

ⓘ Getting There & Away

AIR

Cinnamon Air (☎Colombo 011-247 5475; www.cinnamonair.com) runs scheduled flights once or twice daily to and from Colombo for US$172 one-way.

Sri Lankan Airlines (Map p146; ☎223 2495; 17 Temple St; ⏱8.15am-6pm Mon-Fri, to 1pm Sat) Ticket reservations can be made here.

BUS

Kandy has one main bus station (the manic Goods Shed) and a series of bus stops near the **clock tower** (Map p146). The **Goods Shed bus station** (Map p146) has long-distance buses, while local buses, such as those to Peradeniya (Rs 20), Ampitiya (Rs 17), Matale (Rs 50) and Kegalle (Rs 64), leave from near the clock tower. However, some private intercity express buses (to Negombo and Colombo, for example) leave from Station Rd between the clock tower and the train station. If you're still confused, ask someone to point you the right way.

For Sigiriya you must change in Polonnaruwa and for Dalhousie you normally have to go to Hatton and change there. During pilgrimage season, some buses run direct from Kandy. For details of some of the buses from Kandy, see the boxed table below.

TAXI

Many long-distance taxi drivers hang around the Temple of the Sacred Tooth Relic. Your guest-house or hotel can organise taxi tours, but you may be able to get a cheaper deal if you organise it through these guys. Cars can generally be hired, with a driver and petrol, for approximately Rs 6500 per day.

Some guesthouses advertise day trips to all three Cultural Triangle destinations (Sigiriya, Anuradhapura and Polonnaruwa), but this is an exhausting itinerary for both driver and passengers, and one that encourages manic driving. An overnight stay in Anuradhapura, Sigiriya or Polonnaruwa is a saner and safer option.

Blue Haven Tours & Travels (Map p146; ☎077 737 2066; www.bluehaventours.com; 25 DS Senanayake St) is one of a number of car-hire and tour companies. They charge US$50 per day for a car and driver.

TRAIN

Kandy is a major railway station. Tickets can be bought and reserved up to 10 days in advance at the station (open 5.30am to 6.30pm). Tickets reserved in advance cost a set Rs 600 in second class.

Seats are very popular in the 1st-class observation saloon on the Badulla-bound train. This train originates in Colombo and after Kandy stops in Hatton (near Adam's Peak), Nanu Oya (for Nuwara Eliya), Haputale, Ella and a number of other Hill Country stations. Observation-class tickets cost a set Rs 1000 for anywhere between Kandy and Nanu Oya and Rs 1250 for any of the stations east of there.

If you are unable to reserve a seat at the ticket window, enquire with the stationmaster, who can sometimes release further seating for tourists.

Trains run to the following (prices are for unreserved tickets):

Badulla 2nd/3rd class Rs 270/145

Bandarawela 2nd/3rd class Rs 230/125

Colombo 2nd/3rd class Rs 190/105

Ella 2nd/3rd class Rs 240/130

Haputale 2nd/3rd class Rs 210/115

Hatton 2nd/3rd class Rs 110/65

Nanu Oya (for Nuwara Eliya) 2nd/3rd class Rs 160/90

BUSES FROM KANDY

DESTINATION	BUS STATION	LUXURY FARE (RS)	REGULAR FARE (RS)	TIME (HOURS)
Anuradhapura	Goods Shed	360	190	3-4
Colombo	Station Rd	240	155	3-4
Negombo	Station Rd	-	153	3-4
Nuwara Eliya	Goods Shed	220	120	2
Polonnaruwa	Goods Shed	272	180	3½
Ratnapura	Goods Shed	-	173	6

ⓘ Getting Around

BUS
Buses to outlying parts of Kandy and nearby towns such as Peradeniya, Ampitiya, Matale and Kegalle leave from near the clock tower.

TAXI
With metered air-con taxis, **Radio Cabs** (☎ 223 3322) is a comfortable alternative to three-wheelers. You may have to wait some time for your cab, especially if it's raining and demand is heavy. With taxis (vans) that are not metered, settle on a price before you start your journey.

THREE-WHEELER
The standard cost for a three-wheeler from the train station to the southeast end of the lake is Rs 100 to Rs 150. Drivers will ask foreign tourists for much more, but if you stick to your guns you'll get something approximating the local price.

Around Kandy

☑ 081

There are a few things worth seeing around Kandy that can be done as a half-day trip.

◎ Sights & Activities

★ **Peradeniya Botanic Gardens**   GARDENS
(Map p159; www.botanicgardens.gov.lk; adult/child Rs 1100/550; ☉ 7.30am-5pm) At one time these beautiful botanical gardens were reserved exclusively for Kandyan royalty. Today even commoners are allowed into what are, at 60 hectares, the largest and most impressive botanic gardens in Sri Lanka.

The many highlights include a fine collection of orchids and a stately avenue of royal palms. Another big hit is the giant Javan fig tree on the great lawn. Covering 2500 sq metres, it's like a giant, living geodesic dome.

On weekends and holidays the gardens are packed with romantically inclined local tourists, and it can be hard to move without tripping over yet another canoodling young couple.

If food is more a priority than love, you'll find an overpriced cafeteria (mains Rs 550 to Rs 1000) about 500m north of the entrance, serving Western and Sri Lankan food on a roofed verandah. A better option is to stock up on picnic items. Just keep a close eye on the insistent posse of local dogs.

Bus 644 (Rs 15) from Kandy's clock-tower bus stop goes to the gardens. A three-wheeler from Kandy is around Rs 700 return; a van is around Rs 1500. Many taxi drivers incorpo-rate a visit to the gardens with the Pinnewala Elephant Orphanage (p144) or the Kandy temple loop.

Kandy War Cemetery   CEMETERY
(Map p159; Deveni Rajasinghe; by donation; ☉ 10am-noon & 1-6pm) This small and beautifully melancholic cemetery is maintained by the Commonwealth War Graves Commission. It is the final resting place for those who died defending Sri Lanka during WWII.

Temples
There are several interesting temples around Kandy. Visiting them provides not just an insight into Sri Lankan religious culture but also a jolly good excuse for a romp around some exquisitely pretty countryside. This loop takes in three 14th-century Hindu-Buddhist temples and you'll pass by the entrance to the botanic gardens, allowing you to slot them into your busy day as well. If exclusively using public transport there's a lot of walking involved, so you could narrow down your visit to one or two of the temples. Many people rent a three-wheeler for the day; expect to pay around Rs 3000 from Kandy. If you're combining walking and public transport you'll need to ask the way occasionally, as the loop is not signposted.

Embekka Devale   HINDU TEMPLE
(Map p159; admission Rs 300) Dedicated to the worship of the Hindu deity Mahasen, this beautiful temple with its finely carved wooden pillars depicting swans, eagles, wrestling men and dancing women, was constructed in the 14th century. The best carvings are in the so-called drummers hall.

To get here by public transport catch the frequent bus 643 (to Vatadeniya via Embekka) from near the Kandy clock tower (Rs 38). The village of Embekka is about 7km beyond the botanic gardens (about an hour from Kandy). From the village it's a pleasant rural stroll of about 1km to the temple.

Lankatilake Temple   BUDDHIST, HINDU TEMPLE
(Map p159; admission Rs 300) This temple, mounted on a rocky bluff, is divided into two halves – one half Buddhist and one half Hindu. It features a Buddha image, Kandy-period paintings, rockface inscriptions and stone elephant figures. A caretaker or monk will unlock the shrine if it's not already open. A *perahera* takes place in August. The setting is as impressive as the temple.

From Embekka Devale to here is a 3km stroll beside rice paddies; you'll see the

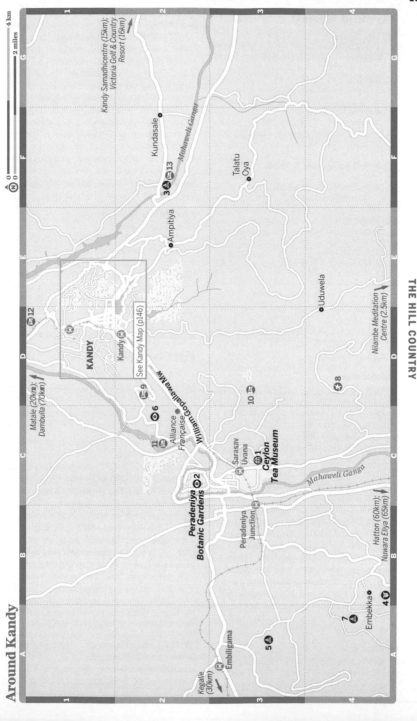

Around Kandy

THE HILL COUNTRY

0   2 miles
0   4 km

Kandy Samadhicentre (15km);
Victoria Golf & Country
Resort (16km)

Mahaweli Ganga

Kundasale

3 △ 13

Talatu
Oya

Ampitiya

12

KANDY

Uduwela

Kandy

See Kandy Map (p146)

Matale (20km);
Dambulla (70km)

Nilambe Meditation
Centre (2.5km)

9

8

6

10

Alliance
Française

11

William Gopallawe MW

Sarasav
Uvana

1
Ceylon
Tea Museum

Peradeniya
Botanic Gardens

2

Mahaweli Ganga

Peradeniya
Junction

Hatton (60km);
Nuwara Eliya (65km)

Embilligama

5 △

7 △

4

Embekka

Kegalle (30km)

Around Kandy

temple on the left. From Kandy you can go directly to the Lankatilake Temple on bus 644 heading towards Pilimatalawa. Get off at Dawulagala Rd from where it's about a 750m walk to the temple.

Gadaladeniya Temple

BUDDHIST, HINDU TEMPLE

(Map p159; admission Rs 200) This Buddhist temple with a Hindu annex dates from the 14th century and the main shrine room contains a seated Buddha. Built on a rocky outcrop and covered with small pools, the temple is reached by a series of steps cut into the rock.

At the time of research, scaffolding and a tin roof covered this temple in an effort to protect it from further rain-induced erosion.

It's a 3km walk to Gadaladeniya Temple from the Lankatilake Temple, or you can catch a bus from Kandy; bus 644 (Rs 28), among others, will take you there. The main Colombo–Kandy road is less than 2km from Gadaladeniya Temple – you reach the road close to the 105km post. It's a pleasant stroll, and from the main road almost any bus will take you to the Peradeniya Botanic Gardens or on to Kandy.

Meditation

There are a couple of well-regarded meditation centres close to Kandy.

Nilambe Buddhist Meditation Centre

MEDITATION

(✆777 804 555; www.nilambe.net) This meditation centre offers daily meditation classes spread over a minimum of three- to five-day stays. Basic accommodation is available. Reservations should be made through the website at least two weeks in advance.

The centre is close to Nilambe Bungalow Junction, about 13km south of Kandy. It can be reached by bus 633 (catch a Delthota bus via Galaha and get off at Office Junction). From Office Junction, you can walk a steep 3km through tea plantations or take a three-wheeler (Rs 250) to the centre. A taxi from Kandy costs Rs 1400 one way.

Dhamma Kuta Vipassana Meditation Centre

MEDITATION

(Map p159; ✆238 5774; www.kuta.dhamma.org; Mowbray, Hindagala) This centre offers courses from one day to 10 days following the SN Goenka system of meditation. Booking ahead is mandatory. There's dorm accommodation with separate male and female quarters. Take a Mahakanda-bound bus from the clock-tower bus stop in Kandy and get off at the last stop. It's a steep 2km walk.

🛏 Sleeping

If you want quiet days spent wandering along shaded tracks, with views of rolling hills, stay just outside of Kandy. Accommodation skews to midrange and top-end properties, and there are some lovely places worth splashing out for.

★ Baramba House

BOUTIQUE HOTEL $$

(Map p159; ✆220 0173; www.barambalanka.com; 22 Upul Mawatha, Primrose Hill; r incl breakfast US$85-95; 🖥🕸) The Swiss-Sri Lankan owners of this idyllic little three-room 'boutique guesthouse' have created a little slice of bliss here. There are cool, high-ceilinged rooms with fans swishing lazily away above giant four-poster beds, a crystal-clear pool in which to work up a breakfast appetite and terraces with easy-chairs, and views over the jungly hills and chocolate-coloured river. No children under 12 years are allowed. It's out near the Kandy War Cemetery (p158) and a Rs 300 three-wheeler ride from central Kandy.

★ The Kandy House

BOUTIQUE HOTEL $$$

(Amunugama Walauwa; Map p159; ✆492 1394; www.thekandyhouse.com; Amunugama Walauwa, Gunnepana; r incl breakfast from US$355; @🕸🖥) Thanks to masses of exotic tropical flora, the air you breathe at this divine boutique hotel, which was once the family home of a Kandyan chief, literally tastes perfumed. Now fully restored, this divine boutique hotel, which is decorated with colonial Dutch antiques, ticks all the honeymoon requirement boxes. A garden infinity pool segues to emerald-green rice paddies.

Note that rooms do not have air-con and there's a two-night minimum stay. No children under 12 years are allowed.

Kandy Samadhicentre   BOUTIQUE HOTEL $$$
(☑ 447 0925; www.thekandysamadhicentre.com; Kukul Oya Rd, Kandy; r US$100-300) Part boutique ecolodge and part Ayurvedic centre, this could be the most relaxing place to stay around Kandy. Thirteen pavilions dot a forested hillside, and each room is decorated with Asian textiles and four-poster beds. Based on room quality alone we think it's overpriced, but judging by the comments in the guestbook, we're in the minority.

Food is both organic and vegetarian (dinner US$15), and no alcohol is served. Yoga (US$25) and massage (US$40) are also available. A three-wheeler to the lodge (50 minutes east of Kandy) costs Rs 1800; arrange pick-up when making your booking.

Amaya Hills   RESORT $$$
(Map p159; ☑ 447 4022; www.amayaresorts.com; Heerassagala; s/d incl breakfast from US$146/156; ❄ @ ⬚ ☒) Perched in the hills, 20 minutes' drive southwest of Kandy, this 100-room hotel incorporates a stunning open lobby, a clifftop swimming pool, and very comfortable rooms with lots of warm wooden tones and a Kandyan design motif.

East of Kandy

Kandy is an important transport hub, with most travellers going west to Colombo, north to the Ancient Cities, or south to the rest of the Hill Country. But it's also possible to go east to Mahiyangana and Badulla, and to Monaragala en route to Arugam Bay and Gal Oya National Park. Further northeast, Batticaloa can be reached by bus from Kandy.

The Buddha is said to have preached at Mahiyangana; a dagoba marks the spot. There are two roads to Mahiyangana. The A26 north road goes past the Victoria Golf Club and the Victoria Reservoir to Madugoda, before twisting downhill through 18 hairpin bends to the Mahaweli lowlands and the dry-zone plains. It's one of the country's hairiest bus rides. Going up you worry about overheating and going down it's all about the brakes. Many vehicles didn't make it and now lie in the jungle beneath.

Drivers prefer the road along the southern shores of the Victoria and Randenigala Reservoirs, which is much faster and in better condition. To travel from Kandy to the hills of Uva Province (including towns such as Ella and Haputale), it's quicker to take this road and then the route south to Badulla than to go via Nuwara Eliya.

Knuckles Range
ELEVATION 1863M

So named because the range's peaks look like a closed fist, this **massif** is home to pockets of rare montane forest. The area, which offers fabulous hiking and birdwatching possibilities, remains relatively unknown to foreign visitors and is one of the best areas in the Hill Country to get off the beaten tourist path.

If you are coming here in order to hike then you'll need to be well prepared. A knowledgeable guide is virtually essential.

Hotels in the Knuckles Range can organise guided hiking trips. In Kandy, see Sumone and Ravi at Sri Lanka Trekking (p151). A guide for the high peaks is compulsory, and some serious wet-weather gear and some leech protection are essential. For anything more ambitious than a couple of hours' stroll around the foothills, you will need to be totally self-sufficient, with camping equipment and food.

The foothills of the Knuckles are covered in small villages and walking in this area is open to anyone. The high massif, though, is a protected zone and entry costs Rs 650. Tickets cannot be purchased at the gate, but will normally be obtained by your guide from a forestry department office.

🛏 Sleeping & Eating

Brookside Resort   HOTEL $
(☑ 562 4933; www.brooksideresort.lk; Dumbara Valley, Elkaduwa; d with air-con Rs 5250, without air-con Rs 2000-3000; ❄) This place, with its partially obscured mountain views, is a fair choice. Communal areas are chock-a-block full of wicker chairs and shelves of knick-knacks, and the rooms are plain and smart. It often hosts noisy wedding parties. Staff speak very little English and seem a little baffled by foreigners but perhaps that's only fair enough.

THE HILL COUNTRY EAST OF KANDY

Green View HOTEL $

(📞 077 781 1881; www.greenviewholidayresort.com; Karagahinna, Elkaduwa; s/d incl breakfast from Rs 2600/3500; 🗻) This cheery hillside lodge has spectacular views of a forested mountain valley and clean rooms with fake roses providing a shot of colour. It's showing its age a little, but staff will happily lead you on easy low-level strolls or much tougher hikes around the edge of the Knuckles Range. Book ahead and they'll pick you up from Kandy.

A swimming pool was under construction at time of research.

★**Mudulkelle Tea & Ecolodge** BOUTIQUE HOTEL $$$

(📞 380 1052; www.madulkelle.com; Madulkelle Village; d incl full board US$389; 🗻🗻) 🍴 Lie in the infinity pool and gaze out over mountain creases and the deep greens of the surrounding tea estates at this intimate and fabulous boutique hotel. The rooms themselves are actually tents, scattered over the hillside, but fear not, this ain't real camping. These luxury tents come with double beds, fully equipped bathrooms and wooden writing desks.

The main building, containing the restaurant, is filled with polished antiques and leather armchairs set beside a roaring log fire. Superb meals are included in the rates and there's a wealth of activities on offer. The manager speaks French and the lodge is engaged in community-development projects.

Rangala House BOUTIQUE HOTEL $$$

(📞 240 0294; www.rangalahouse.com; 92B Bobebila Rd, Makuldeniya, Teldeniya; half-board s/d US$154/214, 4-person studio US$220; 🗻🗻) This gorgeous former tea planter's bungalow is ensconced on a steep forested hillside surrounded by spice trees. It has just four double rooms and a studio for families. Its large living and dining room has a fireplace and views over mountains, the jungles, and the distant bright lights of Kandy.

It organises very good hiking tours in the Knuckles Range.

Hunas Falls Hotel HOTEL $$$

(📞 494 0320; www.hunasfallskandy.com; Elkaduwa; s/d incl breakfast from US$178/189; ❄️@🗻🗻) Perched on the edge of a working tea plantation and spice garden, this hotel, which is popular with visitors from India and the Middle East, has elegant rooms and a bucolic location. Frankly the building itself is something of an ugly and impersonal blot on an otherwise stunning landscape.

ℹ️ Getting There & Away

A taxi from Kandy to Elkaduwa should cost Rs 1500. Alternatively, take a bus to Wattegama (from near the clock tower in Kandy), and then catch another to Elkaduwa.

VISITING THE VEDDAHS

Sri Lanka was inhabited long before the Sinhalese or Tamils arrived on the scene. These original inhabitants, known as the Veddahs (Hunters), are thought to have first arrived on the island some 18,000 years ago and until fairly recently they have lived alongside their fellow Sri Lankans without too many issues. Today though, as with aboriginal communities across South Asia, the remaining Veddah communities are under intense pressure and only a few hundred pure-blooded Veddah remain.

The last Veddah stronghold is in the countryside around the village of **Dambana**, which is east of the small town of **Mahiyangana**. If you want to meet the Veddah you need to find a translator-guide in Dambulla to take you to the pretty hamlet of **Kotabakina**, the most frequently visited Veddah village. Once here you will (for a fairly substantial sum) most likely be entertained with dancing, singing and a 'hunting' display by the Veddah people. Perhaps not surprisingly the whole experience can feel rather staged, but it should also be borne in mind that the money tourism pumps into the villages, and the tourists' desire to see traditional tribal 'culture', might actually be enough to stop the last of Veddah from being swallowed up by mainstream Sri Lankan culture.

The best base for a visit to this area is Mahiyangana, a sprawling and sparsely settled town. The only highlight in the town itself is the **Mahiyangana dagoba** where, according to legend, the Buddha preached on his first visit to Sri Lanka.

There are a few lodging options in Mahiyangana, none of which are very accustomed to foreign guests, and there are buses to Kandy, Badulla and Polonnaruwa, among other destinations.

Adam's Peak (Sri Pada)

ELEVATION 2243M

Located in a beautiful area of the southern Hill Country, this lofty peak has sparked the imagination for centuries and been a focus for pilgrimage for more than a thousand years.

Variously known as Adam's Peak (the place where Adam first set foot on earth after being cast out of heaven), Sri Pada (Sacred Footprint, left by the Buddha as he headed towards paradise), or perhaps most poetically as Samanalakande (Butterfly Mountain; where butterflies go to die). Some believe the huge 'footprint' crowning the peak to be that of St Thomas, the early apostle of India, or even of Lord Shiva.

The pilgrimage season begins on *poya* day in December and runs until **Vesak festival** in May; January and February are busiest. At other times the temple on the summit is unused, and between May and October the peak is often obscured by clouds. During the season pilgrims and tourists alike make the climb up the countless steps to the top.

Walkers leave from the small settlement of Dalhousie (del-*house*), 33km by road southwest of Hatton, which is situated on the Colombo–Kandy–Nuwara Eliya railway and road. In season, the route is illuminated by a sparkling ribbon of lights which are visible from miles around and from afar look like a trail of stars leading into the heavens. It's a view that cannot but fail to send a quiver of anticipation through most people. Out of season you will need a torch. Many pilgrims prefer to make the longer, more tiring – but equally well-marked and lit – seven-hour climb from Ratnapura via the Carney Estate because of the greater merit thus gained.

As dawn illuminates the holy mountain, the diffuse morning light uncovers the Hill Country rising in the east and the land sloping to the coast to the west. Colombo, 65km away, is easily visible on a clear day.

Adam's Peak saves its most breathtaking moment for just after dawn. The sun casts a perfect shadow of the peak onto the misty clouds down towards the coast. As the sun rises higher this eerie triangular shadow races back towards the peak, eventually disappearing into its base.

🏃 Activities

The Climb

You can start the 7km climb from Dalhousie soon after dark – bring a good sleeping bag to keep you warm overnight at the top – or you can wait until about 2am to start. The climb is up steps most of the way (about 5200 of them), and on a quiet day you'll reach the top in 2½ to four hours. A 2.30am start will easily get you there before dawn, which is around 6.30am. Start on a *poya* day or a weekend, though, and the throng of pilgrims will add hours and hours to your climb.

From the car park, the slope is gradual for the first half-hour, passing under an entrance arch and then by the Japan–Sri Lanka Friendship Dagoba. The pathway gets steeper until it becomes a continuous flight of stairs. There are teahouses all the way to the top; in season they open through the night. A few are open out of season. The authorities have banned litter, alcohol, cigarettes, meat and recorded music, so the atmosphere remains reverential.

The Summit

The summit can be cold, so it's not worth getting there too long before dawn and then sitting around shivering. Definitely bring warm clothes, including something extra for the top, and pack plenty of water. If you're in Dalhousie in the pilgrimage season, stalls at the market sell warm jackets and headgear (although on busy nights the crush of humanity can be so intense that you'll be kept warm merely through close proximity to so many other people). Otherwise stop at the market at Nuwara Eliya for outdoor gear at bargain prices. Some pilgrims wait for the priests to make a morning offering before they descend, but the sun and heat rise quickly, so it pays not to linger.

The Descent

Many people find the hardest part is coming down. The endless steps can shake the strongest knees, and if your shoes don't fit well, toe-jam also kicks in. Walking poles or even just a sturdy stick will make the descent much less jarring on your legs. Take a hat, as the morning sun intensifies quickly. Remember to stretch your legs when you finish, otherwise you'll be walking strangely for a few days.

Between June and November, when the pathway isn't illuminated and there aren't many people around, travellers are urged to do the hike at least in pairs. Expect to pay around Rs 1000 for a guide.

🛏 Sleeping & Eating

Dalhousie is the best place to start the climb and it also has the area's best budget accommodation.

THE HILL COUNTRY ACAM'S PEAK (SRI PADA)

Out-of-pilgrimage-season buses may drop you off in Dalhousie's main square, but during the season buses stop wherever they can find a space.

Most guesthouses are on your left as you reach Dalhousie.

White House   HUT $

(☑ 077 791 2009; www.adamspeakaccommodation. com; Dalhousie; r incl half-board Rs 3000-4500; ☎) The White House has a pretty riverside location next to a swimming hole (or rather a paddling hole when the water level is low), lots of hammocks and easy chairs, and accommodation that ranges from basic to quite smart. It can organise guided walks through the tea estates.

Punsisi Rest   HOTEL $

(☑ 051-492 0313; punsisi.rest@yahoo.com; Dalhousie; r incl breakfast Rs 4000-4500; ☎) Ever expanding and ever improving Punsisi Rest mow automatically assigns foreigners to the smart hilltop bungalows with hot showers and wi-fi, but you do have to climb up about a million steps to reach them and this action might just reduce you to tears after climbing Adam's Peak! It offers free pick-up from Hatton train station if you book ahead.

Green House   HOMESTAY $

(☑ 051-222 3956; Dalhousie; s Rs 800, d Rs 1000-2500, q Rs 3000, all incl breakfast) Across the bridge very close to the start of the walking path, the Green House lives up to its name with a pot-plant–filled garden and a breezy gazebo restaurant. Some of the small rooms share a bathroom and all are pretty basic.

★ Slightly Chilled   GUESTHOUSE $$

(☑ 052-205 5502; www.slightlychilled.tv; Dalhousie; r incl half-board US$60; @☎) Dalhousie's best option is Slightly Chilled in name and very chilled in nature. Spacious and colour-ful rooms with polished wooden floors have great views of Sri Pada, and there's an airy restaurant. Mountain bikes can be hired, there's lots of information on other trails in the area and at night there are occasional big-screen movies.

ℹ Information

There are no banking facilities in Dalhousie. The nearest ATMs are in Hatton.

ℹ Getting There & Away

A taxi from Hatton to Dalhousie costs Rs 2500 and a three-wheeler Rs 2000. On busy pilgrimage nights the roads to Dalhousie can get clogged with traffic in the early evenings and it can take hours to cover the final kilometres into town, so try to set off for Dalhousie as early as you can in the day.

BUS

Buses run to Dalhousie from Kandy (from the Goods Shed bus station), Nuwara Eliya and Colombo in the pilgrimage season. Otherwise, you need first to get to Hatton or to Maskeliya, about 20km along the Hatton–Dalhousie road.

Throughout the year there are services to Hatton from Colombo (Rs 246), Kandy (Rs 110) or Nuwara Eliya (Rs 83). There are also some direct buses from Nuwara Eliya and Colombo to Maskeliya.

There are buses from Hatton to Dalhousie via Maskeliya every 30 minutes in the pilgrimage season (Rs 75, two hours). Otherwise, you have to take a bus from Hatton to Maskeliya (Rs 40, last departure about 6pm) and then another to Dalhousie (Rs 35, last departure about 7pm).

TRAIN

All trains travelling from Kandy to Nanu Oya stop in Hatton, the closest train station to Dalhousie. From Kandy trains cost Rs 110/65 (2nd/3rd class). From Nanu Oya it costs Rs 60/30 (2nd/3rd class). Advance reservations in either of

---

PILGRIMAGE ON A POYA DAY

Thinking of climbing Adam's Peak on a *poya* day or weekend? Go for it! It'll likely turn out to be one of the most memorable things you do in Sri Lanka. But take note: the last time we climbed the mountain on such a night we got within 800m of the summit and then stood in a queue for nearly three hours. We only advanced forward by around a hundred metres before giving up (as did most other tourists there who were not so spiritually enlightened). We've heard of some travellers taking more than nine hours to reach the summit on a *poya* day. This doesn't mean you should avoid climbing on such days. In fact, we actually prefer to go up at these times. There's a real carnival-like atmosphere on the mountain, the tea shops are packed, there's plenty of colour and noise, and some Hindu pilgrims even dress up as Shiva himself – but just don't expect to have a silent moment of reflection as the sun rises above the mountains!

these classes is Rs 600 and an observation-class seat in either direction is Rs 1000.

Kitulgala

📳 036

Kitulgala is the adrenalin-sports capital of Sri Lanka. For the moment most visitors are the young and energetic of Colombo, but more and more foreign visitors are starting to discover the delights of white-water rafting, jungle trekking, birdwatching and cave exploration.

The town's other main claim to fame is that David Lean filmed his 1957 Oscar-winning epic *Bridge on the River Kwai* here. You can walk down a pathway to the filming site along the banks of the Kelaniya Ganga. The pathway is signposted on the main road, about 1km from Plantation Hotel in the direction of Adam's Peak. It is virtually impossible to head down the path without attracting an entourage of 'guides' who expect a few rupees for their troubles. If you know the film you'll recognise some of the places. Apparently the actual railway carriages used in the movie now lie at the bottom of the river, after being sunk in an explosive conclusion. You'll have to bring your own scuba gear if you want a look.

A few kilometres from Kitulgala is a large **cave system** where the 28,500-year-old remains of early humans were discovered. Many hotels in the area can arrange a guide to the caves.

🏃 Activities

White-Water Rafting

The Kelaniya Ganga, the river that runs through Kitulgala, offers the best white-water rafting in Sri Lanka. The typical trip takes in seven Class 2–3 rapids in 7km for US$30 per person, including transport and lunch. You'll be on the water for around two hours. Experienced rafters can opt for more difficult Class 4–5 rapids by special arrangement.

Almost every hotel can organise a rafting trip or there are several activity centres along the main road. All offer pretty much the same package for the same price. However not all of these places have insurance – ask to see their papers first.

Hiking

The sheer hills surrounding Kitulgala are covered in dense forest and the area makes for some decent, but quite strenuous, jungle hikes. You will need a guide, good footwear, waterproofs and leech repellent. Most hotels can arrange a guide and suggest a suitable route; Channa Perera at Rafter's Retreat is the most experienced 'jungle man' in the area and is knowledgeable on the local flora and fauna. A half-day trek costs around US$15.

Birdwatching

The area is famous for birdwatching – 23 of Sri Lanka's 27 endemic bird species inhabit the surrounding forest. Rafter's Retreat (p165) has the best ornithological guides. A half-day of birdwatching is around US$15.

🛏 Sleeping & Eating

Rafter's Retreat   HUT $$
(📳 031-228 7598; www.raftersretreat.com; s/d incl half-board US$70/85; 🛜) This old colonial bungalow serves as the hub for this rafting and birdwatching outfit that sprawls along the riverbank. The 10 ecofriendly, but slightly overpriced riverside cottages are basic but very private, and three rooms near the old house are clean and spacious with unbelievably high ceilings.

The breezy riverside restaurant is a great place for a few beers, and the food is excellent. The jovial owner Channa can organise all manner of tours and activities.

★ Royal River Resort   BOUTIQUE HOTEL $$$
(Plantation Resort; 📳 011-273 2755; www.plantationgrouphotels.com; Eduru Ella; s/d incl half-board Rs 10,650/12,900; ❄🍽) Tucked away in a haze of jungle and tea estates, 6km from Kitulgala, this place is fantastically secluded. It has four old-fashioned (but actually new) timber cottages built around, onto and into a series of boulders and waterfalls. The rooms are pleasantly decorated in colonial shades.

There's a tasty little restaurant and a pool. Ah, yes, the 'pool' – just wait until you see how amazing that is!

Borderlands   CAMPGROUND $$$
(📳 Colombo 011-441 0110; www.discoverborderlands.com; incl full board & 2 activities daily US$110; 🛜) This riverside activities camp offers kayaking, rafting, biking, hiking and more, and is run by a fun-loving, young and international crowd. Accommodation is basic and either open-sided cabanas or large tents with beds. There's a clean bathroom block and a cool terrace and dining area.

ℹ Getting There & Away

It's easy to stop at Kitulgala even if you are travelling by bus. If you're coming from Colombo

WORTH A TRIP

A TEA PLANTER'S LIFE

After ascending Adam's Peak most people take their strained leg muscles straight off for a well-deserved rest, and what better place to do so than in one of the delightful tea-estate bungalows that can be founded dotted about the beautiful countryside near Adam's Peak.

Castlereigh Family Cottages (☑051-222 3607; www.castlereighcottages.com; Norton Bridge Rd, Dikoya; half-board small cottage US$100 per person, big cottage US$45 per person) Two nicely decorated, and secluded, cottages in a lovely spot under eucalyptus trees on the edge of the Castlereigh Reservoir. The smaller cottage sleeps four and the bigger one will handle between six and twelve people (minimum six people). Resident staff prepare meals and are always on hand with a drink at just the right moment.

★**Tea Trails** (☑Colombo 011-774 5700; www.teatrails.com; Dikoya; s/d full board from US$437/600; ❋ ☎ ☒) comprises a collection of four colonial-style bungalows built for British tea-estate managers in the late 19th and early 20th centuries. Completely refurbished, and the very definition of the words 'colonial luxury', the bungalows each have four to six large bedrooms, spacious dining and living areas, and verandahs and gardens with views over rolling tea estates. Rates include Western and Sri Lankan meals prepared by a resident chef, along with complimentary wines and single-estate teas. Also on staff are an experienced guide who leads interesting hikes, and a resident tea expert. If tea's not your tipple, have a single malt whisky or end-of-day gin and tonic around your bungalow's roaring fire. The Tea Trails bungalows are one of Sri Lanka's finest places to savour the luxury and leisure of the British colonial experience.

catch the bus to Hatton and get off at Kitulgala (Rs 180). When you're over Kitulgala, flag a bus on to Hatton from the main road (Rs 70).

Kandy to Nuwara Eliya

The road from Kandy to Nuwara Eliya climbs nearly 1400m as it winds through jade-green tea plantations and past crystalline reservoirs. The 80km of asphalt allow for plenty of stops at waterfalls and tea outlets.

Kothmale Reservoir (also known as Puna Oya Reservoir) can be seen further up the road. It's part of the Mahaweli Development Project and blamed by some locals for climatic quirks in recent years. **Ramboda Falls** (108m), about 1.5km from the road, is a spectacular double waterfall.

On the A5, 5km before Nuwara Eliya, the **Labookellie Tea Factory** (⊙8am-6.30pm) is a convenient factory to visit as it's right on the roadside. Its tours are brief in the extreme and while it's worth stopping if you're passing by it's not worth the effort of a special visit. It is, though, a good place to buy well-priced quality teas and enjoy a cuppa with a slice of chocolate cake. Nearby the **Glenloch** (☑052-225 9646; www.glentea.com) and **Blue Field** (www.bluefieldteagardens.com) tea estates offer a fairly similar deal, but with slightly fewer visitors.

Approaching Nuwara Eliya, roadside stalls overflow with all sorts of vegies – a legacy of

Samuel Baker, who arrived in 1846 and made Nuwara Eliya his summer retreat. The veggie-loving Baker introduced many different varieties, including quite a few you vowed not to eat once you reached adulthood. On the steep roadside approach to Nuwara Eliya watch out for children selling flowers. If you're travelling with a loved one, you know what to do.

🛏 Sleeping & Eating

★**Lavender House**   BUNGALOW $$$
(☑052-225 9928; www.thelavenderhouseceylon. com; Hellboda Estate, Katukitula; s/d incl half-board from US$360/420; ☎ ☒) With grand old four-poster beds and portraits of Churchill hanging above the open log fire there's no doubt that this old planter's bungalow has got the colonial thing down to a tee, but it mixes this with fresh modern art, puffed-up pillows and an infinity pool with a view you won't forget.

It's not far from the Kothmale Reservoir. Advance bookings are essential.

Nuwara Eliya

☑052 / POPULATION 25,966 / ELEVATION 1889M
Nuwara Eliya is often referred to by the Sri Lankan tourist industry as 'Little England'. While most British visitors struggle to recognise modern England in Nuwara Eliya, the

toy-town ambience does have a rose-tinted English country village feel to it, though it comes with a disorienting surrealist edge. Three-wheelers whiz past red telephone boxes. Water buffalo daubed in iridescent dye for the Tamil Thai Pongal festival mingle outside a pink, brick Victorian post office. A well-tended golf course morphs into a rolling carpet of tea plantations. The dusty and bustling centre of town is a thoroughly Sri Lankan tangle, but scratch the surface a little to reveal colonial bungalows, hedgerows and pretty rose gardens.

In earlier times, Nuwara Eliya (meaning 'City of Light') was the favoured cool-climate escape for the hard-working and hard-drinking English and Scottish pioneers of Sri Lanka's tea industry. A rainy-day, misty-mountain atmosphere blankets the town from November to February so don't come expecting tropical climes. But during April's spring release, the town is crowded with domestic holidaymakers enjoying horse racing and sports-car hill climbs, and celebrating the Sri Lankan New Year. The cost of accommodation escalates wildly, and Nuwara Eliya becomes a busy, busy party town. For the rest of the year, the economy is based on tea, cool-climate vegetables, tourism and even more tea. Treat yourself to a night at one of Nuwara Eliya's colonial hotels, play a round of golf and a few frames of billiards, and escape into the town's curious combination of heritage and the here-and-now.

The town has an abundance of touts eager to get a commission for a guesthouse or hotel. They'll intercept you on arrival at Nanu Oya train station with fabricated reports of accommodation being closed, cockroach-infested or just plain crooked. Just ignore them.

History

Originally an uninhabited system of forests and meadows in the shadow of Pidurutalagala (aka Mt Pedro, 2524m), Nuwara Eliya became a singularly British creation, having been 'discovered' by colonial officer John Davy in 1819 and chosen as the site for a sanatorium a decade later.

Subsequently the district became known as a spot where 'English' vegetables and fruits, such as lettuce and strawberries, could be grown for consumption by the colonists. Coffee was one of the first crops grown here, but after the island's coffee plantations failed due to disease, the colonists switched to tea. The first tea leaves harvested in Sri Lanka were planted at Loolecondera Estate, in the mountains between Nuwara Eliya and Kandy. As tea experiments proved successful, the town quickly found itself becoming the Hill Country's 'tea capital', a title still proudly borne.

As elsewhere in the Hill Country, most of the labourers on the tea plantations were Tamils, brought from southern India by the British. Although the descendants of these 'Plantation Tamils' (as they are called to distinguish them from Tamils in northern Sri Lanka) have usually stayed out of the ethnic strife that has rocked Jaffna and the North, there have been occasional outbreaks of tension between the local Sinhalese and Tamils. The town was partially ransacked during the 1983 riots.

At nearby Hakgala, there is a significant Muslim population, but internecine strife is not a problem.

◉ Sights

Victoria Park   PARK
(admission Rs 300; ☺7am-6pm) The lovely Victoria Park at the centre of town is one of the nicest, and best maintained, town parks in South Asia, and a stroll around its manicured lawns is a pleasure indeed. The park comes alive with flowers around March to May, and August and September. It's also home to quite a number of hill-country bird species, including the Kashmir flycatcher, Indian pitta and grey tit.

At the far end of the park is a small children's playground and miniature train.

Pedro Tea Estate   TEA FACTORY
(admission Rs 200; ☺8-5pm) To see where your morning cuppa originates, head to the Pedro Tea Estate, about 3.5km east of Nuwara Eliya on the way to Kandapola. You can take a half-hour guided tour of the factory, originally built in 1885 and still packed with 19th-century engineering. However, due to the type of tea processed here (a very light tea), processing only takes place at night when it's colder, so you're unlikely to see much action.

Overlooking the plantations is a pleasant teahouse. Photography inside the factory is forbidden. A three-wheeler from Nuwara Eliya should cost Rs 350 return, including waiting time. Alternatively you could hop on a Ragalla-bound bus (Rs 13) from the main bus station in Nuwara Eliya.

Galway's Land National Park   PARK
(Hawaeliya; admission US$10 plus overall tax 12% VAT; ☺6am-5pm) One of Sri Lanka's newest

Nuwara Eliya

0 ⎯⎯ 100 m
0 ⎯⎯ 0.04 miles

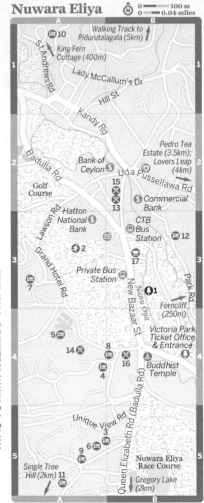

Nuwara Eliya

◎ Sights
1 Victoria Park B3

⊕ Activities, Courses & Tours
Hill Club .... (see 7)
2 Nuwara Eliya Golf Club.........................A3

⊟ Sleeping
3 Alpine Hotel A5
4 Ceybank Rest A4
5 Grand Hotel A4
6 Grosvenor Hotel......................................A5
7 Hill Club A3
8 Hotel Glendower B4
9 Single Tree Hotel A5
10 St Andrew's Hotel A1
11 Teabush Hotel A5
12 The Trevene...B3

⊗ Eating
13 De Silva Food Centre............................B2
Grand Hotel .... (see 5)
14 Grand Indian...A4
Hill Club .... (see 7)
King Prawn Restaurant .... (see 8)
15 Milano Restaurant B2
Nuwara Eliya Golf Club Dining
Room .... (see 2)
16 Restaurant Two......................................B4

⊕ Drinking & Nightlife
High Tea at the Grand .... (see 5)
Lakeview Pub .... (see 3)
17 Victoria Restaurant B3

ways, paddling a swan-shaped paddle **boat** (or a giant helicopter boat) or trotting around on a **pony** are all good reasons to devote an hour or so to Gregory Lake, at the southern end of town. There are also picnic tables, a small restaurant and a snack bar. Boat hire is from the smaller adjoining lake on the opposite side of the road from the main lake.

Lovers Leap   VIEWPOINT
From the Pedro Tea Estate (p167), take a very enjoyable 5km (round-trip) walk to Lovers Leap, an impressive waterfall.

From the tea factory, cross the main road and follow the signs to the tea manager's bungalow along the dirt road. At the first crossroads go left and at the the three-way junction take the middle path until, after about 15 minutes, you hit a dirt parking area. A foot-only track heads left through the tea gardens towards the forest and a rock face. Follow this trail and, just beyond the small Shiva shrine, you'll see the spluttering waterfalls.

(2006) and smallest (29 sq hectares) national parks, Galway's Land is a dense patch of montane forest a few kilometres east of town. It is renowned for its birdlife, including 10 Sri Lankan endemics, as well as wild boar, barking deer and other mammals. Park guides are available by donation from the park office and a 2km walking trail also leaves from here.

Gregory Lake   LAKE
(adult/child Rs 200/20, paddle boat per 30min Rs 500, motorboat per 30min Rs 1500, horse per 15min Rs 300; ⊗8am-6pm) Enjoying the paved walk-

Hakgala Gardens GARDENS
(adult/child Rs 1100/550; ⏲ 7.30am-5.30pm) The pleasantly dishevelled Hakgala Gardens, 10km southeast of Nuwara Eliya (and about 200m lower), are a peaceful retreat. Legend has it that Hanuman, the monkey god, was sent by Rama to the Himalayas to find a particular medicinal herb. He forgot which herb he was looking for and decided to bring a chunk of the Himalayas back in his jaw, hoping the herb was growing on it. The gardens grow on a rock called Hakgala, which means 'jaw-rock'. Planting season is between January and late-March and at these times the gardens don't really look their best.

The Hakgala Gardens are a short bus ride from Nuwara Eliya (take a Welimada-bound bus).

Seetha Amman Temple HINDU TEMPLE
On the way to the Hakgala Gardens, near the 83km post, is the colourful Hindu Seetha Amman Temple at Sita Eliya. It's said to mark the spot where Sita was held captive by the demon king Rawana, and where she prayed daily for Rama to come and rescue her. On the rock face across the stream are circular depressions said to be the footprints of Rawana's elephant.

Tamil wedding parties make it a point to stop here for *puja* (at 8am, 1pm, 2pm and 6pm).

🏃 Activities

The Grand Hotel, St Andrew's Hotel, the Hill Club and Hotel Glendower all have snooker rooms.

Nuwara Eliya Golf Club GOLF
(☎ 223 2835; 18 holes & green fees Rs 5588-6820, 10 holes Rs 4356-5588; ⏲ 8am-6pm) It didn't take the tea planters long to lay out land for drives and putts in their holiday town, and the golf club was founded in 1889. Spreading north from Grand Hotel Rd, Nuwara Eliya Golf Club is beautifully kept and has a retinue of languid sleeping dogs guarding more than a few of the greens.

Temporary members pay Rs 500 per day. Hire golf clubs for Rs 1500 to Rs 2500 per day and golf shoes for Rs 500 per day. As with most golf clubs a certain standard of dress applies (shirts and trousers or shorts of a 're-spectable' length). The club has a convivial wood-lined bar and a billiard room. Dinner in the **dining room** (☎ 222 2835; Nuwara Eliya Golf Club; mains Rs 450-950) includes classic bland English cuisine, such as lamb chops with mint sauce, and an increasing number of Asian dishes.

Hill Club TENNIS
(☎ 222 2653; www.hillclubsrilanka.net; per hour Rs 500) There are four clay tennis courts here. The fee includes balls and racquet hire. Try not to lob a ball into the Sri Lankan president's residence next door.

Cycling

Fat-tyre fans will find plenty of steep dirt trails radiating into the hills from the outskirts of town. Ask at the Single Tree Hotel about **mountain-bike rental** (☎ 222 3009; singletreehtl@sltnet.lk; 178 Haddon Hill Rd; per day Rs 1200). A relatively challenging, but undeniably spectacular, 10km day trip is through the verdant blanket of tea plantations to the Labookellie Tea Factory (p166). There are a few hills to climb, but the reward of swooping downhill makes it worthwhile.

Horse Racing

The **Sri Lanka Turf Club** sponsors horse racing at the 1875-vintage Nuwara Eliya Race Course. The most important event every year is the Governor's Cup race, held over the April Sinhala and Tamil New Year season. The races usually begin around 10.30am.

Hiking

Sri Lanka's highest mountain, **Pidurutalagala** (2524m), rises behind the town. On top stands the island's main TV transmitter; the peak is out of bounds to the public. You can walk about 4km up as far as a concrete water tank; beyond is a high-security zone. Follow the path from Keena Rd, along a ravine through eucalyptus forest (the town's source of firewood) and into the rare, indigenous cloud forest.

An alternative walk is up **Single Tree Hill** (2100m), which takes about 90 minutes. Walk south on Queen Elizabeth Rd, go up Haddon Hill Rd as far as the communications tower and then take the left-hand path. Guesthouses can supply you with a rudimentary map.

For longer hikes, ask at the Single Tree Hotel (p170). Guided walks in the surrounding hills cost from Rs 3000 to 5000. Staff can also arrange longer camping trips.

If you need clothing for cooler weather or trekking, head to the **market** on New Bazaar St for brand-name outdoor gear from Sri Lankan garment factories at bargain prices.

THE HILL COUNTRY NUWARA ELIYA

☞ Tours

Most hotels in town can arrange day trips by car or 4WD to Horton Plains National Park (p173). The standard price for up to five passengers is Rs 4000 (excluding park fees). One of the better 4WD tours organised by a cheap hotel is based at Single Tree Hotel. It's about an hour's drive to the park gates.

Single Tree can also arrange trips to the Pedro Tea Estate (p167) and Lovers Leap (p168) for Rs 1500. For the ultimate waterfall experience, join its waterfall day trip (Rs 3000 to 8000 per van) that takes in between six and 18 different cascades and the Labookellie Tea Factory (p166).

🛏 Sleeping

Nuwara Eliya has masses of places to stay, but many of the budget and midrange places can be on the draughty and dreary side, so it's worth being a little choosy. There's a good range of colonial-style places, but you will pay more for heritage ambience. Unlike other parts of Sri Lanka, there aren't many backpacker-oriented guesthouses. Two exceptions are the Single Tree Hotel and the excellent King Fern Cottage.

You'll need blankets to keep warm at night at almost any time of year. For a fee a few hotels will light a fire in the communal areas on cold nights – you won't find a toastier way to keep warm on a drizzly Nuwara Eliya night.

During the high season, around Sri Lankan New Year in April, rooms are three to five times their normal price. Prices also increase during long-weekend holidays and in August, when package tours descend from abroad.

Single Tree Hotel   GUESTHOUSE $
(☑ 222 3009; singletreehtl@sltnet.lk; 178 Haddon Hill Rd; s/d from Rs 3500/4500; 🛜) The most popular backpacker guesthouse in town has a main building with a sociable vibe and loads of warm timber trim. The rooms in the annex building are a little darker, but usually a lot quieter. The switched-on owners are rather tour pushy, but the tours they offer are generally pretty good.

★ Hotel Glendower   HISTORIC HOTEL $$
(☑ 222 2501; www.hotelglendower.com; 5 Grand Hotel Rd; r incl breakfast from US$85; 🛜) This rambling colonial building has bundles of ye-olde-worlde English charm to it (or a South Asian version of it anyway) with period-style rooms that have the sweet smell

of wood polish. There's a pretty garden (complete with croquet set), a cosy bar lined with bottles of spirits and a billiards room.

It's one of the best value midrange heritage options in town.

Ceybank Rest   HISTORIC HOTEL $$
(☑ 222 3855; s/d incl breakfast Rs 7800/8900; 🛜) This was once a British governor's mansion and has huge rooms from the time when smart travellers journeyed with at least three steamer trunks. The lounge area is beautiful, and the teak furniture and a fine old bar make time travel to the 19th century very easy. At current rates it's a bargain.

Grosvenor Hotel   HISTORIC HOTEL $$
(☑ 222 2307; 6 Haddon Hill Rd; s/d incl breakfast Rs 5500/6500; 🛜) It's a century since it did service as the residence of the colonial governor, and the Grosvenor, with its creaky charm, has expansive hallways, spacious rooms and period furniture that make it one of Nuwara Eliya's best-value colonial options. It's a good idea to take a look at a few rooms, as some are in decidely better condition than others.

Alpine Hotel   HOTEL $$
(☑ 222 3500; www.alpineecotravels.com; 4 Haddon Hill Rd; s/d US$82/91; ✻ @ 🛜) The exterior of this inn is all twee wood panelling and glass, and looks very impressive. The 25 rooms are decent enough but some can be musty. An open wood fire is lit in the lounge every evening, lending a cosy atmosphere to the place. There's a time-warp bar and billiards room too.

The Trevene   HISTORIC HOTEL $$
(☑ 222 2767; www.hoteltrevenenuwaraeliya.com; 17 Park Rd; r incl breakfast Rs 4000-8000; 🛜) This is a very pleasant colonial villa set in flowering gardens and filled with little hideaways where you can curl up with a book on a wet afternoon. Rooms are a mixed bag and it definitely pays to check out a few first. Bigger rooms can accommodate a family. The manager speaks fluent French.

King Fern Cottage   GUESTHOUSE $$
(☑ 077 358 6284; 203/1A St Andrews Dr; r Rs 3000-6000; @ 🛜) Hands down Nuwara Eliya's funkiest place to stay, King Fern combines immaculate, artistic rooms with huge handmade beds, warm-as-toast bedspreads and a laid-back ambience that sometimes sees the owner breaking out his drums for an after-dark, fireside session. It's all wrapped up in a timber pavilion beside a bubbling stream.

★ Ferncliff   BOUTIQUE HOTEL **$$$**
(☑ 072 231 9443; 7/10 Wedderburn Rd; r incl breakfast US180; ☎) This delightful place truly ticks all the 'unique' boxes. Set in spacious grounds, the colonial-era bungalow is straight out of a period drama – even the sprucely turned out staff hovering in the background play their parts perfectly. It is filled with furnishings that are not just reminiscent of 1899 but actually are from 1899.

Everything is perfectly maintained and there's barely a speck of dirt anywhere. All up, this is a wonderful time capsule.

St Andrew's Hotel   HERITAGE HOTEL **$$$**
(☑ 222 3031; www.jetwinghotels.com; 10 St Andrews Dr; r incl breakfast from US$135; ☎) North of town on a beautifully groomed rise overlooking the golf course, this Georgian manor house was once a planters' club. Today it's the most luxurious, and carefully renovated, of the colonial-style hotels. Highlights include a graffiti-stained cocktail bar, a library filled with dusty books and a roaring log fire, a billiards room and a decent restaurant.

The rooms themselves are a melange of the old and the new. It's worth splashing out on a deluxe room which has more character and better sound insulation. There's an in-house naturalist who leads excellent guided nature walks in and around the hotel grounds. Talking of which, the gardens, with their terraced lawns and white cast-iron furniture, seem custom-designed for an afternoon cup of tea.

Grand Hotel   HERITAGE HOTEL **$$$**
(☑ 222 2881; www.tangerinehotels.com; Grand Hotel Rd; s/d incl breakfast from US$201/214; ✳ @ ☎) Right by the golf course, this vast mock-Tudor edifice has immaculate lawns, a reading lounge and a wood-panelled billiards room. The rooms are spacious and comfortable, but if it all feels a bit plastic and forced; that's because much of it is – the original building was considerably smaller than the current one.

Book online for frequent big discounts.

Hill Club   HERITAGE HOTEL **$$$**
(☑ 222 2653; www.hillclubsrilanka.lk; 29 Grand Hotel Rd; r incl breakfast US$160-180; @ ☎) The stone-clad Hill Club is the most profound evidence of Nuwara Eliya's colonial past. The rooms look as if they've had nothing done to them since the last of the stiff-upper-lipped British colonial types checked out. While some people find the time-warp atmosphere enchanting, others just see slightly shabby and overpriced rooms.

Up until 1970 the club was reserved for British males, and one of its bars remained resolutely 'men only' until a few years ago. It's now open to Sri Lankans and, golly gosh old chap, even ladies are allowed in. Tennis courts are available to guests and nonguests, and the lawns and gardens are immaculate. Dinner at the Hill Club is a thoroughly retro and unique experience. Temporary members pay Rs 100 per day.

Teabush Hotel   HISTORIC HOTEL **$$$**
(☑ 222 2345; www.teabush-hotel.com; 29 Haddon Hill; s/d incl breakfast from US$110/120; ☎) Lots of antique furniture pepper this 140-year-old tea planter's bungalow. The heritage charm of the shared, public areas is tempered by slightly more prosaic rooms, but the restaurant views are superb. The cheaper rooms in the old building have more character than those in the new block.

Around Nuwara Eliya

Stashed away among the tea estates around Nuwara Eliya are a couple of fabulous places to stay. Ideally you'll have your own transport if staying at one of these.

★ Heritance Tea Factory   BOUTIQUE HOTEL **$$$**
(☑ 555 5000; www.heritancehotels.com; Kandapola; r incl breakfast from US$176; ☎) One of Sri Lanka's most original hotels, the Heritance, which is built into and around a century old tea factory, blurs the line between museum and luxury hotel. Much of the factory machinery is still in situ and has been incorporated into the design of the hotel. Rooms are stately and plush, activities numerous and the service first rate.

There are two different resturants serving some of the best meals in the hills. One of

---

DON'T MISS

HIGH TEA AT THE GRAND

For the best tea experience in town don't miss afternoon **High Tea at the Grand** (☑ 222 2881; www.tangerinehotels.com; Grand Hotel, Grand Hotel Rd; Rs 800; ⊙ 3.30-6pm). At 3.30pm sharp, waiters in white livery unveil a bulging buffet of perfectly groomed triangular sandwiches and dainty cakes. These are washed down with a vast selection of different teas. High tea is served either outside on the lawn or in the semi-open-air tea lounge.

LOCAL KNOWLEDGE

SOMERSET STRAWBERRIES

Eight kilometres out of Nuwara Eliya town, on the road to Hatton, is the village of Radella. Here you'll find the **Somerset Farm** (☎ 567 5550; Somerset Radella; ⊙ 7.30am-5.30pm) shop and cafe where those in the know buy fresh-from-the-farm strawberries, as well as jam and tea. There are some outdoor tables at which to eat and enjoy them at.

the resturants is inside an old steam-train carriage, which still has its whistle and kind of trundles along the line.

The family rooms, playground, pony rides and babysitting service make it a good bet for those travelling with children.

The Heritance is a 30-minute drive northeast of Nuwara Eliya.

Langdale HOMESTAY $$$
(☎ 492 4959; www.amayaresorts.com; Radetta, Nanu Oya; s/d incl breakfast US$162/172; 🛜 🞸) For the ultimate in luxury 'homestay' try this offering from the Amaya chain. It's a converted old colonial building set, of course, in a tea estate. It all feels like a very posh homestay and the service is first rate, but considering the price we feel it does somewhat lack that 'wow' factor you'd expect. It's 9km west of town on the road to Hatton.

🍴 Eating

For lunch there are plenty of good, cheap options in town, but for dinner you'll probably want to eat at your guesthouse or at one of the ritzier hotel eateries.

Milano Restaurant SRI LANKAN $
(94 New Bazaar St; mains Rs 180-380; ⊙ 7.30am-10pm) With friendly service and a reliable menu of Sri Lankan, Western and Chinese dishes, this is a decent place for a cheap meal in the town centre. After a curry treat yourself to some of their sweet, baked goodies.

Restaurant Two SRI LANKAN $
(Grand Hotel Rd; mains Rs 200-500) Cheap, simple, semi-open-air place with a quiet setting next to the golf course. The food here can be fiery – you've been warned!

De Silva Food Centre SRI LANKAN $
(90 New Bazaar St; mains Rs 200-350; ⊙ 7am-10pm) This inexpensive eatery located along a busy main street serves Sri Lankan and Chinese fare as well as what it claims are the 'town's best burgers'. A few vegetarian *rotti* make a good lunchtime snack.

★ Grand Indian INDIAN $$
(Grand Hotel Rd; mains Rs 600-700; ⊙ 11am-11pm) Far and away the town's favourite restaurant, so much so that in the evenings you often have to wait for a table. The food here is the rich, delicious fare of northern India. The service is fast and efficient, and there's an energetic buzz about the place.

King Prawn Restaurant CHINESE $$
(Hotel Glendower, 5 Grand Hotel Rd; mains Rs 500-800; ⊙ noon-2pm & 6-10pm) Chinese is the overriding culinary influence here, all delivered in a dining room transplanted from 1930s England. Thai flavours also linger in some of the dishes, and there's a good array of seafood on offer. While the food isn't that memorable, it does make a nice change from rice and curry.

The menu prices don't include the raft of different taxes.

Hill Club INTERNATIONAL $$$
(☎ 222 2653; 29 Grand Hotel Rd; set menu US$24; ⊙ 7-10.30pm) Dinner at the Hill Club is an event in itself. The five-course set menu focuses on traditional English meals such as roast beef with all the trimmings. The whole thing is carried off with faded colonial panache. Men must wear a tie and jacket; there's a small selection on hand. Women must also dress in a formal manner.

The food doesn't live up to everyone's expectations, especially with such a relatively high price tag, but it's still a great experience. Come along an hour or so before dinner for a drink in the Hill Club's bars. It was only a few years ago that the 'Casual Bar' was resolutely enforced as 'men only'. Now all gender variations are welcome, provided you are smartly dressed, but we have heard reports that Sri Lankans of a certain 'class' are not always allowed. If you're not staying the night here, you'll have to pay a Rs 100 temporary joining fee.

Grand Hotel INTERNATIONAL $$$
(☎ 222 2881; Grand Hotel Rd; dinner Rs 2900) Very high-quality, five-course Asian and Western dinners are dished up by spiffy waiters serenaded by a grand piano. Although the restaurant is open to nonguests, during very busy periods hotel guests get priority. Smart, formal dress only.

🍷 Drinking

Victoria Restaurant CAFE

(off New Bazaar St, Victoria Park; ⊘7am-8pm) A relaxing place for an afternoon tea, or one of the many different coffees, after a bird-watching and plant-admiring session at Victoria Park. It also does simple meals (Rs 300) all served with a prime park view (and quite a lot of road noise).

Lakeview Pub BAR

(Alpine Hotel, 4 Haddon Hill Rd; ⊘4pm-late) Moody, dark timber, billiards, darts and a lakeview terrace make this a popular spot.

ℹ️ Information

Bank of Ceylon (Lawson Rd) Has an ATM and exchange facilities.

Commercial Bank (Park Rd) Has an ATM and exchange facilities.

Hatton National Bank (Badulla Rd) Has an ATM and exchange facilities.

Post Office (Badulla Rd)

ℹ️ Getting There & Away

BUS

The government CTB bus station is by the main roundabout in the town centre. The private bus station is just up the road. There are buses to/from the following:

DESTINATION	FARE	TIME
Colombo	normal Rs 240, intercity express Rs 480	6hr
Ella	Rs 150	3hr
Haputale	Rs 110	2½hr
Kandy	normal Rs 120, intercity express Rs 220	4hr
Matara	Rs 360	7-8hr, morning departures only
Welimada	Rs 80	1hr

TRAIN

Nuwara Eliya is served by the Nanu Oya train station, 9km along the road towards Hatton and Colombo. Most Nuwara Eliya accommodation will pick you up – often for free – if you have already booked. A taxi from the station costs from Rs 1500 to 2000 and a three-wheeler is Rs 800. At time of research, major roadworks were taking place on the road between the station and town. This was making travel between the two very

bumpy and slow, hence the high cost of transport. Once the work is over transport costs to the station are likely to fall dramatically.

Eastbound trains towards Badulla leave at 9.30am, 12.45pm, 3pm and 3.55pm. Westbound trains towards Kandy and Colombo leave at 9.25am, noon and 5.30pm.

Badulla 2nd/3rd class Rs 140/80

Bandarawela 2nd/3rd class Rs 90/50

Colombo 2nd/3rd class Rs 450/270

Ella 2nd/3rd class Rs 110/60

Haputale 2nd/3rd class Rs 80/40

Hatton 2nd/3rd class Rs 60/30

Kandy 2nd/3rd class Rs 160/90

A 1st-class observation carriage seat is Rs 1000 no matter where you get on or off. The limited number of seats in this class are in high demand so try to book ahead. Not all trains have a 1st-class carriage. A 2nd-class reserved seat is Rs 600 to anywhere between Kandy and Badulla.

Horton Plains National Park & World's End

This is one of the few national parks in Sri Lanka where visitors can walk on their own (on designated trails). Although the main focus of the park is on World's End don't underestimate the joy of the walk across the grassland plains. Longer and more challenging walks up Mt Kirigalpotta and Mt Totapola are also possible.

👁️ Sights

⭐ **Horton Plains National Park** PARK

(adult/child Rs 1895/1011, jeep Rs 250, service charge per group Rs 1011 plus overall tax VAT 12%; ⊘6am-6pm) Horton Plains is a beautiful, silent, strange world with some excellent hikes in the shadows of Sri Lanka's second- and third-highest mountains, Kirigalpotta (2395m) and Totapola (2357m). The 'plains' form an undulating plateau over 2000m high, covered by wild grasslands and interspersed with patches of thick forest, rocky outcrops, filigree waterfalls and misty lakes. The surprising diversity of the landscape is matched by the wide variety of wildlife (although many of the larger animals are very elusive).

Get there for a 7am start and you may be lucky enough to have the paths to yourself. The plateau comes to a sudden end at World's End, a stunning escarpment that plunges 880m.

➡️ **Wildlife**

As an important watershed and catchment for several year-round rivers and streams, the Horton Plains hosts a wide range of wildlife. There are a few leopards, sambar deer and wild boar about, but you'd be very lucky to see the boar or leopard. The shaggy bear monkey (or purple-faced langur) is sometimes seen in the forest on the Ohiya road, and occasionally in the woods around World's End (listen for a wheezy grunt). You may also find the endemic toque macaque.

⇒ Birdwatching

The area is popular with birdwatchers. Endemic species include the yellow-eared bulbul, the fan-tailed warbler, the ashy-headed babbler, the Ceylon hill white-eye, the Ceylon blackbird, the Ceylon white-eyed arrenga, the dusky-blue flycatcher and the Ceylon blue magpie. Birds of prey include the mountain hawk-eagle.

⇒ Plants

A tufty grass called *Chrysopogon* covers the grasslands, while marshy areas are home to copious bog moss (sphagnum). The umbrella-shaped, white-blossomed keena (*Calophyllum*) stand as the main canopy over montane forest areas. The stunted trees and shrubs are draped in lichen and mosses. Another notable species is *Rhododendron zeylanicum*, which has blood-red blossoms. The poignant purple-leafed *Strobilanthes* blossoms once after five years, and then dies.

World's End   VIEWPOINT

The walk to World's End is 4km, but the trail loops back to Baker's Falls (2km) and continues back to the entrance (another 3.5km). The 9.5km round trip takes a leisurely three hours. Unless you get there early the view from World's End is often obscured by mist, particularly during the rainy season from April to September.

All you can expect to see from World's End after around 9am is a swirling white wall. The early morning (between 6am and 10am) is the best time to visit, before the clouds roll in. That's when you'll spy toy-town, tea-plantation villages in the valley below, and an unencumbered view south towards the coast.

Try to avoid doing this walk on Sundays and public holidays, when it can get crowded. And despite the signs, weekend groups of young Sri Lankan guys will do their utmost to make noise and inadvertently scare away the wildlife.

Guides at the national-park office expect about Rs 750. There's no set fee for volunteer guides, but expect to donate a similar amount. Some guides are well informed on the area's flora and fauna, and solo women travellers may want to consider hiring one for safety. Two guides who are genuinely enthusiastic about the park and unusually knowledgeable on the area's fauna and flora are **Mr Nimal Herath** (☑ 077 618 9842; hrthnimal@gmail.com) and **Mr Kaneel Rajanayeka** (☑ 077 215 9583; nuwaraeliyatrekkingclub@hotmail.com), who is just Raja to friends. Both normally work as guide/drivers through the Single Tree Hotel in Nuwara Eliya, but are available on a freelance basis as well.

Wear strong and comfortable walking shoes, a hat and sunglasses. Bring sunscreen, food and water. Ask your guesthouse to prepare a breakfast package for you, and reward yourself with an alfresco brekkie once you reach World's End. The weather can change very quickly on the plains – one minute it can be sunny and clear, the next chilly and misty. Bring a few extra layers of warm clothing (it's very cold up here at 7am).

It is forbidden to leave the paths. There are no safety rails around World's End and there have been a couple of accidents where people have fallen to their deaths. If you have young children with you keep a very firm grip on them as you approach the cliff edge.

Farr Inn   LANDMARK

A local landmark, Farr Inn was a hunting lodge for high-ranking British colonial officials, but now incorporates a basic but expensive cafe and visitor centre with displays on the flora, fauna and geology of the park. A small souvenir stand nearby has books on the park's flora and fauna.

It can be reached by road from Ohiya or Nuwara Eliya and is a three-hour walk uphill from Ohiya train station. It is situated next to the car park from which almost all visitors start the walk to World's End.

☞ Tours

Almost every guesthouse in Nuwara Eliya and Haputale operates trips to Horton Plains and World's End. Expect to pay around Rs 4000 per van and guide (park fees not included).

🛏 Sleeping & Eating

There are two basic Department of Wildlife Conservation bungalows in which you can stay: Giniheriya Lodge and Mahaeliya Lodge. Foreign tourists stay here so rarely (read: never) that nobody appears to have any idea what the rates are. Enquiries should be made through the **Department of Wildlife Conservation** (☑ 011-288 8585; 382 New Kandy Rd, Malambe) in Colombo.

SIR THOMAS LIPTON – ONE VERY CANNY SCOTSMAN

His name lives on in the hot-beverage aisle of your local supermarket, but Sir Thomas Lipton was a major success in business even before he became the biggest player in the global tea industry.

From 1870 to 1888 he grew his parents' single grocery shop in Glasgow to a nationwide chain of 300 stores. Recognising the potential of tea, he cannily bypassed the traditional wholesale markets of London, and went straight to the source by purchasing his own tea plantations in Sri Lanka. His network of 300 stores provided him with guaranteed distribution to sell tea at lower prices to an untapped working-class market. It also inspired the winning advertising slogan, 'Direct from the tea gardens to the tea pot'.

Lipton's planet-spanning ambition wasn't only limited to trade. In 1909 he donated the Thomas Lipton Trophy for an international football competition 21 years before the first World Cup, and he was tireless in his (unsuccessful) attempts to win yachting's America's Cup. His well-publicised interest in the two sports ensured his brand became a household name on both sides of the Atlantic.

ⓘ Information

National Park Office (⊙ 6am-6pm) This is where you buy entrance tickets. Last tickets are sold at 4pm. It's near Farr Inn.

ⓘ Getting There & Away

Most people come from Nuwara Eliya, a trip taking about an hour one way (around Rs 4000 return by van). If taking a tour from Nuwara Eliya you can ask to be dropped afterwards at Pattipola train station to catch the afternoon train to Haputale and Ella (1.20pm; to Ella Rs 90).

You can also get to Farr Inn from Haputale. It takes about 1½ hours by road (Rs 4500 return). From Ohiya the road rises in twists and turns through forest before emerging on the open plains. Keep your eyes peeled for monkeys.

Belihul Oya

☑ 045

Belihul Oya is a pretty hillside region worth passing through on your way to or from the Hill Country – it's 35km from Haputale and 57km from Ratnapura. From here you can walk up to Horton Plains, a seriously strenuous, seven-hour return trip. The path starts from near the Bambarakanda Falls and it's a very good idea to arrange a guide through one of the towns hotels.

◉ Sights

Bambarakanda Falls   WATERFALL
About 14km towards Haputale, near Kalupahana, are the Bambarakanda Falls. Ask the bus driver to let you off at Kalupahana Junction. From the main road it's another Rs 500 by three-wheeler up a barely-there track. A return ride with an hour wait costs Rs 800. From the town centre it's Rs 800 one way.

At 240m, the Bambarakanda Falls are the highest in Sri Lanka. March and April are the best months for viewing the falls, but any visit after heavy rainfall should be worthwhile. At other times the water may be reduced to a disappointing trickle.

🛏 Sleeping

**Bambarakanda
Holiday Resort**   GUESTHOUSE $
(☑ 057-357 5699; www.bambarakanda.com; r incl full board Rs 2500-4000) A few hundred metres before the Bambarakanda Falls is this rustic guesthouse. If you're looking to get off the map for a few days, here's your chance. The rooms are very basic and a bit dingy, but with a setting like this it hardly matters because you'll be outside the whole time enjoying nature in all its glory.

Ideally you'll need your own transport to get here.

Belihul Oya Rest House   HISTORIC HOTEL $$
(☑ 052-280 156; www.ceylonhotelscorporation.com; Ratnapura-Haputale Rd; s/d incl breakfast US$61/67; ✱ 🅰) This resthouse is pleasantly situated next to the crashing river. It has very faded rooms, but the place as a whole has a slight colonial vibe to it and the garden setting is enjoyable. Watch out for the monkeys and don't leave windows open.

Haputale

☑ 057 / POPULATION 5238 / ELEVATION 1580M

Perched at the southern edge of the Hill Country, the largely Tamil town of Haputale clings to a long, narrow mountain ridge with the land falling away steeply on both sides. On a clear day you can view the south coast

Haputale

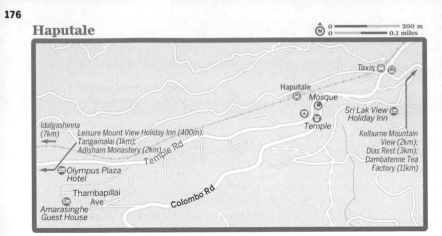

from this ridge, and at night the Hambantota lighthouse pulses in the distance. On a not-so-clear day, great swaths of mist cling magnetically to the hillsides. Either way, it's a spectacular part of the country.

The town centre itself is a dusty ribbon of traffic, three-wheelers and small-scale commerce. But take a short walk and you'll be rewarded with extraordinary views. The railway hugs one side of the ridge in a minor victory for 19th-century engineering.

Haputale now mainly shows the influence of the Sinhalese and Tamil cultures, but the legacy of the British tea planters also lives on. Tea estates blanket the hillsides, punctuated by graceful planters' bungalows, all enveloped in a damp and heavy climate that must have made the British settlers feel right at home. The pretty Anglican church (St Andrew's) on the Bandarawela road has a graveyard filled with poignant memories of earlier times.

In recent years Haputale's popularity with tourists seems to have mysteriously diminished, but the town has an array of good, cheap accommodation and makes an excellent base for visiting Horton Plains National Park, exploring other places in the area or just taking pleasant walks in cool mountain air. It also has a more authentic Sri Lankan air to it than that of nearby Ella and its international traveller feel. Guesthouses arrange vans and 4WDs to Horton Plains for Rs 4500.

See the privately run website www.haputale.de for more information.

⊙ Sights & Activities

★ Dambatenne Tea Factory   TEA FACTORY
(admission Rs 250; ⊙7.30am-6pm) A few tea factories in this area are happy to have vis-

itors. The most popular, Dambatenne, was built in 1890 by Sir Thomas Lipton, one of the most famous figures in tea history. The tour through the works is an education on the processes involved in the fermentation, rolling, drying, cutting, sieving and grading of tea. The tea-factory tour here is probably the most comprehensive around, and afterwards you can sip on a cuppa. On Sundays no processing takes place so there's little to see.

Although it's 11km from Haputale, the factory is easily accessible. Get a bus from the bus station to Bandarawela and get off at the tea factory (buses both ways are every 30 minutes, Rs 23). A three-wheeler there and back costs between Rs 500 to 600.

★ Adisham Monastery   MONASTERY
(adult/child Rs 100/50; ⊙9am-12.30pm & 1.30-4.30pm Sat & Sun, poya days & school holidays) This beautiful Benedictine monastery once belonged to tea planter Sir Thomas Lester Villiers. To recreate his English lifestyle he developed some English country-cottage gardens which are still enchanting visitors today. Inside, visitors are allowed to see the living room and library, which is filled from floor to ceiling with dusty tomes – the *Love Affairs of Mary Queen of Scots* was the raciest book we could find. If that makes you blush try the *History of the Tory Party 1640–1714*.

Today, Adisham is one of only 18 monasteries in the world belonging to the Sylvestrine Congregation, a suborder of the Benedictine fraternity founded in the 13th century.

There's a small shop selling produce from the monastery's lovely gardens and orchards. Buy some real strawberry jam or wild guava jelly to enliven your next breakfast.

The monastery is about 3km west of Haputale. Follow Temple Rd along the ridge until you reach the sign at the Adisham turnoff. A taxi should cost Rs 500 return, including waiting time. Before you reach Adisham the road passes through **Tangamalai**, a bird sanctuary and nature reserve, but there are no facilities.

Hiking

For more spectacular views – weather permitting – take the train to **Idalgashinna**, 8km west of Haputale. Walk back beside the train tracks, enjoying a spectacular view with the terrain falling away on both sides.

Near the Dambatenne tea factory, the **Lipton's Seat** lookout rivals the views from World's End (and it's free). The Scottish tea baron Sir Thomas Lipton used to survey his burgeoning empire from here. Take the signed narrow paved road from the tea factory and climb about 7km through lush tea plantations to the lookout. From the tea factory the ascent should take about 2½ hours. The earliest bus leaves Haputale at 6.30am. Look forward to the company of Tamil tea pickers going off to work as you walk uphill to Lipton's Seat.

Some visitors hike along the train lines from Haputale to **Pattipola** (14km, an all-day hike), the highest train station in Sri Lanka. From Pattipola you can continue via foot or taxi to Ohiya train station, and from there to the Horton Plains.

Sleeping & Eating

Accommodation in Haputale represents fantastic value compared with nearby, busier tourist towns. You're best off eating in your guesthouse, but there are a number of OK places for short eats, dosas (paper-thin pancakes), *rotti*, rice and curry in the town centre.

Sri Lak View Holiday Inn HOTEL $
(226 8125; www.srilakviewholidayinn.com; Sherwood Rd; s/d incl breakfast from Rs 1200/1500; @) Haputale's best-value place to stay combines spotless rooms split across two buildings. Views stretch a few hundred kilometres from the decent restaurant and from some rooms. Multiple reader recommendations mean they must be doing something right. It has plenty of traveller services too. It's worth booking ahead.

Leisure Mount View Holiday Inn GUESTHOUSE $
(226 8327; 163/3 Temple Rd; s incl breakfast Rs 1200-1800; d Rs 2000-2500;) This is a good-value new guesthouse a couple of kilometres west of the town centre. The older, cheaper and more basic rooms are in the family house, while the newly constructed block adjoining the house contains very nice 'deluxe' rooms with beds decorated in flower petals and amazing towel art creations. Views are breathtaking.

Light-sensitive sleepers (or privacy seekers) should know that there are no curtains at the windows. There's a cosy in-house restaurant.

Amarasinghe Guest House HOMESTAY $
(226 8175; Thambapillai Ave; r Rs 2500;) This simple, well-run guesthouse in a tranquil location has been in business for decades. Some people report a somewhat cold welcome. The owner, Mr Amarasinghe, will pick you up from the train station at no charge. If you walk, follow the directions to Bawa Guest House but continue on down the flight of steps, turn left and it's 10m away.

Dias Rest GUESTHOUSE $
(White Monkey; 568 1027; Thotulagala; r/cottages Rs 1600/2000; @) Dias Rest is surrounded by a tea plantation 3km east of the train station. It has a local atmosphere, fairly basic (and chilly) rooms and a family cottage – all with superb views that rival that of World's End on a clear day. The owner is an experienced guide and can advise on interesting local treks.

Olympus Plaza Hotel HOTEL $$
(226 8544; www.olympusplazahotel.com; Temple Rd; s/d incl breakfast Rs 5600/8100;) This multistorey place brings a snazzy feel to sleepy Haputale, and its modern rooms with abstract art on the walls, thick mattresses, hot-water showers and stellar views (from most rooms) offer good value if you're hanging out for a few away-from-home comforts. On weekends it's a popular wedding venue.

★Kelburne Mountain View BOUTIQUE HOTEL $$$
(011-257 3382, 226 8029; www.kelburnemountainview.com; Kelburne Tea Estate; bungalows Rs 19,000-21,000) About 2km east of Haputale train station, Kelburne is a wonderful spot to relax for a few days. It has accommodation in immaculately renovated former tea-planter's bungalows and dapper white-suited waiters attending to your needs. What really makes the property stand out though are the beautiful flower gardens, the surrounding tea estates and stupendous views.

Bungalows sleep between four and six people, which makes this a real bargain if travelling as a group or family. Meals are also available from a resident cook. Advance bookings are essential.

Melheim Resort BOUTIQUE HOTEL $$$
(☑Colombo 011-585 0227; www.melheimresort.com; Lower Blackwood, Beragala; s/d incl breakfast US$140/150; ❄🛜🏊) This upmarket lodge, built into and around giant granite boulders, has great views over the burning lowlands (although not as good as those from Haputale town) and large, very plush cottages. There's a nice pool and good restaurant, and the bath towels are folded and moulded into towel-art elephants, swans and other creatures, which almost make it worth the cost alone! It's 8km downhill from Haputale and 2km from the village of Beragala.

❶ Getting There & Away

BUS
Destinations include Bandarawela (Rs 32, one hour) and Nuwara Eliya (Rs 99, 3½ hours). For Ella, change in Bandarawela. To get to Tangalla or Embilipitiya, change in Wellawaya (Rs 93). All buses depart from the town centre opposite the Risara Bakery.

TRAIN
Haputale is on the Colombo–Badulla line, so you can travel directly by train to and from Kandy or Nanu Oya (for Nuwara Eliya). A 1st-class observation ticket is Rs 1000 for anywhere between Badulla and Nanu Oya and Rs 1250 from Nanu Oya to Kandy. A 2nd-class reservation is Rs 600 to any of the following locations.

East bound trains to Ella and Badulla leave at 12.05pm and 2.15pm. West bound trains towards Kandy leave at 10.25am and 2.25pm.

DESTINATION	FARE	TIME
Bandarawela	2nd/3rd class Rs 20/15	30min
Colombo	Rs 330/180	8½-9hr
Ella	Rs 50/25	1hr
Kandy	Rs 210/115	5½hr
Nanu Oya	Rs 80/40	1½hr
Ohiya	Rs 30/20	40min

TAXI
Private minibus taxis gather in the town centre and will take you to Horton Plains (Rs 4500 return trip including waiting time), Ella (Rs 2000) and Uda Walawe National Park (Rs 6500).

Bandarawela
☑ 057 / POPULATION 7880 / ELEVATION 1230M
Bandarawela, 10km north of Haputale but noticeably warmer, is a busy market town that makes a good base for exploring the surrounding area. Due to its agreeable climate, it's a popular area to retire to. Each Sunday morning the town has a lively market. Otherwise Bandarawela has little to attract tourists. It's a good transport hub if you're heading east or further into the Hill Country.

Bandarawela ⊛ N 0 — 200 m / 0 — 0.1 miles

Bandarawela

⬤ Sleeping
1 Bandarawela Hotel B2

⊗ Eating
2 Mlesna Tea Centre................................A2

❶ Transport
3 Buses to Ella, Badulla & Wellawaya..B2
4 Buses to Haputale & Colombo............B2
5 Buses to Welimada............................B2
6 Long-Distance Buses A1
7 Taxis B2
8 Taxis B3
9 Three-Wheeler Stand..........................B2

◉ Sights & Activities

Dowa Temple   BUDDHIST TEMPLE
(Map p184; Badulla Rd; admission Rs 100) The highlight of the charming Dowa Temple, 6km east of town, is a 4m-high standing Buddha cut into the rock face. The walls of the adjacent cave shrine, carved from solid rock, are covered with excellent Sri Lankan-style Buddhist murals. It's said that King Valagamba (Vattajamini Ahhya) took refuge here in the 1st century BC during his 14-year exile from Anuradhapura. Legend also has it that a secret underground tunnel stretches from this temple all the way to Kandy.

The temple, which is on the road to Badulla, is easy to miss (and the tunnel even easier) if you're coming by bus, so ask the bus conductor to tell you when to alight. A three-wheeler or taxi from Bandarawela should cost Rs 500 return.

🛏 Sleeping & Eating

★ Bandarawela Hotel   HISTORIC HOTEL **$$$**
(📷 222 2501; www.aitkenspencehotels.com; 14 Welimada Rd; s/d incl breakfast US$90/106; 🛜) Around 80 years ago they wisely stopped updating the furniture at this venerable tea planters' club. Now, in the 21st century, this hotel is a jolly fine show. So don your pith helmet, walk shorts, gloves and long socks and ease into one of the relax-at-all-costs easy chairs.

There's nothing forced about this place. It's a genuine time capsule and as such is high on atmosphere but low on modern amenities. For colonial buffs it's worth the trip to Bandarawela alone.

Mlesna Tea Centre   CAFE **$**
(Welimada Rd; tea Rs 70-100; ⊘ 8.30am-5.30pm Mon-Fri, to 6pm Sat & Sun) You're deep in tea country so buy some at this superb tea shop and cafe, which has high-quality leaves from across the hills and a selection of daily cakes.

ℹ Getting There & Away

BUS
Buses run to the following destinations:

DESTINATION	FARE	TIME
Badulla	Rs 64	1¼hr
Ella	Rs 34	30min
Haputale	Rs 32	30min
Nuwara Eliya	Rs 77	2¼hr
Welimada	Rs 53	1hr

TRAIN
Bandarawela is on the Colombo–Badulla railway line. First-class observation tickets through the hills cost Rs 1000 for anywhere between Nanu Oya and Badulla. From Nanu Oya to Kandy is Rs 1250. A reserved 2nd-class ticket is Rs 600.

Trains heading east to Ella and Badulla leave at 12.50pm and 2.45pm.

Trains heading west towards Kandy leave at 7.15am, 9.57am and 1.10pm.

DESTINATION	FARE	TIME
Badulla	2nd/3rd class Rs 60/30	1½hr
Colombo	2nd/3rd class Rs 340/185	8-9hr
Ella	2nd/3rd class Rs 30/15	30min
Haputale	2nd/3rd class Rs 20/15	25min
Kandy	2nd/3rd class Rs 230/125	6hr
Nanu Oya (for Nuwara Eliya)	2nd/3rd class Rs 90/50	2-2½hr

Ella
📷 057

Welcome to everyone's favourite hill-country village and the place to ease off the travel accelerator with a few leisurely days resting in your choice of some of the country's best guesthouses. The views through Ella Gap are stunning, and on a clear night you can even spy the subtle glow of the Great Basses lighthouse on Sri Lanka's south coast. Don't be too laid-back though; definitely make time for easygoing walks through tea plantations to temples, waterfalls and viewpoints. After building up a hiking-inspired appetite, look forward to Sri Lanka's best home-cooked food and the minisplurge of an extended Ayurvedic treatment.

In recent years the popularity of Ella has soared and seemingly every month yet another new guesthouse or hotel opens. Sadly, some of these newer hotels have been built in a hurry by people with little knowledge of the desires and requirements of the average foreign tourist in Ella, resulting in some large, multistorey, cheaply made blots of ugliness scarring the hills of the village. Fortunately, the rumour of a cable-car running between Little Adam's Peak and Ella Rock does (we dearly hope) appear to be just a rumour.

Ella

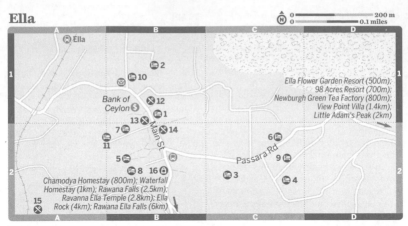

Ella

😴 Sleeping

1 Dream Café Guest House	B1
2 Eeshani Guest Inn	B1
3 Freedom Guest Inn	C2
4 Green Hill	C2
5 Hill Top Guest House	B2
6 Little Folly	C2
7 Okreech Cottages	B2
8 Rawana Holiday Resort	B2
9 Sita's Heaven	C2
10 Sun Top Inn	B1
11 Zion View	B2

🍽 Eating

12 Cafe Chill (Nescoffee Shop)	B1
13 Curd Shop	B1
14 Down Town Rotti Hut	B2
Dream Café	(see 1)
15 Garden View Restaurant	A2
Little Folly Restaurant	(see 6)

🛍 Shopping

16 T-Sips	B2

👁 Sights & Activities

Newburgh Green Tea Factory   TEA FACTORY
(Map p184; Newburgh Tea Estate, Passara Rd; adult/child Rs 300/free; ⊙8am-6pm Mon-Sat) The tours at this green-tea factory are fairly rushed, but you can make interesting comparisons to those factories producing black tea. Newburgh is owned by Finlays, one of the world's larger tea producers, and there is a notable difference in how the factory is run and organised compared to the private factories. It's a half-hour walk from town.

Hiking

Ella is a great place for walking. Most accommodation can give you a hand-drawn map of local paths. Kick off with a stroll to what is locally dubbed **Little Adam's Peak**. Go down the Passara road until you get to the Ella Flower Garden Resort on your right, just past the 1km post. Follow the track to the left; Little Adam's Peak is the biggest hill on your right and is clearly signposted. Take the second path that turns off to your right and follow it to the top of the hill. Part of this path passes through a tea estate. The approximately 4.5km round trip takes about 45 minutes each way. The final 20 minutes or so is uphill, but otherwise it's an easy walk. Get an early start from your guesthouse – around 7am – and you'll meet Tamil families heading off to work in the tea plantations along the way. From atop Little Adam's Peak, waterfalls and a couple of tea factories shimmer from out of the mist that's often welded persistently to the surrounding hills.

Walking to **Ella Rock** is more demanding and a guide is a very good idea (it's easy to miss the turn-off from the railway track and get lost in the forest that covers the upper slopes). Most guesthouses can organise a guide for Rs 1500 per group. It's a three- to four-hour round trip and the views from the top are extraordinary. If you do decide to attempt it yourself, go in a group. Follow the train tracks in the direction of Banarawela for 45 minutes. Just after the black bridge there's a small shrine on the left. Turn left a metre or so after this and down a short embankment. Cross a concrete bridge over the Rawana Falls and then go right up the dirt track immediately after the bridge. Now start climbing uphill. From here on it's easy to get lost, especially on misty or cloudy days. Watch for the occasional faded blue way-marker. There's often someone selling overpriced tea and other drinks at the summit.

For an easier walk (2.5km from town) without a guide, follow the route to Ella Rock but only go as far as the small **Rawana Falls**.

🛏 Sleeping

Touts might approach you on the train with tales that the hotel of your choice is too expensive, closed down or rat-infested. In fact, Ella has a high standard of accommodation (but higher prices than many other Hill Country towns), especially for guesthouses, so they're most likely telling fibs.

During the peak Christmas/New Year period, prices can double from the standard high-season prices.

★**Ella Flower Garden Resort**   GUESTHOUSE **$**
(Map p184; ✆205 0480; www.ellaresort.com; Passara Rd; s/d Rs 3000/4000; ☎) Appropriately named, this place, which sits right beside the trail to Little Adam's Peak, is a horticultural paradise with blooming flower gardens all around and cages filled with paraquets, budgies and cooing love birds. Rooms are spacious, well maintained and very good value, and the family who runs it always has time for a good chat.

Sita's Heaven   GUESTHOUSE **$**
(Map p180; ✆205 0020; off Passara Rd; r Rs 2500-4000; ☎) Down a quiet forested lane five minutes' walk from central Ella, Sita's Heaven offers the best of both worlds, with privacy and great views. It's the kind of place where visitors end up staying longer than they planned.

Sun Top Inn   GUESTHOUSE **$**
(Map p180; ✆222 8673; suntopinn@yahoo.com; r incl breakfast Rs 3500-4500; ☎) The owners of this sunset-orange guesthouse extend such a warm welcome you might feel they've been waiting all their lives for your arrival. Rooms are small and well-kept, and bikes are available for cycling adventures (Rs 1500 per day).

Freedom Guest Inn   GUESTHOUSE **$**
(Map p180; ✆071 689 7778; freedomguestinn@ gmail.com; 132/1 Passara Rd; r incl breakfast Rs 4000; ☎) This is a sweet little three-room homestay with comfortable mattresses and roses on the beds (yeah okay so they're plastic, but it's the thought that counts), and a pretty covered terrace to eat breakfast on.

Little Folly   CHALET **$**
(Map p180; ✆222 8817; littlefolly@hotmail.com; Passara Rd; cottages Rs 3500-4500; @☎) Quaint Little Red Riding Hood wooden cottages squirreled away in a forest that, if not the home of a big bad wolf, is probably home to a monkey or two. The cottages are airy, bright and clean and everything is made of wood. There's a top-notch roadside tea-and-cake shop.

Chamodya Homestay   HOMESTAY **$**
(Map p184; ✆357 5432; r incl breakfast Rs 3400, without bathroom Rs 2500) This is a cute, little, hidden-away homestay fringed by jungle, bathed in peace and run by a lady who barely stops smiling. There are only two rooms (one of which has a shared bathroom) so try and book ahead. A three-wheeler ride from town costs Rs 200.

Eeshani Guest Inn   HOMESTAY **$**
(Map p180; ✆222 8703; eeshaniguestinn@ yahoo.com; r Rs 2000-4500; ☎) This five-room homestay is run by an endearing old couple who'll bustle you in and sit you down for a nice cuppa and a chat. The house is filled with sepia photos of the couple's sons and daughters on their wedding days and there's a pretty flower-filled garden.

Okreech Cottages   COTTAGES **$**
(Map p180; ✆077 238 1638, 077 779 4007; r Rs 4000; ☎) We have to thank the trees for sacrificing themselves in order to create these rough-wood, timbered cottages, each of which contains two comfortable rooms of unusually good value. It's very new and so the gardens still need time to mature before the guesthouse really comes into its own. Not much English is spoken.

Rawana Holiday Resort   GUESTHOUSE **$**
(Map p180; ✆222 8794; nalankumara@yahoo.com; r Rs 2500-3500; ☎) Perched high on a hillside overlooking Ella, this family-run guesthouse contains six fairly basic balcony rooms with views, plus four less-expensive interior rooms. Good food (rice and curry Rs 500) is served in the spacious open restaurant.

★**Planters Bungalow**   HISTORIC HOTEL **$$**
(Map p184; ✆077 127 7286, 492 5902; www.planters bungalow.com; 10 Mile Post, Wellawaya Rd; d/family incl breakfast US$80/120) Just stepping over the threshold into this divine converted tea-planters bungalow, with gardens constantly on the verge of blossoming out of control, brings on a sense of total calm. The three rooms have been impeccably renovated and are filled with religious imagery, fine antiques and works of art (the English owner used to work in art publishing).

For families there's a suite-like room that can accommodate up to six people. At the time of research, a swimming pool and two more rooms were under construction. At current rates this is one of the best deals in the Hill Country.

★ **Waterfall Homestay** GUESTHOUSE **$$**
(Map p184; ☑ 567 6933; www.waterfalls-guest house-ella.com; s/d incl breakfast Rs 5000/6000; ☺ closed 10-19 Apr & first 3 days of every other month; 🛜) Delightfully secluded four-room homestay run by an Australian couple with a flair for art and design. The building melds into the hillside and offers views over the Rawana Falls, which seem to be perfectly framed by the trees surrounding the guesthouse. Each flamboyantly decorated room is different from the last and all the furnishings are of a high standard.

Memorable meals are served on the terrace. It's 1.5km from town; walk along the train tracks or up the dirt road, or a Rs 200 three-wheeler ride.

Zion View GUESTHOUSE **$$**
(Map p180; ☑ 072 785 5713; www.ella-guest house-srilanka.com; r incl breakfast US$80-95; 🛜) This is a first-rate little boutique guesthouse. Rooms have enormous glass-panel windows and Mediterranean-style terraces strewn with hammocks and easy chairs. Eating breakfast on the sunny terrace with views down through the Ella Gap is as good as Ella moments get. Owner Sena, who trained in Switzerland, and his charming wife Rashinika will go out of their way to help.

The in-house restaurant (open to outside guests) serves a delicious rice and curry (Rs 850 to 1150). If you're travelling with young kids, then this is a good bet as they have all the gear, a big play area, as well as a playmate for your little 'un. There's also a nice little Ayurveda centre. They were about to finish work on some large family apartments at the time of research.

Dream Café Guest House HOTEL **$$**
(Map p180; ☑ 222 8950; www.dreamcafeandguest houseella.com; Main Rd; d Rs 5500; 🛜) Located above the busy restaurant of the same name, this hotel's rooms are immaculate and ideal for families. Each room is more of a mini-apartment split into two bedrooms: one with a double bed and one with a couple of sofa beds. Children under 12 years are accommodated for free in their parent's room and those aged between 12 and 20 years cost Rs 1000.

View Point Villa COTTAGE **$$**
(Map p184; ☑ 077 357 3851; www.viewpoint-villa-ella.com; 8 Mile Post, Passara Rd; cottages Rs 3500-9200; 🛜) View Point, a delightfully isolated 8km from Ella, has bright villas that combine soaring ceilings with a tacky overdose – we suggest beheading the pink teddy bears found in each bed. Afterwards, clean yourself of your crime in the shower (read: space station), which comes with built-in lights, radio, massage functions, seats and even water!

A three-wheeler from Ella should cost between Rs 400 and 500. Motorcycles can be rented for Rs 1000 per day for off-the-beaten-path exploring.

Green Hill GUESTHOUSE **$$**
(Map p180; ☑ 205 0022; off Passara Rd; s/d Rs 4000/5850; 🛜) This guesthouse is a short walk from the town centre down a quiet country lane. The rooms are a little overpriced based on quality alone, but when you're on the terrace, relaxing on a bean bag and enjoying the view you probably won't care about such things. There is positive feedback about the food in the guestbook.

Hill Top Guest House GUESTHOUSE **$$**
(Map p180; ☑ 222 8780; r incl breakfast Rs 4500-5600; 🛜) Sprucely maintained rooms, views of Ella Gap to die for, and a welcoming family add up to one of Ella's best. The house is surrounded by verdant gardens, giving a sense of privacy. Good Sri Lankan meals are available.

98 Acres Resort RESORT **$$$**
(Map p184; ☑ 205 0050; www.resort98acres. com; Uva Greenland Tea Estate; s US$170-200, d US$180-210, incl breakfast; 🛜🏊) Set in tea gardens a short way out of town, the 12 stilted cottages here have fabulous views towards Little Adam's Peak. Rooms are of the earthy, rustic-luxury type and the tea-bush-hemmed swimming pool is a huge bonus. Service can be a little curt and it's perhaps not quite as special as the price tag indicates. There's an in-house spa and Ayurveda centre.

✖ Eating & Drinking

Ella's guesthouses are great places to try excellent home-cooked food, perhaps some of the best eating you'll discover in all of Sri Lanka. All the guesthouses and hotels serve meals; they ask for around four hours' notice. Especially good is the food at Rawana Holiday Resort (p181), Zion View, Waterfall Homestay and Ella Flower Garden Resort (p181) – in some guesthouse restaurants you can even join the chef in the kitchen for a rice- and curry-making class. At Rawana Holiday Resort you can look forward to around eight different dishes, including sweet-and-sour eggplant, spicy potato curry, and Rawana's signature garlic curry, made with whole cloves of the 'stinking rose' (it tastes much better than it sounds). Just let them know by midafternoon. Any of the places listed here will normally let interested visitors join them in the kitchen to learn the secrets of their culinary brilliance.

In recent years, the sleepy village has spawned a couple of places that stay open for a few beers later at night. If you've been walking in the surrounding hills and tea plantations, you've probably earned a cooling end-of-the-day ale.

Curd (made with buffalo milk) and treacle (syrup from the *kitul* palm; sometimes misnamed 'honey') is a much-touted local speciality.

Curd Shop INTERNATIONAL $
(Map p180; Main St; meals Rs 200-350; ⊙7am-9pm) Tiny hole-in-the-wall spot near the bus stand that's good for a cheap breakfast before or after an early-morning stroll to Little Adam's Peak. It's a classic backpacker-style place and, as the name suggests, is *the* spot to try curd and honey or *kotthu* (*rotti* chopped up and mixed with vegies etc). It's also handy for picking up sandwiches if you're walking.

Garden View Restaurant SRI LANKAN $
(Map p180; mains Rs 300-600; ⊙7am-10pm) A wooden treehouse-like place with friendly staff, great tasting local meals and cheap prices. You'll pass it as you walk along the railway tracks between town and Ella Rock.

Little Folly Restaurant CAFE $
(Map p180; Passara Rd; cakes Rs 150) It's 3pm, you're in the Hill Country; that must mean it's time to have a nice cup of tea and a slice of homemade lemon or chocolate cake. What better place to do so than this delightful forest-side cafe?

Down Town Rotti Hut SRI LANKAN $
(Map p180; Main St; rotti Rs 190-450; ⊙8am-9pm) The most popular place in town for a fast lunch (they also do a takeaway service) is this place. Its deliciously tasty *rottis* come in a wealth of flavours and are among the mostly amply proportioned we've ever encountered.

Cafe Chill
(Nescoffee Shop) INTERNATIONAL $$
(Map p180; Main St; meals Rs 500-800; ☎) This cool roadside cafe-bar has the traveller-scene thing down to a tee – there are minty mojitos, cool tunes and easy conversations around the table. Oh, and the food? Well, that's pretty good as well, and you shouldn't leave without trying the *lamprais* (meat and vegetables wrapped in a banana leaf and cooked very slowly).

It also has a small selection of second-hand paperbacks.

Dream Cafe INTERNATIONAL $$
(Map p180; Main St; mains Rs 400-900; ☎) Multiple reader recommendations fly the flag for this main-drag place with a cool, shady garden. It's a cosmopolitan wee spot with good espresso coffee, well-executed Western dishes such as tortilla chicken wraps, and smoothies and salads for the healthy traveller. Don't be too pious, though: the beers are nice and cold.

🛍 Shopping

T-Sips TEA
(Map p180; ☑077 788 3434; www.expoteas.com; Wellawaya Rd; ⊙8am-7.30pm) 🌿 This fair-trade tea shop (selling leaves rather than cups of tea) was established by a Sri Lankan tour guide to help local tea-estate children. It donates 5% of all money made to community projects. They sell an array of local teas and infusions.

ℹ Information

There's a post office and the **Bank of Ceylon** has an ATM. Almost every guesthouse and some bigger restaurants have internet access (normally wi-fi).

ℹ Getting There & Away

BUS
The road to Ella leaves the Bandarawela–Badulla road about 9km out of Bandarawela. Buses change schedule fairly often, so ask for an update at the Curd Shop (where many buses stop to collect passengers).

Buses go to Badulla (Rs 53), Bandarawela (Rs 34) and Wellawaya (Rs 67).

Whether you're going to or from Kandy, you must change first at Badulla. Buses to Matara (Rs 240 to Rs 275 depending on bus quality) stop at Ella approximately every hour from about 6.30am until about 2.30pm. The buses are likely to be quite full by the time they reach Ella, though the buses at around noon are usually less busy. You can always catch a bus to Wellawaya and change there for a service to the south coast or for Monaragala (for Arugam Bay). A bus heads to Galle every morning at 8am (Rs 310).

TAXI

Private minibus taxis gather on the roadside close to the Dream Cafe and charge the following:

Galle Rs 14,500
Horton Plains Rs 8500
Mirissa Rs 12,500
Nuwara Eliya Rs 7500
Tangalla Rs 9500
Tissamaharama Rs 6500

If you're heading to Horton Plains you're much better off taking a van from Haputale or Nuwara Eliya instead, both of which are considerably closer.

TRAIN

Ella is an hour from Haputale and Badulla on the Colombo–Badulla line. The stretch from Haputale (through Bandarawela) has particularly lovely scenery. Roughly 10km north of Ella, at Demodara, the line performs a complete loop around a hillside and tunnels under itself at a level 30m lower.

Ella's train station is so quaint it won the 'Best Kept Station' award in 2013. The station manager, Mr Ashendria Disanayake, deserves mention for winning the 'Most Helpful Station Manager' award. It's like Thomas the Tank Engine come to life. Fares and timetables are well posted. You'll probably be met by a few touts spinning fictional tales; Ella's guesthouse fraternity is perhaps the most competitive in all of Sri Lanka. Touts sometimes board the train a few stops before Ella. Observation class is Rs 1000 for anywhere between Nanu Oya and Badulla and Rs 1250 to Kandy and Colombo. A 2nd-class advance reservation is Rs 600 to any of the following destinations.

Eastbound trains to Badulla leave at 6.05am, 1.25pm and 3.15pm. Westbound trains to all other stations are at 6.40am, 9.25am, 10.55am and 12.05pm.

Sample train fares:

DESTINATION	FARE	TIME
Badulla	2nd/3rd class, Rs 40/20	1hr
Bandarawela	2nd/3rd class, Rs 30/15	35min
Colombo	2nd/3rd class, Rs 350/190	9hr
Haputale	2nd/3rd class, Rs 50/25	1-1½hr
Kandy	2nd/3rd class, Rs 240/130	6-10hr
Nanu Oya (for Nuwara Eliya)	2nd/3rd class, Rs 110/60	2½-3hr

Around Ella

There are a number of interesting sights and activities in the vicinity of Ella. You can also easily visit the **Dowa Temple** from Ella.

**Uva Halpewaththa
Tea Factory**　　　　　　　　　　TEA FACTORY
(adult/child Rs 200/100; ☉tours 8am-4pm) The Uva Halpewaththa Tea Factory, not far from Ella, runs very informative tours. After you've enriched yourself with knowledge, enrich your taste buds by trying a sample of the estate's different teas. There's also a small shop (7.30am to 5pm) selling leaves and tea-related paraphernalia. Tours take place throughout the day but tour frequency times vary slightly

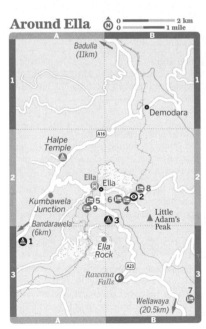

Around Ella 　　　　 0 —— 2 km / 0 —— 1 mile

Around Ella

◉ **Sights**
1 Dowa Temple..A3
2 Newburgh Green Tea Factory.............B2
3 Ravanna Ella Temple...........................B2

🛏 **Sleeping**
4 98 Acres Resort.....................................B2
5 Chamodya Homestay...........................A2
6 Ella Flower Garden Resort..................B2
7 Planters Bungalow................................B3
8 View Point Villa.....................................B2
9 Waterfall Homestay..............................A2

depending on the kind of tea being processed. To be safe, visit in the morning.

To get there catch a bus towards Bandarawela, get off at Kumbawela junction, and flag a bus going towards Badulla. Get off just after the 27km post, near the Halpe Temple. From here you have a very steep 2km walk to the factory. A three-wheeler from Ella will charge Rs 500 return.

Rawana Ella Falls
WATERFALL

(Wellawaya Rd) The 19m-high Rawana Ella Falls are about 6km down Ella Gap towards Wellawaya. During rainy months the water comes leaping down the mountainside in what is claimed to be the 'wildest-looking' fall in Sri Lanka, but during the dry season it may not flow at all. There are vendors selling food and trinkets. Catch any bus heading towards Wellawaya.

Ravanna Ella Temple
BUDDHIST, HINDU

(Map p184) This little temple and cave are associated with the Ramayana story. The cave, located in a cleft in the mountain that rises to Ella Rock, is reputed to be where the king of Lanka lived before capturing Sita. To get here, approach Ella from the direction of Wellawaya, then veer off shortly before the town along a side road. Boys will show you where the steep, overgrown and slippery track up to the cave starts.

Badulla

📞 055 / POPULATION 42,572 / ELEVATION 680M

Badulla marks the southeast extremity of the Hill Country and is a transport gateway to the east coast. It is one of Sri Lanka's oldest towns, occupied briefly by the Portuguese, who torched it upon leaving. For the British it was an important social centre, but beyond the pretty gardens and clock tower, any vestiges of a past – including a racecourse and cricket club – are lost in Badulla's typical Sri Lankan bustle. The railway through the Hill Country from Colombo terminates here. In British times, it was an important hub for transporting plantation products to Colombo.

◉ Sights

Most Sri Lankans visiting Badulla stop at either Muthiyagana Vihara or Kataragama Devale.

Muthiyagana Vihara
BUDDHIST

(off Passara Rd) A large Buddhist complex that includes a whitewashed dagoba in spacious grounds in the southeast of town. During festivals the resident elephant may be paraded around.

Badulla

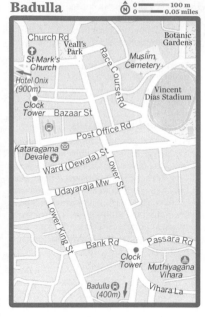

Kataragama Devale
HINDU

(Lower King St) The main objects of veneration are statues of the gods Kataragama, Saman and Vishnu. Uniquely, the *devale* was constructed in Kandyan style rather than South Indian Tamil style, with a long wooden shrine hall painted with murals depicting a *perahera*.

St Mark's Church
CHURCH

(Church Rd) If you're a history buff, take a look through St Mark's Church and peruse the old headstones. Inside is a plaque commemorating the elephant hunter Major Rogers, who was killed by lightning.

Legend has it that following a particularly severe thunderstorm in Haputale in 1845, Rogers stepped onto his veranda and proclaimed, 'It's all over now' to his wife. Ahh, not so fast, matey: one last bolt struck him dead. Relatives of the 1500 elephants he killed in a four-year stint probably trumpeted in glee. Rogers' actual gravestone near Nuwara Eliya is now cracked in half, reputedly by another bolt of celestial energy.

Dunhinda Falls
WATERFALL

(adult/child Rs 200/100; ⊙ 6.30am-5pm) Five kilometres north of Badulla are the 63m-high

Dunhinda Falls. The best time to see them is June and July, but they're worth a visit at any time. From the entrance gate the falls are about 1.5km along a clearly defined, but muddy, path.

There are many snack places along the trail. A three-wheeler from Badulla costs Rs 300 one-way. Buses leave every 30 minutes from Badulla (Rs 30).

Sleeping & Eating

Very few tourists stay overnight in Badulla and in recent years the town's cheaper guesthouses have developed a reputation for being hire-by-the-hour kinds of places. Pricier places tend to be used as wedding-reception venues and can be noisy. A few cheaper places hover around the train station if you're really counting your rupees. There are many local eateries along Lower St, near the intersection with Bazaar St.

Hotel Onix   HOTEL $$
(☏ 222 2426; 69 Bandaranayake Mawatha; d with/ without air-con, incl breakfast Rs 4500/3500; ✳️ 🛜 🖼️) This popular wedding-venue place has spacious rooms that are about the best Badulla has to offer – which frankly isn't much!

ℹ️ Getting There & Away

BUS
Colombo Rs 320 to 465 depending on bus type
Ella Rs 53

OFF THE BEATEN TRACK

RAKKHITHTHAKANDA LEN VIHARAYA CAVE TEMPLE

When travelling between Ella and Wellawaya a fun side-trip can take you to the **Rakkhiththakanda Len Viharaya Cave Temple** (off Wellawaya Rd). The outside of this remote and little-visited cave temple, which is signed off the road to Wellawaya, is covered in faded Kandyan-era paintings including one of the British Royal coat of arms. Inside, the paintings are in far better condition and completely cover all the walls. There's also a reclining Buddha. On *poya* (full moon) days, a large number of monks and villagers come here to meditate but outside these times it's very quiet with just one monk in residence. Entrance is by donation.

Kandy Rs 170 to 240 depending on bus type
Monaragala Rs 113
Nuwara Eliya Rs 120

TRAIN
Observation class is Rs 1000 to anywhere between Badulla and Nanu Oya and Rs 1250 for anywhere beyond Nanu Oya. Reserved 2nd-class tickets are Rs 600. Trains head to Colombo (2nd/3rd class, Rs 370/205) and Kandy (2nd/3rd class, Rs 270/145).

Koslanda

📍 057

Koslanda is a blink-and-it's-gone village. It's on the road between Bandarawela and Wellawaya and is situated at the point where you've dropped far enough out of the hills to see the vegetation turn outrageously tropical.

⊙ Sights

Diyaluma Falls   WATERFALL
Five kilometres east of Koslanda the road passes the 171m-high Diyaluma Falls, Sri Lanka's third-highest waterfall. Cascading down an escarpment of the Koslanda Plateau, the stream is fairly small, but it quickly escalates after a downpour. The falls leap over a cliff face and fall in one clear drop to a pool below.

Sleeping

Living Heritage Koslanda   BOUTIQUE HOTEL $$$
(☏ 077 935 5785; www.koslanda.com; Koslanda; r incl breakfast US$250-300; 🛜 🖼️) Set within 80 acres of grounds that include manicured lawns, tangled forest and even a waterfall, the imitation planters-style bungalows here are cool, calm and impeccably decorated. To this you can add open-air bathrooms (for three of the rooms), private jacuzzis in the shade of banana trees and an infinity pool we're still fantasising about.

There's an array of activities on offer and good western and eastern meals. It's imperative that you call ahead to let them know you're coming and for instructions on how to find the place (it's very well hidden and there are no sign boards), but it's just 600m west of the waterfalls.

Wellawaya

📍 055

By Wellawaya you have left the Hill Country and descended to the dry plains that were once home to the ancient Sinhalese kingdom of Ruhunu. Wellawaya is simply a small crossroads town and, apart from the nearby Buduruwagala carvings, there's not much of interest in the area. Roads run north through the spectacular Ella Gap to the Hill Country, south to Tissamaharama and the coast, east to the coast and west to Colombo.

⊙ Sights

★ Buduruwagala
MONUMENT

(admission Rs 200; ⊙ 6.30am-6pm) About 5km south of Wellawaya, a side road branches west off the Tissa road to the beautiful, 1000-year-old, rock-cut Buddha figures of Buduruwagala. Surrounded by smaller carved figures, the gigantic standing Buddha (at 15m, it is the tallest on the island) in the centre still bears traces of its original stuccoed robe, and a long streak of orange suggests it was once brightly painted.

➡ **The Central Figures**

The central of the three figures to the Buddha's right is thought to be the Mahayana Buddhist figure Avalokiteśvara (the bodhisattva of compassion). To the left of this white-painted figure is a female figure thought to be his consort, Tara. Local legend says the third figure represents Prince Sudhana.

➡ **The Other Figures**

Of the three figures on the Buddha's left-hand side, the crowned figure at the centre of the group is thought to be Maitreya, the future Buddha. To his left stands Vajrapani, who holds a vajra (an hourglass-shaped thunderbolt symbol) – an unusual example of the Tantric side of Buddhism in Sri Lanka. The figure to the left may be either Vishnu or Sahampath Brahma. Several of the figures hold up their right hands with two fingers bent down to the palm – a beckoning gesture.

The name Buduruwagala is derived from the words for Buddha (Budu), images (ruva) and stone (gala). The figures are thought to date from around the 10th century and belong to the Mahayana Buddhist school, which enjoyed a brief heyday in Sri Lanka during this time.

An ancient stupa has recently been uncovered halfway along the road from the junction to the carvings.

➡ **Practical Tips**

You may be joined by a guide, who will expect a tip. A three-wheeler from Wellawaya costs about Rs 500 return. Some people walk from the junction of the main road, which is very pleasant but also long and very hot. The route crosses a series of delicate lakes. Keep an eye out for local birdlife, including many egrets and herons.

Archaeological Museum
MUSEUM

(⊙ 8am-4.30pm Wed-Mon, closed poya days & public holidays) **FREE** This museum, on the corner of the main road from Wellawaya and the road to the Buduruwagala Buddhas, has stone and terracotta artefacts from nearby Buduruwagala. The artefacts are interesting, but signage is generally in Sinhalese only – and someone needs to replace the blown light bulbs!

🛏 Sleeping & Eating

There's a flurry of restaurants and snack stands across the road from the bus station.

Little Rose
GUESTHOUSE $

(☏ 567 8360; www.littlerosewellawaya.com; 101 Tissa Rd; incl breakfast, s with/without air-con Rs 3000/2000, d with/without air-con Rs 4000/2500; ❋ 🎧) Just 500m from the bus station, this is your best option if you're staying overnight to wait for onward transport. This country home is in a quiet rural setting, surrounded by rice paddies and run by a welcoming family. Good, inexpensive meals are available. A three-wheeler from the bus station costs about Rs 120.

ℹ Getting There & Away

Wellawaya is a common staging point between the Hill Country and the south and east coasts. You can usually find a connection here until midafternoon. For Tissamaharama, change at Pannegamanuwa Junction (Rs 88).

Buses leave when full.

DESTINATION	FARE	TIME
Ella	Rs 67	1hr
Embilipitiya	Rs 118	2½hr
Monaragala	Rs 74	1hr
Tangalla	Rs 160	3½hr

Embilipitiya

☏ 047

Embilipitiya is sometimes used as a base for tours to Uda Walawe National Park, as it's only 23km south of the park's ticket office. However, with the increasing range of accommodation around the park itself, there's much less reason to stay in this otherwise busy agricultural town.

Buses leave regularly for most destinations from, or near, the bus station; destinations include Tangalla (Rs 50), Matara (Rs 100) and Ratnapura (Rs 100).

If you're staying at Embilipitiya and wish to organise a tour of Uda Walawe park, catch a bus to Tanamalwila (Rs 75) and ask to be dropped at the gate to the park.

🛏 Sleeping

Centauria Tourist Hotel HOTEL $$
(📞 223 0514; www.centauriahotel.com; s Rs 8350-9620, d Rs 9700-11,050 incl breakfast; ❋ 🛜 ☀) Around 1.5km south of the town centre, this hotel combines a languid ambience with, from the standard rooms, front-row views over a lake. These standard rooms are actually better value and more spacious than the deluxe rooms in the main building.

ℹ Getting There & Away

Buses leave from the bus station (which is right in the town centre) frequently to the following:

DESTINATION	FARE	TIME
Matara	Rs 125	3hr
Ratnapura	Rs 129	3-4hr
Tangalla	Rs 80	2hr
Uda Walawe	Rs 46	½hr

Uda Walawe National Park

This is one of the best places in Sri Lanka to see elephants. According to the 2011 census there are about 600 in the park in herds of up to 50. There's an elephant-proof fence around the perimeter of the park, (supposedly) preventing elephants from getting out and cattle from getting in. The best time to observe elephant herds is from 6.30am to 10am and again from 4pm to 6.30pm.

◉ Sights

Uda Walawe National Park PARK
(admission Rs 1945, service charge per group Rs 1038, vehicle charge per group Rs 250, plus overall tax VAT 12%; ⏱ 6am-6pm) With herds of elephants, wild buffalo, sambar deer and leopards, this Sri Lankan national park rivals the savannah reserves of Africa. In fact, for elephant-watching, Uda Walawe often surpasses many of the most famous East African national parks. The park, which centres on the 308.2-sq-km Uda Walawe Reservoir, is lightly vegetated but it has a stark beauty and the lack of dense vegetation makes game-watching easy. It's the one park in Sri Lanka not to miss.

The entrance to the park is 12km from the Ratnapura–Hambantota road turn-off and 21km from Embilipitiya. Visitors buy tickets in a building a further 2km on. Most people take a tour organised by their guesthouse or hotel, but a trip with one of the 4WDs waiting outside the gate should be around Rs 3500 for a half-day for up to eight people with driver. Last tickets are usually sold at 5pm. A park guide is included in the cost of admission and these guys, who all seem to have hawk-like wildlife-spotting eyes, are normally very knowledgeable about the park and its animals. A tip is expected.

Besides elephants, sambar deer and wild buffalo (although most buffalo you'll see in the park are domesticated), there are also mongooses, jackals, water monitor lizards, lots of crocodiles, sloth bears and the occasional leopard. There are 30 varieties of snakes and a wealth of birdlife – 210 species at last count; northern migrants join the residents between November and April.

Elephant Transit Home ZOO
(adult/child Rs 500/250; ⏱ feedings 9am, noon, 3pm & 6pm) This home, helping to care for the area's injured elephants, is on the main road about 5km west of the Uda Walawe National Park entrance. Supported by the **Born Free Foundation** (www.bornfree.org.uk), the complex is a halfway house for orphaned elephants. After rehabilitation, the elephants are released back into the wild, many into the Uda Walawe National Park. Although you can't get up close and personal with the elephants, a visit at feeding time is still a lot of fun.

At the time of research 98 elephants had been rehabilitated at the Elephant Transit Home and subsequently released. A boisterous group of around 40 juvenile and teenage pachyderms are currently there. Most 4WD operators include a visit here on their trips.

🛏 Sleeping & Eating

Options for staying in and around Uda Walawe have mushroomed in the last couple of years and although much of it is more expensive than you might pay for similar elsewhere, there are still some good places to stay.

Superson Family Guest GUESTHOUSE $
(📞 047-347 5172; 90B CDE Place, Uda Walawe; s Rs 1200, d with/without air-con Rs 3000/1700; ❋) This guesthouse has simple accommodation, a nice garden and good home-cooked food. Prices seem to be very flexible.

UDA WALAWE UNDER THREAT

Wildlife in Uda Walawe is under threat for several reasons, including illegal settlement and the associated grazing of cattle. Another problem is poaching and the use of 'Hakka Patas', small explosive devices that are concealed in food and left on the banks of the Uda Walawe Reservoir, where wild boar graze. Though the explosives target wild boar, several elephants have been severely injured in recent years.

All along the main road fringing the park, shops sell fruit to passing motorists who then attempt to hand feed the wild elephants that gather along the edge of the park fence. Be aware that feeding the elephants encourages dependence and erodes their fear of humans. This frequently leads to human-elephant conflict, with the elephants coming out worse off. While the park rivals East Africa for its elephants, the Sri Lankan National Park authorities fall behind their competitors in Kenya and Tanzania when it comes to good conservation practice.

★**Athgira River Camping**　　CAMPGROUND **$$**
(📞 047-223 3296; www.nilukasafari.com; off Army Camp Rd; half-board s/d US$70/85; 🛜) The most appealing and best value place near Uda Walawe National Park. It has 15 heavy canvas safari tents strung along the river bank. The tents are comfortable rather than luxurious, but all have attached (cold-water) bathrooms and proper beds. It's a social place and the friendly staff organise frequent riverside barbecue nights.

If arriving by public transport, hop off the bus at the Elephant Transit Home and go to the Athgira Restaurant opposite; they'll provide onward transport.

Elephant Lane　　GUESTHOUSE **$$**
(📞 071 525 8280; www.elephantlane.com.lk; Army Camp Rd; with/without air-con Rs 5000/3500, d with/without air-con Rs 5500/4000; ❄🛜) Rather ordinary rooms but it represents real value for money in these expensive parts. All prices include breakfast.

Elephant Safari Hotel　　LODGE **$$$**
(📞 047-567 8833; www.elephantsafarihotel.lk; 60 Aloka Mawatha; half-board s/d Rs 14,960/18,301) Set in spacious gardens filled with people, this place has a warm welcome and seven huge, stylish cottages that feel genuinely luxurious. It's down a maze of muddy rural lanes but is well-signed. The turn-off is a couple of kilometres west of the park gate close to the bridge.

Grand Uda Walawe　　RESORT **$$$**
(📞 047-223 2000; www.grandudawalawe.com; 912 Thanamalwila Rd; s/d half-board US$140/180; ❄🛜🏊) This large, resort-like place centres on an impressive pool complex; it's every tour group's favourite place to stay. Although it doesn't blend seamlessly into the environ-

ment, it's slickly run and offers smart business luxury for those who need it.

🛈 Getting There & Away

Buses from Embilipitiya, the launch pad for the park, cost Rs 46. Most of the cheaper accommodation is in or close to the village of Uda Walawe. More upmarket places can be found strung along the road between the park entrance and Uda Walawe village. Ask the bus driver to either drop you off outside your hotel of choice or as close as possible – some places are stuffed way down alternately dusty and mussy side lanes. If you're just going straight to the park entrances ask to be dropped off there. Jeeps are available for safari from the gates.

Sinharaja Forest Reserve

Sinharaja Forest Reserve　　PARK
(adult/child Rs 644/325, compulsory guide per person from Rs 1000, video camera Rs 560; ⏰ 6.30am-6pm, ticket office to 4.30pm) The last major undisturbed area of rainforest in Sri Lanka, this forest reserve occupies a broad ridge at the heart of the island's wet zone. On most days the forest is shrouded by copious rainclouds that replenish its deep soils and balance water resources for much of southwestern Sri Lanka. Recognising its importance to the island's ecosystem, Unesco declared the Sinharaja Forest Reserve a World Heritage Site in 1989.

The only way to get about the reserve is by foot, and excellent park guides, or freelance guides available through many hotels, can lead you along slippery trails pointing out the wealth of stunning plant, bird and animal life.

➡ **Landscape & History**

Sinharaja (Lion King) is bordered by rivers: the Koskulana Ganga in the north and the

THE HILL COUNTRY SINHARAJA FOREST RESERVE

Gin Ganga in the south. An old foot track that goes past the Beverley Estate marks the eastern border, close to the highest peak in the forest, Hinipitigala (1171m). Towards the west the land decreases in elevation.

The reserve comprises 189 sq km of natural and modified forest, measuring about 21km east to west and 3.7km north to south. It was once a royal reserve, and some colonial records refer to it as Rajasinghe Forest. It may have been the last redoubt of the Sri Lankan lion.

In 1840 the forest became British crown land, and from that time some efforts were made towards its preservation. However, in 1971 loggers moved in and began selective logging. The logged native hardwoods were replaced with mahogany (which does not occur naturally here), logging roads and trails snaked into the forest and a wood-chip mill was built. Following intense lobbying by conservationists, the government called a halt to all logging in 1977. Machinery was dismantled and removed, the roads gradually grew over and Sinharaja was saved. Much of the rest of Sri Lanka's rainforest stands on mountain ridges within a 20km radius of the forest.

There are 22 villages around the forest, and locals are permitted to enter the area to tap palms to make jaggery (a hard brown sweet) and treacle, and to collect dead wood and leaves for fuel and construction. Medicinal plants are collected during specific seasons. Rattan collection is of more concern, as the demand for cane is high. Sinharaja attracts illegal gem miners, too, and abandoned open pits pose a danger to humans and animals, and cause erosion. There is also some poaching of wild animals.

➡ **Wildlife & Plants**

Sinharaja has a wild profusion of flora. The canopy trees reach heights of up to 45m, with the next layer down topping 30m. Nearly all the subcanopy trees found here are rare or endangered. More than 65% of the 217 types of trees and woody climbers endemic to Sri Lanka's rainforest are found in Sinharaja.

The largest carnivore here is the leopard. Its presence can usually be gauged only by droppings and tracks, and it's seldom seen. Even rarer are rusty spotted cats and fishing cats. Sambar, barking deer and wild boar can be found on the forest floor. Groups of 10 to 14 purple-faced langurs are fairly common. There are three kinds of squirrels: the flame-striped jungle squirrel, the dusky-striped jungle squirrel and the western giant squirrel. Porcupines and pangolins waddle around the forest floor, mostly unseen. Civets and mongooses are nocturnal, though you may glimpse the occasional mongoose darting through the foliage during the day. Six species of bats have been recorded here.

Sinharaja has 45 species of reptiles, 21 of them endemic. Venomous snakes include the green pit viper (which inhabits trees), the hump-nosed viper and the krait, which lives on the forest floor. One of the most frequently found amphibians is the wrinkled frog, whose croaking is often heard at night.

There is a wealth of birdlife: 160 species have been recorded, with 18 of Sri Lanka's 20 endemic species seen here.

Sinharaja has leeches in abundance. In colonial times the British, Dutch and Portuguese armies rated leeches as their worst enemy when they tried to conquer the hinterland (which was then much more forested), and one British writer claimed leeches caused more casualties than all the other animals put together. These days you needn't suffer as much because all guides carry antileech preparations.

➡ **Practical Information**

Tickets are sold at the main Forest Department office at Kudawa and at Deodawa, 5km from Deniyaya on the Matara road. The drier months (August and September, and January to early April) are the best times to visit.

See www.sinharaja.4t.com for detailed information on the history, flora and fauna, and the challenges faced by the Sinharaja Forest Reserve.

⊙ Sights

Kotapola, 6km south of Deniyaya, has a superb early-17th-century **rock temple**. It's well worth the climb. The **Kiruwananaganga Falls**, some of the largest in Sri Lanka (60m high and up to 60m wide), are 5km east of Kotapola on the road towards Urubokka. The **Kolawenigama Temple**, 3km from Pallegama (which is 3km from Deniyaya), is of modest proportions but has a unique structure that resembles Kandy's Temple of the Sacred Tooth Relic. It was built by King Buwanekabahu VII in recognition of the protection given to the tooth relic by the villagers. The shrine has Kandyan-style frescoes.

🛏 Sleeping & Eating

It's most convenient to visit the reserve from Deniyaya if you don't have your own wheels and accommodation is much better value here than around the northern Kudawa entrance.

Deniyaya

Deniyaya Rest House HOTEL $

(☎ 041-227 3600; r Rs 2000) Like most former government rest houses in Sri Lanka, this place has the best location in town, with great views over the countryside. The large, good-value rooms are ageing gracefully, and there's a bar-restaurant where you can tally up your leech bites over a stiff drink. It's just off the main road in the town of Deniyaya.

Sinharaja Rest GUESTHOUSE $

(☎ 041-227 3368; sinharaja_rest@yahoo.com; Temple Rd; r incl breakfast Rs 3500-4000; ☎) Brothers Palitha and Bandula Rathnayaka are both certified forest guides, so staying here makes it easy to maximise your time. The six rooms at their home are fairly basic, but there's good home-cooking and a lovely private garden. Day trips to the Sinharaja Forest Reserve cost Rs 4000 per person and include transport, guiding and lunch (but exclude park entrance fees).

Trips are also open to nonguests. If you give the brothers a week's notice, they can arrange overnight stays in forest bungalows. The same family also have some smarter cottages a short way up the road that sleep four (US$90 to $100 including breakfast).

Rainforest Lodge HOTEL $$

(☎ 041-492 0444; www.rainforestlodge-srilanka. de; s €25-49, d €44-61, incl breakfast; ☎) Located in perfect isolation in a tea plantation a few minutes' walk from the road, Rainforest Lodge has sparkling and spacious rooms with high-quality bathrooms. The views include a green trifecta of rainforest, rice paddies and tea gardens, and good food is served.

Forest trips cost Rs 4500 for one person or Rs 6500 for two people, including food, transport and guiding fees.

The Rainforest BOUTIQUE HOTEL $$$

(☎ Colombo 011-558 8714; www.rainforest-ecolodge. org; s/d incl breakfast US$170/205) ✎ Seventeen and a half rather tortuous kilometres north of Deniyaya, and at the very top of a mountain, is this luxury hideaway, which might well be the remotest hotel in Sri Lanka. Highly original rooms with stupendous views have been created out of metal shipping containers and recycled railway sleepers. It is tucked away in a jungle-hemmed valley.

Water comes from nearby springs and is solar heated. There's also an impressive recycling scheme. It sits right on the edge of Sinharaja reserve; good forest tours are available.

Kudawa

Rock View Motel HOTEL $$

(☎ 045-567 7990; www.rockviewmotel.com; Weddagala; s/d incl breakfast Rs 4750/6500) Functional and airy rooms with views over rolling hills of forest and tea bushes. It's 2km east of Weddagala and about the best value deal in these parts. It can be noisy at weekends when it often hosts wedding parties.

Blue Magpie Lodge GUESTHOUSE $$

(☎ 077 320 6203; www.bluemagpie.lk; Kudawa; s/d incl breakfast US$75/88) Just a short walk from the park entrances this friendly lodge has clean and basic rooms. Electricity is only available by generator in the evenings and early mornings. It's expensive, even considering the remote location. There are good forest and birding guides available.

Boulder Garden BOUTIQUE HOTEL $$$

(☎ 045-225 5812; www.bouldergarden.com; Sinharaja Rd, Koswatta; s/d US$146/259; ☀) This brilliantly designed but somewhat damp and down-at-heel ecoresort offers 10 rustic rooms – two of them in actual caves – built among boulders and streams.

Meals are available in a beautiful garden restaurant, but be aware that their 'Western' breakfast costs an astronomical US$62 for a single traveller.

Rainforest Edge LODGE $$$

(☎ 045-567 9238; www.rainforestedge.com; Balwatukanda, Weddagala; s/d incl breakfast US$136/199; ☀) Tucked into the hills a few hundred metres from Weddagala, these seven rustic huts are a bit too rustic for the high prices they charge. Still, the views from the terrace are stunning. At the time of research it was about to close for a major refurbishment, which might make it a very different beast altogether.

ℹ Information

Tickets are sold at the main Forest Department office at Kudawa and at Deodawa, 5km from Deniyaya on the Matara road.

In Deniyaya, the **Commercial Bank** has an ATM and exchange facilities, and internet access is also available in the village.

WORTH A TRIP

RATNAPURA

Sitting in well-irrigated valleys between Adam's Peak and Sinharaja Forest Reserve, busy Ratnapura ('City of Gems' in Sanskrit) is a famous trading centre for the area's ancient wealth of gem stones. The region's wet and humid climate encourages the formation of riverbeds, which are the perfect environment for gem stones to develop.

There are several 'gem museums' that contain modest displays on gem lore, along with less-than-modest showrooms where you're encouraged to purchase 'local' gems at 'local' prices.

The outskirts of town are dotted with **gem mines** and, although none cater specifically to tourists, most guesthouses can arrange visits.

You can also observe **gem merchants** selling their wares along Saviya St northeast of the clock tower. The biggest local gem market, however, convenes most mornings (*poya* full-moon days being an exception) in **Newitigala**, a 40-minute drive away. Both markets are usually over by 3pm.

Another reason to visit Ratnapura is that it's the take-off point for one of the oldest routes up **Adam's Peak**. Peak-baggers and pilgrims pick up the Gilimalai pilgrimage route from the road head at Carney Estate, 15km, or one hour, away from Ratnapura by bus. It takes six to eight hours to reach the top of the peak, and five to seven hours to descend. Leeches are a particular menace on this trail.

ⓘ Getting There & Away

There are several park access points, but the most relevant to travellers are those via Kudawa in the northwest and via Mederapitiya (reached from Deniyaya) in the southeast. The Mederapitiya entrance is the easiest to reach by public transport.

BUS

From Ratnapura to Deniyaya there are buses (Rs 185; five hours) roughly every hour from 6.45am until the afternoon. There are also several buses to and from Galle (Rs 120; three hours).

For Kudawa you can get a bus from Ratnapura to Kalawana (Rs 74) and from there to Weddagala (4km before Kudawa, Rs 32), and then, finally, hop on one to Kudawa (Rs 30). A three-wheeler from Weddagala to Kudawa is around Rs 500.

CAR

If you have a car, the road through Hayes Tea Estate, north of Deniyaya en route to Madampe and Balangoda (for Belihul Oya, Haputale or Ratnapura), is very scenic. Trying to loop from the north to the south entrances of the park is also very scenic, but slow and painful.

The Ancient Cities

Best Places to Stay

➡ Rice Villa Retreat (p212)
➡ Lion Lodge (p203)
➡ Jim's Farm Villas (p196)
➡ Kalundewa Retreat (p199)
➡ The Sanctuary at Tissawewa (p222)
➡ Lakeside at Nuwarawewa (p221)

Best Places to Eat

➡ Heritance Kandalama Hotel (p199)
➡ The Sanctuary at Tissawewa (p222)
➡ A&C Restaurant (p197)

Why Go?

Crumbling temples, lost cities and sacred sites are reason enough to head up country to the cultural heartland of Sri Lanka. It was here on the hot central plains that ancient Sinhalese dynasties set up their capitals and supported massive artistic and architectural endeavours. Eventually these kingdoms fell, giving nature a chance to reclaim the land.

For more than a century archaeologists have been slowly shedding the many layers of history from this overgrown landscape. The rock fortress at Sigiriya, the monumental dagobas of Anuradhapura and refined carvings of Polonnaruwa are but a few of the sites now considered national treasures.

This region is commonly called the 'Cultural Triangle'. Besides the amazing ruins, save time for the national parks, which teem with elephants and outstanding birdlife. Plan on spending several days here making new discoveries daily.

When to Go
Dambulla

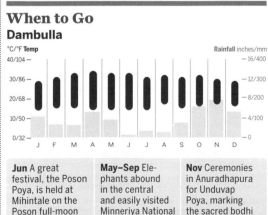

Jun A great festival, the Poson Poya, is held at Mihintale on the Poson full-moon night.

May–Sep Elephants abound in the central and easily visited Minneriya National Park.

Nov Ceremonies in Anuradhapura for Unduvap Poya, marking the sacred bodhi tree's arrival.

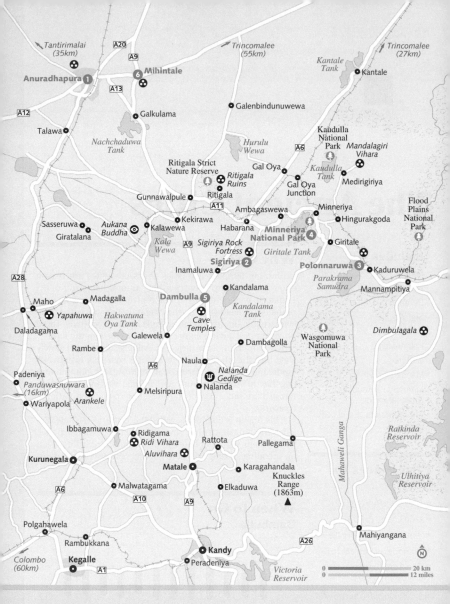

Ancient Cities Highlights

1 Feeling humbled by the epic scale of the monuments and profound spirituality evident at **Anuradhapura** (p215)

2 Scaling the great rock of **Sigiriya** (p200) for epic views, outstanding art and intriguing ruins

3 Admiring the exquisite carvings and temples at the fascinating ruins of the former Sinhalese stronghold of **Polonnaruwa** (p206)

4 Spotting bird and animal life in the lush **Minneriya National Park** (p213)

5 Going Buddha-spotting in **Dambulla** (p197), where hillside rock caves contain some of Sri Lanka's most stunning cultural artefacts

6 Marvelling at the scenery, temples and monuments of **Mihintale** (p223)

ℹ️ Information

Head to **Lonely Planet** (www.lonelyplanet.com/
sri-lanka/the-ancient-cities) for planning advice,
author recommendations, traveller reviews and
insider tips.

CULTURAL TRIANGLE TICKETS

Tickets are needed to visit the major Cultural
Triangle sites as well as a few of the minor ones.
Most are run by the Central Cultural Fund (CCF),
which has a good website (www.ccf.lk).

Round Tickets (which offered substantial savings) are no longer available. Admission tickets
to the main sites are steep, and cost as follows:

Anuradhapura US$25
Dambulla US$10
Medirigiriya Vihara US$10
Mihintale US$4
Polonnaruwa US$25
Ritigala US$10
Sigiriya US$30

ℹ️ Getting Around

The towns and cities of the Cultural Triangle are
well connected by public and private buses, and
in some cases by train. Distances are not great
and most roads are good, so getting around the
main destinations by public transport is relatively
straightforward (although buses can be very
crowded at certain times of day and during holiday periods). Departures between major towns
and tourist sites are fairly frequent.

As always, the easiest way to tour, however, is
with a car and driver. You can reach the area by
train or bus and then arrange for a car and driver
on a daily basis through your accommodation.

For a reliable driver (around Rs 6000 per day)
to cover the sites around the Cultural Triangle,
and beyond, **Let's Go Lanka** (☎ 077 630 2070;
www.letsgolanka.com) and **Nadee Lanka Tours**
(☎ 077 999 8859; www.nadeelankatours.com)
are recommended.

Three-wheelers are readily available for short
hops, too.

Matale

🎵 066 / POP 46,000

This midsize regional city at the heart of
the island lies in a broad, fertile valley at an
elevation of 300m. Matale is a featureless urban sprawl with a congested one-way system
of roads, so you're unlikely to want to linger
long. However, the road north of town is
lined with dozens of spice plantations (which
welcome visitors) where vanilla, rubber, cin-
chona, jackfruit, cocoa and cardamom thrive.
The area is also famous for *kohila* (a type of
watercress) and small, mild chillies.

A drive east through Knuckles Range,
east of Matale, presents some remarkable
mountain views. The B38 heads uphill from
the north end of town to a pass near Ratto-
ta, while other roads head southwest to the
hill villages of Elkaduwa and Karagahandala
before winding down to Kandy and the Victoria Reservoir.

DON'T MISS

SPICE GARDENS

The A9 highway between Matale and Dambulla is famous for its spice gardens, with over 30
dotted along the road. All offer free tours of their gardens with an English-speaking guide
who can explain the merits and health properties of herbs, spices and plants including
cocoa, vanilla, cinnamon, cloves, coriander, coffee, nutmeg, pepper, cardamom, aloe vera,
iriweriya and the henna plant.

Most visitors enjoy the tours and find them educational but note that these spice gardens
are very much commercial operations, surviving on profits from in-house shops that sell
powders and treatments. Some of the prices asked for products range from eye-watering to
rip-off; expect a medium- to hard-sell and some fanciful claims for health properties of the
produce.

Euphoria Spice (☎ 270 9107; www.euphoriaspice.com; ⊗ 8.30am-4pm) Offers very detailed
tours of its spice garden and has a shop selling all kinds of creams, potions and lotions that
are said to help everything from sleeplessness to low sex drive. Staff are welcoming, there's
a cafe, and cooking demonstrations are also performed. Located 15km north of Matale on
the road to Dambulla.

Heritage Spice & Herbs Garden (☎ 205 5150; 130 Center Land, Madawala Ulpotha; ⊗ 8am-
5pm) With an attractive, shady garden, this spice specialist runs informative tours and has a
cafe for snacks and drinks. Around 15km north of Matale.

◉ Sights

Aluvihara MONASTERY
(admission Rs 250, workshop payment by donation; ☻6.30am-6.30pm) Set in a chasm in the hills, surrounded by giant boulders, this monastery is an intriguing site. There's a unique series of monastic caves, some spectacular religious paintings and a stupa or two. It's easily accessible (just off the road, 3km north of Matale).

Legend has it that a giant used three of the rocks as a base for his cooking pot, and the name Aluvihara (Ash Monastery) refers to the ashes from the cooking fire.

➤ **Reclining Buddha Cave**

The first cave you come to contains a 10m reclining Buddha and impressive lotus-pattern murals on the ceiling. Another is filled with cartoon-like murals of the realms of hell – if you're considering straying from the straight and narrow, you may think twice after seeing the statues of devils meting out an inventive range of punishments to sinners in the afterlife. One scene shows a sexual sinner with his skull cut open and his brains being ladled out by two demons.

➤ **Buddhaghosa Cave**

Up a flight of rock steps is a cave dedicated to Buddhaghosa, the Indian scholar who is supposed to have spent several years here while working on the Tipitaka. Although histories affirm that Buddhaghosa lived in Anuradhapura in the 6th century AD, there's no clear evidence he stayed at Aluvihara. Nonetheless the cave walls are painted with scenes showing Buddhaghosa working on *ola* (palm-leaf) manuscripts.

➤ **Summit**

Stairs continue to the summit of the rock bluff, where you'll find a dagoba and sweeping views of the surrounding valley. To the west, atop a rocky outcrop 150m above the monastery, is a seated golden Buddha offering protection and blessings with an *abhaya* (palm facing-outward) gesture.

➤ **Workshop**

The Tipitaka was first transcribed from oral and Sinhalese sources into Pali text by a council of monks held at Aluvihara in the 1st century BC. Two thousand years later, in 1848, the monks' library was destroyed by British troops putting down a revolt. The long process of replacing the *ola* manuscripts still occupies monks, scribes and craftspeople today. You can see their workshop (a donation includes having your name inscribed on a small length of *ola*).

A three-wheeler from Matale to Aluvihara will cost about Rs 500 return, including waiting time; the bus fare is Rs 10.

Matale Heritage Centre CULTURAL CENTRE
(☏222 2404; 33 Sir Richard Aluvihara Mawatha; ☻9am-4pm Mon-Sat) **FREE** This crafts centre draws on the rich traditions of the area, producing quality batik, embroidery, carpentry and brasswork. It occupies a sprawling compound of bungalows, workshops and gardens up in a forest. The centre's kitchen does meals for groups of four (book by phone a day ahead); it costs Rs 1000 per person for a banquet of many rices and curries.

It's located 2km north of Matale, up a side road off the A9 highway. A three-wheeler from Matale will cost about Rs 400 return, including waiting time.

**Sri Muthumariamman
Thevasthanam** HINDU TEMPLE
(admission Rs 200; ☻6am-1pm, 4-8pm) Just north of the bus stop for Kandy (at the north end of town) is this interesting Hindu temple. A priest will show you the five enormous, colourful ceremonial chariots pulled along by people during an annual festival.

🛏 Sleeping & Eating

There's no compelling reason to stay in Matale but there are a couple of decent options.

Sesatha Hotel GUESTHOUSE **$**
(☏223 1489; h.sesatha@gmail.com; 40 Kohombiliwela; r Rs 2800-4000; ❋ ����) An elegant, modern place with rice-field views from the balconies of the rooms. The gardens are a delight, dotted with palm trees and overlooked by the restaurant tables. Sesatha is 1.5km south of town, about 200m off the main road.

★ **Jim's Farm Villas** LODGE **$$$**
(☏077 782 8395; www.jimsfarmvillas.com; 3km west of Madawala Ulpotha; s/d/tr US$100/125/150; ❋ ⬤ ⬤) ✦ In the misty, verdant hills north of Matale, at an elevation of 450m, this working organic farm (harvesting coconuts, mangoes, bananas and papaya) is owned by an Englishman and run on an environmentally sustainable basis. Rooms (divided between two villas, with a third under construction) are beautiful, with attractive wooden furniture, Egyptian-cotton bed linen and generous balconies or verandahs.

The cooking is exceptional and meals (US$10 to US$20) are eaten communally. It's 20km north of Matale.

Surathura Spice Garden
SRI LANKAN $

(🖉222 2338; 3 Thotagamuwa; buffet Rs 450; ⊙11am-3.30pm) Around 4km north of Matale, this is a pretty run-of-the-mill spice garden but the lunchtime buffet is worth investigating with tasty vegetarian curries made from breadfruit and jackfruit. Try a cardamom-infused coffee afterwards.

★ A&C Restaurant
SRI LANKAN $$

(🖉367 4501; 3/5 Sir Richard Aluvihara Mawatha; mains Rs 600-1100; ⊙11am-3pm) For a step up in class from your standard-issue rice and curry, this atmospheric place offers delicious Sri Lankan meals that are varied and flavourful, with lots of choice. It's on the same turnoff as the Matale Heritage Centre, but then take a sharp left rather than the road to the centre.

❶ Getting There & Away

Bus 593 runs from Kandy to Matale (normal/intercity express Rs 48/68, 1½ hours) every 10 minutes. Buses to Dambulla or Anuradhapura will drop you at Aluvihara (Rs 10) or the spice gardens. There are six trains daily on the pretty spur line between Matale and Kandy (1st/2nd/3rd Class Rs 25/50/100, 1½ hours).

Nalanda Gedige

Nalanda Gedige
HINDU

(⊙7am-5pm) The venerable Nalanda Gedige is built in the style of a South Indian Hindu temple and enjoys a wonderfully peaceful location next to a tank (artificial lake) with prolific local birdlife.

The temple consists of an entrance hall connected to a taller *shikara* (holy image sanctuary), with a courtyard for circumambulations. There is no sign of Hindu gods, however, and the temple is said to have been used by Buddhists. It's one of the earliest stone buildings in Sri Lanka.

The temple's richly decorated stone-block walls, reassembled from ruins in 1975, are thought to have been fashioned during the 8th to 11th centuries. The plinth bears some Tantric carvings with sexual poses – the only such sculptures in Sri Lanka – but before you get excited, the carvings are weather-beaten and it's difficult to see much in the way of action.

❶ Getting There & Away

Nalanda Gedige is about 25km north of Matale and 20km before Dambulla, 1km east of the main road; look out for the sign near the Km 49 post.

Anuradhapura buses from Kandy or Matale will drop you at the turnoff.

Dambulla

🖉066 / POP 72,500

Dambulla's famed Royal Rock Temple is an iconic Sri Lankan image – you'll be familiar with its spectacular Buddha-filled interior long before you arrive in town. Despite its slightly commercial air, this remains an important holy place and should not be missed.

The town of Dambulla is of no interest, cursed by heavy traffic heading for one of Sri Lanka's biggest wholesale markets. A night here is tolerable, but consider visiting the site as a day trip from the more relaxing environs of Kandy or Sigiriya.

⊙ Sights

★ Cave Temples
BUDDHIST

(adult/child US$10/free; ⊙7.30am-12.30pm & 1-6pm) FREE The beautiful Royal Rock Temple complex sits about 160m above the road in the southern part of Dambulla. Five separate caves contain about 150 absolutely stunning Buddha statues and paintings, some of Sri Lanka's most important and evocative religious art. Buddha images were first created here over 2000 years ago, and over the centuries subsequent kings added to and embellished the cave art.

From the caves there are superb views over the surrounding countryside; Sigiriya is clearly visible some 20km distant.

Dambulla is thought to have been a place of worship since 1st century BC, when King Valagamba (also known as Vattagamani Abhaya), driven out of Anuradhapura, took refuge here. When he regained his throne, he had the interior of the caves carved into magnificent rock temples. Further paintings were made by later kings, including King Nissanka Malla, who had the caves' interiors gilded, earning the place the name Ran Giri (Golden Rock).

This process of retouching original and creating new artwork continued into the 20th century. Remarkably, the overall impact is breathtakingly coherent to the eye.

From the highway, Dambulla's entrance looks pretty grim – the Disneyesque concrete Buddha, monstrous Golden Temple and vast car park are distinctly off-putting. But things improve markedly as you climb the hillside, leaving the commercialism behind, and ascend a vast, sloping rock face that leads to the caves.

THE ANCIENT CITIES NALANDA GEDIGE

Dambulla

N 0 ———— 200 m
0 ———— 0.1 miles

inside the cave collects water that constantly drips from the ceiling of the temple – even during droughts – which is used for sacred rituals.

➡ Cave III (Maha Alut Viharaya)

This cave, the New Great Temple, was said to have been converted from a storeroom in the 18th century by King Kirti Sri Rajasinghe of Kandy, one of the last Kandyan monarchs. It is also filled with Buddha statues, including a beautiful reclining Buddha, and is separated from Cave II by only a masonry wall.

➡ Cave IV (Pachima Viharaya)

The relatively small Western Cave is not the most westerly cave – that position belongs to Cave V. The central Buddha figure is seated under a *makara torana,* with its hands in *dhyana mudra* (a meditative pose in which the hands are cupped). The small dagoba in the centre was broken into by thieves who believed that it contained jewellery belonging to Queen Somawathie.

➡ Cave V (Devana Alut Viharaya)

This newer cave was once used as a storehouse, but it's now called the Second New Temple. It features a reclining Buddha; Hindu deities, including Kataragama (Murugan) and Vishnu, are also present.

Golden Temple   BUDDHIST TEMPLE
(www.goldentemple.lk) **FREE** At the foot of the cave temples hill stands the modern Golden Temple, a kitschy structure completed in 2000 using Japanese donations. On top of the cube-shaped building sits a Buddha image in

➡ Cave I (Devaraja Viharaya)

The first cave, the Temple of the King of the Gods, has a 15m-long reclining Buddha. Ananda, the Buddha's loyal disciple, and other seated Buddhas are depicted nearby. A statue of Vishnu is held in a small shrine within the cave, but it's usually closed.

➡ Cave II (Maharaja Viharaya)

The Temple of the Great King is arguably the most spectacular of the caves. It measures 52m from east to west and 23m from the entrance to the back wall; the highest point of the ceiling is 7m. This cave is named after the two statues of kings it contains. There is a painted wooden statue of Valagamba on the left as you enter, and another statue further inside of Nissanka Malla. The cave's main Buddha statue, which appears to have once been covered in gold leaf, is situated under a *makara torana* (archway decorated with dragons), with the right hand raised in *abhaya mudra* (pose conveying protection). Hindu deities are also represented. The vessel the *dhammachakka mudra* (wheel-turning pose) and a huge neon sign.

Dambulla Museum   MUSEUM
(adult/child Rs 250/130; ☉ 7.30am-4.30pm) Re-creations of art from the cave temples, artefacts and detailed English-language explanations are presented in a large building some 500m south of the main caves' parking area. The displays are a good primer on Sri Lankan art – from cave paintings to 18th-century frescoes. Staff are keen to show you around.

Dambulla Produce Market   MARKET
(Matale Rd; ☉ noon-3am) Even if you're not looking to buy a truckload of bananas, this vast wholesale market south of the centre offers a fascinating look at the vast range of produce grown in Sri Lanka. What you see being carted about with manic energy (be careful and stay out of everybody's way) will be sold in Colombo tomorrow.

🛏 Sleeping & Eating

Trucks on Highway A9, which cuts through the heart of Dambulla, thunder across town night and day, so bear this in mind when choosing a room. Guesthouses tend to be near the cave temples, while many tour-group-geared hotels are north of town. Some of the best places are way out in the lush countryside by the Kandalama lake.

Nature Tourist Inn   GUESTHOUSE $
(☎ 077 912 0855; naturetouristinn@gmail.com; Kandy Rd; d/tr incl breakfast Rs 1600/1950; 🛜) A sound little guesthouse managed with love and attention by Thomz and his family, who dote on their guests and can provide good local information and help with transport. All three simple rooms have private hot-water bathrooms, mosquito nets and fans. Yes, it's close to the road, but the cave temples are on your doorstep.

Healey Tourist Inn   HOMESTAY $
(☎ 228 4940; 172 Kandy Rd; s/d Rs 1200/1600; 🛜) This family-run place, within walking distance of the caves and bus station, has five basic, clean-if-Spartan rooms that have mosquito nets and a piece of furniture or two. You'll find common areas for chilling and the owners are helpful and welcoming.

Sundaras   GUESTHOUSE $$
(☎ 072 708 6000; www.sundaras.com; 189 Kandy Rd; dm US$15-20, r US$30-60, deluxe US$70-115; ✻ @ 🛜) This smart, modern converted villa offers comfort and space and is within a short stroll of the caves and museum. Staff are attentive and the rooms are kept clean and well-presented, the best sharing a terrace which overlooks a slim garden. Two 'deluxe' dorms (one is a four-bed female-only option) have recently been added, embracing the backpacker market.

It's a good place, but perhaps not the best value, as prices are a tad steep across the board. All rates include breakfast.

Dambulla Heritage Resthouse   HOTEL $$
(☎ 228 4799; http://ceylonhotelscorporation.com; Kandy Rd; s/d/tr US$64/70/82; ✻ 🛜) This former government rest house has been given the full Heritage treatment, and now boasts very classy interiors – the dark-wood furniture and elegant fabrics make more than a nod to colonial times. There's a great cafe-restaurant too. But, and this is a considerable but, it's close to the dreaded highway and traffic noise is omnipresent.

Arika Boutique Villa   BOUTIQUE HOTEL $$
(☎ 493 5045; www.arikavillas.com; Puwakattawala Road; r from US$72; ✻ 🛜 ≋) A small, hip hotel with spacious, stylish rooms with a nice blend of natural materials and a splash of contemporary art on the walls. It's 12km south of Dambulla, just off the Kandy Rd.

★ Kalundewa Retreat   HOTEL $$$
(☎ 077 307 6341; www.kalundewaretreat.com; r from US$144; ✻ @ 🛜 ≋) The attention to detail at Kalundewa Retreat is impressive, with a stunning range of accommodation units that feature polished-concrete floors, modern art and stylish wooden furniture; some have lovely arched roofs and private jacuzzis. The forest setting, lake, paddy fields, birdsong and undisturbed natural environment adds up to a wonderful experience.

Hiking, biking, birding (with a resident ornithologist), bathing (in a spring-fed pool) and kayaking on the lake can be arranged and there's lots of wildlife around the hotel (including peacocks and monitor lizards). Service and meals are excellent too, but note that no alcohol is sold – guests can BYO though). It's 7km east of Dambulla.

★ Heritance Kandalama Hotel   RESORT HOTEL $$$
(☎ 555 5000; www.heritancehotels.com; r from US$166; ✻ @ 🛜 ≋) Designed by renowned architect Geoffrey Bawa, this is one of Sri Lanka's signature hotels. The hotel emerges from the forest like a lost city, its walls and roofs covered in vines that allow it to blend into the natural environment. Light floods into the

beautifully appointed rooms and there's an infinity pool overlooking the Kandalama Wewa.

Seriously consider dropping by for a meal if you're not a guest; the setting and dining experience are what memories are made of. Wildlife encountered in the hotel grounds includes monkeys and deer, and birdwatching walks can be organised. It's 11km east of Dambulla.

Amaya Lake RESORT HOTEL **$$$**
(☑ 446 8100; www.amayaresorts.com; villas from US$130; ✳ @ 🖥 ☎) The Amaya Lake complex has over a hundred stylish villas set in magnificent landscaped grounds. The scale of the place will suit those looking for the full resort hotel experience, as the facilities are superb (including tennis courts, a gorgeous pool and a spa). Expect evening entertainment and buffet banquets. It's 9km east of Dambula.

Bentota Restaurant SRI LANKAN **$**
(Anuradhapura Rd; mains from Rs 300; ☺ 8am-8pm; ✳) In the town centre, this ever-reliable local chain offers good short eats, and tasty rice and curry.

Dambulla Heritage Resthouse Cafe CAFE **$$**
(Kandy Rd; mains Rs 600-1000; 🕿) A lovely cafe-restaurant, all monochrome photographs and period furniture, that's perfect for everything from a cappuccino and a piece of gateau to delicious meals like pot-roasted chicken (Rs 595) and lake fish (Rs 550). There's a good wine selection.

ⓘ Getting There & Around

Dambulla is 72km north of Kandy on the road to Anuradhapura. The junction with the Colombo–Trincomalee road (A6) is in the centre of town.

The closest train station is in Habarana, 23km north. Frequent buses run from the bus terminal:
Anuradhapura Rs 88, two hours, every 45 minutes
Colombo Rs 150, five hours, every 30 minutes
Kandy Rs 80, two hours, every 30 minutes
Polonnaruwa Rs 78, 1¾ hours, every 45 minutes
Sigiriya Rs 30, 45 minutes, every 45 minutes

Three-wheelers cost Rs 100 to 150 around town. Be aware that commission-hungry drivers will attempt to steer you to favoured places to stay.

Sigiriya

☑ 066 / POP 1800
Rising from the central plains, the iconic rocky outcrop of Sigiriya is perhaps Sri Lanka's single most dramatic sight. Near-vertical walls soar to a flat-topped summit that contains the ruins of an ancient civilisation, thought to be once the epicentre of the short-lived kingdom of Kassapa, and there are spellbinding vistas across mist-wrapped forests in the early morning.

Sigiriya refuses to reveal its secrets easily, and you'll have to climb a series of vertiginous staircases attached to sheer walls to reach the top. On the way you'll pass a series of quite remarkable frescoes and a pair of colossal lion's paws carved into the bedrock. The surrounding landscape – lily-pad-covered moats, water gardens and quiet shrines – and the excellent site museum, only add to Sigiriya's rock-star appeal.

History

Peppered with natural cave shelters and rock overhangs – supplemented over the centuries by numerous hand-hewn additions and modifications – Sigiriya may have been inhabited in prehistoric times.

The established historical theory is that the rock formation served royal and military functions during the reign of King Kassapa (AD 477–495), who built a garden and palace on the summit. According to this theory, King Kassapa sought out an unassailable new residence after overthrowing and murdering his own father, King Dhatusena of Anuradhapura. However, in recent years some archaeologists have challenged this viewpoint and believe Sigiriya was not a fortress-palace but a monastery and religious site.

After the 14th century the complex was abandoned. British archaeologist HCP Bell rediscovered the ruins in 1898, which were further excavated by British explorer John Still in 1907.

Unesco declared Sigiriya a World Heritage Site in 1982.

⊙ Sights

Sigiriya (www.ccf.lk/sigiriya.htm; adult/child US$30/15; ☺ tickets 8.30am-5.30pm) is an archaeological site. Shorts are fine and a sarong is not necessary. Expect a visit to take at least half a day.

To avoid the fiercest heat, get as early a start as possible. A good strategy is to head straight for the rock itself so you're climbing Sigiriya in the relative cool of the morning. The ascent involves steep climbs, so if you're not fit it may be tough. There's no shade on the exposed summit so a hat is recommended. Then later in the morning you can amble around the gardens and tour the museum.

Sigiriya

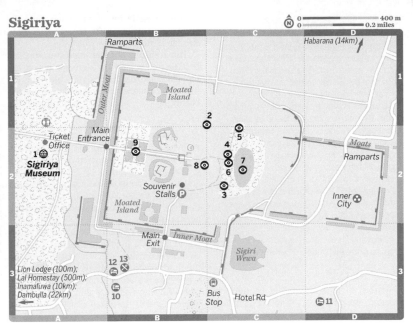

Hopeful guides hang around the entrance and will also approach you once you're inside. If you decide to use their services, negotiate very carefully.

Bring plenty of water (there are drink vendors near the entrance and exit).

Royal Gardens   GARDENS

The lowest section inside the Sigiriya complex is a beautifully landscaped area dotted with water gardens, then as you approach the rock its foothills contain boulder gardens (home to numerous Buddhist shrines) and terraced gardens. It's a beautiful place to explore away from the crowds (but perhaps better to experience at leisure after you've completed the hard yards of ascent and descent). Find a quiet spot and listen to the gentle gurgle of water and the songs of birds.

From the main entrance you pass symmetrical **water gardens**, which extend from the foot of the rock; bathing pools, little islands with pavilions that were used as dry-season palaces, and trees.

The **boulder gardens**, closer to the rock itself, feature rocks that once formed the bases of buildings. The steplike depressions in the sides of boulders were the foundations of brick walls and timber columns. The cistern and audience-hall rocks are impressive.

The rock rises sheer and mysterious from the jungle. A series of steps leads up through the boulders at its base to the western face, and then ascends it steeply.

The base of Sigiriya has been landscaped to produce the **terraced gardens**.

Frescoes   ART

Halfway up the rock there's an open-air spiral stairway leading up from the main route to a long, sheltered gallery in the sheer rock face.

THE ANCIENT CITIES SIGIRIYA

PALACE OR MONASTERY?

Though the established view is that Sigiriya's summit was the site of Kassapa's palace, some (including Dr Raja de Silva, Sri Lanka's former archaeological commissioner) are not convinced. In particular the absence of stone bases, post holes, visible foundations for cross walls or window sashes, and a lack of lavatory facilities has caused doubt and provoked heated academic debate as to the purpose of the structures. For de Silva, this site was a vast Buddhist monastery, embracing both Theravada and Mahayana practices, and existing for many centuries before and after Kassapa's rule. The summit was a sanctuary for meditation, containing *kutis* (cells) for monks and paved paths for Buddhist perambulation.

In this niche is a series of paintings of buxom, wasp-waisted women, popularly believed to represent either *apsaras* (celestial nymphs) or King Kassapa's concubines.

Protected from the sun in the sheltered gallery, the paintings remain in remarkably good condition, their colours still glowing. They're at their best in the late-afternoon light.

Modern theory suggests the female forms represent aspects of Tara – a bodhisattva and one of the most important figures in Tantric Buddhism. They are similar in style to the rock paintings at Ajanta in India, but have a specific character in their classical realist style. No one knows the exact dates of the impressive frescoes, though it's unlikely they date as far back as the 5th century (when King Kassapa reigned).

Mirror Wall   ART

Beyond the fresco gallery detour, the path clings to the sheer side of the rock and is protected on the outside by a 3m-high wall.

This wall was coated with a smooth glaze upon which visitors felt impelled to note their impressions of the women in the gallery above – or so says local legend. The graffiti was inscribed between the 6th and 14th centuries.

You'll have to look hard beyond the modern mess to see the ancient messages. One typical graffito reads, 'The ladies who wear golden chains on their breasts beckon me. As I have seen the resplendent ladies, heaven appears to me as not good.' Another reads, 'A deer-eyed young woman of the mountainside arouses anger in my mind. In her hand she had taken a string of pearls and in her looks she has assumed rivalry with us.'

The graffiti is of great interest to scholars because they show the development of the Sinhala language and script, and because they demonstrate an appreciation of art and beauty.

Lion's Paws   CARVINGS

At the northern end of the rock, the narrow pathway emerges on to the large platform from which the rock derived its later name – the Lion Rock (Sigiriya). HCP Bell, the British archaeologist responsible for an enormous amount of archaeology in Sri Lanka, found the two enormous lion paws when excavating here in 1898.

At one time a gigantic brick lion sat at this end of the rock, and the final ascent to the top commenced with a stairway that led between the lion's paws and into its mouth. The lion symbolism serves as a reminder to devotees ascending the rock that Buddha was Sakya-Simha (Lion of the Sakya Clan) and that the truths he spoke of were as powerful as the sound of a lion's roar.

The 5th-century lion has since disappeared, apart from the first steps and the paws. Reaching the top means clambering up across a series of grooves cut into the rock; fortunately there is a handrail.

Summit   SUMMIT

The spectacular terraced summit of the rock covers 1.6 hectares. This is thought to be the site chosen by King Kassapa for his fortified capital after he had assassinated his father. Today only the low foundations of structures exist, and the remains are visually unimpressive. Still, it's hard not to be captivated by the astonishing views from this lofty perch, which extend for miles across an emerald ocean of forest canopy.

A smooth stone slab (the so-called king's throne, possibly a meditation spot) sits 30m away from the ruins of a dagoba. The 27m-by-21m tank, hewn out of the rock, looks for all the world like a modern swimming pool, although it was probably used for water storage.

Cobra Hood Cave   CAVE

This rocky projection earned its name because the overhang resembles a fully opened cobra's hood. Generally you pass by this cave after descending the rock on your way to the south gate and the car park. Below the drip ledge is an inscription from the 2nd century BC that indicates it belonged to Chief Naguli, who would have donated it to a monk. The plastered interior of the cave was once embellished with floral and animal paintings.

★ Sigiriya Museum   MUSEUM

(⊙ 8.30am-5.30pm) This superb museum uses detailed and engaging displays and has a fine diorama of the site, providing an excellent overview and explaining Sigiriya's cultural importance beyond the obvious natural beauty.

The theory that Sigiriya was a Buddhist monastery is given here, although the established position that it was a palace or fortress prevails. Trade routes are explained, showing Sigiriya's connections with the Gulf, China, India and the Roman empire. Among the artefacts, the large buxom stone deity stands out.

The museum is near the main ticket booth. No photographs are permitted inside.

☞ Tours

The land around the rock is loaded with animals and natural features. The large resorts – including Elephant Corridor, Hotel Sigiriya and Jetwing Vil Uyana – all offer various nature tours from about Rs 2000. These are open to non-guests and usually include the services of a naturalist.

🛏 Sleeping & Eating

New hotels are opening all the time in the area around Sigiriya. It's easy to understand the appeal: the village is a mellow little place, off the main highway, and a far more preferable base than Dambulla.

There are a few traveller-geared cafe-restaurants in Sigiriya village, and virtually all guesthouses and hotels offer meals. For a spellbinding setting consider dining at Jetwing Vil Uyana.

★ Lion Lodge   GUESTHOUSE $

(☎ 071 479 3131; www.sigiriyalionlodge.com; r Rs 2200-4500; ❄ 🛜) An outstanding place to stay, thanks to the genuine welcome and attention paid to guests – it seems nothing is too much trouble for Agith and Ramya, the owners, who are constantly offering tea and snacks. Rooms are divided between the main building and a separate block (which are larger), all are immaculately clean and spacious.

It's up a little lane, a short walk west of the village. If you need air-conditioning, there's an extra charge.

Fresco Lion Villa   GUESTHOUSE $

(☎ 071 780 7634, 077 630 2070; www.letsgolanka. com; Sigiriya Rd; s Rs 3500-4000, d 4000-4500; ❄ 🛜) This well-run place (formerly Ancient Villa) has been totally renovated and now offers fine cottages with new fixtures and fittings in a leafy, rural compound about midway between Sigiriya and the Inamaluwa junction. At the rear there's a lovely little stream, which is often visited by thirsty elephants. Regular torch-lit barbecue dinners under the stars make for a memorable evening.

There's an extra charge (Rs 1000) for aircon. Bike (Rs 350) and scooter (Rs 1500) hire can be arranged. It's 7km west of the village centre.

Lal Homestay   GUESTHOUSE $

(☎ 228 6510, 077 704 5386; lalhomestay@gmail. com; 209 Ehelagala; r Rs 2000; ❄) For that living-with-a-family experience, Lal's is perfect. Your host family could not be more welcoming or friendly, offering home-cooked meals (try the delicious jackfruit curry) and useful travel info. The three rooms, each with verandah and hot-water bathroom, are kept clean and tidy.

Flower Inn   GUESTHOUSE $

(☎ 567 2197, 568 9953; r Rs 2500-3500; ❄ 🛜) This centrally located guesthouse bursts with plants, both plastic and genuine. The nine rooms at the rear are a little chintzy but fair value and maintained by a friendly family. Meals are not usually available but tea and coffee are.

Nilmini Lodge   GUESTHOUSE $

(☎ 077 306 9536, 567 0469; nilmini_lodge@yahoo. com; r Rs 1500-2500; ❄ 🛜) Old-school guesthouse owned by a family who have been

THE ANCIENT CITIES SIGIRIYA

DON'T MISS

EXPLORING AROUND SIGIRIYA

With a bike or scooter you can explore the entire region around Sigiriya, which has a wealth of lush forests, wild elephants, hundreds of bird species and no end of archaeological sites. One of the best places to start is **Pidurangala Rock**. About 1km north of the Sigiriya site, this important cultural spot includes a temple, a tiny museum and never any crowds. Most rewarding is the climb up the rock, where there are amazing views of the more famous rock looming to the south.

Another good ride follows backroads for 25km to Dambulla via the Amaya Lake hotel and Kandalama Wewa, the large tank (reservoir).

hosting travellers for years and can provide lots of useful tips about the rock and region. Rooms are basic (some share bathrooms), but adequate enough and certainly inexpensive. It's close to both the rock and village centre.

The Hideout Sigiriya LODGE **$$**
(077 771 6088; http://sigiriyahideout.com; r incl breakfast US$58-79; ✱ ☎ ⊠) The aptly named Hideout is indeed a real escape, tucked away at the end of a dirt road surrounded by fields and with viewing treehouses for spotting birds (including eagles and peacocks). It's extremely peaceful here. Rooms are spacious but perhaps a little prosaic for the prices asked. Still, the setting is lovely and the welcome is warm.

Upali, the charming elderly owner is a worldly gent who lived in Japan for years and has travelled the globe. Located 7km west of the village.

Fresco Water Villa HOTEL **$$**
(228 6160; www.frescowatervilla.com; r US$85; ✱ ☎ ⊠) A new three-storey modern hotel with minimalist rooms kitted out with stylish furniture and finished in subdued colours. It's set off the road and the 25m pool is heaven after a hard day tackling the rock. However the in-house restaurant is pricey. It's 5km west of the village centre.

Hotel Sigiriya HOTEL **$$**
(228 6821; www.serendibleisure.com; Hotel Rd; r from US$87; ✱ @ ⊠) There are truly remarkable views of the rock from the dining and pool areas at this hotel. Rooms are spacious enough but the decor could perhaps use an update. Lots of tour groups stay here and it's also popular with twitchers, lured by its resident naturalist who leads much-lauded bird-watching trips (Rs 2000).

Jetwing Vil Uyana LUXURY HOTEL **$$$**
(228 6000; www.jetwinghotels.com; Kibissa; r US$163-370; ✱ @ ☎ ⊠) For natural-world immersion – crocodiles in the pond, monitor lizards in the grass and occasional visiting elephants – the Jetwing is a great choice. The huge, individual chalets (book a 'water' or 'forest' dwelling for the best views) have a rustic look outside but inside are equipped with all mod cons (including Bose sound systems).

A resident naturalist is on hand to give walking tours, there's a yoga instructor, and the cuisine (and dining room setting) are superb. It's 7km west of the village.

Elephant Corridor LUXURY HOTEL **$$$**
(228 6951; www.elephantcorridor.com; Kibissa; r from US$220; ✱ @ ☎ ⊠) Set in over 80 hectares of unfenced grasslands, this high-end hotel is a terrific place to spot wildlife. Iguanas, monitor lizards and mongooses are all regularly encountered and wild elephants wander through the area. The villas are spectacular and incredibly spacious, all with private indoor plunge pools and there's a good spa and pool set in a forest clearing.

Rack rates are steep but web deals can drop tariffs to around US$100 a night. Located 7km west of the village.

Chooti SRI LANKAN **$**
(mains Rs 180-300; ☻ 7am-9pm; ☎) Cooking up a *rotti* storm, this likeable shop-cum-restaurant serves up delicious, freshly cooked sweet and savoury *rotti* bread by the roadside (and good meals too). Suck on a fresh coconut or slurp on a fruit shake and you're sated. It's in the centre of the village.

🛍 Shopping

Sigiriya Crafts Complex HANDICRAFTS
(Sigiriya Rd; ☻ 8am-6pm) Artisans and craftspeople, including wood carvers and sculptors, are based at this government-run crafts village about midway between Inamaluwa and Sigiriya.

ℹ Information

Stock up on cash elsewhere as there are no banks in Sigiriya and the nearest ATM is in tiny Kimbissa, 5km west of the village. You'll find plenty of banks in Dambulla, the nearest town.

Head to **Lonely Planet** (www.lonelyplanet.com/ sri-lanka/the-ancient-cities/sigiriya) for planning advice, author recommendations, traveller reviews and insider tips.

ℹ Getting There & Around

Sigiriya is about 10km east of the Inamaluwa junction on the main road between Dambulla and Habarana. Buses to/from Dambulla run about every 30 minutes from 6.30am to 6.30pm (Rs 28, 45 minutes). A three-wheeler between Dambulla to Sigiriya is around Rs 800.

Sigiriya and its surrounds are ideally explored by bike (Rs 300 per day) or scooter (Rs 1500); most guesthouses can organise rentals.

Habarana

066 / POP 8700
This small town serves as a base for Sigiriya and safaris to Minneriya and Kaudulla National Parks. There's a fast-expanding range of accommodation in the surrounding area, including lots of new luxury places. Transport

links are excellent: Habarana has the nearest train station to both Dambulla and Sigiriya and sits on a busy crossroads.

Elephant rides around the tank can be arranged for a pricey US$20 to US$30 per person per hour. In the creek near town you can watch mahouts scrubbing down their elephants; guides and most locals can point the way.

🛏 Sleeping & Eating

In the last few years many new upmarket places have opened around Habarana. The town itself also has some good hotels, though budget places are limited.

Habarana Inn   GUESTHOUSE $
(📞 227 0010; www.habaranainnsrilanka.com; Dambulla Rd; r Rs 3000; ❄ 🛜) An aging structure that still has some charm, but is really starting to show its (40) years. The rooms, all with mosquito nets and fans, are clean and simply furnished (book either 1 or 2, which face a very pretty rear garden). Meals are available.

Galkadawala   LODGE $$
(📞 077 373 2855; www.galkadawala.com; s/d incl breakfast from US$77/84; ❄ @ 🛜) Harmoniously built in a forest setting from recycled materials, this remote eco-lodge is perfect for wildlife enthusiasts, with nature (outstanding birdlife and the odd elephant) very much on your doorstep – which is the local tank. Maulie, your amiable and intelligent host, is very knowledgeable about the area and Galkadawala's vegetarian (only) food is a real highlight.

It's at the end of a dirt track, 11km west of Habarana.

The Heritage Habarana   HOTEL $$
(📞 227 0003; www.ceylonhotelscorporation.com; s/d incl breakfast US$66/72; ❄ 🛜) Formerly the Rest House, this attractive historic structure has been very sensitively renovated and offers high comfort levels and an excellent location in the heart of town. Its four rooms boast original (turquoise) window shutters and are fronted by a long shaded verandah. Dining in the excellent in-house Mini-Avanhala cafe-restaurant is a pleasure too.

Mutu Village   GUESTHOUSE $$
(📞 077 269 4579; www.mutuvillage.com; Kashyapagama; s/d US$40/48; ❄ 🛜) This new guesthouse is run by a very accommodating couple: Mutu is a superb cook and Ajith takes good care of guests. The environment is great, with a lovely garden to enjoy, away from the hubbub and traffic in town. Guides for wildlife spotting

and birding can be organised, as well as drivers for exploring the region. It's a ten-minute walk south of the main junction.

The Other Corner   LODGE $$$
(📞 011 739 9500, 077 374 9904; www.tocsrilanka.com; s/d incl breakfast US$85/110; ❄ @ 🛜 ☒) An earthy alternative to stark modernist hotels and minimalist rooms, the Other Corner is an excellent new (solar-powered) eco-lodge. It's set in extensive, shady grounds with herb gardens; the nine gorgeous mud-brick, thatched cabanas are linked by sandy trails. All food is prepared freshly to order (no buffets!). The excellent resident naturalist leads birdwatching walks. It's 1.5km south of the centre.

Aliya   LUXURY HOTEL $$$
(📞 204 0400; www.aliya-resort-and-spa-sigiriya-sri-lanka.en.ww.lk; r from US$121; ❄ @ 🛜 ☒) A bombastic new temple of luxury that's raised the bar very high indeed. The layout – a dramatic entrance, an elevated lobby overlooking Sigiriya, a lovely open-sided restaurant and village-like collection of stylish chalets – has been meticulously planned. The 30m infinity pool (with rock views at the end of each lap!) is breathtaking. Service and food are superb.

Rates are actually very reasonable considering the facilities. Be aware that such is the scale of the place (96 rooms and suites) it's not for those seeking an intimate experience. Located 4km southwest of town.

Cinnamon Lodge   LUXURY HOTEL $$$
(📞 227 0012; www.cinnamonhotels.com; r from US$135; ❄ @ 🛜 ☒) A very classy and professionally run hotel, with a Portuguese colonial design and 11 hectares of lush landscaping. A nature trail leads to a treehouse platform for viewing birds, deer and monkeys. Rooms are tastefully presented and comfortable. Cinnamon is rightly renowned for its food (everything from sushi to Sri Lankan) and the lunchtime buffet spread (Rs 2500) is exceptional.

The elegant main restaurant area is quite something, with tables overlooking the lovely pool.

Mini-Avanhala   CAFE, WESTERN $$
(www.ceylonhotelscorporation.com; The Heritage Habarana; mains Rs 600-1100; 🛜) The Heritage's cafe-restaurant is perched opposite the main junction in town, so is perfect for people-watching. There's a classy, turn-back-the-years ambience and a wide choice of food: local-style curries, Western breakfasts (Rs 490), sandwiches, grilled meats and 'devilled' dishes. Those with a sweet tooth must check

out the cake cabinet (try a piece of *rulang*, made from coconut and toffee).

❶ Getting There & Away

BUS

Buses stop at the crossroads outside the Heritage Habarana hotel. Frequent services:

Anuradhapura Rs 88, 2½ hours, every 30 minutes

Dambulla regular/air-con Rs 25/40, 30 minutes, every 30 minutes

Polonnaruwa Rs 40, one hour, every 30 minutes

TRAIN

The train station is 1km north of town on the Trincomalee road. The infrequent train services include the following:

Batticaloa 1st/2nd/3rd class Rs 380/210/115, 3½ hours, 1 daily

Colombo 1st/2nd/3rd class Rs 620/380/240, six hours, 2 daily

Polonnaruwa 1st/2nd/3rd class Rs 160/90/50, one to two hours, 2 daily

The station at Palugaswewa, 6km west, is served by more and faster trains.

Polonnaruwa

📷 027 / POP 15,800

Kings ruled the central plains of Sri Lanka from Polonnaruwa 800 years ago, when it was a thriving commercial and religious centre. From here, free-marketeers haggled for rare goods and the pious prayed at any one of its numerous temples. The glories of that age can be found in archaeological treasures which give a pretty good idea of how the city looked in its heyday. You'll find the archaeological park a delight to explore, with hundreds of ancient structures – tombs and temples, statues and stupas – in a compact core. The Quadrangle alone is worth the trip.

The fact that Polonnaruwa is close to elephant-packed national parks only adds to its popularity. And the town itself makes a pleasant base for a day or two, fringed by a huge, beautiful tank with a relaxed ambience.

History

For three centuries Polonnaruwa was a royal capital of both the Chola and Sinhalese kingdoms. Although nearly 1000 years old, it's much younger than Anuradhapura and generally in better repair (though smaller in scale).

The South Indian Chola dynasty made its capital at Polonnaruwa after conquering Anuradhapura in the late 10th century: Polonnaruwa was a strategically better place to guard against any rebellion from the Ruhunu Sinhalese kingdom in the southeast. It also, apparently, had fewer mosquitoes! When the Sinhalese King Vijayabahu I drove the Cholas off the island in 1070, he kept Polonnaruwa as his capital.

Under King Parakramabahu I (r 1153–86), Polonnaruwa reached its zenith. The king erected huge buildings, planned beautiful parks and, as a crowning achievement, created a 25-sq-km tank, which was so large that it was named the Parakrama Samudra (Sea of Parakrama). The present lake incorporates three older tanks, so it may not be the actual tank he created.

Parakramabahu I was followed by Nissanka Malla (r 1187–96), who virtually bankrupted the kingdom through his attempts to match his predecessors' achievements. By the early 13th century Polonnaruwa was beginning to prove as susceptible to Indian invasion as Anuradhapura was, and eventually it, too, was abandoned and the centre of Sinhalese power shifted to the western side of the island.

In 1982, Unesco added the ancient city of Polonnaruwa to its World Heritage list.

❂ Sights

Most visitors will find a day is enough time to explore the ruins, which can be conveniently divided into five groups: the Royal Palace group; the Quadrangle; the Northern Group (spread over a wide area); a small group near the Polonnaruwa Heritage Hotel on the banks of the tank; and the small Southern group, towards the New Town. There are also a few

---

NAVIGATING POLONNARUWA

Polonnaruwa has three distinct areas:

Old Town has a small commercial centre, hotels, the main museum and is close to the archaeological site. It borders the waters of Topa Wewa (Topa Tank) and has a relaxed, tropical vibe.

New Town is south of Old Town and also has hotels but is otherwise not very densely developed and has little of interest.

Kaduruwela is 4km east of Old Town and is the main commercial strip for the region. It has the main bus and train stations, banks and services, a lot of traffic and little beauty.

Polonnaruwa

Polonnaruwa

Archaeological Museum   MUSEUM
(⊙9am-6pm) This excellent museum is comprised of several rooms, each dedicated to a particular theme: the citadel, the outer city, the monastery area (check out the model of the monks' hospital and medical instruments) and Hindu monuments. The latter room contains a wonderful selection of bronzes, including some outstanding Shiva statues. One depicts Shiva, ringed by an *aureole* (celestial arch), performing a cosmic dance while trampling on a dwarf; another depicts a seated, four-armed Shiva bearing a battle axe.

◉ Royal Palace Group

This group of buildings dates from the reign of Parakramabahu I. It's the logical place

other scattered ruins. The main structures all have useful information plaques.

A bike is an ideal way to explore the area. There's plenty of shade around the monuments and vendors sell drinks (including iced coconuts) and snacks.

to start a tour of the site, before continuing north to see the other principal monuments.

Royal Palace
RUIN

The Royal Palace constructed by Parakramabahu was a magnificent structure measuring 31m by 13m, and is said to have had seven storeys. Today its crumbling remains look like giant cavity-ravaged molars.

The 3m-thick walls have holes to receive the floor beams for two higher floors; however, if there were another four levels, these must have been made of wood. The roof in this main hall, which had 50 rooms in all, was supported by 30 columns.

Audience Hall
RUIN

Parakramabahu's Audience Hall is notable for the frieze of elephants, each of which is in a different position. There are fine lions at the top of the steps.

Bathing Pool
RUIN

In the southeast corner of the palace grounds, the Bathing Pool (Kumara Pokuna) has two of its crocodile-mouth spouts remaining.

◉ Quadrangle

Only a short stroll north of the Royal Palace ruins, the area known as the Quadrangle is literally that – a compact group of fascinating ruins in a raised-up area bounded by a wall. It's the most concentrated collection of buildings you'll find in the Ancient Cities – an archaeologist's playpen. Besides the ruins described here, look for the **recumbent image house**, the **chapter house**, the **Bodhisattva shrine** and the **bodhi tree shrine**.

Polonnaruwa Quadrangle

Vatadage
BUDDHIST

In the southeast of the Quadrangle, the *vatadage* (circular relic house) is typical of its kind. Its outermost terrace is 18m in diameter, and the second terrace has four entrances flanked by particularly fine guardstones. The moonstone at the northern entrance is reckoned to be the finest in Polonnaruwa. Four separate entrances lead to the central dagoba with its four Buddhas. The stone screen is thought to be a later addition, probably added by Nissanka Malla.

Thuparama Gedige
BUDDHIST

At the southern end of the Quadrangle, the Thuparama Gedige is the smallest *gedige* (hollow Buddhist temple with thick walls) in Polonnaruwa, but is also one of the best: it's the only one with its roof intact, supported by corbel arch-style supports. The inner chamber is delightfully cool and contains eight beautifully executed Buddha statues.

The building shows a strong Hindu influence and is thought to date from the reign of Parakramabahu I.

Hatadage
MONUMENT

Erected by Nissanka Malla, the Hatadage monument is said to have been built in 60 hours. It's in poor condition today but was originally a two-storey building (and may have once housed the Buddha Tooth Relic). Stand at the entrance and admire the symmetry of the pillars receding into the distance.

Latha-Mandapaya
RUIN

The busy Nissanka Malla was responsible for the Latha-Mandapaya. This unique structure consists of a latticed stone fence – a curious imitation of a wooden fence with posts and railings – surrounding a very small dagoba. The dagoba is encircled by stone pillars shaped like lotus stalks, topped by unopened buds. It is said that Nissanka Malla sat within this enclosure to listen to chanted Buddhist texts.

Gal Pota
MONUMENT

The Gal Pota (Stone Book) is a colossal stone representation of an *ola* book. It is nearly 9m long by 1.5m wide, and 40cm to 66cm thick. The inscription on it, the longest such stone inscription in Sri Lanka (and there are many!), indicates that it was a Nissanka Malla publication. Much of it extols his virtues as a king, but it also includes the footnote that the slab, weighing 25 tonnes, was dragged from Mihintale, a mere 100km away.

Satmahal Prasada
MONUMENT

In the northeast corner stands the unusual ziggurat-style Satmahal Prasada, which consists of six diminishing storeys (there used to be seven), shaped like a stepped pyramid. Check out the figurines set in niches within its crumbling walls.

Atadage
MONUMENT

A shrine for the tooth relic, the Atadage is the only surviving structure in Polonnaruwa dating from the reign of Vijayabahu I.

Velaikkara Slab Inscription
MONUMENT

Just in case you thought that bureaucrats have evolved through the years, check out this 12th-century memorial slab with an equally lifeless slab of text tossing off credits in all directions.

◉ Around the Quadrangle

Dotted around the fringes of the Quadrangle there's a number of structures, including Shiva Devales (Hindu temples), relics from the South Indian invasion of the 10th century.

Shiva Devale No 1
HINDU

Just south of the Quadrangle, the 13th-century Hindu temple Shiva Devale No 1 displays the Indian influence that returned after Polonnaruwa's Sinhalese florescence. It is notable for the superb quality of its stonework, which fits together with unusual precision. The domed brick roof has collapsed, but when this building was being excavated a number of excellent bronzes, now in the Archaeological Museum, were found.

Shiva Devale No 2
HINDU

Shiva Devale No 2 is the oldest structure in Polonnaruwa and dates from the brief Chola period, when the Indian invaders established the city. Unlike so many buildings in the Ancient Cities, it was built entirely of stone, so the structure today is much as it was when built.

Pabula Vihara
BUDDHIST

Also known as the Parakramabahu Vihara, Pabula Vihara is a typical dagoba from the period of Parakramabahu I. This brick stupa is the third-largest dagoba in Polonnaruwa, and set in a woodland clearing.

◉ Northern Group

These ruins, all north of the city wall, start about 1.5km north of the Quadrangle. They include the impressive **Alahana Pirivena group** (consisting of the Rankot Vihara, Lankatilaka, Kiri Vihara, Buddha Seema Prasada and the other structures around them.) The name of the group means 'crematory college' – it stood in the royal cremation grounds established by Parakramabahu.

Further north is Gal Vihara, probably the most famous group of Buddha images in Sri Lanka.

We've organised the sites below in a south to north direction, the way you'll approach them from the Quadrangle. A bike makes exploration a lot easier.

Rankot Vihara
BUDDHIST

The 54m Rankot Vihara dagoba, the largest in Polonnaruwa and the fourth largest on the island, has been ascribed to the reign of King Nissanka Malla. Like the other major dagobas in Anuradhapura and Polonnaruwa, the dome consists of earth fill covered by a brick mantle and plaster. The construction clearly imitates the Anuradhapura style. Surgical instruments found in a nearby ruined 12th-century hospital are said to be similar to those used today.

Buddha Seema Prasada
RUIN

The highest building in the Alahana Pirivena group, this was the monastery abbot's convocation hall. This building features a fine *mandapaya* (raised platform with decorative pillars).

★ Lankatilaka
BUDDHIST

One of the most evocative structures in Polonnaruwa, the Lankatilaka temple was built by Parakramabahu and later restored by Vijayabahu IV. This huge *gedige* has 17m-high walls, although the roof has collapsed. The cathedral-like aisle leads to a huge standing (headless) Buddha. Offerings of incense, and the structure's columns and arches add to the distinctly ecclesiastical, devotional atmosphere.

The outer walls, decorated with bas-reliefs, show typical Polonnaruwa structures in their original state.

Kiri Vihara
BUDDHIST

Construction of the dagoba Kiri Vihara is credited to Subhadra, King Parakramabahu's queen. Originally known as the Rupavati Chetiya, the present name means 'milk white'. It was renamed when the overgrown jungle was cleared away after 700 years of neglect and the original lime plaster was found to be in perfect condition. It is still the best-preserved unrestored dagoba at Polonnaruwa.

★ **Gal Vihara**   MONUMENT
This is a group of beautiful Buddha images that probably marks the high point of Sinhalese rock carving. They are part of Parakramabahu's northern monastery. The Gal Vihara consists of four separate images, all cut from one long slab of granite. At one time each was enshrined within a separate enclosure.

The **standing Buddha** is 7m tall and is said to be the finest of the series. The unusual position of the arms and sorrowful facial expression led to the theory that it was an image of the Buddha's disciple Ananda, grieving for his master's departure for nirvana, since the reclining image is next to it. The fact that it had its own separate enclosure, along with the discovery of other images with the same arm position, has discredited this theory and it is now accepted that all the images are of the Buddha.

The **reclining Buddha** depicted entering parinirvana (nirvana-after-death) is 14m long. Notice the subtle depression in the pillow under the head and the wheel symbol on the pillow end. The other two images are both of the seated Buddha. The one in the small rock cavity is smaller and of inferior quality.

Nelum Pokuna   POND
A track to the left from the northern stretch of road leads to unusual Nelum Pokuna (Lotus Pond), nearly 8m in diameter, which has five concentric, descending rings of eight petals each. The pool was probably used by monks.

Tivanka Image House   MONUMENT
The northern road ends at Tivanka Image House. Tivanka means 'thrice bent', and refers to the fact that the Buddha image within is in a three-curve position normally reserved for female statues. The building is notable for the carvings of energetic dwarfs cavorting around the outside, and for the fine frescoes within – the only Polonnaruwa murals to have survived. Some of these date from a later attempt by Parakramabahu III to restore Polonnaruwa, but others are much older.

◎ Southern Group

The small southern group is close to the compound of top-end hotels. By bicycle it's a pleasant ride along the bund of the Topa Wewa. You'll likely find more cows (and their friends, the cattle egret) than you will people here.

Potgul Vihara   MONUMENT
Also known as the library dagoba, the Potgul Vihara is an unusual structure. A thick-walled, hollow, dagoba-like building, it is thought to have been used to store sacred books. It's effectively a circular *gedige*, and four smaller solid dagobas arranged around this central dome form the popular Sinhalese quincunx arrangement of five objects in the shape of a rectangle (one at each corner and one in the middle).

Statue   STATUE
Standing nearly 4m high, this statue displays an unusually lifelike human representation, in contrast to the normally idealised or stylised Buddha figures. Exactly whom it represents is a subject of some debate. One theory is that it's the Indian Vedic teacher, Agastya, holding a book. Or alternatively, it could be the bearded, stately figure is Parakramabahu I clasping the 'yoke of kingship'. Or some say that the king is simply holding a piece of papaya.

You'll find it at the northern edge of the group.

◎ Rest House Group

Concentrated a few steps to the north of the Polonnaruwa Heritage Hotel are the ruins of **Nissanka Malla's palace**, which have almost been reclaimed by the earth. The **Royal Baths** are the ruins nearest to Polonnaruwa Heritage Hotel.

King's Council Chamber   MONUMENT
This is where the king's throne, in the shape of a stone lion, once stood (it's now in Colombo's National Museum). Inscribed into each column in the chamber is the name of the minister whose seat was once beside it. The mound nearby becomes an island when the waters of the tank are high; on it are the ruins of a small summer house used by the king.

⌂ Sleeping

The Old Town is far less frenetic than the New Town (whose hotels are generally rather tired). Nearby Giritale is a good alternative, rural base.

Leesha Tourist Home   HOMESTAY $
(☏ 072 334 0591; leeshatourist@hotmail.com; 105/A New Town Rd; r with fan/air-con Rs 1800/2800; ❄ ☎) Good vibes are guaranteed at this fine guesthouse thanks to the efforts of genial owner Upali and his family. Rooms are well-priced and sparkling clean, all with mosquito nets and sprung matresses (though those abutting the main road suffer some traffic noise). It's a sociable place with tables for

playing Parcheesi or sampling the delicious home cooking.

Jeep safaris to Minneriya and Kaudulla can be organised, and bikes are available (Rs 300 per day).

Devi Tourist Home HOMESTAY $
(✆222 3181; devitouristhome@aol.com; Lake View Watte; r Rs 2200-3000; ❄@) Down a quiet, leafy suburban lane this well-run, inviting and orderly homestay is a good choice, with rooms (the cheapest are fan-only) arranged around a pretty garden. Meals are filling (don't miss string hoppers for breakfast), bicycles are available (Rs 200 per day) and they have their own tuk-tuk for pick-ups.

Samudra Guest House GUESTHOUSE $
(✆222 2817, 077 692 8813; Habarana Rd; r Rs 2000-3500; ❄🛜) Budget rooms (the cheapies have fans and cold water) are pretty good value in this rambling old house, though the owner is often not around – call for service. The rear garden is lovely, and meals are offered. Bicycles can be hired for Rs 300.

Thisara Guest House GUESTHOUSE $
(✆222 2654, 077 170 5636; www.thisaraguesthouse. com; r with fan/air-con Rs 2500/3000; ❄🛜) About 100m off the main road south of the Old Town, this place has clean, spacious rooms in two blocks, those at the rear with rice-paddy views are better and the ones to book. Bikes cost Rs 300 per day. Call for a pick-up from the bus or train station.

Manel Guest House GUESTHOUSE $
(✆222 2481; http://manelguesthouse.com; New Town Rd; r Rs 2500-3000; ❄@) Appearances are somewhat deceptive at this ugly-looking concrete structure (watch your head as you climb the stairs) as the rooms are actually fine for a night or two and are decent value. Wi-fi is only available in the restaurant area; meals are served.

Jayaru Guest House GUESTHOUSE $
(✆071 563 6678, 444 4263; jayaru.guest@yahoo. com; Circular Rd; r Rs 1200; 🛜) If you're looking for a really inexpensive room, this simple guesthouse is worth considering, as it's located in a quiet area and has a pleasant garden with tables and chairs for chilling. Rooms are simple, clean and have fans and mossie nets; bathrooms are cold water.

Siyanco Holiday Resort HOTEL $$
(✆222 6868; www.siyancoholidayresort.com; 1st Channel Rd; r Rs 4000-8500; ❄🛜🏊) Very central, this established hotel has an older block where rooms are basic and inexpensive (though you have to pay extra for air-conditioning). The new wing offers modern, spacious, inviting rooms with fridges and TVs. It's a short walk from the ruins and close to the tank.

The Lake HOTEL $$$
(✆011-558 5858; www.the-lake-polonnaruwa-sri-lanka.en.ww.lk; Potgul Vihara; s/d/tr 112/118/139; ❄@🛜🏊) Right by the lakeshore, this elegant, renovated two-storey hotel offers sublime views of the tank (and buffalo and birdlife) from its beautifully presented rooms, restaurant and pool area. The atmosphere is relaxing, with classical music in the lobby, monochrome photographs and attentive service.

🍴 Eating

There's little reason to venture far from your hotel or guesthouse for a meal as there are no stand-out selections locally.

Sathosa GROCERY STORE
(⏰24hr) This store is the place to buy snacks and picnic items for a shady spread at some far corner of the archaeological site.

The Lake Restaurant SRI LANKAN, WESTERN $$
(www.the-lake-polonnaruwa-sri-lanka.en.ww.lk; The Lake hotel, Potgul Vihara; mains Rs 400-1400; 🛜) This hotel's dining room enjoys a terrific perspective over the azure waters of the tank, and it's air-conditioned, so it offers a lunchtime respite from the tropical heat. Menuwise you can grab a bowl of noodles with vegies for Rs 350 or fine-dine for much more.

ℹ Information

The site's **ticket desk** (✆222 4850; www.ccf. lk/polonnaruwa.htm; adult/child US$25/12.50; ⏰7.30am-6pm), located at the museum, has some information.

The main archaeological site closes at 6pm. You'll enter from Habarana Rd, about 500m north of the museum. Tickets are not usually checked at the Polonnaruwa Heritage or Southern groups.

Although tickets technically allow you only one entrance, you can ask a ticket collector to sign and date your ticket so you can return. This way you could visit the site in the morning, take a break around midday and return in the late afternoon.

Old Town and Kaduruwela have ATMs.

KIT PC Computer Shop (70 Habarana Rd; per hr Rs 70; ⏰7.30am-10pm) Internet access.

Post Office (Batticaloa Rd) In the centre of the Old Town.

Tourist Police (⌨ 222 3099; Batticaloa Rd) In the Old Town at the main traffic circle.

❶ Getting There & Away

BUS

Polonnaruwa's main bus station is in Kaduruwela, 4km east of Old Town on Batticaloa Rd. Buses to and from the west pass through Old Town, but to make sure you get a seat, start at Kaduruwela.

Buses are frequent until about 4pm on main routes, which include:

Anuradhapura Rs 128, three hours

Colombo regular/air-con Rs 250/440, six hours

Dambulla via Habarana Rs 77, 1½ hours

Kandy regular/air-con Rs 88/175, three hours

TRAIN

Polonnaruwa is on the Colombo–Batticaloa railway line and is about 30km southeast of Gal Oya, where the line splits from the Colombo–Trincomalee line. The train station is in Kaduruwela.

Trains include the following:

Batticaloa 1st/2nd/3rd class Rs 280/150/85, 2½ hours, five daily

Colombo 1st/2nd/3rd class Rs 700/420/265, six to seven hours, two daily

❶ Getting Around

Frequent buses (Rs 10) link Old Town and Kaduruwela. Three-wheeler drivers ask for Rs 200 or more.

Bicycles are great for getting around Polonnaruwa's monuments, which are surrounded by shady woodland. Most guesthouses rent bikes for Rs 200 to 350 per day, or scooters for Rs 1500.

The waterside Potgul Mawatha (Lake Rd) is a beautiful ride, taking you along the shores of the Parakrama Samudra tank.

Giritale

⌨ 027 / POP 8200

Northwest of Polonnaruwa on the Habarana road, Giritale is a sleepy, spread-out settlement alongside the impressive 7th-century Giritale Tank. It's essentially a rural community, with a few places to stay (all 7km to 15km from Polonnaruwa). It makes a good base for visiting both the ruins of Polonnaruwa and Minneriya National Park.

🛏 Sleeping

There's a growing selection of accommodation in the Giritale area.

Lak Nilla HOMESTAY $
(⌨ 077 911 5265, 224 6808; shurlywt@yahoo.com; r Rs 2500; ✳ 🛜) A very simple but hospita-

ble homestay with three clean rooms in a friendly local's house, in a village setting off the highway. A sumptious dinner costs Rs 650 and bikes can be hired and safaris set up. It's around 10km northwest of Polo.

★ **Rice Villa Retreat** GUESTHOUSE $$
(⌨ 077 630 2070; www.letsgolankatours; 21 mile post, Polonnaruwa Rd, Jayanthipura; s Rs 4000-4500, d Rs 4500-5000; ✳ @ 🛜) A memorable place to stay, this beautifully located guesthouse enjoys an idyllic position overlooking an expanse of rice paddies. Bungalows are well-appointed, with modern bathrooms and contemporary design touches. After a hot day travelling, the spa – offering treatments and massages – is very tempting indeed. But best of all, the hospitality from the family owners is warm and genuine.

Add Rs 1000 if you want air-conditioning. Meals are excellent and cooking classes are offered. Reserve in advance and arrange a pickup from the Giritale bus stop, which is 3.5km to the east.

Nikawewa Eco Lodge LODGE $$
(⌨ 077 630 2070; www.letsgolankatours; r Rs 4500-5500; 🛜) A new venture by the owner of the excellent Rice Villa Retreat nearby, these stilted treehouses with private bathroom and forest views are the perfect escape for those that yearn for a rustic, natural environment. Wild elephants pass close by (rainy season is the best time to view them). Forest treks, walking and cycling trips and cooking classes are offered. Meals are a highlight, with Sri Lankan and Western breakfasts (Rs 500) and many local dishes to sample for dinner (from Rs 750). Call for a pickup.

Giritale Hotel HOTEL $$
(⌨ 224 6311; www.giritalehotel.com; r from US$82; ✳ @ 🛜 ✉) There was lots of updating going on when we dropped by this large hotel, so comfort levels in the (previously) dated rooms should have improved. It enjoys unmatched views over a forest to the tank – see if you can spot elephants across the water. It's mainly set up for buffet-style dining.

Deer Park RESORT $$$
(⌨ 224 6272; www.deerparksrilanka.com; r from US$108; ✳ @ 🛜 ✉) A large resort-style property, deep in the trees by the tank , is being steadily renovated. All cottages have lovely garden sitting areas, some have outdoor showers and the top units have views of Giritale Tank. Nature tours can be arranged and there is a spa and gym.

ℹ️ Getting There & Away

Frequent buses on the road between Polonnaruwa and Habarana (and other towns to the west) stop in Giritale village. None of the places to stay is especially near the stop, so arrange for a pickup.

Mandalagiri Vihara

This *vatadage* (circular relic house) is virtually identical to the one at Polonnaruwa, but while Polonnaruwa's is ringed by many other structures, this one stands alone atop a low hill. A granite flight of steps leads up to the *vatadage*, which has concentric circles of 16, 20 and 32 pillars around the dagoba and is noted for its fine stone screens. Four large Buddhas face the four cardinal directions. The site is uncrowded and accessed via a pretty country-road drive.

An earlier structure may have been built here around the 2nd century, but the one that stands today was constructed in the 7th century by Aggabodhi IV. There was once a hospital next to the *vatadage* – look for the bath shaped like a coffin.

ℹ️ Information

Admission tickets cost adult/child US$10/5, but it's rare for anyone to check your ticket.

ℹ️ Getting There & Away

Near Medirigiriya, about 30km north of Polonnaruwa, Mandalagiri Vihara is best visited as a half-day trip from Giritale. There are no places to stay or eat nearby. Without your own transport, this trip is a nearly impossible odyssey.

Minneriya & Kaudulla National Parks

With their proximity to Polonnaruwa and Habarana, the Minneriya and Kaudulla National Parks offer an excellent chance of seeing elephants and other animals without the crowds of Yala National Park. On some days you won't need to enter the parks to view elephants as they freely roam the countryside.

ℹ️ Information

If you want to see herds of elephants, first speak to locals (guesthouse staff, tour companies or guides) as they'll know which of these two parks have the greatest concentration at any one time.

To visit the parks you must be accompanied by a licensed guide and you must enter and leave by vehicle (which will be your guide's 4WD or truck). Both parks are well served by tours: during busy times you'll find guides in jeeps waiting at the park gates. Typically, however, you'll arrange a trip with your guesthouse or hotel (or you can hire a guide from those waiting at the main crossroads in Habarana). With guide fees – and the many park fees – two people can expect to pay around US$90 for a four-hour safari.

Besides the guide you hire, a park ranger will accompany you. Although this service is technically free, each group should tip the ranger a small amount. The parks are open dawn to dusk. Fees are as follows:

Minneriya National Park adult/child Rs 1950/1050, service charge Rs 1100, charge per vehicle Rs 250

Kaudulla National Park adult/child Rs 1200/700, service charge Rs 1000, charge per vehicle Rs 250

A VAT of 12% will be added to the figures above.

Minneriya National Park

This national park is one of the best places in the country to see wild elephants, which are often present in huge numbers, and wading birds. Dominated by the ancient Minneriya Tank, the park has plenty of scrub, forest and wetlands in its 88.9 sq km to also provide shelter for toque macaques, sambar deer, buffalo, crocodiles and leopards (the latter are very rarely seen however).

The dry season, from May to September, is reckoned to be the best time to visit (as by then water in the tank has dried up, exposing grasses and shoots to grazing animals). Elephants, which can number 200 or more, come to feed and bathe during what is known as 'the Gathering' (see page 214), and flocks of birds, such as little cormorants, painted storks, herons and large pelicans all fish in the shallow waters. However, it's also possible to see large numbers of elephants here at other times of year, too. We saw more than 100 in February when we visited.

The park entrance is on the Habarana–Polonnaruwa road. A visitor centre near the entrance sells tickets and has a few exhibits about the park's natural history. The initial 40-minute drive (along a very poor dirt road) into the heart of the park is through dense forest, where wildlife sightings are rare. But then the landscape opens up dramatically, and the views across the tank are superb.

Kaudulla National Park

This park stands on the fringe of the ancient Kaudulla Tank. It established a 66.6-sq-km elephant corridor between Somawathiya

THE GATHERING

One of Asia's great wildlife spectacles occurs at Minneriya National Park in August and September. Known as 'the Gathering', 200 or more elephants gather for several weeks in one concentrated spot. Long thought to be driven by thirst during the dry season, only recently has it been learned that the natural factors behind the Gathering are much more complex.

The elephants surround the Minneriya Tank, the huge reservoir first built in the 3rd century AD. It was assumed that they were there for the water, as it remains wet even when smaller water holes dry up. However, biologists have discovered that the water's retreat from the land is what really lures the elephants. As the tank shrinks, it leaves behind vast swaths of muddy earth that are soon covered in rich, tender grass. It's a tasty feast for the elephants and they come in droves.

Unfortunately, recent actions by the water authority (which manages irrigation for local farmers) have threatened the Gathering in recent years. When the tank is full, new grasses won't emerge. The result can be a lot of elephants standing around looking for their food. Other pressing issues include illegal encroachment inside the park and the poaching of wildlife.

Chaitiya National Park and Minneriya National Park. Just 6km off the Habarana–Trincomalee road at Gal Oya junction, it is also a popular safari tour from Polonnaruwa and Habarana because of the good chance of getting up close and personal with elephants. In October there can be up to 250 elephants in the park, including herds of juvenile males. There are also leopards, fishing cats, sambar deer, endangered rusty-spotted cats and sloth bears. The best months for a visit are October to March.

Ritigala Ruins

Deep inside the **Ritigala Strict Nature Reserve** are the sprawling, jungle-covered ruins of an extensive monastic and cave complex. The broken stone structures, fallen carvings and once-sacred caves lie on a 766m hill, a striking feature that looms above the dry central flatlands.

Ritigala was probably a place of refuge (as long ago as the 4th century BC) and also has mythological status. It's claimed to be the spot from which Hanuman (the monkey god) leapt to India to tell Rama that he had discovered where Sita was being held by the king of Lanka.

Monks found Ritigala's caves ideal for an ascetic existence, and more than 70 have been discovered. Royals proved generous patrons, especially King Sena I, who in the 9th century made an endowment of a monastery to the *pamsukulika* (rag robes) monks.

Ritigala was abandoned following the Chola invasions in the 10th and 11th centuries, after which it lay deserted and largely forgotten until it was rediscovered by British surveyors in the 19th century.

◉ Sights

The ruined structures that remain are not that visually impressive to the casual observer and there are none of the usual icons: no bodhi tree, no relic house and no Buddha images. The only embellishments are on the urinals at the forest monastery – it's been conjectured that by urinating on the fine stone carving the monks were demonstrating their contempt for worldly things.

Near the Archaeology Department bungalow are the remains of a *banda pokuna* (artificial pond), which apparently fills with water during the rainy season. It's an evocative location, with the steep green mountain providing a backdrop like a verdant amphitheatre. From here it's a scramble along a forest path via a donations hall to a **ruined palace** and the **monastery hospital**, where you can still see the grinding stones and huge stone baths. A flagstone path leads upwards; a short detour takes you to what is often described as a stone fort – or, more accurately, a lookout.

The next group of ruins of note are the double-platform structures so characteristic of forest monasteries. Here you can see the **urinal stones**. Scholars think they were used for meditation, teaching and ceremony.

❶ Information

Few people make it to Ritigala; it's a steep, punishing climb through the forest (allow at least three hours to see the site). Individual tickets cost US$10/5 per adult/child.

There are some Archaeology Department staff based here. At least one will insist on accompanying you on a tour of the ruins (a tip of Rs 500 or so per group is sufficient).

ⓘ Getting There & Away

Ritigala is 14km northwest of Habarana, the turnoff from the Anuradhapura–Habarana road is near the 14km post. It's then 6.2km on a good paved road followed by a rough track for 2.3km. It may be impassable after heavy rains.

Anuradhapura

📑 025 / POP 64,000

The ruins of Anuradhapura are one of South Asia's most evocative sights. The sprawling complex contains a rich collection of archaeological and architectural wonders: enormous dagobas, soaring brick towers, ancient pools and crumbling temples, built during Anuradhapura's thousand years of rule over Sri Lanka. Today several of the sites remain in use as holy places and temples; frequent ceremonies give Anuradhapura a vibrancy that's a sharp contrast to the ambience at Polonnaruwa.

Current-day Anuradhapura is a rather pleasant albeit sprawling city. Mature trees shade the main guesthouse areas, and the main street is orderly compared to the ugly concrete agglomerations elsewhere.

History

Anuradhapura first became a capital in 380 BC under Pandukabhaya, but it was under Devanampiya Tissa (r 247–207 BC) – during whose reign Buddhism reached Sri Lanka – that it first rose to great importance. Soon Anuradhapura became a great and glittering city, only to fall before a South Indian invasion – a fate that was to befall it repeatedly for more than 1000 years. But before long the Sinhalese hero Dutugemunu led an army from a refuge in the far south to recapture Anuradhapura. The 'Dutu' part of his name, incidentally, means 'undutiful' because his father, fearing for his son's safety, forbade him to attempt to recapture Anuradhapura. Dutugemunu disobeyed him, and later sent his father a woman's ornament to indicate what he thought of his courage.

Dutugemunu (r 161–137 BC) set in motion a vast building program that included some of the most impressive monuments in Anuradhapura today. Other important kings who followed him included Valagamba (r 109–103 BC), who lost his throne in another

Indian invasion but later regained it, and Mahasena (r AD 276–303), the last 'great' king of Anuradhapura, who was the builder of the colossal Jetavanarama Dagoba. He also held the record for tank construction, building 16 of them in all, plus a major canal. Anuradhapura was to survive for another 500 years before finally being replaced by Polonnaruwa, but it continued to face incursions from South India again and again – made all the easier by the cleared lands and great roads that were a product of Anuradhapura's importance.

◉ Sights

You'll need a couple of days to properly explore the Unesco-recognised **Anuradhapura Heritage Site** (www.ccf.lk/anuradhapura.htm; US$25; ⏱24hr).

The scale of the ruins is huge. You can appreciate individual areas such as the Citadel on foot but a bicycle is an ideal way to get around. There are pretty rides on car-free trails and walkways that link the main sites. The four main areas of interest are Mahavihara, the spiritual centre of Anuradhapura, home to the Sri Maha Bodhi; Abhayagiri Monastery, arguably the most evocative part of the entire site, with several temples and dagobas more than 2000 years old, spread over a large, forested area; the Citadel, a compact collection of structures about 1000 years old; and Jetavanarama, a huge dagoba and important museum in a small area.

◉ Mahavihara

This is the heart of ancient Anuradhapura and is often the scene of religious ceremonies, which draw masses of people dressed in their finest. Relics here date from the 3rd century BC to the 11th century AD.

★**Sri Maha Bodhi**　　SACRED TREE
(admission Rs 200) The sacred bodhi tree is central to Anuradhapura in both a spiritual and physical sense. It was grown from a cutting

ⓘ TEMPLE ETIQUETTE

Because so many of Anuradhapura's important sites are still considered holy it is important to be prepared to remove your shoes, wear a sarong or otherwise don modest dress as required.

Sri Lankan pilgrims wear white, which is considered a holy colour, a mode you might choose to copy out of respect (and also as it reflects strong sunlight).

Anuradhapura

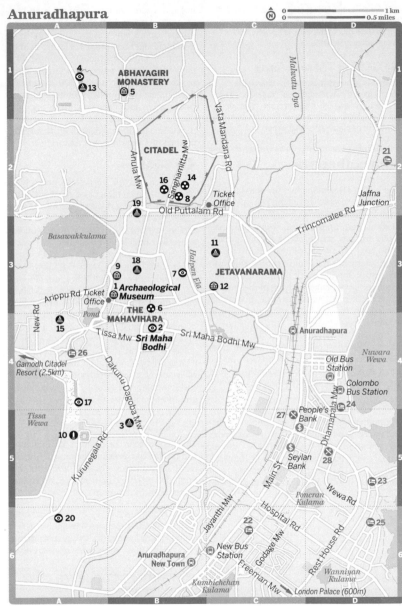

brought from Bodhgaya in India and is said to be the oldest historically authenticated tree in the world; tended by an uninterrupted succession of guardians for over 2000 years, even during the periods of Indian occupation.

Today thousands of devotees come to make offerings, particularly on *poya* (full-moon) days and weekends. Sunset is a magical time to visit.

The faithful believe it was Princess Sangamitta, sister of Mahinda (who introduced the Buddha's teachings to Sri Lanka) who brought the cutting from India so it has a

Anuradhapura

connection to the geographical heart of the Sinhalese religion.

There is not one but many bodhi trees here; the oldest and holiest stands on the top platform. Railing and other structures around the trees are festooned with prayer flags.

April and December are particularly busy months as pilgrims converge on the site for *snana puja* (offerings or prayers).

Brazen Palace RUIN

So called because it once had a bronze roof, the ruins of the Brazen Palace stand close to the bodhi tree. The remains of 1600 columns are all that is left of this huge palace, said to have had nine storeys and accommodation for 1000 monks and attendants.

It was originally built by Dutugemunu more than 2000 years ago, but through the ages was rebuilt many times, each time a little less grandiosely.

The current stand of pillars (now fenced off) is all that remains from the last rebuild – that of Parakramabahu around the 12th century.

Ruvanvelisaya Dagoba BUDDHIST

This magnificent white dagoba is guarded by a wall with a frieze of hundreds of elephants standing shoulder to shoulder. Apart from a few beside the western entrance, most are modern replacements for the originals from 140 BC.

Today, after incurring much damage from invading Indian forces, it rises 55m, considerably less than its original height; nor is its form the same as the earlier 'bubble' shape. Its lowest circumference is usually wrapped in a strip of dazzlingly coloured cloth.

Ruvanvelisaya was commissioned by King Dutugemunu, but he didn't live to see its completion. However, as he lay on his deathbed, a false bamboo-and-cloth finish was placed around the dagoba so that Dutugemunu's final sight could be of his 'completed' masterpiece. A limestone statue south of the great dagoba is popularly thought to be of Dutugemunu.

The land around the dagoba is rather like a pleasant green park, dotted with patches of ruins, the remains of ponds and pools, and collections of columns and pillars, all picturesquely leaning in different directions. Slightly southeast of the dagoba you can see one of Anuradhapura's many monks' refectories. Keeping such a large number of monks fed and happy was a full-time job for the lay followers.

Thuparama Dagoba BUDDHIST

In a beautiful woodland setting north of the Ruvanvelisaya Dagoba, the Thuparama Dagoba is the oldest dagoba in Sri Lanka – indeed, probably the oldest visible dagoba in the world. It was constructed by Devanampiya Tissa in the 3rd century BC and is said to contain the right collarbone of the Buddha. Its 'heap-of-paddy-rice' shape was restored in 1862 to a more conventional bell shape and to a height of 19m.

The slender, capital-topped pillars of the surrounding *vatadage* (circular relic house), perhaps the dagoba's most unique feature, enclose the structure in four concentric circles. Impressions on the dagoba pediments indicate the pillars originally numbered 176, of which 41 still stand. Although some Sri Lankan scholars believe these once supported a conical wooden roof, there is no archaeological evidence for this theory, nor does it follow any known antecedent in South India, whose dagobas were the prototypes for virtually all Sinhalese dagobas.

⦿ Abhayagiri Monastery

For the sheer delight of exploring an ancient city, much of it still enveloped in tropical forest, the 2000-year-old Abhayagiri Monastery area can't be beat.

★ Abhayagiri Dagoba   BUDDHIST

Dating back to the 1st century BC, this colossal dagoba was once the ceremonial focus of a 5000-strong monastery. Originally over 100m high, it was one of the greatest structures in the ancient world, its scale only matched by the pyramids of Giza (and nearby Jetavanarama). Today, after several reconstructions, Abhayagiri Dagoba soars 75m above the forest floor. Visually, it's stunning, and your first glimpse of this brick monument (which is shielded by surrounding forest) through a gap in the trees is breathtaking.

The name means 'Hill of Protection' or 'Fearless Hill'. In the Saddarma Rathnawaliya scripture it says a statue of a golden bull containing relics of the Buddha was buried in the core of the stupa.

Abhayagiri Dagoba has some interesting bas-reliefs, including one near the western stairway of an elephant pulling up a tree. A large slab with a Buddha footprint can be seen on the northern side, and the eastern and western steps have unusual moonstones made from concentric stone slabs.

Moonstone   MONUMENT

A ruined 9th-century school for monks northwest of the Abhayagiri Dagoba is notable for having the finest carved moonstone in Sri Lanka; see how many species of animals you can find in its elaborate carvings. This is a peaceful wooded area full of butterflies, and makes a good place to stop and cool off during a tour of the ruins (there are drinks and snack stands close by). Look for the fine steps featuring plump little figures.

It forms part of a structure often mistakenly described as Mahasena's Palace or the Queen's Pavilion.

Ratnaprasada   RUIN

Most of the 8th-century Ratnaprasada or 'Gem Palace' lies in ruins today, though it was originally five stories high with a graceful, tiered roof. At its entrance, however, you'll find a beautifully carved *mura gala* (guardstone), which depicts the Cobra King holding a vase with a flowering branch, with a dwarf attendant at his feet and his head framed by a cobra hood.

In the 8th century a new order of *tapovana* (ascetic) monks settled in the fringes of the city, among the lowest castes, the rubbish dumps and the burial places. These monasteries were large but unadorned structures; ornamentation was saved for toilets, now displayed at the Archaeological Museum. The monks of Ratnaprasada monastery gave sanctuary to people in trouble with the authorities, and this led to a major conflict with the king. When court officials at odds with the king took sanctuary in the Ratnaprasada, the king sent his supporters to capture and execute

---

ANURADHAPURA'S NEW STUPA

Two thousand years after the first of the great dagobas was constructed, a huge new stupa, **Sandahiru Seya** (Moon-Sun Temple), is emerging on the south side of Anuradhapura. Commissioned by President Rajapaksa, work started in 2010.

Designed to reach 85m in height, with a circumference of 244m, it will rise above the ancient dagobas of Jetavanarama and Abhayagiri (but will not surpass the original height of these two monuments). Sandahiru Seya is being constructed from brick (mor than 30 million) and will be plastered then whitewashed when finished.

Controversially, this is just one of nine new stupas planned, on orders of the president 'in appreciation of the noble service rendered by the armed forces and police to defeat terrorism and bring lasting peace to the country'. However, some have objected to the principle of dedicating a religious monument to the actions of the Sri Lankan military. The government's position is that most citizens have backed the scheme (and many have made donations to the project).

Sandahiru Seya is scheduled to be completed by 2016.

them. The monks, disgusted at this invasion of a sacred place, departed en masse. The general populace, equally disgusted, besieged the Ratnaprasada, captured and executed the king's supporters and forced the king to apologise to the departed monks in order to bring the monks back to the city and restore peace.

To the south of the Ratnaprasada is the **Lankarama**, a 1st-century-BC *vatadage*.

Abhayagiri Museum   MUSEUM

(◎10am-5pm) `FREE` The Chinese-funded Abhayagiri Museum, just south of the Abhayagiri Dagoba, commemorates the 5th-century visit of Chinese Buddhist monk Faxian to Anuradhapura. Faxian spent some time living at the Abhayagiri monastery translating Buddhist texts, which he later brought back to China. The museum, arguably the most interesting in Anuradhapura, contains a collection of squatting plates, jewellery, pottery and religious sculpture from the site. There's a lot of information (in English and Sinhala) about the many monuments of Anuradhapura and a bookshop.

Samadhi Buddha   MONUMENT

This 4th-century statue, seated in the meditation pose, is regarded as one of the finest Buddha statues in Sri Lanka. Pandit Nehru, a prominent leader in India's independence movement, is said to have maintained his composure, while imprisoned by the British, by regular contemplation of a photo of this statue.

Kuttam Pokuna (Twin Ponds)   WATER FEATURE

These swimming-pool-like ponds were likely used by monks from the monastery attached to Abhayagiri Dagoba. Water entered the larger pond through the mouth of a *makara* (mythical multispecies beast) and then flowed to the smaller pond through an underground pipe. Note the five-headed cobra figure close to the *makara* and the water-filter system at the northwestern end of the ponds.

Although they are referred to as twins, the southern pond, which is 28m in length, is smaller than the 40m-long northern pond.

Eth Pokuna (Elephant Pond)   WATER FEATURE

Surrounded by jungle, the magnificent *eth pokuna* (elephant pond) is thought to be an ancient water storage pool for the Abhayagiri monastery, rather than a swimming pool for pachyderms. However such is its scale – 159m long, 53m wide and 10m deep – a whole herd could undoubtedly bathe here.

Underground channels from the Periyamkulama Tank keep the pond topped up, and are still in working order – during very heavy rains water pours into the pond from inlets.

◎ Citadel

Time has not been kind to the Citadel and its once-great walls have almost entirely been re-absorbed by the earth.

Royal Palace   RUIN

Built in 1070 (some 12 centuries after Anuradhapura's fall) this palace was an attempt by King Vijayabahu I to link his reign with the glories of the ancient Sinhalese capital. Little remains today except two fine guardstones.

Mahapali Refectory   RUIN

The Mahapali refectory is notable for its immense trough (nearly 3m long and 2m wide) that the lay followers filled with rice for the monks.

Dalada Maligawa   RUIN

In the Royal Palace area you can also find the Dalada Maligawa, a temple that may have been the first Temple of the Tooth. The sacred Buddha's tooth originally came to Sri Lanka in AD 313.

◎ Jetavanarama

Jetavanarama Dagoba   BUDDHIST

The Jetavanarama Dagoba's massive dome rises above the entire eastern part of Anuradhapura. Built in the 3rd century by Mahasena, it may have originally topped 120m, but today is about 70m – similar to the Abhayagiri. When it was built it was almost certainly the third-tallest monument in the world, the first two being Egyptian pyramids.

Its vast, bulbous form is unplastered and said to consist of more than 90 million bricks.

A British guidebook from the early 1900s calculated that Jetavanarama contained enough bricks to make a 3m-high wall stretching from London to Edinburgh.

Behind it stand the ruins of a monastery that housed 3000 monks. One building has door jambs over 8m high still standing, with another 3m underground.

Jetavanarama Museum   MUSEUM

(◎8.30am-5.30pm) A 1937 British colonial building provides a suitably regal venue for some of the treasures found at Jetavanarama. The objects displayed here show great artisanship and detail. Look for the elaborate carved urinal in Room 1. In the fittingly named Treasure Room there are beautiful examples of jewellery, necklaces, carvings and pottery. Look for the 7th-century gold Buddhas.

Buddhist Railing   HISTORIC SITE
A little south of the Jetavanarama Dagoba, on the other side of the road, there is a stone railing built in imitation of a log wall. It encloses a site 42m by 34m, but the building within has long disappeared.

◉ Museum Quarter

Anuradhapura has one main museum, the Archaeological Museum, which covers most of the local sites. Two other museums, the Abhayagiri Museum and Jetavanarama Museum, are closely tied to their namesake sites.

★ Archaeological Museum   MUSEUM
(entrance included with Sri Maha Bodhi ticket; ⊘ 8am-5pm Wed-Mon, closed public holidays) The old British colonial administration building has recently been renovated and has an interesting collection of artwork, carvings and everyday items from Anuradhapura and other historic sites around Sri Lanka.

Exhibits include a restored relic chamber, as found during the excavation of the Kantaka Chetiya dagoba at nearby Mihintale, and a large-scale model of Thuparama Dagoba's *vatadage* as it might have been if a wooden roof (for which there is no physical or epigraphic evidence) had existed. In the museum's grounds are the carved squatting plates from Anuradhapura's western monasteries, whose monks had forsaken the

---

TANKS
....
Anuradhapura has three great tanks. **Nuwara Wewa**, on the east side of the city, is the largest, covering about 12 sq km. It was built around 20 BC and is well away from most of the old city. The 160-hectare **Tissa Wewa** is the southern tank in the old city.

The oldest tank, probably dating from around the 4th century BC, is the 120-hectare **Basawakkulama** to the north. Northwest of here are the ruins of the western monasteries, where the monks dressed in scraps of clothing taken from corpses and, it's claimed, lived only on rice.

All are good for quiet bike rides and walks.

---

luxurious monasteries of their more worldly brothers. To show their contempt for the effete, luxury-loving monks, the monks of the western monasteries carved beautiful stone squat-style toilets, with their brother monks' monasteries represented on the bottom. Their urinals illustrated the god of wealth showering handfuls of coins down the hole. Look for other interesting and characterful sculptures scattered about the grounds.

Folk Museum   MUSEUM
(admission Rs 100; ⊘ 8.30am-5pm Sat-Wed, closed public holidays) A short distance north of the Archaeological Museum there's a Folk Museum with dusty exhibits of country life in Sri Lanka's North Central Province.

◉ Other Sites

South and west of the main historic and sacred areas are several more important sites.

Mirisavatiya Dagoba   BUDDHIST
(Rs 250) This huge dagoba was the first built by Dutugemunu after he captured the city in the 2nd century BC. The story goes that Dutugemunu went to bathe in the tank, leaving his ornate sceptre implanted in the bank. When he emerged he found his sceptre, which contained a relic of the Buddha, impossible to pull out. Taking this as an auspicious sign, he had the dagoba built.

Mirisavatiya Dagoba is one of three very interesting sites that can be visited in a stroll or ride along the banks of the Tissa Wewa.

Royal Pleasure Gardens   ROYAL GARDENS
Known as the Park of the Goldfish, these extensive royal pleasure gardens cover 14 hectares and contain two ponds skilfully designed to fit around the huge boulders in the park. The ponds have fine reliefs of elephants on their sides. It was here that Prince Saliya, the son of Dutugemunu, was said to have met a commoner, Asokamala, whom he married, thereby forsaking his right to the throne.

Isurumuniya Vihara   MONUMENT
(admission Rs 200; ⊘ 8am-6pm) The rock temple, dating from the reign of Devanampiya Tissa (r 247-207 BC), has some very fine carvings. Best known of the sculptures is the 'lovers', which dates from around the 5th century AD and is built in the artistic style of the Indian Gupta dynasty of the 4th and 5th centuries. There is a lovely lotus pond in front. Other images (including one of elephants playfully splashing water) remain in situ on the rock

face but most carvings have been moved into a small museum within the temple.

Vessagiriya
HISTORIC SITE

South of the Isurumuniya Vihara are extensive remains of the Vessagiriya cave monastery complex, which dates from much the same time.

🎊 Festivals & Events

Unduvap Poya
RELIGIOUS

(☉Nov) Each November, thousands of pilgrims flock to Anuradhapura for Unduvap Poya, which marks the arrival of the sacred bodhi tree from India, and there are impressive ceremonies.

☞ Tours

Most places to stay can arrange for licensed guides if you'd like – useful if you want a deep understanding of Anuradhapura and its rich history. Rates start at about Rs 1500 for two hours with you providing the transport.

One of the best local guides is **Charitha Jithendra Jith** (☑ 077 303 7835; charithjith@ yahoo.com).

🛏 Sleeping

Hotels and guesthouses are scattered around town and many new places are opening in the countryside around the city. The greatest concentration of places is in the pleasant leafy neighbourhood between Main St and the Nuwara Wewa tank.

Note that commission-seeking hotel touts often board trains a few stations outside of town and hassle visitors. Three-wheeler drivers are equally pushy. Many places offer a free pick-up from transport terminals.

★ Milano Tourist Rest
HOTEL $

(☑ 222 2364; www.milanotouristrest.com; 40/596 JR Jaya Mawatha; r Rs 1500-3500; ❄@🛜) An excellent place to stay, Milano is a professionally run place in an elegant late-1950s house, with period furnishings and a touch of class that belie the moderate prices. All rooms have thick mattresses, fridges, satellite TV and modern bathrooms. The restaurant is good and there's a lovely garden for al fresco dining.

Miano has expanded operations to a second villa a short walk away, which offers the same high standards.

French Garden Tourist Rest
GUESTHOUSE $

(☑ 222 3537; www.frenchgardenanuradhapura.com; 488/4 Maithnipala Senanayake Mawatha; r Rs 1500-2500; ❄🛜) Close to the New Bus Station, this two-storey guesthouse is well set up for travellers. Its seven rooms are clean and have mosquito nets; filling meals are served and the efficient team in charge are on-the-money.

Andorra Tourist Rest
GUESTHOUSE $

(☑ 071 406 6932; 10/2/L Nuwarawewa Watte; r with fan/air-con 1000/1500; ❄🛜) New in 2014, this neat little, cheap guesthouse enjoys a near-rural location with many peacocks seen in the mornings (and fireflies at night). Rooms are smart and modern, very clean and have TVs; one has a balcony with rice-paddy views. It's about 3km east of the ruins.

★ Lakeside at Nuwarawewa
HOTEL $$

(☑ 222 3265; www.lakeside-at-nuwarawewa-anuradhapura-sri-lanka.en.ww.lk; Dhamapala Mawatha; s/d/tr US$70/80/90; ❄@🛜) Renovated from top to tail, this hip modernist hotel, built in 1957, has a sublime, utterly beguiling location on the banks of the lovely Nuwara Wewa tank. All rooms are immaculately presented and have a balcony or verandah (7 to 18 have tank views). It's great value, and the restaurant is excellent too.

Gamodh Citadel Resort
HOTEL $$

(☑ 492 8906; www.gamodhcitadelresort.com; Lolugaswewa, Elayapaththuwa; r Rs 5000-8000; ❄🛜) A terrific rural hotel, offering rooms with very high comfort levels in the two new blocks and comfortable-enough (if smallish) rooms in the old one. The landscaped grounds are wonderful, with tables dotted around a lawn that stetches down to a generously sized pool, and meals are very flavourful. It's 2.5km west of the Tissa Wewa tank.

London Palace
GUESTHOUSE $$

(☑ 223 5070; www.londonpalacesl.com; 119/29r Malagas Jen; r Rs 3500-6000; ❄@🛜) Impressive new two-storey place ('palace' is a little ambitious!) with ten lovely, clean, bright and airy rooms with high-quality furnishings, TV, minibar, neutral-colour schemes and balcony (except the single). The location is a little way from the centre, but bikes are available (Rs 400). It's owned by the efficient people behind Milano Tourist Rest.

Hotel Randiya
HOTEL $$

(☑ 222 2868; www.hotelrandiya.com; 19A/394 Muditha Mawatha; r incl breakfast Rs 4500-6250; ❄@🛜) This hotel looks good from the outside, with its *walawwa* (minor palace) style architecture. Inside, rooms are well-maintained but showing their age now. Still, staff are sweet and there's a great

THE AUKANA BUDDHA

According to legend, the magnificent 12m-high standing **Aukana Buddha** (admission Rs 500) was sculpted during the reign of Dhatusena in the 5th century, though some sources date it to the 12th or 13th century. Aukana means 'sun-eating', and dawn – when the first rays light up the huge statue's finely carved features – is the best time to see it.

Note that although the statue is still narrowly joined at the back to the rock face it is cut from, the lotus plinth on which it stands is a separate piece. The Buddha's pose, *ashiva mudra*, signifies blessings, while the burst of fire above his head represents the power of total enlightenment.

You'll need a sarong to visit the statue; the ticket office is at the top of the first set of steep steps. A couple of vendors sell drinks near the parking area.

Getting There & Away

The Aukana Buddha is 800m from the village of Aukana. It's hard to visit this site by public transport. Buses between Dambulla and Anuradhapura stop at the junction town of Kekirawa (Rs 30, 30 minutes, every 30 minutes), from where there are infrequent services to Aukana, so you may be hanging around for some time. A three-wheeler from Kekirawa to Aukana is around Rs 1000 with waiting time.

Alternatively, Aukana is on the Colombo to Trincomalee rail line. Four daily trains stop here: the station is 1km from the statue.

---

wood-panelled bar for drinks. A pool was under construction when we dropped by.

The Sanctuary at Tissawewa
HISTORIC HOTEL **$$$**

(☑ 222 2299; www.the-sanctuary-at-tissawewa-anuradhapura-sri-lanka.ww.lk; s/d incl breakfast US$106/118; ❄ 🛜) For sheer colonial class this Raj-era relic (formerly a British governor's residence) can't be matched. It's been beautifully and respectfully restored – the stylish rooms boast all mod cons and the verandahs are a delightful place to enjoy a peaceful afternoon, overlooking the mature gardens dotted with mahogany and teak trees and home to peacocks and monkeys.

Service is excellent and the in-house restaurant is among the best in town.

Palm Garden Village Hotel
HOTEL **$$$**

(☑ 222 3961; www.palmgardenvillage.com; Old Puttalam Rd, Pandulagama; r from US$105; ❄ 🛜 🏊) Set in leafy gardens with a lovely pool area, this resort hotel has spacious, if slightly dated, rooms set in 38 hectares of gardens. Extras include tennis courts, an Ayurvedic spa and the occasional visiting elephant. It's 6km west of town.

🍴 Eating

Dining choices are surprisingly limited in Anuradhapura. Several hotels have good restaurants, including The Sanctuary at Tissawewa.

Walkers
SRI LANKAN **$**

(Harischandra Mawatha; mains Rs 200-350; 🛜) Just east of the 'elephant' roundabout this modern cafe-restaurant-store is a popular spot for egg, curry and noodle dishes. There's a side terrace for dining and staff are friendly.

Family Super
SUPERMARKET **$**

(279 Main St; meals Rs 100-250; ⊘ 7am-8.30pm) Anuradhapura's best supermarket has imported foods, sunscreen, mosquito repellent and a separate bakery area with good short eats and ice cream.

Casserole
CHINESE **$$**

(279 Main St; mains Rs 500-700; ⊘ 7am-8.30pm; 🛜) It's nothing that special but if you're in urgent need of some air-con and non-local food this large 2nd-floor restaurant has lots of Chinese, East Asian (try the nasi goreng) and Western dishes.

⭐ The Sanctuary at Tissawewa
INTERNATIONAL, SRI LANKAN **$$$**

(www.the-sanctuary-at-tissawewa-anuradhapura-sri-lanka.en.ww.lk; mains Rs 800-1600; 🛜) There are few better situations for an enjoyable meal or drink than the verandahs and dining room in this beautiful colonial hotel. Try the chilli-marinated grilled pork chops, a seafood platter or one of their sandwiches. If you're touring the ruins in the daytime heat, drop by for a coffee (the best in town, served in white embossed china cups) or juice. No alcohol is served but you can BYO.

ℹ️ Information

Main St and Dhamapala Mawatha in the centre have banks and ATMs as well as shops selling anything you might need.

Head to **Lonely Planet** (www.lonelyplanet.com/sri-lanka/the-ancient-cities/anuradhapura) for planning advice, author recommendations, traveller reviews and insider tips.

TICKETS FOR ANURADHAPURA

Entrance tickets for the main sites of Anuradhapura cost US$25/15 per adult/child.

Unfortunately the Anuradhapura ticket is valid for only one day. To avoid having to buy more than one, you'll need to be strategic. Tickets are most closely inspected in the Abhayagiri, Citadel and Jetavanarama collections of sites and museums plus the main Architecture Museum. You could try to squeeze your touring of these important sites into one day and then use a second day for sites with their own entrance fees, such as Sri Maha Bodhi and Mirisavatiya Dagoba. You can buy the Anuradhapura ticket at the Abhayagiri, Jetavanarama and Architecture museums. There's also a handy ticket office just east of the Citadel.

ℹ️ Getting There & Away

BUS

Confusingly, Anuradhapura has three bus stations. Unless noted otherwise, daytime service in all directions is frequent (every 30 minutes or so).

Colombo Bus Station Private air-con and 'semi comfortable' (larger seats, no air con) buses leave from this small station near the Old Bus Station. Services include the following:

Colombo Rs 390-540, six hours

Dambulla Rs 170, 1½ hours

Kandy Rs 360, four hours

New Bus Station Buses heading to points east and north start here. Services include the following:

Jaffna Rs 328, six hours, eight daily

Mihintale Rs 30, 30 minutes

Polonnaruwa Rs 120, three hours

Trinco Rs 170, 3½ hours, three daily

Old Bus Station Southbound buses start here and stop at the New Bus Station, by which time seats may be few. Services include the following:

Colombo via Dambulla Rs 274, six hours

Colombo via Negombo Rs 253, six hours

Dambulla Rs 95, 1½ hours

Kandy Rs 190/360 normal/air-con, four hours

TRAIN

Anuradhapura's main train station is an art-deco gem. Train services include the following:

Colombo 1st/2nd/3rd class Rs 600/370/240, five hours, five daily

Kandy, changing at Polgahawela 1st/2nd/3rd class Rs 485/275/150, six hours, four connections daily

Pallai (for Jaffna) 1st/2nd/3rd class Rs 420/230/130; 3½ hours; two daily

ℹ️ Getting Around

The city is too spread out to investigate on foot. A three-hour taxi tour costs about Rs 1500 and a three-wheeler about Rs 1200. Bicycles are the best local means of transport and can be rented at most hotels and guesthouses (Rs 300 to 500 per day).

Mihintale

📵 025

This somnolent village and temple complex, 13km east of Anuradhapura, holds a special place in the annals of Sri Lankan lore. In 247 BC King Devanampiya Tissa of Anuradhapura was hunting a stag on Mihintale Hill when he was approached by Mahinda, son of the great Indian Buddhist emperor, Ashoka. Mahinda tested the king's wisdom and, considering him to be a worthy disciple, promptly converted the king on the spot. Mihintale has since been associated with the earliest introduction of Buddhism to Sri Lanka.

Each year a great festival, the **Poson Poya**, is held at Mihintale on the Poson full-moon night (usually in June).

◎ Sights

Exploring **Mihintale** (US$4; ⏱ 24hr) involves a steep climb, so you may wish to visit it early in the morning or late in the afternoon to avoid the midday heat.

Wannabe guides charge about Rs 800 for a two-hour tour that is exhaustive in detail. If the guide follows you up the steps, you're committed, so make your decision clear before setting out. Single women are advised not to tour alone with a guide.

Stairway STAIRWAY
In a series of flights, 1843 ancient granite slab steps lead majestically up the hillside (if you lose count, you have to go back to the bottom and start over). The first flight is the widest and shallowest. It's possible to avoid more than half the steps by driving up Old Rd.

Kantaka Chetiya BUDDHIST
At the first landing a smaller flight of steps leads to this partly ruined dagoba off to the right, one of the oldest at Mihintale. It's 12m high (originally more than 30m) and 130m

Mihintale

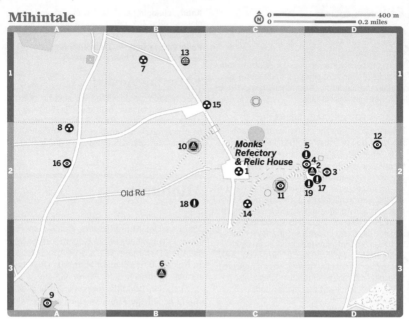

Mihintale

around its base. A Brahmi inscription found nearby records donations for the dagoba. It's noteworthy for its friezes. Four stone flower altars stand at each of the cardinal points, and surrounding these are well-preserved sculptures of dwarfs, geese and other figures.

While exactly who built it is open to conjecture, Devanampiya Tissa (r 247–207 BC) had 68 cave monasteries built, and the dagoba would have been constructed near these. King Laji Tissa (r 59–50 BC) enlarged it. So the dagoba was built sometime in between.

South of the Kantaka Chetiya, where a big boulder is cleft by a cave, if you look up you'll see what is thought to be the oldest inscription in Sri Lanka, predating Pali in Sri Lanka. The inscription dedicates the mountain's shelters to meditation, now and for eternity. Through the cave, ledges on the cliff face acted as meditation retreats for the numerous monks once resident here. There are around 70 different sites for contemplation.

★ Monks' Refectory
& Relic House   RUIN

On the second landing is the monks' refectory with huge stone troughs that the lay followers kept filled with rice for the monks.

Nearby, at a place identified as the monastery's relic house, are two inscribed stone slabs erected during the reign of King Mahinda IV (r 975–91). The inscriptions laid down the rules relating to the relic house and the conduct of those responsible for it.

One inscription clearly states that nothing belonging to the relic house shall be lent or sold. Another confirms the amount of land to be given in exchange for a reliable supply of oil and wicks for lamps and flowers for offerings. Also known as the Mihintale tablets, these inscribed stones define the duties of the monastery's many servants: which servants gather firewood and cook, which servants cook but only on firewood gathered by others, and so on.

There are also rules for monks: they should rise at dawn, clean their teeth, put on their robes, meditate and then go to have their breakfast (boiled rice) at the refectory, but only after reciting certain portions of the scriptures.

Assembly Hall   MONUMENT
On the same level as the relic house, this hall, also known as the convocation hall, is where monks met to discuss matters of common interest. The most senior monk would have presided over the discussions, and the raised dais in the middle of the hall was apparently where this person sat. Sixty-four stone pillars once supported the roof. Conservation of this site began in 1948. The main path to the Ambasthale Dagoba leads from here.

Sinha Pokuna   MONUMENT
Just below the monks' refectory on the second landing, and near the entrance if you are coming via Old Rd, is a small pool surmounted by a 2m-high rampant lion, reckoned to be one of the best pieces of animal carving in the country. Anyone placing one hand on each paw would be right in line for the stream of water from the lion's mouth. There are some fine friezes around this pool.

Ambasthale Dagoba   BUDDHIST TEMPLE
(admission Rs 500) The final steep stairway, lined with frangipani trees, leads to the place where Mahinda and the king met. The Ambasthale Dagoba is built over the spot where Mahinda stood. Nearby stands a **statue of the king** in the place where he stood. On the opposite side of the dagoba from the statue is a cloister and behind that, a large, white sitting **Buddha statue**. Stone pillars surround the dagoba and may once have been used to hold offerings.

The name Ambasthale means 'Mango Tree' and refers to a riddle that Mahinda used to test the king's intelligence.

Nearby is the **Sela Chetiya**, which has a stone rendering of the Buddha's footprint. It's surrounded by a railing festooned with prayer flags left by pilgrims, who have also scattered coins here.

Mahaseya Dagoba   ANCIENT TEMPLE
This dagoba (arguably the largest at Mihintale) is thought to have been built to house relics of Mahinda. The **bodhi tree** to the left of the base of the steps is said to be one of the oldest surviving ones. From here there is a view over the lakes and trees to Anuradhapura, a horizon studded with the domes and spikes of all the massive dagobas.

A small **temple** at the foot of the dagoba has a reclining Buddha and Technicolor modern frescoes – donations are requested. A room at the side is a **devale** (a complex designed for worshipping a Hindu or local Sri Lankan deity) with statues of major gods – Ganesh, Vishnu, Murugan (Skanda) and Saman.

THE ANCIENT CITIES MIHINTALE

SCULPTURAL SYMBOLISM

The four *vahalkadas* (solid panels of sculpture) at the Kantaka Chetiya are among the oldest and best preserved in the country and are the only ones to be found at Mihintale.

Vahalkadas face each of the four cardinal directions and comprise a series of bands, each containing some sort of ornamentation. The upper part usually contained niches in which were placed sculptures of divine beings. At either end of each *vahalkada* is a pillar topped with the figure of an animal, such as an elephant or a lion. How or why these sculptural creations came into being is subject to speculation, but one theory is that they evolved from simple flower altars. Others suggest they were an adaptation from Hindu temple design.

The cardinal points in traditional sculptural work are represented by specific animals: an elephant on the east, a horse on the west, a lion on the north and a bull on the south. In addition to these beasts, sculptures also feature dwarfs (sometimes depicted with animal heads), geese (said to have the power to choose between good and evil), elephants (often shown as though supporting the full weight of the superstructure) and *naga* (serpents, said to possess magical powers). Floral designs, apart from the lotus, are said to be primarily ornamental.

Mahinda's Cave
CAVE

There is a path leading northeast from the Ambasthale Dagoba down to a cave where there is a large flat stone. This is said to be where Mahinda lived and the stone is claimed to be where he rested. The track to the cave is hard on tender bare feet.

Aradhana Gala
VIEWPOINT

To the east of Ambasthale Dagoba is a steep path over sun-heated rock leading up to a point with great views. A railing goes up most of the way. Aradhana Gala means 'Meditation Rock'.

Naga Pokuna
RUIN

Halfway back down the steep flight of steps from the Ambasthale Dagoba, a path leads to the left, around the hill topped by the Mahaseya Dagoba. Here you'll find the Naga Pokuna (Snake Pool), so called because of a five-headed cobra carved in low relief on the rock face of the pool. Its tail is said to reach down to the bottom of the pool. Continuing on from here, you eventually loop back to the second landing.

Et Vihara
BUDDHIST

At an even higher elevation (309m) than the Mahaseya Dagoba are the remains of a dagoba called Et Vihara (literally, 'Elephant Monastery'). The origin of the name is open to conjecture, but it may have been named after the monastery nearby. The Mihintale tablets mention Et Vihara and its image house.

Museum
MUSEUM

There is a small museum on the road leading to the stairs; however, it is shut for an interminable refurbishment. It normally has a small collection of interesting artefacts.

Hospital
RUIN

A ruined hospital and the remains of a **quincunx** of buildings, laid out like the five dots on a die, flank the roadway before the base of the steps to the temple complex. The hospital consisted of a number of cells. A *bat oruwa* (large stone trough) sits among the ruins. The interior is carved in the shape of a human form, and the patient would climb into this to be immersed in healing oils.

Inscriptions have revealed that the hospital had its specialists – there is reference to a *mandova*, a bone and muscle specialist, and to a *puhunda vedek*, a leech doctor.

Indikatu Seya Complex
RUIN

Back on the road leading to Old Rd and outside the site proper are the remains of a monastery enclosed in the ruins of a stone wall. Inside are two dagobas, the larger known as Indikatu Seya (Dagoba of the Needle). Evidence suggests that this monastery was active in fostering Mahayana Buddhism. The main dagoba's structure differs from others in Mihintale; for example, it's built on a square platform.

Nearby is a hill that's been dubbed **Rajagirilena** (Royal Cave Hill) after the caves found here with Brahmi inscriptions in them. One of the caves bears the name of Devanampiya Tissa. A flight of steps leads up to the caves.

Kaludiya Pokuna
WATER FEATURE

Further south along the same road is the Kaludiya Pokuna (Dark Water Pool). This artificial pool was carefully constructed to look realistic, and features a rock-carved bathhouse and the ruins of a small monastery.

🛏 Sleeping & Eating

Hotel Mihintale
HOTEL **$$**

(📞 226 6599; www.ceylonhotels.com; Trincomalee Rd; r Rs 5000-6500; ❇ @ 🛜) As Mihintale is so close to Anuradhapura few people stay in the area, but this attractive hotel has a pleasing open-sided lobby lounge and very spacious rooms that are a little dated but have nice features like parquet floors. The pavilion cafe serves a set lunch for Rs 600.

ℹ Getting There & Away

Mihintale is 13km east of Anuradhapura. Buses run often (Rs 30, 30 minutes) from Anuradhapura's New Bus Station. A return taxi, with two hours to climb the stairs, costs about Rs 1500; a three-wheeler is about Rs 1200. It takes less than an hour to cycle here.

Yapahuwa

⭐ **Yapahuwa Rock Fortress**
ROCK FORTRESS

(Fire Rock; admission Rs 500; ☉ 6am-6pm) Rising 100m from the surrounding plain, the impressive granite outcrop of Yapahuwa (pronounced yaa-pow-a) has some fascinating features and history. Between 1272 and 1284, King Bhuvanekabahu I used the rock fortress as his capital and kept Sri Lanka's sacred Buddha tooth relic here. Indians from the Pandavan dynasty captured Yapahuwa in 1284 and carried the tooth relic to South India, only for it to be recovered in 1288 by King Parakramabahu I.

Yapahuwa's steep **ornamental staircase**, which led up to the ledge holding the tooth temple, is one of its finest features. One of the lions near the top of the staircase appears on the Rs 10 note. The porches on the stairway had extraordinarily beautiful pierced-stone windows, one of which is now in the National Museum in Colombo; the other is in the museum right here.

The **museum** is off a parking area about 300m beyond the entrance to the steps. On display are stone sculptures of Vishnu and Kali, fragments of pottery and the carved stone screen. There are excellent, illuminating displays in English.

Past the museum you can wander through the remains of the **ancient fortress**. It's a beautiful area, with little waterways and stone ruins. Near the stairs entrance, a **cave temple** contains some 13th-century frescoes and images of the Buddha made from wood and bronze. At various junctures monks or staff for the site may open things for you; a tip of Rs 100 is a worthy offering of thanks.

❶ Getting There & Away

Yapahuwa is 9km east of the Anuradhapura–Kurunegala highway, which buzzes with buses. Three-wheelers charge about Rs 1000 return (including waiting time) from the junction of Daladagama on this road.

The site is also 6km from Maho railway junction, where the Trincomalee line splits from the Colombo–Anuradhapura line.

Panduwasnuwara

Panduwasnuwara   RUIN
Almost abandoned, the 12th-century ruins of the temporary capital of Parakramabahu I are spread over a wide area.

Near the entrance is a moat, the massive citadel wall and the remains of a palace. Further on are image houses, dagobas and monks' living quarters. Follow the road past the school and veer left; you'll shortly come to a restored tooth temple with a bodhi tree and, beyond that, the remains of a round palace (apparently once multistoreyed) enclosed in a circular moat.

There are many stories about who lived in this palace and why it was built. Legend has it that it kept the king's daughter away from men who would desire her; it had been prophesied that if she bore a son, he'd eventually claim the throne. Another story is that it was built to house the king's wives and, intriguingly, that there was once a secret tunnel that led from the king's palace and under

PADENIYA

About 85km south of Anuradhapura and 25km northwest of Kurunegala, where the Puttalam and Anuradhapura roads branch off, is the Kandyan-style **Padeniya Raja Mahavihara** (donations appreciated), which is worth popping into if you're passing by. It's a pretty, medieval temple with 28 carved pillars and a stunning elaborate door (said to be the largest in Sri Lanka) to the main shrine. There is also a clay-image house and a library, as well as a preaching hall with an unusual carved wooden pulpit.

the moat to the queens' palace. However attractive these stories are, historians have not been able to conclude why the palace was built.

❶ Getting There & Away

Panduwasnuwara is about 17km southwest of Padeniya on the road between Wariyapola and Chilaw. The turnoff to the site is at Panduwasnuwara village, where there is a tiny museum that's a dusty cliché. It's best visited with your own transport.

Ridi Vihara

Ridi Vihara   BUDDHIST
(donation Rs 200; ⏰7am-4pm) Literally the 'Silver Temple', Ridi Vihara is so named because it was here that silver ore was discovered in the 2nd century BC. It makes for an interesting detour to see its wonderful frescoes and the unusual Dutch tiles from Neduntivu (Delft).

The primary attraction is the golden statue in the main cave, called the **Pahala Vihara** (Lower Temple), which also houses a 9m recumbent Buddha resting on a platform decorated with a series of blue-and-white tiles.

The tiles were a gift from the Dutch consul and depict scenes from the Bible, including Adam and Eve being banished from the Garden of Eden.

The nearby **Uda Vihara** (Upper Temple) was built by King Kirti Sri Rajasinghe. The entrance has a Kandyan-period moonstone. Some clever visual tricks were used by the fresco artists; in one case, what appears to be an elephant reveals itself on closer inspection to be a formation of nine maidens. Hindu deities and images of the Buddha are represented in the caves.

Outside the temple complex you can see an abandoned **dagoba** at the top of a smooth rocky outcrop. On the way up, to your right, is an ancient inscription in the stone, said to have been etched on King Dutugemunu's behalf. An easy 10-minute walk starts to the right of this abandoned dagoba (as you are walking up to it). Head past a modern pavilion to an abandoned bungalow; nearby, on the top of the cliff there are the most magnificent views.

❶ Getting There & Away

Ridi Vihara is situated east of the Kurunegala–Dambulla road, 2km from Ridigama village.

Kurunegala

🖉 037 / POP 34,500

Kurunegala is a busy, congested market town and transport hub between Colombo and Anuradhapura, and Kandy and Puttalam. The town itself is not interesting, but there are a few diversions nearby.

◉ Sights

The large, smooth rocky outcrops that loom over the town are a striking feature of this city. Named for the animals they appear to resemble (Tortoise Rock, Lion Rock etc), the outcrops are, unsurprisingly, endowed with mythological status. It's said that they were formed when animals that were endangering the free supply of water to the town were turned into stone.

There's a road going up **Etagala**, a large black boulder on the eastern side of the city. The views are extensive from here. On the way up you pass a small shrine, **Ibbagala Vihara**, and at the head of the road there is a **temple** named after the rock itself.

🛏 Sleeping & Eating

Few travellers stay here but there are a couple of accommodation and dining options.

Hotel Viveka   HOTEL **$**
(🖉222 2897; www.hotelviveka.com; 64 North Lake Rd; r fan/air-con Rs 2200/2500; ❄) An elegant whitewashed villa with a verandah overlooking the lake in a shady part of town. Its five rooms have been recently renovated and have modern bathrooms. Viveka doubles as Kurunegala's most convivial bar and restaurant (mains Rs 300 to 500).

Littlemore Estate Bungalows   LODGE **$$**
(🖉072 231 9443; reservations@ferncliff.lk; 3km west of Pellandeniya village; r US$60; ❄ 🛜 ❄) An intriguing new accommodation option, Littlemore Estate is a 50-hectare coconut plantation bordered by paddy fields and woodland with a healthy local peacock population. There are three very tastefully presented modern rooms, and staff will show you around the estate and explain all about coconut harvesting. Meals are traditional Sri Lankan.

It's 9km northwest of Kurunegala, the turnoff is at the village of Pellandeniya on the A10 highway.

In & Out   SRI LANKAN **$**
(18 Puttalam Rd; mains Rs 150-400; ⊙7am-10pm; ❄) An unexpectedly modish cafe-restaurant close to the bus station with good Sri Lankan and Western dishes. Omelettes, sandwiches, and Chinese-style meals are available, as well as rice 'n' curry and some good desserts.

❶ Getting There & Away

Buses depart from a chaotic, fume-filled bus station in the very centre of town. Frequent services include the following:

Anuradhapura express Rs 270, three hours
Colombo express Rs 340, 3½ hours
Kandy express Rs 90, one hour
Negombo Rs 170, 3½ hours

Trains depart from a station 2km southwest from the town centre.

The East

Best Places to Eat

➡ Hideaway (p236)

➡ Crab (p253)

➡ Coconut Beach Lodge (p253)

➡ RN Buffet & Take Away (p244)

Best Places to Stay

➡ Stardust Beach Hotel (p235)

➡ Uga Jungle Beach Resort (p255)

➡ Roy's Inn (p246)

➡ Sandy Beach Hotel (p235)

➡ Nandawanam Guesthouse (p246)

Why Go?

Welcome to a different Sri Lanka. You've probably experienced the booming beach resorts in the south and west. Maybe you're searching for somewhere a little less developed, a coastline that retains a more earthy, local feel. Well, the East might just be that place.

A mellow, emerging region, there's near-zero package tourism here – most places to stay are family-run guesthouses and small hotels. Still a little raw around the edges, the East remains primarily a land of fishing villages, sandy lanes, chickens in the yard and tradition. It's a culturally fascinating combination of ocean-orientated Muslim communities, astonishing Hindu temples, crumbling colonial forts, dazzling markets and a coastline of killer surf, hidden bays and stretch-for-miles white sand beaches.

Sure, there's the odd blot on the landscape. But with vastly improved infrastructure – upgraded highways, new bridges and better train and air links – the East will not remain a country cousin for long.

When to Go
Trincomalee

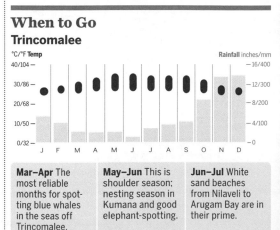

Mar–Apr The most reliable months for spotting blue whales in the seas off Trincomalee.

May–Jun This is shoulder season; nesting season in Kumana and good elephant-spotting.

Jun–Jul White sand beaches from Nilaveli to Arugam Bay are in their prime.

The East Highlights

1 Hanging ten on the endless rights of chilled-out surf mecca **Arugam Bay** (p232)

2 Seeking out blue whales and spinner dolphins on boat trips from **Uppuveli** (p251) and **Nilaveli** (p253)

3 Chasing a skittish leopard – or monitoring the treetops for sleeping cats – in **Kumana National Park** (p239)

4 Snorkelling or diving with reef sharks around **Pigeon Island National Park** (p253)

5 Venturing up a lost highway past empty sandy beaches, lagoons and mangroves **north of Nilaveli** (p255)

6 Listening to the quiet ripple of the water and watching rainbow-coloured kingfishers flit around mangroves on **Pottuvil Lagoon** (p237)

7 Napping in a hammock on a hill overlooking the sea at **Lighthouse Point** (p238)

8 Exploring the fortress, Hindu temples and sights in the historic port of **Trincomalee** (p247)

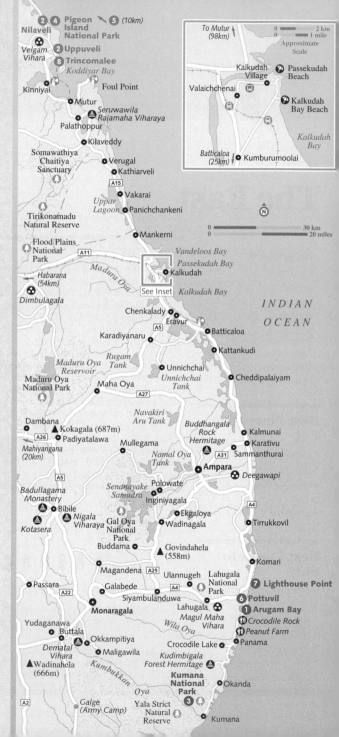

Monaragala

🗂 055

If you're coming from the touristy Hill Country, then Monaragala will probably be your first stop in the East. A bustling place with a huge Sunday market, it's a good introduction to the region. The town nestles beneath Peacock Rock, a round-topped forest-covered mountain. Upgraded roads and improved transport connections mean that few travellers now break their journey in Monaragala these days, but the town's unhurried ambience and leafy avenues have a certain appeal.

◉ Sights & Activities

An easy but beautiful hike starts near the bus station. Walk five minutes past a colourful little Hindu **Ganesh Temple** to the ageing rubber factory, then veer left to a rock-paved footpath that climbs between attractive boulder fields through Monaragala's famous rubber plantations. A much more demanding trek is the full-day round trip to the summit of the densely forested **Maragala Rock**. There is no set trail up the mountain and you'll need a guide, which can be organised through guesthouses (including Kanda Landvilka) for around Rs 2000 per day. From the summit you can check the surf at Arugam Bay on a clear day.

🛏 Sleeping & Eating

For cheap meals there are various stalls around the bus station.

★ **Kanda Landvilka**   GUESTHOUSE $
(YMCA; ☑ 227 6925; raxawa@yahoo.com; Araliya Rd; s/d Rs 1000/2000; ✳) Run by Uva, a hospitable English-speaking licensed tour guide and his family, this excellent guesthouse (in the old YMCA building) has five spacious rooms and a lounge, and is the best place to hook up with other travellers. Hiking to Maragala rock and a rubber plantation are offered, the latter involving a night in a hilltop mountain lodge. There's good food too: rice and curry costs Rs 300.

Victory Inn   HOTEL $
(☑ 227 6100; www.victoryinnmonaragala.com; 65 Wellawaya Rd; s Rs 1500, d with/without air-con Rs 4500/3500; ✳🖢) The smartest place in town, though that's not saying much – the Victory's smoked-glass facade and lobby are looking pretty dated. Rooms here (some with balconies) and most with wooden trim, are also old-fashioned, though comfortable enough.

For a filling meal, the Rs 350 lunch buffet is a great deal, and the restaurant serves both Western and local dishes.

Sunshine Guesthouse   HOTEL $
(☑ 227 6313; Wellawaya Rd; s Rs 1500, d with/without air-con Rs 3250/2750; ✳🖢) This hotel was being renovated at the time of research. It offers spartan but clean tiled rooms with mossie nets.

Pavilion   SRI LANKAN $
(61 Pottuvil Rd; ⊘ meals in canteen/restaurant from Rs 200/300) In the heart of town on a busy junction, the Pavilion is a tale of two halves. The smart, air-conditioned restaurant has posh tables and makes a civilised setting for dinner, with well-presented fish, vegetable and noodle dishes. For more casual dining, the neighbouring canteen has lots of excellent rice-and-curry options and is great for lunch.

ℹ Information

Commercial Bank (Bus Station Rd) and several others along Wellawaya Rd have ATMs. In the market area, **Samudura Communications** (☑ 227 6765; per hr Rs 50; ⊘ 8am-6.30pm) is the best internet cafe.

Wijayawardana (VJ) is a friendly English-speaking **guide** who charges Rs 4000 per day for leading hikes or trips in a three-wheeler; call him on ☑ 077 649 1117.

ℹ Getting There & Away

Monaragala is a convenient junction town between the east, the south and the hills. Some handy bus routes include the following:

Ampara Rs 110, 2½ hours, hourly
Colombo Rs 415, seven hours, hourly
Ella Rs 105, two hours, six daily
Kandy Rs 210, five hours, five daily
Kataragama Rs 85, two hours, two daily
Nuwara Eliya Rs 175, four hours, 9.15am and 2.30pm
Pottuvil (for Arugam Bay) Rs 120, 2½ hours, seven daily
Siyambulanduwa (for Ampara and Arugam Bay) Rs 50, one hour, frequent
Wellawaya (via Buttala; for the Hill Country) Rs 50, one hour, every 20 minutes

Around Monaragala

Yudaganawa

In a forest clearing near the village of Buttala, the ancient, ruined dagoba (stupa) of

WORTH A TRIP

SLEEPING IN THE TREES

Tree Tops (☏077 703 6554; www.tree topsjunglelodge.com; per person all-inclusive US$145) is the antidote to concrete resort hotels and national parks overrun with hundreds of jeeps. Tree Tops offers a true back-to-nature experience. Beautifully isolated at the base of the Weliara Ridge, 10km from Buttala, this wilderness lodge offers the chance to marvel at the dawn chorus, listen for wild elephants and be dazzled by the stars of the night sky.

Accommodation is in three spacious, canvas 'chalets' (tented huts on a raised, sand-filled platform with bathrooms). Unfortunately all this comes at a considerable cost, but food (mostly vegetarian), drinks and guided hikes with expert local trackers around the area, including to Arhat Kanda, the scenic 'Hills of Enlightenment', are included. Reservations are essential.

The owners also plan to open a second wilderness lodge in the Habessa area, 6km south of Tree Tops close to Yala National Park (block 4).

Yudaganawa (admission Rs 100; ☉6am-6pm) is an enigmatic and powerful site. Only the bottom third remains, but the setting is evocative and your imagination can run riot with thoughts of how amazing it must have looked back in its day. It's thought to have been an earthen stupa built 2300 years ago, though various alterations over the years – including an ongoing renovation that began in the 1970s – have obscured its history.

The small building in front houses 300-year-old carved-wood Buddhas and some exquisite faded paintings; it probably dates to the 7th century.

Just before reaching the main site you'll pass the charming, moss-encrusted ruins of the much smaller 12th-century **Chulangani Vihara**, with a lovely, compact dagoba and fragments of a 7th-century Buddha.

Buses from Monaragala to Buttala (Rs 30, 25 minutes) run every 30 minutes, and a three-wheeler from Buttala costs Rs 300 return. A three-wheeler from Monaragala costs Rs 1200 return, or around Rs 2800 for both the Yudaganawa sites and Maligawila.

Maligawila & Dematal Vihara

Tucked away in a shady forest glade in Maligawila (mali-ga-wila) are the extensive 7th-century remnants of **Pathma Vihara** (☉dawn-dusk) FREE and its two stunning Buddha statues. A little walk through the woods (bearing left) brings you to a magnificent 15m-tall **Buddha statue**, carved from a single piece of stone and weighing 100 tons. The figure was only discovered in the 1950s and restored (and reheaded) a few decades later. At its feet are usually offerings of flower petals left by pilgrims.

A few minutes' walk in the opposite direction is the 10m-high **Maitreya Bodhisattva** (Avalokitesvara), sitting high atop five stone terraces. It was found in pieces in the 1950s, then blown up by treasure-seeking looters, but reconstituted in 1991. It's a beautiful statue despite the scaffolding harness and corrugated canopy.

Frequent buses run to Maligawila from both Monaragala (Rs 50, 40 minutes) and Buttala (Rs 30). The journey to Maligawila from Monaragala, past jungles and paddy fields, is as much a highlight as the ruins themselves. If you're heading towards Buttala it's possible to hop off the bus at **Dematal Vihara**, a gorgeous temple lost in a sea of picturesque paddy fields.

A three-wheeler from Monaragala costs Rs 1800 return, or Rs 2800 return to do the Maligawila–Yudaganawa loop.

Arugam Bay

☏063

Lovely Arugam Bay, a moon-shaped curl of soft sand, is home to a famed point break that many regard as the best surf spot in the country. It's a tiny place, with a population of a few hundred, and everything is dotted along a single road, which parallels the coast.

If you're not a surfer, there are plenty of other draws: beachfront guesthouses, oceanside restaurants and a mellow, swing-another-day-in-a-hammock kind of vibe that's totally removed from the brash west-coast beach resorts. Arugam Bay also makes a great base for several adventures in the surrounding hinterland. During the low season (November to April) things get very quiet and some places shut up shop altogether, but it can also be a beautiful time to visit, with few tourists and glistening green landscapes.

Arugam Bay

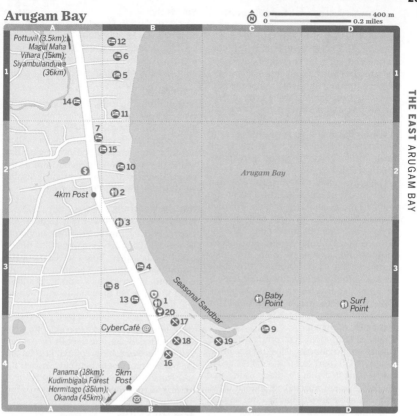

Arugam Bay

⊕ Activities, Courses & Tours
1 A-Bay Surf Shop	B3
2 Aloha	B2
3 Safa Surf School	B3
Surf N Sun	(see 13)

⊖ Sleeping
4 Bay Vista	B3
5 Beach Hut	B1
6 Galaxy Beach	B1
7 Happy Panda Homestay & Very Small Café	A2
8 Hideaway	B3
9 Mambo's	C4
Nice Place	(see 15)
10 Samantha's Folly	B2
11 Sandy Beach Hotel	B1

12 Stardust Beach Hotel	B1
13 Surf N Sun	B3
14 The Danish Villa	A1
15 Tropicana Beach Hotel	B2

⊗ Eating
Hideaway	(see 8)
16 Meena	B4
17 Perera Restaurant	B4
18 Samanthi's Restaurant	B4
19 Siripala Place Surf Cafe	C4
Stardust Restaurant	(see 12)
Surf N Sun	(see 13)

⊙ Drinking & Nightlife
20 Siam View Hotel	B3

🏃 Activities

Surfing

The famous, long right point break at the southern end of Arugam Bay offers consist-

ent surf from April to September, with some good (and much quieter) days until November. (Some other points don't get going until May or June.)

Locals, as well as some travelling surfers, tend to overhype Arugam Bay as a world-class spot, which is slightly fanciful, to say the least. However, it consistently produces long and fairly fat slow-breaking waves that are ideal for intermediate surfers. Surf averages 1m to 1.5m, with a few rare 2m days. On small days it can be very shallow and sectiony while at any size there can be lots of boils and bumps to deal with. In season it can get dangerously busy, and learners should stick to the gentle beach break further inside the point, also known as Baby Point.

There are many more breaks of similar quality, most of which need a decent-size swell. To the north, these include **Pottuvil Point**, which is a slow right-hander, ideal for learners (it tends to be better later in the season), **Whiskey Point** and **Lighthouse Point**, which are both also good for beginners. To the south is **Crocodile Rock**, **Elephant Rock** and **Peanut Farm** – the latter has two breaks (one of which is advanced) – **Panama**, which gets bad reviews, and **Okanda**, which is rumoured to be the best of the lot.

Several surf shops rent out boards, give lessons and do camping trips to some of the further points. Surf camp tours allow you to start surfing first thing in the morning, and you don't have to worry about food or transport, but some surfers find it's just as easy, and cheaper, to make their own way.

A-Bay Surf Shop SURFING
(bodyboards & surfboards per day from Rs 600, lessons per hr Rs 3000; ⊗8am-8pm) A good selection of old boards suitable for learners, plus expert ding-repair service, wax and sunscreen.

Aloha SURFING
(☑224 8379; www.aloha-arugambay.com; short/long boards per day Rs 1000/1300, lessons per hr Rs 2500; ⊗6am-7pm) This guesthouse and surf school has newish boards and will hold beginners' hands to get them started. Sells fins, wax and leashes.

Safa Surf School SURFING
(☑077 955 2268; www.safaarugambay.com; short & long boards/body boards per day €5.50/3, lessons from €32) Well-organised surf shop run by local surfer Fawas Lafeer, offering lessons from native instructors, good quality board hire and repairs.

Surf N Sun SURF SHOP
(☑224 8600; www.thesurfnsun.com; short/long boards per day Rs 800/1000) The savvy owners here organise excursions to surf spots around A-Bay. However, the hire boards aren't ideal for learners.

Swimming

Seas are rough but OK for swimmin. However, alsways ask locals before plunging in at lesser-known beaches, where rips might be strong. There's safe swimming in shallow water at the southern end of Arugam Bay, where the beach bends around towards the point. However, this is essentially a fishing beach so not ideal for lounging on.

Nature-Watching

Mangrove tours on Pottuvil Lagoon, just north of the bay, are superb and should not be missed. They are best organised directly via the boatmen. Tours to **Kumana National Park**, home to leopards, elephants, wild buffalo, crocodiles and outstanding birdlife can be set up by many guesthouses and hotels.

There's a good chance of seeing crocodiles and elephants around Crocodile Rock on Pasarichenai Beach, just south of Arugam Bay. For **birdwatching** Pottuvil Lagoon and the ponds and lagoons between Arugam Bay and Panama are prime areas, and home to waterfowl and waders.

🛏 Sleeping

All the following hotels and guesthouses are on the beach or nearby. Many places have a kind-of homespun charm and remain family-owned. The term 'cabana' refers to anything from ultra basic plank or *cadjan* (coconut-frond matting) huts to luxurious full-facility bungalows. Low-season discounts of 20% to 35% are common.

Beach Hut CABANA $
(☑224 8202, 077 160 6203; www.arugambay beachhut.com; huts from Rs 600, cabanas Rs 1000-1500; ☜) A quirky, locally-owned beachside place with loads of atmosphere and a loyal clientele of backpackers and surfers. There's a choice of digs (all built from timber, bamboo and thatch) including treehouse-style cabanas and A-frame huts - most are only steps from the ocean. The restaurant to the rear has a large table for socialising, a shady terrace and good-value meals (Rs 400 to 700).

Laundry and good local tours, including boat trips on the lagoon, are offered too.

Nice Place GUESTHOUSE $
(📞 077 341 2240; r with fan/air-con Rs 3500/6000; ❄️🛜) Run by a lovely lady (who'll whip up everything from an espresso to a fish curry), this fine guesthouse has immaculate rooms with lovely touches, including attractive floor mats and curtains, that face a little garden compound. The fan options are fine value. It's beachside, around 100m from the sand.

Samantha's Folly CABANA $
(📞 077 338 7808; www.samanthasfolly.com; follies Rs 2000, tents Rs 4000, cabanas Rs 3500-4500; @🛜) Highly popular with travellers, thanks to its gregarious vibe, guest kitchen and communal dining. Samantha's pioneered the 'folly' (a bamboo frame topped with a thatch roof) though there are also cabanas and an Arabian-style tent. The restaurant offers good grub (meals Rs 400 to 900) and it's a good place to hook up with others for a safari.

Also offers board rental.

Galaxy Beach CABANA $
(📞 224 8415; www.galaxysrilanka.com; cabanas Rs 3000-4000; ❄️🛜) A sociable place where many of the spacious cabanas are raised on stilts, and hammocks abound between the shoreside trees. Galaxy has charm and ambience: its posher cabanas are attractive, but budget options are bare and the worn bedding needs replacing. Still, the beachfront location is superb, and the book exchange, board games and regular barbecues are bonuses.

Happy Panda Homestay & Very Small Café GUESTHOUSE $
(📞 077 299 0779; www.happypandahotel.com; r Rs 2200; 🛜) Tiny place 50m from the beach with three simple, clean, arty rooms and a very inviting porch-lounge area, complete with hammocks. Happy Panda is also famous for its breakfasts (Rs 400 to 500): the French toast and tropical fruit salad with local curd both rock.

Tropicana Beach Hotel GUESTHOUSE $
(📞 077 127 2677; d_asmin@yahoo.com; tw Rs 1800) It's right on the road but the aquamarine cottages are simple and cute. Rooms only have table fans, but the grounds boast blooming flowers and parakeets are commonly seen. The nice couple who run Tropicana will involve you in family life.

★ **Sandy Beach Hotel** HOTEL $$
(📞 224 8403; www.arugambay-hotel.com; s/d Rs 7500/8000; ❄️🛜) This fine new beachside hotel has 13 rooms – all beautifully presented, immaculately clean and most boasting minibars, desks and very attractive furniture – and one simpler A-frame cabana. Owner Mr Badur Khan is totally charming, an educated and well-travelled gentleman who goes the extra mile to ensure your stay is comfortable and loves chatting with his guests.

Rooms 1 and 2 have balconies with sea views. A restaurant is planned; rates drop considerably off-season.

★ **Stardust Beach Hotel** HOTEL, CABANA $$
(📞 224 8191; www.arugambay.com; cabanas s/d US$35/43, r US$70-80, apt US$95-110; 🛜) Exuding beach chic, this wonderful Danish-run place sits pretty at the far end of the bay. There's a simply magnificent open-sided restaurant-lounge-terrace facing the ocean. It's perfect for languid meals or a relaxed drink and browsing the owners' books and magazines. Rooms and apartments are charming, with elegant furnishings (though they have cold-water bathrooms) while cabanas are simple, neat and well-designed.

Yoga classes and massages are offered in season.

Surf N Sun CABANA $$
(📞 224 8600; www.thesurfnsun.com; cottages incl breakfast US$30-45; 🛜) Deservedly popular place that definitely wins the 'garden of the year' award, with a lush, verdant Eden complete with pond and bursting with tropical greenery. The cottages, some with crazy trees growing out of the showers, are cosy too, if slightly overpriced. It's a well-designed place with lots of lounge space for chilling with a book and good food too.

Discounts are readily available at quiet times.

Mambo's CABANA $$
(📞 077 782 2524; www.mambos.lk; s/d US$45/60, bungalows US$85-130; ❄️🛜) Surfer favourite, right next to the main point, allowing you to tumble out of bed and land in the lineup. Offers attractive fan-only rooms in the guesthouse and excellent bungalows with window screens, earthy, simple decor and little porches in a delightful garden setting. The bar-restaurant has hammocks, tasty, filling meals (Rs 400 to 1000) and Saturday-night parties. Prices vary a lot according to the season.

The Danish Villa
HOTEL $$

(☎695 7936; www.thedanishvilla.dk; r with fan/
air-con from Rs 3600/6300; ❈🖥) Yes, it's on
the landside of the beach road but you've a
lovely peaceful garden (except when the odd
troop of monkeys whoops by) and incredi-
bly classy, colonial-style ambience to enjoy.
There's a good choice of rooms, friendly staff
and fine Western and Asian food available.

Bay Vista
HOTEL $$

(☎224 8577; www.bayvistahotel.com; r US$55-
80; ❈🖥) Inviting new modern hotel with
a prime beachfront location (you can watch
the fishermen come and go from the sea-
view rooms) and immaculately presented
minimalist accommodation equipped with
quality furnishings and bed linen in a whitewashed interior. The restaurant serves very
tasty local and Italian food.

Hideaway
CABANA $$$

(☎224 8259; www.hideawayarugambay.com; r/
bungalows from US$50/100; ❈🖥) A fine place
with atmospheric, boho accommodation
scattered around a huge, shady garden plot.
Stylistically, think hand-painted window
shutters, tribal textiles and a nod to *Elle Dec-
oration*. At the rear is a colonial-style villa
draped in bougainvillea with four rooms
(these lack privacy, though) and a restau-
rant. Very tasteful, but, as it's not beachside,
a bit pricey.

Hideaway's restaurant offers lovingly pre-
pared meals and has a relaxed vibe.

Kottukal
Beach House
BOUTIQUE HOTEL $$$

(☎011-234 5700; www.jetwinghotels.com; r US$147;
❈🖥) Intimate, secluded new beachfront
villa hotel, 5km north of Arugam Bay, managed by Jetwing, the renowned hotel group.
Perfectly located for sybaritic surfers as it's
right by the Pottuvil Point break. As there are
just four rooms (all very well-presented and
appointed) it's perhaps best for couples who
want to get away from it all.

🍴 Eating & Drinking

You'll find a great range of places to eat,
with cosmopolitan menus in many restaurants offering everything from Italian to
Indonesian dishes, including lots of seafood.
For inexpensive local grub many guesthouse
owners (including Nice Place) will whip up
a mean rice and curry given a little notice.

Mambo's, Galaxy Beach and Beach Hut
all organise beach and full-moon parties in
season, and are good spots for a drink on
any night. Beach raves at Whiskey Point's
SaBaBa Surf Café can be wild in season, with
dancing under the stars.

Most restaurants in Arugam Bay serve
alcohol.

Meena
SRI LANKAN $

(meals Rs 200-500) For a very authentic local
meal, this small place pumps out all the usual faves including string hoppers, rice and
curry, *kotthu* (*rotti* chopped up and mixed
with vegies) and fried rice. Sip on a tropical
fruit juice while you savour the flavours.

Perera Restaurant
SRI LANKAN $

(mains Rs 250-400) Simple roadside joint that
works well for a decent rice and curry and
genuine Sri Lankan meals at affordable prices. Also serves some Western food, including
breakfasts.

Samanthi's Restaurant
SRI LANKAN $$

(☎077 175 9620; Freedom Beach Cabanas; mains
Rs 250-675; 🖥) 🖉 Samanthi's, at Freedom
Beach Cabanas, is run by a family of strong,
cheerful local women. Order ahead for rice
and curry (around Rs 350); other dishes
are the standard A-Bay mix of Western and
modified Sri Lankan. Try the fresh fruit with
honey and buffalo curd: the yoghurt is a re-
gional speciality.

Siripala Place
Surf Cafe
SRI LANKAN, SEAFOOD $$

(mains Rs 400-850) Right next to the spot
where the fish are first hauled out of the
deep blue, so the seafood at this place is surf-
fresh. The views and breezes are the perfect
backdrop.

★Hideaway
INTERNATIONAL $$$

(☎224 8259; www.hideawayarugambay.com;
mains Rs 900-1500; 🖥) A delightful environ-
ment for a meal, this classy hotel restaurant
features a menu that changes daily and lots
of fresh, locally sourced ingredients. Staff
are professional and welcoming. Many dish-
es feature Mediterranean and East Asian
influences (like jumbo prawn risotto with
lemon grass, lime leaves and fresh coconut
milk). There are also lots of vegetarian, ve-
gan and gluten-free choices.

Check out their garden Hide & Chill bar
(evenings only, in season) for divine cock-
tails (two for one during happy hour, 6pm to
7pm) and also Hideaway Blue cafe for coffee,
panini sandwiches, juices and smoothies.

Stardust Restaurant
INTERNATIONAL $$$

(☑224 8191; www.arugambay.com; meals Rs 800-1800; 🛜) For a memorable setting for a meal, this superb beachfront hotel restaurant is just the ticket, with expertly executed European and Asian dishes, wine by the bottle (and glass) as well as terrific juices, lassis and espresso coffee. There's a lovely terrace and garden as well as an open-sided dining area that catches the ocean breeze. Not cheap, but worth it.

Surf N Sun
SEAFOOD, SRI LANKAN $$$

(www.thesurfnsun.com; mains Rs 600-1200; 🛜) Enjoy a great setting for your meal on the gorgeous outdoor deck lounge, with low-slung cushions, throw pillows, and candles and lanterns. Good food too, including seafood, pizza and the occasional barbecue.

Siam View Hotel
BAR

(www.arugam.com; 🛜) After the government demolished their wildly popular (but illegally built) beachside bar in 2011, the action shifted inland to this ungainly-looking roadside party HQ. Hosts a slew of party nights, with everything from tech-house DJs to local reggae bands rocking the dance floor. As there's a microbrewery on the premises you'll find a selection of interesting beers to sample.

Look for the classic British phone box outside.

ℹ️ Information

There's only one **ATM** (located on the main drag) in Arugam Bay, but many more a short ride away in Pottuvil.

Arugam Bay Information (www.arugam.info) Travel and local info.

CyberCafé (wi-fi/internet per hr Rs 100/150; ⊙9am-10pm) Offers fast connections.

Pasarichenai Sub Post Office (⊙8am-noon & 1-5pm Mon-Sat)

Tourist Police (☑011-308 1044) This Colombo number connects to the beach police station. Policemen are usually here during daylight hours to assist tourists.

DANGERS & ANNOYANCES

Locals are used to seeing Western women in swimwear on the beach, but as this is a conservative Muslim community, consider wearing a T-shirt over your swimsuit, or even a T-shirt and shorts to avoid unwanted attention. It's considered respectful, for both men and women, to dress modestly; when off the beach, don't wander around in swimwear.

ℹ️ SIYAMBULANDUWA

Buses to Pottuvil – from anywhere – aren't frequent. But buses to Siyambulanduwa (a market town 37km to the west) are, and so are buses from Siyambulanduwa to Pottuvil. You can get to Arugam Bay most of the time if you head to Siyambulanduwa. Pottuvil buses run only until around 5pm, but the well-run **Nethmini Hotel** (☑055-355 0891; www.nethminihotel.com; Ampara Rd; r with fan/air-con US$17/27; ✳) is 1km from the bus stand.

There have been cases of attempted sexual assault in secluded areas, particularly south behind the surf point. There is a tourist-police post on the beach.

ℹ️ Getting There & Around

BUS & THREE-WHEELER

Nearby Pottuvil is the gateway to Arugam Bay, from where you'll need to get a three-wheeler (Rs 200). The only exceptions are the rare buses from Pottuvil to Panama, which pass by Arugam Bay (one continues to Monaragala). Three-wheeler fares to local surf spots are given in the relevant sections.

CAR

Private air-con taxis to Colombo cost around Rs 18,000.

MOTORCYCLE & BICYCLE

Virtually all guesthouses can find you a bicycle (Rs 350 to 500) or scooter (Rs 1000 to 1500) for the day .

North of Arugam Bay

Pottuvil
☑063

For most tourists the small town of Pottuvil is simply the transport hub for Arugam Bay, 3km further south. But Pottuvil has several ATMs, a decent market, a few low-key sights and a lovely lagoon to explore.

⊙ Sights & Activities

Pottuvil Lagoon
LAGOON

The mangroves, islands and waterways of Pottuvil Lagoon are a rich ecosystem teeming with giant monitor lizards, crocodiles, kingfishers, the occasional elephant (who does not like to be disturbed), eagles,

Pottuvil

peacocks, egrets and monkeys. Birdlife includes spoonbills, stilts, several kinds of kingfisher, sea eagles, pelicans and herons. Seeing them as you cruise along on a two-hour **mangrove ecotour** (4-person boat Rs 2500; ⊙departs 6am & 4pm), with only the sounds of the fisherman's pole in the water and animals in the trees, is both exciting and serene.

The tours were designed to help conserve the mangrove forests and support local fishers: they fund a community-managed credit banks which provides low-interest loans to locals. You can arrange a tour through most hotels in Arugam Bay, but if you can manage the language barrier (most boat conductors do not speak English), it's best for the fishers if you organise with them directly. Their **Hidiyapuram Fishermen's Cooperative Society** (☑072 660 8560, 077 861 9959; two-hour boat trip Rs 3000; ⊙6am-6pm) has an office on the south side of the lagoon; call and reserve as best you can, and someone will meet you there. A three-wheeler from Arugam Bay costs Rs 800 return.

Mudu Maha Vihara   RUIN
Hidden away in Pottuvil's backstreets are the ancient ruins of Mudu Maha Vihara. This lovely little site, partly submerged in the encroaching sand dunes, features a fine 3m-high standing Buddha statue flanked by two bodhisattva figures. The **beach** just behind is wide, beautiful and undeveloped, but not safe for swimming.

Pottuvil Point   SURFING
About 2km past the Cooperative Society's office, at the end of a scenic peninsula-like stretch of sand, is beautiful Pottuvil Point, which is a slow right-hander ideal for learners. There's a very rustic **restaurant** (mains Rs 200 to 350) here and the very luxurious Kottukal Beach House. Pottuvil Point is Rs 800 return by three-wheeler from Arugam Bay.

❶ Getting There & Away
Three-wheelers to Arugam Bay cost Rs 200.

Whiskey Point

Whiskey Point is a three-minute beach walk from Pottuvil Point but further by road. The point's good for beginners, and the waves are consistent from late April on. **SaBaBa Surf Café** (☑077 711 8132; mains Rs 350-900; ⊙7am-10pm) is a gorgeous space to hang out, with cushioned seating around its huge wooden deck, great grub, beds on the beach and regular parties in surf season (usually Wednesdays and Fridays) with DJs playing full-on house and electronica till dawn (and beyond). If you like the scene so much you want to stay, you can do so at one of the attractive thatched bungalows in the neighbouring **Whiskey Bay Surf Resort** (☑071 288 9289; http://surfwhiskey.com; bungalows s/d US$35/50), which are well set up for surfers, with boards available for hire.

Three-wheelers charge around Rs 1500 return, including three hours' waiting, from Arugam Bay (a 20-minute trip).

Lighthouse Point

Lighthouse Point, another beginner/medium right-hander, is 23km north of Arugam Bay. It's a lovely, isolated spot and its fine sandy beach is little visited. The surf season is late April to September.

Green House, another point further north, is a 15-minute walk along the beach. Three-wheelers charge Rs 2000 return from Arugam Bay.

There are a couple of good places to stay.

Hilltop Beach Cabanas   CABANA $
(☑077 374 1466; http://hilltopcabanas.com; cabanas Rs 1500-4000) Gorgeous place that gets

rave reviews thanks to the kindness and cooking (most meals Rs 300 to 550) of owner Dilani. Of the cabanas, the one on stilts is best, with million-dollar views shining through seashell garlands. Rooms have minimal solar-powered electricity (lights only), and bathrooms are outside under the trees.

They have a dongle for internet use, which guests can borrow.

Lighthouse CABANA $
(☎075 283 5544; www.arugambaybeachhut. com/lighthouse; cabanas Rs 2000-4000) New in 2012, these eight rustic cabanas sit easy in their rural surrounds right by the break. Kanthan, the owner, worked at Beach Hut in Arugam Bay for years, and is well versed to travellers' needs, preparing great local food (meals from Rs 250). It's solar powered, and there are often yoga classes during the main season.

South of Arugam Bay

Arugam Bay to Panama

Kilometres of untouched sandy beaches stretch south of Arugam Bay. Close-by surf points, reached via the coast road, include **Crocodile Rock** (Rs 500 return by three-wheeler), **Elephant Rock** (Rs 800) and **Peanut Farm** (around Rs 1000). The road to Panama stays somewhat inland but intersects with lagoons where you can spot waterfowl, wading birds, water buffalo and even elephants. It's a beautiful, savannah-like landscape.

Panama (12km south of Arugam Bay) is a farming village with an end-of-the-world atmosphere, whose only sights are an attractive white **dagoba** and a stunning, untouched (but shade-free) sandy beach a kilometre east of town. If there's heavy seas, swimming is usually unsafe (and surfers won't have any joy on these dumpy shore breaks). At the northern end of the beach, close to the jellyfish-processing plant (jellyfish are sent to the Far East for use in cooking), is a fairly lame right-point break that is good for novice surfers. Arugam Bay three-wheelers charge Rs 1500 return, or you can wait for a rare bus.

Panama to Okanda

The superb 47-sq-km site of **Kudimbigala Forest Hermitage** is a jumble of forgotten Sigiriya-style outcrops set in dense jungle. Over 200 shrines and hermits' lodgings are set in caves or sealed rocky overhangs and six Buddhist monks still live here. While none is individually especially interesting, the atmosphere is fantastic and the dagoba-topped summit of the highest rock offers vast panoramas across the eccentric landscape and forest canopy. There are glimpses of lagoon and sandbars towards the shore, and the far southwestern horizon is distantly serrated by the spiky Weliara Ridge. Kudimbagala is usually visited along with Kumana or Okanda; three-wheelers charge Rs 2500 return (prepare yourself for the rough dirt track). As this is an active hermitage, quiet and modest dress are requested.

The Arugam–Okanda road ends at the entry gate for Kumana National Park. Immediately east of the gate is **Okanda**, a seasonal settlement for local fishermen and home to the **Okanda Sri Murugan Kovil**. Though relatively small, the main temple has a colourful *gopuram* (gateway tower) and is a major point on the Pada Yatra pilgrimage to Kataragama. Thousands of pilgrims gather here during the two weeks before the July *poya* (full moon) before attempting the last, and most dangerous, five-day leg of the 45-day trek from Jaffna. The temple is of great spiritual importance as it marks the supposed point at which Murugan (Skanda) and his consort Valli arrived in Sri Lanka on stone boats.

Just five minutes' walk from the temple is a sweeping beige-white beach with an excellent right-point break, popular with surfers fleeing the crowds at Arugam Bay.

Kumana National Park & Kumana Reserve

This 357-sq-km **park** (☎063-363 5867; adult US$12, plus per jeep Rs 250, service charge per group US$8, VAT 12%; ☻6am-6.30pm), often still referred to by its old name, Yala East, is much less frequently visited than its busy neighbour, Yala National Park. Consequently, it's a far less 'zoolike' experience and it never feels too crowded here, even during high season. Yes, the density of animals is lower but it's not rare to spot a leopard, along with elephants, crocodiles and turtles, white cobras, wild buffalo and tons of birds. About a dozen bears live in the park, but they're rarely seen.

The park's best-known feature is the 200-hectare **Kumana bird reserve**, an

WORTH A TRIP

MAGUL MAHA VIHARA & AROUND

About 12km west of Pottuvil lies this evocative 5th-century-BC ruin, set in a peaceful forested spot. Built by King Dhatusena (473–453 BC), the site was probably part of a royal compound. At the foot of a former shrine is a beautiful and well-preserved moonstone; ringed with elephants, it's unusual for having little riders atop some of them. The site is 1km south of the A4 between the 308 Km and 309 Km posts.

There's also an elevated stupa, in good condition and guarded by stone lions, a *vatadage* (circular relic house) on a cross-shaped platform that – in a stroke of ancient trompe l'oeil – is 'supported' by the stone pillars and crouched lions around its base, and a crudely patched up headless Buddha. Note the streamlined elephant-trunk railings along the site's staircases.

A little further west, between the 309 Km and 310 Km posts is Kotawehera, the ruined remains of an ancient brick stupa, which enjoys a magnificent situation upon a hilltop. On a clear day there are spectacular vistas over forests to the wetlands around Pottuvil Lagoon.

ornithologically rich mangrove swamp 22km beyond Okanda. May to June is nesting season. There have been sightings of Sri Lanka's very rare black-necked stork, but more commonly spotted, even outside the bird reserve, are Malabar pied hornbills, green bee-eaters, blade-headed orioles and painted storks, among others. Watchtowers provide a terrific perspective for birdwatchers. Visitors regularly report seeing dozens of peacocks here.

Entry fees are myriad, and can really add up. A mandatory guide (who may not speak English) accompanies each vehicle. Guesthouses in Arugam Bay can help arrange for a jeep and driver; the going rate is around Rs 10,000 per day. (It's not as expensive as it seems given the park's rough roads.) Guide **Siddiq** (☑ 077 481 7774) gets rave reviews for animal-spotting.

You can arrange **camping trips** within the park, which allow you to watch animals at dusk and dawn – the two best times. For this, the algorithm becomes even more complicated: US$20 per person, US$27 per group, Rs 250 per jeep, plus 12% tax.

Drivers in Arugam Bay charge US$300 for two people, which includes the transport, evening and morning safaris, equipment and meals. **Aliya** (www.aliyasafari.com), very professional safari specialists based near Buttala, are strongly recommended.

Ampara

☑ 063

Laid-back Ampara sits in the midst of countryside dappled with paddy fields, lakes and palm groves. Though the town itself won't hold you, the area has a couple of low-key sights.

◉ Sights

Japanese Peace Pagoda   BUDDHIST
(Sama Chaitya) This pagoda, 4km west of town, is a graceful stupa with a twist or two, including a vaguely Roman-looking colonnade ringing its lower level. Niches containing gilded Buddhas contrast superbly with the whitewashed body of the temple. The incense-smoked image room near the entrance, with its Buddha statues and colourful altar, is also fascinating, especially when the friendly resident monk and nun are drumming and chanting.

The main reason for coming here, though, is the chance of seeing herds of passing **wild elephants**, but they've been shy in recent years and don't come by like they used to. Try your luck: at around 5pm to 6pm, the elephants may pass through a narrow passageway in front of the pagoda, or in the field behind it. Birdwatchers will also find the pagoda platform a handy perch for spotting hundreds of waterbirds that flit about the facing lake.

To reach the temple follow DS Senanayake Rd from the clock tower, which heads towards Inginyagala, passing scenic Ampara Tank. After 4km, a short right turn brings you to the pagoda.

Sri Manika Pillaiyar   HINDU
(Inginyagala Rd) The Sri Manika Pillaiyar, which boasts an array of Hindu statuary illuminated by fairy lights, gives Ganesh a lovely view across Ampara Tank.

🛏 Sleeping & Eating

Ambhasewana Guest GUESTHOUSE $
(✒222 3865; 51st Ave; r with/without air-con Rs 1800/850; ❄) Run by a welcoming family, this simple lilac-and-white guesthouse occupies a shady plot on a quiet side street, a couple of blocks from the town centre. The nine airy rooms are a great option if you're on a tight budget.

Monty Guest House HOTEL $$
(✒222 2169; www.montyhotel.com; 1st Ave; s/d Rs 2500/3000, r with air-con Rs 5000-9000; ❄ 🛜 ⊠) In a leafy suburb 1km south of the centre, the likeable Monty is a well-run place to stay. Design-wise it's slightly quirky: some communal areas resemble a multistorey car park, while the contemporary lobby is very tasteful. Fan rooms are functional and a tad dark, but air-con options boast modern furniture and clean lines.

The restaurant serves a range of excellent local and Western dishes (mains Rs 280 to 650) on its inviting outdoor terrace or in the dining room.

**Chinese & Western
Food Court** CHINESE, SRI LANKAN $$
(✒222 2215; terrelb@gmail.com; Stores Rd; mains Rs 250-650; ⊙11am-10pm; 🛜) A bustling, attractive place with tables set in a central garden and an open-sided dining room. Features lots of Chinese-style mains including delicious Manchurian chicken and salad (Rs 775), and several dishes with *kankun,* a leafy green related to morning glory. C&W also has chintzy rooms that are overpriced considering their size.

The hotel can set up safari trips to national parks including Gal Oya National Park; contact owner Terrel, who has 4WDs.

New City SRI LANKAN $
(Keells New City Supermarket; meals Rs 150-300) A good bet for a lunchtime rice and curry, *kotthu* in the evening or quick eats (deep-fried snacks and other small bites) for the times in between. It's close to the clock tower in the heart of town.

ℹ Information

Commercial Bank (DS Senanayake Rd) Has an ATM.

SabeeCom.Net & Bookmart (✒492 1455; Regal Junction; per hr Rs 50; ⊙8.30am-6.30pm Sun-Fri) Has reasonably fast internet connections.

ℹ Getting There & Away

Ampara's bus stand has CTB and private services. For Arugam Bay you can also take a bus to Siyambulanduwa (Rs 78, three hours, 10 daily) and change there, or minibus-hop via Akkaraipattu (Rs 50, hourly) to Pottuvil. For Batticaloa, you can minibus-hop via Kalmunai (Rs 48, frequent). Other useful services:

Batticaloa Rs 90, three hours, four daily
Colombo ordinary/semi-luxury Rs 385/525, 10 hours, nine/four daily
Kandy ordinary/air-con Rs 240/420, 5½ hours, hourly
Nuwara Eliya Rs 298, eight hours, 6.30am
Pottuvil (for Arugam Bay) Rs 121, three hours, 2pm

Around Ampara

**Buddhangala
Rock Hermitage** BUDDHIST
(donations accepted; ⊙6am-8pm) Rising above the forest north of Ampara, this 150m-high hill offers panoramic views from its rocky summit (including, occasionally, wild elephants at dusk). The site is said to be 1800 years old, and when the old temple, whose remains are to the left of the main shrine, was excavated in 1964, a gold casket containing a tooth of the Buddha was discovered. It's now housed inside the dagoba and is on view every June for three days around *poya* day.

Within an ancient cave overhang, interesting museum-style treasures include a human skeleton, used in meditation. The site is beautiful, but without a guide or English signage, its spiritual relevance is somewhat lost; English-speaking monks may be around to chat. Three-wheelers from Ampara, 7km away, cost Rs 800 return including waiting time.

Deegawapi RUIN
(Dighavapi Cetiya) According to legend, Deegawapi is the one place in southeastern Sri Lanka that the Buddha visited. The stupa was built during the reign of King Saddhatissa (137–119 BC) and patched up in the 2nd and 18th centuries AD before becoming lost in the jungle.

Rediscovered in 1916, for decades it has been at the centre of disputes; many Sinhalese say the area's predominantly Muslim population deliberately settled on ancient dagoba (read: Sinhalese) land, while many Muslims, who have lived in the region for centuries, see the claim as a bridgehead for Sinhalese colonisation.

The site might not be interesting enough to warrant the lengthy detour: the vast central red-brick dagoba stub is massive, but it lacks a particularly scenic setting. An excavation is ongoing. The small **archaeological museum** (⊘8am-5pm) **FREE** has potential.

Batticaloa

🖉 065

Historic Batticaloa (Batti for short) enjoys a spectacular position surrounded by lagoons with palm-filtered sunlight glancing off the water. There's a mellow vibe to the town, and though there are no dramatic or must-see sights, a morning exploring the compact centre and its huge fortress and many churches is time well spent. It's not a large place and ideal to explore on foot. Sandy beaches are close by, but these were hit hard by the 2004 tsunami.

◉ Sights & Activities

There are three distinct areas of interest, each divided by the waters of the Batticaloa lagoon. The most atmospheric quarter is **Puliyanthivu**, actually an island, and home to the fort, several colonial-era churches and the bus stands. Across the lagoon to the north is the **new town**, the commercial hub whose broad streets lined with shops and banks. Southeast of here, via a bridge, is the leafy suburb of **Kallady**, home to midrange hotels, and a sandy beach.

Dutch Fort   FORT
(Bazaar St, Puliyanthivu; ⊘8.30am-4.15pm) **FREE** This once-mighty fort is now home to administrative offices, and though large sections of the structure are crumbling it's still an evocative sight. It was built by the Portuguese in 1628, but the Dutch took over after just 10 years, followed by the Brits. Access is controlled, so you're likely to be escorted around the 6m-thick ramparts by a policeman or soldier, who'll point out the English canons, surviving watchtowers and ruined belltower. Views across the lagoon are magnificent.

There's a tiny **museum** with several intriguing items labelled, alas, only in Tamil, and you can glimpse the old jail (now a store).

For a great perspective of the fort, head to the tiny **Auliya Mosque** (Lady Manning Dr) over the water with its curious green minaret.

Thiruchendur
Murugan Alayam Temple   HINDU
(Navalady Rd, Kallady) Built in 1984 as a stopping point on the Pada Yatra pilgrimage to Kataragama, the temple has a Murugan image said to have opened its own eyes before the painter could do the job. The structure was slammed by the tsunami, leaving its small *gopuram* leaning at an alarming angle. The colourful leaning tower sits near the beach between Third and Fourth Cross Sts in Kallady.

Kallady &
Navalady Peninsula   BEACH
This long, beach-edged peninsula is home to the Kallady and Navalady neighbourhoods. Kallady has a lovely near-deserted strip of beach that's fine for a swim, though there's still plenty of tsunami damage evident and not that much shade.

St Mary's Cathedral   CHURCH
(St Mary's St, Puliyanthivu) The grand, turquoise-coloured St Mary's Cathedral is one of the most eye-catching churches in Batti. St Mary's was rebuilt in 1994 following its partial destruction during fighting between local Tamils and Muslims.

Anipandi
Sitivigniswara Alayar   HINDU
(Hospital Rd, Puliyanthivu) Of the many Hindu temples, Anipandi Sitivigniswara Alayar is visually the finest, with a magnificent *gopuram* that's decorated with a riotous festival of intertwined god figures.

Batticaloa Market   MARKET
(Lloyds Ave) Stock up with tropical fruit as well as gifts for back home, like spoons made from coconut shells and palmyra palm jaggery (raw sugar) in laid-back, hassle-free environs.

Imperial Saloon   SHRINE
(Trinco Rd; ⊘8.30am-8.30pm, to 1pm Sun) Consider a haircut and head massage (Rs 400) at this utterly bizarre salon, a monument to kitsch. Every inch is covered in decorative painting, fake flowers, sequins, filigree, stained glass or tinsel garlands, and at the back of the salon, up towards the faux-sky ceiling, is an interfaith shrine, from where Durga, Mary and the Buddha keep an eye on things.

Batticaloa

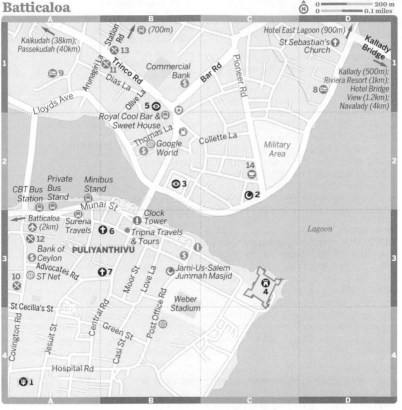

St Anthony's CHURCH

(St Anthony's St, Puliyanthivu) The vaguely Mexican-looking, earth-toned St Anthony's is one of the most eye-catching churches in Puliyanthivu.

Sri Lanka Diving Tours DIVING

(☎ 077 061 5205, 031-371 7451; www.srilanka-divingtours.com; Navalady; ⊙ Mar-Sep) This professional dive school specialises in wrecks, and Batticaloa has a world-class one: the HMS *Hermes*, a British aircraft carrier that was sunk by Japanese bombers in 1942. This dive is for tec divers only (the five-day certification course, for very advanced divers, is also offered here), but there are several other dives in the area for those less advanced. Two dives cost US$70; it's US$120 for tec dives. The dive school also operates a guesthouse here, but rooms are seriously overpriced.

🛏 Sleeping

The Kallady area is a bit of a hike from the sights of Puliyanthivu as you have to cross two bridges.

Many travellers opt to stay by the beach in the Kalkudah area 30km to the north.

Treatooo   GUESTHOUSE $
(☑ 222 7600; www.treatooo.com; 103 Lady Manning Drive; s/d/tr Rs 1500/2000/2500, with air-con Rs 2200/2800/3500; 🌡 🤝) This welcoming guesthouse has nine spacious and tidy rooms, some boasting balconies with lagoon views. The family owners look after travellers well, offering tasty local, Chinese and Western dishes (Rs 250 to 500) as well as good transport information and laundry. Its waterside location is superb.

Hotel Bridge View   HOTEL $
(☑ 222 3723; www.hotelbridgeview.com; 63/24 New Dutch Bar Rd, Kallady; s/d/tr from Rs 1120/1300/1560; 🌡 🤝) This garden hotel 1km from the bridge is ageing but worth considering. Rooms are surrounded by greenery; oddly, those in the old wing are better than the newer ones. Any bridge views are imagined. The restaurant serves decent seafood and curries, though service could be snappier.

Riviera Resort   HOTEL $
(☑ 222 2164, 222 2165; www.riviera-online.com; New Dutch Bar Rd, Kallady; s/d from Rs 1342/2440, d with air-con from Rs 4885; 🌡 @ 🤝) Perched at the water's edge with views of Kallady Bridge and the lagoon, the Riviera is certainly a peaceful, relaxing place to stay. The accommodation has some old-fashioned charm, but would benefit from a makeover; expect somewhat dark rooms and a slightly faded feel. Still, there's a well-stocked bar and restaurant offering good local cooking.

Kayaks are available for hire (singles/doubles Rs 500/800) for exploring the lagoon and there are also bikes.

YMCA   GUESTHOUSE $
(☑ 222 2495; Boundary Rd; s/d/tr from Rs 800/1150/1500, with air-con Rs 1725/2300/2875; 🌡) If you're really watching the rupees, the Y is so cheap it's worth considering. The location is central yet quiet and the staff are friendly, but the large impersonal block offers near-zero ambience; rooms are bare and bathrooms are cold-water only. No food is served, but drinks are available.

Hotel East Lagoon   HOTEL $$
(☑ 222 9222; www.hoteleastlagoon.lk; Munai Lane, Uppodai Lake Road; r/ste from Rs 7100/16,800; 🌡 🤝 🔲) Now top dog in town, this new colonial-style place enjoys a serene lagoonside setting 1km northeast of the centre with fine views over the water to Kallady from its plush, spacious rooms. There's a good restaurant with an excellent lunch buffet (Rs 900) for great local foods including lots of vegetarian choices.

🍴 Eating & Drinking

TD Foods & Takeaway   SRI LANKAN $
(15 Covington Rd; meals Rs 180-380) Tiny TD is strung with coloured lights and Chinese lanterns and is next to a Tamil music shop, so eating here is a full sensory experience. Serves excellent biryanis, noodles and *kotthu*.

Sun Shine Fast   SRI LANKAN $
(315 Trinco Rd; meals Rs 180-400) Sun Shine has quite a reputation, and it's easy to see why. This modern, clean and welcoming place covers all bases with an amazing display of biriyanis, curries (try the mutton), and pilau rice as well as burgers, cakes and snacks (samosas for Rs 25), juices and lassis. There are two locations across the street from each other.

Seven Star   SRI LANKAN $
(New Kalmunai Rd, Kallady; rice & curry Rs 150-250) Scores strongly for genuine rice and curry – as the lunchtime crowds will attest. Seven Star is just north of the clock tower.

★ RN Buffet & Take Away   SRI LANKAN $$
(☑ 222 2684; 42 Covington Rd; meals Rs 120-600; ⊘ 7.30am-6pm, lunch buffet 11am-3.30pm) A wonderful find, this hyper-busy little eatery run by a delightful, industrious couple has an excellent takeaway section (vegie/meat meals Rs 120/200) popular with office workers. Upstairs is a buffet restaurant; the lunchtime spread (Rs 600) includes fish, chicken and lots of vegetarian dishes. Western food (like pasta) can also be prepared; call ahead and espresso coffee is available.

Riviera Resort   SRI LANKAN $$
(☑ 222 2165, 222 2164; www.riviera-online.com; New Dutch Bar Rd, Kallady; meals Rs 350-800; ⊘ noon-3pm & 5-10pm; 🤝) Dining here evokes memories of colonial times, as waiters fix you up with a drink (ideally a gin and tonic)

on the verandah, take your order and beck-on you into the dining room, set up with all manner of dishes and white-cloth napkins. The food is worth the wait, including excellent crab curries and seafood.

Tomato Restaurant   WESTERN, SRI LANKAN $$
(136 Trinco Rd; meals Rs 300-600; ☉10am-10.30pm; ☎) When the tropical heat becomes too much, the sanctity of air-conditioned Tomato is refreshingly welcome. This refined restaurant has Western food (pasta, sandwiches, salads, seafood and grilled lamb chops) as well as Northern Indian specials from the tandoori oven (after 6pm) including naan bread and tikkas. No alcohol is served, but there's a good choice of juices.

It's above Sun Shine Fast.

Café Chill   CAFE
(9 Pioneer Rd; drinks & snacks Rs 50-200; ☉9.30am-8.30pm; ☎) A meeting point for Batti's bright young things, this hip little cafe serves coffee, tea (including herbal varieties), juices and lassis in a relaxed semi-alfresco setting close to the lagoon. Snacks such as French fries and samosas are also available.

ⓘ Information

Bank of Ceylon (Covington Rd) Has an ATM.

Commercial Bank (Bar Rd) Has an ATM

Google World (Thomas La; internet per hr Rs 40; ☉8.30am-8.30pm) Fast internet.

Post Office (Post Office Rd; ☉7am-8pm Mon-Fri, to 6pm Sat, to 5pm Sun)

ST Net (27 Covington Rd; internet per hr Rs 50) Quick connections and friendly staff.

Tourist Information Booth (Bazaar St; ☉9am-5pm)

Tripna Travels & Tours (St Anthony's St; ☉9am-5.30pm Mon-Fri, to 1pm Sat)

ⓘ Getting There & Away

AIR

Batticaloa's airport is 2km southwest of the bus stand. **SriLankan Airlines** (☑1979; www.sri lankan.lk) flies to/from Colombo's Bandaranaike International Airport four times a week (one way US$258). The Sri Lankan Air Force's **Helitours** (☑011-314 4244, 011-314 4944; www.helitours. lk) has flights on military planes to/from Colombo's Ratmalana airport on Tuesdays (one way Rs 4650).

BUS

CTB buses, private buses and minibuses have adjacent bus stations on Munai St, but many head out from the police station area; inquire

in advance. Buses north to Trinco and south to Pottuvil do not divert inland anymore as the coastal highway is now in excellent condition and new bridges are open. Combined CTB and private departures include the following:

Ampara Rs 92, three hours, three daily

Badulla Rs 236, six hours, five daily

Colombo Rs 322, nine hours, three daily

Jaffna (via Vavuniya) Rs 380, eight hours, four daily

Polonnaruwa Rs 130, two hours, every 30 minutes

Pottuvil (for Arugam Bay) Rs 147, three hours, 12 daily

Trincomalee Rs 200, four hours, every 30 minutes

Valaichchenai (for Passekudah and Kalkudah) Rs 50, 50 minutes, every 20 minutes

Most people prefer the private buses to Colombo:

Surena Travels (☑222 6152; Munai St; ☉4.30-8.30pm) For Colombo (ordinary/air-con Rs 650/1000, nine hours, 6.15pm, 8.30pm and 9pm).

Royal Cool Bar & Sweet House (Trinco Rd; ☉6am-10pm) For Colombo (ordinary/air-con Rs 600/900, nine hours, 9pm and 9.30pm).

TRAIN

Book well in advance at the helpful **railway office** (☑222 4471; ☉8.30am-4pm) for trains to Colombo 3rd/2nd/1st class Rs 310/500/840, 8½ hours, 7.15am and 8.15pm

Around Batticaloa

Batticaloa Lighthouse   LIGHTHOUSE
(Palameenmadu; boat trips Rs 400-3000; ☉boat trips 8am-7pm) At the end of a sandbar, surrounded by lagoons and mangroves, this lighthouse dates from 1913. The coastline around here is a popular family excursion (avoid weekends) and there's a play area for kids. Swimming in the calm water, surrounded by islands and inlets, is the main draw, though **boat trips** can be good for bird- and crocodile-watching.

Three-wheelers charge Rs 350 from Batticaloa.

Kalkudah & Passekudah Beaches

☑ 065

These spectacular back-to-back beaches, 34km north of Batticaloa, present as stark a juxtaposition as you could imagine.

On one side of a narrow peninsula, the breathtaking white sands of sickle-shaped **Passekudah beach** are being developed as a kind of mini-Cancun, a government-driven 'Special Economic Zone' with 14 luxury hotels ultimately planned to ring the bay. Fishermen have also been ordered to move their boats away from the main beach. Sure, it's a glorious stretch of sand, but for the next few years the immediate surrounds are a mess, resembling a building site, as edifices in various stages of construction emerge from scrubland.

Passekudah's extremely shallow water heats up to bathtub temperatures on sunny days (you'll have to wade out some distance for a good swim). There's also lots of sharp coral mixed in with the sand, so take care if barefoot. You'll often find busloads of Sinhalese tourists here; try walking north along the shore to avoid the crowds.

In contrast, **Kalkudah beach**, 2km away over the headland to the south, is deserted, save the odd fisherman and his boat. This fabulous stretch of golden sand *was* once lined with hotels, but these were destroyed in the civil war and 2004 tsunami. There's little shade, but it's a delight to explore; just wander along the shore until you find your own private patch of sand.

Coconut Cultural Park
PARK

(Beach Rd, Passekudah; admission Rs 250; ☺ 8am-5pm) Just behind the hotels, this impressive new attraction is dedicated to the coconut, surely the world's most remarkable plant, and inexorably linked with the Sri Lankan nation (their cultivation is mentioned in the Mahavamsa) and diet. You can wander under coconut groves and learn all about the coconut palm's many uses – timber for housing and shelter, coir rugs and rope, cooking oil and toddy. Beauty creams sold here make great souvenirs and coconut ice cream is the ideal post-tour treat.

🛏 Sleeping & Eating

Luxury hotels line the Passekudah shoreline. Budget guesthouses and midrangers are concentrated along the Valaichchenai–Kalkudah Rd and in the sandy lanes inland from Passekudah beach.

No matter where you stay, both beaches are very accessible. All the hotels listed here are no more than 2km from either beach.

Most people dine in hotels as there are no specific restaurants.

Victoria Guest House
GUESTHOUSE $

(☑ 957 8968; victoriaghouse@yahoo.com; Valaichchenai–Kalkudah Rd; s/d from Rs 2000/2500, ❋ 🛜) This is where you stay if you want to experience down-to-earth Sri Lankan hospitality. Cleanliness standards are high. It's run by Mercy and her family, who prepare delicious home-cooked meals (using vegetables from their garden; mains Rs 250) for their guests, rent out bikes and are generous with smiles and laughter.

Victoria (the owner's mum) drops by most days and is an expert on natural medicine.

Moni Guesthouse
GUESTHOUSE $

(☑ 365 4742; Valaichchenai–Kalkudah Rd; d with/without air-con Rs 2800/1700; ❋ 🛜) Moni is in the midst of things, but has a good family feel. The five rooms are basic but kept tidy and the family owners prepare filling meals (Rs 250 to 400), including lot of fish curries and huge breakfasts.

New Land Guesthouse
GUESTHOUSE $

(☑ 568 0440; 283 Valaichchenai–Kalkudah Rd; r Rs 1000-1500, with air-con Rs 2500; ❋ 🛜) A well-run, welcoming family-run place with a selection of very clean rooms that have mosquito nets and wood furnishings; those in the new block are a bit smaller. Mains cost Rs 200 to 250.

★ Roy's Inn
GUESTHOUSE $$

(☑ 205 0223; www.roysinnguesthouse.com; Mariyamman Kovil Rd, Passekudah; s/d Rs 5000; ❋ 🛜) Delightful new place, with gorgeous, well-constructed cottage-style accommodation dotted around a pretty, peaceful garden. All the units are immaculately clean, boast high ceilings, mozzie nets and good-quality beds and mattresses. Staff are extremely helpful and there's a little restaurant for great-value meals (Rs 250 to 400).

It's signposted down a sandy lane, 300m inland from Passekudah beach.

Nandawanam Guesthouse
GUESTHOUSE $$

(☑ 225 7258; www.nandawanam.blogspot.co.uk; Valaichchenai–Kalkudah Rd; r Rs 3300-5500; ❋ 🛜) This green villa is set well back from the road in beautiful gardens. Rooms vary – those on the ground floor are more traditional, while upstairs they're modern – but all are very clean and tidy, and boast good thick mattresses and cable TV. Meals are excellent and staff are sweet and helpful: you'll feel right at home here.

Uga Bay
HOTEL $$$

(☑ 567 1000; www.ugaescapes.com; Passekudah beach; r/ste from US$142/196; ✿ ☎ ⊠) On a huge beachside plot, this luxury resort hotel offers beautifully finished rooms and suites (all with sea views) that combine dark wood, marble and contemporary detailing to achieve a pleasing vision of tropical chic. All are equipped with an iPod dock, huge flat-screen TV and DVD player. Kids will love the massive pool, and there's a spa and gym.

Book on the hotel's website at least a week in advance for the best rates.

Anilana Pasikuda
RESORT HOTEL $$$

(☑ 203 0900; www.anilana.com/pasikuda; r/chalets from US$138/165; ✿ ☎ ⊠) Tasteful beachfront hotel where ultra modernity is tempered with thatched roofs and natural materials. All accommodation (in the main building or shoreside) features hip lighting and modish bathrooms and is set around a lovely pool that's perfect for laps. There's a well-regarded spa (try the hydrotherapy treatments) and fine restaurant (grilled or barbecued fish is superb).

❶ Getting There & Away

The small town of Valaichchenai on the A15 coastal highway is the gateway to Passekudah and Kalkudah. Buses (Rs 50, 50 minutes, every 20 minutes) connect Valaichchenai with Batticaloa. Heading north, there are services to Trincomalee (Rs 152, three hours, every 30 minutes).

Three-wheelers charge Rs 150 for the short hop between Valaichchenai and Passekudah or Kalkudah.

Trincomalee

☑ 026 / POPULATION 59,000

Trincomalee (Trinco) had a rough time in the war, but this fascinating town is beginning to thrive again. Sitting on one of the world's finest natural harbours, Trincomalee is old almost beyond reckoning: it's possibly the site of historic Gokana in the Mahavamsa (Great Chronicle), and its Shiva temple the site of Trikuta Hill in the Hindu text Vayu Purana. Most people just pass through the city on their way to the nearby beaches of Uppuveli and Nilaveli, but the town has some charm, lots of history and an interesting melange of people.

Trincomalee's superb deep-water port has made it the target for all manner of attacks over the centuries: by the British takeover in 1795, the city had changed colonial hands

seven times. Today the Sri Lankan armed forces control Fort Frederick, along with the British-built airfield, China Bay, to the south.

◉ Sights & Activities

Fort Frederick
FORTRESS

(Konesar Rd) FREE Occupying the neck of a narrow peninsula, Fort Fredrick has been a defensively important site for centuries. A fortress was initially constructed here by the Portuguese in 1623 and later rebuilt by the Dutch. The British took over in 1782 (look out for royal insignias crowning the tunnel-like gateway that pierces the fort's massively stout walls).

The fortress is occupied today by the Sri Lankan military, but you're able to wander around substantial parts of this once huge garrison.

Assorted cannons and artillery are dotted around the enclave, which also contains a small number of spotted deer.

The impressive Georgian-style mansion (not open to visitors) is **Wellesley House**, named after a Duke of Wellington. It dates from the late 1700s.

There's also a big standing **Buddha statue** at the **Gokana Temple**, from where there are fine views of Trinco and the coastline.

Kandasamy Kovil
HINDU

(Kandasamy Kovil Rd) This revered temple at the summit of a rocky outcrop is one of Sri Lanka's *pancha ishwaram*, five historical Hindu temples dedicated to Shiva and established to protect the island from natural disaster. It houses the *lingam* (Hindu phallic symbol) known as the Swayambhu Lingam. It's an ancient place of worship, but

---

A WHALE WATCHTOWER

Jutting into the ocean on the east side of the city of Trincomalee, **Swami Rock** has been declared the world's greatest vantage point for blue whale spotting by oceanographers.

Blue whales are present in the seas off Trinco all year round, though sightings are most frequent between the months of February and November. Sperm whales also regularly cruise by.

So while you're exploring the Kandasarny Kovil temple, spare some time to gaze at the big blue offshore for spouting cetaceans. And bring binoculars if you can.

THE EAST TRINCOMALEE

Trincomalee

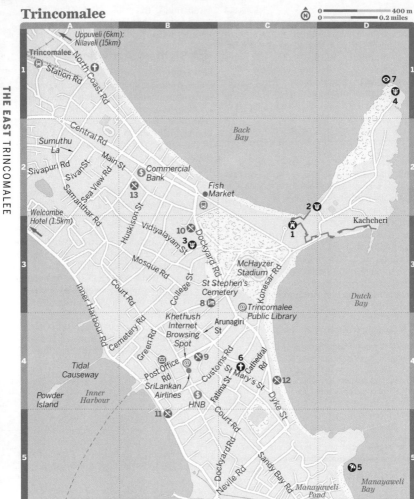

Trincomalee

the current structure dates to 1952. Pilgrims from across the nation flock here; its *puja* (prayers) at 6.30am, 11.30am and 4.30pm are always well attended.

The site is thought to have been a place of worship for at least two millennia. There was certainly a temple here by 300 AD, which was later built up over the years by everyone from the Cholas to the Jaffna Kingdom (its *gopuram* was said to be visible to sailors at sea), until being destroyed by the Portuguese.

One one side of the temple compound is **Swami Rock**, a 130m-high cliff nicknamed Lovers' Leap. It's associated with Francina van Reede, a Dutch woman who is said to have jumped from here in the late 17th century.

St Mary's Cathedral   CHURCH

(St Mary's St) Of the city's churches, the 1852 Catholic St Mary's Cathedral is particularly attractive, with a sky-blue neo-baroque frontage and a tiled, towered rear.

Kali Kovil   HINDU

(Dockyard Rd) Kali Kovil has the most impressive, eye-catching *gopuram* of Trinco's many Hindu temples.

Trincomalee Beaches   BEACH

Trinco's most famous beaches are at nearby Uppuveli and Nilaveli, but picturesque **Dutch Bay** isn't bad. It's more a place for strolling, but swimming is possible (watch out for the undertow). **Manayaweli Cove** is an appealing curl of fishing beach where you can also swim; reach it by strolling past **Manayaweli Pond**, aka Dhoby Tank, where local washers do their laundry. **Inner Harbour** and **Back Bay** are too polluted for swimming.

🛏 Sleeping

Most travellers (rightly) prefer the beachside accommodation in Uppuveli, just 6km north.

Sunshine Hotel   HOTEL $

(☑ 222 0288; http://sunshinehotelhall.com; 4 Green Road; r with fan Rs1200-1800, with air-con Rs 4000-4500; ✳) The garish banana-yellow and salmon-pink paintwork may be in-your-face loud but Sunshine's location on a quiet, suburban street is mellow. Fan rooms are quite spacious, clean and simple while air-con options come with all the trimmings including flat-screen TV, minibar and even an ironing board – perfect for those who like to keep their creases nice and sharp.

Service is a little spotty but friendly enough.

Welcombe Hotel   HOTEL $$

(☑ 222 3885, 222 3886; www.welcombehotel. com; 66 Orr's Hill Lower Rd; s/d from US$78/88; ✳ 🖥 🏊) Ageing hilltop hotel with a slightly bizarre, quasi-Japanese design, fading pink paint and a blue roof. Rooms are generously proportioned, some with bay views from their balconies, and staff are friendly, but it's only fair value.

🍴 Eating & Drinking

Anna Pooram
Vegetarian Restaurant   SOUTH INDIAN $

(415 Dockyard Rd; snacks Rs 15-80, rice & curry Rs 120-150) Bustling vegie eatery excelling in Tamil dishes, it's always packed at lunchtime. Famous for its *sambar* (soupy lentil dish with veg) and rice and curry. It has a couple of tables but is hugely popular for its take-away trade.

Ajmeer Hotel   SRI LANKAN $

(65 Post Office Rd; mains Rs 100-250; ⊙ 5.30am-10.30pm) Excellent rice and curry (Rs 120 to 200) – even the veg version rocks. The refills seem to never end, portions are enormous and the vibe is friendly.

RAWANA & THE SWAYAMBHU LINGAM

The radio-mast hill opposite Swami Rock is considered to be the site of the mythical palace of the 10-headed demon king Rawana. He's the Hindu antihero of the Ramayana, infamous for kidnapping Rama's wife, Sita. Along with Sita, he supposedly carried to Lanka the powerful Swayambhu Lingam, taken from a Tibetan mountaintop. This *lingam* became the object of enormous veneration. However, in 1624 the proselytising Catholic-Portuguese destroyed the surrounding clifftop temple, tipping the whole structure, *lingam* and all, into the ocean. It was only retrieved in 1962 by a scuba-diving team that included writer Arthur C Clarke, who described the discovery in *The Reefs of Taprobane*. For cameraman Mike Wilson, who first spotted the *lingam*, the experience proved so profound that he renounced his career and family to become Hindu Swami Siva Kalki (see http://kataragama.org/sivakalki.htm).

TRINCO TO BATTI

New bridges and the upgraded A15 highway between Trincomalee and Batticaloa have cut travel times considerably, and this scenic coastal route now begs to be explored.

Heading out of Trinco the A15 loops around the fringes of giant bite-shaped Trincomalee Bay, passing the airport. After 17km there's a turnoff on the left (signposted just before the Kinniya bridge) for **Marble Beach** (☑ 026-302 1000; www.marblebeach.lk; Marble Beach; chalets US$120-150, villas from US$250 incl full board; ❉ ☎), a glorious cove bookended by wooded headlands. There's a strip of golden sand, no trash and a drinks stand. School groups descend on the beach from time to time (afternoons are quieter), but otherwise it's a lovely place to kick back with sheltered swimming and a little snorkelling. On the north side of the bay a section of the beach is reserved for guests of the resort (but diners are welcome to use the restaurant; book ahead). Marble Beach is managed by the Sri Lankan Air Force and you have to pay an entrance fee of Rs 20/50 per person/car.

Continuing south over the Kinniya beach the A15 hugs the coastline then crosses another bridge before the Muslim town of **Mutur** where the roadside **MNU Hotel & Restaurant** (☑ 077 350 2377; Batticaloa Rd) provides Chinese, local, and even some Arabic food and has clean, good-value rooms.

Pushing on south, there's a turnoff at the Km 101 post for the important stupa **Seruwawila Rajamaha Viharaya**, one of the holiest Buddhist monuments in Sri Lanka, founded in the 2nd century BC, but only rediscovered (and reconstructed) in the 1920s. It deteriorated badly in the civil-war years, but was renovated in 2009.

Continuing south, the A15 cuts through an ocean of rice paddies and then a very sparselypopulated region of scrub bush and wetlands.

Just after the Panichchankeni bridge, at the Km 58 post, **Tranquility Coral Cottages** (☑ 011-262 5404; http://tccvakaraisl.com; Sallithievu Rd, Panichchankeni; cottages incl meals Rs 4000-8000) is 2km from the highway and offers an unplugged, off-the-grid beach experience. Here you can enjoy empty white sands, explore the Panichchankeni lagoon, snorkel the reefs around Sallithievu (an islet connected by a sandbar to the mainland) and taste home-style cooking. The wooden cottages are spacious but perhaps a little pricey for true Robinson Crusoes.

From here it's 27km south to the twin beaches of Kalkudah and Passekudah.

New Parrot Restaurant SRI LANKAN **$**
(96 Main St; mains Rs 100-400; ⊘ closed Sun evening) Head up the stairs to this simple place that offers reliably good noodles, rice, *kotthu*, soup and 'devilled' dishes. Try the special fried rice with chicken or omelette.

Dutch Bank Cafe CAFE, INTERNATIONAL **$$**
(88 Inner Harbour Rd; meals Rs 400-800; ☎) A beautifully designed new (air-conditioned) cafe-restaurant in a historic building that combines dramatic architectural features – check out those exposed stone arches – with contemporary design. Menu-wise there's everything from pasta, sandwiches and noodle dishes to Sri Lankan specials. Drinkswise you'll find espresso and cappuccino (Rs 300), good juices and shakes. It faces the Inner Harbour.

Green Park Beach Hotel INDIAN, INTERNATIONAL **$$**
(☑ 222 2369; 312 Dyke St; meals Rs 350-650; ☎) This slightly dated hotel on Dutch Bay has a vast menu that includes local, Western (pasta, pizza and salads) and recommended North Indian dishes, including tasty biriyanis and kormas. They also offer espresso (but no alcohol).

❶ Information

Commercial Bank (Central Rd) and **HNB** (Court Rd) both have ATMs.

Khethush Internet Browsing Spot (380 Court Rd; internet per hr Rs 40; ⊘ 8am-8pm Mon-Sat)

Post Office (Post Office Rd; ⊘ 7am-7pm Mon-Sat, 8.30am-4.30pm Sun)

Trincomalee Public Library (Dockyard Rd; internet per hr Rs 40; ⊘ 8am-5.30pm Tue-Sun) Fast internet in spacious bright surrounds.

ⓘ Getting There & Away

AIR

Helitours (☑ 011-314 4944, 011-311 0472; www.helitours.lk), the Sri Lankan Air Force airline, conducts passenger flights on military planes between China Bay airfield, 13km south of town, and Colombo's Ratmalana Air Force Base. Flights operate three times a week (one way Rs 4650, one hour).

Cinnamom Air (operated by **SriLankan Airlines** ☑ 222 7775; www.srilankan.com; 328 Court Rd) flies between Colombo and Trincomalee (US$254) three times a week.

BUS

The A15 coast road to Batticaloa is well and truly open and in excellent condition. CTB and private bus departures include the following:

Anuradhapura Rs 210, four hours, four daily

Batticaloa (via Habarana and Polonnaruwa) Rs 200, four hours, every 30 minutes

Colombo from Rs 345, eight hours, every 45 minutes

Colombo (air-con; book in advance) from Rs 600, 6½ hours, four evening departures

Jaffna (via Vavuniya) Rs 320, seven hours, nine daily

Kandy Rs 265, 5½ hours, hourly, plus three air-con (Rs 430) buses daily

Uppuveli/Nilaveli Rs 14/26, 20/30 minutes, every 20 minutes

TRAIN

There are two trains daily between Trincomalee and Colombo Fort, including a direct overnight sleeper service. Reserve at **Trincomalee station** (☑ 222 2271; ☺ bookings 8am-noon). You can also travel to Polonnaruwa and Batticaloa via a change in Gal Oya.

Colombo sleeper 3rd-/2nd-/1st-class sleeper Rs 270/450/750, 8½ hours, 7.30pm

Colombo unreserved (transfer in Gal Oya) 3rd/2nd class Rs 205/370, 8½ hours, 7am

Uppuveli & Nilaveli

☑ 026

North of Trinco, the indented coastline is blessed with fine beaches. Development is contained to two villages at the moment: the pretty palm-lined sands of Uppuveli, and the more exposed beach of Nilaveli, which is far more spread out. The ambience is very mellow at both places, but in season a sociable backpacking scene is developing at Uppuveli.

This is a poor region of fishing communities that was hit hard in wartime and the 2004 tsunami, but the coastal scenery more than compensates. The ocean is the main attraction: there's some surf, and the snorkelling and scuba diving around Pigeon Island (a pretty island ringed by coral reef just offshore from Nilaveli) is an increasing draw.

Uppuveli

Uppuveli, 6km from Trincomalee, is an engaging little coastal community consisting of a fine beach of golden sand, a few hundred locals, a dozen or so places to stay and a seemingly unlimited supply of fresh seafood.

Uppuveli's not exactly drop-dead gorgeous, but it does have a distinctly local charm, an intimate feel and some good-value accommodation. It's many travellers' favourite hangout in the East.

◉ Sights & Activities

Commonwealth
War Cemetery   CEMETERY
(Nilaveli Rd; ☺ dawn-dusk) For a break from the beach, stroll up to this beautifully kept cemetery. This is the last resting place for hundreds of Commonwealth servicemen who died at Trinco during WWII, most of them during a 1942 Japanese raid that sank more than a dozen vessels.

You'll be shown around by the amiable caretaker, whose knowledge of the cemetery is incredible – he'll lead you to specific graves, or those of the many nationalities buried here.

Salli
Muthumariamunam Kovil   HINDU
The beachfront Salli Muthumariamunam Kovil temple is 4km by road from Uppuveli, but only a short wade (or hop by boat if the tide is high) from the north end of Uppuveli beach. It's across Fishermen's Creek, masked from view by green-topped rocks.

Sri Lanka
Diving Tours   DIVING, WATERSPORTS
(☑ 077 068 6860, 071 132 3974; www.srilanka-divingtours.com; Aqua Inn Hotel, 12 Alles Gardens) Dive professionals, offering thorough and enjoyable courses (PADI Open Water is US$425) and fun dives (US$40) to Pigeon Island, Swami Rock in Trincomalee and the Irakkandy shipwreck. Snorkelling trips are also excellent.

Water-skiing and wakeboarding are possible when conditions are suitable, and kayaks (US$5), body boards and snorkelling gear (US$5) are available for rent.

Uppuveli

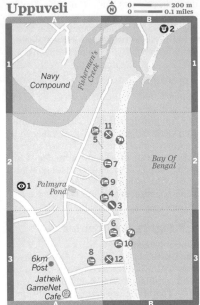

In season (April to September), whale-spotting (US$40 per person) and dolphin-watching (US$30) trips are also popular.

🛏 Sleeping

Aqua Inn　　　　　　　BUDGET HOTEL **$**
(📞077 854 6139; www.aquahoteltrincomalee. com; 12 Alles Garden; s/d Rs 2000/2500, with air-con Rs 4500/5000; ❄🕸📶) It's difficult to be too positive about Aqua as it could be so much better. First the good points: it's cheap, sociable and the beachfront location is superb. However, prepare yourself for the fearsomely ugly concrete accommodation block and distinctly grim budget rooms (with a dim, bare lightbulb for 'decor'); air-conditioned options are slightly better.

Backpackers are pushed here by commission-hungry tuk-tuk drivers in Trinco, so it's always busy. As a place simply to crash and meet others it's doable, and the bar-restaurant is undeniably a great place to hang out for a drink, even if the food is forgettable.

Shiva's Beach Resort　　　　　HOTEL **$**
(📞320 4882; goldenbeachtrinco24@gmail. com; 178/32 Alles Garden; r with fan/air-con Rs 2500/5000; ❄📶) Initial appearances are a little deceptive here as the slab-like concrete design looks rather soulless from the outside, but the spacious, neat rooms are actually a good deal. You can usually get a bed if everywhere else is booked.

Palm Beach　　　　　　　GUESTHOUSE **$**
(📞222 1250; d with/without air-con Rs 4500/4000, annex s with shared bathroom Rs 1800, d Rs 2700; ⏱Feb-Oct; ❄📶) Italian-owned hotel with tasteful, though slightly dated, rooms, all with dark-wood furniture and little porches, though bathrooms are cold-water and mattresses are foam slabs. The shady gardens are a short stroll from the beach and there's excellent food. For a bargain, check out the budget annex with charmingly monastic rooms.

★Coconut Beach Lodge　　　GUESTHOUSE **$$**
(📞222 4888, 492 5712; coconutbeachlodge@gmail. com; r with/without air-con from Rs 7700/3300; ❄📶) Locally owned place with a blissful beachfront location. The garden compound is a delight; at its rear is an elegant villa-style structure for home-cooked meals and hanging out with other guests. Standard rooms are superb value and very popular, with nice touches like artwork in the bathroom, while the air-con rooms have high ceilings and all mod cons.

The welcoming owners are real characters, and very knowledgeable about the region. They cook superb local food (order by 3.30pm) and can set up boat trips and transport.

Golden Beach Cottage GUESTHOUSE $$
(🕿 721 1243; r Rs 2500-6000; ✳ 🛜) Offering good rates for its inexpensive rooms, which have a few homey touches (wardrobes, mirrors and little front porches) and are surprisingly spacious. Fancier options here are overpriced. The cottages are located on a beautiful patch of beach south of Chaaya Blu.

★**Chaaya Blu** RESORT $$$
(🕿 222 1611; www.cinnamonhotels.com; s/d incl breakfast US$215/230, chalets s/d incl breakfast US$245/260; ✳ @ 🛜 ⛱) Beautifully designed hotel that makes the most of its prime beachside plot, where all rooms face the ocean. Colour schemes – whitewashed walls and cobalt blues – are offset with punchy orange throw pillows, textiles and mosaic art. The expansive lawn is a delightful base for a day's lounging, with a lovely 30m pool, and both restaurants are superb.

Sea Lotus Park RESORT $$$
(🕿 222 5327; www.sealotuspark.com; s/d Rs 9600/10,400, bungalows s/d Rs 6800/7390; ✳ @ 🛜 ⛱) Worth considering, this beachfront hotel has two classes of rooms: those that are recently renovated, spacious and modern (though set back from the sea in a concrete block) and dated cabanas that are poorly maintained but boast unmatched shorefront views. Meals and service standards are pretty average.

✕ Eating & Drinking

Coconut Beach Lodge SRI LANKAN $$
(🕿 492 5712, 222 4888; meals Rs 350-650; 🛜) Coconut Beach is the best place in town for Sri Lankan-style home cooking. Rice and curry, grilled seer fish and giant prawns, plus vegie delights are all prepared with love and served on a pretty candlelit patio. Reserve by 3.30pm.

Silver Beach SEAFOOD, SRI LANKAN $$
(Beachside; meals Rs 500-900) A casual locally owned beachside restaurant with a welcoming owner. There's always fresh fish (around Rs 1200 will easily feed two people), which is served with salad and fries, and the battered calamari is superb too.

★**Crab** INTERNATIONAL $$$
(Chaaya Blu; meals Rs 1000-2500; ◔ noon-11pm) A wonderful setting for a meal, this casual hotel restaurant is perfect for a lazy lunch by the waves or a romantic evening meal. You'll find a wide selection of dishes, all competitively priced, with everything from Indonesian spicy rice with satay to succulent seafood (and a particularly fine crab curry). For dessert, try the delicious berry cheesecake.

There's an open kitchen, full bar and good service.

Palm Beach ITALIAN $$$
(🕿 222 1250; meals Rs 1300-2600; ◔ 6.30-9pm, closed Nov-Jan; 🛜) Authentic Italian food, including fine pasta and seafood, prepared by chef Donatella; the menu changes daily but always includes a special or two. Enjoys a good reputation, but as it's the only game in town for Western cuisine, there's very little competition. Expect pleasant but hardly memorable surrounds (it's well off the beach). Reserve essential.

ⓘ Information

Uppuveli has no ATMs or banks; head to Trinco.
Jatheik GameNet Cafe (Nilaveli Rd; internet per hr Rs 50; ◔ 8.30am-8pm Mon-Sat)
St Joseph's Medical Service (Nilaveli Rd; ◔ 24hr) Around-the-clock medical services.

ⓘ Getting There & Away

Irakkandy–Trincomalee buses run every 20 minutes; flag one down on the main road for Trincomalee (Rs 14, 20 minutes) or Nilaveli (Rs 14, 10 minutes). Three-wheelers cost Rs 350 to Trinco and Rs 500 to Nilaveli.

Nilaveli

Nilaveli, the Trinco region's other beach resort, is far less intimate than Uppuveli, with hotels scattered up and down little lanes off the coastal highway – it's around four kilometres from one end of the village to the other. If you're looking for some serious beach time, then Nilaveli could be just the ticket, for the sands are golden and the ocean inviting. Offshore, Pigeon Island offers fine diving and snorkelling.

⊙ Sights & Activities

★**Pigeon Island National Park** DIVING, SNORKELLING
(adult/child US$10/5, plus boat fee Rs125, service charge per group US$8, VAT 12%; ◔ 7am-5.30pm) Floating in the great blue 1km offshore, Pigeon Island, with its powdery white sands and glittering coral gardens, tantalises with possibilities. A nesting area for rock pigeons, the island is beautiful enough, with rock pools and paths running through thickets,

but it's the underwater landscape that's the real star. The reef here is shallow, making snorkelling almost as satisfying as diving, and it's home to dozens of corals, hundreds of reef fish (including blacktip reef sharks) and turtles.

Note that the recent surge in tourism has damaged the reef to a degree, so don't expect a pristine marine environment. Close to the shore, some daytrippers stomp all over shallow coral.

The Pigeon Island National Park ticket office is on the beach in front of the Anilana hotel. As with all national parks in Sri Lanka, the various fees and charges are myriad and really add up. And this excludes boat charter and snorkelling gear rental costs!

Dive shops, including Poseidon Diving School and Sri Lankan Diving Tours, offer trips here, as do many hotels.

Note that the navy base in Trincomalee has a decompression chamber that can (allegedly) be reached by ambulance in 10 minutes.

★ Poseidon Diving School   DIVING

(☏ 077 706 9442; www.divingsrilanka.com; at Pigeon Island View Guest House; whale-watching trips per 3 people €130; ☉ Apr-Nov) This well-organised school offers lots of scuba action, including PADI open water certification courses (€300), fun dives and snorkelling trips to Pigeon Island. Whale-watching boat trips searching for blue whales and sperm whales are also offered.

Nilaveli Private
Boat Service   BOAT TRIP, SNORKELLING

(☏ 071 593 6919; fishing trips Rs 2500, whale-watching trips per 4 people Rs 12,000) The local boatmen's association has set prices for the Pigeon Island trip – Rs 1700 per boat – while snorkelling gear costs Rs 600 per day to rent. Boat hire costs the same whether it's a full day (7am to 5.30pm) or a couple of hours. You'll find captains at the beach by the ticket office. Fishing trips and whale-watching excursions are also offered.

🛏 Sleeping & Eating

Nilaveli has around a dozen or so places to stay, most in the midrange and top-end categories. There are a couple of budget places but they're poor value and not worth it. Note that off-season things are very quiet in Nilaveli.

If you're searching for a place to stay, a tuk-tuk is definitely worth hiring – accom-

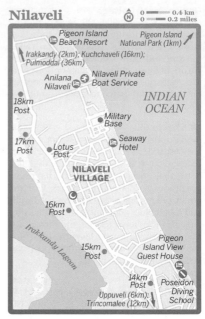

modation is very spread out. All of the following serve food.

Seaway Hotel   HOTEL $$

(☏ 223 2212; r with fan Rs 4500, with air-con 7500-10,000; ❄☏) Set just off the beach, the inviting Seaway offers a wide choice of accommodation in a huge grassy compound (which could do with some landscaping). There are three classes of rooms, from smallish but clean fan-cooled budget digs with cold-water bathrooms and front porches to very attractive modern options with attractive furnishings, minibar, hot water and balconies.

Staff are friendly and helpful and there's a thatched roof restaurant for good breakfasts (Rs 400) and Sri Lankan and Western meals (Rs 450 to 750).

Pigeon Island
View Guest House   GUESTHOUSE $$

(☏ 223 2238; www.pigeon-island.com; d/tr from Rs 4000/5000; ❄☏) Thanks to its peaceful beachside location, this place is an excellent choice. The three-storey pink structure is somewhat functional and rooms are a little spartan, but they are airy and clean. Eager, helpful staff enhance the welcoming vibe and local meals are moderately priced (Rs 400 to 800) and plentiful. Located at the end of a lonely dirt road.

WORTH A TRIP

NORTH OF NILAVELI

The beautiful B424 coastline road north of Nilaveli follows the shore, with the ocean on one side and lagoons inland. It's a great day out on a motorbike, or for those with the lung power, a bicycle (it's very flat). Public transport is limited on this route.

Heading north there's little of interest for the first 6km, but after you cross the river estuary at Kumpurupiddi the road runs very close to the beach, and then skirts a huge shallow lagoon on the west. A system of dykes and channels here enables sea water to be pumped into **salt pans** and salt to be harvested in the dry season. Rows and rows of identical houses are grouped around these salt flats, constructed by Indian charities to house communities hit by the tsunami and civil war.

Continuing north, you'll find the intriguing (signposted) archaeological site of **Kuchchaveli** at the Km 34 marker on the highway. Occupying a rocky point that juts into the Indian Ocean are the modest remains of a brick stupa. From the stupa's elevated position there are spectacular views over a turquoise sea, across the white foam of the rollers, with stunning sandy beaches to the north and south. The land here is controlled by the Navy but open to the public, and the two or three officers based at this lonely spot are usually very welcoming.

Around the Km 40 post the road traverses another lovely river estuary, the sandy shoreline dotted with colourful fishing boats. Then you pass through an area of dense mangrove forests, home to monitor lizards and prolific birdlife (including herons, storks and waders) before reaching an army checkpoint. From here it's a short trip to the isolated but friendly village of **Pulmoddai** at Km 54, which sits just inland from the Kokkilai Lagoon, an important bird sanctuary. Here the **Asam Hotel** (meals Rs 150-250) is your best bet for lunch, a popular place with rice and curry, and drinks.

Buses (Rs 75, 1½ hours, six daily) connect Pulmoddai with Trincomalee, passing through Nilaveli and Uppuveli en route. Services (Rs 88, two hours, three daily) also head to Mullaitivu, opening up an intriguing route to the north.

Uga Jungle Beach Resort
RESORT **$$$**

(📞 011-567 1000; www.jungle-beach-resort-trinco malee-sri-lanka.en.ww.lk; Km 27, Kuchchaveli; cabins from US$130; ❄🛜🏊) 🏖 Eco-style resort built from natural materials (timber and thatch) that enjoys a wonderful location just off a truly spectacular virgin beach. All the magnificent rooms have been sensitively constructed (only two trees were cut when the hotel was developed) so there's lots of shade, greenery and resident birdlife. The pool area is gorgeous, ringed by foliage and bordering the restaurant.

You'll find excellent Western and local food at surprisingly moderate prices. Guests can enjoy free yoga sessions and there's a spa. It's 9km north of Nilaveli.

Anilana Nilaveli
HOTEL **$$$**

(📞 011-203 0900; www.anilana.com/nilaveli; r/ ste from US$139/157; ❄🛜@🏊) Setting new standards in Nilaveli, this hip hotel (which opened in April 2014) ticks all the right contemporary boxes with sleek accommodation finished in subtle shades of cream: all with gorgeous bathrooms and a balcony facing the beach (or one of the two huge pools). There's a wonderful deck for languid alfresco meals, and excellent Asian and Western food.

Check out the spa for Ayurvedic treatments to revitalise the skin and senses.

Pigeon Island Beach Resort
HOTEL **$$$**

(📞 492 0633; www.pigeonislandresort.com; s/d/tr with air-con incl breakfast from US$120/150/203; ❄🛜🏊) Beachside hotel with rooms in a long two-storey building that are attractive but pricey (only suites have sea views). Worth a visit for lunch or dinner as the food is great (meals Rs 700 to 2000) and the dining and lounge areas, with their antique furniture, wicker lamps and breezes, are charming.

🛈 Getting There & Away

Flag down any passing bus for Trincomalee (Rs 26, 30 minutes, every 20 minutes). A three-wheeler will cost around Rs 800 or Rs 500 to Uppuveli.

Jaffna & the North

Best Places to Eat

➡ Mangos (p269)
➡ Cosy Restaurant (p269)
➡ Malayan Café (p269)
➡ Fort Hammenhiel (p276)

Best Places to Stay

➡ Morgan's Residence (p267)
➡ Jaffna Heritage Hotel (p268)
➡ Fort Hammenhiel (p276)
➡ Theresa Inn (p267)
➡ Baobab Guest House (p261)

Why Go?

With towering, rainbow Hindu temples, sari-clad women on bicycles and a spectacular coastline fringed with palmyra and coconut palms, the North is a different world. Here the climate is arid for most of the year and the fields sun-baked. The light is stronger: surreal and white-hot on salt flats in the Vanni, bright and lucid on coral islands and northern beaches, and soft and speckled in Jaffna's leafy suburbs and its battle-scarred centre.

And, of course, there are the cultural differences. From the language to the cuisine to religion, Tamil culture has its own rhythms, and people here are proud of their heritage. Inevitably, given that this region was a war zone until very recently, there's still a noticeable military presence. But the ambience is far more relaxed than you'd expect, as locals focus on healing, rebuilding and reviving the rich traditions of northern life.

When to Go
Jaffna

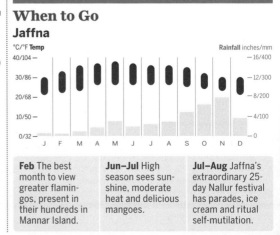

Feb The best month to view greater flamingos, present in their hundreds in Mannar Island.

Jun–Jul High season sees sunshine, moderate heat and delicious mangoes.

Jul–Aug Jaffna's extraordinary 25-day Nallur festival has parades, ice cream and ritual self-mutilation.

See Jaffna Peninsula Map (p272)

20 km
12 miles

BAY OF BENGAL

Palk Strait

Palk Bay

The Vanni

A35

A32

A34

A9

A14

A30

A29

Giant's Tank

Wahalkada Tank

Gulf of Mannar

Rokkilai Lagoon

Nanthi Kadal Lagoon

Jaffna & the North Highlights

❶ Marvelling at the spectacular seascapes and surreal light exploring **Jaffna's Islands** (p274)

❷ Slipping into a trance during *puja* (prayers) at **Nallur Kandaswamy Kovil** (p263) and investigating the charming **market** (p269) and its textiles, tropical fruit and cigars

❸ Observing the war's destruction of homes, temples and communities and appreciating the strength of its survivors

❹ Discovering ancient baobab trees, a historic fort and remote bays at **Mannar Island** (p260)

❺ Riding along coastal

roads in the **Jaffna Peninsula** (p271), fringed by fishing boats, calm seas and quiet beaches

❻ Learning about Hindu traditions at **Maviddapuram Kanthaswamy Kovil** (p271), **Thirukketeeswaram Kovil** (p261) or **Thurkkai Amman Kovil** (p271)

History

The north has always existed a bit apart from the rest of the island; even under colonial regimes the region remained highly autonomous. Jaffna, especially, has always been an important city, and one of the defining moments on the path to war came in 1981 when a group of Sinhalese burnt down Jaffna's library. This was seen as a violent affront to the Tamils' long and rich intellectual tradition.

The war began two years later, and Jaffna continued to be a hotspot for violence. For two decades the North was synonymous with death and destruction as the Liberation Tigers of Tamil Eelam (LTTE) and Sri Lankan military contested control. With the war's ending on the shores of Mullaittivu in 2009, a sense of calm and stability is at last returning to the North, though there is still much rebuilding to be done, both in terms of infrastructure and community relations.

Climate

The north is made up of two distinct areas: the low-lying Jaffna peninsula and its islands, and the vast Vanni, a flat scrubby area. The region is extremely dry most of the year, except after the October to January northeastern monsoon, when the green erupts.

Vavuniya

☎ 024 / POPULATION 78,000

A transport hub, the bustling town of Vavuniya (*vow*-nya) has few sights but an afternoon spent here isn't unpleasant. With road and rail links to Jaffna much improved, few travellers stop in Vavuniya these days, though there are adequate hotels and restaurants.

⊙ Sights

The town arcs around an attractive **tank** that's best observed from **Kudiyiruppu Pillaiyar Kovil**, a sprawling Ganesh temple.

Archaeological Museum   MUSEUM
(☎222 4805; Horowapatana Rd; ⊙9am-5pm)
FREE This museum is unlikely to impress if you're arriving from the ancient cities, but some of the pinched-faced terracotta figures from Kilinochchi (4th to 5th century) are delightfully primitive, while the central hexagonal chamber has some fine 5th-to-8th-century Buddha statues in Mannar limestone.

Madukanda Vihara   BUDDHIST
(Horowapatana Rd) The quietly charming Madukanda Vihara is a Rs 200 three-wheeler ride from central Vavuniya, beyond the 3km post southeast on the A29. It was reputedly the fourth resting point in the journey of the

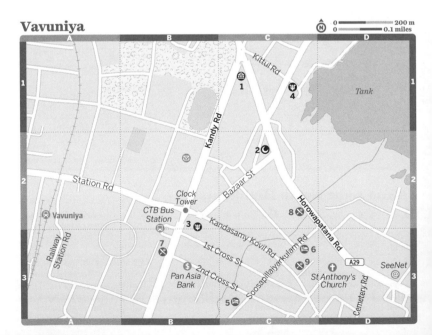

Vavuniya

sacred Buddha tooth relic from Mullaittivu to Anuradhapura during the 4th-century reign of King Mahsen.

Kandasamy Kovil   HINDU
(Kandasamy Kovil Rd) This photogenic Murugan (Skanda) temple has a very ornate, if faded, *gopuram* (gateway tower) and a gold-clad image in its sanctum.

Grand Jummah Mosque   MOSQUE
(Horowapatana Rd) A grand mosque awash in aqua tiling, with shiny gold onion domes.

🛏 Sleeping & Eating

Hotel Nelly Star   HOTEL $
(☑ 222 4477; www.nellystarhotel.com; 84 2nd Cross St; r with fan/air con from Rs 2000/2800, VIP r Rs 3950; ❄ 🛜 🛁) The Nelly Star has a somewhat bizarre colour scheme and an ungainly appearance, but its wide choice of rooms offer decent value. We didn't spot any celebs in the 'VIP' options, but they're extremely spacious, each with two double beds. Eating and drinking choices are excellent: a poolside cafe for snacks, a formal restaurant (mains Rs 220-600) and a well-stocked bar.

Hotel Swarkka   GUESTHOUSE $
(☑ 222 1090; Soosapillaiyarkulam Rd; s/d/tr with fan Rs 1750/2250/2750, with air-con Rs 2250/2750/3000; ❄) If you're on an economy drive, this dated hotel might suffice for a night. Rooms, with TV and mossie nets, are spacious but ageing. On the plus side the family owners are very welcoming and there's a restaurant at the front for meals (Rs 200-400).

Neethan's Hotel   SRI LANKAN $
(45 Kandy Rd; meals Rs 180-280) Just south of the clock tower and very handy for the bus terminals, this busy little place is a top spot for lunchtime rice and curry.

Ryana Restaurant   SRI LANKAN $
(47/8 Kandasamy Kovil Rd; meals Rs 150-270) A bustling, ever-popular little eatery famed for its spicy *kotthu* (*rotti* chopped up and mixed with vegies). Staff are friendly.

Royal Garden Restaurant   INDIAN, PIZZERIA $
(☑ 492 2677; 200 Horowapatana Rd; meals Rs 180-550; ⊙ 10.30am-10pm) This large restaurant looks impersonal from the street (thanks to its huge wedding hall) but persevere and you'll find a rear dining area that's unexpectedly intimate, with tables set in alcoves around a little garden. The menu covers all bases with delicious Indian dishes, and decent Chinese and pizza, though no booze is served. Call for a delivery.

ℹ Information

Vavuniya is full of transient characters, and the streets get very quiet after dark. Solo women should exercise caution when going out at night.

Banks with ATMs include **Pan Asia Bank** (2nd Cross St).

Post Office (Kandy Rd; ⊙ 8am-8pm Mon-Sat)

SeeNet (395/1 Horowapatana Rd; internet per hr Rs 50; ⊙ 8.30am-8pm Mon-Sat) Reliable internet access is available here.

ℹ Getting There & Away

The highway to Jaffna is now in excellent condition. You may be asked to present your passport at army checkpoints but there are no other security concerns.

Many of Vavuniya's three-wheelers are equipped with meters, so prices for short hops around town are very reasonable.

BUSES

Vavuniya's Central Tourist Board (CTB) **bus station** is by the clock tower. Less organised private buses, with similar fares, line 2nd Cross St.

Anuradhapura Rs 76, one hour, every 20 minutes

Colombo CTB/private 'semi-luxury' Rs 270/390, seven hours, every 30 minutes

Jaffna Rs 164, four hours, every 30 minutes

Kandy Rs 191, five hours, 12 daily

Mannar Rs 114, 2½ hours, hourly

Trincomalee Rs 138, 3½ hours, hourly

TRAINS

Call or visit Vavuniya's **railway booking office** (☑ 222 2271; ⊙ 7-10am & 4-5pm) for current services. At the time of research, the railway north to Jaffna was terminating at Pallai, 30km before Jaffna, but trains should be running all the way to Jaffna by the time you read this. Similarly, a branch line under construction from the town of Medawachchiya (25km south of Vavuniya) will soon open up rail travel to Mannar Island, scheduled sometime in late 2014 or 2015.

Anuradhapura 3rd/2nd/1st class Rs 50/90/160, one hour, six daily

Colombo 3rd/2nd/1st class Rs 265/410/680, seven hours, six daily

Mannar Island & Around

♪ 023

Sun-blasted Mannar Island is a dry near-peninsula with lots of white sand and palm trees, gulls and terns, wild donkeys and fishing boats. Culturally, it's an intriguing place: dotted with ancient baobab trees (native to Africa and said to have been planted by Arab merchants centuries ago) and crumbling colonial edifices built by the Portuguese, Dutch and Brits.

Once a prosperous pearling centre, today Mannar is one of the poorest, least fertile and most isolated corners of Sri Lanka. The island was hard hit by the war: it was a major exit and entry point to India, just 30km away, and continues to host many refugees. Thousands of Muslims were driven out by the LTTE in 1990.

In many ways the island still feels like it's in recovery mode, with dusty streets, a slightly forlorn appearance and more than its share of trash and mosquitoes. That said, the people are welcoming and there's a good choice of budget accommodation.

Mannar Town

Reached via a 3km-long causeway from the mainland, Mannar Town is a somewhat scruffy transport hub. There's not that much for tourists, but as virtually all accommodation is based here, this is where most travellers gather.

Star Fortress FORT
An imposing Portuguese-Dutch construction, this star-shaped fortress is situated right by the causeway to the island and ringed by a moat. It's desperately in need of renovation, but the ruins are atmospheric and contain the roofless remains of a chapel, dungeon and Dutch belltower. Climb the ramparts for an impressive perspective of the town and Gulf of Mannar.

The Fort was built in a quadrangular layout by the Portuguese in 1560, but captured in 1658 by the Dutch, who rebuilt it in 1695, adding four bastions. A century later, the colonial merry-go-round turned again as the British, drawn to Mannar by the pearl banks offshore, occupied the structure.

Baobab Tree LANDMARK
(Palimunai Rd) An offbeat attraction, this ancient baobab tree was allegedly planted by Arab traders. It has a circumference of 19.5m and is believed to be over 700 years old. In Africa the baobab is sometimes called the upside-down tree (because its branches look like roots); locals in Mannar refer to it as the *ali gaha* (elephant tree) since its tough, gnarled bark resembles the skin of an elephant. It's 1.2km northeast of the town centre.

Around the Island

The island is not endowed with beautiful dream-style stretches of sand, but attractive **Kiri beach** has good swimming, though no shade. Expect some trash. It's fringed by a small palmyra palm forest that's home to monkeys. It's located 6km west of Mannar Town.

PEARL ISLAND

The shallow seas around Mannar have been associated with **pearls** since antiquity. Ancient Greek and Roman texts mention pearling here, and the Chinese monk Fa-hsien (Faxian) documented Mannar's exceptional pearls in 411, as did Marco Polo. Arab sailor Ibn Batuta (who passed by in 1344) reported seeing precious collections of pearls in the Mannar royal treasury.

The British also benefited substantially from pearl profits. Between 1796 and 1809, £517,481 (a vast sum in those days) was credited as revenue into the Ceylon treasury from pearls. Over 200 pearling boats would set sail each day to comb the shallow waters of the Gulf of Mannar, each boat containing a government-employed 'shark charmer' who would perform ceremonies to safeguard divers against underwater attack.

Profits from pearling declined steeply in the late 19th century, possibly due to dredging, over-exploitation and the emergence of cultured pearls. The last pearling season in Sri Lanka, in 1906, was a commercial failure.

Mannar's one main east–west highway is paved and in good condition. Heading west from Mannar Town you'll pass a cluster of **baobab trees** after about 3km. Around the 8 Km marker is **Our Lady of the Martyrs**, a church and huge meditation hall where many hundreds gather to pray and meditate (Thursdays, 4–7pm).

Continuing west you'll pass a vast lagoon (look out for flamingos in February) and the small town of Pesalai before approaching the port of **Talaimannar**, 38km from Mannar Town. Until 1990 ferries departed from here to Rameswaram, India, and it's hoped connections might again resume when the rail track across the island is completed, perhaps in late 2014.

The island's western extreme is marked by a lonely lighthouse on land occupied by the navy. Offshore is **Adam's Bridge** – a chain of reefs, sandbanks and islets that nearly connects Sri Lanka to the Indian subcontinent. In the Ramayana these were the stepping stones that the monkey king Hanuman used in his bid to help rescue Rama's wife Sita from Rawana, the demon king of Lanka. Boat trips (operated by the navy, leaving from Talaimannar) to the first of the bridge's sandbars were suspended at the time of research but may again resume.

There's good swimming at the village of **Urumale**, 1km before the lighthouse, where fishermen specialise in catching stingrays – you'll see (and smell) chunks drying in the sun here. Boats line the beach in front of the village, but there are empty sands a short walk away to the east.

🛏 Sleeping & Eating

Baobab Guest House GUESTHOUSE $
(☏222 3155; 70 Field St, Mannar Town; s/d with fan & shared bathroom Rs 750/1000, with air-con & private bathroom Rs 1750/3000; ✳🛜) A cheerful, welcoming place, Baobab has a quiet location, and an attractive living/dining room for socialising and tasty meals (order ahead). The traditional red-oxide floors and window screens add a touch of class. It's a 10-minute walk from the centre of town. As there are only four rooms, book well ahead.

Mannar Guest House GUESTHOUSE $
(☏222 2006; www.mannarguesthouse.com; 55/12 Uppukulam, Mannar Town; s/d with fan Rs 2000/2500, with air-con Rs 2500/3000; ✳🛜) In a mixed Hindu/Muslim residential neighbourhood, this well-run guesthouse has eight small rooms, all with twin beds and

WORTH A TRIP

THIRUKKETEESWARAM KOVIL

On the mainland, 13km east of Mannar Town, Thirukketeeswaram Kovil is one of the *pancha ishwaram*, the five historical Sri Lankan Shiva temples established to protect the island from natural disaster. It's an imposing site, with a towering, colourful *gopuram*. Ranged around the temple are pavilions containing five gigantic floats, called juggernauts, that are wheeled out each February for the impressive Maha Sivarathiri festival.

Thirukketeeswaram Kovil is 4.5km down a side road off the Mannar–Vavuniya road between the 76km and 77 Km markers. Buses from Mannar are frequent; three-wheelers charge Rs 1000 for the round trip.

private bathrooms. The English-speaking owner's family live at the rear of the compound and can usually provide meals if organised in advance.

Four Tees Rest Inn LODGE $
(☏077 557 1206, 323 0008; Station Rd; s/d/tr with fan & shared bathroom Rs 1000/1500/2000, r with air-con Rs 3000; ✳) Nine kms west of Mannar Town, this likeable lodge offers a quiet, rural base including a lovely garden dotted with mature trees. Particularly popular with birders, manager Mr Lawrence has lots of tips to ensure you make the most of your stay and can organise birdwatching excursions. Very good value meals (around Rs 300) are available.

It's best suited to those with their own transport, though when the train line reopens there will be a station on its doorstep.

Shell Coast Resort HOTEL $$$
(☏077 144 9062; www.shellcoastresort.com; 6km southwest of Pesalai; s/d Rs 6250/14,250, cabana Rs 14,250-19,000; ✳🛜🏊) Offering the only beachside accommodation in Mannar, this new resort offers impressive octagonal wooden cabanas with terraces and attractive rooms with shared verandahs. The rustic setting will suit those searching for a back-to-nature vibe, however the beach is in need of a clean-up. Rates include breakfast.

Palmyrah House HOTEL $$$
(☏011-259 4467; www.palmyrahhouse.com; Karisal; s/d/tr from US$113/144/174; ✳🛜🏊) Offers

WORTH A TRIP

OUR LADY OF MADHU CHURCH

This church (⊙ 6am-8pm) is Sri Lanka's most hallowed Christian monument (though it's thought to be have been constructed over an ancient Hindu shrine). Its walls shelter Our Lady of Madhu, a diminutive but revered Madonna-and-child statue brought here in 1670 by Catholics fleeing Protestant Dutch persecution in Mannar.

The statue rapidly developed a reputation for miracles – it was particularly revered as offering protection from snake bites – and Madhu has been a place of pilgrimage ever since. The vast Madhu compound also served as a refuge for those fleeing the civil war when refugee camps ringed the complex.

The present church dates from 1872 and is quite plain but has soaring central columns. Outside, the most striking feature is the elongated portico painted cream and duck-egg blue. The church attracts huge crowds of pilgrims to its 10 annual festivals, especially the one on 15 August.

Our Lady is 12km along Madhu Rd, which branches off the Vavuniya–Mannar road at Madhu Junction on the 47 Km marker. Vavuniya–Mannar buses (and trains from Medawachchiya, a station on the Jaffna–Colombo main line) both stop at Madhu Junction. From here three-wheelers cost Rs 800 return including waiting time.

tasteful, colonial-style rooms in a tranquil location around 12km west of Mannar Town; the ambience and service are very refined. Rates include all meals.

Colombo Pilawoos　　　　SRI LANKAN $
(Grand Bazaar, Mannar Town; meals Rs 140-300) Pilawoos, right at the main roundabout, has lots of rice and curries, *kotthu* and delicious hoppers (bowl-shaped pancakes; be sure to get the 'sugar sambar' to go with them).

City Hotel　　　　　　　SRI LANKAN $
(42 Grand Bazaar, Mannar Town; meals Rs 180-300) A hospitable restaurant just south of the causeway with a good-value range of curry dishes, grilled fish and spicy chicken.

ⓘ Information

Mannar has a **post office** (Field St) and a few banks with ATMs, including **Commercial Bank** (Main St).

ⓘ Getting There & Around

The railway connection from Colombo to Mannar, via Medawachchiya, was almost restored at research time. It's possible that ferries to Rameswaram (India) will resume when the railway reopens. Buses from Mannar include the following:

Colombo Rs 378, eight hours, seven daily

Jaffna Rs 196, 3½ hours, 10 daily

Tallaimannar Rs 52, one hour, hourly

Thirukketeeswaram Kovil Rs 21, 20 minutes, nine daily

Vavuniya Rs 114, 2½ hours, hourly

Jaffna

📵 021 / POPULATION 116,000

Slowly but surely reemerging as a bastion of Hindu tradition, art and creative culture, Jaffna is once again welcoming visitors and looking to rise again. It's an intriguing, unimposing and mostly untouristed place that's a thoroughly rewarding place to invest a few days discovering Sri Lankan Tamil culture.

Inescapably, decades of war, emigration, embargoes and loss of life and property have deeply affected this historic Tamil town. If you've just arrived from the south, the impact of all this is all too evident, with ruined homes, bombed churches, and civic buildings pockmarked by bullets and shrapnel very much part of the scene. Around one in five of the city's structures suffered war damage. The military retain a strong presence and locals complain about harassment and infringement of property as well as livelihood. Peace and reconciliation are still works in progress.

As refugees and exiles return to rebuild the city, confidence and finance is returning. The city is surprisingly green and leafy, with attractive palm-shaded colonial-era suburbs and beautiful temples and churches. Physically, new structures (including the city's first shopping mall) and upgraded road, rail and air connections are inspiring optimism. But you'll appreciate Jaffna more for its insights into the Tamil people and their struggle than for any specific points of interest.

The city is also an ideal base for forays to the idyllic islands just to the west, and trips along the coastline and lagoons of the surrounding peninsula.

History

For centuries Jaffna has been Sri Lanka's Hindu-Tamil cultural and religious centre – especially during the Jaffna kingdom, the powerful Tamil dynasty that ruled from Nallur for 400 years beginning in the 13th century. But the Portuguese tried hard to change that. In 1620 they captured Cankili II, the last king (his horseback statue stands on Point Pedro Rd, near the Royal Palace ruins), then set about systematically demolishing the city's Hindu temples. A wave of mass Christian conversions followed.

Following a bitter three-month siege, the Portuguese surrendered their 'Jaffnapattao' to the more tolerant Dutch a few decades later, and Dutch Jaffna, which lasted for almost 140 years, became a major trade centre. Jaffna continued to prosper under the British, who took over in 1795 and sowed the seeds of future inter-ethnic unrest by 'favouring' the Jaffna Tamils.

The city played a crucial role in the lead-up to the war, and by the early 1980s escalating tensions overwhelmed Jaffna; for two decades the city was a no-go war zone. Variously besieged by Tamil guerrillas, Sri Lankan Army (SLA) troops and a so-called peacekeeping force, the city lost almost half of its population to emigration. In 1990 the LTTE forced Jaffna's few remaining Sinhalese and all Muslim residents to leave. Jaffna suffered through endless bombings, a crippling blockade (goods, including fuel, once retailed here for 20 times the market price – one reason so many residents ride bicycles) and military rule after the SLA's 1995 recapture of the town.

Then in the peace created by the 2002 accords, the sense of occupation was relaxed and Jaffna sprang back to life: domestic flights began; refugees, internally displaced persons (IDPs) and long-absent émigrés returned; and new businesses opened and building projects commenced. Hostilities recommenced in 2006 and tension continued through the end of the war in 2009.

Today a sense of stability has returned and a mood of hopefulness is evident across the city. The population of the Jaffna peninsula, however, is still well below its prewar figure.

◉ Sights

Jaffna is dotted with Hindu temples, easily identified by their red-and-white-striped walls, ranging from tiny shrines to sprawling complexes featuring *mandapaya* (raised platforms with decorated pillars), ornate ponds and towering *gopuram*.

The city also has an abundance of churches, many located on shady streets east of the centre. Commercial activity is crammed into the colourful hurly-burly of Hospital, Kasturiya and Kankesanturai (KKS) Rds.

If you can get your hands on some wheels, Jaffna is perfect for bicycle rides.

Nallur Kandaswamy Kovil HINDU
(Temple Rd; donations accepted; ◎ 4am-7pm) This huge Hindu temple, crowned by a towering god-encrusted, golden-ochre *gopuram,* is one of the most significant Hindu religious complexes in Sri Lanka. Its sacred deity is Murugan (or Skanda), and at cacophonic *puja,* at 5am, 10am, noon, 4.15pm (small *puja*), 4.30pm ('special' *puja*), 5pm and 6.45pm, offerings are made to his brass-framed image and other Hindu deities like Ganesh,

---

ℹ STAYING SAFE

Foreigners visiting the north and the towns of Jaffna, Kilinochchi, Mullaittivu, Mannar and Vavuniya no longer need to get permission from the Sri Lankan Ministry of Defence. Travellers will encounter the odd army checkpoint and road closure, and there are several High Security Zones, including the area around Jaffna airport where access is tightly controlled.

At the time of research the situation on the ground was calm, but politically active locals (and foreigners) still face state intimidation. Harassment, detentions and occasional disappearances continue, and the root reasons for the civil unrest are far from resolved. Keep an eye on regional news and politics.

Although NGOs have made enormous progress clearing land mines, some remain, along with tonnes of unexploded ordnance. Walk only on roads or very well-trodden paths. Do not wander on deserted beaches.

Locals may not want to speak openly about politics or the war; use sensitivity and tact. Also be careful not to take photographs of soldiers, military posts or potentially strategic sites like ports and bridges.

For two very different perspectives, try www.defence.lk and www.tamilnet.com.

Jaffna

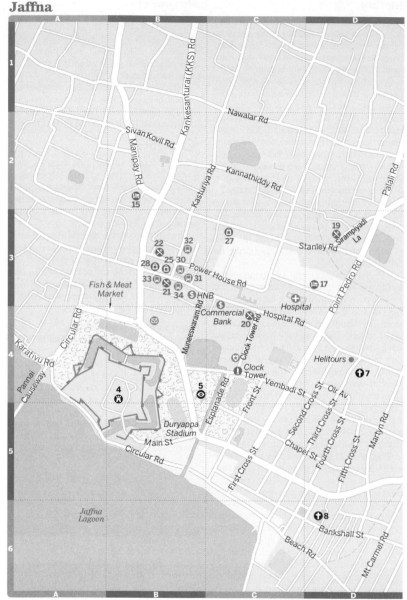

in shrines surrounding the inner sanctum. It's about 1.5km northeast of the centre.

The kovil's current structure dates from 1734, and its huge compound shelters brasswork, larger-than-life murals, pillared halls and a colonnaded, stepped holy pool.

Several friendly priests, some of whom speak English, can answer questions about the temple and its traditions. Visitors must remove their shoes; men need to remove their shirts as well. You can also say a prayer at the sacred tree in the temple's

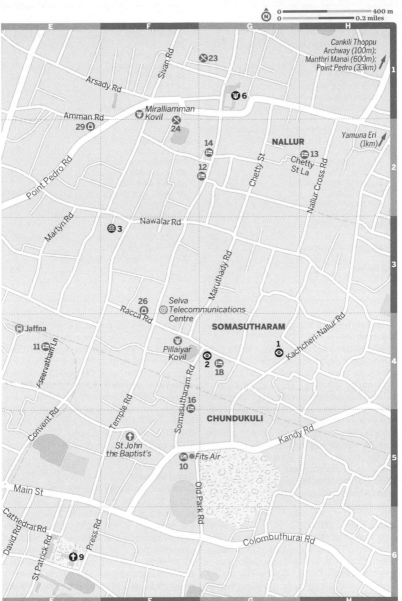

southern courtyard anytime: get a piece of gold-threaded cloth from outside the temple, wrap some coins in it, and tie it to the tree along with a prayer. Afterwards, ring the big brass bell. The temple is the focus of the enormous and spectacular Nallur Festival in mid-summer.

Jaffna Fort FORT

(Main St) FREE Overlooking the Jaffna lagoon, sections of this vast complex (once one of the greatest Dutch forts in Asia) have been recently restored, though it remains largely in ruins. It was built in 1680 over an earlier Portuguese original, and defensive triangles were added

Jaffna

in 1792 to produce the classic Vaubanesque star form.

Jaffna's fort has been fought over for centuries. Today you're free to explore its walls, admire its gateways and moats and view the city from its ramparts.

Long the gatehouse of the city, this citadel once housed thousands of troops and civilians. Many of its walls (constructed from coral, stone, brick and mortar) are still hidden beneath overgrown slopes.

During the war, government forces used it as an encampment, and in 1990 the LTTE – at the time in control of the rest of Jaffna – forced out government troops after a grisly 107-day siege.

Jaffna Public Library   LIBRARY
(http://english.jaffnalibrary.lk; Esplanade Rd; ⊙9am-7pm) Tellingly, one of the first major buildings to be rebuilt after the 2002 ceasefire was Jaffna's Public Library. The earlier library was burnt down by pro-government mobs (some say forces) in July 1981, a destruction deemed a cultural attack by many Tamils – few acts were more significant in the build-up to civil war. In its reconstruction, architects kept true to the elegant original neo-Mughal design. Today it's a bright spacious place that's very actively used by Jaffna's citizens.

Jaffna residents had long considered their city to be one of Asia's finest intellectual capitals, and the library was an important Tamil cultural centre and historic institution (it was inaugurated in 1841). The world-renowned collection included more than 90,000 volumes, including irreplaceable Tamil documents such as the one surviving copy of *Yalpanam Vaipavama*, a history of Jaffna. All of this went up in flames.

There's a statue of Saraswati – Hinduism's goddess of knowledge – out front.

Royal Palace   RUIN
(Chemmani Rd) Nallur was the capital of the Jaffna Kingdom for 400 years, and a few weathered structures remain. They're worth the excursion if you have a good imagination. Yamuna Eri, a U-shape pool made of carved stones, is neglected but still intact – it's thought to have been the royal family's women's bathing pool. The tank is behind a playground on Chemmani Rd, about 500m from Kachcheri–Nallur Rd.

Around the corner on Point Pedro Rd are **Cankili Thoppu archway**, one of the palace's original entrances, and the beautifully crumbling **Manthri Manai** (Minister's Quarters).

Jaffna Archaeological Museum   MUSEUM
(Nawalar Rd; donations accepted; ⊙8am-4.45pm Wed-Mon) This unkempt but interesting

museum is hidden away at the end of a messy garden behind a concrete events hall. At the door are a rusty pair of Dutch cannons from the fort and a set of whale bones. Inside, the most interesting items are some 15th-century Buddha torsos found at Kantarodai and a 14th-century 'seven-mouthed pot.'

St Mary's Cathedral
CHURCH

(Cathedral Rd) Built by the Dutch along classical lines, St Mary's Cathedral is astonishingly large, but it's curious to see corrugated-iron roofing held up by such a masterpiece of wooden vaulting.

Our Lady of Refuge Church
CHURCH

(off Hospital Rd) This unusual structure looks like a whitewashed version of a Gloucestershire village church.

St James'
CHURCH

(Main St) This is the grandest church in Jaffna, a classical Italianate edifice.

British Council
CULTURAL CENTRE

(☑ 752 1521; www.britishcouncil.lk; 70 Rakka Rd; ⊙ Wed-Sun 9am-5pm) Opened in 2014, the British Council has a library stocked with magazines, newspapers and English literature and hosts cultural events including art exhibitions.

Alliance Française
CULTURAL CENTRE

(☑ 222 8093; alliancejaffna@yahoo.com; 61 Kachcheri-Nallur Rd; ⊙ 9am-5pm) Has a comfy lounge with English- and French-language newspapers and a library with books in French and English. Offers occasional film screenings.

✫✫ Festivals

Nallur Festival
RELIGIOUS

Spread over a period of 25 days in July and/or August, this Hindu festival climaxes on day 24 with parades of juggernaut floats and gruesome displays of self-mutilation by entranced devotees.

Jaffna Music Festival
MUSIC

(www.jaffnamusicfestival.org) In addition to Jaffna's religious festivals, the city hosts the biennial Jaffna Music Festival in March of odd-number years. This festival showcases both local and international musicians and performers from countries as far off as Brazil and Norway.

European Film Festival
CINEMA

(www.europeanfilmfestsrilanka.com) The excellent European Film Festival is held in Jaffna, Kandy, Colombo and Galle in October and November.

🛏 Sleeping

Jaffna has a decent selection of budget guesthouses, though good midrangers are harder to come by.

Most places are located in the leafy eastern suburbs of the city.

★ Morgan's Residence
GUESTHOUSE $

(Maria's; ☑ 222 3666; 103 Temple Rd; s/d with aircon Rs 3000/4000; ❄ 🛜) A wonderful four-roomed guesthouse in an elegant villa with four-posters, beamed ceilings and a grand dining table. It's a great place to socialise with others over tea or beer in the courtyard garden and manager Maria is a delight, going the extra mile to welcome guests (including Angelina Jolie, no less!). Book ahead.

Theresa Inn
GUESTHOUSE $

(Do Drop Inn; ☑ 222 8615, 071 856 5375; calistusjoseph89@gmail.com; 72 Racca Rd; s/d/tr Rs 1500/2000/2250, with air-con Rs 2750/2250/3000; ❄ 🛜) A good choice, located on a leafy plot on a quiet street, with eight clean and airy rooms that represent good value. The family

---

THE ROAD TO JAFFNA

During the war, the A9 – when it was open at all – was often the only permitted land route across **Tamil Eelam**, the LTTE-controlled Vanni region. This flat, savannah-like area, sometimes nicknamed Tigerland, was effectively another country. Travellers stutter-stepped through Sri Lanka Army (SLA) and LTTE checkpoints, complete with customs and 'immigration' for LTTE-controlled territory, and the trip from Vavuniya to Jaffna took up to 16 hours.

Today the trip takes around four hours, and the nearest thing to a checkpoint is a little shack where government soldiers may ask to see your passport.

Kilinochchi, once the administrative capital of Tigerland, is the only sizeable town en route. The most dramatic scenery is around the **Elephant Pass**, an eerily beautiful 1km-long causeway that anchors the Jaffna peninsula to the rest of Sri Lanka. Possession of it was viciously fought over during the war.

owners are helpful, offer tasty meals and can organise bikes (Rs 350 per day), scooters (Rs 1500) or a car and driver (from Rs 5000).

Pillaiyar Inn
HOTEL $$

(☑ 222 2829; www.pillaiyarinn.com; 31 Manipay Rd; s/d/tr from Rs 2200/2700/3500, with air-con Rs 3000/4000/5000; ✵ @) Close to the centre, this Jaffna institution is set back from the road in a pretty garden. Friendly, old-fashioned and professionally run, it has a run-down old wing (avoid) and a good, if slightly bland, new wing (book). The food is excellent.

Sarras Guest House
GUESTHOUSE $

(☑ 222 3627, 567 4040; jaffnasarras@gmail.com; 20 Somasutharam St; r with/without air-con from Rs 2500/2000; ✵ 🛜) Ageing colonial mansion with some (faded) character, including polished old floorboards and red-oxide flooring, though maintenance could be a little better. The very spacious top-floor rooms are best; avoid the last-resort annex. The family running the place can prepare meals and advise on transport options.

Green Grass
HOTEL $

(☑ 222 4385; www.jaffnagreengrass.com; 33 Aseervatham Ln, Hospital Rd; r with air-con Rs 3000/3300/3850; ✵ 🛜 ✈) Architecturally it's a mess, but thanks to its attractive gardens and pool this place has some charm. The cheap rooms are worn and have thin foam mattresses; the more expensive options are comfortable. There's a rather gloomy restaurant.

★ Jaffna Heritage Hotel
BOUTIQUE HOTEL $$

(☑ 222 2424; www.jaffnaheritage.com; Temple Rd; s/d/tr Rs 9000/11,000/13,000; ✵ 🛜 ✈) A superb new modern hotel where the ten rooms tick all the contemporary design boxes, with clean lines, high ceilings and stylish fittings. The expansive hotel grounds are fringed by coconut palms. Staff are very welcoming and meals are excellent, though no meat, eggs or alcohol are served. It's rightfully the top choice in town for those who have a generous accommodation budget.

Subhas
HOTEL $$

(☑ 222 4923; www.subhasgroup.com; 49 Victoria Rd; s/d Rs 3500/4500, r with air-con Rs 4000–7900; ✵ 🛜) Straight out of the Soviet school of architecture, this concrete hotel is actually a pretty good bet if you want a central location. There are four classes of rooms, from dark and few-frills to modern and spacious with fancy furnishings.

The dining room is a bit of an afterthought at the rear of the compound; there are better places to eat in town close by.

Lux Etoiles
HOTEL $$

(☑ 222 3966; www.luxetoiles.com; 34 Chetty St Ln; d with air-con Rs 4070-6270; ✵ 🛜 ✈) Set on a quiet suburban street, initial impressions are good – there's a vintage Austin automobile in the lobby that seems to be more an art statement than a representation of a place to park. However, the smallish tiled rooms are plain and pretty overpriced for what you get.

The large pool is big enough for laps, but not really the place to lounge with a cocktail.

Fits Pavilion
HOTEL $$

(☑ 222 3790, 077 234 8888; www.fitsair.com; 40 Kandy Rd; s/d/tr incl breakfast Rs 8500/10,348/12,200; ✵ 🛜) A stylish converted villa, with seven tastefully decorated rooms that feature handsome dark wood furniture and ochre paintwork, and a lovely lounge with tribal artefacts. However, it lacks somewhat in terms of atmosphere and service. Excellent food is available, including filling Western breakfasts.

It's on a main road, but set back from traffic. The airline Fits Air has an office here.

Fits Margosa
HISTORIC HOTEL $$$

(☑ 224 0242; www.fitsair.com; Station Rd, Urelu North; s/d incl breakfast from US$111/123; ✵ 🛜) This stunning 19th-century colonial manor house in landscaped gardens has beautifully presented accommodation, most with open-air bathrooms. Perhaps a little overpriced, it's nonetheless worth a splurge; the restaurant has great local and Western food.

As it's 10km north of the city, it's only really a good option for those with their own transport.

🍴 Eating & Drinking

Jaffna is a good place to try South Indian-style cuisine. Red-hued *pittu* (rice flour and coconut, steamed in bamboo), *idiyappam* (string hoppers or steamed noodles) and *vadai* (deep-fried doughnut-shaped snacks made from lentil flour and spices) are local favourites. Booze-wise, there are limited watering holes as Jaffna is a conservative town; hotel bars are your best bet.

Jaffna Market (p269) is the best place to buy fresh food, but if you need a supermarket **Food City** (Cargills Sq, Hospital Rd; ⊙ 7am-9pm) stocks both international and local foods.

THE PALMYRA

Symbolising the North of the nation, the towering, fan-leafed palm tree known as the **palmyra** is abundant across the region, its graceful crown of leaves defining many a horizon at sunset. Of the estimated 11 million or so palmyra trees in Sri Lanka, 90% are found in the three provinces of Jaffna, Mannar and Kilinochchi.

Making an essential contribution to Tamil culture, palmyra uses are many: timber for construction; leaves for fencing, roofing and woven handicrafts; fibre for rope; and sap for drinking. If left to ferment for a few hours, the sap becomes a mildly alcoholic, fragrant toddy. Young palmyra roots are high in calcium and eaten as a snack and also ground to make flour for a porridge called *khool*. In markets across the North you'll find great blocks of jaggery (delicious golden-coloured unrefined palm sugar) from unfermented palmyra toddy.

The Palmyrah Development Board (www.katpahachcholai.com) promotes a range of products, from shopping bags to shampoo, made from the palmyra.

★ Mangos
SOUTH INDIAN $

(☑ 222 8294; Nallalaxmy Ave, 359 Temple Rd; meals Rs 200-400; ☺ 10.30am-10pm) With an open kitchen, lots of space and outdoor seating area, Mangos is an atmospheric place to dine and wildly popular with extended Tamil families. The South Indian food is exceptional with around 20 dosas (try the ghee masala), great *parotta* (Keralan-style flat bread) and *idiyappam*. For lunch, the thali (Rs 200) can't be beat.

It's located around 2km northeast of the centre, but is walkable from the guesthouses in the Nallur district.

Malayan Café
SRI LANKAN $

(36 38 Grand Bazaar; meals Rs 120-220; ☺ 6.30am-9pm) Highly authentic and atmospheric old-school eatery in the market district with marble-topped tables, wooden cabinets, swirling fans and photos of holy men illuminated by lime-coloured fluorescent tubes gazing down on diners. The cheap, tasty vegetarian fare (dosas, rice and curry for lunch and light meals) is served on banana leaves and eaten by hand.

Hotel Rolex
SRI LANKAN $

(☑ 222 2808; 340 Hospital Rd; meals Rs 80-250) On the main drag, this local eatery is usually bustling and has friendly management, a good range of food options and 'nuts ice cream'.

Rio Ice Cream
ICE CREAM $

(448A Point Pedro Rd; ice creams & sundaes Rs 60-250; ❄) For a typical Jaffna treat, head to the trio of popular ice-cream parlours behind the Nallur Kandaswamy Kovil. Rio is the local favourite, though local tastes are very sweet.

★ Cosy Restaurant
NORTH INDIAN $$

(☑ 222 5899; 15 Sirampiyadi Ln, Stanley Rd; meals Rs 240-700; ☺ 11am-11pm; ❄ 🖐) Cosy now has two locations. This (non-vegie) branch has a lovely open courtyard seating and subdued lighting. The big attraction here is the tandoori oven, which fires up at 6pm daily and pumps out delicious naan bread, tikkas and tandoori chicken. The Jaffna crab (combo with naan and a drink Rs 699) is outstanding too, and beer is available.

Green Grass
INDIAN $$

(www.jaffnagreengrass.com; 33 Aseervatham Ln, Hospital Rd; mains Rs 300-500; ☺ 10am-10pm; 🖐) The garden restaurant here, with tables under a mango tree and around the pool, is a good spot for Tamil, Indian (try the crab curry) and Chinese dishes, and also for an evening beer. Avoid the unappealing indoor dining room.

Jaffna Heritage Hotel
INDIAN, WESTERN $$

(Temple Rd; meals Rs 600-1200; 🖐) For a refined ambience, the restaurant at the Jaffna Heritage Hotel is perfect. Offers excellent (veg-only) Indian and Sri Lankan food including wonderful coconut *rotti* and delicately spiced currries. Also a good choice for a healthy, if pricey, Western breakfast (Rs 900) which includes tropical fruit, cereals, toast and tea/coffee (but no eggs).

Morgan's
BAR

(103 Temple Rd; ☺ 6-10pm; 🖐) By far the nicest place for a beer in Jaffna, the garden courtyard bar of this unsigned but characterful guesthouse draws a good mix of travellers and NGO workers most nights. Beers are cold and the wi-fi is fast.

🛍 Shopping

Jaffna Market
MARKET

(Hospital Rd) Jaffna's colourful fruit and vegetable market is west of the bus stand, but the greater market area encompasses several glorious blocks beyond that. In the market itself,

Mr M Chandresakaran's stall, by the bananas, sells traditional Jaffna cigars.

Art Gallery ARTS & CRAFTS
(Racca Ln) Jaffna's first art gallery is in a striking white structure and showcases work by contemporary Sri Lankan artists.

Rosarian Convent WINE
(Thoma Monastery; 48 Colombuthurai Rd; ☺ 8.30am-1pm & 2-5.30pm Mon-Sat) The convent makes Rosetto 'wine' (Rs 300 per bottle). Sweet and laced with cinnamon and cloves, it tastes like German *gluhwein*. There's also startlingly coloured grape 'juice' and 'nelli crush' (Rs 180), both nonalcoholic, flavourful fruit cordial concentrates.

Ms Ruby Sorupan CLOTHING
(☎ 320 5358; 89 Point Pedro Rd; ☺ 10am-5pm) A kindly and competent seamstress, Ms Ruby Sorupan will whip you up a *salwar kurta* (dress-like tunic and trouser outfit) or *choli* (sari blouse) for about Rs 200 or so. Only Mr Sorupan speaks English, so try to visit when he's around.

Anna Coffee COFFEE
(No 4, Modern Market; ☺ 8.30am-6pm Mon-Sat) Sri Lankan coffee (Rs 750 per kg) and tea (from Rs 380 per kg) from a venerable old shop in the market district.

Future World ELECTRONICS
(☎ 221 9655; www.futureworld.com.lk; 70-72 Stanley Rd; ☺ Mon-Sat 9.30am-5pm) Genuine Apple computers and accessories and a service centre for repairs.

ℹ Information

Jaffna's many ATMs include **Commercial Bank** (Hospital Rd) and **HNB** (Hospital Rd & Stanley Rd).
Eelavar.com (www.eelavar.com/jaffna) Informative website with good sections on Jaffnese history, culture and arts.
Post Office (Postal Complex, KKS Rd; ☺ 7am-5pm Mon-Sat)
Selva Telecommunications Centre (124 Temple Rd; internet access per hr Rs 60; ☺ 7.30am-8.30pm) Fast connections, with booths for international calls.

ℹ Getting There & Away

AIR
Jaffna's Palali Airport is 17km north of town, deep within a high-security military zone. It's not served by public transport but both airlines offer shuttle bus connections.
Fits Air (☎ 222 3790; www.fitsair.com; 40 Kandy Rd) Flies to/from Ratmalana airport, south of Colombo (Rs 18,000, 75 minutes, daily), and also to Trincomalee (Rs 5000, 35 minutes, weekly). Free drop-offs and pick-ups to your hotel are included.
Helitours (☎ 011-314 4944, 011-314 4244; www.helitours.lk; Hospital Rd; ☺ 10am-1pm) Passenger flights – on air -orce planes – to/from Palali Airport and Colombo's Ratmalana airport (Rs 7750, three weekly, 75 minutes). Also offers a service from Trincomalee (Rs 3750, three weekly, 30 minutes). An obligatory shuttle bus departs from Helitours' town office. You need to arrive two hours ahead.

BUS
Long-Distance
From the **CTB bus stand** (☎ 222 2281) and neighbouring **private bus stand** (Kasturiya Rd) there are frequent long-distance services:
Anuradhapura Rs 252, five hours, three daily
Colombo Rs 670, 12 hours, eight daily
Kandy Rs 352, nine hours, nine daily
Mannar Rs 200, 3½ hours, 10 daily
Trincomalee Rs 324, seven hours, five daily
Vavuniya Rs 198, four hours, every 30 minutes

Numerous private bus companies offer **overnight services** to Colombo. Around a dozen offices are all grouped together on Hospital Rd, including **VT Express** (Hospital Rd). Rates are Rs 700/900/1300 for an ordinary/semi-luxury/luxury bus and the journey time is 10 to 12 hours.

Jaffna Peninsula
Destinations around the peninsula (including the islands) are served by both CTB and private minibuses from the CTB bus stand and stops close by on **Powerhouse Rd**. Be warned that local buses are slow and can be infrequent; check return times before you head out. Services include the following:
Kairanagar via Vaddukkodai (782, 786) Rs 48, 1½ hours, every 30 minutes
Kayts (777) Rs 45, one hour, every 30 to 60 minutes (bus 780 also goes here but takes longer)
Keerimalai spring (private minibuses 82, 87, 89) Rs 40, one hour, every 20 minutes
Kurikadduwan (KKD; 776) Rs 74, 1½ hours, hourly
Point Pedro via Nelliady (750) Rs 69, 1½ hours, every 30 minutes
Point Pedro via Valvettiturai (VVT; 751) Rs 73, 1½ hours, every 30 to 60 minutes
Tellippalai via Chunnakam (for Thurkkai Amman Kovil, Kantarodai, Keerimalai spring; 769) Rs 36, every 30 minutes

CAR & MOTORBIKE
Many travellers prefer the freedom of renting a motorbike or car to explore the peninsula and islands. Traffic is light and roads are now in

good condition. Scooters cost Rs 1500 per day (excluding petrol); a car with driver around Rs 6000 per day. Most guesthouses and hotels can arrange bike and car hire.

❶ Getting Around

Jaffna is not a large city and the central area is easily explored on foot or by bicycle (Rs 250 per day from guesthouses).

Few travellers bother with city buses (Rs 8) but you can take bus 769 for the Chundukuli district or bus 750 for the Nallur via Point Pedro Rd. Buses are much safer – in terms of both groping and theft – and less crowded than minibuses.

Three-wheelers are very common and cost Rs 150 to 250 for most trips. At night, locals recommend calling one (or having someone call one for you) for security reasons. Recommended drivers include **Baskar** (☑ 077 921 8122) and **Suman** (☑ 077 079 0317).

Jaffna Peninsula

☑ 021

Once you get beyond Jaffna's already rustic outer boroughs, you're plunged into fields of palmyra palms, technicolor temples, holy springs and miles of coastline. Few of the sights are individually outstanding, but together they make an interesting day trip or two, especially if you hire your own transport.

There's a distinctly eerie vibe to much of the peninsula, which was fought over for decades during the war. You'll pass shelled buildings and long-abandoned houses left roofless, with nature reclaiming the terrain as trees, roots and shoots overwhelm the ruins. Unexploded ordnance has been cleared from most parts, but some undoubtedly remains and you'll pass (marked) minefields on many roads. Never stray from roads and tracks, and avoid deserted beaches too.

To the North Coast & Keerimalai Spring

Though a lot of the surrounding area is a military zone and off limits, the road to Keerimalai spring is open. Kankesanturai (KKS), its endpoint, however, is still restricted. For bus details see popposite.

From Jaffna, it's a straight road north to the small town of Chunnakam, from where there's a 3km squiggle of lanes leading west to the beautiful and mysterious **Kantarodai Ruins** (⊘ 8.30am-5pm). Two dozen or so dagobas, 1m to 2m in height, in a palm-fringed field, their origins are the subject of fierce controversy: part of the raging 'who was here first?' histor-

ical debate. Originally flat-topped and low to the ground, the stone structures were built upon by Sri Lanka's Department of Archaeology in 1978 – some say to restore the original dagoba shape that the ancient Buddhist community here had created; others say to impose a Buddhist history on an ancient culture that had its own set of traditions (maybe for burials). It's hardly a mind-blowing vista, especially as it's all behind a wire fence, but the structures are quite otherworldly-looking.

Beside the KKS road at the 13 Km marker and close to the 'new' village of **Tellippalai**, the vast **Thurkkai Amman Kovil** (⊘ 5.30am-7pm, closed 1-3pm some days) is set behind a fairly deep, stepped pool. The temple celebrates the goddess Durga and draws relatively large crowds, of women especially, on Tuesdays and Fridays, when devotees pray for a good spouse. *Puja* is at 8am, 11am, noon and 4pm, and the priests are welcoming. The temple also runs an orphanage for 150 kids.

East of here lies the vast **Palali KKS Military Camp**, one of Sri Lanka's largest and perhaps most controversial High Security Zones. This zone is also the site of Jaffna's Palali Airport. Between 1983 and 1993, the entire population (more than 25,000 families) was evicted from 58.5 sq km of prime agricultural land. Everything within the zone was either destroyed or converted for military use. Since the war, the SLA has been returning small tracts of lands back to their owners, though some local families have been reluctant to move back.

There's no access to KKS and the Keerimalai spring via the main highway, so you'll have to loop around via some country lanes to the west and then back east again. The route is well signposted. Located right at the main turnoff on the highway, **Maviddapuram Kanthaswamy Kovil** survived bombings and looting in the war and is now flourishing again. The priests here are very friendly and will probably do a *puja* for you if you like (otherwise, it's at 11.30am).

Just before the spring is the 6th-century-BC **Naguleswaram Shiva Kovil**, one of the *pancha ishwaram*, five temples dedicated to Lord Shiva in Sri Lanka. Before the civil war, this was a thriving Hindu pilgrimage site with several temples and six *madham* (rest homes for pilgrims) and *samadhi* shrines for holy men. Only traces of the original buildings survived, and the temple was bombed by the army in 1990.

But since 2011 there's been a lot of reconstruction with support from the All Ceylon

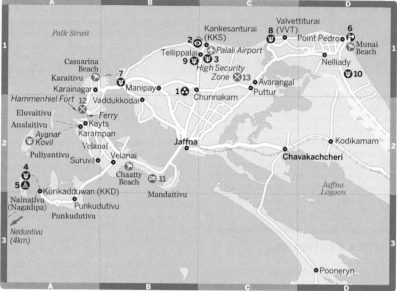

Hindu Congress, and the Naguleswaram temple has reopened, along with a new *madham* for pilgrims. Work is ongoing to revive the complex further, and ensure Naguleswaram and its sacred spring is once again a place of pilgrimage and prayer.

Legend has it that the sacred **Keerimalai spring** became famous after the 7th-century visit by a Chola princess: not only was her digestive disorder instantly healed when she bathed in the waters and prayed to Murugan, but so was her facial deformity, which, according to one source, had the 'likeness of a horse's head'. Even if your face doesn't look like a horse, the spring is a beautiful little spot: the men's side has a picturesque stepped pool of bright aquamarine water set against the sea, while the women have a smaller pool nearby surrounded by tall walls (for the best, really). The waters are supposed to be healing, and there are changing rooms on-site; women should bathe in something modest. Jaffna buses/minibuses are Rs 30 to the spring, or get a three-wheeler from the Tellippalai bus stand for Rs 350/600 one way/round trip.

If you're heading east after Keerimalai you'll have to first return south along the AB16 highway to Chunnakam before you can cut across via Puttur towards Valvettiturai and Point Pedro. You'll pass the excellent, old-fashioned **Sri Murugan Café** (Vakaiadi; rice & curry Rs 180; ⊙5am-9pm) for rice and curry 3km west of Puttur.

For a more scenic drive, consider heading west along the newly upgraded coastal road from Keerimalai spring, which hugs a palm-fringed shoreline. There are no real sights this way, but the scenery is sublime, with a sparkling ocean offshore. Inevitably there are also plenty of reminders of the war, including bombed churches and battle-ravaged buildings. The navy now occupies a lot of the coastal land in these parts, and is busy developing a couple of hotels for tourism. At the tiny settlement of Ponnalai, 16km from Keerimalai, you'll reach the causeway for the island of Karainagar.

Valvettiturai

On the way to Valvettiturai (VVT) is the charming, waterfront **Selvachannithy Murugan Kovil** (also known as Sella Sannathy Kovil) in Thondaimanaru. Like so many places on the peninsula it was severely damaged during the war, but today the important Murugan temple is a scenic stop, with a lively *puja*.

The gorgeous coast road leads east to VVT, once a rich smuggling town but now most famous as the birthplace of LTTE leader Vellupillai Prabhakaran. Known for his

Jaffna Peninsula

extraordinary ruthlessness, charisma and single-minded strength of purpose, Prabhakaran's personality was considered by many to be the reason that the LTTE – of all the militant Tamil-rights groups that emerged in the 1970s – rose to prominence. Prabhakaran's death was reported during the final days of the war. Today there's nothing left of the Prabhakaran family home. The army demolished it in 2010, an action which many observers thought was to prevent it from becoming a tourist attraction, or even a kind of shrine.

Point Pedro & Around

From VVT, the coast road curves east to Point Pedro. This area was devastated by the 2004 tsunami; locals say fishing boats were found 1km inland. The shoreline is beautiful, with a narrow white-sand beach and a coral reef offshore – the sea is too shallow for good swimming however. You'll pass a succession of tiny fishing hamlets, where large rays and sharks, as well as snapper and barracuda, are harvested from the ocean, their flesh sun-dried in neat rows by the road.

Ramshackle **Point Pedro** is the Jaffna peninsula's second town; it has a few faint hints of a lingering colonial style and was hit hard by the 2004 tsunami. It's still a very poor settlement and you'll struggle to find anywhere to eat. From Point Pedro bus station walk 100m south and then east, passing a curious stone **tollgate** that locals claim dates from the Dutch era. Some 500m beyond, turn left towards the sea up St Anthony's Lane and past the town's two finest **churches**. The coast road continues 1km east to **Point Pedro Lighthouse** (off limits; no photos), beyond which the fishermen's beach becomes wider. The nicest area of **Munai Beach** is nearly 2km further on, as are some attractive views of Vadamaraadchi Lagoon. Three-wheelers from central Point Pedro charge Rs 200 one-way to Munai Beach.

Further southeast is the much-revered **Valipura Kovil**, 5km from central Point Pedro. Its *gopuram* is painted in an unusually restrained colour palette and the temple interior has some very pretty Krishnas. It's famous for the boisterous, recently revived water-cutting festival in October, which attracts thousands of pilgrims. *Puja* is at 7am, 9.30am, noon, 4.15pm and, on Sunday, 6pm.

To Elephant Pass and the Northeast Shore

A wonderful day trip from Jaffna on a motorbike (or hired car/three-wheeler), this trip takes in a famous battle site and some spectacular coastal scenery. Don't stray from roads and marked tracks as this region was fought over for many years.

Some 52km southeast of Jaffna, via the fast, smooth A9 highway, is **Elephant Pass**, a narrow causeway that connects Jaffna peninsula to the rest of the island. You'll pass war reminders along the entire route, with bombed buildings and (marked) minefields lining the highway.

The actual pass gets its name from the hundreds of elephants which were herded through here en route to India between 300 BC and the 19th century.

For most Sri Lankans the name is inexorably linked with the civil war; for decades the government and Tamil Tigers contested control of this strategic spot – the gateway to Jaffna – with particularly bloody battles waged in 1991, 2000 and 2009.

Today virtually all war reminders have been cleared except for a grandiose, vaguely stupa-like **monument** which glorifies the role of the Sri Lankan armed forces in defeating the enemy within and lauds the role of President Rajapaksa ('who was born for the grace of the nation') in triumphalist language.

The wetlands surrounding the monument are unexpectedly beautiful, an aquamarine

TAMIL TIGER BURIAL GROUNDS

Although bodies of the deceased are generally cremated in Hindu tradition, those of LTTE fighters were buried instead, beneath neatly lined rows of identical stones. The fallen Tigers were called *maaveerar* – 'martyrs' or 'heroes' – and their cemeteries Maaveerar Thuyilum Illam (Martyrs' Sleeping Houses). The tradition of burial began in the 1990s, not long after the 1989 initiation of Maveerar Naal (Heroes Day), held each year on 27 November. The cemeteries were controversial: many saw them as a natural way to honour those who died; for others, they were a propaganda tool.

When the Sri Lankan Army (SLA) took control of the Jaffna peninsula in 1995, it destroyed many of the cemeteries, only to have the LTTE build them up again after the 2002 ceasefire. But when the SLA conquered areas in the East in 2006 and 2007, and then again after the war's end in 2009, all cemeteries (and other LTTE monuments) across the North and East were bulldozed anew – to the distress of many Tamils, especially family members of the deceased. The SLA went further in early 2011 by building a military base on the site of a cemetery at Kopay, just a few kilometres northeast of Jaffna. According to the BBC, the army claimed to be unaware of any 'unhappiness' over the site.

An online Maaveerar Thuyilum Illam, including the names and burial places of many Tigers, is maintained at www.maaveerarillam.com.

sea fringed by patches of white sand and mangroves, with lots of wading birds in evidence.

From the monument it's a short hop south over the causeway to the Elephant Pass restaurant, which has good-value meals (Rs 200-400), and then on to the town of **Kilinochchi**, 15km away.

Returning 9km back towards Jaffna there's a turnoff which heads north to the coast, 8km away. It's a gloriously isolated road, which traverses a couple of villages and a long slender lagoon before hitting the shore at **Chempiyanpattu**. There's a stunning beach here, a classic tropical picture of white sand, azure ocean and swaying coconut palms, though absolutely no facilities – perfect if you really want to get away from it all. Most of the abandoned houses visible from here all the way up the entire shoreline to Point Pedro, were destroyed by the 2004 tsunami.

If you head back from Chempiyanpattu beach, you can follow a lonely coastal road which heads northwest up the narrow peninsula, with the shore to your east and a beautiful lagoon on your west side. The first 7km or so is paved, then there's a 15km stretch which is well-maintained dirt track, while the final 7km or so is paved before you hit Point Pedro. Sections of the coastal land are controlled by the army and minefields were being cleared here when we passed through, so don't stray from the road. Expect to encounter monkeys, monitor lizards and lots of birdlife on the way.

You'll eventually arrive in **Point Pedro**, a humdrum port of little interest, from where you can loop back to Jaffna.

Jaffna's Islands

The highlight of the entire region, Jaffna's low-lying islands are a blissful vision of the tropics. The main pleasure is not any specific sight, but the hypnotic quality of the waterscapes and the escapist feeling of boat rides to end-of-the-earth villages.

As the sea here is very shallow (only a metre or so deep in places) the light is very special indeed, with sunlight bouncing off the sandy seafloor. The islands are all dotted with palmyra palms – their fronds are used for fencing and roofs, while their sap produces a mildly alcoholic toddy.

Causeways and boat connections link the islands, making a number of idyllic daytrips possible. One option is to head from Jaffna city to Velanai and then to the island of Punkudutivu, ferry-hopping from here across to the temples of Nainativu and then returning by Kayts and Karaitivu island to the mainland. The second option is an excursion to remote, idyllic Neduntivu (Delft).

The LTTE was once active on these waters, and the Sri Lankan Navy presence continues to be strong; in fact, the Navy itself conducts most ferry services.

The islands' beaches may not be quite as beautiful as those on the South coast, but they do offer pleasant swimming in balmy water. Women should swim in T-shirts and shorts.

Bus connections to the islands are not that frequent, for details see p270. The ideal way to explore these islands is on two wheels, giving you the freedom to pull over when and where you want. The terrain is very flat so it's perfect for cycling or covering by scooter; both can be loaded onto ferries between islands.

Velanai

Velanai island, connected by a causeway to Jaffna, is sometimes referred to as Leiden, its Dutch name, or Kayts, after the village on its northeast coast. A beautiful but sparsely populated place, it has a deserted feel thanks to the war, and many structures remain in ruins.

If you approach Velanai from Jaffna, you'll pass a turnoff for the half-built **Sabins Blue Ocean Resort** (jj@legendtrading.com; r US$15), which has a slightly forgotten air (don't expect much in the way of service) and a few basic rooms, but a lovely beachside location.

A few clicks further on, **Chaatty Beach** is no white-sand wonder, but it's passable for swimming and has changing rooms, picnic gazebos and snack vendors. It's just 11km from Jaffna.

If you approach Velanai from Karainagar, the ferry will drop you at the eerie, tumbleweed settlement of **Kayts**, between a dozen scuttled fishing boats. This lonely place had far more bustle in centuries past as this was the port from where elephants were shipped to India. Kayts today is tiny but has some noteworthy colonial buildings, including three churches near the jetty. Walk straight up Sunuvil Rd and take your first right to get to the Portuguese **St James'**; if you turn left instead you'll hit **St Joseph's**; and if you continue up Sunuvil Rd, you'll see **St Mary's** on the left. Just beyond St Mary's, the first asphalt lane to the right leads 600m to a placid waterfront **cemetery** with views of offshore **Fort Hammenhiel** (now a luxury hotel). At the island's northwest is **Karampan**, where

Navy-operated ferries depart for Analaitivu and Eluvaitivu.

Punkudutivu

A long, delightful causeway links Velanai to the island of Punkudutivu. Notice the lagoon fishermen who use wade-out traps and sail little wind-powered canoes. **Punkudutivu village**, the scene of minor riots in December 2005, has one of Jaffna's most screechingly colourful Hindu temples, while many old houses lie in various stages of decay. Smaller causeways link Punkudutivu to the ferry port at **Kurikadduwan** (KKD) for Navy-run boats to Neduntivu and Nainativu.

Nainativu (Nagadipa)

Known as Nainativu in Tamil and Nagadipa in Sinhalese, this 6km-long lozenge of palmyra groves is holy to both Buddhist and Hindu pilgrims.

Right in front of you as you step off the jetty is the **Naga Pooshani Amman Kovil** complex, an airy Hindu temple set amid mature neem trees. The main temple deity is the *naga* goddess Meenakshi, a consort of Shiva. (The term *naga* refers variously to serpent deity figures and to the ancient inhabitants of the island.) Women wishing to conceive come here seeking blessings, delivered during the trance-inducing midday *puja*. An impressive festival is held in June or July every year.

Walk 10 minutes south along the coast road to find the **Nagadipa temple**, the North's only major Buddhist pilgrimage site. According to legend, the Buddha came to the island to prevent war between a *naga* king and his nephew over ownership of a gem-studded throne. The solution: give it to the temple

---

THE MILITARY & TOURISM IN THE NORTH

Sri Lanka has a heavily militarised society, particularly in the north of the country, which was a war zone for decades and where 16 of the 19 army divisions are still stationed.

Since the end of the war in 2009, the military has taken over large chunks of coastal land. The government considers this necessary to safeguard national security; protest groups deem many actions land grabs for profiteering. What's not in dispute is that villagers have been removed from their ancestral land and the military is increasingly involved in tourism in the north.

Some hotels, such as Fort Hammenhiel (p276), are located on well-established military bases and are less contentious. Others, including the **Thalsevana Resort** (www.thalsevanaresort.com) near Kankesanturai in the Jaffna peninsula, have been built on land previously held by villagers. The Navy controls all ferry services around Jaffna's islands and boat trips to Adam's Bridge, off Mannar. Airline Helitours (p270) is owned and operated by the Sri Lankan Air Force.

Where possible, we have attempted to indicate which businesses are military-owned.

instead. The precious chair and original temple disappeared long ago, but today there is an attractive silver-painted dagoba. Just behind, three happy-looking Buddhas sit in a domed temple.

Poya (full-moon) days are observed by both Hindus and Buddhists on the island; expect crowds. Navy-run ferries (Rs 50, 20 minutes) depart KKD on Punkudutivu island for Nainativu every 15 minutes or so from 6.30am to 5.30pm.

Neduntivu (Delft)

The intriguing, windswept island of Neduntivu (Delft) is 10km across the water southwest of KKD on Punkudutivu island. Around 6000 people live here, but it feels deserted, with dirt roads running through coconut-palm groves, aquamarine water and white sand, and a rich diversity of flora that includes neem, a rare, ancient **baobab tree**, and vines that you can swing from. Hundreds of field-dividing walls are hewn from chunks of brain and fan corals, while Delft ponies descended from Dutch mounts roam barren fields edged by rocky coral shores. There is a **giant rock** that is said to be growing and is therefore worshipped, and a small, very ruined **Dutch fort** a short walk from the ferry dock.

Manal Kanuttadi is a pretty beach 1km from the dock where you could camp with permission from the Navy. (There's a small shop near the dock selling water and snacks but little in the way of real food available.)

In 2011 Basil Rajapaksa (the president's brother and economic development minister) announced plans to 'beautify the island into a magnificient tourist attraction' with resorts and roads. However, there's been no movement on this as yet (possibly as Neduntivu is a military-declared High Security Zone).

It's impossible to explore Neduntivu without transport. Three-wheelers/pick-ups (Rs 1500/3000 for three hours) can be rented for island tours from the dock.

A crowded Sri Lankan Navy-operated ferry (free, one hour) departs KKD daily at 9am, returning at 2.30pm. Arrive 30 minutes before (or earlier) to secure somewhere to sit, and

expect an uncomfortable, if memorable trip. If you're travelling by bus from Jaffna you'll need to catch the 6.40am departure to KKD to make the ferry connection.

Karaitivu

Karaitivu has two main things going for it: access to Kayts and the trippy crossing from Jaffna across a long, water-skimming **causeway**, with views of wading fishermen and shrimp traps. Look right at the start of the causeway to spy the towering *gopuram* of **Ponnalai Vishnu Kovil** through the palms.

Karaitivu's **Casuarina Beach** is an attractive stretch of sand with good swimming and, as the name indicates, a shoreline backed by mature casuarina trees. It's popular with folk from Jaffna on weekends and has a couple of snack bars for a bite to eat and a drink. Half-hourly buses from Jaffna to **Karainagar** pass within 2km of the beach. There are three-wheelers available for onward transport.

The southern tip of the island is home to a naval zone, from where the **Kayts ferry** (free, 10 minutes, half-hourly except 12.30pm to 2pm, last at 5.30pm) departs.

A kilometre west of the jetty, inside the naval base itself (present a copy of your passport for access), is part of the spectacular new resort **Fort Hammenhiel** (meals Rs 400-800). Right on the shoreline, with amazing sunset views, the large modern restaurant here offers excellent meals, including lots of seafood, and has a full bar. There's a pretty white-sand beach with shallow water (and a muddy sea bottom) that diners are welcome to use.

Offshore, the tiny islet in the bay is home to the pocket-sized **Fort Hammenhiel** (☑ 381 8216; http://forthammenhielresort.lk; r US$110; ❄ 🛜), a 17th-century Dutch structure that's now been sensitively converted into a luxury hotel. Owned and operated by the Navy, it's only open to paying guests, with access by boat. There are only four rooms, and meals can be ordered from the restaurant over the water. Spending a night here is undoubtedly one of Sri Lanka's unique experiences.

Understand
Sri Lanka

Sri Lanka Today

Tourists continue to pour into Sri Lanka in ever greater numbers. But even as the physical and economic consequences of the long war recede, the country is embroiled by the international attention focused on its president, Mahinda Rajapaksa.

Best in Print

On Sal Mal Lane Ru Freeman weaves together the many strands of Sri Lankan society in a beautiful novel set down a Colombo lane.

Running in the Family A comic and reflective memoir by Michael Ondaatje of his Colombo family in the 1940s.

Monkfish Moon Nine short stories, by Booker Prize–nominated Romesh Gunesekera, provide a diverse glimpse of Sri Lanka's ethnic conflict.

Wave A searing memoir by Sonali Deraniyagala opens on the morning of 26 December 2004, right before the tsunami kills her husband, children and parents.

Human Rights Groups

Sri Lanka Campaign for Peace and Justice (www.srilankacampaign. org) A global nonpartisan movement calling for humanitarian relief, an end to human rights abuses and a repeal of the government's anti-terror regulations.

Human Rights Watch (www.hrw.org) Researches and publishes regular reports about human rights conditions in Sri Lanka.

Investigations Resisted

Sri Lanka is likely to be dogged by allegations about its behaviour during the long civil war for years to come – at least as long as the current government rejects calls for an investigation by the United Nations Human Rights Council (UNHRC). It is generally agreed that human rights abuses were committed by all sides in the final months of the 26-year war, which ended in May 2009. But the contention that the Sri Lankan military killed 40,000 Tamil civilians in its final push to victory simply won't go away. Two documentaries, *Sri Lanka's Killing Fields: War Crimes Unpunished* and *No Fire Zone: In the Killing Fields of Sri Lanka*, by the UK's Channel 4 have stoked calls for investigations. A report by the UNHRC says that there is enough evidence of civilian slaughter to require a full investigation.

The Sri Lankan government, led by President Mahinda Rajapaksa, has denied human rights abuses and fought against any official investigation. It's a strategy that has kept the issue in the headlines internationally. The 2013 Commonwealth Heads of Government Meeting should have been a triumph for Rajapaksa; instead, there was intense pressure on governments to boycott the meeting and Canada, India and Mauritius refused to attend.

In 2014 Sri Lanka's parliament formally rejected any investigation by the Sri Lankan government or the UN, although the vote was not overwhelming. Meanwhile, human rights groups worldwide seem determined to keep the matter alive and the UN regularly votes for investigations.

Omnipresent President

You can't avoid him: the grinning face of President Mahinda Rajapaksa is everywhere in Sri Lanka. He gazes out from huge billboards and signs on the sides of buildings, in countless publications and more. It's a cult of personality that he hopes will allow him to stay in power beyond the next election, which must happen by 2016. His extended family can be found throughout the government and business; one of his brothers, Gotabhaya, is Secretary of Defence.

Along with Rajapaska's domination of Sri Lanka's official life has come a wide range of allegations of abuses of power. In 2013 alone, Human Rights Watch said the government 'targeted civil society through threats, surveillance, and clampdowns on activities and free speech'. Navi Pillay, the UN Commissioner for Human Rights, denounced 'a climate of fear' that is undermining democracy and eroding the rule of law. Amnesty International said flatly: 'There are no human rights in Sri Lanka.' Rajapaksa and his circle deny all these claims but life can be hard for those inside the country who disagree.

Journalists who go beyond the docile coverage in the main newspapers have suffered much abuse. Opposition politicians have faced pro-government mobs when they've tried to investigate Rajapaska's massive Chinese-financed construction schemes around his hometown of Hambantota. Even Sarath Fonseka, who was Rajapaksa's military chief during the final victory over the LTTE, ended up in jail after he challenged his former boss for the presidency in 2010.

In 2014 a radical band of Buddhist monks attacked Muslims while the police and military looked on. Sri Lanka's Minister of Justice, Rauff Hakeem, himself a Muslim, condemned this even as he admitted the government had done nothing to prevent it. Given that many Sri Lankans say they are willing to overlook Rajapaska's alleged misdeeds because the prospect of a return to war is worse, the stoking of ethnic tensions ahead of elections looked suspicious to many.

Welcome Tourists!

The many allegations of official misdeeds so far don't seem to have affected Sri Lanka's tourism. Visitor numbers are booming, even if the numbers themselves are a bit fuzzy. About 1.2 million people visited the island in 2013, an approximate 20% increase on 2012 figures. These kinds of numbers are fuelling a boom in tourist construction that can be seen across the nation. New hotels are rising up on previously unspoilt beaches while families are building guesthouses near popular tourist sites.

Predictably, a host of environmental concerns have been raised about all the development, but with most Sri Lankans anxious to better their lot and the government calling for tourism to contribute 7.5% to the country's GDP, such worries are easily ignored.

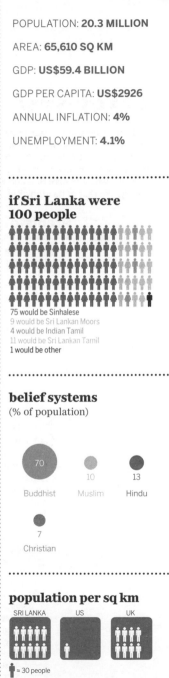

POPULATION: **20.3 MILLION**

AREA: **65,610 SQ KM**

GDP: **US$59.4 BILLION**

GDP PER CAPITA: **US$2926**

ANNUAL INFLATION: **4%**

UNEMPLOYMENT: **4.1%**

if Sri Lanka were 100 people

75 would be Sinhalese
9 would be Sri Lankan Moors
4 would be Indian Tamil
11 would be Sri Lankan Tamil
1 would be other

belief systems
(% of population)

70 Buddhist
10 Muslim
13 Hindu
7 Christian

population per sq km

SRI LANKA   US   UK

≈ 30 people

History

Sri Lanka's location – near India and along hundreds of ancient trade routes – has for ages made it attractive to immigrants, invaders, missionaries, traders and travellers from India, East Asia and the Middle East. Many stayed on, and over generations they assimilated and intermarried, converted and converted back. Although debates still rage over who was here first and who can claim Sri Lanka as their homeland, the island's history, like that of its ethnicities, is one of shifting dominance and constant flux.

The indigenous Veddahs were called Yakshas, or nature spirits, by the island's early arrivals. No one knows if this is because the Veddahs were so at home in nature or because they prayed to their departed ancestors – spirits known as *nae yaku*.

Prehistory & Early Arrivals

Sri Lanka's history is a source of great pride to both Sinhalese and Tamils, the country's two largest ethnic groups. The only problem is, they have two completely different versions. Every historical site, religious structure, even village name, seems to have conflicting stories about its origin, and those stories are, in turn, blended over time with contrasting religious myths and local legends. The end results are often used as evidence that the island is one group's exclusive homeland; each claims first dibs.

Did the Buddha leave his footprint on Adam's Peak (Sri Pada) while visiting the island that lay halfway to paradise? Or was it Adam who left his footprint embedded in the rock while taking a last look at Eden? Was the chain of islands linking Sri Lanka to India the same chain that Rama crossed to rescue his wife Sita from the clutches of Rawana, demon king of Lanka, in the epic Ramayana?

Whatever the legends, the reality is that Sri Lanka's original inhabitants, the Veddahs (or, as they refer to themselves, Wanniyala-aetto: 'forest dwellers'), were hunter-gatherers who subsisted on the island's natural bounty. Much about their origins is unclear, but anthropologists generally believe that they are descended from people who migrated from India, and possibly Southeast Asia, and existed on the island as far back as 32,000 BC. It's also likely that rising waters submerged a land bridge between India and Sri Lanka in around 5000 BC.

Historians and archaeologists have differing interpretations of its origins, but a megalithic culture emerged in the centuries around 900 BC

TIMELINE	Pre-6th century BC	6th century BC	4th century BC
	The island is inhabited by Veddahs (Wanniyala-aetto), a group of hunter-gatherers who anthropologists believe were descendants of a society that existed on Sri Lanka since 32,000 BC.	Vijaya, a shamed North Indian prince, is cast adrift, but makes landfall on Sri Lanka's west coast. He settles around Anuradhapura and establishes the island's first recorded kingdom.	India's first poet pens the Hindu epic the *Ramayana*, in which the god Rama conquers Lanka and its demon-god Rawana. The sandbars off Mannar Island are described as Rama's Bridge.

with striking similarities to the South Indian cultures of that time. Also during this Early Iron Age, Anuradhapura grew as a population centre.

Objects inscribed with Brahmi (an ancient 'parent' script to most South Asian scripts) have been found from the 3rd century BC; parallels with both North Indian and South Indian Brahmi styles have been noted, though Tamil words are used in many of those found in the north and east of the island. Sri Lankan historians debate these details fiercely, as do many Sri Lankans, but rather than there being two distinct ethnic histories, it is more likely that migrations from West, East and South India all happened during this time and that those new arrivals all mixed with the indigenous people.

Anuradhapura

The 5th-century-AD Pali epic, the Mahavamsa, is the country's primary historical source. Although it's a somewhat faithful record of kingdoms and Sinhalese political power from around the 3rd century BC, its historical accuracy is shakier – and indeed full of beautiful myths – before this time. Nonetheless, many Sinhalese claim they're descended from Vijaya, an immoral 6th-century-BC North Indian prince who, according to the epic, had a lion for a grandfather and a father who had lion paws and married his own sister. Vijaya was banished for bad behaviour, with a contingent of 700 men, on dilapidated ships from the subcontinent.

Landing near present-day Mannar, supposedly on the day that the Buddha attained enlightenment, Vijaya and his crew settled around Anuradhapura, and soon encountered Kuveni, a Yaksha (probably Veddah) who is alternately described as a vicious queen and a seductress who assumed the form of a 16-year-old maiden to snag Vijaya. She handed Vijaya the crown, joined him in slaying her own people and had two children with him before he kicked her out and ordered a princess – and wives for his men – from South India's Tamil Pandya kingdom. (That, by this account, the forefathers of the Sinhalese race all married Tamils is overlooked by most Sri Lankans.) His rule formed the basis of the Anuradhapura kingdom, which developed there in the 4th century BC.

The Anuradhapura kingdom covered the island in the 2nd century BC, but it frequently fought, and coexisted with, other dynasties on the island over the centuries, especially the Tamil Cholas. The boundaries between Anuradhapura and various South Indian kingdoms were frequently shifting, and Anuradhapura was also involved in conflicts in South India. A number of Sinhalese warriors arose to repel South Indian kingdoms, including Vijayabahu I (11th century AD), who finally abandoned Anuradhapura and made Polonnaruwa, further southeast, his capital.

For centuries the kingdom was able to rebuild after its battles through rajakariya, the system of free labour for the king. This free labour provided the resources to restore buildings, tanks and irrigation systems and to

Veddah Place Names

Gal Oya National Park

Nanu Oya

Kelaniya Ganga

Possible Early Iron Age Sites

Sigiriya

Kantarodai

Tissamaharama

3rd century BC	205–161 BC	103–89 BC	1st century BC
Indian emperor Ashoka sends his son and daughter to spread Buddha's teachings. Anuradhapuran King Devanampiya Tissa accepts them, beginning Sri Lankan ties between government and religion.	Reign of Chola King Elara, described in the Mahavamsa as a just leader. Although Tamil and Hindu, he offers alms to Buddhist monks and employs both Sinhalese and Tamils.	Five Tamil kings from India invade Anuradhapura and rule for 14 years. King Valagamba is forced to flee and shelters in the caves around Dambulla.	The Fourth Buddhist council is held in Aluvihara. The collection of the Buddha's teachings, previously preserved by oral tradition, is written down for the first time.

TANK-BUILDING

The science of building tanks, studying gradients and constructing channels is the key to early Sri Lankan civilisation. The tanks, which dot the plains of the ancient dominions of Rajarata (in the north-central part of the country) and Ruhuna (in the southeast), probably started as modest structures. But by the 5th century BC they reached such dimensions that local legends say they were built with supernatural help. It is claimed that Giant's Tank near Mannar Island was built by giants, while other tanks were said to have been constructed by a mixed workforce of humans and demons.

The irrigation system, developed on ever-greater scales during the millennium before the Common Era, ranks with the ancient *qanats* (underground channels) of Iran and the canals of Pharaonic Egypt in sophistication. These dry-zone reservoirs sustained and shaped Sri Lanka's civilisation for more than 2500 years, until war and discord overtook the island in the 12th to 14th centuries AD.

develop agriculture. The system was not banished from the island until 1832, when the British passed laws banning slavery.

The Buddha's Teaching Arrives

Buddhism arrived from India in the 3rd century BC, transforming Anuradhapura and possibly creating what is now known as Sinhalese culture. Today the mountain at Mihintale marks the spot where King Devanampiya Tissa is said to have first received the Buddha's teaching. The earliest Buddhist emissaries also brought to Sri Lanka a cutting of the bodhi tree under which the Buddha attained enlightenment. It survives in Anuradhapura, now garlanded with prayer flags and lights. Strong ties gradually evolved between Sri Lankan royalty and Buddhist religious orders. Kings, grateful for monastic support, provided living quarters, tanks (reservoirs) and produce to the monasteries, and a symbiotic political economy between religion and state was established – a powerful contract that is still vital in modern times.

BODHI

The bodhi tree in Anuradhapura has a 2000-year history of human care and custody, making it the world's oldest tree of this kind.

Buddhism underwent a further major development on the island when the original oral teachings were documented in writing in the 1st century BC. The early Sri Lankan monks went on to write a vast body of commentaries on the teachings, textbooks, Pali grammars and other instructive articles, developing a classical literature for the Theravada (doctrine of the elders) school of Buddhism that continues to be referenced by Theravada Buddhists around the world. The arrival of the Buddha's tooth relic at Anuradhapura in AD 371 reinforced the position of Buddhism in Sinhalese society, giving a sense of national purpose and identity and inspiring the development of Sinhalese culture and literature.

4th century AD	5th century	5th century	5th century
Buddhism is further popularised with the arrival in Anuradhapura of the sacred tooth relic of the Buddha. It becomes a symbol of both religion and sovereignty over the island.	After engineering his father's death and expelling his older brother Mugalan, King Kassapa constructs the rock fortress at Sigiriya. With the help of Indian mercenaries, Mugalan finally retakes the throne.	The Mahavamsa (Great Chronicle) epic poem is written by Buddhist monks. It recounts the Buddhist and royal history of the island, interwoven with supernatural tales.	Indian scholar-monk Buddhaghosa arrives in Sri Lanka and writes the Visuddhimagga, a manual for the Buddha's teachings. His explications become part of the Theravada canon and are still studied today.

Polonnaruwa

The next capital, at Polonnaruwa, survived for over two centuries and produced two more notable rulers. Parakramabahu I (r 1153–86), nephew of Vijayabahu I, expelled the South Indian Tamil Chola empire from Sri Lanka, and carried the fight to South India, even making a raid on Myanmar. He also constructed many new tanks and lavished public money to make Polonnaruwa a great Asian capital.

His benevolent successor, Nissanka Malla (r 1187–96), was the last king of Polonnaruwa to care for the well-being of his people. He was followed by a series of weak rulers, and with the decay of the irrigation system, disease spread and Polonnaruwa was abandoned. The lush jungle reclaimed the second Sinhalese capital in just a few decades.

After Polonnaruwa, Sinhalese power shifted to the southwest of the island, and between 1253 and 1400 there were another five different capitals, none of them as powerful as Anuradhapura or Polonnaruwa. Meanwhile, the powerful kingdom of Jaffna expanded to cover a huge part of the island; when Arab traveller Ibn Batuta visited Ceylon in 1344, he reported that it extended south as far as Puttalam.

With the decline of the Sinhalese northern capitals and ensuing Sinhalese migration south, a wide jungle buffer separated the northern, mostly coastal Tamil settlements and the southern, interior Sinhalese settlements. For centuries, this jungle barrier kept Sinhalese and Tamils largely apart, sowing the seeds for Sri Lanka's ethnic dichotomy.

Trade & Conquest
Enter the Portuguese

At the heart of the Indian Ocean, Sri Lanka had been a trading hub even before Arab traders arrived in the 7th century AD with their new Islamic faith. Gems, cinnamon, ivory and elephants were the valued items of commerce. Early Muslim settlements took hold in Jaffna and Galle, but the arrival of a European power, focused as much on domination as trade, forced many Muslims inland to flee persecution.

When the Portuguese arrived in 1505, Sri Lanka had three main kingdoms: the Tamil kingdom of Jaffna and Sinhalese kingdoms in Kandy and Kotte (near Colombo). Lourenço de Almeida, the son of the Portuguese Viceroy of India, established friendly relations with the Kotte kingdom and gained a monopoly on the valuable spice trade. The Portuguese eventually gained control of the Kotte kingdom.

Tamil–Portuguese relations were less cordial, and Jaffna successfully resisted two Portuguese expeditions before falling in 1619, at which point the Portuguese destroyed Jaffna's many beautiful Hindu temples and its

Descendants of Mozambican slaves brought to Sri Lanka by the Portuguese are almost totally assimilated. Their most obvious contributions to modern Sri Lankan culture are the folk tunes called *bailas*, love songs founded on Latin melodies and African rhythms.

7th–15th century	11th century	1216	1505
Arab traders settle in Sri Lanka, marrying locally and establishing Islam on the island. They maintain trade with the Middle East and coexist peacefully with both Tamils and Sinhalese.	Weary of continued conflict with Tamil neighbours, King Vijayabahu I defeats the Cholas and moves the Sinhalese capital southeast to Polonnaruwa; a brief golden age follows.	As Polonnaruwa declines, the Tamil kingdom of Jaffna is established and briefly becomes a feudatory of South India's Pandya kingdom before gaining independence. It survives for four centuries.	Following Polonnaruwa's decline, Sinhalese power is with the Kotte in the southwest. The Portuguese arrive and conquer the entire west coast, but Kandy defeats their advances.

European-Era Forts

Batticaloa

Jaffna

Matara

Trincomalee

royal library. Portugal eventually took over the entire west coast, then the east, but the Kandyan kingdom in the central highlands steadfastly resisted domination.

The Portuguese brought religious orders, including the Dominicans and Jesuits. Many coastal communities converted, but other resistance to Christianity was met with massacres and the destruction of temples. Buddhists fled to Kandy and the city assumed its role as protector of the Buddhist faith, a sacred function solidified by another three centuries of unsuccessful attempts at domination by European powers.

The Dutch

In 1602 the Dutch arrived, just as keen as the Portuguese on dominating the lucrative traffic in Indian Ocean spices. In exchange for Sri Lankan autonomy, the Kandyan king, Rajasinha II, gave the Dutch a monopoly on the spice trade. Despite the deal, the Dutch made repeated unsuccessful attempts to subjugate Kandy during their 140-year rule.

The Dutch were more industrious than the Portuguese, and canals were built along the west coast to transport cinnamon and other crops. Some can be seen around Negombo today. The legal system of the Dutch era still forms part of Sri Lanka's legal canon.

The British

The British initially viewed Sri Lanka in strategic terms, and considered the eastern harbour of Trincomalee as a counter to French influence in India. After the French took over the Netherlands in 1794, the pragmatic Dutch ceded Sri Lanka to the British for 'protection' in 1796. The British moved quickly, making the island a colony in 1802 and finally taking over Kandy in 1815. Three years later, the first unified administration of the island by a European power was established.

Sunil S Amrith's *Crossing the Bay of Bengal: The Furies of Nature and the Fortunes of Migrants* tells the human, economic and environmental history of the bay whose 'western gateway' was once Ceylon.

The British conquest unsettled many Sinhalese, who believed that only the custodians of the tooth relic had the right to rule the land. Their apprehension was somewhat relieved when a senior monk removed the tooth relic from the Temple of the Sacred Tooth Relic, thereby securing it (and the island's symbolic sovereignty) for the Sinhalese people.

Sinhalese angst grew further when British settlers began arriving in the 1830s. Coffee and rubber were largely replaced by tea from the 1870s, and the island's demographic mix was profoundly altered with an influx of Tamil labourers – so called 'Plantation Tamils' – from South India. (These 'Plantation Tamils' were – and still are – separated by geography, history and caste from the Jaffna Tamils.) Tamil settlers from the North made their way south to Colombo, while Sinhalese headed to Jaffna. British colonisation set the island in a demographic flux.

1658	1796	1802	1815
Following a treaty with the Kandyan kingdom, the Dutch, who arrived in 1602, establish a monopoly on the spice market and wrest control of coastal Sri Lanka from the Portuguese.	The Netherlands, under French control, surrenders Ceylon to the British. The shift is initially thought to be temporary, and the British administer the island from Madras, India.	After the decline of the Dutch, Sri Lanka becomes a British colony. The island is viewed as a strategic bulwark against French expansion, but its commercial potential is soon recognised.	Determined to rule the entire island, the British finally conquer the Kandyan kingdom. It's the first (and only) time all of Sri Lanka is ruled by a European power.

The Road to Independence

Growing Nationalism

The dawning of the 20th century was an important time for the grass-roots Sri Lankan nationalist movement. Towards the end of the 19th century, Buddhist and Hindu campaigns were established with the dual aim of making the faiths more contemporary in the wake of European colonialism, and defending traditional Sri Lankan culture against the impact of Christian missionaries. The logical progression was for these groups to demand greater Sri Lankan participation in government, and by 1910 they had secured the minor concession of allowing Sri Lankans to elect one lonely member to the Legislative Council.

By 1919 the nationalist mission was formalised as the Ceylon National Congress. The Sinhalese-nationalist activist Anagarika Dharmapala was forced to leave the country, and the mantle for further change was taken up by a variety of youth leagues, some Sinhalese and some Tamil. In 1927 Mahatma Gandhi visited Tamil youth activists in Jaffna, providing further momentum to the cause.

Further reform came in 1924, when a revision to the constitution allowed for representative government, and again in 1931, when a new constitution finally included the island's leaders in the parliamentary decision-making process and granted universal suffrage. Under the constitution no one ethnic community could dominate the political process, and a series of checks and balances ensured all areas of the government were overseen by a committee drawn from all ethnic groups. However, both Sinhalese and Tamil political leaders failed to thoroughly support the country's pre-independence constitution, foreshadowing the problems that were to characterise the next eight decades.

From Ceylon to Sri Lanka

Following India's independence in 1947, Ceylon (as Sri Lanka was then called) became fully independent on 4 February 1948. Despite featuring members from all of the island's ethnic groups, the ruling United National Party (UNP) really only represented the interests of an English-speaking elite. The UNP's decision to try to deny the 'Plantation Tamils' citizenship and repatriate them to India was indicative of a rising tide of Sinhalese nationalism.

In 1956 this divide increased when the Sri Lankan Freedom Party (SLFP) came to power with an agenda based on socialism, Sinhalese nationalism and government support for Buddhism. One of the first tasks of SLFP leader SWRD Bandaranaike was to fulfil a campaign promise to make Sinhala the country's sole official language. Under the British,

Sir James Emerson Tennent's affable nature shines through in his honest and descriptive writing about 19th-century Sri Lanka, now serialised at www.lankaweb.com/news/features/ceylon.html.

Not an easy read but an important one, *When Memory Dies*, by A Sivanandan, is a tale of the ethnic crisis and its impact on one family over three generations.

1832	1843–59	1870s	Late-19th century
Sweeping changes in property laws open the door to British settlers. English becomes the official language, state monopolies are abolished and capital flows in, funding coffee plantations.	Unable to persuade the Sinhalese to labour on plantations, the British bring in almost one million Tamil labourers from South India. Today 'Plantation Tamils' are 4% of the population.	The coffee industry drives the development of roads, ports and railways, but leaf blight decimates the coffee industry and plantations are converted to growing tea or rubber.	The Arwi language, a combination of Tamil and Arabic that evolved among Sri Lankan Moors, is at its peak, with the publication of several important religious works.

MEMOIRS

Enemy Lines: Warfare, Childhood, and Play in Batticaloa, by Margaret Trawick, is a poignant memoir of living and working in eastern Sri Lanka and witnessing the recruitment of teenagers to the LTTE cause.

Tamils became capable English speakers and were overrepresented in universities and public-service jobs, which created Sinhalese resentment, especially during the slow economy of the 1950s. The main political parties played on Sinhalese fear that their religion, language and culture could be swamped by Indians, perceived to be natural allies of Sri Lankan Tamils. The Tamils, whose Hindu identity had become more pronounced in the lead-up to independence, began to find themselves in the position of threatened minority.

The Sinhala-only bill disenfranchised Sri Lanka's Hindu and Muslim Tamil-speaking population: almost 30% of the country suddenly lost access to government jobs and services. Although tensions had been simmering since the end of colonial rule, this decision marked the beginning of Sri Lanka's ethnic conflict.

A similar scenario played out in 1970, when a law was passed favouring Sinhalese for admission to universities, reducing numbers of Tamil students. Then, following an armed insurrection against the government by the hardline anti-Tamil, student-led People's Liberation Front (Janatha Vimukthi Peramuna or JVP), a new constitution (which changed Ceylon's name to Sri Lanka) gave Buddhism 'foremost place' in Sri Lanka and made it the state's duty to 'protect and foster' Buddhism.

Unrest grew among northern Tamils, and a state of emergency was imposed on their home regions for several years from 1971. The police and army that enforced the state of emergency included few Tamils (partly because of the 'Sinhala only' law), creating further division and, for Tamils, an acute sense of oppression.

Birth of the Tigers

In the mid-1970s several groups of young Tamils, some of them militant, began advocating for an independent Tamil state called Eelam (Precious

1919	1931	1948	1956
Following the British arrest in 1915 of Sinhalese leaders for minor offences, the Ceylon National Congress unifies Sinhalese and Tamil groups to further nationalist and pro-independence goals.	A new constitution introduces power sharing with a Sinhalese-run government. Universal suffrage is introduced as the country is the first Asian colony to give women the right to vote.	Ceylon becomes an independent member of the Commonwealth six months after India. The United National Party (UNP) consolidates power by depriving Plantation Tamils of citizenship.	The Sri Lankan Freedom party (SLFP) defeats the UNP on a socialist and nationalist platform. Protests, ethnic riots and conflict break out after a 'Sinhala only' language law is passed.

Land). They included Vellupillai Prabhakaran, a founder of the Liberation Tigers of Tamil Eelam (LTTE), often referred to as the Tamil Tigers.

Tamil had been elevated to the status of 'national language' for official work, but only in Tamil-majority areas. Clashes between Tamils and security forces developed into a pattern of killings and counter-reprisals, all too often with civilians in the crossfire. Passions on both sides rose, and a pivotal moment came in 1981, when a group of Sinhalese rioters (some say government forces) burnt down Jaffna's library, which contained, among other things, various histories of the Tamil people, some of which were ancient palm-leaf manuscripts.

Small-scale reprisals followed, but the world only took notice two years later, in 1983, when, in response to the Tigers' ambushing and killing of 13 soldiers in the Jaffna region, full-scale anti-Tamil massacres erupted in Colombo. In a riot now known as Black July, up to 3000 Tamils were clubbed, beaten, burned or shot to death, and Tamil property was looted and burned. Several Tamil-majority areas, including Colombo's Pettah district, were levelled, and violence spread to other parts of the country.

The government, the police and the army were either unable or unwilling to stop the violence; some of them assisted. Hundreds of thousands of Tamils left the country or fled to Tamil-majority areas in the North or East – and many joined the resistance. (Many Sinhalese, meanwhile, moved south from the North and East.) The horror of Black July prompted a groundswell of international sympathy for Tamil armed resistance groups, and brought funding from fellow Tamils in southern India, as well as from the government of Indira Gandhi.

Revenge and counter-revenge attacks continued, and grew into atrocities and massacres – on both sides. The government was widely condemned for acts of torture and disappearances, but it pointed to the intimidation and violence against civilians, including Tamils and Muslims, by the Tamil fighters. Implementation of a 1987 accord, offering limited Tamil autonomy and officialising Tamil as a national language, never happened, and the conflict escalated into a 25-year civil war that eventually claimed upwards of 100,000 lives.

William McGowan's *Only Man is Vile* is an incisive, unrelenting account of ethnic violence in Sri Lanka, penetrating deeply into its complexities.

War & Attempts at Peace

Indian Peacekeeping

In 1987 government forces pushed the LTTE back into Jaffna as part of a major offensive. India pressed the Sri Lankan government to withdraw, and the two heads of state, JR Jayawardene and Rajiv Gandhi, negotiated an accord: the Sri Lankan government would call off the offensive, Tamil rebels would disarm, and an Indian Peace Keeping Force (IPKF) would protect the truce. Tamil regions would also have substantial autonomy, as Colombo devolved power to the provinces.

1958	1959	1959	1972
The country sees its first island-wide anti-Tamil riot. It lasts for days, leaves more than 200 people dead in violent attacks (and some revenge attacks) and displaces of thousands of Tamils.	Despite coming to power in 1956 with a Sinhalese-nationalist manifesto, SWRD Bandaranaike begins negotiating with Tamil leaders for a federation, leading to his assassination by a Buddhist monk.	Widow Sirimavo Bandaranaike assumes her late husband's SLFP post, becoming the world's first female prime minister. She is appointed prime minister several more times before her death in 2000.	A new constitution is created. It changes Ceylon's name to Sri Lanka, declares, once again, Sinhalese to be the official language and gives Buddhism 'foremost place' among the island's religions.

It soon became clear the deal suited no one. The LTTE complied initially but ended up in battle with the IPKF when it refused to disarm. Opposition to the Indians also came from the Sinhalese, a revived JVP and sections of the sangha (community of Buddhist monks and nuns), leading to violent demonstrations.

In 1987 the JVP launched a second revolution with political murders and strikes, and by late 1988 the country was terrorised, the economy crippled and the government paralysed. The army struck back with a ruthless counter-insurgency campaign. The insurrection was put down, but not before tens of thousands died.

By the time the Indian peacekeepers withdrew, in March 1990, they had lost more than 1000 lives in just three years. But no sooner had they left than the war between the LTTE and the Sri Lankan government escalated again. By the end of 1990 the LTTE held Jaffna and much of the North, although the East was largely back under government control. In May 1991 Rajiv Gandhi was assassinated by a suicide bomber; it was blamed on the LTTE, presumably in retaliation for consenting to the IPKF arrangement.

The 2002 Ceasefire

Although most Tamils and Sinhalese longed for peace, extremists on both sides pressed on with war. President Premadasa was assassinated at a May Day rally in 1993. The LTTE was suspected but never claimed responsibility. The following year, the People's Alliance (PA) won the parliamentary elections; its leader, Chandrika Bandaranaike Kumaratunga, the daughter of former leader Sirimavo Bandaranaike, won the presidential election. The PA had promised to end the civil war, but the conflict continued in earnest.

In 2000 a Norwegian peace mission brought the LTTE and the government to the negotiating table, but a ceasefire had to wait until after the December 2001 elections, which handed power to the UNP. Ranil Wickremasinghe became prime minister, and economic growth was strong while peace talks appeared to progress. Wickremasinghe and President Chandrika Bandaranaike Kumaratunga, however, were from different parties, and circled each other warily until 2003, when Kumaratunga dissolved parliament and essentially ousted Wickremasinghe and his UNP.

In 2002, following the Norway-brokered ceasefire agreement, a careful optimism reigned. In the North, refugees, internally displaced persons and long-absent émigrés began to return, bringing an economic boost to devastated Jaffna. Nongovernmental organisations started tackling, among other things, an estimated two million land mines.

But peace talks stumbled, and the situation was ever more fraught. Accusations of bias and injustice were hurled from all sides. In October

---

At least one million land mines were laid during Sri Lankan hostilities in the 1990s. Efforts to clear the mines have meant that thousands of displaced people have been resettled.

Anil's Ghost, by Booker Prize–winner Michael Ondaatje, is a haunting novel about human rights amid the turmoil of late-20th-century Sri Lanka. The book has received international commendation and some local condemnation.

1970s	1979	1981	1983
Young Tamils begin fighting for an independent Tamil state called Eelam (Precious Land) in Sri Lanka's north. The Liberation Tigers of Tamil Eelam (LTTE) emerge as the strongest group.	Sri Lanka enacts the Prevention of Terrorism Act. Police may detain for up to 18 months anyone thought to be connected with unlawful activities. The Act is still in effect.	Jaffna's Public Library, home to many ancient Tamil works and a symbol of Tamil culture and learning, is burnt down by Sinhalese mobs, galvanising the Tamil separatist movement.	The ambush of an army patrol near Jaffna ignites widespread ethnic violence. Up to 3000 Tamils are estimated killed by Sinhalese rioters in what is now known as Black July.

2003 the US listed the LTTE as a Foreign Terrorist Organization. Some believed this to be a positive move; others saw it as an action that would isolate the LTTE, causing further strain and conflict. In early 2004 a split in LTTE ranks added a new dynamic, and with killings, insecurity, accusations and ambiguities, the Norwegians left. At that stage almost all of Sri Lanka, including most of the Jaffna peninsula, was controlled by the Sri Lankan government. The LTTE controlled a small area south of the Jaffna peninsula and pockets in the East, but it still had claims on land in the Jaffna peninsula and in the island's northwest and northeast.

After the Tsunami

An event beyond all predictions struck on 26 December 2004, affecting not only the peace process but also the entire social fabric of Sri Lanka. As people celebrated the monthly *poya* (full moon) festivities, the waves of a tsunami cast their fury, killing 30,000 people and leaving many more injured, homeless and orphaned. Initial optimism that the nation would come together in the face of catastrophe soon faded into arguments over aid distribution, reconstruction, and land tenure and ownership.

Meanwhile Kumaratunga, seeking to extend her presidential term, sought to alter the constitution. Thwarted by a Supreme Court ruling, presidential elections were set for 2005. Among the contenders, two candidates were the most likely victors – the then prime minister, Mahinda Rajapaksa, and opposition leader, Ranil Wickremasinghe. With an LTTE voting boycott, Rajapaksa narrowly won. The LTTE's motives for the boycott were unclear, but their actions cost Wickremasinghe an expected 180,000 votes and the presidency and, perhaps, a better chance at peace.

President Rajapaksa pledged to replace Norwegian peace negotiators with those from the UN and India, renegotiate a ceasefire with the LTTE, reject Tamil autonomy and refuse to share tsunami aid with the LTTE. Such policies didn't auger well for future peace. Meanwhile LTTE leader Prabhakaran insisted on a political settlement during 2006, and threatened to 'intensify' action if this didn't occur. Tensions were high, and again Sri Lanka was perched on a precipice. Killings, assaults, kidnappings and disappearances occurred on both sides, and commentators predicted the worst.

The End of the War

An Elusive Ceasefire

Another ceasefire was signed in early 2006, but cracks soon appeared and by mid-year the agreement was in tatters. Major military operations by both sides resumed in the north and east, and a wave of disappearances and killings in 2006 and 2007 prompted human-rights groups and the international community to strongly criticise all belligerents. By

The 2004 Indian Ocean tsunami killed more than 225,000 people in 14 countries. The waves, which were in some places more than 30m tall, travelled as far as the East African coast.

July 1987	1987	1987–89	1991
An accord is signed, with India's involvement, granting Tamils an autonomous province in the country's north, but disagreements over its implementation prevent it from going into effect.	Government forces push the LTTE back into Jaffna. An Indian Peace Keeping Force (IPKF) attempts to establish stability, but is also dragged into conflict with the LTTE.	The JVP launches a second Marxist insurrection, and attempt a Khmer Rouge–style peasant rebellion in the countryside. When the uprising is finally crushed, up to 60,000 people have died.	A Black Tiger (an LTTE fighter trained in suicide missions) kills former Indian Prime Minister Rajiv Gandhi, presumably to protest the IPKF, in the world's first female suicide bombing.

TAMIL
TIGER

Although its authorship and veracity have been disputed, *Tamil Tigress*, by Niromi de Soyza, tells the engrossing story of a former Tamil Tiger child soldier who left school at 17 to join the movement.

August the fighting in the northeast was the most intense since the 2002 ceasefire, and peace talks in Geneva failed again. The optimistic days of negotiation and ceasefire seemed more distant than ever.

In January 2008 the Sri Lankan government officially pulled out of the ceasefire agreement, signalling its dedication to ending the 25-year-old civil conflict by military means. Later in the year the LTTE offered a unilateral 10-day ceasefire in support of the South Asian Association for Regional Cooperation (SAARC) summit being held in August in Colombo. The government, suspicious that the LTTE planned to use the ceasefire as a time to shore up its strength, responded with an emphatic no.

Cornering the LTTE

A change in military strategy saw the Sri Lankan security forces fight fire with fire with an increase in guerrilla-style attacks, and by August the Sri Lankan Army (SLA) had entered the LTTE's final stronghold, the jungle area of the Vanni. The Sri Lankan government stated that the army was on track to capture the LTTE capital Kilinochchi by the end of 2008. Faced with a series of battleground defeats, the LTTE struck back with another suicide bomb in Anuradhapura, killing 27 people.

In September 2008 the Sri Lankan government ordered UN agencies and NGOs to leave the Vanni region, saying it could no longer guarantee their safety. This may have been true, but their withdrawal denied a beleaguered population of Tamils access to humanitarian support and the security of a human-rights watchdog. The departure of the NGOs and the barring of independent journalists from the conflict region made (and continues to make) it impossible to verify claims made by either side about the final battles of the war.

Government and LTTE forces remained dug in around Kilinochchi – the de facto capital of the unofficial Tamil Eelam state since 1990 – until the SLA declared victory there in January 2009. This was followed rapidly

A FLAG FOR COMPASSION

Sri Lanka's flag was created in 1948 and took on many changes over the years. The core element was the lion on a crimson background, which had been used on flags throughout Sri Lankan history, beginning with Prince Vijaya, who is believed to have brought a lion flag with him from India. The lion, then, represented the Sinhalese people, and the gold is said to signify Buddhism. The flag was adopted in 1950, and as Sri Lanka settled into independence, it evolved: in 1951 green and orange stripes were added to signify Sri Lanka's Muslims and Hindus, respectively, and in 1972 four bodhi-tree leaves were added to represent *metta* (loving-kindness), *karuna* (compassion), *upekkha* (equanimity) and *muditha* (happiness).

1994	1995–2001	2002	2004
President Chandrika Kumaratunga comes to power pledging to end the war with the LTTE. Peace talks are opened, but hostilities continue. In 1999 she survives a suicide-bomb attack.	Hostilities between the Sri Lanka military and the LTTE intensify; following more failed attempts at negotiation, the LTTE bombs Kandy's Temple of the Sacred Tooth Relic in 1998.	After two years of negotiation, a Norwegian peace mission secures a ceasefire. Sri Lankans, especially in the north and east, return to a new normal; many émigrés return.	A tsunami devastates coastal Sri Lanka, leaving 30,000 people dead. It's thought the disaster will bring unity, but the government and LTTE are soon wrangling over aid distribution and reconstruction.

by claims of control throughout the Vanni, and by February, the LTTE had lost 99% of the territory it had controlled just 12 months earlier.

Government advances pushed remaining LTTE forces and the 300,000 Tamil civilians they brought with them to an increasingly tiny area in the northeast near Mullaittivu. Amid growing claims of civilian casualties and humanitarian concerns for the noncombatants hemmed in by the fighting, foreign governments and the UN called for an immediate ceasefire in February 2009. Military operations continued, but escape routes were opened for those fleeing the fighting to move to no-fire zones, where there was to be further transport to welfare centres. The military, claiming that attacks were being launched from within the safe zones, then shelled them for days.

With claims that the SLA was bombing civilians in 'safe areas', and counter-claims that the LTTE was using Tamil civilians as human shields and stopping them from leaving the conflict zone, the UN High Commissioner for Human Rights Navi Pillay accused both sides of war crimes. But the international community remained largely quiet.

The Bitter End

By April, tens of thousands of Tamil civilians along with LTTE fighters were confined to a single stretch of beach, where they were bombarded from all sides. The LTTE offered the Sri Lankan government a unilateral ceasefire, but given that the Sri Lankan military's objectives were so close to being fulfilled, it was dismissed as 'a joke' by the Sri Lankan Defence Secretary. Other efforts by Swedish, French and British diplomats to inspire a truce were also dismissed by a Sri Lankan government with ultimate battleground success in its sights after three decades.

The government forces finally penetrated the LTTE and implored trapped war refugees to move to safe areas. The Tigers allegedly blocked many from leaving and killed others; refugees reported that government forces raped and executed many who surrendered.

The end finally came in May when the Sri Lankan military captured the last sliver of coast and surrounded the few hundred remaining LTTE fighters. The LTTE responded by announcing they had 'silenced their weapons' and that the 'battle had reached its bitter end'. Several senior LTTE figures were killed, including leader Vellupillai Prabhakaran, and the war that terrorised the country for 26 years was finally over.

In *Crucible of Conflict: Tamil and Muslim Society on the East Coast of Sri Lanka,* Dennis McGilvray argues that peace in Sri Lanka requires recognising the country's cultural diversity.

2005	2008	2008–2009	May 2009
Sinhalese nationalist Mahinda Rajapaksa wins presidential elections. Before the election Rajapaksa signs a deal with the Marxist JVP party, rejects Tamil autonomy outright and denies tsunami aid to the LTTE.	The government pulls out of the 2002 ceasefire agreement, signalling a single-minded focus on a military solution. From 1983 to 2008, an estimated 70,000 people have died in the conflict.	In the war's final months, up to 40,000 civilians are killed, according to a later report by a UN special panel. The Sri Lankan government denies any civilian deaths.	After almost 30 years, Asia's longest-running war ends in May when the LTTE concedes defeat after a bloody last battle at Mullaitivu. Legitimate Tamil aspirations and grievances remain.

Environmental Issues

At first glance Sri Lanka looks like a Garden of Eden. The country positively glows with greens and is filled with the noise of endlessly chirping, cheeping, buzzing, growling and trumpeting animals. Add to that the sheer diversity of landscapes and climatic zones and you get a place that appears to be a natural wonderland – and indeed it is. But it's one that is under serious threat thanks to a combination of deforestation, rapid development, pollution and human-wildlife conflict.

Largest Surviving Tracts of Rainforest

Sri Pada Peak Wilderness Reserve (224 sq km)

Knuckles Range (175 sq km)

Sinharaja Forest Reserve (189 sq km)

Pear-shaped Treasure

Looking a lot like a plump pear, the island country of Sri Lanka dangles into the Indian Ocean off the southern end of India. At roughly 66,000 sq km it's slightly smaller than Ireland, but sustains 4.5 times as many people. That's 22 million in a space stretching 433km from north to south and only 244km at its widest point – like the entire population of Australia taking up residence in Tasmania.

Thrust up out of the encircling coastal plains, the southern centre of the island – the core of the pear – is dominated by mountains and tea-plantation-covered hills. The highest point is broad-backed Mt Pidurutalagala (Mt Pedro; 2524m), rising above the Hill Country capital city of Nuwara Eliya. However, the pyramid profile of 2243m-high Adam's Peak (Sri Pada) is better known and far more spectacular.

Hundreds of waterways channel abundant rain from the south-central wet-zone uplands – haven of the country's surviving rainforests – down through terraced farms, orchards and gardens to the paddy-rich plains below. The Mahaweli Ganga, Sri Lanka's longest river, has its source close to Adam's Peak and runs 335km to Koddiyar Bay, the deep-sea harbour of Trincomalee.

North-central Sri Lanka is home to high, rolling hills, including some fantastically dramatic landscapes, such as the area around the Knuckles Range. These hills give way to plains that extend to the northern tip of the island. This region, portions of the southeast and most of the east comprise the dry zone.

Sri Lanka's coastline consists of hundreds of mangrove-fringed lagoons and marshes – some now protected wetlands – interspersed with fine white-sand beaches, the most picturesque of which are on the southwest, south and east coasts. A group of low, flat islands lies off the Jaffna peninsula in the north.

BIOLOGICAL HOTSPOT

Sri Lanka's superlatives extend to its natural world. Conservation International has identified Sri Lanka as one of the planet's 25 biodiversity hotspots, which means the island is characterised by a very high level of 'endemism' (species unique to the area). Sure enough, Sri Lanka tops the charts, with endemism in 23% of the flowering plants and 16% of the mammals. On the other hand, hotspots are targeted as habitats seriously at risk and that's very much the case with Sri Lanka.

In terms of animals, it's not just elephants – although they are awesome; Sri Lanka has a huge range of animals for such a small island. And where Africa has its famous 'Big Five' (lion, leopard, elephant, rhino and Cape buffalo), Sri Lanka has a 'Big Four' plus one (leopard, elephant, sloth bear and wild Asiatic water buffalo, plus the ginormous blue whale found offshore).

Plants

The southwestern wet zone is home to the country's surviving tropical rainforest, characterised by dense undergrowth and a tall canopy of hardwood trees, including ebony, teak and silkwood. The central hill zone has cloud forests and some rare highland areas populated by hardy grasslands and elfin (stunted) forests.

Other common trees are the banyan, bodhi (also known as bo or peepu), flame, rain, Ceylon ironwood and neem, an assortment of names as colourful as their barks, leaves and especially flowers. There are traditional medicinal uses for almost all of them. In the Hill Country don't be surprised by the eucalypts planted to provide shade at tea estates.

Native fruit trees such as mangoes, tamarinds, wood apples and bananas grow in many private gardens, supplemented by introduced species like papayas and guavas. The jackfruit and its smaller relative, the *del* (breadfruit), will certainly catch your eye. The jackfruit tree produces the world's largest fruit; green and knobbly skinned, it weighs up to 30kg and hangs close to the trunk.

> *What Tree Is That?*, by Sriyanie Miththapala and PA Miththapala, contains handy sketches of common trees and shrubs in Sri Lanka, and includes English, Sinhala and botanical names.

Sri Lanka's Elephants

Elephants occupy a special place in Sri Lankan culture. In ancient times they were Crown property and killing one was a terrible offence. Legend has it that elephants stamped down the foundations of the dagobas (stupas) at Anuradhapura, and elephant iconography is common in Sri Lankan art. Even today elephants are held in great affection. Of those in captivity, the Maligawa tusker, who carries the sacred tooth relic for the Kandy Esala Perahera, is perhaps the most venerated of all. In the wild, one of Sri Lanka's most incredible wildlife events is 'the Gathering' in Minneriya National Park.

Despite being held in high regard, Sri Lanka's elephant population has declined significantly. Their plight has become a powerful flashpoint in the ongoing debate about human–animal conflict.

Dwindling Numbers

At the end of the 18th century an estimated 10,000 to 20,000 elephants lived unfettered across Sri Lanka. By the mid-20th century small herds of the decimated population (perhaps as few as 1000) were clustered in the low-country dry zone. Natural selection had little to do with that cull: under the British, big-game hunting delivered a mighty blow to elephant life expectancy. Today experts disagree about whether numbers are increasing or diminishing, but the population is believed to be between 3000 and 4000 in the wild, half of which live on protected land, plus about 300 domesticated animals.

Human–Elephant Conflict

Farmers in elephant country face an ever-present threat from animals that may eat or trample their crops, destroy their buildings and even take their lives. During the cultivation season, farmers maintain round-the-clock vigils for up to three months to scare off unwelcome raiders. For farmers on the breadline, close encounters with wild elephants are a luxury they can't afford.

> **Save the Elephants**
>
> Don't feed them in the wild.
>
> Don't patronise places where they're in chains.
>
> Do visit them in national parks to support conservation.

ENDANGERED SPECIES

The International Union for Conservation of Nature's Red List of Threatened Species counts more than 60 species in Sri Lanka as either critically endangered or endangered. They include the Asian elephant, purple-faced langur, red slender loris and toque macaque. All five of Sri Lanka's marine turtle species are threatened, as are the estuarine crocodile and the mild-mannered dugong, all of which are killed for their meat. Also under threat are several species of birds, fish and insects.

Meanwhile, elephants, which need about 5 sq km of land each to support their 200kg-per-day appetites, no longer seem to have sufficient stock of food staples in the small wildlife safety zones where they are protected. Hunger (and perhaps curiosity) is driving them to seek fodder in other areas – manmade ones abutting their 'secure' habitats. The resulting conflict pits elephants against farmers – both just trying to secure their own survival.

Sri Lanka's Natural Unesco World Heritage Sites

Sinharaja Forest Reserve (p189)

Central Highlands, encompassing the Sri Pada Peak Wilderness Reserve (p163), Horton Plains National Park (p173) and Knuckles Range (p161)

Contributing to the vicious circle is unfortunate behaviour on both sides. Electric fences installed in the national parks to contain elephants have been knocked down by farmers seeking to graze their cattle illegally on park land. Elephants leave the parks through the compromised fences and bedevil the farmers. Also, as can be seen at Uda Walawe National Park, vendors have set up fruit stands where the park borders the highway, so that tourists can feed the elephants. An increasing number of elephants now hang out all day by the roadside waiting for their tasty handouts. The idea of actually foraging for their normal diet is soon forgotten.

Possible Solutions

Some people are looking for long-term solutions to the conflict. One involves fencing *humans in;* or, rather, fencing elephants out of human areas. This approach has been proven effective by the Sri Lanka Wildlife Conservation Society, an award-winning wildlife conservation group. Another is to give farmers alternative livelihood solutions and land practices that incorporate elephants. The collection and commercial use of elephant dung is one such possible enterprise (you can see the resulting products at the Cottage Craft shop in Colombo). Spreading around the economic benefits that come from scores of visitors coming to see elephants is another solution.

The sacred bodhi tree was brought from India when Mahinda introduced the teachings of the Buddha to Sri Lanka in the 3rd century BC. Most Buddhist temples have a bodhi tree, but the most famous is the Sri Maha Bodhi of Anuradhapura, the oldest historically authenticated tree in the world.

Deforestation & Overdevelopment

Arguably Sri Lanka's biggest environmental threat is from deforestation and over-development leading to serious habitat loss. At the beginning of the 20th century about 70% of the island was covered by natural forest. By 2005 this had shrunk to about 20%. Worse, in recent years Sri Lanka has had one of the highest recorded rates of primary-forest destruction in the world: an 18% reduction in forest cover and 35% loss of old-growth tracts. You only need to see the huge old-growth trees being cut up at the roadside lumber mills between Matale and Dambulla to understand that threats to the rainforest are ongoing.

Chena (shifting cultivation) is blamed for a good part of this deforestation, but irrigation schemes, clearance for cultivation and land 'development', armed conflict, and, obviously, illegal logging have all been contributing factors.

The boom in Sri Lanka's economy after peace is also bound to put even more pressure on the environment. With tourism increasing rapidly, new construction projects are proliferating. And the track record is not good: after the 2004 tsunami, laws were put in place that banned construction of hotels and restaurants within 100m of the high-tide line, yet at Unawatuna and many other coastal areas, new buildings were built virtually at the water's edge.

Responsible Travel in Sri Lanka

The best way to responsibly visit Sri Lanka is to try to be as unintrusive as possible. This is of course easier than it sounds, but consider the following tips.

➡ **Demand green** Sri Lanka's hotel and guesthouse owners are especially accommodating and as visitor numbers soar, most are keen to give the customers what they want. Share your environmental concerns and tell your hosts that their green practices – or lack thereof – are very important to you.

➡ **Watch your use of water** Travel in the Hill Country of Sri Lanka and you'll think the island is coursing with water, but demand outstrips supply. Take up your hotel on its offer to save itself big money, er, no, to save lots of water, by not having your sheets and towels changed every day. Also, stay at places without pools. If you want a dip, stay at the beach; tell your host that you appreciate there *not* being a pool.

➡ **Don't hit the bottle** Those bottles of water are convenient, but they add up and are a major blight. Still, you're wise not to refill from the tap, so what to do? Ask your hotel if you can refill from their huge containers of drinking water.

➡ **Conserve power** Sure you want to save your own energy on a sweltering afternoon, but using air-con strains an already overloaded system. Electricity demand in Sri Lanka is soaring. Try to save as much energy as possible and act as if you are paying your own electricity bill.

➡ **Don't drive yourself crazy** Can you take a bus or, even better, a train, instead of a hired car? Even Colombo is more walkable than you think, it's a very interesting stroll all the way from Cinnamon Gardens to Fort and it's better for the environment than a ride in an exhaust-spewing three-wheeler. And encourage the recent trend of hotels and guesthouses providing bikes for guests. Large swaths of Sri Lanka are best toured during the day on two wheels.

➡ **Bag the bags** Just say no to plastic bags (and plastic straws too). The clerk might look at you funny but you'll be doing your bit.

For information on environmental issues in Sri Lanka, see the following websites.

➡ **Environment Sri Lanka** (www.environmentlanka.com) The Department of Forestry & Environmental Science at the University of Sri Jayewardenepura has info on Sri Lankan wildlife and essays on key environmental issues.

➡ **Green Movement of Sri Lanka** (www.gmsl.lk) A consortium of 150 groups that are involved in natural-resource management. Among the projects highlighted are the ongoing reports of the environmental threats posed by Sri Lanka's massive road-building schemes.

➡ **Lakdasun** (www.lakdasun.org) Visit the helpful forums on this website to get up-to-date information from knowledgeable Sri Lankan locals on how to 'Discover, explore and conserve the natural beauty of Sri Lanka'.

➡ **Sri Lanka Wildlife Conservation Society** (SLWCS; www.slwcs.org) Recognised by the UN in 2008 for community-based projects that made a tangible impact on poverty, the SLWCS has opportunities for volunteering.

MULLAITIVU

ENVIRONMENTAL ISSUES RESPONSIBLE TRAVEL IN SRI LANKA

In 2010 the site of the Liberation Tigers of Tamil Eelam's last stand, Mullaitivu, in the far north-east, was turned from a former theatre of war into Sri Lanka's newest protected area: Mullaitivu National Park.

The Nature of Sri Lanka, with stunning photographs by L Nadaraja, is a collection of essays about Sri Lanka by eminent writers and conservationists.

People of Sri Lanka

Every day in Sri Lanka, families bring flowers to white-domed dagobas (stupas), women in bright saris walk to rainbow-coloured Hindu temples with offerings for their gods, and whitewashed mosques call the faithful to prayer in the cool dawn. Of course, the country has seen decades of war and violence, and tensions remain. But the traditions continue, and Sri Lankans somehow manage to find moments of peace, all the while greeting visitors with warmth and hospitality as they've done for millennia.

VEDDAH

Tradition & Ethnicity

Traditional Sri Lankan life was centred on the *gamma* (village), a highly organised hub of activity, where everyone fulfilled specific roles. Agriculture was the mainstay, and some villages focused on particular products – even today you might pass through a 'cane-furniture *gamma*'. Every village had a protector deity (or several), usually associated with aspects of nature.

Veddahs

The Veddahs (Hunters), or, as they refer to themselves, Wanniyala-aetto (People of the Forest), are Sri Lanka's original inhabitants. Each wave of migration to Sri Lanka left the Veddahs with less forest on which to subsist. Today they are so few in number that they don't even make the census, and only a tiny percentage of those retain a semblance of their old culture, which comprises a hunter-gatherer lifestyle and close relationships to nature and their ancestors. The Kele Weddo (jungle-dwelling Veddahs) and Can Weddo (village-dwelling Veddahs) live mainly in the area between Badulla, Batticaloa and Polonnaruwa.

To learn more about historical and contemporary Veddah life and customs, see www.vedda.org.

Sinhalese

The predominantly Buddhist Sinhalese sometimes divide themselves into 'low country' and 'high country' (ie Kandyan). The Kandyan Sinhalese are proud of the time when the Hill Country was a bastion of Sinhalese rule, and still consider Kandy to be the island's spiritual hub. Although the Buddha taught universalism, the Sinhalese have a caste system, with everyone falling somewhere along the spectrum between aristocrat and itinerant entertainer.

Tamils

Most Tamils are Hindu and have cultural and religious connections with South Indian Tamils across the water, though they generally see themselves as discrete groups. The same is true of Jaffna Tamils, who live mostly in the North and East, and 'Plantation Tamils', who were brought by the British from India in the 19th century to work on tea farms. For most Hindus, caste is very important. Jaffna Tamils are mainly of the Vellala caste (landlords and blue bloods), while Plantation Tamils mainly come from lower castes. Times are changing, however, and traditional caste distinctions among both Sinhalese and Tamils are gradually eroding.

Moors

The island's Muslims – called Sri Lankan Moors – are descendants of Arab or Indian traders who arrived around 1000 years ago. To escape Portuguese persecution, many moved into the Hill Country and the east coast, and you'll still see predominantly Muslim towns like Hakgala near Nuwara Eliya. Most Moors speak Tamil.

Burghers

The Burghers are descendants of the Portuguese, Dutch and British. Even after independence, Burghers had a disproportionate influence over political and business life, but when growing Sinhalese nationalism reduced their role, many Burghers emigrated. Look out for surnames such as Fernando, de Silva and Perera.

Multifaith Pilgrimages
Adam's Peak
Kataragama
Nainativu

PEOPLE OF SRI LANKA RELIGION

Religion

Religion has been the cause of much division in Sri Lanka, but the often-overlooked reality is that Sri Lanka's many religions mix openly. Buddhists, Hindus, Muslims and Christians visit many of the same pilgrimage sites, a Catholic may pay respect to a Hindu god, and Sri Lankan Buddhism has Hindu influences and vice versa.

Buddhism

Buddhism is the belief system of the Sinhalese and plays a significant role in the country, spiritually, culturally and politically. Sri Lanka's literature, art and architecture are all strongly influenced by it. Strictly speaking, Buddhism is not a religion but a practice and a moral code espoused by the Buddha. Although 'Buddhist' now is a deeply entrenched cultural and ethnic identifier, the Buddha taught meditation to people of various religions, and emphasised that no conversion was necessary (or even recommended) to benefit from his teachings, also known as the Dhamma.

Born Prince Siddhartha Gautama in modern-day Nepal around 563 BC, the Buddha abandoned his throne to seek a way out of suffering. After years of rigorous training, the Buddha discovered the Four Noble Truths: existence itself is suffering; suffering is caused by craving for sensual and material pleasures as well as existence itself; the way out of suffering is through eliminating craving; and craving can be eliminated by following a path of morality and the cultivation of wisdom through meditation. After many states of spiritual development – and, probably, many lifetimes – nirvana (enlightenment, or *nibbana* in Pali) is achieved, bringing freedom from the cycle of birth and death.

Historical Buddhism

King Devanampiya Tissa's acceptance of the Buddha's teaching in the 3rd century BC firmly implanted Buddhism in Sri Lanka, and a strong relationship developed between Sri Lanka's kings and the Buddhist clergy.

Worldwide there are two major schools of Buddhism: Theravada and Mahayana. Theravada ('way of the elders') scriptures are in Pali, one of the languages spoken in North India in the Buddha's time, while Mahayana ('greater vehicle') scriptures are in Sanskrit. Theravada is regarded as more orthodox, and Mahayana more inclusive of later traditions.

Mahayana Buddhism is practised in Sri Lanka, but the Theravada tradition is more widely adopted. Several factors have consolidated Buddhism, especially the Theravada stream, in Sri Lanka. Sinhalese Buddhists attach vital meaning to the words of the Mahavamsa (Great Chronicle; one of their sacred texts), in which the Buddha designates them protectors of the Buddhist teachings. This commitment was fuelled

BUDDHIST BELIEFS

In *Buddhism: Beliefs and Practices in Sri Lanka*, Lynn de Silva combines lucid writing, fascinating information and a scholarly (but accessible) approach to shed light on the island's Buddhist tradition.

by centuries of conflict between the Sinhalese (mainly Buddhist) and Tamils (mainly Hindu). For some Sinhalese, Mahayana Buddhism resembled Hinduism – and indeed was followed by many Tamils in early times – and therefore defence of the Theravada stream was considered crucial. Many Buddhist sites in India were destroyed in the 10th century AD, around the time of a Hindu resurgence (and a popular Hindu text that described the Buddha as a wayward incarnation of Vishnu), further reinforcing the Sinhalese commitment to protect the tradition.

In Hindu mythology elephants are seen as symbols of water, life and fortune. They also signify nobility and gentleness, the qualities achieved when one lives a good life. In Sri Lanka, only the elephant parades with sacred Buddhist relics and Hindu statues.

Buddhist Nationalism

Since the late 19th century an influential strand of 'militant' Buddhism has developed in Sri Lanka, centred on the belief that the Buddha charged the Sinhalese people with making the island a citadel of Buddhism in its purest form. It sees threats to Sinhalese Buddhist culture in Christianity, Hinduism and, more recently, Islam. Sri Lankan Buddhism is historically intertwined with politics, and it was a Buddhist monk who assassinated Prime Minister SWRD Bandaranaike's in 1959 because of his 'drift' from a Sinhala-Buddhist focus, in contradiction of the very first Buddhist precept against killing. Many Buddhist monks have also strongly opposed compromise with the Tamils.

In 2007, hardline Sinhalese-nationalist monks achieved leverage in the Sri Lankan government through the Jathika Hela Urumaya (JHU; National Heritage Party). In 2012, a group of monks who felt the JHU was not aggressive enough in protecting Buddhism, founded the Bodu Bala Sena (BBS; Buddhist Power Force), which has, along with other radical groups, been implicated in several protests and attacks against Muslim and Christian communities in recent years. At a 2013 opening for a BBS training school, Defense Secretary (and brother of the president) Gotabhaya Rajapaksa said in a speech that 'it is the monks who protect our country, religion and race'.

For more information on Hinduism, see www.bbc.co.uk/religion/religions/hinduism.

Hinduism

Tamil kings and their followers from South India brought Hinduism to northern Sri Lanka, although the religion may have existed on the island well before the arrival of Buddhism, as a result of the island's proximity to India and the natural cultural exchange that would have taken place. Today, Hindu communities are most concentrated in the north, the east and tea plantation areas.

POYA DAYS

Poya (or uposatha) days fall on each full moon and have been observed by monks and laypeople since the time of the Buddha as times to strengthen one's practice. Devout Buddhists visit a temple, fast after noon and abstain from entertainment and luxury. At their temple they may make offerings, attend teachings and meditate. Poya days are public holidays in Sri Lanka and each is associated with a particular ritual.

Durutu (January) Marks the Buddha's first supposed visit to the island.

Vesak (May) Celebrates the Buddha's birth, enlightenment and parinibbana (final passing away).

Poson (June) Commemorates Buddhism's arrival in Sri Lanka.

Esala (July/August) Sees the huge Kandy festival, which observes, among other things, the Buddha's first sermon.

Unduwap (December) Celebrates the visit of Sangamitta, who brought the bodhi tree sapling to Anuradhapura.

Hinduism is a complex mix of beliefs and gods. All Hindus believe in Brahman: the myriad deities are manifestations of this formless being, through which believers can understand all facets of life. Key tenets include belief in ahimsa (nonviolence), samsara (the cycle of births and deaths that recur until one reaches a pure state), karma (the law of cause and effect) and dharma (moral code of behaviour or social duty).

Hindus believe that living life according to dharma improves the chance of being born into better circumstances. Rebirth can also take animal form, but it's only as a human that one may gain sufficient self-knowledge to escape the cycle of reincarnation and achieve moksha (liberation).

For ordinary Hindus, fulfilling one's ritual and social duties is the main aim of worldly life. According to the Hindu text Bhagavad Gita, doing your duty is more important than asserting your individuality.

The Hindu pantheon is prolific: some estimates put the number of deities at 330 million. The main figures are Brahma, who created the universe, and his consort Saraswati, the goddess of wisdom and music; Vishnu, who sustains the universe and is lawful and devout, and his consort Lakshmi, the goddess of beauty and fortune; and Shiva, the destroyer of ignorance and evil, and his consort, Parvati, who can be the universal mother or the ferocious and destructive Kali. Shiva has 1008 names and takes many forms: as Nataraja, lord of the *tandava* (dance), his graceful movements begin the creation of the cosmos.

Islam

Sri Lanka is home to almost two million Muslims – descendants of Arab traders who settled on the island from the 7th century, not long after Islam was founded in present-day Saudi Arabia by the Prophet Mohammed. Islam is monotheistic, and avows that everything has been created by Allah.

After Mohammed's death the movement split into two main branches, the Sunnis and the Shiites. Sunnis emphasise following and imitating the words and acts of the Prophet. They look to tradition and the majority views of the community. Shiites believe that only imams (exemplary leaders) can reveal the meaning of the Quran. Most of Sri Lanka's Muslims are Sunnis, although small communities of Shiites have migrated from India.

All Muslims believe in the five pillars of Islam: the *shahada* (declaration of faith: 'there is no God but Allah; Mohammed is his prophet'); prayer (ideally five times a day); the *zakat* (tax, usually a donation to charity); fasting during the month of Ramadan; and the *hajj* (pilgrimage) to Mecca.

Christianity

Christianity in Sri Lanka potentially goes back to the Apostle Thomas in the 1st century AD, and it's certain that in the early centuries AD small numbers of Christians established settlements along the coast.

With the Portuguese in the 16th century, Christianity, specifically Roman Catholicism, arrived in force, and many fishing families converted. Today, Catholicism remains strong among western coastal communities. The Dutch brought Protestantism and the Dutch Reformed Church, mainly present in Colombo, while evidence of the British Christian denominations include stone churches that dot the Hill Country landscape.

Religious Hubs

Nallur Kandaswamy Kovil, Jaffna

Temple of the Sacred Tooth Relic, Kandy

Kechimalai Mosque, Beruwela

Our Lady of Madhu Church, Madhu

PEOPLE OF SRI LANKA RELIGION

NAMES

Want to understand more about people's names in Sri Lanka? It's all revealed at http://asiarecipe.com/srinames.html.

Sri Lankan Tea

Sri Lanka is the world's fourth-largest tea-producing nation. The Dutch may have come to the island for spices, but the country is now more associated with an imported plant – tea. Today, even the national cricket team's shirts bear sponsorship by Ceylon Tea.

Shaping the Nation

Tea came to Sri Lanka when extensive coffee plantations were decimated by disease in the 19th century. The first Sri Lankan tea was grown in 1867 at the Loolecondera Estate southeast of Kandy. Plantation owners discovered that the Hill Country combines a warm climate, altitude and sloping terrain: a winning trifecta that's perfect for growing tea.

Shipments of Ceylon tea began filling London warehouses in the 1870s. The public's thirst for a cuppa proved nearly unquenchable. Fortunes were made by the early growers, which included a name still famous worldwide today: Thomas Lipton. By the 1890s, Lipton's tea plantations were exporting around 30,000 tons of tea back to London.

Tea production continued to spiral upwards in the 20th century. Forests were cleared and plantations greatly expanded. A running war was fought with various pests and diseases that afflicted the crops, and all manner of chemicals were created to keep the tea plants healthy.

Today Sri Lanka is the world's fourth-biggest tea-producing nation, with an annual figure of 340 million kilos in 2013. Sri Lankan tea (branded internationally as 'Ceylon' tea) enjoys a premium positioning and its sale prices are well above those of rival nations. The annual value of the Sri Lankan tea crop is over US$1.5 billion.

Despite the British roots of the industry, most Ceylon tea today is exported to the Middle East and North Africa (53% of all exports in 2012), followed by Eastern Europe and Russia (24%).

Besides the various forms of ubiquitous black tea, in 2013 Sri Lanka produced 3.69 million kilos of green tea, which is known for its more pungent flavour, and white tea, which is among the most premium of teas and is often called 'silver tips'.

Quality

The many varieties of tea are graded by size (from cheap 'dust' through fannings and broken grades to 'leaf' tea) and by quality (with names such as flowery, pekoe or souchong). Obviously, tea sized as dust is rather inferior. Anything graded in the leaf category is considered the minimum designation for respectable tea. In terms of quality designations, whole leaves are best and the tips (the youngest and most delicate tea leaves) are the very top tier.

The familiar name pekoe is a superior grade of black tea. Interestingly, there is no definitive record of where the 'orange' in the popular orange pekoe moniker comes from. It definitely has nothing to do with flavour but rather is either an artefact of a designation used by early Dutch tea traders or a reference to the colour of the leaves when dried. Either way, orange pekoe is a very superior grade of Ceylon black tea.

PLANTATIONS

Tea plantations cover about 1900 sq km. This is primarily in the hill country and adjoining regions, especially in the south.

Altitude

Altitude is another vital indication of tea quality. Udawatte (high-grown tea) is considered the finest; it grows slowly but has a delicate, subtle flavour that makes it greatly sought after – Dimbula, Nuwara Eliya and Uva are three prime growing districts. Udawatte is grown above 1200m.

Medawatte (mid-grown tea) has floral and malty notes and a fullness of body but is less refined; Kandy is the main centre of production. It's picked at altitudes of 600m to 1200m, and occupies the middle ground in price and quality.

Yatawatte (low-grown tea) is stronger, higher in caffeine and more robust, but it's not considered as complex; it's found below 600m. The foothills inland of the coast are centres of low-grown production: Ratnapura and Galle are two important districts.

Cultivation

Tea bushes are typically planted a metre or so apart on contoured terraces to help irrigation and to prevent erosion. A tea bush is around 1m (3 ft) in height, and is regularly pruned to encourage new shoots, prevent flowering and fruit formation and maximise leaf production. Adequate rainfall is essential, as is fertilisation.

Tea leaves are plucked by hand every seven to 14 days, a task traditionally carried out by Tamil women in Sri Lanka. The pluckers have a daily target of between 20kg and 30kg (44 to 66 pounds). After plucking, the tea leaves are taken to a factory where they are left to wither (demoisturised by blowing air at a fixed temperature through them). You'll spot the huge factory buildings throughout tea-growing country. Many are more than 100 years old.

The partly dried leaves are then crushed, starting a fermentation process. The green leaves quickly turn a coppery brown as additional heat is applied. The art in tea production comes in knowing when to stop the fermentation, by 'firing' the tea at an even higher heat to produce the final, brown-black leaf that will be stable for a reasonable length of time. Finally the tea is separated and graded according to leaf size.

The workers who regulate the myriad variables to take a day's pickings and produce proper tea, which will demand the premium prices Sri Lankan tea producers count on, are high up the ladder on the plantations. There is a definite art to the process, which has been refined over decades.

It only takes 24 hours from the time tea is picked to process it and load it in bags for shipment.

All the island's teas are branded with a 'Lion Logo', which denotes that the tea was produced in Sri Lanka.

In a (probably unintentional) bit of honesty the nation's main tea producers funded a marketing arm in 1932: the Ceylon Tea Propaganda Board.

DRINKING BLACK TEA

Although black tea is usually forgiving, there are still right and wrong ways to prepare a cup. For maximum enjoyment, keep the following points in mind.

➡ Store tea in an airtight container, whether it is loose or in tea bags. It's prone to absorbing odours, which are especially harmful to some of the delicate blends or flavoured teas.

➡ Use fresh water and boil it (water that's been boiling for a while or which was previously boiled gives you a flat-tasting cup of tea).

➡ Too accustomed to tea bags? With loose tea, it's one teaspoon per average-sized cup plus one extra if you're making a pot.

➡ Let the tea brew. It takes three to five minutes for tea to fully release its flavour.

➡ Conversely, once the tea is brewed, toss the tea leaves, whether they were loose or in a tea bag. Tea leaves quickly get bitter once brewed.

➡ For milk tea, pour the milk into the cup and then add the tea: the flavours mix better.

Tea Workers

Sri Lanka's tea industry is responsible for more than one million jobs – about 5% of the entire population. At around US$4 per day, wages for tea pickers remain very low. Compulsory pension and funeral payments erode them further.

Most families live in seriously substandard housing, barracks-like buildings (known as 'lines') on the fringes of plantations. Few have running water or electricity, and wood and coal stoves used for cooking and heating cause respiratory diseases.

The vast majority of tea workers are Tamils. Originally the British tea barons intended to hire Sinhalese workers but the labour was unappealing to the locals, so the plantation owners looked to India. Huge numbers of Tamils were brought over. Today they remain one of the most marginalised groups in the nation. Most are landless, classified as 'Indian Tamils', and disadvantaged by linguistic and cultural differences (including a caste system).

After water, tea is the world's most popular drink. More tea is drunk every day than every other drink – including coffee, soft drinks and alcohol – put together.

Visiting Tea Plantations

A great introduction to the endless rolling green fields of the Hill Country's tea plantations is riding the train from Ella to Haputale. In just a few hours you'll see dozens of plantations and their emerald-green carpets of plants. Amid it all you'll see sari-clad pluckers toiling under the sun, busily meeting their quotas for the day.

Tea factories and plantations throughout the Hill Country provide tours to explain the process, usually using machinery and technology that are largely unchanged since the 19th century. Some of our favourite places to get up close and smell the tea include:

Ceylon Tea Museum (p149) Near Kandy. An informative early stop in your tea tour.

Labookellie Tea Factory (p166) A factory well positioned by the Nuwara Eliya road if you're in a hurry.

Hundungoda Tea Estate (p121) Near Koggala. Produces over 25 varieties of tea.

Pedro Tea Estate (p167) Near Nuwara Eliya. Has tours of the factory, which was originally built in 1885.

Dambatenne Tea Factory (p176) Near Haputale. Built by Sir Thomas Lipton in 1890 and offers full-on tours.

Activities

There are all manner of hikes, treks and rides through the Hill Country's tea regions. Here are three of our favourites.

➡ A 10km bicycle ride through tea plantations that begins in Nuwara Eliya.

➡ A 7km walk through tea plantations to the lookout Lipton's Seat near Haputale.

➡ A 4.5km walk through verdant hills to the lookout Little Adam's Peak near Ella.

In the Hill Country you can stay in a variety of colonial-era cottages that were used by tea-plantation managers. Located in beautiful settings, they are attractive and evocative places to sleep.

Buying Tea

Tea is inexpensive, easy to pack and much loved by almost everyone so it makes an excellent gift for others at home – or yourself. The tea factories and plantations in the Hill Country have a bewildering array of options on offer. There are also many good shops in Colombo.

Ceylon black tea is the best known and is famous for its citrusy taste. Green Ceylon is characteristically pungent, with a slightly nutty flavour. Ceylon Silver Tips tea is produced from very young buds that are silvery white, have a delicate flavour and command premium prices.

Survival Guide

Directory A–Z

Accommodation

Sri Lanka has all types of accommodation ranging from rooms in family homes to five-star resorts. With tourism booming, prices have been increasing rapidly. Wherever you stay be sure to bargain over the price as negotiation is common.

Rates are very seasonal, particularly at beach resorts. The prices quoted in this guide are typical high-season rates; look for good discounts in the low season. The high season is December to April on the west and south coasts, and April to September on the east coast.

Note that there are reports of a few hotels refusing to honor prepaid reservations made on sites such as agoda. com. They'll tell you that if you want to stay you'll need to pay rack rate (always inflated) and that you will then need to get your money back from the booking website. This is usually a scam. Bring printed confirmations and have the local contact number for the booking website. One call should sort things

out as the hotel won't want to be banned from the booking website.

Some midrange and top-end hotels quote room prices in US dollars or euros, but accept the current rupee equivalent. Note that a service charge of 10% will usually be added to the rate you're quoted. At many hotels an additional Value Added Tax (VAT) of 14.25% is added, which can make for a big surprise at check-out. Reviews in this guide include the addition of both service charge and VAT.

Types of Accommodation

Guesthouses and hotels provide the majority of places to sleep in Sri Lanka. In rural areas, almost every place is a guesthouse. The difference is that hotels will usually be larger and offer more services beyond a person minding the desk. Often guesthouses are family-run.

Almost every place to stay will serve meals. Note that it's easy to stumble upon places that are quite inferior, whether it's a guesthouse renting rooms by the hour

or top-end hotels that have ossified. There are almost always better choices nearby, so look around.

BUDGET

There are budget guesthouses and a few budget hotels across Sri Lanka; they vary widely in standards and price.

Expect the following amenities:

➡ fans in most rooms, air-con in only one or two (fans are fine in the Hill Country and right on the beach)

➡ maybe hot water

➡ private bathroom with shower and sit-down flush toilet

➡ wi-fi (in many cases)

➡ simple breakfast

➡ laissez-faire but cheery staff.

LUXURY RENTALS

Sri Lanka has some beautiful rental villas, old colonial mountain retreats and other luxurious and exclusive accommodation options. Three good places to start browsing:

➡ www.villasinsrilanka.com

➡ www.lankarealestate.com

➡ www.vrbo.com

MIDRANGE

Midrange guesthouses and hotels are the most common choices throughout Sri Lanka. Most provide a decent level of comfort, although some can be quite nice, with a range of services and views. Choices include well-run colonial-era hotels (that haven't turned far upmarket) and stylish places on or near a beach.

Expect the following amenities:

➡ maybe a balcony, porch or patio

➡ satellite TV

➡ small fridge

➡ air-con in most if not all rooms

➡ wi-fi (in most cases)

➡ maybe a pool.

TOP-END HOTELS

Top-end hotels range from small stylish boutique affairs in colonial mansions to lavish five-star resorts.

Expect the following amenities:

➡ good service

➡ usually enticing views – ocean, lush valleys and rice fields or private gardens

➡ usually a pool

➡ spa.

Villa rentals are taking off in beachy areas, especially along the south coast. Specialty accommodation includes the former homes of British tea-estate managers in the Hill Country, which have been converted into guesthouses or hotels, often with beautiful gardens and antique-stuffed living rooms.

Customs Regulations

Sri Lanka has the usual list of prohibited imports, including drugs, weapons, fresh fruit and anything remotely pornographic.

Items allowed:

◆ 0.25L of perfume

◆ 1.5L of alcohol.

There are duty-free shops in the arrivals area before you reach baggage claim at the airport. Besides booze they include appliances such as blenders and refrigerators.

For more details, see **Sri Lanka Customs** (www.customs.gov.lk).

Discount Cards

An International Student ID Card is not widely recognised in Sri Lanka.

Electricity

The electric current is 230V, 50 cycles. Plugs come in a bewildering range of variations. Besides the primary plug type shown here, you may well find US, EU and British-style plugs in your room.

Adaptors are readily available at markets, supermarkets and tourist shops for under Rs 500.

230V/50Hz

Embassies & Consulates

It's important to realise the limits of what your embassy can do if you're in trouble. Generally speaking, their hands are tied if you've broken Sri Lankan law. In real emergencies you might get some assistance, but only if all other channels have been exhausted. Embassies can recommend hospitals, doctors and dentists.

Unless indicated, the following embassies are in Colombo:

Australian High Commission (Map p64; ☎011-246 3200; www.srilanka.embassy.gov.au; 21 RG Senanayake Mawatha/Gregory's Rd, Col 7)

Canadian High Commission (Map p64; ☎011-532 6232; www.srilanka.gc.ca; 33-A 5th Lane, Col 3)

French Embassy (Map p64; ☎011-263 9400; www.ambafrance-lk.org; 89 Rosmead Pl, Col 7)

German Embassy (Map p64; ☎011-258 0431; www.colombo.diplo.de; 40 Alfred House Ave, Col 3)

Indian High Commission
(Map p64; 011-232 7587; www.hcicolombo.org; 36-38 Galle Rd, Col 3)

India Visas (011-255 9435; www.ivsvisalanka.com) Indian visas are issued by an independent contractor with offices in Colombo, Kandy and Jaffna. Check the website for details and to download forms in advance.

Maldivian High Commission (Map p68; 011-258 7827; www.maldiveshighcom.lk; 25 Melbourne Ave, Col 4)

Netherlands Embassy (Map p64; 011-251 0200; srilanka.nlambassade.org; 25 Torrington Ave, Col 7)

UK High Commission (British High Commission; Map p64; 011-539 0639; ukin srilanka.fco.gov.uk; 389 Bauddhaloka Mawatha, Col 7)

US Embassy (Map p64; 011-249 8500; srilanka. usembassy.gov; 210 Galle Rd, Col 3)

EATING PRICE RANGES

The following price ranges refer to a standard main course.

$ less than Rs 450

$$ Rs 450 to 1200

$$$ more than Rs 1200

Food

See Eat and Drink Like a Local (p34) for information about Sri Lankan food.

Gay & Lesbian Travellers

Same-sex sexual activity is illegal in Sri Lanka and the subject is rarely discussed publicly. No one has been convicted for more than 60 years, but it pays to be discreet. There is no legislation to protect LGBT people from harassment.

The situation is changing, and Colombo has a low-key scene. You can be more open in cosmopolitan areas such as Col 1, Col 3 and Col 7.

Equal Ground (011-567 9766; www.equal-ground.org), a Colombo-based organisation supporting gay and lesbian rights, sponsors pride events, offers counselling services and has useful online resources.

Health

While the potential dangers of Sri Lankan travel may seem worrisome, most travellers experience nothing more serious than an upset stomach. Travellers tend to worry about contracting infectious diseases, but infections rarely cause *serious* illness or death in travellers. Note that hygiene standards are casual at best and downright bad at worst in many kitchens throughout the country.

Availability & Cost of Health Care

Medical care is hugely variable in Sri Lanka. Colombo has some good clinics aimed at expats; they're worth using over options aimed at locals because a superior standard of care is offered. Embassies and consulates often have lists of recommended medical providers.

Self-treatment may be appropriate if your problem is minor (eg traveller's diarrhoea). If you think you may have a serious disease, especially malaria, do not waste time: travel to the nearest quality facility to receive attention. It is always better to be assessed by a doctor than to rely on self-treatment.

Before buying medication over the counter, always check the use-by date and ensure the packet is sealed. Colombo and larger towns all have good pharmacies; most medications can be purchased without a prescription.

Health Insurance

Even if you're fit and healthy, don't travel without health insurance: accidents do happen. A travel or health insurance policy is essential. You may require extra cover for adventure activities, such as scuba diving. If your normal health insurance doesn't cover you for medical expenses abroad, get extra insurance. If you're uninsured, emergency evacuation is expensive, and bills of more than US$100,000 are not uncommon.

Vaccinations

Specialised travel-medicine clinics stock all available vaccines and can give specific recommendations for your trip. The doctors will consider factors including your vaccination history, your trip's duration, activities you may be undertaking and underlying medical conditions such as pregnancy.

REQUIRED VACCINATIONS

The only vaccine required by international regulations is yellow fever. Proof of vaccination will only be required if you have visited a country in the yellow-fever zone within the six days before entering Sri Lanka.

RECOMMENDED VACCINATIONS

The US Centers for Disease Control (CDC) recommends travellers consider the following vaccinations for travellers to Sri Lanka (as well as being up to date with measles, mumps and rubella vaccinations).

Adult diphtheria and tetanus Single booster recommended if none in the previous 10 years.

Hepatitis A Provides almost 100% protection for up to a year.

Hepatitis B Now considered routine for most travellers.

Japanese Encephalitis Recommended for rural travel, people who will be doing outdoor activities, or anyone staying longer than 30 days.

Polio Incidence has been unreported in Sri Lanka for several years but must be assumed to be present.

Rabies Three injections in all. A booster after one year will then provide 10 years' protection.

Typhoid Recommended for all travellers to Sri Lanka, even if you only visit urban areas.

Varicella If you haven't had chickenpox, discuss this vaccination with your doctor.

Water

Tap water is not safe to drink. Use bottled or filtered water; for the former, look for the small round 'SLSI'

AYURVEDA

Ayurveda (eye-your-veda) is an ancient system of medicine using herbs, oils, metals and animal products to heal and rejuvenate. Influenced by the system of the same name in India, Ayurveda is widely used in Sri Lanka for a range of ailments.

Ayurveda postulates that the five elements (earth, air, ether, water and light) are linked to the five senses, which in turn shape the nature of an individual's constitution – his or her *dosha* (life force). Disease and illness occurs when the *dosha* is out of balance. The purpose of Ayurvedic treatment is to restore the balance.

For full-on therapeutic treatments, patients must be prepared to make a commitment of weeks or months. It's a gruelling regimen featuring frequent enemas and a bare minimum diet of simple vegetable-derived calories.

Much more commonly, tourists treat themselves at Ayurvedic massage centres attached to major hotels and in popular tourist centres. Full treatments take up to three hours and include the following relaxing regimens.

➡ Herbal saunas (Sweda Karma) are based on a 2500-year-old design. The plaster walls are infused with herbal ingredients, including honey and sandalwood powder. The floor of the sauna is covered with herbs. Like a European sauna, a steady mist of medicinal steam is maintained with water sprinkled onto hot coals.

➡ The steam bath (Vashpa Swedanam) looks like a cross between a coffin and a torture chamber. Patients lie stretched out on a wooden platform, and a giant hinged door covers the body with only the head exposed. From the base of the wooden steam bath, up to 50 different herbs and spices infuse the body.

➡ The so-called Third Eye of the Lord Shiva treatment (Shiro Dhara) is the highlight for many patients. For up to 45 minutes, a delicate flow of warm oil is poured slowly onto the forehead and then smoothed gently into the temples by the masseuse.

While there are numerous spas with good international reputations, the standards at some Ayurvedic centres are low. The massage oils may be simple coconut oil and the practitioners may be unqualified, except in some instances where they may even be sex workers. As poisoning cases have resulted from herbal treatments being misadministered, it pays to enquire precisely what the medicine contains and then consult with a conventional physician.

For massage, enquire whether there are both male and female therapists available; we've received complaints from female readers about sexual advances from some male Ayurvedic practitioners. In general it's not acceptable Ayurvedic practice for males to massage females and vice versa.

logo, which shows the water has been tested by the government's Sri Lanka Standards Institution (the majority of local brands).

Insurance

Unless you are definitely sure that your health coverage at home will cover you in Sri Lanka, you should take out travel insurance – bring a copy of the policy as evidence that you're covered.

Worldwide travel insurance is available at www.lonelyplanet.com/travel-insurance. You can buy, extend and claim online anytime – even if you're already on the road.

Internet Access

Internet facilities are available across Sri Lanka. In the smallest of towns, look around the bus stand. Access costs Rs 100 to Rs 150 per hour.

Wi-fi in guesthouses and hotels is common in Colombo and touristed areas of the coasts and inland areas. It's often free, except at some top-end places, which can charge excessive rates. Connection speeds are acceptable – but don't expect to stream a film. Also, reception in rooms may not work.

Legal Matters

Sri Lanka's legal system is a complex, almost arcane mix of British, Roman-Dutch and national law. The legal system tends to move slowly, and even a visit to a police station to report a small theft can involve a whole lot of time-consuming filling out of forms. The tourist police in major towns and tourist hotspots should be your first point of contact in the case of minor matters such as theft.

Drug use, mainly locally grown marijuana, but also imported heroin and meth-amphetamine, occurs in tourist centres such as Hikkaduwa, Negombo and Unawatuna. Dabbling is perilous; you can expect to end up in jail if you're caught using anything illegal.

Maps

Digital maps, online and in apps by Apple, Bing and Google, are usually up to date.

Money

The Sri Lankan currency is the rupee (Rs), divided into 100 cents; pricing in cents is rare. Rupee coins come in denominations of one, two, five and 10 rupees. Notes come in denominations of 10, 20, 50, 100, 200, 500, 1000, 2000 and 5000 rupees.

ATMs

ATMs are easily found in towns and cities of any size. ATMs often issue Rs 5000 notes. Try and break a few as soon as possible as small vendors may not accept large notes: you can usually do this inside the bank that operates the ATM.

Cash

Any bank or exchange bureau will change major currencies in cash, including US dollars, euros and British pounds. Change rupees back into hard currency at the airport (before security, there are no exchange counters after) prior to leaving, as even nearby countries may not exchange Sri Lankan currency.

Credit Cards

MasterCard and Visa are the most commonly accepted credit cards. Cards are generally accepted at some midrange and most top-end hotels and restaurants.

Moneychangers

Moneychangers can be found in Colombo and major tourist centres. Their rates are competitive but choose carefully, as money-exchange scams abound. Stick to banks or reputable offices, such as those at the airport. ATMs are safer and more reliable.

Tipping

Although a 10% service charge is added to food and accommodation bills, this usually goes straight to the owner rather than the worker.

➡ **Restaurants and bars** Up to 10% in cash to servers beyond the 'service charge'

➡ **Drivers** 10% of total fee

➡ **Room cleaners** Up to Rs 100 per day

➡ **Bag carriers/porters** Rs 50 per bag

➡ **Shoe minders at temples** Rs 20

➡ **Guides** Varies greatly; agree to a fee in parks and religious sites *before* you set out

Opening Hours

Generally you'll find the following opening hours in Sri Lanka, although variations exist. Outside of tourist areas much is closed on Sunday.

Banks 8am to 3pm Monday to Friday

Bars Usually close by midnight, last call is often a sobering 11pm.

Government and private offices, post offices 8am to 4.30pm Monday to Friday (but they are not standardised)

Restaurants and cafes 7am to 9pm daily, later in areas popular with travellers

Shops 10am to 7pm Monday to Friday, 10am to 3pm Saturday

Shops and services catering to visitors 9am to 8pm

PRACTICALITIES

➡ Sri Lanka has several daily newspapers in English; they can be entertaining reads, whether intentionally so or not. Try a few to find your favourite.

➡ Sri Lankan government-run stations dominate the radio and TV broadcast channels. Midrange and more expensive hotels usually have satellite TV with international networks.

➡ Sri Lanka uses the international metric system, though some Sri Lankans still express distance in yards and miles. The term *lakh* is often used in place of '100,000'.

➡ Smoking is not common in Sri Lanka. Smoking is outlawed on buses, trains and public places. Bars and restaurants are legally required to have separate smoking and nonsmoking sections, although these often merge.

➡ Alcohol is not sold on *poya* (full moon) days; this includes hotel bars.

Photography

➡ Most Sri Lankans love getting their picture taken, but it's common courtesy to ask permission. A few business-oriented folk, such as the stilt fishermen at Koggala or the mahouts at the Pinnewala Elephant Orphanage, will ask for payment.

➡ It's forbidden to film or photograph dams, airports, road blocks or anything associated with the military.

➡ Never pose beside or in front of a statue of the Buddha (ie with your back to it) as this is considered extremely disrespectful.

➡ Flash photography can damage age-old frescoes and murals, so respect the restrictions at places such as Dambulla and Sigiriya.

Public Holidays

With four major religions, Sri Lanka has a lot of public holidays; also, all *poya* days are public holidays and much is closed.

New Year's Day 1 January

Tamil Thai Pongal Day 14 January, Hindu harvest festival

Independence Day 4 February

Good Friday March/April

Sinhala and Tamil New Year 14 April

Labour Day 1 May

Id-Ul-Fitr July, end of Ramadan

Christmas Day 25 December

Safe Travel

Sri Lanka is open for travel, though you can check the security situation in advance at government websites. Parts of the North may remain sensitive for some time, so you may still encounter a few road blocks and security zones.

Sri Lanka does not present any extraordinary concerns about safe travel, although women will want to read about certain concerns.

Telephone

Sri Lanka country code	☑94
International access code	☑00

Mobile Phones

Mobile coverage across Sri Lanka is good in built-up areas and cheap. You can get a SIM card that has data and voice credit for as low as Rs 1500.

The main mobile companies have booths in the arrivals area of Bandaranaike International Airport; compare prices as there are wide variations in rates. Major providers include the following:

Dialog (www.dialog.lk)

Hutch (www.hutch.lk)

Mobitel (www.mobitel.lk)

Phone Codes

All regions have a three-digit area code followed by a six- or seven-digit number. Mobile numbers usually begin with ☑07 or ☑08 and have up to 12 digits.

Time

Sri Lanka's time, being 30 minutes off the top of the hour used in much of the world, bedevils many a traveller. Sri Lanka is 5½ hours ahead of Greenwich Mean Time (the same as India), 4½ hours behind Australian Eastern Standard Time and 10½ hours ahead of American Eastern Standard Time.

Toilets

All top-end and midrange accommodation will have sit-down flush toilets. Only budget places that don't get a lot of tourists will have squat toilets and lack toilet

SHOPPING

Sri Lanka has a wide variety of attractive handicrafts on sale. Markets in major towns are good places to start. Top-quality vanilla beans, for example, are sold very cheaply.

Colombo offers a great and growing range of places to shop. Elsewhere, interesting shops and boutiques can be found in tourist areas, especially Galle. Laksala, a government-run store found in most cities and tourist towns, has items of reasonable quality.

Bargaining

Unless you are shopping at a fixed-price shop, you must bargain. Before you hit the open markets, peruse the prices in a fixed-price shop for an idea of what to pay. Generally, if someone quotes you a price, halve it. The seller will come down about halfway to your price, and the last price will be a little higher than half the original price. Try and keep a sense of perspective. Chances are you're arguing over less than US$1.

Batik

Originally introduced by the Dutch in colonial times, the Indonesian art of batik is very popular in Sri Lanka. Some of the best and most original batik is made in the west-coast towns of Marawila, Mahawewa and Ambalangoda, and there are also several worthwhile outlets in Kandy.

Gems

You'll find showrooms and private dealers all across Sri Lanka. In Ratnapura, the centre of the gem trade, it seems that everybody is a part-time gem dealer. Your challenge is the same here as elsewhere in the world: make sure what you're being offered is not worthless glass. The best way to avoid the myriad gem scams is to avoid buying any.

Masks

Sri Lankan masks are a popular collector's item. They're carved at a number of places, principally along the southwest coast. Look for shops from Galle and to the East.

Spices

Spices are integral to Sri Lanka's cuisine and Ayurvedic traditions. A visit to a spice garden is an excellent way to discover the alternative uses of familiar spices.

paper. Public toilets are scarce (and are grim when they exist); use restaurants, hotels and attractions such as tea-plantation visitor centres.

Tourist Information

The Colombo main office of the **Sri Lanka Tourist Board** (SLTB; Map p64; ☑243 7059; www.srilanka.travel; 80 Galle Rd, Col 3; ◷9am-4.45pm Mon-Fri, to 12.30pm Sat) has useful glossy brochures and staff can help with hotel bookings.

Travellers with Disabilities

Sri Lanka is a challenge for travellers with disabilities, but the ever-obliging Sri Lankans are always ready to assist. If you have restricted mobility, you may find it difficult, if not impossible, to get around on public transport. Buses and trains don't have facilities for wheelchairs. Moving around towns and cities can also be difficult for those in a wheelchair and for the visually impaired because of the continual roadworks and often-poor quality roads; don't expect many smooth footpaths. The chaotic nature of Sri Lankan traffic is also a potentially dangerous challenge. A car and driver is your best transport option. If possible, travel with a strong, able-bodied person.

Apart from some top-end hotels, accommodation is not geared for wheelchairs. However, many places can provide disabled travellers with rooms and bathrooms that are accessible without stairs.

Visas

You can now obtain your tourist visa for Sri Lanka in advance via the web.

Obtaining a Visa

Before visiting Sri Lanka, do the following to get a 30-day visa:

➡ Visit the **Sri Lanka ETA** (Electronic Travel Authorization; www.eta.gov.lk) website several days before arriving.

➡ Follow the online application process and pay with a credit or debit card.

➡ Once approved, print out the visa confirmation.

You can still obtain visas at Sri Lankan embassies abroad and there is a counter at Bandaranaike International Airport for people who arrive without a visa, although you'll have to wait with the other visa-less masses and pay a small penalty.

Visa Fees

The visa fees are as follows:

➡ Transit visas good for 48 hours are free

➡ Standard 30-day tourist visas cost US$30

Visa Extensions

You can renew a 30-day tourist visa twice, for 30 days each time. Contact the **Department of Immigration and Emigration** (☏011-237 5972; www.immigration.gov.lk). Extensions are not hard to get but require jumping through some bureaucratic hoops and downloading some forms.

Volunteering

Following the tsunami in 2004, Sri Lanka became a focus for many volunteer efforts and organisations. Many volunteer opportunities continue.

International Volunteer HQ (IVHQ; www.volunteerhq. org) Organises a wide-range of volunteer experiences, including teaching, medical care and temple renovation.

Millenium Elephant Foundation (www.millennium elephantfoundation.com) Located near Pinnewala, the group cares for elephants rescued from abusive situations. Volunteers assist with animal care.

Sewalanka Foundation (www.sewalanka.org) Uses short-term volunteers with business development and agricultural expertise.

Volunteer Sri Lanka (www. volunteersrilanka.net) Has short-term volunteer positions, especially for teachers.

Women Travellers

Women travelling alone may experience uncomfortable levels of male attention. Outside of Colombo, it is a good idea to cover your legs and shoulders, though you'll be stared at no matter what you wear. Tight tops are a bad idea. And away from the tourist beaches of the South and West, consider swimming in a T-shirt and shorts.

In Colombo and popular tourist areas you can relax the dress code. 'Are you married?' could be the snappy conversation starter you hear most often, so consider wearing a fake wedding ring and carrying a few pics of your imaginary partner back home.

Women travelling alone may be hassled while walking around day and night, or while exploring isolated places. Physical harassment (grabbing and groping) can occur anywhere. Single women may be followed, so try to be connected with larger groups of people. There have also been cases of solo women being attacked by guides at heritage sites; again, don't go alone.

However, travelling in Sri Lanka is not one long hassle. Unpleasant incidents are the exception, not the rule. But remember there are many social environments that are almost exclusively male in character – local bars, for example.

Stock up on tampons as they can be very hard to find.

Bus & Train Travel

Women travelling solo will find buses and trains trying at times. In Colombo ordinary buses are so packed that sometimes it's impossible to avoid bodily contact with other passengers. Stray hands on crowded buses and trains happen; this is something that local women are also subjected to. Change your seat or sit with a local woman. If you gesture to a local woman to sit next to you, she'll understand.

Women travelling solo should avoid night trains.

Transport

GETTING THERE & AWAY

Air service to Sri Lanka is increasing right along with tourism numbers.

Flights, tours and rail tickets can be booked online at lonelyplanet.com/bookings.

Entering the Country

Immigration at Bandaranaike International Airport is straightforward.

Passport

You must have your passport with you at all times in Sri Lanka. Before leaving home, check that it will be valid for at least six months after you plan to return home.

Air

Airports & Airlines

Sri Lanka's primary international airport is **Bandaranaike International Airport** (CMB; www.airport.lk) at Katunayake, 30km north of Colombo. There are 24-hour moneychanging facilities in the arrivals and departures halls as well as ATMs, mobile phone dealers and more.

Arriving is fairly hassle-free as touts are mostly kept away. Transit passengers and those checking in early should note, however, that the terminals remain quite spartan in terms of amenities.

Major airlines serving Sri Lanka include the following:

Air Asia (www.airasia.com)

British Airways (www.britishairways.com)

Cathay Pacific (www.cathaypacific.com)

Emirates (www.emirates.com)

Etihad (www.etihadairways.com)

Indian Airlines (www.indian-airlines.nic.in)

Malaysia Airlines (www.malaysia-airlines.com)

Qatar Airways (www.qatarairways.com)

Singapore Airlines (www.singaporeair.com)

SriLankan Airlines (www.srilankan.aero)

Thai Airways (www.thaiairways.com)

Turkish Airlines (www.turkishairlines.com)

Tickets

ASIA

Sri Lanka is well served by major Asian carriers, including Malaysian budget favourite Air Asia. Service from India is competitive between several carriers. Many visitors combine a visit to Sri Lanka with the Maldives. SriLankan Airlines and Emirates fly between Colombo and Malé.

AUSTRALIA & NEW ZEALAND

Connections are on Asian carriers such as Singapore Airlines and Thai Airways. Using Emirates requires major backtracking.

EUROPE

SriLankan Airlines links Colombo nonstop with major European airports. Connecting through on a carrier such as British Airways, Emirates, Etihad Airways, Qatar Airways and Turkish Airlines is common.

NORTH AMERICA

You're literally going halfway around the world from Canada and the USA; from the west coast connect through Asia, from the east coast connect through the Middle East or India.

MATTALA RAJAPAKSA INTERNATIONAL AIRPORT

Opened in 2013, **Mattala Rajapaksa International Airport** is 15km north of Hambantota near the south coast. Although it can handle the largest jets, it has yet to attract many flights – but it has attracted criticism.

CLIMATE CHANGE & TRAVEL

Every form of transport that relies on carbon-based fuel generates CO_2, the main cause of human-induced climate change. Modern travel is dependent on aeroplanes, which might use less fuel per kilometre per person than most cars but travel much greater distances. The altitude at which aircraft emit gases (including CO_2) and particles also contributes to their climate change impact. Many websites offer 'carbon calculators' that allow people to estimate the carbon emissions generated by their journey and, for those who wish to do so, to offset the impact of the greenhouse gases emitted with contributions to portfolios of climate-friendly initiatives throughout the world. Lonely Planet offsets the carbon footprint of all staff and author travel.

Sea

Plans to resume ferry services between Mannar in northwest Sri Lanka and India have been rumoured for many years, but have yet to materialise. A service linking Colombo and Tuticorin (Tamil Nadu) in India lasted only a few months.

GETTING AROUND

Domestic flights in Sri Lanka are quite limited, distances are not vast and new expressways are shrinking travel times.

Travelling on public transport is mostly a choice between buses and trains: both are cheap. Trains can be crowded, but it's nothing compared with the seemingly endless numbers of passengers that squash into ordinary buses. Even standing on a train is better than standing on a bus.

On the main roads from Colombo to Kandy, Negombo and Galle, buses cover around 40km to 50km per hour. On highways across the plains, it can be 60km or 70km an hour. In the Hill Country, it can slow to just 20km an hour.

All public transport gets crowded around *poya* (full moon) holidays and their nearest weekends, so try to avoid travelling then.

Air

Options for flying within Sri Lanka are limited. Connecting air service at Bandaranaike International Airport is provided by **Cinnamon Air** (☑011-247 5475; www.cinnamonair.com), which caters to well-heeled travellers. Destinations include Batticaloa, Dickwella, Sigiriya and Trincomalee. Service is on small planes, some using floats.

Very limited domestic service operates at times from Ratmalana Air Force Base, 15km south of Fort. Flights to Jaffna are operated by **Fits Air** (☑011-255 5156; www.fitsair.com).

Bicycle

Cycling around historic areas such as Anuradhapura and Sigiriya are the best and most enjoyable ways to see these important sites. More and more hotels and guesthouses have bicycles guests can hire (rent).

Hire

➡ Simple, cheap mountain bikes make up much of the rentals you'll find in guesthouses and hotels. Rates average about Rs 500 per day.

➡ If your accommodation doesn't hire bikes, they can usually hook you up with someone who does. Many places rent bikes to nonguests.

➡ Bikes available for day use typically are not suitable for long-distance riding. Bike-rental shops offering quality long-distance machines are rare. Consider bringing your bike from home if you plan on serious cycle touring.

Bike Tours

Tour and outfitting companies organise cycling tours of Sri Lanka and may also help you get organised for independent travel.

Action Lanka (www.actionlanka.com)

Eco Team (www.srilankaecotourism.com)

SpiceRoads Cycling Tours (www.spiceroads.com)

Long-Distance

➡ Keen long-distance cyclists will enjoy Sri Lanka, apart from the steeper areas of the Hill Country and the busy roads exiting Colombo. When heading out of Colombo in any direction, take a train to the edge of the city before you start cycling.

➡ Start early in the day to avoid the heat, and pack water and sunscreen. Your daily distances will be limited by the roads; be prepared for lots of prudent 'eyes down' cycling as you negotiate a flurry of obstacles from potholes to chickens. Remember, too, that speeding buses, trucks and cars use all parts of the roadway and shoulder, so be very cautious and wear very visible clothing.

➡ If you bring your own bicycle, also pack a supply of spare tyres and tubes. These suffer from the poor road surfaces, and replacement parts can be hard to obtain. The normal bicycle tyre size in Sri Lanka is 28in by 1.5in. Some imported 27in tyres for 10-speed bikes are available, but only in Colombo.

➡ Keep an eye on your bicycle at all times and use a good lock.

➡ When taking a bicycle on a train, forms must be filled out, so deliver the bicycle at least half an hour before departure. At Colombo Fort train station you may want to allow up to two hours. It costs about twice the 2nd-class fare to take a bicycle on a train.

Purchase

Expect to pay US$125 to US$500 for a new bike, depending on the quality. Most are made in India or China. There are bike shops (rentals not available) along Dam St in the Pettah market area of Colombo. Also try:

Lumala (www.lumala.lk)

Bus

Bus routes cover about 80% of the nation's 90,000km of roads. There are two kinds of bus in Sri Lanka:

Central Transport Board (CTB) buses These are the default buses and usually lack air-con; they ply most long-distance and local routes. You'll also see buses with a Sri Lanka Transport Board (SLTB) logo.

Private buses Independent bus companies have vehicles ranging from late-model Japanese coaches used on intercity-express runs to ancient minibuses on short runs between towns and villages. Private air-con intercity buses cover some major routes. For long-distance travel they are more comfortable and faster than other bus services. Note that completion of the Southern Expressway

has sparked the introduction of express services in fully modern air-con coaches between Colombo's suburbs and Galle.

General Tips

Bus travel in Sri Lanka can be interesting and entertaining. Most locals speak at least some English, so you may have some enjoyable interactions. Vendors board to sell snacks, books and gifts on long-distance routes.

Important considerations for bus travel:

➡ Major routes will have service several times an hour during daylight hours.

➡ Finding the right bus at the chaotic bus stations of major cities and towns can be challenging, although almost all buses now have part of their destination sign in English.

➡ There is usually no central ticket office; you must locate the right parking area and buy your bus ticket either from a small booth or on board the bus.

➡ You may be able to reserve a seat on a bus in advance; check at the station.

➡ 'Semi-comfortable' (or 'semi-luxe') buses are run by private companies and have larger seats and window curtains compared to CTB buses, but lack the air-con of the best intercity buses.

➡ Most people at bus stations and on buses will help you with your questions.

➡ Luggage space is limited or non-existent; you may have to buy a ticket for your bag.

➡ The first two seats on CTB buses are reserved for clergy (Buddhist monks).

➡ To guarantee a seat, board the bus at the beginning of its journey.

➡ When you arrive at your destination, confirm the departure details for the next stage of your journey.

Costs

In most cases, private bus companies run services parallel to CTB services. Intercity expresses charge about twice as much as CTB buses, but are more than twice as comfortable and usually faster. Fares for CTB buses and ordinary private buses are very cheap.

Car & Motorcycle

➡ Self-drive car hire is possible in Sri Lanka, though it is far more common to hire a car and driver. If you're on a relatively short visit to Sri Lanka on a midrange budget, the costs of hiring a car and driver can be quite reasonable.

➡ When planning your itinerary, you can count on covering about 35km/h in the Hill Country and 55km/h in most of the rest of the country.

➡ Motorcycling is an alternative for intrepid travellers. Distances are relatively short and some of the roads are a motorcyclist's delight; the trick is to stay off the main highways. The quieter Hill Country roads offer some glorious views, and secondary roads along the coast and the plains are reasonably quick. But you will have to make inquiries as motorcycle and motorbike rental is nowhere near as commonplace as it is in much of the rest of Asia.

➡ New expressways are revolutionising how people get around Sri Lanka.

➡ Throughout Sri Lanka, Mw is an abbreviation for Mawatha, meaning 'Avenue'.

Driving Licence

An International Driving Permit (IDP) can be used for driving in Sri Lanka; it's pricey, valid for three months to one year and is sold by auto clubs in your home country. Note that many travellers never purchase an IDP and have no problems.

Hiring a Car & Driver

A car and a driver guarantee maximum flexibility in your travels and while the driver deals with the chaotic roads, you can look out the window and – try to – relax.

You can find taxi drivers who will happily become your chauffeur for a day or more in all the main tourist centres. Guesthouses and hotels can connect you with a driver, which may be the best method. Travel agencies also offer various car and driver schemes, although these can cost considerably more.

COSTS

Various formulas exist for setting costs, such as rates per kilometre plus a lunch and dinner allowance and separate fuel payments. The simplest way is to agree on a flat fee with no extras. Expect to pay Rs 7000 to 9000 per day (US$60 is a good average), excluding fuel, or more for a newer air-con vehicle. Other considerations:

➡ Most drivers will expect a tip of about 10%.

➡ Meet the driver first as you may sense bad chemistry.

➡ Consider hiring a driver for only two or three days at first to see if you fit.

➡ You are the boss. It's great to get recommendations from a driver but don't be bullied. Drivers are known

to dissuade travellers from visiting temples and other sights where there are no commissions.

➡ Unless you speak absolutely no English or Sinhala, a guide in addition to the driver is unnecessary.

Drivers make a fair part of their income from commissions. Most hotels and guesthouses pay drivers a flat fee or a percentage, although others refuse to. This can lead to disputes between you and the driver over where you're staying the night, as the driver will wish to steer you literally to where the money is. Some hotels have appalling accommodation for drivers; the smarter hotels and guesthouses know that keeping drivers happy is good for their business, and provide decent food and lodgings.

Recommended drivers include the following (there are many more; the Lonely Planet Thorn Tree forum is a good source of driver recommendations):

Milroy Fernando (✆077 727 2780; milroy@ancientlanka. com)

Dimuthu Priyadarshana (✆077 630 2070; dimuthu81@ hotmail.com)

Nilam Sahabdeen (✆081-238 4981; http://srilankatour. wordpress.com/)

Self-Drive Hire

Colombo-based company **Shineway Rent A Car**

(✆258 3133; www.rentalcar srilanka.com; Colombo) offers self-drive car hire. You'll find other local firms as well as very small operations in tourist towns. You can usually get a car for about US$30 per day with 100km of included kilometres. But it is still uncommon to see visitors driving themselves in Sri Lanka.

Road Conditions

You may see a number of accidents; driving requires constant attention to the road. Country roads are often narrow and potholed, with constant pedestrian, bicycle and animal traffic to navigate. Note, however, that Sri Lanka's massive road-building program is improving roads across the nation.

Punctures are a part of life here, so every village has a repair expert.

It's dangerously acceptable for a bus, car or truck to overtake in the face of oncoming smaller road users. Three-wheelers, cyclists, or smaller cars and vans simply have to move over or risk getting hit. To announce they are overtaking, or want to overtake, drivers sound a shrill melody on their horns. If you're walking or cycling along any kind of main road, be very alert.

Road Rules

➡ Speed limit 56km/h in towns, 72km/h in rural areas and 100km on the new expressways.

SRI LANKA'S NEW HIGHWAYS

Various new expressways are opening over the next few years. Most will be toll roads, with relatively cheap tolls. Besides new expressways in and around Colombo (see p for more information), other new routes include:

Colombo–Kandy Expressway Approved in 2012, this road is expected to reduce travel time to close to an hour. There is no set opening date.

Southern Expressway The first new expressway completed. It is 161km long and runs from Colombo's southern suburb of Kottawa, near Maharagama, to Matara via an exit near Galle. Until linking roads are complete, it can take as long to get from Fort to the expressway entrance as it does from there to Galle – or even longer. Plans call for the road to eventually reach Hambantota.

➡ Driving is on the left-hand side of the road, as in the UK and Australia.

Hitching

Hitching is never entirely safe in any country in the world, and we don't recommend it. In any case, Sri Lanka's cheap fares make it an unnecessary option.

Local Transport

Many Sri Lankan towns are small enough to walk around. In larger towns you can get around by bus, taxi or three-wheeler.

Bus

Local buses go to most places, including villages outside main towns, for fares from Rs 10 to 50.

Taxi

Sri Lankan taxis are common in all sizable towns, and even some villages. Only some are metered (mostly in Colombo), but over longer distances their prices are comparable to those of three-wheelers, and they provide more comfort and security. Radio taxis are available in Kandy and Colombo. You can count on most taxi rides costing between Rs 60 and 100 per kilometre.

Three-wheeler

Three-wheelers, known in other parts of Asia as tuk-tuks, *bajajs* or autorickshaws, are literally waiting on every corner. Use your best bargaining skills and agree on the fare before you get in. Some keen drivers will offer to take you around Mars and back, and we've heard of travellers who have gone from Kandy to Nuwara Eliya in a three-wheeler, which would be a slow five hours or so.

As a rule of thumb, a three-wheeler should cost no more than Rs 150 per kilometre, but this can prove elusive depending on your negotiating skills. Note that three-wheelers with meters are becoming popular in Colombo.

Three-wheelers and taxis waiting outside hotels and tourist sights expect higher-than-usual fares. Walk a few hundred metres to get a better deal.

Tours

Sri Lanka has many inbound travel companies providing tours. Many of the tours are focused on a particular interest or activity.

Action Lanka (☎011-279 1584; www.actionlanka.com; 366/3, Rendapola Horagahakanda Lane, Talangama, Koswatta) Arranges outdoor activities including white-water rafting, kayaking, diving, mountain biking and walks.

Baurs (www.baurs.com) Wildlife-watching tours.

Boutique Sri Lanka (www.boutiquesrilanka.com) Specialises in interesting accommodation, Ayurvedic retreats and luxury resorts, guesthouses and small heritage hotels.

Eco Team Sri Lanka (www.srilankaecotourism.com) Wide range of wilderness-based active adventures, including white-water rafting, hiking and wildlife safaris.

Hoi An Motorbike Adventures (www.motorbiketours-hoian.com; 9-day tours from US$2000) Excellent guided motorbike tours along scenic back roads in some of the less-visited parts of the island, all featuring safari excursions.

Jetwing Eco Holidays (☎011-238 1201; www.jetwingeco.com) Wildlife and birdwatching tours.

Red Dot Tours (www.reddottours.com) Everything from golf and cricket to wildlife and wellness.

Sri Lanka Expeditions (www.srilankaexpeditions.com) Activity-based tours, including rock climbing, trekking, mountain biking and white-water rafting.

Sri Lanka In Style (www.srilankainstyle.com) Splurge-worthy and unique accommodation.

World Expeditions (www.worldexpeditions.com) Wildlife, culture and adventure tours, often guided by experts.

Train

Sri Lanka's railways are a great way to cross the country. Although they are slow, there are few overnight or all-day ordeals to contend with. A train ride is almost always more relaxed than a bus ride. Costs are in line with buses: even 1st class doesn't exceed Rs 1000.

There are three main lines:

South from Colombo A scenic delight. Recently renovated, runs past Aluthgama and Hikkaduwa to Galle and Matara.

East from Colombo To the Hill Country, through Kandy, Nanu Oya (for Nuwara Eliya) and Ella to Badulla. A beautiful route, the portion from Haputale to Ella is one of the world's most scenic train rides.

North from Colombo Through Anuradhapura to Mannar and also to Jaffna on rebuilt and renovated tracks. One branch reaches Trincomalee on the east coast, while another serves Polonnaruwa and Batticaloa.

Other Lines The Puttalam line runs along the coast north from Colombo, although rail buses run between Chilaw and Puttalam. The Kelani Valley line winds 60km from Colombo to Avissawella.

General Tips

➡ Trains are often late. For long-distance trains, Sri Lankans sometimes measure the lateness in periods of the day: quarter of a day late, half a day late and so on.

➡ Most stations have helpful information windows.

GETTING AROUND OPTIONS

Your options for getting around Sri Lanka are many. Broadly, the options and considerations are as follows:

	PROS	CONS
Bus	cheap, frequent, go everywhere	very crowded, uncomfortable, no room for luggage, slow
Car & Driver	comfortable, flexible, efficient	more expensive than buses and trains
Train	tickets in all classes are cheap, some routes beautiful, 1st class comfortable	not frequent, slow, 2nd and 3rd class crowded and uncomfortable, limited destinations

➡ The **Sri Lankan Railways website** (www.railway.gov.lk) has a useful trip planner.

Classes

There are three classes on Sri Lankan trains:

1st class Comes in three varieties: coaches, sleeping berths and observation saloons (with large windows). The latter are used on the line east from Colombo and are the preferred means of travelling this scenic line. Some have large rear-facing windows and vintage interiors.

2nd class Seats have padding and there are fans. On some trains (but not to Galle) these seats can be reserved in advance.

3rd class Seats have little padding and there are no reservations. The cars accommodate as many as can squeeze in and conditions can be grim.

In addition private companies have begun running comfortable train cars, which are attached to regular trains (routes include Colombo to Badulla, Ella, Kandy and Mathara, fares average US$12). Although the 1st-class observation cars are more charming – and cheaper – these private cars offer air-con, snacks and may have seats available when regular trains are already fully booked.

Private car operators:

Expo Rail (☎011-522 5050; www.exporail.lk)

Rajadhani Express (☎071-453 6840; www.rajadhani.lk)

Reservations

➡ You can reserve places in 1st class and in 2nd class on many intercity expresses.

➡ Always make a booking for the 1st-class observation saloons, which are very popular.

➡ Reservations can be made at train stations up to 10 days before departure. You can book a return ticket up to 14 days before departure.

➡ If travelling more than 80km, you can break your journey at any intermediate station for 24 hours without penalty. You'll need to make fresh reservations for seats on the next leg.

Language

WANT MORE?

For in-depth language information and handy phrases, check out Lonely Planet's Sinhala Phrasebook and India Phrasebook. You'll find them at **shop.lonelyplanet. com**, or you can buy Lonely Planet's iPhone phrasebooks at the Apple App Store.

Sinhala and Tamil are national languages in Sri Lanka, with English commonly described as a lingua franca. It's easy to get by with English, and the Sri Lankan variety has its own unique characteristics – 'You are having a problem, isn't it, no?' is one example. However, while English may be widely spoken in the main centres, off the beaten track its spread thins. In any case, even a few words of Sinhala or Tamil will go a long way.

SINHALA

Sinhala is officially written using a cursive script. If you read our coloured pronunciation guides as if they were English, you shouldn't have problems being understood. When consonants are doubled they are pronounced very distinctly, almost as separate sounds. The symbols t and d are pronounced less forcefully than in English, th as in 'thin', dh as the 'th' in 'that', g as in 'go', and r is more like a flap of the tongue against the roof of the mouth – it's not pronounced as an American 'r'. As for the vowels, a is pronounced as the 'u' in 'cup', aa as the 'a' in 'father', ai as in 'aisle', au as the 'ow' in 'how', e as in 'met', i as in 'bit', o as in 'hot', and u as in 'put'.

Basics

Hello.	aayu-bowan
Goodbye.	aayu-bowan
Yes.	owu
No.	naha
Please.	karuna kara
Thank you.	istuh-tee

Excuse me.	samah venna
Sorry.	kana gaatui
Do you speak English?	oyaa in-ghirisih kata karenawa da?
What's your name?	oyaaghe nama mokka'da?
My name is ...	maaghe nama ...

Accommodation

Do you have any rooms available?	kaamara thiyanawada?
How much is it per night?	ek ra-yakata kiyada
How much is it per person?	ek kenek-kuta kiyada
Is breakfast included?	udeh keh-emath ekkada?
for one night	ek rayak pamanai
for two nights	raya dekak pamanai
for one person	ek-kenek pamanai
for two people	den-nek pamanai
campsite	kamping ground eka
guesthouse	gesthaus eka
hotel	hotel eka
youth hostel	yut-hostel eka

Eating & Drinking

Can we see the menu?	menoo eka balanna puluvandha?
What's the local speciality?	mehe visheshayen hadhana dhe monavaadha?

I'd like rice and curry, please.	bahth denna
I'm a vegetarian.	mama elavalu vitharai kanne
I'm allergic to (peanuts).	mata (ratakaju) apathyayi
No ice in my drink, please.	karunaakarala maghe beema ekata ais dhamanna epaa
That was delicious!	eka harima rasai!

Please bring a/the...	... karunaakarala gennah
bill	bila
fork	gaarappuvak
glass of water	vathura veedhuruvak
knife	pihiyak
plate	pingaanak

bowl	vendhuwa
coffee	koh-pi
fruit	palathuru
glass	co-ppuwa
milk	kiri
salt	lunu
spoon	han-duh
sugar	seeni
tea	thay
water	vathura

NUMBERS – SINHALA

0	binduwa
1	eka
2	deka
3	thuna
4	hathara
5	paha
6	haya
7	hatha
8	atta
9	navaya
10	dahaya
100	seeya
200	deh seeya
1000	daaha
2000	deh daaha
100,000	lakshaya
1,000,000	daseh lakshaya
10,000,000	kotiya

Emergencies

Help!	aaney!/aaeeyoh!/ammoh!
Call a doctor!	dostara gen-nanna!
Call the police!	polisiyata kiyanna!
Go away!	methanin yanna!
I'm lost.	maa-meh nativelaa

Shopping & Services

What time does it open/close?	ehika kiyatada arinneh/vahanneh?
How much is it?	ehekka keeyada?
big	loku
medicine	behe-yat
small	podi/punchi

bank	bankuwa
chemist/pharmacy	faahmisiya
... embassy	... embasiya
market	maakat eka
my hotel	mang inna hotalaya
newsagency	pattara ejensiya
post office	tepal kantohruwa
public telephone	podu dura katanayak
tourist office	sanchaaraka toraturu karyaalayak

Time & Dates

What time is it?	velaave keeyada?
morning	udai
afternoon	havasa
day	davasa
night	raah
week	sumaanayak
month	maasayak
year	avuurudeh
yesterday	ee-yeh
today	ada (uther)
tomorrow	heta

Monday	sandu-da
Tuesday	angaharuwaa-da
Wednesday	badaa-da
Thursday	braha-spetin-da
Friday	sikuraa-da
Saturday	senasuraa-da
Sunday	iri-da

SIGNS – SINHALA

ඇතුල්වීම	Entrance
පිටවීම	Exit
විවෘතව ඇත.	Open
වසා ඇත.	Closed
තොරතුරු දැන්වුම	Information
තහනම් වේ.	Prohibited
පොලීස් ස්ථානය	Police Station
කාමර ඇත.	Rooms Available
කාමර නැත.	No Vacancy
වැසිකිළි	Toilets
පුරුෂ	Men
ස්තී	Women

Transport & Directions

When does the next ... leave/arrive?	meelanga ... pitaht venne/paminenne?
boat	bohtuwa
bus (city)	bus eka
bus (intercity)	bus eka nagaraantara
train	koh-chiya
I want to get off.	mama methana bahinawa
I'd like a one-way ticket.	mata tani gaman tikat ekak ganna ohna
I'd like a return ticket.	mata yaam-eem tikat ekak ganna ohna
1st class	palamu veni paantiya
2nd class	deveni paantiya
3rd class	tunveni paantiya
bus stop	bus nevathuma
ferry terminal	totu pala
timetable	kaala satahana
train station	dumriya pala
I'd like to hire a ...	mata ... ekak bad-dhata ganna ohna
bicycle	baisikeleya
car	kar (eka)
Where is a/the ...?	... koheda?
Go straight ahead.	kelinma issarahata yaanna
Turn left.	wamata harenna
Turn right.	dakunata harenna
near	lan-ghai
far	durai

TAMIL

The vocabulary of Sri Lankan Tamil is much the same as that of South India – the written form is identical, using the traditional cursive script – but there are marked differences in pronunciation between speakers from the two regions. In this section we've used the same pronunciation guides as for Sinhala.

Basics

Hello.	vanakkam
Goodbye.	poytu varukirehn
Yes.	aam
No.	il-lay
Please.	tayavu saydhu
Thank you.	nandri
Excuse me.	mannikavum
Sorry.	mannikavum
Do you speak English?	nin-gal aangilam paysu-virhalaa?
What's your name?	ungal peyr en-na?
My name is ...	en peyr ...

Accommodation

Do you have any rooms available?	ingu room kideikkumaa?
How much is it per night/person?	oru iravukku/aalukku evvalavur?
Is breakfast included?	kaalei unavum sehrtha?
for one/two nights	oru/irandu iravukku
for one/two people	oruvarukku/iruvarukku

SIGNS – TAMIL

வழி உள்ளே	Entrance
வழி வெளியே	Exit
திறந்துள்ளது	Open
அடைக்கப்பட்டுள்ளது	Closed
தகவல்	Information
அனுமதி இல்லை	Prohibited
காவல் நிலையம்	Police Station
அறைகள் உண்டு	Rooms Available
காலி இல்லை	No Vacancy
மலசலகூடம்	Toilets
ஆண்	Men
பெண்	Women

campsite	mukhaamidum idahm
guesthouse	virun-dhinar vidhudheh
hotel	hotehl
youth hostel	ilainar vidhudheh

Eating & Drinking

Can we see the menu?	unavu pattiyalai paarppomaa?
What's the local speciality?	ingu kidaikkak koodiya visheida unavu enna?
I'd like rice and curry, please.	sorum kariyum tharungal
I'm a vegetarian.	naan shaiva unavu shaappidupavan
I'm allergic to (peanuts).	(nilak kadalai) enakku alejee
No ice in my drink, please.	enadu paanaththil ais poda vendaam
That was delicious!	adhu nalla rushi!

Please bring a/the...	... konda varungal
bill	bill
fork	mul karandi
glass of water	thanni oru glass
knife	kaththi
plate	oru plate

bowl	kooppai
coffee	kahpee
fruit	paadham
glass	glass
milk	paal
salt	uppu
spoon	karandi
sugar	seeree
tea	te-neer/plan-tea
water	than-neer

Emergencies

Help!	udavi!
Call a doctor!	daktarai kuppidunga!
Call the police!	polisai kuppidunga!
Go away!	pohn-goh!/poi-vidu!
I'm lost.	naan vali tavari-vittehn

Shopping & Services

What time does it open/close?	et-thana manikka tirakhum/mudhum?

NUMBERS – TAMIL

0	saifer
1	ondru
2	iranduh
3	muundruh
4	naan-guh
5	ainduh
6	aaruh
7	ealluh
8	ettu
9	onbaduh
10	pat-tuh
100	nooruh
1000	aayirem
2000	irandaayirem
100,000	oru latcham
1,000,000	pattuh lat-chem
10,000,000	kohdee

How much is it?	adhu evvalavu?
big	periyeh
medicine	marunduh
small	siriyeh
bank	vanghee
chemist/pharmacy	marunduh kadhai
... embassy	... tudharalayem
market	maarket
my hotel	enadu hotehl
newsagency	niyuz paper vitku-midam
post office	tafaal nilayem
public telephone	podhu tolai-pessee
tourist office	toorist nilayem

Time & Dates

What time is it?	mani eth-tanai?
morning	kaalai
afternoon	pit-pahel
day	pahel
night	iravu
week	vaarem
month	maadhem
year	varudem
yesterday	neh-truh
today	indru
tomorrow	naalay

Monday	tin-gal
Tuesday	sevvaay
Wednesday	budahn
Thursday	viyaalin
Friday	vellee
Saturday	san-nee
Sunday	naayiru

Transport & Directions

When does the next ... leave/arrive?	eththanai manikku aduththa ... sellum/varum?
boat	padakhu
bus (city)	baas naharam/ul-loor
bus (intercity)	baas veliyoor
train	rayill

I want to get off.	naan iranga vendum
I'd like a one-way ticket.	enakku oru vahly tikket veynum
I'd like a return ticket.	enakku iru vahlay tikket veynum

1st class	mudalahaam vahuppu
2nd class	irandaam vahuppu
bus/trolley stop	baas nilayem
luggage lockers	porul vaikku-midam
timetable	haala attavanay
train station	rayill nilayem

I'd like to hire a ...	enakku ... vaadakhaikku vaynum
bicycle	sai-kul
car	car

Where is it?	adhu en-ghe irukkaradhu?
Where is a/the ...?	... en-ghe?
Go straight ahead.	neraha sellavum
Turn left.	valadhur pakkam tirumbavum
Turn right.	itadhu pakkam thirumbavum
near	aruhil
far	tu-rahm

SRI LANKAN ENGLISH

Greetings & Conversation
Go and come. – farewell greeting, similar to 'See you later' (not taken literally)
How? – How are you?
Nothing to do. – Can't do anything.
What to do? – What can be done about it? (more of a rhetorical question)
What country? – Where are you from?
paining – hurting
to gift – to give a gift

People
baby/bubba – term used for any child up to about adolescence
batchmate – university classmate
peon – office helper
uncle/auntie – term of respect for elder

Getting Around
backside – part of the building away from the street
bajaj – three-wheeler
bus halt – bus stop
coloured lights – traffic lights
down south – the areas south of Colombo, especially coastal areas
dropping – being dropped off at a place by a car
get down – to alight (from bus/train/three-wheeler)

normal bus – not a private bus
outstation – place beyond a person's home area
petrol shed – petrol/gas station
pick-up – 4WD utility vehicle
seaside/landside – indicates locations, usually in relation to Galle Rd
two-wheeler – motorcycle
up and down – return trip
up country/Hill Country – Kandy and beyond, tea plantation areas
vehicle – car

Food
bite – snack, usually with alcoholic drinks
boutique – a little, hole-in-the-wall shop, usually selling small, inexpensive items
cool spot – traditional, small shop that sells cool drinks and snacks
hotel – a small, cheap restaurant that doesn't offer accommodation
lunch packet/rice packet – rice/curry meal wrapped in plastic and newspaper and taken to office or school for lunch
short eats – snack food

Money
buck – rupee
last price – final price when bargaining
purse – wallet

GLOSSARY

ambalama – wayside shelter for pilgrims

Aurudu – Sinhalese and Tamil New Year, celebrated on 14 April

Avalokitesvara – the *bodhisattva* of compassion

Ayurveda – traditional system of medicine that uses herbs and oils to heal and rejuvenate

bailas – folk tunes based on Portuguese, African and local music styles

baobab – water-storing tree *(Adansonia digitata),* probably introduced to Mannar Island and the Vanni in northern Sri Lanka by Arab traders

bodhi tree – large spreading tree *(Ficus religiosa);* the tree under which the Buddha sat when he attained enlightenment, and the many descendants grown from cuttings of this tree

bodhisattva – divine being who, although capable of attaining *nirvana*, chooses to reside on the human plane to help ordinary people attain salvation

Brahmi – early Indian script used from the 5th century BC

bund – built-up bank or dyke surrounding a *tank*

Burgher – Sri Lankan Eurasian, generally descended from Portuguese-Sinhalese or Dutch-Sinhalese intermarriage

cadjan – coconut fronds woven into mats and used as building material

Ceylon – British-colonial name for Sri Lanka

chetiya – Buddhist shrine

Chola – powerful ancient South Indian kingdom that invaded Sri Lanka on several occasions

CTB – Central Transport Board, the state bus network

dagoba – Buddhist monument composed of a solid hemisphere containing relics of the Buddha or a Buddhist saint; a *stupa*

devale – complex designed for worshipping a Hindu or Sri Lankan deity

dharma – the word used by both Hindus and Buddhists to refer to their respective moral codes of behaviour

eelam – Tamil word for precious land

gala – rock

ganga – river

gedige – hollow temple with thick walls and a corbelled roof

gopuram – gateway tower

guardstones – carved stones that flank doorways or entrances to temples

Hanuman – the monkey king from the *Ramayana*

Jataka tales – stories of the previous lives of the Buddha

juggernaut – decorated temple cart dragged through the streets during Hindu festivals (sometimes called a 'car')

kachcheri – administrative office

kadé – Sinhalese name for a streetside hut (also called boutiques); called *unavakam* by Tamils

Karava – fisherfolk of Indian descent

karma – Hindu-Buddhist principle of retributive justice for past deeds

Kataragama – see *Murugan*

kiri bath – dessert of rice cooked in coconut milk

kolam – meaning costume or guise, it refers to masked dance-drama; also the rice-flour designs that adorn buildings in Tamil areas

kovil – Hindu temple dedicated to the worship of Shiva

kulam – Tamil word for *tank*

lakh – 100,000; unit of measurement in Sri Lanka and India

lingam – phallic symbol; symbol of Shiva

LTTE – Liberation Tigers of Tamil Eelam, also known as the Tamil Tigers; separatist group fighting for an independent Tamil Eelam in the North and the East

Maha – northeast monsoon season

Mahaweli Ganga – Sri Lanka's longest river, starting near Adam's Peak and reaching the sea near Trincomalee

Mahayana – later form of Buddhism prevalent in Korea, Japan and China; literally means 'greater vehicle'

Mahinda – son of the Indian Buddhist emperor Ashoka, credited with introducing Buddhism to Sri Lanka

mahout – elephant master

Maitreya – future Buddha

makara – mythical beast combining a lion, a pig and an elephant, often carved into temple staircases

makara torana – ornamental archway

mandapaya – a raised platform with decorative pillars

masala – mix (often spices)

moonstone – semiprecious stone; also a carved 'doorstep' at temple entrances

mudra – symbolic hand position of a Buddha image

Murugan – Hindu god of war; also known as *Skanda* and *Kataragama*

naga – snake; also applies to snake deities and spirits

nirvana – ultimate aim of Buddhists, final release from the cycle of existence

nuwara – city

ola – leaves of the talipot palm; used in manuscripts and traditional books

oruva – outrigger canoe

oya – stream or small river

Pali – the language in which the Buddhist scriptures were originally recorded

palmyra – tall palm tree found in the dry northern region

perahera – procession, usually with dancers, drummers and elephants

pirivena – centre of learning attached to monastery

poya – full-moon day; always a holiday

puja – 'respect', offering or prayers

rajakariya – 'workers for the king', the tradition of feudal service

Ramayana – ancient story of Rama and Sita and their conflict with *Rawana*

Rawana – 'demon king of Lanka' who abducts Rama's beautiful wife Sita in the Hindu epic the *Ramayana*

relic chamber – chamber in a *dagoba* housing a relic of the Buddha or a saint and representing the Buddhist concept of the cosmos

Ruhunu – ancient southern centre of Sinhalese power near Tissamaharama that survived even when Anuradhapura and Polonnaruwa fell to Indian invaders

samudra – large *tank* or inland sea

Sangamitta – sister of *Mahinda;* she brought the sacred *bodhi tree* sapling from Bodhgaya in India

sangha – the community of Buddhist monks and nuns; in Sri Lanka, an influential group divided into several nikayas (orders)

Sanskrit – ancient Indian language, the oldest known member of the Indo-European languages

sari – traditional garment worn by women

Sinhala – language of the Sinhalese people

Sinhalese – majority population of Sri Lanka; principally Sinhala-speaking Buddhists

Skanda – see *Murugan*

stupa – see *dagoba*

Tamils – a people of South Indian origin, comprising the largest minority population in Sri Lanka; principally Tamil-speaking Hindus

tank – artificial water-storage lake or reservoir; many of the tanks in Sri Lanka are very large and ancient

Theravada – orthodox form of Buddhism practised in Sri Lanka and Southeast Asia, which is characterised by its adherence to the *Pali* canon

unavakam – Tamil name for a streetside hut; called kadé or boutiques by the Sinhalese

vahalkada – solid panel of sculpture

vatadage – circular relic house consisting of a small central *dagoba* flanked by Buddha images and encircled by columns

Veddahs – original inhabitants of Sri Lanka prior to the arrival of the Sinhalese from India; also called the *Wanniyala-aetto*

vel – trident; the god *Murugan* is often depicted carrying a *vel*

vihara, **viharaya** – Buddhist complex, including a shrine containing a statue of the Buddha, a congregational hall and a monks' house

Wanniyala-aetto – see *Veddahs*

wewa – see *tank*

Yala – southwest monsoon season

Behind the Scenes

SEND US YOUR FEEDBACK

We love to hear from travellers – your comments keep us on our toes and help make our books better. Our well-travelled team reads every word on what you loved or loathed about this book. Although we cannot reply individually to your submissions, we always guarantee that your feedback goes straight to the appropriate authors, in time for the next edition. Each person who sends us information is thanked in the next edition – the most useful submissions are rewarded with a selection of digital PDF chapters.

Visit **lonelyplanet.com/contact** to submit your updates and suggestions or to ask for help. Our award-winning website also features inspirational travel stories, news and discussions.

Note: We may edit, reproduce and incorporate your comments in Lonely Planet products such as guidebooks, websites and digital products, so let us know if you don't want your comments reproduced or your name acknowledged. For a copy of our privacy policy visit lonelyplanet.com/privacy.

OUR READERS

Many thanks to the travellers who used the last edition and wrote to us with helpful hints, useful advice and interesting anecdotes:

A Annele Keller, Alex Jones, Alexa Vlaming, Andrea Meier, Andrew Crouch, Anette Czepulowski, Angelique Braat, Anne Catrien Gielens, Annemarie Robertsen, Annette Elben, Asit Mukhopadhyay **B** Binia Fraser, Birgit Malin, Blanc Nadine, Brat Caroline, Brian Woodgate **C** Catharian Kaffenberger, Cecilia Jensen, Cecilia Rovelli, Cheng Huang Leng, Chris Oey, Christopher Rowland, Colleen Mavris **D** Dani Carranza, David Bruce-Steer, David Dimasi, David Eisenrauch, David Engstrand, David Taylor, Dilsiri Welikala **E** Elad Wexler, Elisa Janszen, Erich Malter, Ernesto Sanchez Beaumont, Esther Hermans-Spijker **F** Floris and Marcella, Frans van Assendelft **G** Gabriel Corens, Gary Heiden, Gemma Stewart, George Fogh, Geraldine Plas **H** Hans Ohrt, Herman Boerrigter **I** Irene Söding **J** James Smith, Jan Joost, Jane Mason, Javi Molina, Jean-Marc Legras, Jeroen Derichs, Jessy Nourrit, Joelle Abi Chaker, Joep van Schalkwijk, John Evans, John Moore, John Turner, Jon McGowan, Jonathan Meyer Harrison, Julia Antonova **K** Karel Jan van den Heuvel Rijnders, Kathryn Smyth, Kathryn Stanczyszyn, Katia Begall, Kevin Callaghan, Krupa Thakrar **L** Léa Deswarte, Lin Chia Ying, Louisa Johnsson Zea & Mario Zea, Luis Navas **M** Maarten Bavinck, Marc-Olivier Bergeron, Marieke Holl, Marius Muraska, Mariusz Lewicki, Mark Rimer, Markus Lindner, Matthew Ashbolt, Meike Sier, Melissa Lazell, Michael Konefal, Moana Mutscheller **N** Nadine Blanc, Natalie Hedges, Neil Hankinson, Neil Hart, Noor van Hapert **O** Olle Klint **P** Paul Buxton **R** Randi Johnbeck, Rita Mensink, Roger Race, Ronnie Dunetz, Rose Hawke **S** Sarah Parish, Saskia Beijering, Saskia Fernando, Shirin Reuvers, Shirley Sim, Siegfried Schoen, Soeren Finkbeiner, Søren & Grethe Iversen, Steve Jones, Stine Porsbjerg, Suzanne Hamilton **T** Thomas Winther Andersen, Tim Giesberts, Tobias Vishvabaratha, Tony Knight, Tuomo Huuskonen **V** Véronique D'haens, Virginia Scott

AUTHOR THANKS

Ryan Ver Berkmoes

Thanks to all who made my time in Sri Lanka a delight and shared valuable insights: Milroy Janaka and my old pal Juliet Coombe were extremely helpful. Thanks to the myriad others who answered questions and offered advice to a seemingly confused traveller who did a lot of note taking and always had one more question. Off island, love and thanks to former Sri Lanka resident Alexis Averbuck, who gave me reason to leave.

Stuart Butler

First and foremost I must, once again, thank my wife, Heather, and children, Jake and Grace, for putting up with my extended periods away while working on this project and (to Heather) for coping so admirably with two small children on her own. As always massive thanks to my Sri Lankan friends Dimuthu Priyadarshana and family, HA Anura, Milroy Fernando, Sena and Rashinika Kolambahewage, Stephanie and Palitha, Ramyadava Gunasekara, Juliet Coombe, Jai and Sumana and Sue and Faiesz, at Sharon Inn. Finally, thanks to all the other nameless Sri Lankans I pestered with questions about bus schedules and so on.

Iain Stewart

Thanks to Somey for scenic rides and great company, Mark Wyndham and the crew for the bike trip, Dimuthu for his hospitality and all in Mannar and Jaffna. And to James Smart, Joe Bindloss and the Lonely Planet team for their professionalism and help on this title.

ACKNOWLEDGMENTS

Climate map data adapted from Peel MC, Finlayson BL & McMahon TA (2007) 'Updated World Map of the Köppen-Geiger Climate Classification', Hydrology and Earth System Sciences, 11, 1633¬44.

Cover photograph: Stilt fishing, near Weligama. Jon Hicks/Corbis

THIS BOOK

This 13th edition of Lonely Planet's *Sri Lanka* guidebook was researched and written by Ryan Ver Berkmoes, Stuart Butler and Iain Stewart. The previous two editions were written by Brett Atkinson, Stuart Butler, Ethan Gelber, Amy Karafin and Ryan Ver Berkmoes.

Destination Editors Joe Bindloss, James Smart
Product Editor Amanda Williamson
Senior Cartographer David Kemp
Book Designer Jessica Rose
Assisting Editors Victoria Harrison, Kate Kiely, Kellie Langdon, Rosie Nicholson, Christopher Pitts, Erin Richards

Assisting Cartographers Mick Garrett, Corey Hutchison, Rachel Imeson
Cover Researcher Naomi Parker
Language Content Branislava Vladisavljevic
Thanks to Ryan Evans, Claire Naylor, the Kates, Karyn Noble, Angela Tinson, Samantha Tyson, Lauren Wellicome

Index

C
canals 86, 87
canoeing 43

NOTES

Map Legend

Sights
- Beach
- Bird Sanctuary
- Buddhist
- Castle/Palace
- Christian
- Confucian
- Hindu
- Islamic
- Jain
- Jewish
- Monument
- Museum/Gallery/Historic Building
- Ruin
- Sento Hot Baths/Onsen
- Shinto
- Sikh
- Taoist
- Winery/Vineyard
- Zoo/Wildlife Sanctuary
- Other Sight

Activities, Courses & Tours
- Bodysurfing
- Diving
- Canoeing/Kayaking
- Course/Tour
- Skiing
- Snorkelling
- Surfing
- Swimming/Pool
- Walking
- Windsurfing
- Other Activity

Sleeping
- Sleeping
- Camping

Eating
- Eating

Drinking & Nightlife
- Drinking & Nightlife
- Cafe

Entertainment
- Entertainment

Shopping
- Shopping

Information
- Bank
- Embassy/Consulate
- Hospital/Medical
- Internet
- Police
- Post Office
- Telephone
- Toilet
- Tourist Information
- Other Information

Geographic
- Beach
- Hut/Shelter
- Lighthouse
- Lookout
- Mountain/Volcano
- Oasis
- Park
- Pass
- Picnic Area
- Waterfall

Population
- Capital (National)
- Capital (State/Province)
- City/Large Town
- Town/Village

Transport
- Airport
- Border crossing
- Bus
- Cable car/Funicular
- Cycling
- Ferry
- Metro/MRT/MTR station
- Monorail
- Parking
- Petrol station
- Skytrain/Subway station
- Taxi
- Train station/Railway
- Tram
- Underground station
- Other Transport

Note: Not all symbols displayed above appear on the maps in this book

Routes
- Tollway
- Freeway
- Primary
- Secondary
- Tertiary
- Lane
- Unsealed road
- Road under construction
- Plaza/Mall
- Steps
- Tunnel
- Pedestrian overpass
- Walking Tour
- Walking Tour detour
- Path/Walking Trail

Boundaries
- International
- State/Province
- Disputed
- Regional/Suburb
- Marine Park
- Cliff
- Wall

Hydrography
- River, Creek
- Intermittent River
- Canal
- Water
- Dry/Salt/Intermittent Lake
- Reef

Areas
- Airport/Runway
- Beach/Desert
- Cemetery (Christian)
- Cemetery (Other)
- Glacier
- Mudflat
- Park/Forest
- Sight (Building)
- Sportsground
- Swamp/Mangrove

OUR STORY

A beat-up old car, a few dollars in the pocket and a sense of adventure. In 1972 that's all Tony and Maureen Wheeler needed for the trip of a lifetime – across Europe and Asia overland to Australia. It took several months, and at the end – broke but inspired – they sat at their kitchen table writing and stapling together their first travel guide, *Across Asia on the Cheap*. Within a week they'd sold 1500 copies. Lonely Planet was born.

Today, Lonely Planet has offices in Franklin, London, Melbourne, Oakland, Beijing and Delhi, with more than 600 staff and writers. We share Tony's belief that 'a great guidebook should do three things: inform, educate and amuse'.

OUR WRITERS

Ryan Ver Berkmoes

Coordinating Author, Colombo, The South. Ryan first visited Sri Lanka in 2005 after the tsunami when he covered the aftermath as a journalist. Impressed then at Sri Lanka's resilience, he's only more impressed now as the island emerges from its long time in the shadows. On his visits since he has criss-crossed this beautiful island looking for the best rice and curry ever. He's had some great ones but this sort of quest should never end. Ryan writes about travel and more at ryanverberkmoes.com and @ryanvb

Read more about Ryan at:
lonelyplanet.com/members/ryanverberkmoes

Stuart Butler

The West, The Hill Country. Originally from Devon in the UK, Stuart first made it to Sri Lanka during a long trans-Asia surf trip back in the early 1990s. One wave and one curry later and he was hooked. Since then the food, beaches, wildlife, waves, people and hills have called him back dozens of times. His travels have also taken him across South Asia and beyond, from the savannah of East Africa to the Arctic tundra. He now lives with his wife and two small children on the beaches of southwest France. Stuart also wrote Beaches & Activities, National Parks & Safaris, Travel with Children and Environmental Issues. His website is www.stuartbutlerjournalist.com

Read more about Stuart at:
lonelyplanet.com/members/stuartbutler

Iain Stewart

The Ancient Cities, The East, Jaffna & the North. Iain has been captivated by Sri Lanka for years but this was his first writing assignment in the country. Highlights on this trip were a 1000km motorbike journey through the hill country and tea plantations, the majesty of Anuradhapura, hanging out with Mark in Jaffna, blue whales offshore and elephants on land, fresh seafood in Mirissa and good old rice and curry by the roadside. Iain also wrote Eat & Drink Like a Local and Sri Lankan Tea.

Read more about Iain at:
lonelyplanet.com/members/iainstewart

Published by Lonely Planet Publications Pty Ltd
ABN 36 005 607 983
13th edition – January 2015
ISBN 978 1 74220 802 2
© Lonely Planet 2015   Photographs © as indicated 2015
10 9 8 7 6 5 4 3 2 1
Printed in China